THE KEDGE-ANCHOR

OR

YOUNG SAILORS' ASSISTANT

William Brady

DOVER PUBLICATIONS, INC.
Mineola, New York

Dedicated
to the
UNITED STATES' NAVY
and
MERCHANT SERVICE

Bibliographical Note

This Dover edition, first published in 2002, is an unabridged republication of the text and illustrations from the fourth, enlarged edition (1849) of the work originally published by the author in 1847 in New York.

Library of Congress Cataloging-in-Publication Data

Brady, William, d. 1887.
The kedge-anchor : a young sailors' assistant / William Brady.
p. cm.
Originally published: New York : W. Brady, 1847.
Includes index.
ISBN-13: 978-0-486-41992-3 (pbk.)
ISBN-10: 0-486-41992-4 (pbk.)
1. Seamanship—Handbooks, manuals, etc. I. Title.

VK541 .B82 2002
623.88—dc21

2001028697

Manufactured in the United States by LSC Communications
41992404 2017
www.doverpublications.com

THE

KEDGE-ANCHOR;

OR,

YOUNG SAILORS' ASSISTANT.

APPERTAINING TO THE PRACTICAL EVOLUTIONS OF MODERN SEAMANSHIP, RIGGING, KNOTTING, SPLICING, BLOCKS, PURCHASES, RUNNING-RIGGING, AND OTHER MISCELLANEOUS MATTERS, APPLICABLE TO SHIPS OF WAR AND OTHERS.

Illustrated with Seventy Engravings.

ALSO,

TABLES OF RIGGING, SPARS, SAILS, BLOCKS, CANVASS, CORDAGE, CHAIN AND HEMP CABLES, HAWSERS, &c., &c., RELATIVE TO EVERY CLASS OF VESSELS.

BY WILLIAM BRADY, SAILING MASTER, U. S. N.

FOURTH EDITION.

IMPROVED AND ENLARGED, WITH ADDITIONAL MATTER, PLATES, AND TABLES.

NEW YORK:
PUBLISHED BY THE AUTHOR.
SOLD AT R. L. SHAW'S NAUTICAL STORE, NO. 222 WATER ST., AND THE PRINCIPAL NAUTICAL AND STATIONERS' STORES THROUGHOUT THE UNITED STATES.

1849

PREFACE.

In offering the following work to the public, the author deems no apology necessary, as it was written for the use of the Naval and Merchant Service of the United States, as a ready means of introducing Young Sailors to the theory of that art by which they must expect to advance in the profession they have chosen. He flatters himself, however, that it will be found useful to many old and experienced seamen, as well as to those who have just entered the sailors' life, and particularly to those destined for the Navy. Should it fall into the hands of the learned, they will bear in mind that he is better versed with the marlinespike than the pen, and that it was composed in the hours of relaxation from official duties. He therefore hopes that it may be received for that which it is intended to be, A Kedge-Anchor, for the youthful sailor. The work has been submitted to the inspection of a number of experienced officers, both in the Navy and Merchant Service, who have given it their decided approbation;—some of whose names are appended to the work. With these few remarks, he submits it to a discerning public, to stand or fall on its own merits.

W. N. Brady, Master U.S.N.

RECOMMENDATIONS.

I have examined the manuscript of Mr. Brady and approve of it, as a very useful Book for young officers and others, in the Naval and Merchant service.

JOHN GALLAGHER, *Captain U. S. Navy.*

I fully concur in the above.

E. PECK, *Commander U. S. Navy.*

I have examined the within treatise on Seamanship, and other miscellaneous matter appertaining to ships and vessels of war (written by William Brady, Master U. S. Navy). It affords me much pleasure to recommend the same to the junior officers of the Navy, and others who may be disposed to learn the profession of Seamanship.

W. C. WETMORE, *Commander U. S. Navy.*

Examined and approved as a work that will be useful to the Service.

J. D. L. SAUNDERS, *Commander U. S. Navy.*
J. MATTISON, *Commander U. S. Navy.*

This I conceive to be a valuable work, and well calculated to be useful to the Service.

JOSHUA R. SANDS, *Commander U. S. Navy.*

I have closely examined the within work, and think it well calculated for the instruction of young officers and others in the Navy.

JAMES RENSHAW, *Captain U. S. Navy.*

I fully concur in the above.

FRANCIS O. ELLISON, *Master U. S. Navy.*

I have carefully examined the within work on Seamanship, and think it one well calculated for the instruction of young officers, and others. C. G. HUNTER, *Lieutenant U. S. Navy.*

We cheerfully recommend this work of William Brady, S. Master U. S. Navy, to the maritime community, and think it well calculated for the instruction of all who may be disposed to learn the profession of Seamanship.

ISAAC McKEEVER, Captain U. S. Navy.
JAMES McINTOSH, Commander U. S. Navy.
WILLIAM L. HUDSON, " "
HENRY EAGLE, " "
A. G. GORDON, Lieutenant U. S. Navy.
CADWALDER RINGGOLD, " "
WILLIAM F. LYNCH, " "
HENRY W. MORRIS, " "
FRANCIS B. ELLISON, " "
JAMES H. ROWAN, " "
JOHN COLHOUN, " "
T. TURNER, " "
T. A. HUNT, " "
HENRY MOORE, " "
JOHN J. GLASSON, " "
CHARLES HEYWOOD, " "
CHARLES S. BOGGS, " "
ALEXANDER GIBSON, " "
ALEXANDER M. PENNOCK, " "
MONTGOMERY HUNT, " "
FRANCIS HAGGERTY, " "
J. R. McMULLANY, " "

CAPT. HENRY D. HUNTER, Commanding U. S. Rev. Steamer Polk.
JOHN McGOWAN, 1st Lieutenant U. S. Rev. Marine.
WILLIAM H. BROWN, Lieutenant U. S. Rev. Marine.
JOSEPH C. NOYES, Lieutenant U. S. Rev. Marine.
CAPT. E. RICHARDSON, President American Seamen Friend Society.
" AUGUSTUS PROAL, Reviewer of the Work.

CAPT. SAMUEL YEATON, Commanding Packet ship Oxford.
" D. G. BAILEY, " " Yorkshire.
" GEORGE B. CORNISH, " " Sheridan.
" E. G. FURBER, " " Europe.
" A. B. LOWBER, " " Montezuma.
" J. A. WOTTEN, " " Admiral.
" JOSEPH HAMILTON, Commanding Packet ship So. Carolina.
' CHARLES R. GRIFFITH, Commanding Ship Southport.
" JAMES RENNE, " " Gondola.
" IRA BURSLEY, " " Hottenger.
" GEORGE W. HOWE, Commanding Packet ship Bavaria.

United States Ship of-the-Line OHIO. 84 guns

United States' Razee or Frigate Independence, at Anchor. 56 guns

CONTENTS.

PART I.

PART II.

PART III.

PART IV.

PART V.

PART VI.

PART VII.

PART VIII.

PART IX.

PART X.

PART XI.

THE KEDGE-ANCHOR.

We shall first commence with knotting a rope-yarn.

1.—TO KNOT ROPE-YARNS.

Take the two ends of the yarns, and split them open about two inches from the end; and if to make a smooth knot, you may scrape down a little with a knife, so as to make the ends lay smooth; you then crutch them together as you see in Plate No. 1. Take two opposite ends (leaving the other two dormant), pass one of the ends *under*, and the other *over* the standing part of the yarn, connecting them together at the same side you took them from at first; then jam your knot taut, and see if it will stand test by stretching the yarn from knee to knee, and hauling on it; if it stands without drawing, you may trim the ends, and go on.

2.—TO MAKE A FOX.

Take two or three rope-yarns and make them fast to a belaying-pin; stretch them out taut, and twist them together on your knee; then rub it down smooth with a piece of old tarred parcelling. This is called a Fox, and is used for many purposes, such as making gaskets, mats, plats, temporary seizings, bending studding-sails, &c.

3.—TO MAKE A SPANISH FOX.

Take a single rope-yarn and make one end fast as before to a belaying-pin, and untwist and twist it up again the contrary way, and rub it smooth. This is used for small seizings, &c.

4.—TO MAKE A KNITTLE.

A Knittle is made of two or three rope-yarns laid up together by hand, twisting them between the thumb and finger, and laying them up against the twist of the yarn. They are used for many purposes on board a ship, particularly for hammock clews.

5.—OVERHANDED KNOT.

To make an overhanded knot, you pass the end of the rope over the standing part and through the bight.

6.—FIGURE OF EIGHT KNOTS.

Take the end of your rope round the standing part, under its own part and through the lower bight, and your knot is made.

7.—TWO HALF-HITCHES.

Pass the end of your rope round the standing part, and bring it up through the bight—this is one half-hitch; two of these, one above the other, completes it.

8.—REEF, OR SQUARE KNOT.

First make an overhanded knot round a yard, spar, or anything you please; then bring the end being next to you over the left hand and through the bight; haul both ends taut, and it is made.

9.—A BOWLINE KNOT.

Take the end of the rope in your right hand, and the standing part in the left—lay the end over the standing part, then with your left hand turn the bight of the standing part over the end part, so as to form a cuckold's neck on the standing part; then lead the end through the standing part *above*, and stick it down through the cuckold's neck, and it will appear as in the Plate.

10.—BOWLINE ON THE BIGHT.

Take the bight of the rope in your right hand, and the standing part in the other; throw a cuckold's neck over the bight with the standing parts, then haul enough of the bight up through the cuckold's neck to go under and over all parts; jam all taut, and it will appear as in the Plate.

11.—A RUNNING BOWLINE.

Take the end of the rope round the standing part, through the bight, and make a single bowline upon the running part, and the knot is made.

12.—A TIMBER HITCH.

Take the end of a rope round a spar; pass it under and over the standing part then pass several turns round its own part and it is done.

13.—A FISHERMAN'S BEND.

With the end of a rope take two round turns round a spar, or through the ring of a kedge-anchor; take one half hitch around the standing parts, and under all parts of the turns; then one half hitch around the standing part above all, and stop the end to the standing part; or you can dispense with the last half hitch, and tuck the end under one of the round turns, and it becomes a studding-sail bend.

14.—A ROLLING BEND.

A rolling bend is something similar to a fisherman's bend. It is two round turns round a spar as you see in the plate, two half hitches around the standing part, and the end stopped back.—(*See Plate.*)

15.—A CARRICK BEND.

This bend is more used in bending hawsers together than for any other purpose. In forming this bend you will take the end of the hawser, and form a bight, by laying the end part on the top of the standing part, so as to form a cross; take the end of the other hawser, and reeve it down through this bight, up and over this cross; then pass the end down through the bight again on the opposite side, from the other end, for one end must be on the top, and the other underneath, as you see in the plate.

If both end parts come out at the top it will be a granny's knot. (*Remember this.*)

16.—A CAT'S-PAW.

This is generally used in the ends of lanyards, to hook the tackle to, in setting up rigging; to form it, you first lay the end part of the lanyard across the standing part, which will form a bight; then lay hold of the bight with one hand on each side ot it, breaking it down, and turning it over *from you* two or three times; clap both bights together, and hook on to both parts.—(*See Plate.*)

17.—A SHEET OR BECKET BEND.

Pass the end of a rope through the bight of another rope, or through the becket of a block; then round both parts of the bight, or becket, and take the end under its own part, as you see in the plate. It is sometimes put under twice, and the end stopped back to the standing part.

18.—A BLACK-WALL HITCH.

This is used with a lanyard, in setting up rigging, to hook a luff tackle to, instead of a cat's paw, where the end of the lanyard is not long enough to form a paw; but a strap and toggle is preferable to both.

To make a black-wall over a hook, you form a bight, or rather a *kink* with the end of the lanyard, having the end part underneath, and the standing part on the top; stick the hook through the bight, keeping the bight well up on the back of the hook (as you see in the plate), until you set taut the tackle.

Note.—You can learn it much better by practice than explanation.

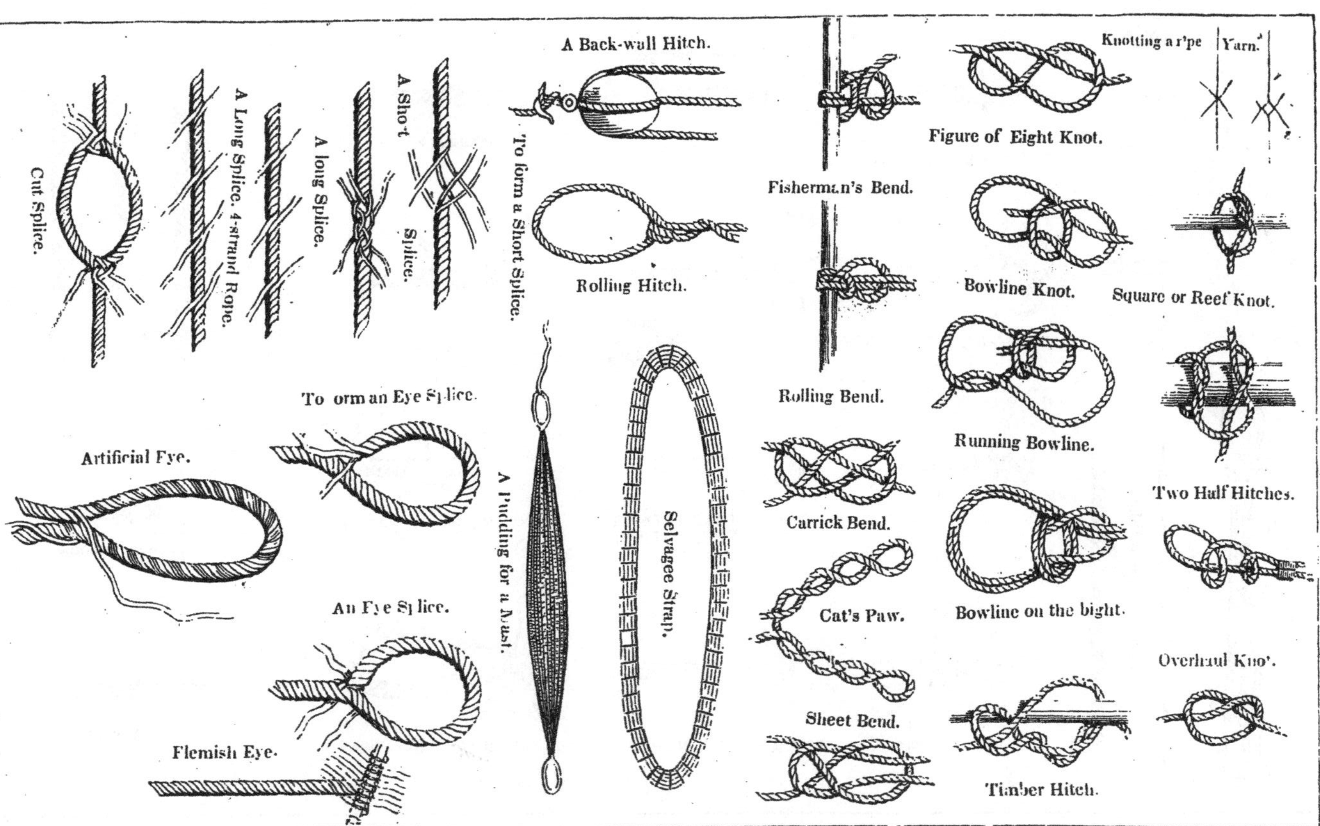

Knotting a Rope Yarn.
Figure of Eight Knot.
Fisherman's Bend.
Bowline Knot.
Square or Reef Knot.
Rolling Bend.
Running Bowline.
Two Half Hitches.
Carrick Bend.
Cat's Paw.
Bowline on the bight.
Overhaul Knot.
Sheet Bend.
Timber Hitch.
A Back-wall Hitch.
Rolling Hitch.
To form a Short Splice.
A Short Splice.
A long Splice.
A Long Splice. 4-strand Rope.
Cut Splice.
Selvagee Strap.
A Pudding for a Mast.
To form an Eye Splice.
Artificial Eye.
An Eye Splice.
Flemish Eye.

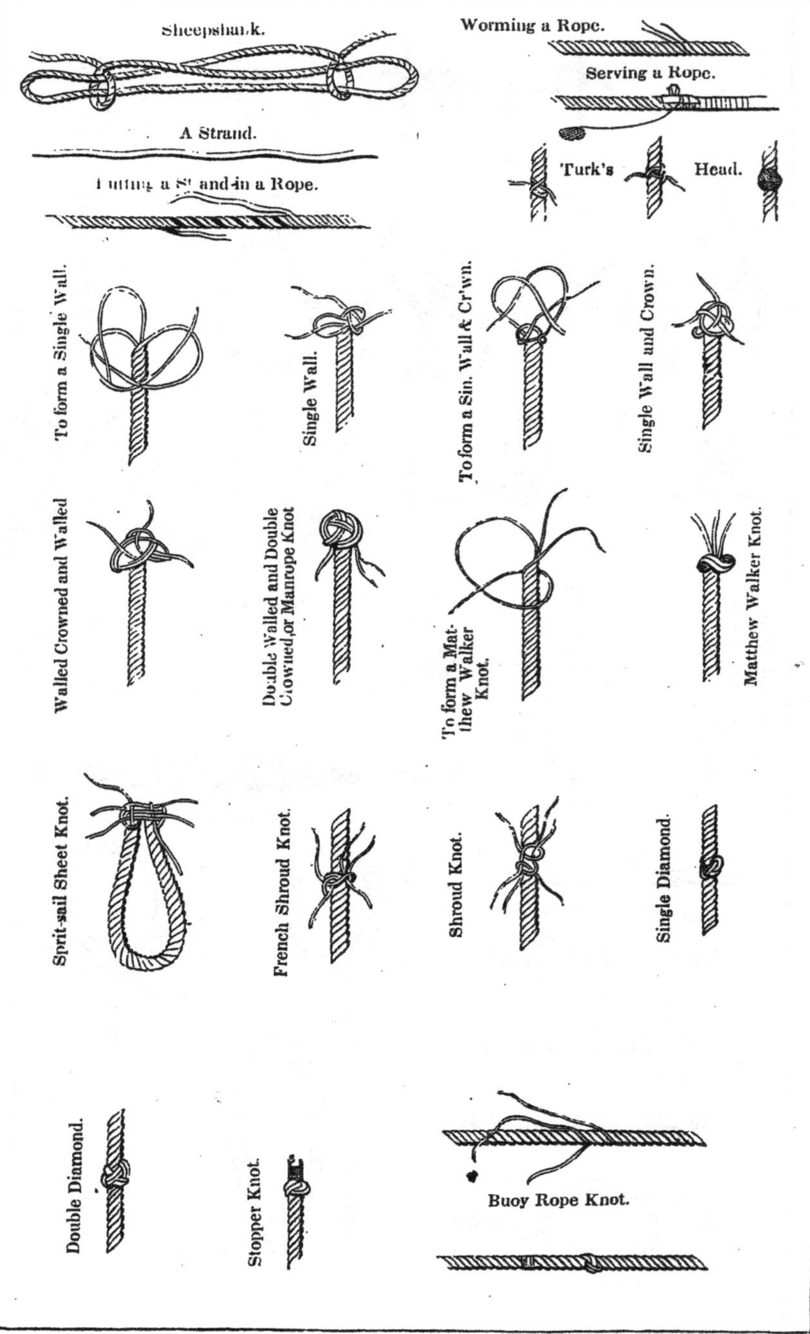
Sheepshank.
Worming a Rope.
Serving a Rope.
A Strand.
Putting a Strand in a Rope.
Turk's
Head.
To form a Single Wall.
Single Wall.
To form a Sin. Wall & Cr'wn.
Single Wall and Crown.
Walled Crowned and Walled
Double Walled and Double Crowned, or Manrope Knot
To form a Matthew Walker Knot.
Matthew Walker Knot.
Sprit-sail Sheet Knot.
French Shroud Knot.
Shroud Knot.
Single Diamond.
Double Diamond.
Stopper Knot.
Buoy Rope Knot.

19.—A ROLLING HITCH.

With the end of a rope take a half-hitch around the standing part; then take another through the same bight, jaming it in above the first hitch and the upper part of the bight, then haul it taut, and dog your end above the hitch, around the standing part, or you may take a half-hitch around the standing part and stop the end back with a yarn.

20.—A SALVAGEE STRAP.

To make a salvagee strap, you may get a couple of spike nails, and drive them into an old piece of plank, or whatever you can find convenient to answer the purpose, or get two hooks, lash them to any convenient place, as far apart as the length you intend to make the strap; take the end of the ball of rope-yarns, and make it fast to one of the spikes or hooks, then take it round the other one, and keep passing the rope-yarn round and round in this manner, hauling every turn taut as you pass it, until it is as stout as you wish it to be.

If it is to be a very large strap, marl it down with stout spun-yarn; if of middling size, marl with two single rope-yarns; if a small strap, a single rope-yarn.

21.—A PUDDING FOR A MAST OR YARD.

Take a piece of rope of the required length, and splice an eye in each end; get it on a stretch, worm it, and then parcel it according to the shape you want it. They are generally made as you see in the Plate, large in the middle, tapering gradually toward the ends, and made flat on the side that goes next the yard or mast. When you have got it the size required, marl it down, commencing in the middle and marling both ways until you come to the eye; if it is intended for a yard it is generally covered with thick leather or green hide; if for a mast, it is pointed over for neatness.

22.—A SHORT SPLICE.

To splice the two ends of a rope together, you first unlay the rope to a sufficient length, then crutch them together as you see in the plate; you must then lay hold of the three strands next to you in your left hand, holding them solid around the other part until you stick the three upper ends, or, if it is a large rope, you may stop the ends with a yarn; then take the upper or middle end, pass it over the first strand next to it, stick it underneath the second strand, and haul it taut in the lay of the rope; turn the rope a little towards you, and stick the second end as you did the first; the third in the same manner, hauling them taut along the lay of the rope;—turn the rope round, stick the other three ends in the same manner, and it will appear as in the plate.

Note.—If you intend to serve over the ends, you need not stick them but once; but if not you must stick them twice, and cross-whip them across the strands so as to make them more secure. If the ends are to be served, take a few of the underneath yarns, enough to fill up the lay of the rope for worming, then scrape or trim the outside ends, and marl them down ready for serving.

23.—A LONG SPLICE.

To make a long splice, unlay the ends of two ropes to a sufficient length, crutch them together in the same manner as a short splice; unlay one strand for a considerable length, and fill up the space which it leaves with the opposite strand next to it; then turn the rope round and lay hold of the two next strands that will come opposite their respective lays, unlay one and fill up with the other as before; then cut off the long strands, and it will appear as in the Plate.

To complete this splice, you will split the strands equally in two, then take the two opposite half strands and knot them together, so as to fill up the vacant lay; then you stick the ends twice under two strands with all six of the half strands, leaving the other six neutral; then stretch the splice well before you cut the ends off, and it is finished.

24.—EYE-SPLICE.

An eye-splice is made by opening the end of a rope, and laying the strands at any distance upon the standing part of the rope, according to the size of the eye-splice you intend to make; you then divide your strands by putting one strand on the top and one underneath the standing part, then take the middle strand, (having previously opened the lay with a marlinespike,) and stick it under its respective strand, as you see in the Plate. Your next end is taken over the first strand and under the second; the third and last end is taken through the third strand on the other side.

25.—A CUT SPLICE.

Cut a rope in two, and according to the size you intend to make the splice or collar—lay the end of one rope on the standing part of the other, and stick the end through between the strands, in the same manner as an eye-splice, and it will appear as in the plate. This forms a collar in the bight of a rope, and is used for pendants, jib-guys, breast-backstays, odd shrouds, &c.

26.—A FLEMISH EYE.

Unlay the end of a rope, open the strands and separate every yarn, divide them in two halves, then take a piece of round wood the size you intend to make the eye, and half-knot about one-half of the inside yarns over the piece of wood; scrape the remainder down over the others; marl, parcel, and serve, or if preferable, hitch it with hambro-line. This makes a snug eye for the collars of stays. (*See Plate.*)

27.—AN ARTIFICIAL EYE.

Take the end of a rope and unlay one strand to a certain distance, and form the eye by placing the two strands along the standing part of the rope and stopping them fast to it; then take the odd strand and cross it over the standing part, and lay it into the vacant place you took it from at first; work around the eye, filling up the vacant strand until it comes out at the crutch again, and lies under the other two strands; the ends are tapered, scraped down, marled, and served over with spun-yarn.

28.—TO WORM AND SERVE A ROPE.

Worming a rope, is to fill up the vacant space between the strands of the rope with spun-yarn; this is done in order to strengthen it, and to render the surface smooth and round for parceling.

Parceling a rope is wrapping old canvass round it, cut in strips from two to three inches wide, according to the size of the rope; the strips of canvass to be well tarred and rolled up in rolls before you commence to lay it on the rope. The service is of spun-yarn, clapped on by a wooden mallet such as you see in the plate, called a serving mallet; it has a large score cut in the under part of it, so as to fay on the rope, and a handle about a foot long, or according to the size of the mallet. The service is always laid on against the lay of the rope; a boy passes the ball of spun-yarn at some distance from the man that is serving the rope, and passes it round as he turns the mallet; when the required length of service is put on, the end is put under the three or four last turns of the service and hauled taut.

Note.—It has always been customary to put on parceling with the lay of the rope in all cases; but rigging that you do not intend to serve over, the parceling ought to be put on the contrary way.

29.—TO CLAP ON A THROAT AND QUARTER SEIZING.

Splice an eye in one end of the seizing, and take the other end round both parts of the rope that the seizing is to be put on; then reeve it through the eye, pass a couple of turns and heave them hand-taut; then make a *marlinespike-hitch* on the seizing, by taking a turn with the seizing over the marlinespike, and laying the end over the standing part; push the marlinespike down through, then under the standing part and up through the bight again. Heave taut the two turns of the seizing with the spike; pass the rest and heave them taut in the same manner, making six, eight, or ten turns, according to the size of the rope; then pass the end through the last turn, and pass the riding turns, five, seven, or nine, always laying one less of the riding than of the first turns; these should not be hove too taut—the end is now passed up through the seizing, and two cross-turns taken between the two parts of the rope, and round the seizing; take the end under the last turn and heave it taut; make an overhanded knot on the end of the seizing, and cut off close to the knot.

Note.—When this is put on the end of a rope, and round the standing part, it is called an end-seizing; if on the two parts below the end, a middle or quarter-seizing. A throat-seizing is passed the same way, but is not crossed with the end of the seizing.

30.—TO MAKE A TURK'S HEAD.

Turk's heads are made on man-ropes, and sometimes on the foot-ropes of jib-booms in place of an overhanded knot, as the Turk's head is much neater than the knot, and considered by some an ornament. It is generally made of small white line. Take a round turn round the rope you intend to make the Turk's head on,—cross the bights on each side of the round turn, and stick one end under one cross, and the other under the other cross; it will then be formed like the middle figure in the plate, after which follow the lead until it shows three parts all round, and it is completed.

31.—TO SHEEPSHANK A ROPE OR BACKSTAY.

This is intended for shortening a backstay; the rope is doubled in three parts, as you see in the Plate, and a hitch taken over each bight with the standing part of the backstay and jamed taut.

32.—TO PUT A STRAND IN A ROPE.

This is done in case of one strand of a rope getting chafed or magged, and the other two remaining good. To perform this, you take your knife and cut the strand at the place where it is chafed, and unlay it about a couple of feet each way; then take a strand of a rope as near the size as possible, and lay it in the vacancy of the rope, (as you see in the Plate,) and stick the ends the same as a long splice.

33.—TO WALL AND CROWN.

Unlay the end of a rope, and with the three strands form a wall knot, by taking the first strand and forming a bight; take the next strand, and bring it round the end of the first, the third strand round the second, and up through the bight of the first—this is a wall. (*See Plate.*)

To crown this, lay one end over the top of the knot, which call the first, then lay the second over it, the third over the second, and through the bight of the first. It will then appear as you see in Plate No. 3.

34.—TO MAKE A MATHEW WALKER.

A Mathew Walker is made by opening the end of a rope, and taking the first strand round the rope and through its own bight; then take the second end round the rope underneath, through the bight of the first, and through its own bight; the third end take round the same way, underneath and through the bights of all three. Haul the ends well taut, and it will appear as in the Plate. This is a good lanyard knot, if well made.

35.—A SPRITSAIL SHEET KNOT.

Unlay two ends of a rope, and place the two parts which are unlaid together; form a bight with one strand, and wall the six together against the lay of the rope, (which is hawser-laid,) the same as you would a single wall with three ends; after you have walled with the six ends, haul them taut; you must then crown with the six ends, and it will appear as in the Plate. To complete it, you must follow the lead of the parts, and double wall and crown it.

This knot is frequently used in old-fashioned ships as a stopper knot.

36.—A SHROUD KNOT.

Unlay the ends of two ropes and place them one within the other, the same as you commence to make a short splice; then single wall the ends of one rope round the standing part of the other, and then wall the other three ends in the same manner; the ends are opened out, tapered down, and served over with spun-yarn. This knot is used when a shroud is either shot or carried away.

37.—A FRENCH SHROUD KNOT.

Place the ends of two ropes as before, drawing them close together; then lay the first three ends back upon their own part, and single wall the other three ends round the bights of the other three and the standing part; it will then appear like the figure in the Plate. The ends are tapered as the other. This knot is much neater than the common shroud knot.

38.—SINGLE DIAMOND KNOT.

Unlay the end of a rope a sufficient length to make the knot, and with the three strands form three bights, holding the ends fast down the side of the rope in your left hand, with the standing part of the rope; then take the first strand over the bight of the second strand and through the bight of the third; then take the second over the third and through the bight of the first; then the third, over the first and through the second. Haul these taut and lay the ends of the strands up again, and it will appear as in the Plate. This knot is used for jib-boom foot-ropes, man-ropes, &c.

39.—DOUBLE DIAMOND KNOT.

To make this, you make a single one as before; then take a marlinespike and open the strands, and follow the lead through two single bights, the ends coming out at the top of the knot; lay the ends of the strands up as before, and it will appear as in the Plate.

40.—A STOPPER KNOT

Is made by double-walling and crowning, which has been described before on another page. The ends, if very short, are whipped without being laid up; but if long they are laid up and stopped.

41.—A BUOY-ROPE KNOT.

Unlay the strands of a cable-laid rope, take one strand out of the large ones, and then lay the three large ones up again as before; take the three small ones which were left out, single and double them round the standing part of the rope; then take your spare ends, worm them along the lay and stop them.

42.—COMMON SENNIT.

Sennit is made by plaiting rope-yarns together. (*See Plate No.* 4.)

43.—A SEA GASKET.

A sea gasket is made by taking three or four foxes, according to the size you intend to make the gasket. Middle them over a belaying-pin, and plait three or four together, long enough to make the eye; then clasp both parts together to form the eye; then plait it by bringing the outside foxes on each side alternately over to the middle; the outside one is laid witb the right hand, and the remainder held steadily—work the whole together, adding a fox when necessary. When you have got it a sufficient length, diminish by dropping a fox at proper intervals. To finish it, you must lay one end up, leaving its bight down; then plait the others through this bight about one inch; haul the bight taut to secure all parts—cut the ends off, whip it, and it is completed.

44.—A PANCH, OR WROUGHT MAT.

A piece of six or nine-thread stuff is stretched in a horizontal direction, and the foxes (according to the breadth you intend to make the mat) are middled and hung over it; then take the fox nearest the left hand and twist a turn in the two parts, and one part give to the man opposite (two men being employed to work the mat); the next fox has a turn twisted in its two parts, and one part given back to your partner; the remainder are twisted round the first which are given back, and then again round its own part, and so on with the remainder of the foxes, until you get it the breadth you wish. At the bottom of the mat selvedge it by taking a piece of nine-thread stuff, the same as you used for the top. The two parts of the foxes which are twisted together at the bottom are divided, and the nine-thread put between them; the foxes are hitched round it, and the end put through its own lay with a marlinespike; trim the ends off, and thrum it with pieces of old strands of rope, cut in pieces about three or four inches long; open the lays of the foxes with a marlinespike, push the thrums through the lays, and open the ends out.

45.—HARBOR GASKET, OR FRENCH SENNIT.

A harbor gasket is made with foxes, something similar to the common sea gasket,—but instead of taking the outside fox over all the rest, and bringing it into the middle, you interweave it between them by taking the outside fox of both sides, and taking it over one and under the other, working it towards the middle, the same as common sennit.

46.—POINTING A ROPE.

Unlay the end of the rope a sufficient length for pointing, and stop it; open the strands out into yarns, and take out as many as you think it will require to make the knittles, by splitting the yarns and making one knittle out of every outside yarn; when they are made, stop them back on the standing part of the rope; then form the point with the rest of the yarns, by trimming and scraping them down to a proper size, and marl it down with twine—divide the knittles, taking every other one up and every other one down; then take a piece of twine, called the warp, and with it pass these turns very taut, taking a hitch with the last turn every time you pass the warp, or filling. Then take the knittles which are up and bring them down, and the ones which are down, up; hauling them taut, and passing the warp every time over the lower knittles; proceed in this manner until you get almost to the end, reserving enough of the knittles to finish it with; leave out every other bight of the knittles of the last lay, and pass the warp through the bight, haul them taut and cut them off. A becket is sometimes worked in the end.

Note.—Knittles are made by laying rope-yarns together, with your finger and thumb, against the twist of the yarn.

Snaking is for the better securing of a seizing, which is passed round the single part of the rope and therefore cannot be crossed. It is done by tucking the end part of the seizing *under* and *over* the lower and upper turns of the seizing.

47.—TO MAKE A GROMMET.

A grommet is made by unlaying a strand of a rope and placing one part over the other; with the long end follow the lay, until it forms a ring, with three parts of the strand all round; finish it by knotting and sticking the ends the same as a long splice. (*See plate No.* 4.)

48.—TO PASS A ROSE LASHING.

It is used in lashing a strap or pudding round a mast or yard or the parral lashing of a top-gallant yard; this lashing is passed crossways over and under one eye, then under and over the other; the end part is afterwards taken in a circular form round the crossing, and the end tucked under the last part.

Note.—This circular part is done to expend the end, instead of cutting it off, so that it will answer again for the same purpose.

49.—TO WEAVE A SWORD MAT.

A piece of wood called a sword is used; this is put alternately between the parts of the spun-yarn or sennit, stretched over two round iron bolts (as you see in the figure); the warp of marline is placed through the parts which the sword has opened, and jamed by it close to the head; a piece of spun-yarn is put slack through the same division at the opposite end and left there; the sword is taken out, passed under and over the parts as before, and each end of the warp passed and jamed taut. The piece of spun-yarn which was left at the opposite end, is now lifted up, and brings the parts as they were first divided by the sword; the warp is passed as before, and so on until the mat is completed.

50.—A LASHING CLEAT

Is shaped like the figure in the Plate, having scores for the seizings which are marked, and a groove cut in the part that fits next to the shroud.

BLOCKS.

51.—A SHELL, PIN, AND SHEAVE.

Blocks are of different kinds, shapes, and sizes, according to the several purposes for which they are intended.

A block consists of a shell, sheave, and pin; and from the number of these sheaves it derives its name, viz.: a block with one sheave is called single; with two sheaves, double; with three, treble; and with four sheaves it is called a four-fold block. The shell of a block is made of ash, and has one or two scores cut at each end, according to its size; these scores are for the purpose of admitting a strap, which goes round the block, in the centre of which is a hole for the pin; the shell is hollow inside to admit the sheave. The sheave is a solid wheel, made of lignum vitæ, iron, or brass; in the centre is a hole for the pin, on which it turns. The lignum vitæ sheave is bushed with brass or iron; round the circumference a groove is cut, that the rope which goes over it may play with ease. The sheave is placed in the shell, and the pin is put through both shell and sheave, which constitute a block.

52.—SINGLE, DOUBLE, AND TREBLE BLOCKS.

What is termed a single block has but one sheave, and if intended for a double strap there are two scores on the outside of the shell. Single blocks are more used than any other kind on board of a ship.

A double block has an additional sheave; it is otherwise the same as a single block.

A treble block is made in the same manner as a double, with one more sheave. Treble blocks are generally used as purchase blocks, and strapped in the manner you see in the Plate.

53.—A SHOULDER BLOCK.

A shoulder block is the same as a single block, with the exception that it has a projection at the bottom of the shell, called

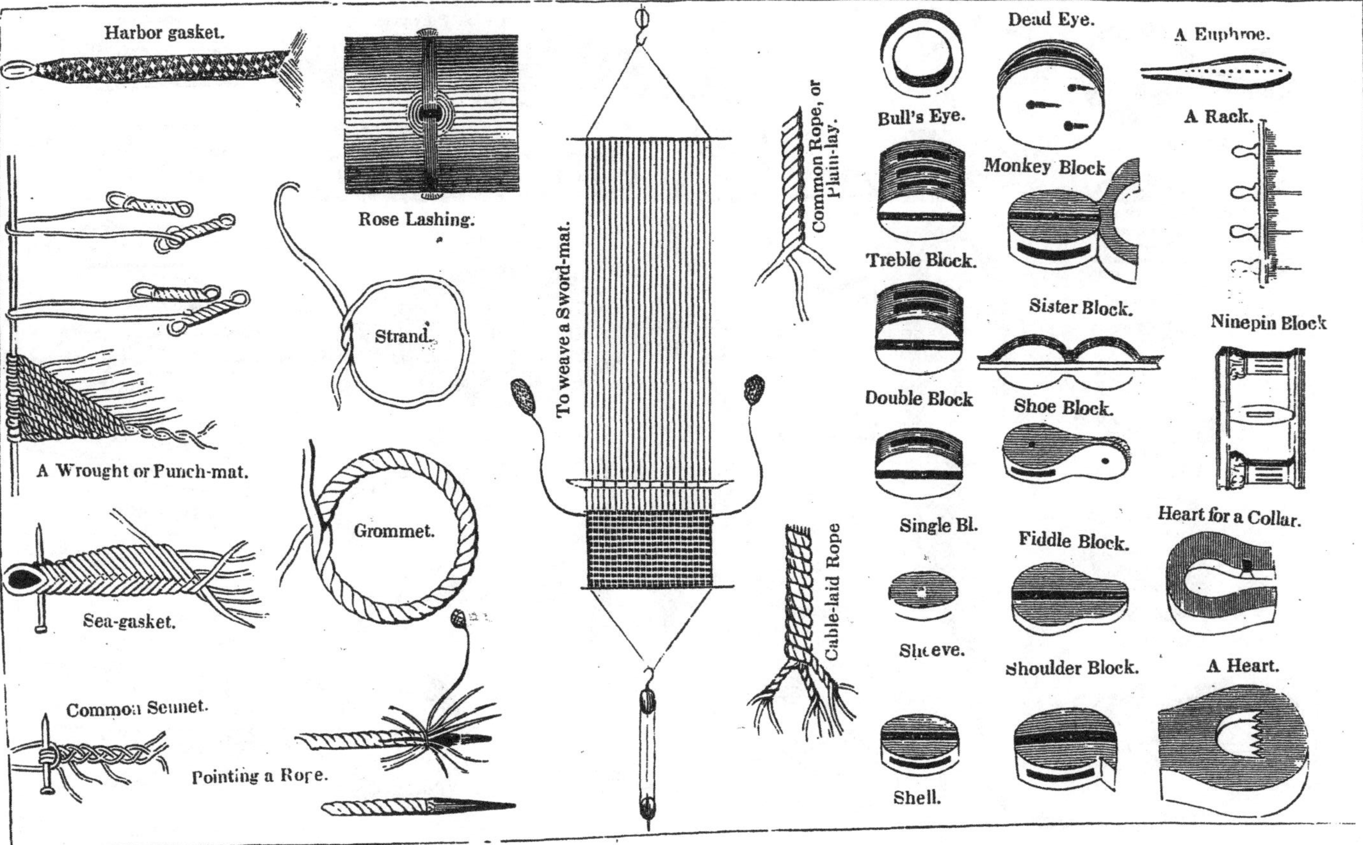
Harbor gasket.
Rose Lashing.
Strand.
A Wrought or Punch-mat.
Grommet.
Sea-gasket.
Common Sennet.
Pointing a Rope.
To weave a Sword-mat.
Common Rope, or Plain-lay.
Cable-laid Rope
Bull's Eye.
Dead Eye.
A Euphroe.
A Rack.
Monkey Block
Treble Block.
Sister Block.
Ninepin Block
Double Block
Shoe Block.
Single Bl.
Fiddle Block.
Heart for a Collar.
Sheeve.
Shoulder Block.
A Heart.
Shell.

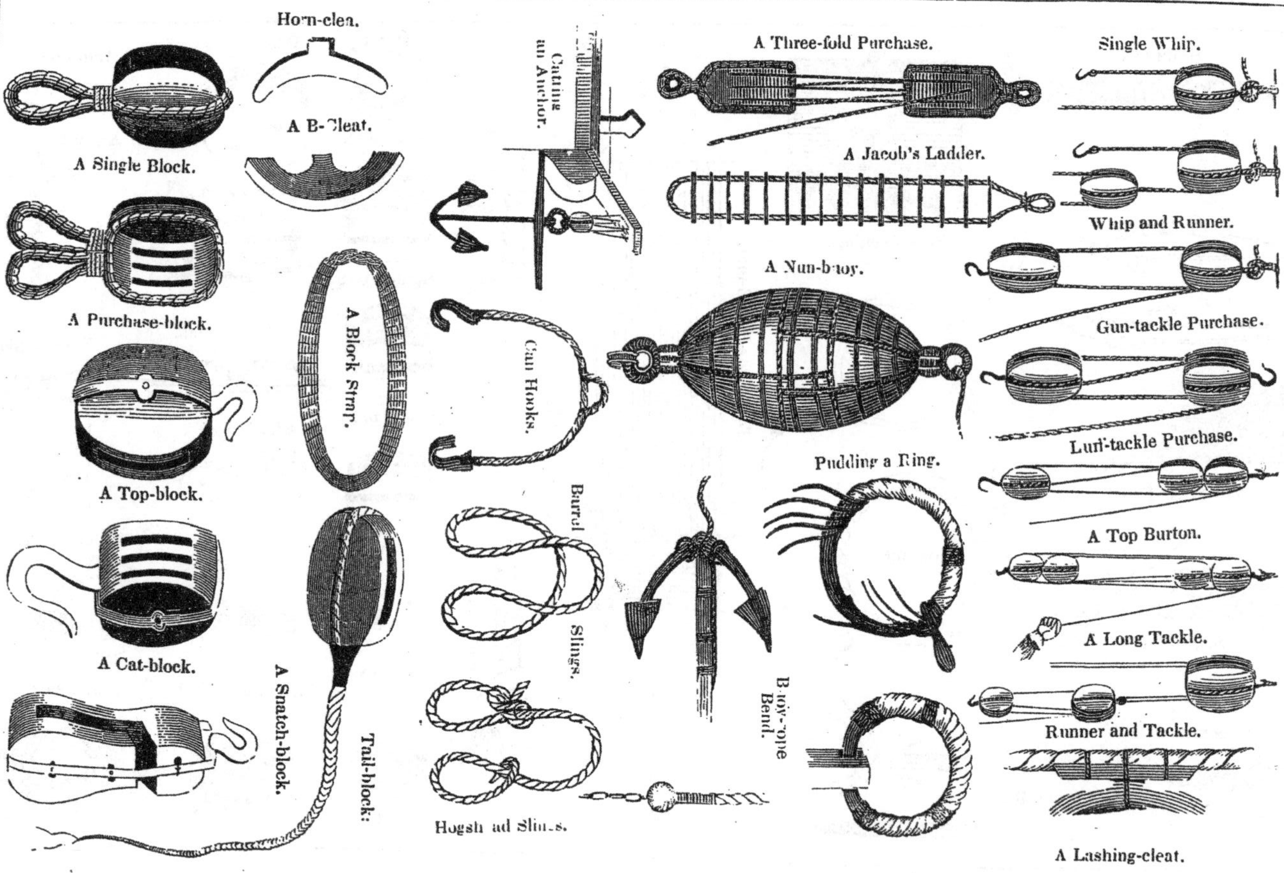
Single Whip.
Whip and Runner.
Gun-tackle Purchase.
Luff-tackle Purchase.
A Top Burton.
A Long Tackle.
Runner and Tackle.
A Lashing-cleat.
A Three-fold Purchase.
A Jacob's Ladder.
A Nun-buoy.
Pudding a Ring.
Buoy-rope Bend.
Catting an Anchor.
Can Hooks.
Barrel Slings.
Hogshead Slings.
Horn-cleat.
A B-Cleat.
A Block Strap.
Tail-block.
A Snatch-block.
A Single Block.
A Purchase-block.
A Top-block.
A Cat-block.

a shoulder, to prevent the rope that reeves through it from jamming between the block and the yard. These blocks are mostly used for bumkin or lift blocks on lower vards.

54.—A FIDDLE BLOCK

Is made like two single blocks one above the other, the upper one being the largest so as to allow the rope which is rove in the upper sheave, to play clear of the rope in the under one. These blocks are used in places where there is not space enough for a double one, or where it (the double block) would be liable to split by not *canting* fair, or having room to play. These blocks are used for top burtons, &c. &c.

55.—A SHOE BLOCK

Is also made like two single blocks, but the sheave of the upper one lies in a contrary direction to that of the lower one. They are generally used as buntline blocks to courses; the buntline reeving in the upper sheave, and the whip in the lower one.

56.—A SISTER BLOCK

Has two sheave-holes one above the other,—three scores for seizings, one at each end, and one between both sheaves; they are hollowed out on each side of the shell, to take the shroud. These blocks are used as topsail-lift and reef-tackle blocks, and are seized-in between the two forward shrouds of the topmast rigging, above the futtock stave. The lift reeves through the lower sheave, and the topsail reef-tackle through the upper one.

57.—A DEAD-EYE

Is a large round piece of wood with three holes in it, (as you see in the Plate,) and a groove cut round it for the shroud to lie in. It is used to turn in the ends of shrouds and backstays;—the three holes are used to reeve the lanyard through, when setting up the shroud or backstay.

A bull's-eye is a kind of thick wooden thimble, with a hole in the centre, and a groove cut round the outside for the rope o seizing to lay in.

58.—A HEART

Is a block of wood with a large hole in the centre, at the bottom of which are four or five scores, and round the outside is a groove cut to admit a rope called a stay; there are other hearts called collar-hearts, which are open at the lower ends, opposite to which the lanyard is passed. This heart has a double score cut round the outside, and two grooves cut on each side for the seizings to lay in, which keeps the collar in the scores of the heart. Hearts intended for bobstays should be made of lignum vitæ; those made of ash being liable to split.

59.—A BELAYING-PIN RACK

Is a piece of wood with a number of holes through it, in which belaying-pins are stuck; on the back part are several scores for the shrouds to lie in to which it is seized.

60.—A EUPHROE

Is a long piece of wood, having a number of holes, through which the legs of the crowfoot is rove,—a score is cut round it to admit of a strap. This is used for the ridge of an awning.

61.—A HORN CLEAT.

Horn cleats are used for different purposes; some are made to seize on to the shrouds; they are called *lashing cleats;* others are made to nail on to different parts of the bulwarks. They are of different shape and size, and used to belay various ropes to, in all parts of the ship.

62.—A B-CLEAT

Is a piece of wood scored out inside, something like the letter B, and rounded off outside; they are used for leading a rope through, or for keeping it in its place on the masts, bowsprit, &c.

63.—A STRAP FOR A BLOCK.

Straps are fitted in various ways, according to the use they are intended for, and according to the size of the block.

A common strap is fitted in the following manner:—

First, cut the rope once-and-a-half the round of the block, then get it on a stretch,—worm, parcel, and serve as near the end as possible, not to interfere with splicing; then splice the ends together with a short splice, and finish serving snug up to the splice. Stretch it and cut the ends off, or you may serve over the ends, and it will appear as in the Plate. If there is a number of those straps required, it would be best to get the rope on a stretch, and serve off the required number before cutting.

64.—A TAIL BLOCK

Is strapped with an eye-splice, snug round the block; the ends are stuck but once; then scraped down, and served over with spun-yarn. Clap on a stout whipping about six inches from the splice; open the ends out, twist them into foxes, and plait them together, as mentioned for gaskets; or, the strands may be opened out and marled down salvagee fashion; tapering it a little towards the end of the tail.

Note.—Blocks used for jiggers, have a double tail made in the same manner.

65.—A PURCHASE BLOCK

Is double strapped, having two scores in the shell for that purpose; the strap is wormed, parceled, and served, (sometimes only wormed and parceled,) and spliced together. It is then doubled so as to bring the splice at the bottom of the block. The seizing is put on the same as any other; the only difference is, that it is crossed both ways, through the double parts of the strap.

These block-straps are so large and stiff, that it requires a purchase to set them securely in the scores of the block, and bring them into their proper place.

66.—A TOP BLOCK

Is a single iron-bound hook-block, with (generally) a brass sheave; it hooks to an eye-bolt in the cap. The top-pendants are rove through the top-blocks when swaying up topmasts.

67.—A CAT BLOCK.

The cat block is three-fold, iron-bound, with a large iron hook attached to it, for the purpose of hooking the ring of the anchor when catting it.

On the forward side of the shell of this block are two small eye-bolts, for the purpose of fitting a small rope, called the back-rope bridle, used in hooking the cat.

68.—A SNATCH BLOCK

Is generally iron-bound, with a swivel hook; an iron clasp is fitted on the iron band, or strap, with a hinge to go over the snatch, and toggles on the opposite side, as you see in the Plate. The bight of a hawser or large rope is placed in this block, when warping the ship, &c.

Note.—There has been of late years several different improvements made on these blocks.

Blocks of this description, and of a large size, are generally termed "viol, or rouse-about blocks."

69.—A NUN BUOY.

Buoys are used when a ship is riding at anchor, to denote the position of the anchor. They are a kind of a cask, large in the middle, and small at both ends; hooped close with iron hoops, and strapped with rope well served. A buoy-strap is cut *nine times* the length of the buoy; this is sufficient to make the slings and hoops; the slings have an eye spliced in each end, the hoops are rove through these eyes, spliced together, and fitted on the buoy, as you see in the Plate.

70.—TO BEND A BUOY-ROPE.

The buoy rope is made fast with a clove-hitch round the arms of the anchor, close up to the crown, and the end part stopped along the shank, with one or two stops.

Some are fitted with a running eye, and when used this way the running eye is rove round one arm, a hitch taken over the other. and seized in the cross.

In large ships they are fitted with pendants and slip buoy-ropes; the pendants have a large thimble spliced in one end, large enough to receive a stout hawser, in case you should want to purchase the anchor by the buoy-rope. The size for the slip buoy-rope is one-third the size of the proper buoy-rope.

71.—TO PUDDING THE RING OF AN ANCHOR.

The ring of the anchor is well tarred, and parceled with tarred canvass; then a number of lengths of old rope are cut three times the diameter of the ring; these are laid on the ring, and stopped by a temporary seizing in the middle; they are then placed fair by hand round the rings, as you see in the Plate.

When one or two turns of rattling-stuff is taken round all parts, and a heaver put through it, it is hove well round, which stretches all parts snug round the ring. After it is all hove on neatly, put on the seizings, four in number. (*See Plate.*)

72.—A JACOB'S LADDER.

These ladders are used in many different parts of a ship of war; they are used for stern ladders, rigging ladders, and on the swinging booms in harbor, &c. There are several different ways of making them; some are made salvagee fashion, and covered; others are made of four-stranded rope, and have the rounds put through between the strands of the rope. But the most general way of making these ladders, is to take some small rope, (about two-inch stuff,) and make two straps the length you intend to make the ladder, and splice them together with a short-long-splice. The straps being made, get them on a stretch both together, and see if they bear an equal strain; if not, shorten one strap, so as to make both alike. Take a piece of chalk and mark off where you intend the rounds to go, about fifteen inches apart.

The *rounds* are pieces of round wood, about two inches in diameter, of the length required, with a score on each end, for the rope to lay in. Put the rounds in between both parts of the rope, exactly at the chalk mark; having got them all placed, commence and seize them in, by putting on a snug seizing of marline on each side of the round; you may parcel, leather, or serve in the nips, just as may be preferred.

73.—CAN HOOKS

Are broad flat iron hooks, in the eyes of which thimbles are inserted. What is termed a pair of can hooks, is a piece of rope four or five feet long, or long enough to span a cask from chime to chime. When fitted, one of these hooks are spliced into the end of this rope; it is then got on a stretch, wormed, parceled and served, and a thimble is sometimes seized in the bight, to hook on to, when lifting a cask.

Note.—Some are fitted with chain, with a large iron ring in the middle.

74.—HOGSHEAD SLINGS

Is a piece of rope about five fathoms long, and from five to six inches in circumference, with a large thimble spliced in one end, and the other end well whipped. They are used to sling large casks, being more secure than can hooks. They are put on in this manner:—pass the bight over one end of the cask, reeve the end through the thimble, and haul it well taut; then take the end round the other end of the cask, and take two half-hitches round the standing part, and it is done. (*See Plate.*)

75.—BARREL SLINGS

Are generally made of three inch rope, and of sufficient length to go round the barrel. They are similar to a long strap, spliced together with a short splice; it is passed round the barrel and one bight rove through the other.

They are sometimes made long enough to sling two or three barrels at a time.

76.—A SINGLE WHIP.

A single whip is the smallest and most simple purchase in use. It is made by reeving a rope through a single block, as you see in the Plate.

77.—A GUN-TACKLE PURCHASE

Is made by reeving a rope through a single block, then through another single block, and make the end fast to the one it was first rove through, or splice it into the bottom of the block for neatness. (*See Plate.*)

78.—A LUFF-TACKLE PURCHASE

Consists of a double and single block; the rope is rove through one of the sheave holes of the double block, then through the single one, through the double one again, and the end made fast to the single block, with a becket bend, to a becket in the bottom of the block. (*See Plate.*)

79.—A TOP BURTON

Is rove in the same manner as a luff-tackle purchase; the only difference is, that the upper block of the burton is a fiddle block, while that of the luff is a double one. (*See Plate.*)

80.—WHIP AND RUNNER.

If a rope is rove through a single block, it is called a whip, as before mentioned; and if the fall of this whip be spliced round the block of another whip, it becomes whip on whip, or whip and runner. (*See Plate.*)

81.—A RUNNER AND TACKLE

Is the same purchase as a luff-tackle applied to a runner. A runner is a large rope rove through a single block, with a hook spliced in one end. (*See Plate.*)

82.—A TWO-FOLD PURCHASE

Consists of two double blocks; the fall is first rove through one sheave of the upper block, then through one of the lower ones; through the upper one again, then through the lower one, and make the end fast to the upper block.

83.—A THREE-FOLD PURCHASE.

A three-fold purchase is rove in this way, the blocks having one more sheave, only that you commence to reeve the fall in the middle sheave first,—instead of one of the side ones, which brings a cross in the fall. The reason of its being rove in this manner, is, that the heaviest strain comes first on the fall part, and if it was rove in the side sheave, it would have a tendency to *cant the block in the strap*, split the shell of the block, and cut the fall; but when it is in the middle sheave it draws all down square alike.

84.—NAMES OF ROPES.

The different kinds of ropes are designated as follows:—

Hawser-laid and cable-laid rope is all the same; it is composed of nine strands, each strand having an equal number of yarns. These nine strands are laid into three, by twisting three small ones into one large one; then the three large ones are laid up, or twisted together left-handed, which makes the nine strands; this is a hawser-laid, or cabled, rope.

A common or plain rope is composed of three strands, of an equal number of yarns twisted together.

Shroud-laid rope is made in the same manner, only that it consists of four strands instead of three, and a small strand which runs through the middle, termed the heart of the rope. When plain-laid rope is laid up left-handed, it is called *back-laid rope.* There is also four stranded hawser-laid rope, which is used for stays, &c. &c.

PART II.

85.—LAUNCHING A SHIP.

After the carpenters have completed the hull of the vessel, the necessary preparations for launching are commenced as follows :—

Get an anchor on each bow ; get the cables on board and bend them to the anchors ; range and bitt the cables ; bend the buoy ropes, and see everything clear for letting go the anchors.

It will then be necessary to get four stout hawsers on the spar deck, two on each side ; bend one to the other, and have them coiled down clear for running. This being done, pass the ends of two hawsers out forward, through the warping chocks on each bow ; pass the ends aft, one on each side, and make them fast to some secure place, on their respective sides of the launching slip, as clear of the ways as possible. Stop the bights of the hawsers with a single rope-yarn up along the ship's sides, so as not to interfere with the ways, or interrupt the progress of the carpenters while knocking away the shores previous to launching.

Have men stationed to attend to veering the hawsers and cables when the ship is off the ways, and also to letting go the anchors, if necessary. Have a few buckets of water ready to throw on the bitts, to prevent any danger that might occur from fire while veering the hawsers and cables.

The ways being well greased, and the necessary preparations for launching completed, all the blocks and wedges by which the ship was formerly supported, are driven out from under her keel, until the whole weight gradually subsides upon the sliding ways, or cradle ; a few shores, or stanchions, remain, by which she is retained on the stocks until the period for launching arrives, which is generally at high water ; they are then cut away, and all obstructions removed, with the exception of the *dogshore* (a representation of which is given in the Plate). The word is given "to *launch*"—the dogshore is then knocked away, which causes her to advance down the inclined plane into the water.

If the ship should *hang* after the dogshore is removed, it will be necessary to apply screws under the fore-foot, which will cause her to move immediately along the ways. The ways generally extend a sufficient depth under the surface of the water to float the vessel when she arrives at the extreme ends.

When the ship is off the stocks "veer away roundly," and do not attempt to check her until she begins to *deaden her way*, then check her "handsomely" with the hawsers so as not to part them; if, however, they should part, let go an anchor immediately; if that should not bring her up, let go the other anchor, and veer gradually on both *cables* until she is brought up.

Note.—When a ship is to be launched it is always customary to hoist the ensign, jack, and pennant; the jack forward, ensign aft, and the pennant amidships. Flagstaffs are erected for that purpose previous to launching, as represented in the Plate, where you see a ship of war ready to be launched from the stocks.

86.—CUTTING OUT STANDING RIGGING.

Lower Rigging.—Measure the distance from the larboard side of the mast-head to the foremost dead-eye in the starboard channels, which distance set off on the floor of the rigging loft and stick in a marlinespike at each extremity. The shroud stuff being stretched, stop one end to one of the marlinespikes; take the bight round the other and back again: this is the first pair of shrouds; pass it round again, *outside at each end*, for the second pair, and continue in this manner until one gang of rigging is completed. Mark the length of the eyes straight across at the *opposite end*, to the one stopped to the marlinespike; cut at the latter in an angular direction (so that the after-legs will be a little longer than the forward ones), and the inside pair will be the first pair of shrouds. Hitch a piece of spun-yarn round each shroud, in the centre of the eye, making knots on it according to the number of the shroud, commencing the inside pair with one knot. The mark for the length of the eye gives the place for the eye-seizing; the round of the rope giving their place on the mast-head. (*Old fashion.*)

The proportion for the eye is the round of the mast-head above the bolsters; I have also seen the breadth of the seizing added (some allow five squares of the mast-head, which is the best rule), supposing it would lay fairer on the side of the bolsters than too close to the mast-head. This precaution is hardly necessary, as the rigging will stretch sufficiently in pulling up to bring the seizing down, no matter how much it may have been stretched before being warped round for cutting.

Rigging cut on the above old plan, causes great waste in squaring off the ends, after fitting the eyes, previous to turning-in the dead-eyes. I would therefore recommend (if not in a great

A Ship ready for Launching.

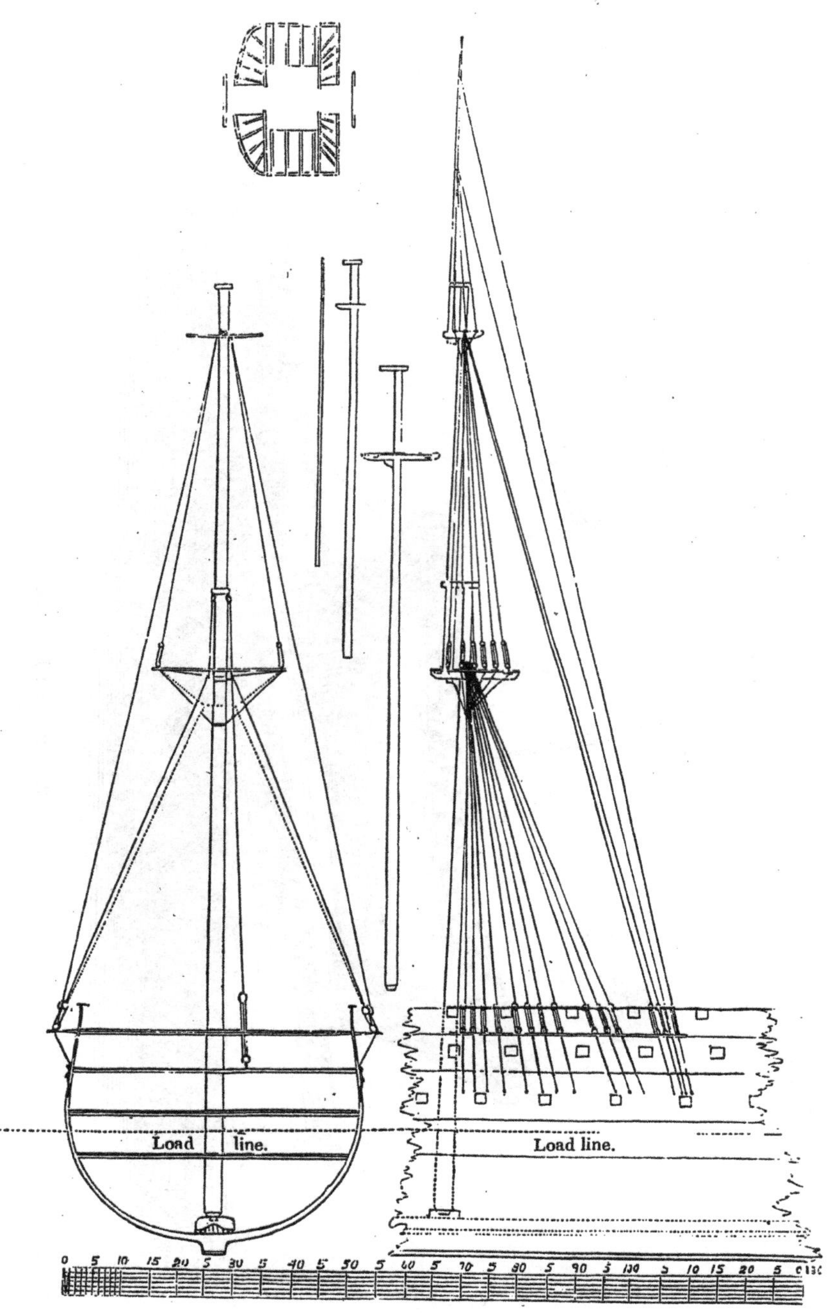

Sketch of a draft for cutting rigging.

hurry) a more economical plan. Get the shroud-warp on a stretch, or rather one end of it, long enough for one pair of shrouds; mark off the distance for the required service, and when completed—being wormed, parceled, and served, while on a taut stretch—measure the length with a tape-line, from *draft* of first pair of shrouds, No. 1 starboard; when measured and chalked the required length, "come up the stretch," and cut at the chalk-mark; middle the shroud at the centre of the service, and lay it on the loft floor. Continue fitting, and cutting, in this way until you get the number of shrouds required for the gang, allowing each pair of shrouds to lap over the diameter of the rope at the eye, as they are laid on the loft floor; alternately making due allowance at the ends, before cutting, for the carry aft, or the jump of a port, if required. (*See Plate.*)

Note.—In measuring the length of the shrouds, some prefer the distance from the opposite side of the mast-head to the partners, added to half the breadth of the deck, from the mast to the side.

In parceling, begin at each end where the service is to leave off, and parcel upwards to the middle of the eye, where commence serving downwards on each leg. The eye seizings are round ones, and when put on, the whole eye is neatly covered with parceling. A half-sister block is sometimes put between the two forward shrouds, for the lower boom topping lift to lead through.

87.—TOPMAST AND TOP-GALLANT RIGGING

Is cut in the same manner. In fitting the topmast rigging, always seize-in a sister-block between the two forward shrouds, for the topsail lift and reef tackles. The swifters are generally served the whole length.

The eyes of the top-gallant rigging are made to fit exactly around the cylinder; if there is an odd topmast, or top-gallant shroud, on each side, they are either fitted with a horse-shoe-eye, or go together with a cut splice.

88.—BREAST AND STANDING BACKSTAYS.

These may be cut by the same rule; the eyes of the breast backstays are fitted in different ways. They are sometimes spanned together, making a square, the size of the mast-head; sometimes they have an eye like the shrouds, made to fit close; and others have a small eye seized in the bight, and lashed round the mast-head. The eyes of the standing backstays are fitted like those of the shrouds.

89.—CAT HARPEN LEGS, AND FUTTOCK SHROUDS.

Take one-third the breadth of the top, and lay of that distance from the eye-seizing, down upon the shrouds, each side; draw a line across which will represent the cat harpens, and measured on the scale, will give their length; splice in eyes at each end; worm, parcel, serve, and leather them. The distance from the extremity of the top and this line upon the shroud, will give the length of the futtock shrouds, which must have a hook and thimble in their upper ends, and a thimble in their lower ends.

90.—FORE-AND-AFT STAYS.

Measure from the after parts of the mast-head to where the stays set up, and to this distance add the length of the mast-head, for collars.

Collars for stays are the length of their respective mast-heads. The mousings are raised once-and-a-half the size of the stays, and at a distance equal to twice the length of the mast-head from the mousing. A Flemish eye is worked on the end, and the stay rove through it; or they may be fitted with lashing eyes, in which case each leg is the length of the mast-head; the service is continued the length of the eye below the mousing, the collars leathered, and the hearts turned in with the lay of the rope. Stays are wormed, parcelled, served, and leathered in the wake of all nipps, such as the bees, bullock-blocks, and sheave-holes.

91.—CUTTING LOWER MAST HEAD-PENDANTS.

The forward pair should be twice the length of the mast-head —the after pair twice-and-a-half; thimbles are spliced in the ends, and they are wormed or spanned together, so as to form a span to fit the mast-head.

92.—BOBSTAYS.

The bobstays are cut twice the length from the collars, on the bowsprit, to their respective holes on the cutwater. They are wormed, parceled, and served the whole length, and leathered in the nipp, after which they are rove through the holes, spliced together, and the dead eyes turned in, in the wake of a splice.

93.—BOWSPRIT SHROUDS.

The length from the bowsprit to the eye-bolts in the bows; a dead-eye or heart is spliced into one end, and a hook and thimble in the other.

94.—JIB AND FLYING JIB GUYS.

Take the distance from the boom-end to the bows, making a small allowance for reeving through the straps on the spritsail yard. They are generally fitted with a cuckold's neck over the boom end, and set up with dead-eyes to the bows. The cuckold's neck is served or covered with canvass. The guys in the wake of the spritsail yard are leathered. The martingales must be cut, and fitted to the manner in which they are rove.

95.—CUTTING RUNNING RIGGING.

The greater part of the running rigging may be cut as it is rove, making due allowance for the hands to clap on. The length and size may also be got from the rigging table for all classes in the navy (see rigging tables). The most proper way to ascertain the length of a rope is from the *draft*, or rigging plan of the vessel you are employed upon, making the proper allowance for leading out, &c., &c.

96.—RIGGING SHEERS, AND TAKING IN MASTS AND BOWSPRIT.

In cases where there is neither sheers nor wharf to have recourse to, in order to get the lower masts on board, it becomes necessary to get such spars as can be procured, and erect a pair of sheers on board for that purpose.

In doing this proceed as follows:—Take in a sufficiency of ballast to steady the ship and shore the decks from the skin up, particularly abreast of the partners. Sling skids up and down the sides; reeve the parbuckles, and bring the sheer legs alongside, with their small ends aft; parbuckle them on board, raise one leg over the capstan, and their heads or after ends resting either on the taffrail, the break of the poop, or a spar placed in the most convenient spot, the more elevated the better. Square the heels exactly one with the other, so that when they come to be raised the legs may be found of equal height.

As near the after ends of the spars as may be considered necessary, when crossed, put on the head-lashing of new, well-stretched rope (*figure-of-*8 *fashion*), similar to a racking seizing, and cross with the ends. Open out the heels, carrying one over to each gangway, and placing it on a solid piece of oak or shoe, previously prepared for the purpose. Clap stout tackles on the heels, two on each, one leading forward, the other aft; set taut the after ones, and belay them. Lash a three or four-fold block, as the upper one of the main purchase, over the main lashing (so that it will hang plumb under the cross), with canvass underneath to prevent chafing; and in such a manner that one-half the turns of the lashing may go over each horn of the sheers, and divide the strain equally; also sufficiently long to secure the free action of the block. Lash the small purchase block on the after horn of the sheers, sufficiently high for the falls to play clear of each other, and a girtline block above all.

Middle a couple of hawsers, and clove-hitch them over the sheer heads—having two ends leading forward, and two abaft, led through viol blocks, and stout luffs clapped on them. These should be sufficiently strong to secure the sheers while lifting the masts.

The lower purchase block is lashed forward (perhaps round the cut-water), and the fall being rove, the sheers are raised by heaving upon it, and preventing the heels from slipping forward, by means of the heel tackles previously mentioned.

Sometimes a small pair of sheers are erected for the purpose of raising the heads of the large ones; in which case care must be taken to place them so as to allow the heads or horns of the other pair to pass through.

When the sheers are up, or nearly perpendicular, *cleat the shoes*, so as to confine the heels to their places upon them. They can then be transported along the deck by means of the heel-tackles and guys to the situation required, taking care to make them rest upon a beam, and to have the deck properly shored up below.

Finally, give the sheers the necessary rake by means of the guys, and set taut all the guys and heel-tackles. Also, five or six feet above the deck, on each leg, put two cleats, for the purpose of applying two stout lashings from *them above*, to the dead-eyes in the channels *below*, in order to give greater security; this being done, the sheers may be considered ready. (*See Plate*).

Note.—The skids which are slung up and down the sides, are for the purpose of keeping the sheer-legs clear of the channels, and from thence to the plank shear. Mats should also be placed over the quarter galleys to prevent injury.

Parbuckles are hawsers which are middled ; the ends of which are taken through two ports which are about five or six ports apart, from outside, in ; down over the rail, under the sheer legs ; up again through snatch blocks, in the opposite water-ways, and luffs clapped on them. The counter parbuckles are used to ease the sheer legs down on deck, and are rove through the gun-deck ports. Mats should be placed in the wake of the chafe, where the parbuckle leads over the rail, or up through the gun-deck ports.

The parbuckling on board of heavy spars for sheers may be much facilitated at times, and injury to the ship avoided, by attending to circumstances, and getting them in at slack water, or over the bows or stern.

When a ship is confined to her own resources, the lower yards are the best spars for sheers ; the heels (or yard-arms resting on the deck) being strengthened where they taper by a temporary fish, *woolded on*, and the woolding set up by wedges.

In a brig, the main yard and main boom are the best spars for sheers (if other spars are not available).

The shoes are made of either stout oak plank or beam timbers of pine, and long enough to extend over at least three beams, with a saucer in them for the heels to rest in ; likewise, mortices or bolts in each end for lashing. The spare caps will be found very handy for placing the heels of the spars in, and the eye-bolts in them convenient for hooking the heel-tackles, and transporting along the decks.

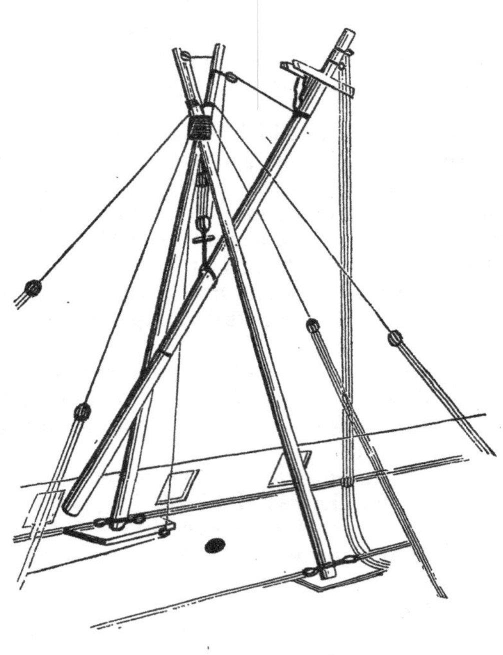

97.—TO TAKE IN THE MIZEN-MAST.

Tow the mizen-mast alongside, with the head aft, and the garland* lashed on to the forward part of the mast, at the distance from the tennon to just above the spar deck partners; lash a pair of girtline blocks on the mast-head, and reeve the girtlines; bend the sheer-head girtline to the mast below the bibbs to *cant* it. Overhaul the main purchase down abaft, thrust the strap through the eyes of the garland, toggle it, and secure the toggle by a back-lashing. Take the fall to the capstan and "heave round;" when the heel rises near the rail, hook on a heel-tackle to ease it inboard. Get the mast fair for lowering by means of the girtlines, have carpenters attending below, wipe the tennon dry, and white lead both it and the step, "lower away," and step the mast.

Pass a couple of straps around the mast; to each of these hook the double blocks of the pendant tackles—the single ones

---

* Garlands are made of new rope, well stretched (salvagee fashion), marled together and parceled. They are laid on the forward part of the mast, a stout lashing put on over all, and crossed between the garland and the mast;—a good dogging also, if necessary, passed downward.

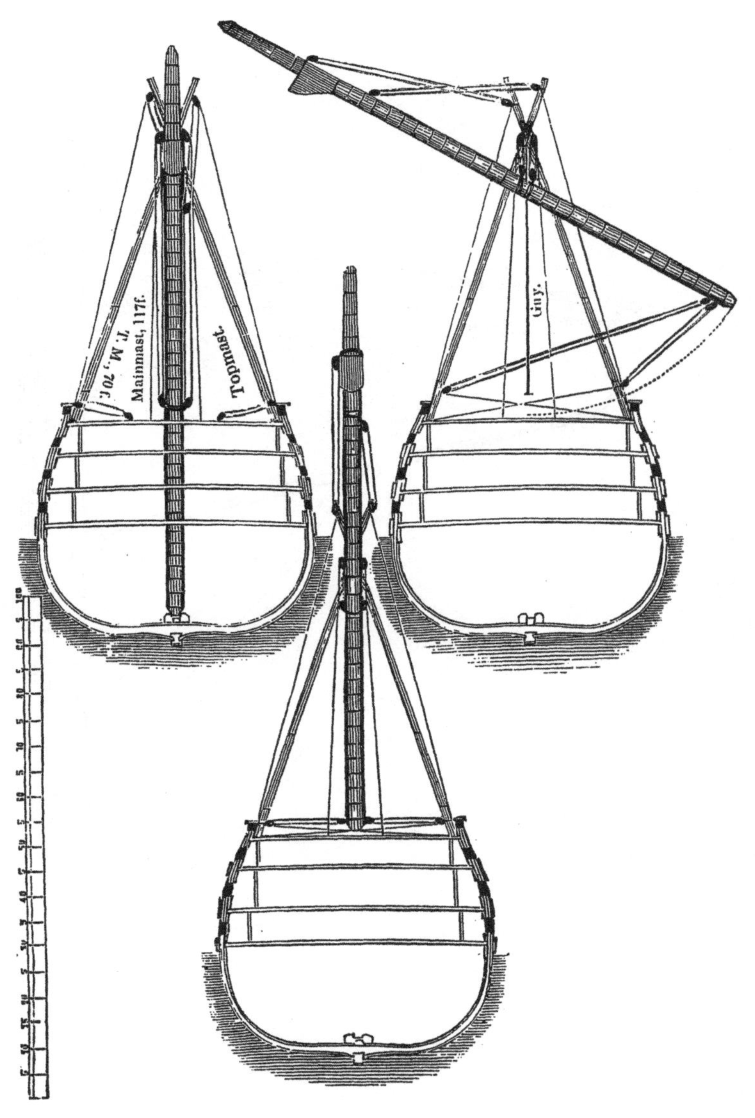

Masting and Dismasting.

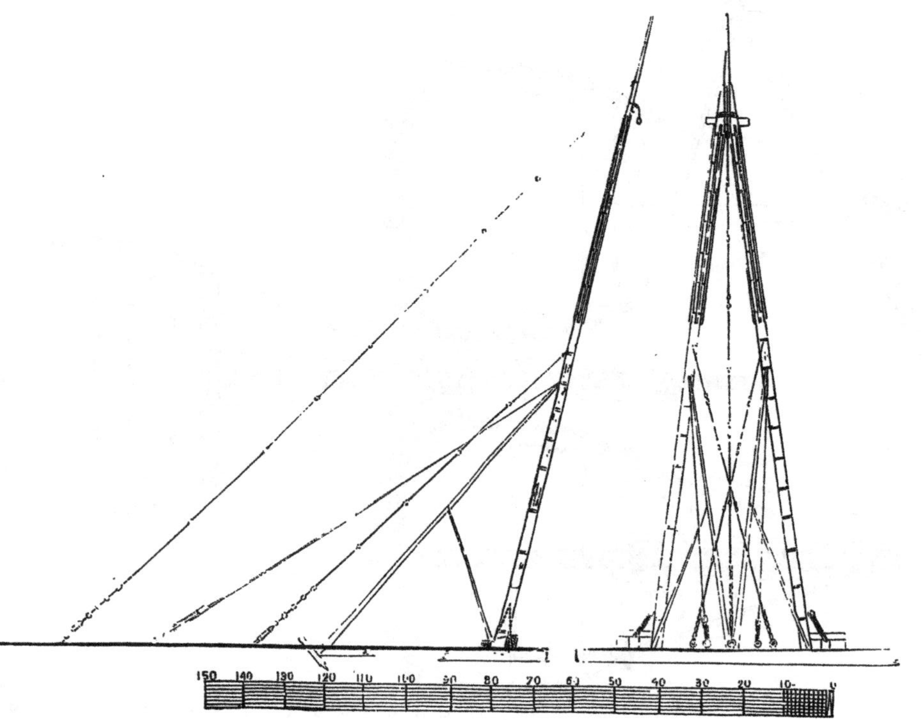

A Representation of the Masting Shears in the New York Navy Yard, for the Masting and Dismasting of large Ships.

to the sides, and hauled taut; wedge the mast temporarily, "come up" the purchases, man the guy and heel tackles, wet the decks, and transport the sheers forward for taking in the main-mast.

The object of taking in the mizen-mast first is, because the breadth of beam is less aft than forward; and the heels of the sheers being spread more as they go forward, the head lashing consequently becomes tauter; moreover, if the mizen-mast was taken in *last*, the bowsprit must be got in *first*, and thus the *advantage* of securing the sheers to the foremast-head, when getting in the bowsprit, would be lost.

98.—TO TAKE IN THE MAIN AND FOREMAST.

Proceed in the same manner as in getting in the mizen mast. The garland for the small purchase should be lashed about the diameter of the mast, *above* the main purchase.

In taking in either of the masts, if the sheers should be found to be a few inches short, the difficulty may be remedied by manning the forward guy-falls, and bringing the sheers perpendicular to the deck. Some distance may also be saved by using no garlands and having the purchase blocks lashed to the mast. If in lowering there should still be a difficulty, chocks might be placed on the kelson until the tennon rested on them; then steady the mast by means of the small purchase and sheer-head girtlines, while the main purchase is unlashed, and lashed again on the mast sufficiently high to step it.

If the ship has a top-gallant forecastle, it would be well to step the mast forward of the sheer legs, for the brake of the forecastle comes abreast of the partners; and, in a case of this kind, it would be well to take in the foremast first.

99.—TO TAKE IN THE BOWSPRIT.

Transport the sheers as far forward as possible, or as the bows will permit; send a hand to the sheer-head, bend on the girtlines to the small purchase block to light it up, unlash it, and lash it again to the forward fork or horns of the sheers, pass a strap round the foremast-head, to which hook a large tackle, carry it well aft, and haul it taut, for the purpose of staying the mast. Lash a couple of large single blocks to the foremast-head, middle a hawser, and clove-hitch it over the sheer-head; reeve the ends through the blocks at the mast-head, down on deck, carry them well aft, and take a turn. Hook the after heel-tackles forward, and take the after-guys aft; pass a bulwark lashing round eacn heel, rake the sheers over the bows sufficiently for the main purchase to hang directly over the gammoning scuttle, and make all fast.

The bowsprit being brought under the bows, with the head forward, and the garlands lashed on, the main one a little more than one-third from the heel, the smaller one between the cap and bees, having guys leading from the bowsprit to the cat-heads, and a couple of straps round the heel for hooking the bedding tackles. Overhaul down the purchases and toggle them; "sway away," attending it by the guys, until nearly perpendicular; hook on the bedding tackles, which are taken from the bitts on the main deck, and led up through the partners; wipe the tennon dry, and white-lead both it and the mortice; "lower away," bouse upon the bedding tackles, and bring it into its place; come up purchases, guys, unlash garlands, and proceed to dismantle the sheers.

If the ship has a topgallant forecastle, you will be unable to take in the bowsprit with the sheers without the assistance of a *derrick*,* on account of the brake of the forecastle, it not being prudent to step sheers on the top of it.

When the ship is masted, and alongside the yard, commence getting on board and stowing ballast and tanks; fit the rudder, gammon the bowsprit, fit and set up the bobstays and bowsprit shrouds; fit fore stay collars; get on board tops, caps, cross-trees, topmasts and topgallant masts, placing lower yards athwart ships, topsail and topgallant yards amidships; also, have ready tackles and luffs for setting up the rigging and staying the masts, top-blocks with lashings for top-ropes, and all the rigging at hand and in order.

100.—GAMMONING THE BOWSPRIT.

In rigging a stage under the bowsprit for this purpose, make use of two small spars, such as topgallant studding-sail booms, with their heels lashed to the head-rail, their heads frapped together, and slung from the bowsprit end, and boards laid across from one to the other.

The gammoning is of new, well-stretched rope, generally water-laid. One end of the gammoning being whipt, is passed through the hole in the cutwater, and over the bowsprit with a round turn, then clenched round the bowsprit close against the stop or cleats; the other end passes through the forepart of the hole in the cutwater, again round the bowsprit (but before the

---

* See Derrick. in Miscellaneous Articles.

clinch), and again through the hole in the cutwater, abaft the first turn. All the succeeding turns go in the same way, laying forward on the bowsprit and aft in the cutwater, and all are passed inside of the first turns; by which means the outer turns on the bowsprit which bear the most strain are more preserved from chafing than the inner ones.

The turns are then hove taut as follows:—A leading block is made fast to the holes for the bobstays by a strap long enough to admit of the pendant, which is then rove through it, leading straight through the hawse-hole to the capstan. In one end of this pendant an eye is spliced, through which a bight of the gammoning is passed, and retained by means of a toggle, while to the other end is hooked a long tackle, and the fall led to the capstan. As each turn is hove taut, it is, by some, nailed to the bowsprit, and by others, racked in several places, which is preferable to nailing.*

When all the turns are passed and hove taut, they are frapped together by as many crossturns as are passed on the bowsprit. The end is then whipped and seized to one of the turns.

In ships with two gammonings, the outer one is hove taut first, as it would otherwise slack the inner one.

Note.—Iron gammoning is now allowed for vessels of all classes in the service. (*See Rigging Table.*)

101.—FITTING RIGGING.

The shroud is hove well taut, with a tackle clapped on one end, and the other secured to a sampson post. It is wormed, parceled, and served a third down from the seizing; the swifter or foremost shroud all the way, except where the dead-eye is turned in. A sword mat is sometimes laced on the foremost shroud, which, I think, answers much better, as it can be taken off and the rope dried; and, from the different ropes I have seen rotted under the service, I feel convinced, the less on rigging, unless where absolutely necessary, the better.

In parceling the eyes, commence from each end of the service and finish in the centre, and pass several riding parts, as in breaking the shroud to form the eye, the service gets opened, which allows the wet to get in; and if the service is begun in the centre, doubled, and then passed toward each end, it will prevent the wet getting to the rope.

In forming the eye, take a good strand, knot both ends together, and lay it across both parts of the shroud; having brought them as close together as possible, pass both bights of the strand

---

* See Gammoning the Bowsprit, in Miscellaneous Articles.

under the shroud clear of each other; then place a long bolt across, close to the strand on the upper side; take a round turn round the bolt with each bight of the strand on each side of the shroud, put a smaller bolt through each eye in the strand, and *heave it round* the long bolt, and as the turns accumulate on the bolt, both parts of the shroud come together; when quite close pass the eye seizing, the shroud being previously parceled in the way of it.

When there is an odd on each side, it is fitted horse-shoe fashion to fit the mast-head; parceled, and served over a third down the same as the other shrouds. I have seen the odd shroud put on the mast-head first (after the pendants), instead of last; and then the others put on in rotation: No. 1 starboard, No. 2 larboard, No. 3 starboard, &c. &c.

102.—FITTING MAST-HEAD PENDANTS.

The long leg, when two, should be a third of the shroud. The eye is formed the same as the shroud: wormed, parceled, &c. A thimble is spliced in each end, the ends put in once and a-half, marled down, and served over. The formost leg is once and a-half the round of the rope shorter than the after one. The thimbles are well parceled before being spliced in.

Small ships have only one pendant on each side; when this is the case, the rope is cut to the proper length, the starboard pendant is spliced into the larboard, and the larboard into the starboard, with a cut splice forming an eye, or span, to fit the square of the mast-head; a thimble is spliced into each end, and they are wormed, parceled and served;—they are the same length as a long leg, when a pair on each side.

103.—LOWER AND TOPMAST STAYS.

Stays are four stranded, and are now both the same size, and lashed abaft the mast-heads. The legs are made for the collar in laying up. When sufficient length is laid up for the stay, from whence the collar commences to the end for setting up, two strands, one for each, are left sufficiently long to double back, and are then laid up as four strands, forming the lashing eyes and legs. The ends of the strands are then unlaid, the inside ones wormed into the lay of the rope; the other strands are divided, laid up, and worked in alongside the first strands; then some more yarns are twisted smaller and used as backing; some inside yarns from each strand should be wormed into the stay their whole length, below the crotch; the legs are then wormed, so as to completely fill the rope, commencing from the centre of the eyes for lashing, which should be well opened with a large seting fid, and worming carried into the stay as far down as the worming of the legs. The outside yarns of the legs are then marled down, over all, round the stay, tapering the ends. The legs are well parceled and served, and likewise the stay, sufficiently far down to take the lower yards, and covered with tanned hide.

The stays should be hove well out with purchases, and allowed to hang, pulling up occasionally. I have known a line-of-battle ship's stays (cable laid rope) to stretch out twelve feet, and after a two month's cruise were long enough to allow nearly two feet to be taken off the fore-stays.

Stays fitted with lashing eyes are decidedly preferable, as they are easier shifted; the collars not being so long the yards can be slung higher up, and consequently braced further forward.

In the merchant service the stays are also fitted on the bight, or two in one, as follows: the bight is put over the mast-head and both ends taken forward and set up in their respective places. Others again put the bight under the bowsprit and set them up abaft the mast head, with lashing eyes, putting on a seizing at the proper place to form the collar. This last plan would not answer for a ship of war.

104.—TO RIG THE FOREMAST.

White-lead the mast-head in the wake of the trestle-trees, overhaul down the girtlines, bend on the trestle-trees and sway them on board; take out the after chock, wipe them dry, bend the girtlines to the forward part and stop the girtlines to the after part; bend the main girtline to the after part also; "sway away," having a steadying-line forward to keep the trestle-trees from catching under the bibbs, for if they should be heavy, one man aloft will not be able to bear them off; when above the bibbs, send a hand aloft to slip the stops, one at a time, so as to let them come down gradually. "Lower away," bouse on the after girtlines, and get the trestle-trees in their places; send aloft the after chock, ship and bolt it. Tar the mast-head in the way of the rigging; overhaul down the girtlines for the bolsters, which are tarred and parceled; sway them aloft and stop them; lash the girtline blocks to the after part of trestle-trees.

The rigging is then sent up by the girtlines in the following manner:—

Mast head pendants.—Foremost pair of shrouds, starboard side; foremost pair of shrouds, larboard side; second pair of shrouds, starboard side; second pair of shrouds, larboard side, and so on until all the shrouds are over, after which send up the stay, and last of all the preventer or spring-stay.

Placing the rigging.—The girtlines being overhauled down send aloft the lower pendants, which have got a long and short leg, fitted together with a span, or square, the size of the mast-head; the long leg is placed abaft, so that in case of the forestay being shot away, the pendant tackles can be hooked in them without being in the way of the fore-yard in bracing; while the leg being abaft, the mast affords them good security. As soon as the mast-head pendants are placed they ought to be lashed abaft, the tackles hooked, and the mast stayed by them. Overhaul down the girtlines, bend the mast-head one on the shroud, with a timber-hitch, or toggle, four or five feet below the seizing, and stop it to the centre of the eye; take the girtline from the after trestle-tree, and bend it half way down the shroud; "sway away," on the lower girtline, and lift the weight of the shroud. When high enough, the stop in the eye is cut, and it will fall over the mast-head; the men on the trestle-tress placing it fair on the bolsters, beating it well down, with commanders, and observing to have the eye-seizing come as near the centre of the mast-head as possible. The larboard pair is got up in the same manner, and so on until all are placed. Reeve the lanyards, if prepared with a knot on the end; a double-wall and crowned is preferable, a mathew-walker being liable to capsize; the lanyard should be rove through the hole under the end of the shroud, because in setting it up, the strain comes on the shroud first, and keeps the dead-eye in its place; if put under the standing part, the strain coming on the end first, the dead-eye would *slue round.*

Setting up the lower rigging.—The rigging is often placed and then set up, but I would prefer (if time would permit) having it pulled up as placed. When the first pair on each side are over and placed, and the lanyards rove through both dead-eyes, clap a selvagee strap on each shroud well up; to this hook the single block of a luff tackle; the double, to a blackwall hitch in the lanyard; then take the lower blocks of the pendant tackles and hook them to both the falls of the luffs on each side; reeve the tackle falls through the leading blocks, and pull up, setting up both pair of shrouds at the same time, the men on the trestle-trees beating the shroud down as pulled up; when well up, place two pair more, and proceed in this manner until the mast is rigged.*

The advantage of pulling up a pair at each side, instead of singly, is evident from the fact that pulling up singly injures the seizing; as it is first dragged *forward* and then *aft* by the after

* See note on lower rigging.

leg, it is liable to slack the seizing, and perhaps snap the inside turns.

In rigging the lower masts, I have seen the after swifter go over first; a plan that is now adopted in small vessels. In staying the mast these swifters should be set taut, the mast being previously wedged, and the stays set steadily up. I have heard some old sailors dispute this plan, it being new, but for my own part I think well of it.

Note.—The trestle-trees might be got over without knocking out the after-chocks, by running up a derrick abaft the mast, well lashed abaft below the bibbs, having chocks placed between it and the mast, sufficient to admit of the free passage of the after chock of the trestle-trees. They are sometimes got on before getting in the mast, but they then bring in an additional and unnecessary weight upon the mast-head, and moreover, in lowering, catch over the shear-head.

N. B. The blocks for *topmast stays* should be put on *after* the second pair of shrouds (on foremast).

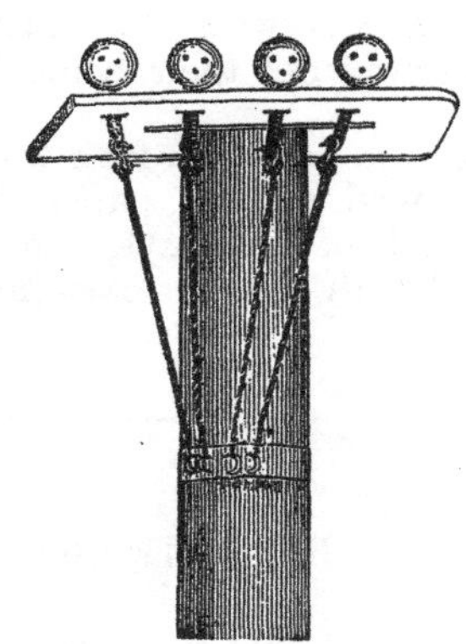

105.—FUTTOCK SHROUDS

Are now fitted, and hooked to the futtock plates in the top, and set up to an iron band round the mast. In small vessels these are iron, and set up with turnbuckles, or screws. Cat-harpens are seldom used, being considered unnecessary lumber aloft.

Note.—The futtock shrouds are hooked to their respective plates, ***with the points of the hooks in.***

106.—TO RIG THE MAIN AND MIZEN-MAST.

Proceed in the same manner as directed for the foremast. The mainmast of a frigate has one more pair of shouds than the foremast, and the mizen-mast three less. The mizen-mast has only one pendant on each side, fitted with a cut-splice, and a thimble spliced in each end. The rigging is placed the same as the fore or main; the mast is steadied into its place with a couple of long burtons, one to each pendant, and hooked to straps round the bitts, or to ring-bolts in the fore part of the quarter-deck bulwarks. If the stays are not ready for going up, the tackles can be hooked to a lashing round the mast, the pendants being wanted to pull up the rigging (for placing); the rigging is the same as the fore.

In setting up the main-stays, pass one *under*, the other *over*, around the cross-piece in the four bitts, for the purpose; clap the selvagee straps well up the stay, and two more near the ends; to these hook two luffs; to the falls of the luffs hook the lower blocks of main tackles; reeve their falls through leading blocks, in as direct a line with the stay as possible, and grease the bitts in the way of the stay.

In placing the main stays, in the manner mentioned above, there is sufficient space between tbe stays for a shot to pass through, which often prevents their being both cut away at the same time.

When the rigging is to be set up for a full due, the stays in the way of the bitts are well wormed, parceled, served, and covered with hide; and the ends of the stays, and all the lower rigging whipped, and covered with canvass caps (neatly fitted).

107.—TO RIG THE BOWSPRIT.

Bobstays.—The rope should be well stretched, wormed, parceled, and served, and in the way of the cutwater covered with leather; when none is to be had, pass two parts of parceling, the first against, the second with the lay of the rope; and serve with good stout spun-yarn, or four-yarn plait; then reeve them through the cutwater, splice both ends together, put the strands in once each way, marl down, and serve over. The hearts are then secured in their place (keeping the splice on the upper side) with a round seizing, with parceling under it. They are sometimes fitted to shackle to the cutwater, with iron plates let in flush with the wood, a bolt going through both plates, which is very snug and strong.

Bowsprit Shrouds are single pieces of rope. When cut the required length (a hook and thimble), the latter parceled, is spliced into one end, put in once-and-a-half, marled down and served over; a heart is spliced into the other. After being hooked to eye-bolts in the bows for the purpose, they are set up to their collars on the bowsprit.

A celebrated master (now a commander) in the navy, and a first rate seaman, never served the bowsprit rigging *all over;* it is, certainly, in my opinion, better not to do so, as the water can never lodge, which it may do, by getting in from broken service, which cannot be repaired at sea. They are now fitted one-third chain, on account of the chain cable chafing against them.

It is not unusual, in small vessels, to insert thimbles instead of hearts in the bobstays, bowsprit shrouds, and collars; covering the lanyards neatly afterwards, with canvass.

Placing the rigging.—Tar well the bowsprit; then put on the first forestay collar, first pair bowsprit shroud collars, first bobstay collar; second bobstay collar; second pair of shroud collars; spring-stay collar; and cap bobstay collar; then heave them close up, pass and heave well *on* with a rose-lashing.

The man-ropes are spliced, or hooked into bolts in the bowsprit cap, and in the other end an eye is spliced; ends put in once-and-a-half, and set up with a lanyard to an eye-bolt in knight-heads or stanchions, for the purpose; splices served over, and leathered in the nip.

The goblines* are either clove-hitched, or may be fitted with a cuckold's neck around the end of the dolphin-striker, and set up to the bows, one on each side.

108.—GETTING THE TOPS OVER.

Whole tops.—Overhaul the girtlines for the cross-trees, white-lead the squares in the trestle-trees, and ship them. The girtlines being on each side of the mast-head are then overhauled down for the tops; one end is passed from underneath, and up through the hole for futtock plate and hitched to the standing part; the girtline can be rove down through one of the holes in the edge of lubber's hole; the girtline stopped to the foremost edge, to holes bored for the purpose. A girtline is taken from

* Called back-ropes by some.

the mizen-mast-head, and bent to the foremost part of maintop; bend on a tripping line to the pigeon hole leading from the fore-mast-head. Man the girtlines and "sway away;" when sufficiently high to allow the foremost edge of lubber's hole to clear the mast-head, cut the stops and cant it over by the tripping line, and the top will hang in the girtlines, when it can be lowered, placed, and bolted.

I have seen girtlines bent from the foremost part of the fore-top to the bowsprit end; and from foremast to the forward part of the maintop; and from mainmast to foremost part of mizen-top, to assist in getting the tops over; but if they are properly slung it is not necessary.

The dead-eyes for the topmast rigging can now be hauled up, and put in their places in the top-rims: and also ship the top-rail, and stanchions in their respective places.

109.—GETTING HALF-TOPS OVER.

Unlash the girtline blocks from each side of the mast-head, and lash them on the foremost and after sides; send the end of the foremost girtline down abaft all, the other between the cross-trees.

If the starboard half is to be got over, place it on the deck with its upper side up, or on its edge with the upper side aft. Take the foremost girtline, reeve it down through the foremost hole, by lubber's hole for the purpose, (or from aft forward, if on its edge,) take it underneath the top, and if the hole for the futtock plate will take it, reeve it up, (or from forward, aft, if on its edge,) and half-hitch it to the mast-head, or standing part; then take the mast-head part under the top, (if on its edge, to the foremost side,) and seize it well to the foremost corner with a piece of small rope, through a hole bored for the purpose. Take the after girtline, reeve it the same way through the after hole bored for the purpose in the after part of lubber's hole; pass, and half-hitch it the same way as the fore one, and secure it with a good seizing of small rope, through another hole bored in the foremost corner. If the futtock holes will not take the girtlines, stop them with spun-yarn. The top should be so balanced in the girtlines, as to hang fair when the stops are cut. Reeve the other ends of the girtlines through the leading blocks; man them, and sway up the top with the after girtline; at the same time taking in the slack of the fore one. Have men stationed at the trestle-trees to bear off, cut the stops, and place. When the edge is clear of the cross-trees, cut the after stop and sway on both girtlines; and when the foremost corner is well up, cut the stops; the top will then hang in the girtlines, and can be easily placed. Shift the girtlines for the larboard half, get it up the same way, bolt and secure the top. Shift the girtlines on each side of the mast head, as they were before. A girtline from the mizenmast-head is sometimes bent to the foremost edge of the main-top, to assist in bearing off; (it can be dispensed with;) a rope's end bent to the top and hauled well aft, will answer the same purpose. Half-tops may be swayed up, before the cross trees are sent aloft, and hung to the mast-head, one half on each side, swayed chock up; then send up the cross-trees, and bolt them to the trestle-trees; lower the half tops down on the cross-trees; place and secure them as before.

Note.—In cold weather it would be best to get the tops over before rigging the masts, in order to give the men a more secure place for standing while placing the rigging; and in this case a derrick rigged on the top would be the best way to get the rigging over in a heavy ship. (If the topmast is pointed and swayed about six feet above the lower mast-head, it will make a good derrick for getting the lower rigging over.)

110.—GETTING UP TOP-BLOCKS, &c.

Top-blocks are large single blocks, having iron straps, which are formed after being put round the block, into a large hook. Overhaul down the girtlines through lubber's hole; bend one part through the sheave hole of the block, and stop it to the back part of the hook; hoist it up, and lash it to the mast-head around the hook, with a lashing long enough to allow the block to hang half-mast-head high. Through this block reeve a hawser; send the foremost end down through the square hole in the foremost part of the trestle-trees; the after end through the lubber's hole through a leading block on deck, and round the capstan.

111.—GETTING UP THE TOPMAST.

Take two half-hitches through the fid-hole, with the foremost end of the hawser, and stop the hawser well round the hounds of the topmast with a good lashing. Man the capstan, and heave the mast up and down. Unbend the hawser, reeve it through the sheave-hole in the topmast; send a hauling line down through the trestle-trees for the end of the hawser, which haul up and clinch round the lower mast-head over the block. Overhaul the girtlines down before all, and get the cap into the top.

Note.—Pendant tackles may be used to a greater advantage than a hawser in pointing a topmast, when light handed.

112.—GETTING THE CAP INTO THE TOP.

Bend the foremost end of the girtlines, which were sent down before all, through the round hole in the cap, and stop them along to the after part of the square hole, keeping the bolts in the cap *up*.* Man the girtlines and "sway away," bearing well off the fore part of the top. When high enough, lower, and place the round hole over the square hole in the trestle-trees. Sway the topmast well through and lash it securely to the cap; put a capstan bar in the fid-hole with a hauling line on the end, and heave the topmast up; when the cap is clear of the lower mast-head, haul on the line from the bar in the heel of the topmast, and it will slue the mast and bring the square hole of the cap over the lower masthead; ship the cap-shore, then lower the hawser, or tackle, and place the cap, beating it into its place. Land the mast, unreeve the hawser, unlash the top blocks, and hook them to their proper bolts on each side of the cap; reeve the hawser through one block, through the trestle-trees, through the sheave in the top-mast, up through trestle-trees again, and reeve the end through the foremost bolt in the cap on the opposite side of the block; before reeving it through, parcel it well; take two half-hitches on its own, or standing part, and secure the end with a round seizing of spun-yarn. Bring the hawser to the capstan, heave the topmast up and try the fit; (then lower away, get the topmast on deck, and try the other set); and then lower the mast for rigging. Secure the girtline blocks to eye-bolts in the cap, or to the topmast cross-trees.

Note.—The stop should be taken off the hounds of the topmast, directly it is pointed through the trestle-trees; and when getting on deck, after it is landed, single the hawser the same as when getting up and down, and stop it to the hounds; then have slip ropes on the heel to haul it forward or aft, whether fore or main, and place it on the chocks, for stowing on the booms. A fore-topmast is generally stowed with the head forward; a main with the head aft; both heads are sometimes stowed forward, a practice that is frequently adopted at the present day.

---

* The object of *keeping the bolts up* in getting the cap into the top, is, that they may not catch on the top rim and cause delay, and perhaps injury. (*It is not intended to be shipped so.*)

113.—TURNING IN DEAD-EYES.

If in the loft, get the length from the mast-head to the deck, from the draft, if the masts are not stepped, and place the dead-eye to that length, making due allowance for stretching in setting up. Turn the dead-eye in as near the end as possible, so that all parts of the shroud may be equally stretched, which will prevent its having *a gouty end.*

The principal caution is to keep the lay in the rope, as it prevents the wet getting in. If the shroud is to be wormed, and served in the wake of the dead-eye, the worming should not be hove in too taut, as breaking the shroud round the dead-eye would probably snap it.

The score being well tarred, the end of the shroud is taken underneath, round the dead-eye, inside standing, or mast-head part; a bolt is put in a hole of the dead-eye. Take a good strand, knot both ends together; it is then middled and crossed round the end of the shroud; both bights are taken round the bolt, one on each side of the dead-eye, and a smaller bolt put in each bight, which are hove round the large bolt in the dead-eye. As the turns accumulate, it heaves the shroud taut round. The dead-eye should be secured through one of the holes with spun yarn to the shroud before heaving, where the shroud is marked, for the lower part. When the dead-eye is turned in, in a loft, the shroud is hove in with a jigger, (or dead-eye machine).

When the shroud is hove well round, pass a good throat-seizing. When secured, take out the bolts, get a small jigger, hook one end to a strap round the end of the shroud, and the other to the mast-head part; take a good strand, knot both ends together, take it round the end and standing or masthead part; put a bolt in both bights, and heave it round, pulling up the jigger at the same time; this will bring the end taut up, as heaving on the strap brings both parts close together; then pass a round, or quarter seizing, and a smaller one on the end.

If the rigging is turned in on shore, keep the lay in the rope, and when sent out of the loft, to be placed on the mast-head, keep the ends inside, the shrouds being marked with a knot or a piece of spun-yarn, according to the number. The ends will lay aft on one side, and forward on the other; this is of importance and should be remembered.

Turning in dead-eyes, termed *Cutter stay-fashion.*—The dead-eye being placed to the mark, the end is passed round it as before, but instead of being secured with a throat-seizing, the end is passed round the standing-part and seized to the part round the dead-eye with a round-seizing, and another on the end further round the dead-eye. The same precaution as in the other way, keep the lay in the rope and *end* inside.

Note.—Worming and serving ***shrouds*** in the wake of the dead-eyes is not a common practice in all ships, but I would recommend it as a great preservative to the shrouds, if they were served at least six feet above the dead-eyes. I have known of many gangs of rigging condemned on account of the shrouds being *magged* and *chafed* in the wake of the dead-eyes and throat-seizing, for want of service, when all other parts of the shrouds were found to be good.

114.—GETTING TOPMAST CROSSTREES OVER.

Overhaul a girtline through the round hole in the cap; and if they are to go up from the starboard side, overhaul and send it down, and the after girtline outside the top; hitch that through the round hole in the cap, well out on the starboard foremost horns underneath, and secure the end with a good seizing of spun-yarn; the after one bend on in the same way, to the after starboard horn; then stop both girtlines well with spun-yarn, close to the trestle-trees, and also with two stops, on the larboard horns; "sway away;" having a guy from the deck to clear it of the top, as it goes aloft. When the upper, or larboard horns are well clear of the cap, take two rope's ends from the larboard side of the top, and bend them to the larboard horns, and man them in the top—these are called "steadying lines," and are used to prevent the crosstrees ***falling back***, if a stop is cut too soon, and to assist in getting the crosstrees on the cap, and over the mast-head. "Sway higher," cutting the stops, and hauling on the steadying lines. When the trestle-trees are as high up as possible on the cap, haul on the steadying lines, and cut the stops close to the trestle-trees on the starboard side, and the crosstrees will fall across the cap; then place the after hole between the trestle-trees, over the round hole in the cap—cast off the girtlines and steadying lines—white-lead the mast-head in the wake of the crosstrees, and sway the topmast through; beat the crosstrees well down on the mast-head; and when placed, sway the topmast a few feet higher for rigging. Pass a lashing through the fid-hole, and round the lower mast, to steady it.

The topmasts are sometimes fidded before rigging, to avoid the greater strain upon the top tackles. If a topmast has only one sheave (like a mizen topmast), it is a good precaution to reeve a hawser through the fid-hole, and haul it taut, as the mast goes aloft; unreeving it only when the mast is high enough for fidding, or previous to the squares entering the trestle-trees.

115.—PLACING TOPMAST RIGGING.

Tar the masthead in the wake of the rigging; send the bolsters aloft, and stop them. After the bolsters are on, put over first the mast-head pendants—then the span for ginn blocks; then follows the straps, with thimble in for standing part of the tyes—next, first pair of shrouds on the starboard side, then the larboard; and so on, until all are over; then lash the breast backstay (if single); if a pair, put them over the same as a shroud; next the after backstays; lash the stays, if fitted for it, if not, put them over the same as lower stays, with *mousings*, The collars of the stays go between the cross-trees, and lash over the after one. Some prefer chain spans. The most approved method is an iron plate, with a hook on each end, which lays across the trestle-trees.

116.—TO SEIZE-IN THE SISTER-BLOCKS.

There is a score on each side to take the shroud, and three scores for seizing—one on each end, and one between both sheaves. They are seized-in the length of the hanging block, from the eye-seizing, to prevent any risk of the reef-tackle and lift being jammed between the hanging blocks and the rigging—

one seizing is passed round the shrouds, above the block, another below the block; and a small seizing put on each score, round the block and shrouds. The topsail-lift leads through the lower sheave, and reef tackle through the upper one.

The larboard block should be seized-in once the diameter of the shroud lower than the other, as, if both are seized alike (the starboard shroud going over first) they would not be square when the rigging is placed.

117.—BACKSTAYS, (BREAST,)

When in pairs, are fitted with eyes, the same as the shrouds, and served sufficiently far down to be square with the service of the topmast shrouds. They are also parceled and served in the way of the lower yards, when braced up. When there is only one backstay it is secured round the mast-head with a lashing passed round it, through an eye spliced in;* they are set up to a treble block in the channels. Through these blocks a fall is rove, the standing part being spliced into the strap of the double block, and then led from the treble block through a fair leader in the side, in on deck.

Note.—I have seen ships without breast backstays on any mast, and they carried sail equally well with those who had them; one was the *Independence razee:* her breast backstays were converted into standing ones, and set up a little further aft, or immediately forward of the proper standing backstays.

Breast backstays are generally pulled up in stays when the ship is head to wind, having a quarter-watch of topmen stationed by them. If they should be set up too taut, whch may be the case, especially when the rigging is slack, they are likely to snap and endanger the mast by the sudden jerk; if not set up enough, they can be of no use, and are only an additional weight on the mast-heads, and a useless expenditure of rope. Their being set up to bear an equal strain with the rigging, will not occur with the greatest care once in a year, and I consider them particularly injurious on top-gallant-masts. A good stout *standing backstay* is the main support.

---

* Some are fitted with a cut splice.

118.—STANDING AFTER-BACKSTAYS,

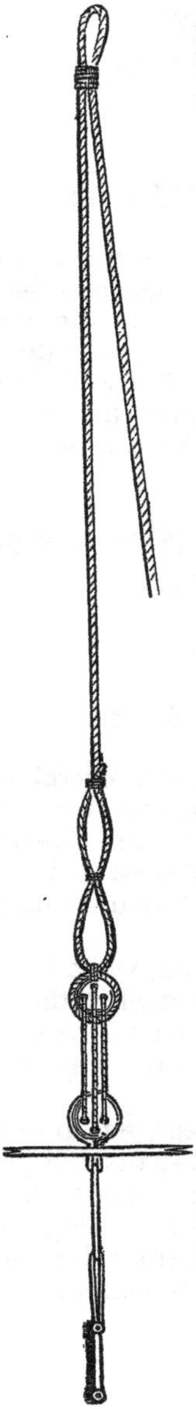

When in pairs, are fitted with an eye the same as topmost rigging. When an odd one on each side, they are fitted with a horse shoe. They are now fitted the same size as lower rigging.

The backstays are set up with a lanyard rove through dead-eyes, the same as shrouds, having service in the wake of the lower yards and tops.

119.—MAIN TOPMAST STAY

Is fitted of the same size as the standing back-stay. A large clump block is strapped round the foremast head, over the eyes of the rigging, and immediately over the square hole in the after part of the trestle-trees. Through this block the main topmast stay is rove down, through the trestle-trees—has a thimble turned in the end, lanyard spliced and rove through it, and set up to a span shackle in the deck, abaft the foremast, for the purpose; or a large bull's-eye hooked to an eye-bolt, and set up on the end.

The spring stay leads through a block strapped round the foremast above the cat-harpens, and sets up in the fore-top.

120.—MIZEN TOPMAST STAY

Is rove through a thimble strapped round the mainmast-head, over the eyes of the rigging; and when set up, is secured to its own part with round seizings. If preferred, it can be set up with a thimble turned into the end, and a lanyard rove through it; but this is not necessary. When the stays are well stretched, the thimbles can be spliced in, but it is not a good plan; for, should it be necessary to unreeve, the splice must be drawn, which will injure the rope. I have seen them fitted in this way, and pointed over for neatness,—but prefer their being turned in, and the end pointed or capped.

Note.—There is no mizen topmast spring-stay.

121.—GETTING THE TOPMAST CAPS ON.

The girtline blocks should be lashed well up to the topmast head. Overhaul down before all the foremost ends, and secure them to the foremost bolts in the cap; stop them to the centre ones, and also to the square hole in the after part; sway the cap up;—when well up, cut the after stops, sway higher, and the cap can be easily placed by the man aloft, and girtlines cast off.

If the cap should be very heavy, use a derrick; a capstan bar will answer the purpose.

Note.—Ship the capshore the same time you place the cap.

122.—MAST-HEAD MAN ROPES, &c. &c.

A piece of rope has an eye spliced in one end, and several over-handed knots made on the bight, at equal distances from each other. They should be long enough to reach a third down the topmast rigging, and seized round the mast-head close to the cap; one on each side is sufficient. They are absolutely necessary in large ships, and should be on all.

I have seen them in some very neat ships; and, when it is recollected the small space the men have for their feet when they get near the crosstrees, and the long mast-head, to get on the cap, it is certainly worth while to sacrifice something in the way of appearance to ensure the safety of a man's life.

Some large ships have ladders with two steps, set up to the eyes of the topmast rigging, from the cap; also, spans and grab-ropes fitted, to go from the swifters abreast of the cap, which will be found very convenient for the topmen, when exercising sails. These may appear trifling matters to some, but ships fitted with them are generally ahead, when exercising in a squadron.

123.—TOP TACKLE PENDANTS, &c.

When cut to the required length, a thimble, *well parceled*, is spliced into one end, and the other pointed, with a becket in it. There are two to the fore, and two to the main topmasts. In the heel of each topmast there is a dumb sheave;—take one pendant and reeve it through the top block, hooked to the cap, through the trestle-trees, through the dumb sheave, or *heel-block*, through an eye-bolt in the foremost part of the cap, on the opposite side to the block; take two half-hitches, and secure the end to its own part, with a spun-yarn seizing; hook the top tackle block to the thimble in the pendant, and the lower one, to a bolt in the deck for the purpose; reeve the fall through a leader, and bring it to the capstan; heave well taut, and unreeve the hawser by which the mast was formerly hove up for rigging.

The other pendant reeves through the other top-block, through the sheave hole in the topmast, and clenched to the other eye-bolt in the fore corner of the cap; hook the blocks, reeve and bring the fall to the capstan, taking the other off, and manning it well. When no capstan, both falls must be well-manned by hand.

Top Tackle Falls and Blocks.—The upper block is double, strapped, which is made into a hook; the lower is also double, and should be iron-strapped, having a swivel; a single one is hooked near the double as a leading block; the fall is rove; the standing part hitched, or clenched, over the block; they are sometimes spliced in, and some have beckets.

To hook the double block, clap a single tail-block well up on the pendant, reeve a whip through it, hitch one end of the whip through one of the sheaves of the double block, hoist it up, and hook it to the pendant.

124.—PREPARING TO FID THE TOPMASTS.

Capshores should be stepped and secured, luff tackles clapped on all the stays and backstays. Lower blocks should not be hooked on to the lanyards, but to bolts in the deck, and eye-bolts or straps in the chains; capstans and falls manned, topmast rigging quite clear, and hove over the sides of the tops, and the topmasts hove up and fidded, *mast stayed, rigging set up &c.*

125.—RATTLING THE LOWER AND TOPMAST RIGGING.

Cat-harpen legs and futtock shrouds are seized-on and set up; topmast stayed, rigging and backstays set up, lanyards secured as lower rigging,—then commence rattling down.

Girt the rigging with three fore and aft swifters—one by the shear rail, and the others at equal distances, as follows:—Make one end of a small rope fast round the foremost shroud, take a turn round the next, then the third, and so on, until all are taken in; then back the same way, and half-hitch it round the first. The swifter should be just taut, and not so as to bring the shrouds together,—the object being to make the ratlines a little tauter when let go. Sometimes swifters are not used, but the ratlines are never so square, or look well. Care should be taken that they are not too taut, for, when let go, all the strain will come on the seizing in the eyes of the ratlines, and they will be constantly snapping. Two swifters on each side are sufficient for the topmast rigging.

Spar the rigging down, with spare spars, such as studding-sail yards, boat's oars, boat's masts, handspikes, or anything *light* that will answer, and seize them to the shrouds on the outside, at equal distances, leaving sufficient space for three or four ratlines between each spar.

A coil of small well-stretched rope is placed on each side of the deck, two or three on a side when required to be done quick. Splice an eye in one end of the rattling stuff, seize it to the first shroud, and then commence clove-hitching on the second, and so on to the after, but one; then measure the distance from that to the last, cut it off, and splice an eye in the end. Beat the *hitches* well round each shroud, seize the end to the foremost one, and also the other eye to the after one, and rattle up, taking the shear of the rails. The hitches are formed on the outside, and at equal distances; in three or four places take a ratline to the after swifter;—these are called *shear ratlines*.

When it is necessary to rattle quick, take three ends up at a time. Fifteen inches is a good distance between the ratlines, and their places should be chalked off all the way up and down before commencing. Each man employed should have a measure within his reach, and care should be taken to make the ratlines on one side correspond in a parallel direction with those of the other. This can only be seen from the outside of the ship. Make the hitches neat, and the eyes small; few things tend more to a snug appearance.

If the rigging is to be blacked, after rattling down, it is best to leave the spars on until that is done, taking them off as you black down

126.—FUTTOCK-STAVES IN TOPMAST RIGGING

Are iron bolts parceled and served; are seized to the shrouds the length of the *hounds*, down on the inside; seizings passed as in lower rigging.

Cat-harpen legs on topmast rigging.—Take the length from the starboard foremost shroud round the mast, and to the after one on the same side; get a piece of rope this length, splice an eye in each end, worm, parcel, and serve it. There are two on each mast. Seize the foremost end to the foremost shroud and futtock stave, take it round the mast and seize it to the after one; secure one to the larboard side in the same manner.

I have seen them go from the foremost starboard shroud, straight to the after larboard one, crossing abaft the mast. They are also fitted to set up with thimbles and a lanyard, abaft the mast. When this is done, both eyes are seized to the futtock staves on the starboard side, a thimble seized in the bight, and set up abaft the mast to the larboard one, with a lanyard fitted in the same way. (Vessels with chain topsail ties are fitted with iron *bands*, to go round the mast, with eyes for the topgallant rigging to lead through.)

127.—TO RIG THE JIB-BOOM.

Hoist the jib-boom on board by the hawser or tackle, which was left at the foremast head when getting on board the fore topmast, run the end out on the bowsprit, pointing it through the stays and bowsprit cap. Reeve the heel-rope, and sway the jib-boom out a foot or two beyond the cap. Reeve the jib-stay through the hanks, *traveller if required*, and then through the inner sheave-hole, in the boom end, martingale and necklace, and turn a double block in the inner end; reeve the lanyard or fall through this, and a single block bolted to the bows. To the traveler seize the jib downhaul blocks and traveling guys; tar the boom end, put a grommet over, to which seize the fore top-gallant bowline blocks, one on each side.

Foot ropes.—There is one on each side of the jib-boom. They should be long enough when in their place to allow a man to stand navel-high along the boom, and are fitted as follows: take a piece of rope long enough to make both; cut it in the centre and splice one end into the other with a cut splice, forming an eye to fit the jib-boom end. Four or five overhand knots are taken at equal distances on the rope, from the eye, according to the length of the foot-rope; the knots are for the purpose of preventing the men from slipping. In each end splice a small eye, large enough to take a lashing, by which they are set up to bolts in the bowsprit cap. An eye is sometimes made by taking a round turn round the boom end, and two seizings passed. Also with a span, horse-shoe fashion, and neatly covered with canvass.

Note.—Turk's-heads worked through the strands, may be substituted for knots on the foot-ropes, if time will permit.

128.—JIB-BOOM MARTINGALE STAY

Is a short rope, with an eye in each end to fit the jib-boom, and end of the dolphin-striker. The eyes are well served, and covered with canvass or leather. The martingale is wormed, and a small twine seizing (snaked) put on round the worming at equal distances between the eyes; three, or four, according to the length, which must depend on the way the dolphin-striker is intended to stand, or rake. It looks best when perpendicular to cap or jackstaff.

Chain is sometimes used for the purpose, as also for back-ropes; and is found to answer well, it not being liable to stretch.

129.—JIB-BOOM GUYS.

There is one pair on each side; an eye is made to fit the boom-end by passing a round seizing, when in their place; both ends are rove through thimbles on each yard-arm of spritsail yard (when crossed). Then brought in and both ends set up to bull's eyes in the bow, or fitted with tackles.

Placing the rigging on the jib-boom..—First, the foot-ropes; next, the martingale stay, and guys. In some ships, an iron grummet is fitted with an eye on top and one underneath, neatly leathered, and put over the boom-end first. The martingale stay is hooked to the underneath eye, the jib-tack and downhaul to the upper one.

130.—MARTINGALE BACK-ROPES

Are pendants, middled and served in the centre, the round of the dolphin striker, both parts crossed and secured with a throat seizing. The service should be long enough to take in the seizing. In the ends splice a single or double block; another single one is strapped into a bolt in the bow for the purpose, or fitted in a strap with a hook and thimble (hook moused). A gun tackle, or luff-purchase, is then rove, the standing part of the fall spliced round the pendant, in after end of the block, rove through the one in the bow, over the head rails, back through the one in the pendant, and through a fair leading sheave, in the forecastle bulwark. These falls, after being pulled up, are racked together outside the bulwark. If belayed on the forecastle, they should be seized to their next part, so as not to be let go by mistake.

131.—PLACING THE RIGGING ON A DOLPHIN-STRIKER.

Back-ropes first, and next the martingale; below this rigging, in the end of the dolphin-striker, are two or three sheaves, and one close above it, large enough to admit the jib-stay, which is rove through it; flying jib-stay in the next sheave, and flying martingale stay under all, which will show two ropes leading from each boom end, to the dolphin-striker.

132.—GETTING THE JIB-BOOM OUT.

The flying jib-boom iron is driven on; the heel rope manned (if rigged), and the boom hauled out. The heel strap is placed in a score in the heel for the purpose, and both bights lashed together; then another lashing passed round the strap, between the boom and the bowsprit, and the strap well frapped together. The heel being well secured, set up the back ropes and guys.

Note.—Rigging to be placed same as jib-boom.

133.—SENDING UP TOPGALLANT MASTS.

The topgallant top blocks being hooked, we will suppose the long mast rope is to be rove, from the starboard side of the top-mast-cap; take the end through the square hole in the fore part of the trestle-trees, half-hitch it through the fid-hole, and stop it round the *hounds*, and the royal mast-head; send the hauling part through lubber's hole, and through a leading block or sheave on deck. The topgallant rigging is fitted on a sheet-iron cylinder or funnel, attached to the jack cross-trees (by an order from the former Navy Commissioners), leathered and painted on the outside, and tarred on the inside; put on the grommet or strap for the main royal stay* to reeve through, then put on the topgallant and flying jib-stays, starboard and larboard shrouds, breast and standing backstays, and secure them over the funnel; overhaul the girt-lines down on deck, and bend them on to the rigging, around all parts, about the length of the mast-head below the jack, and a good stop through the funnel; hoist the funnel up and place it, with the rigging on, over the hole in the cap, and take the stays forward and reeve them.

Man the mast-ropes and "sway away," having men stationed to bear off and place the rigging or funnel. When pointed through the funnel, place the royal rigging and truck, reeve the signal halyards, and *attach* the conductor; "sway higher," land the mast on the top or forepart of lower mast-cap, and, if required, reeve the short mast rope; reeve the pointed end through a block hooked to the cap on the larboard side, or the sheave, then through the trestle-trees, through the sheave-hole in the topgallant-mast, up through the trestle-trees, and secure the end to the foremost bolt in the cap, with two half-hitches, and seize the end; to the thimble in the other end, hook the double block of a burton; hook the single one to a strap round the trestle-trees; send the burton fall on deck through lubber's hole, and lead it through a single leading block, and haul it taut; unreeve the long mast rope, and fid the mast; when the fid is in, the mast rope can be unrove, if wished.

Reeve the ends of the shrouds through the horns of the cross-trees, between the topmast rigging, over the futtock staves, and turn a thimble in each end; strap another round a futtock plate, inside the dead-eyes of top-mast rigging; if there is none placed in the top, splice a lanyard into that in each shroud, and take two or three turns through each, stay the mast, and set the rigging and backstays up.

In setting up the backstays the single block of the jigger, which is hooked to the thimble is hooked to a blackwall hitch, in the lan-

* Suppose this to be the fore topgallant-mast.

yard, and when set up, expend the lanyard through the thimbles, and seize the ends. On both shrouds on each side clap on small jiggers, hook the double blocks to straps on the shrouds, the single to Blackwall hitches in the lanyards, and set up and secure the same as the backstays.

The fore topgallant stay reeves through the outer sheave-hole in the jib-boom, and through a bull's-eye hooked to the bows, and when set up, is seized to its own part.

The main topgallant stay is rove through the middle sheave in the after chock of the fore topmast crosstress, or through a block strapped around the fore mast-head, and set up in the fore top.

The mizen topgallant stay is rove through a bull's-eye in the after part of the main cap, and set up in the main top.

134.—ROYAL RIGGING.

There is one breast, and after backstay on each side, seized as the after backstays on topgallant masts. The breast backstay or *shroud*, is pulled up with a gun tackle purchase;* the after leg has a thimble turned in, and sets up in the after part of the chains, with a lanyard.

Royal stays.—As there is no funnel (although it would be a great advantage to have one), splice an eye in the stay to fit the mast-head, cover it, and serve over the splice. It goes on next to the grommet, then the shroud and backstays, spanned together.

The fore royal stay is rove through the outer sheave-hole in the flying jib-boom end, and pulled up through a fair leader on the forecastle.

The main royal stay is rove through a thimble stopped around the foretop gallant mast-head, through another strapped round the eye of a shroud, and when set up is seized to its own part.

Mizen royal stay reeves through a sheave in the after part of the main topmast trestle-trees, through a thimble strapped round the eye of a main shroud, and seized to its own part.

---

* Royal-backstays are set up with a jigger to their respective places in the channels. The shrouds are set up in the top(breast-backstay-fashion.

135.—SHORT AND LONG TOPGALLANT MAST-ROPES.

Short mast ropes have a thimble spliced in one end, and the other end pointed. They are rove when the mast is rigged, and are used for fidding. They should be sufficiently long (when the mast is landed on the top or cap), after being rove through the block and sheave in the heel of the mast, and clenched to the cap, to allow the thimble to hang clear of the cat-harpen legs.

If the topsail-yard is crossed, the mast is landed on it, for rigging; if the topgallant-mast should be too long to allow its being landed on the yard, the mast rope must be lengthened accordingly.

Long mast ropes.—Ropes are often fitted for the purpose; but the topgallant yard rope is generally used. I have seen them fitted as follows, and they answered very well:—

The rope is rove, and stopped to the topgallant-masthead, and royal sheave-hole, leaving a long end over the upper stop, to hitch to the bolt, before cutting the stops. To prevent the rope *slipping*, rack both parts together above the sheave-hole in the heel of the mast.

136.—TO RIG THE FLYING JIB-BOOM.

Sway it on board and point it through the iron at the jib-boom end. A tail block is put on the neck of the iron, or on the jib-stay, close down to the boom. Through this block reeve the heel rope, one end taken in on the forecastle, and the other bent to the heel of the boom. A rope is bent to the heel of the boom to serve as a guy; sway the boom out a foot or two for rigging. Put over the foot ropes, fitted as the jib-boom, the inner ends seized to the jib-boom end, inside the iron. The martingale, when single, is secured round the boom end, clenched, spliced, or with a running eye, rove through a sheave in the dolphin-striker, and in on the forecastle, on the opposite side to the royal stay. When double, a single block is strapped round the boom end, and the standing part spliced round the dolphin-striker; hauling part as when single.

Guys.—One on each side spliced into each other, forming a cut-splice to fit the boom end. The other end rove through thimbles, strapped round the spritsail yard, through fair leaders in the bulwarks, and pulled up on the forecastle, or set up on the bows.

Man the heel rope and get the boom out; the heel is placed in a step formed on the fore side of the bowsprit cap, for the purpose, and secured with a lashing, rove through the end, and passed round the jib-boom. Set up the martingale, stay the fore topgallant and royal mast, (fore and aft,) by the stays and backstays; and if the spritsail yard is crossed, reeve the guys, turn in thimbles, and set them up.

137.—SPRITSAIL LIFTS

Are single; have an eye spliced in one end to fit the yard-arm; splices served over are taken over the jib guys, rove through the bull's-eye in the cap, and set up on the forecastle. Blocks are sometimes strapped into the bolts, but it is quite unnecessary. Bolts are often driven into the fore side of the cap, and the lifts led through; when this is done, they are generally set up there with lanyards and thimbles, spliced into the end, which answers every purpose.

138.—SPRITSAIL BRACES.

A single block is strapped in toa bolt in the cheek of the foremast on each side. The brace has an eye in one end, to fit the yard arm; the other is rove through the single block, on collar of fore-stay, and another single block is spliced into the end; a luff tackle purchase is rove with it, and a double block on the deck, one sheave answering for a leading one.

They are sometimes rove double, but the practice is getting out of date.

139.—STRAPPING THIMBLES FOR GUYS ON SPRITSAIL YARDS.

The thimbles are double-strapped and secured, after being placed round the yard, and in the score of the thimbles, with a round seizing passed between the thimble and the yard; the splices laying in the upper side of the score in the thimbles.

Some fit grummet straps, or a short-long splice, in the strap for neatness.

The use of double straps is to allow the thimbles to lay fair with the yard for the jib guys to lead through; if single, they would stand fore and aft.

140.—CROSSING A SPRITSAIL YARD.

The yard being rigged, prepare for crossing as follows:

Clap a good selvagee strap well up, on the fore topmast stay; to it hook a snatch or leading block large enough to take a hawser; reeve it and timber-hitch it round the starboard quarter of the spritsail yard, (if got out on the starboard side,) stop it along to the larboard quarter, and half way out on the larboard yard-arm. Overhaul down the lifts and braces, and sway out, keeping the larboard yard-arm under the bowsprit; when clear on the larboard side, put over the brace, or block, and lift, and haul out; when nearly out, or before clear of the head rails, put over the starboard brace or block and lift; haul on the hawser, starboard lift, and brace, and cast off the stops. When sufficiently out, pass the parrel, *take a turn or hold well on the end;* hook the tye, and square the yard. Cast off the hawser and unreeve it; reeve the jib-guys through their thimbles on the spritsail yard, turn in dead-eyes or blocks, and set them up to others on the bows; set all up taut and square the yard.

141.—TWO HALF SPRITSAIL YARDS.

Two half spritsail yards, made like dolphin-strikers, are secured to the bowsprit with jaws, (or an iron band fitted round the bowsprit, with a double goose-neck hinge,) to cant or turn in any required direction. When the half spiritsail yard is carried it is rigged as follows:—

The fore guys are made of well stretched rope, and equal in strength to the jib guys together, each fitted with an artificial eye to fit the jib-boom end and half yard-arm. They should be wormed with small rope, parceled and served, or covered in the eyes; four stranded rope is preferable, it being not so liable to stretch as three.

The after guys are fitted with an artificial eye in one end, to fit the yard arm, and a thimble spliced into the other. They are the same size as the fore guys, and wormed in the same manner.

If made on purpose, and four-stranded, the thimble is kept in the bight with a round seizing.

The jumper, or lower guy, is fitted the same as the after, only shorter; the length of this depends on the drop intended to be given to the yard arm, which should never be less than the sprit-sail yard, when well braced up, or, in other words, *canted.*

The jumper is put on the yard arm first, then the after one, next, the foremost, and over the jib-boom. The after one is set up to a bolt by the cat-head, well down; the lower, to an eye-bolt in each side of the cutwater, well out.

For a frigate, the guys are eight-and-a-half-inch, and wormed with twenty-one thread stuff. Four-stranded rope, if made on purpose, can have the eyes formed when laying up in the rope walk. Some fit forward and after guys all in one.

142.—WHISKERS.

Whiskers are iron outriggers from the cathead, with sheaves in them for the guys to reeve through, and set up to the fore chains, the same as when rove through the spritsail yard. This plan is much in use in small vessels, but the boom is supported almost entirely by the martingale, as the guys being considerably above the boom, and its always *topping up*, when the sail is set on a wind, the more wind the greater the strain on the martingale; and should the guys be not carefully pulled up, the boom must depend on the martingale entirely for support.

143.—TO GET ON BOARD AND RIG LOWER YARDS.

Overhaul the hawser from the lower mast-head, bend on to the slings of the yard, and get them nearly up and down; clap selvagees on the quarters, to which hook the pendant tackles. As it comes on board, cut the stops, easing away on the pendant tackle, and bousing on the other, until the yard is athwart-ships; place chocks in the hammock nettings for the yard to rest on; slue them fair, and lash them; come up the tackles, cast off the hawsers, and place a shore under the middle of the yard to prevent its springing. Measure the yard, tar and leather the slings, fit a saddle for the D thimble, which lash on with a piece of well stretched rope, heaving each turn taut with a Spanish windlass, and fitting the score of the D thimble. Cover all with leather, and fit the straps for the preventer slings, &c., &c., &c.

Note.—The iron sling-bands are now used instead of the *old fashioned* D thimble.

Chain is now generally used, and allowed to all ships in the service for the slings (proper), rope ones being used as preventers. (See Rigging Table.)

144.—TRUSS STRAPS.

A large thimble with the score well parceled, is seized into a double strap, which is made by splicing both ends together, and served over; the thimble secured in the strap with a round seizing, the splice laying in the score. The strap should be long enough to go round the yard in the quarter, both eyes lashing together on the fore side. There are two on each yard. One thimble is seized inside the truss pendant, the other outside; and one in the round of the pendant higher up than the other.

145.—TRUSS PENDANTS*

Are wormed, parceled, and served; an eye is spliced in one end large enough to take the pendant when rove through it; in the other an artificial eye is made, large enough to take the single block for truss fall. The pendant should be rove through the small eye before the artificial one is made, boused well taut round the yard, the eye being kept underneath, and one pendant higher than the other. Reeve the upper pendant through the upper thimble, and lower pendant through lower thimble. Being rove in this manner, they will lead perfectly clear of each other.

Hide rope is preferable for pendants, but the iron patent truss is now allowed to all vessels, up to a second class frigate inclusive. (*New regulation*).

146.—QUARTER BLOCKS—LOWER YARDS.

Quarter or topsail sheet blocks are large single blocks, with double straps; the block seized in with a round seizing, and secured round the yard, (inside the cleat, one on each side,) with a rose-lashing passed through both bights on the top of the yard.

* For length and size, see Rigging Table.

Before the lashing is passed, the block should be hove up with heavers, and the eyes of the strap brought as close together as possible. This is done with a good strand passed through both, and hove up with a Spanish windlass. Vessels carrying chain topsail sheets, have iron blocks fitted to the iron bands in the slings of the yard for that purpose. (See Rigging Table).

147.—CLEW GARNET BLOCKS

Are single; seized into a single strap, with an eye spliced in each end, and are secured round the yard with a rose-lashing, the same as the topsail sheet blocks, just outside the cleats. Some ships have all the rigging inside the cleats, which is much neater.

Note.—Iron bound blocks are allowed to all classes of vessels in the navy, by the new regulation, for this purpose.

148.—LIFT BLOCKS—LOWER YARDS

Are single, seized into a single strap, with a round seizing; the strap being long enough to go over the yard arm, after the block is seized in. If both ends are spliced together, the splice should lay in the score of the block, or upper side; but a grummet will answer equally as well, and look snugger.

149.—FOOT ROPES AND STIRRUPS.

The foot ropes are cut once-and-a-half the length of the yard, (excepting lower yards). An eye, to fit the yard arm, is spliced in one end; and a small one, to take a seizing, in the other. The splicing served in the way of chafing (one-third) midship part.

Stirrups are short pieces of rope spliced round the foot rope; eyes spliced in the opposite ends, to go over the jackstay-bolts; splices served over. They are sometimes unlaid at one end and made into plait, and secured to the yard with flat-headed nails, having a small piece of hide or leather placed under their heads before being driven into the yard. Going over the jackstay bolts is preferable; and some seize it to the neck of the bolt, or staple. They hang on the after side of all yards.

Some vessels have their foot ropes fitted to go abaft the mast, and seized to the parrel, which answers a very good purpose, especially in vessels with raking masts, as it gives the men a better opportunity to stand.

150.—JACKSTAYS.—BENDING AND REEFING.

Take a piece of rope of the proper size,* cut off the length of the yard, splice an eye in each end, to fit the yard arm, sufficiently taut to require being driven on. Cut in the centre, and splice a thimble in each end; put the strands for splicing in once-and-a-half, marl down, and serve over. If two jackstays on each arm, (which should always be the case when the sail is reefed to one), the large one, before splicing the thimbles in, is rove through the eye-bolts on the yard for the purpose; this is the reefing jackstay. The bending one is fitted the same way, and after being put over the yard arm, is seized to the neck of the bolts on the after side.

This plan has been generally adopted, as it was found much easier to reef, than when fitted with only one jackstay; there being always difficulty and delay in getting the points between the jackstay and the yard, when the sail was bent to it. When only one jackstay, it is rove through the eye-bolts.

Note.—Iron bending jackstays are now allowed for all vessels in the navy.

151.—BRACE BLOCKS.—LOWER YARDS.

The straps should be fitted sufficiently taut to require being being driven on the yard arm. Two thimbles are fitted, one within the other, called *lock thimbles.* Take a piece of rope, of the proper size, and cut it long enough to go round one thimble and the yard, when spliced together; worm, parcel and serve it, and pass a round seizing round this strap, close to the thimble. Grommet straps are preferable, if time will permit.

The block is a large single one, with two scores. For the strap take a piece of rope the required length, and splice both ends to-

---

* For the length and size of rope, see Rigging Table.

gether; worm, parcel, and serve it; reeve it through the thimble already strapped, and pass both parts round the score of the other thimble; then place both bights in the scores in the brace block, keeping the splice in the after end of the block; pass a round seizing between the block and thimble, crossing it both ways, as in a double strap.

Cross-jack brace-blocks are single, and strapped the same as lower ones. A double block is secured to the after shrouds in the main rigging, the same as main preventer brace blocks. When reeving the cross-jack braces, one end of the brace is clinched, spliced, or half-hitched, and the end seized, just below the block; then rove through the block on the yard, through the inside sheave in double block, and through a fair leading sheave in a rack, in the side or a leading block. I have seen blocks strapped into bolts on the main-mast, for the brace and bowline, which answered well. The brace block should be put on the yard, sufficiently far in to be inside the topmast backstays, when braced up.

Note.—These braces should be well *below* the yard, as it always *tops up* on the wind, which slacks the weather leech; this is partly the reason a mizen-topsail never stands well.

152.—PLACING THE RIGGING ON LOWER YARDS.

Sling bands in the centre, and also on both sides, close to the topsail sheet block, the truss pendants, then truss straps; if the rigging is all within the cleats, a clue garnet block is lashed on each side; if not, they are lashed one on each side, close outside. I have seen them both ways, but inside is preferable.

Tar well the yard arm, close to the cleats and slings, in the wake of the rigging, first jackstay; if two, the bending one, and set it up amidships with a lanyard. Then the foot ropes; after going over the yard arm, and rove through the stirrups, they are lashed together, with a lanyard rove through both thimbles, and are secured with a good seizing to the strap of quarter block. Then the brace, and lift blocks. Rolling tackle straps on the inner quarter of yard, with the eye abaft burton straps on the outer quarter yard-arm, eye on top of yard.

If the stirrups go over the jackstay bolts, they should be put over before the jackstay is rove.

The cross jack-yard has no jackstay, head earings, or yard tackle straps; and the brace blocks, instead of going over the yard-arm, are put on some distance inside of the sheave hole for the mizen-topsail sheets, on the forward side of the yard.

153.—GETTING UP JEER-BLOCKS, AND REEVING JEERS.

Secure two single whip blocks to the after bolts in lower cap. Send the two foremost ends through lubber's hole down on deck; bend them through the shell of the block, with two half-hitches, and seize the end. Stop them along each leg of the strap, the larboard whip to the larboard leg, and the starboard whip to the starboard leg; then stop both legs together with a seizing of spun-yarn in the bights—the hauling part of the whips being through lubber's hole and through a leading block on deck; man them and hoist the blocks into their places. When clear of the top, cut the stop in the bights, haul on the whips, and they will bring the strap into its place, on each side of the mast-head. Then cut the upper stops, on the whips; take a turn and pass the lashing in the bight, securing each end to their next part. When secured, let go, and take off the whips.

Reeving jeers.—The standing part is clenched round the strap of the upper block, rove through the one on the yard, up through another sheave in upper block, and so on, until all rove full. The hauling part is rove through a leading sheave, in fore or main bitts, or through leading blocks. When heaving up, they are either brought to the capstan, or manned by hand.

The jeer blocks are now generally fitted with hooks, as they can be got up and down much quicker. At the present day, few ships are seen to carry their jeers up in their proper places.

154.—LOWER LIFT BLOCKS

Are double; an iron plate is bolted across the upper side of the main or fore cap; it is in the form of a crescent, with the hollow side toward the topmast. In each end of the crescent, or horn, an eye is turned and a thimble put in it. Instead of the eyes being turned, I have seen two eye-bolts driven through the crescent and cap, and secured underneath with a nut; a thimble is also put in the eye-bolt, and the blocks strapped in.

The cross-jack lift blocks are single, one on each side, and can be fitted as the fore or main, or (a chalk) abaft the mast-head, if preferred, for neatness.

155.—REEVING LOWER LIFTS.

Clench one end round the yard outside all, then take the other end up and reeve it through the foremast sheave in the double block in the fore or main cap, then through the block on the yard, through the other sheave in the double block, and through lubber's hole on deck; well up this part, splice a lizard for jigger tackle, or use tails selvageed on the end. The upper block of the jigger can be spliced or turned in to the lift, if preferred.

The cross jack lifts go over the yard arms with an eye spliced in the end to fit them. The other end is rove through the block at the cap, and is set up with two thimbles and a lanyard in the top; one thimble being turned into the end, the other strapped to the eye of one of the lower shrouds.

156.—MAIN BRACES—ON BUMKIN, &c.

A single block is seized into a double strap, with a round seizing crossed both ways; the strap is then put over an iron outrigger, or bumkin on the quarters, fitted for the purpose. The standing part of the brace being parceled, is rove through another bolt in the bumkin, and spliced into it or clenched; the other end rove through the block on the yard arm, from out, in through the block in the bumkin, and through a sheave in the bulwarks (abaft), for the purpose.

Double blocks are sometimes put on the bumpkin, instead of single ones, and also two sheaves inserted in the bulwarks instead of one, both ends of the brace rove, and led in-board—*a great facility in working ship.*

157.—FORE BRACES

Are clove-hitched, and the end seized aft on the collar of the main stay, below the splice; the other end taken forward and rove from in, out, through the block on the yard, through a single block strapped into a bolt in the cheek of the main-mast, with a thimble in it, close up to the trestle-trees; then rove from forward aft, through a sheave in the main fife-rail.

The brace is often middled, and clove-hitched in the bight on the main stay, and both ends taken forward and rove as before. Some have a hole bored in the bibs, or cheeks of the mast, instead of clove-hitching it around the main stay.

158.—CROSSING THE LOWER YARDS.

The jeers being rove, reeve the pendants and falls, hitch the pendants around the quarters of the yard, splice in the lanyard of the D thimble, and take the yard tackles forward to keep the yard clear of the mast. The lifts and braces being rove, man the lifts and jeer falls, "sway away," and when the yard comes abreast of the futtock staves, pass the lashing of the D thimble, parcel it well, over all, frap all parts together, and cover all with canvass; reeve the truss pendants, turn in the blocks, reeve the falls, haul taut the tresses, and square the yard by the lifts and braces.

159.—TO GET ON BOARD THE TOPSAIL YARDS.

A large single block is lashed to the topmast-head, through which a hawser is rove; overhaul it down forward and hitch it to the slings of the yard, stop it along the yard arm, and sway it on board. Cast off the hawser, middle the yard, and prepare it for rigging.

160.—RIGGING TOPSAIL YARDS. (FORE AND MAIN.)

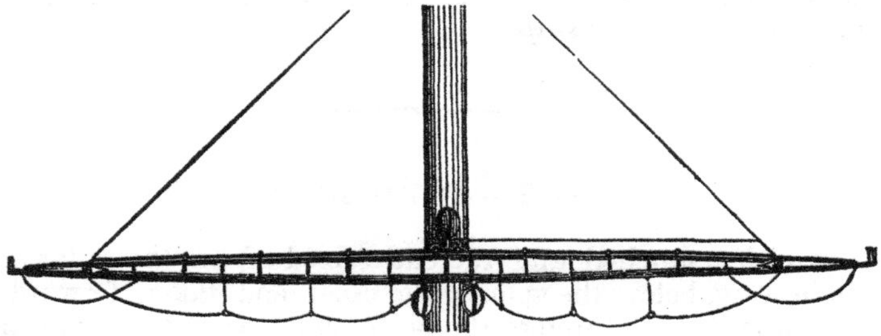

The jackstays, after going over the yard arm, are rove through the eye-bolts or staples, and set up a-midships with a lanyard and thimble spliced in.

Foot ropes round the yard abaft, on their opposite quarters, as follows:—splice the lanyard into the eye in the end; take it over the yard, and round on the fore side, underneath through the eye; again back round the yard on the fore side, through the eye, and back the same way, until sufficient turns are taken to secure it. Then take a half-hitch from the lower edge of the eye, round all parts of the lashing; pass it round before; reeve through the eye on the upper side, take two half-hitches round all, and secure the end.

Tye blocks are now generally iron-strapped, and bolted into *straps* round the yard for the purpose. If fitted with rope, they must have double straps, and secured round the yard, on the upper foremost quarter, with a rose-lashing. If they are single blocks, two on each yard.

Quarter blocks are double blocks, iron strapped, and secured in the same way as tye blocks. Much time is saved by having them fitted in this manner, as in shifting yards, the topgallant sheets, and topsail clewlines need not be unrove, which must be the case if rope-strapped. If rope-strapped they are seized into a single strap, and lashed on top of the yard with a rose-lashing.

Parrel.—Take two pieces of rope, one longer than the other; the long one of sufficient length to go round the mast and yard on each side; the short leg to go round the mast, and lash to the long leg on each side. An eye is spliced in each end, are wormed, parceled, and served; both marled together and covered with leather. A round seizing is passed around both, close to the eye of the short leg, on each side. The long leg is taken round the yard, brought round on the fore side, and secured to the short leg with a lashing of small rope, passed through both eyes. The other eyes are lashed together when the yard is across.

Brace blocks are strapped in the same way as fore or main yard.

Flemish horse is a short piece of rope spliced round a thimble, which is on the neck of the pacific-iron,* it has an eye spliced in the other end, and when the yard is rigged, is secured the same as a foot rope, just inside the brace block, two or three feet, according to the length of the yard. They should be long enough to allow a man to stand on them to pass an earing, &c. They are sometimes fitted to lower and top-gallant yards, for the convenience of reefing, &c.

Jewel-blocks are single blocks, seized into a strap put over a thimble on the neck of the pacific-iron, outside the thimble for the Flemish horse. Some fit them to go over the yard arm. Others fit them with sister hooks, to hook to the pacific iron.

Straps.—Half way out, on each yard arm, a strap is fitted long enough to allow a thimble to be secured in it, with a seizing passed between the yard and thimble,—this is called a rolling tackle

---

* Is what the boom-iron ships on.

strap. Also, straps are put on the yard, with thimbles seized in the same way, inside the lift, to hook a burton to; but a selvagee strap is generally used for that purpose.

161.—THE MIZEN TOPSAIL YARD

Is rigged nearly the same as the others, but the brace blocks are on the fore-side, and the Flemish horses generally spliced into bolts in the ends of the yards, with round thimbles in them. There is seldom more than one tye-block on this yard, and no jewel blocks.

162.—PLACING THE RIGGING ON TOPSAIL YARDS.

Tar the yard arms; first the jackstay, foot ropes, brace, and lift block; if no lift block, the lift; Flemish horses, and jewel-blocks. The quarter blocks should be lashed so as to hang clear of the cap, when the yard is down. See that the boom irons go on, and a small cleat, or saddle, inside of the sheave hole, about two feet on each yard-arm, to keep the topgallant sheets clear of the yard. Also reefing cleats on yard-arms, outside the lift.

163.—CROSSING THE TOPSAIL YARDS.

Reeve a hawser through one of the hanging blocks; send one end down before all, the other through lubber's hole, and through a leading block on deck. Take a round turn, and timber-hitch the hawser round the slings of the yard; stop it along the larboard yard-arm, if got up on the starboard side; if got up on the larboard side, the contrary. Overhaul well down to main or fore rigging, the starboard lifts and braces; the larboard into the top, and stop them ready for rigging. Man the hawser, and "sway away." When the upper yard arm is clear of the top, put over the brace and lift, (or block,) and "sway higher;" rig the lower yard arm, take in the slack of the lifts and braces, then cast off the stops on the upper yard-arm, and when the yard is well up, take two or three turns with the parrel-lashing; bouse well up on the starboard or lower lifts, overhaul the larboard. and the stops being cast off, the yard will fall across. Secure the parrel; square the yard by braces and lifts, and cast off and unreeve the hawser.

Note.—In large ships the lifts and brace blocks are generally placed on the yard arms before the yard is sent aloft. The braces are rove when the yard goes up. I would also recommend double yard ropes in heavy ships in crossing topsail yards; also to use the burtons.

164.—FITTING FLY-BLOCKS FOR TOPSAIL HALLIARDS.

The blocks spliced into the tyes are so called. They are large flat blocks; some double, sometimes single, and often one double and one single to each. The tyes are sometimes spliced taut round them; but this way is bad; as the rope stretches, the blocks cant, and are split. Also a long-eye is sometimes made in the end of the tye, and the fly block kept in its place by a round seizing passed close above the block. The block in general use is seized into a strap, leaving sufficient space above to splice the tye in; or a thimble spliced into the end of the tye, and the fly block strapped with a pair of sister hooks, to hook to the tyes. Either of the latter ways are preferable to the former.

When the yard is on the cap, these blocks should be square with the top rails. Before turning in and setting up for a full due, an iron traveler is put on the topmast backstay, which is seized to the fly-block,—it prevents the block from striking or injuring the top when lowering; it also keeps the turns out of the halliards. There is sometimes a traveling jackstay fitted for this purpose.

Reeving Topsail Halliards.—When rove double, a single block is strapped into, or hooked, to a swivel bolt in the after part of the chains; one end of the halliards is spliced into the upper part of the strap of this block, or bent into a becket put there for the purpose, and the end seized. The other end is then rove through one of the sheaves in the double block in the tye, then through the sheave in the single block in the chains, through the other sheave in the double block, and through a leading block on deck.

The Mizen Topsail Halliards have only one tye. The standing part is clenched or half-hitched to the strap, with the thimble, at the mizen-topmast head, and a single block spliced or secured in the end. Another single block is strapped into a swivel bolt in the mizen chains, and the halliards rove as with two single blocks; the fall rove through a leading block or cheek. (Some ships have a treble fly block).

165.—RIGGING TOPGALLANT YARDS.

They are got on board like the topsail yards. Leather the slings, seize-on the D thimble, parrel, and quarter blocks, rolling tackle straps,—tar the yard arms—foot ropes the same as topsail yards—stirrups one to each foot rope—iron jackstays secured to the yard with staples, fitted the same way as rope. (Iron sling-bands are allowed by the *new regulation.*)

The lifts are single; an eye is spliced to fit the yard-arm; the other end is rove through the thimble, or bull's-eye, or a half sister-block in the topgallant-rigging; a thimble turned into the end, and a lanyard spliced into it, and set up to another thimble strapped round a futtock plate inside the dead-eye in the top, or set up on the end.

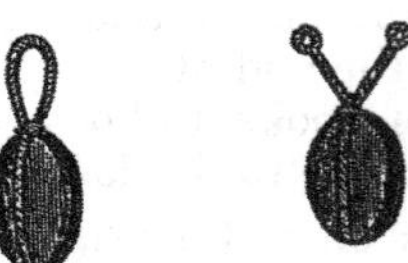

Braces.—A single block is seized into a single strap, having an eye to fit the yard-arm. If a single brace, an eye is spliced to fit the yard-arm, and the lift and brace marled together.

The quarter-blocks are double; are seized into a single strap, an eye being spliced in each end;—they lash together on the top of the yard—the foremost sheave for top-gallant clewline, after one for royal sheet.

Parrel.—A long and short leg. Take a piece of rope, cut it the required length, and splice the ends together round the yard. In one bight seize a thimble, with a round seizing; the other one round the yard; pass a round seizing close to the yard, round the parrel on the after side; splice a lanyard into the thimble, and fit a short strap the same way on the other quarter. These straps are sometimes served, and often covered with leather,—they go inside the cleats. Grommets can be worked if preferred, and dispense with the thimbles, as they are likely to injure the mast. Jaws are also recommended. The patent iron parrels are now in use in the navy, but are found not to answer for ships of war.

Tripping beckets are fitted one on each yard-arm; work grummet straps on quarter of yard, seize a thimble in with a round seizing passed between the yard and thimble. A grommet is put on the yard rope, to fit the yard-arm, when getting ready for crossing. Also, a lizard; a small piece of rope with a thimble spliced in one end, the other whipped. It goes on the yard rope before being bent to the yard.

When ready for going aloft, the yard rope is bent on, and the yard stopped to the lower rigging; the main on the starboard side, fore and mizen on the larboard side.

Note.—Royal yards, opposite sides, to the topgallant yards.

166.—TOPGALLANT BRACES.

Fore.—If double, the standing part is clove-hitched round the first and second shrouds of the main topmast rigging, or crotch of the stay, through the block for the brace, through another single tail block, secured to the first and second shrouds (the same as, and under the standing part), through lubber's hole, and through a fair leading sheave on deck.

They are often led forward from the blocks in the topmast rigging, through a leading block strapped round the eyes of the fore rigging, or after part of the top, and through fair leading sheaves on the forecastle. In ships of war, I prefer them abaft. The block in the topmast rigging is fitted as follows:—

A single piece of rope is spliced round a single block, having a tail about three or four feet long; clove-hitch this tail round the first shroud, then round the second, and seize the end. I have seen a round turn taken round the first, and a clove-hitch round the second; either plan will do, but if neatness is studied, clove-hitch round the second and third; this will bring the block under the rigging, and out of sight. If rove single, the block is secured the same way—an eye made in the end of the brace to fit the yard-arm; the other end rove through the block on deck, as before.

A whip is sometimes put on the brace, the block spliced in close up to the cat-harpens, which answers very well. One end of the whip is spliced into a bolt on deck, the other led through a fair leading sheave or block.

Main.—The main topgallant braces are fitted the same as the fore, with the exception of leading. The standing part is secured in the same manner to the foremost, or second and third shrouds of mizen-topmast rigging; the hauling part before all, through lubber's hole, and through a sheave in the rack, or a leading block, to the side abreast of the mizen-mast.

Mizen.—The mizen topgallant braces are single. An eye is spliced in one end to fit the yard-arm. The other end is rove through a single block; seized into a single strap, and secured to an eye-bolt on each side of the main cap, and through lubber's hole on deck. I have seen these braces led through blocks in main topmast rigging, in harbor, where appearance has been much studied.

167.—CROSSING TOPGALLANT YARDS.

One man stands on the topmast cap; two on the crosstrees (one on each side), one of the latter shoves off the grommet, and rigs the upper yard-arm; the man on the opposite side bears off,—one man stands in the topmast rigging to put on the lower lift and brace; another stands on the topsail yard, ready to bear off; the lower lift should be well manned in the top.

When the order "sway out of the chains," is given, the man standing on the fore part of the top bears the yard rope off, to clear the yard-arm of the top—when clear, "sway away." When the yard-arm is clear of the crosstrees, the grommet is shoved off, the upper lift and brace is put on, and the order "sway higher" is given; then the lower lift and brace is put on, and the lift hauled well taut. The man on the cap has the parrel-lashing in his hand, ready for passing; he reeves a turn, and on the order, "sway cross," he hauls on the lizard. The lower lift is boused on, and the yard falls across; the braces are hauled taut, and the yard squared.

When a ship is going to sea, the lifts and braces are stopt to the jackstay, and the topgallant yard ropes toggled for halliards, or half-hitched over the upper block. To toggle the halliards: Strap two single blocks, with single straps, leaving an eye below the seizing, in one, to take a small lashing; in the other to take the bight of the topgallant yard rope. Lash the block with the small eye, to the eye of a lower shroud, and reeve the yard rope through it. To the strap of the other block secure the toggle with a nettle lanyard.

Note.—Separate halliards may be fitted to dog on to the yard rope, with a double-tailed lizard, and hook the lower block to an eye-bolt in the top, which answers a better purpose.

168.—ROYAL YARDS

Are fitted the same as topgallant yards, and rigged the same, with the exception of the quarter blocks, which are single. In small vessels they have no jackstay, the sail being bent to the yard. Topgallant sails are often bent the same way, but jackstays keep the sail much better up on the yard. Some prefer a wooden batten nailed to the yard. Iron jackstays are now used for all vessels in the navy. (*New Regulation.*)

Fore Royal Braces.—Two blocks fitted in one strap, as span blocks, are lashed round the main topgallant mast-head; the blocks standing on the foremost quarter, on each side. Between the after part of the fore topmast trestle-trees, *a piece of wood with two sheaves*, the same size, and a large one in the centre, is secured.* The braces are single, an eye is spliced in one end to fit the royal yard-arm; the other end rove through the span-blocks, back again through the sheaves in the fore topmast trestle-trees, and into the fore top.

The blocks are often strapped separately, and seized into the strap with a round seizing, leaving room for a seizing to be passed through the strap, and round the eye of the topgallant stay, before going on the funnel, one on each side. This will not look so neat as span blocks, and are not so easily taken off and put on. The blocks for royal braces are often seized on the topgallant stay, with the idea of clearing the foot of the main royal.

Main royal braces are fitted in the same manner as the fore, and led through single blocks on mizen-topgallant mast-head, and back into the main top; or through lubber's hole in the mizen-top on deck. The latter is decidedly the best plan, as they can be much better attended to when under the eye of the officer of the watch, than when left to the topmen.

Mizen royal braces are fitted the same as the others, and lead through sheaves in the after ends of the main topmast crosstrees, and into the top.

Crossing royal yards.—They are crossed the same as the topgallant yards. When they are rigged aloft, the topgallant masts should be fitted with jacks for the men to stand on, not only to expedite the crossing, but also for the safety of the men. They are made of iron, and put on the topgallant mast immediately over the hounds; the jack is made round to fit the mast, and is

---

* This piece of wood is called a fair-leading chock.

put on before the funnel, if used. The horns on each side are of a proportioned length to the mast; an eye is turned in the end of each horn, for the royal rigging to reeve through, and set up as before. When no royal rigging, the breast backstay should be rove through the eye, and set up in the top with a gun tackle purchase, fitted between the two after dead-eyes.

Royal rigging is quite unnecessary, in my opinion, except in large vessels—the breast and standing backstay is sufficient.

Royal sheets are either toggled or bent to the clews, rove through sheaves, in the yard-arms, and through the after-sheave in quarter block, on the topgallant yard; through leading thimbles on the topmast rigging, and into the top, or on deck.

169.—ROYAL AND TOPGALLANT GEAR.

When the topgallant and royal yards are sent on deck, the topgallant sheets are stopped to the topmast-head, and hauled taut on deck. I have seen them in harbor stopt to the tye-blocks close down to the yard. The former is decidedly the best plan, as they are always ready for bending; the clewlines and bowlines, are also stopped at the mast-head.

The lifts and braces are taken outside the topgallant rigging, and the eyes stopt to the rigging at the topmast-head, before all;—hauled taut on deck, and in the top.

Royal gear is stopt at the topgallant mast-head, and hauled taut on deck, or in the top.

170.—SPANKER-BOOM, TRYSAIL-MAST, AND GAFF.

The spanker-boom, trysail-mast, and gaff, may be got on board by the yard and stay-tackle. Put the hoops on the trysail-mast, and stop them; sway away by a pendant tackle, and point the mast through the after chock of the trestle-trees; lash its head to the mizen mast-head; leather the boom in the wake of the crutch; seize on sheet-blocks, and reeve the sheets; tar the boom, put over the foot-ropes, which are set up, just outside the taffrail; boom-guys, which go with a gun-tackle purchase to the quarters. Hook the topping lift to an iron span around the boom; ship and key the boom; seize on a cleat to belay the outhaulers to; then leather the jaws of the gaff, fit throat, and peak-halliard blocks, brail blocks,* vangs and blocks,—reeve throat and peak-halliards, hoist up the gaff, and haul taut the vangs.

The spencer gaff may be rigged nearly in the same manner.

Chocks should be fitted to go in between the lower and trysail mast-heads. Copper the mast, in the way of the jaws.

171.—SPANKER-BOOM SHEET AND GUYS IN ONE.

Into a bolt, with a thimble in each quarter, strap a double block with a single strap; then seize into two grommet-straps, worked round the boom, (wormed and covered,) two single blocks, one on each side, just outside the taffrail, or crutch. Secure these blocks in their straps, with a round seizing passed between the block and the boom. The rope for the guys is middled and cut; then an eye, or cut splice made to fit the boom end. Take the larboard guy, and reeve it through one of the sheaves in the double block on the quarter, through the single block on the boom, through the other sheave in the double block, through a fair leader in the side, and pull it up on deck. The starboard one is rove in the same manner, through the block on the starboard quarter.

172.—SPANKER-BOOM TOPPING-LIFTS.

A cheek with a sheave in it, is bolted on each side of the mizen trestle-trees, under the rigging; instead of this cheek, a single block is often strapped into a bolt, with a thimble in it. On the boom outside the taffrail, is an iron hoop, with an eye-bolt on each side, and thimbles in them. Parcel the thimbles in the outside bolts, and into them splice the topping lifts; the other end reeve down through the cheeks on the trestle-trees, or block, and splice a parceled thimble in the end, for the purpose of hooking the jigger-tackle.

---

* Cheek-blocks are allowed, fitted to all gaffs, by new regulation. (*See Block Table.*)

173.—A BRIG OR SCHOONER'S MAIN-BOOM.

There being so little boom projecting over the stern, guys are unnecessary. On each quarter, strap a double block, and one on each side of the boom, in separate straps: through these reeve the sheet,—the standing-part from the strap of the quarter-block, and hauling part through one of the sheaves of the quarter-block. In working with the watch they are found very useful; one man can ease over, while two more can take in the slack. A boom-tackle is fitted with a pendant, to hook forward to an eye-bolt outside, and used when necessary. (*Also crotch-ropes*).

174.—REEVING PEAK-HALLIARDS.

The standing-part is spliced into an eye-bolt underneath, or bottom of the block; then the other end rove through the inside block on the gaff, from forward, aft; then through a sheave in the double block, through the outer block on the gaff, from forward, aft, and down through the sheave in the double block, and through a leading sheave in the bitts, or block on deck.

You may dispense with one block, and splice the standing-part round the gaff.

175.—REEVING THROAT-HALLIARDS.

The standing-part is spliced into the single block, which is hooked to the gaff, up through the double block under the top, down through the single block, up again through the other sheave in double block, and through a leader, opposite to the peak-halliards.

176.—TO FIT SINGLE VANGS.

Middle the required length of rope, and seize a cuckold's-neck in the bight to fit the gaff-end, and lead one end on each side. The cuckold's-neck should be neatly covered with canvass, and two snug seizings put on each quarter of the neck, showing two parts of the rope on the top of the gaff, and one underneath. Paint the eye the same color as the gaff.

177.—DOUBLE VANGS.

Seize into each bight of a long grommet strap, a single block, and secure the strap round the end of the gaff, outside the rigging cleats, with a lashing passed round the strap underneath the gaff, and over each block. Splice the standing part of the fall into a bolt; reeve the other end through the block on the gaff, and through a single block strapped into a bolt, also in the bulwarks. Blocks fitted in this way are called span-blocks. This is decidedly the best plan, as the purchase can be of use until hauled close down on deck. Pendants are now seldom used.

178.—FITTING GAFFS WITH CHEEKS, OR BRAIL-BLOCKS.

Close to the jaws, outside the single blocks for the throat-brails, secure two double blocks, strapped in the same manner as the outer blocks used for the peak-brails. The peak-brails, after being rove through the outer blocks, are led through the double ones in the jaws, and on deck through leading blocks.

Gaffs are also fitted with cheeks, instead of blocks; and sheaves cut in the jaws for the throat-brails, and fair leaders; which is the approved plan at present, and is very neat. Some ships in the service have their gaffs fitted to hook to an iron band, with a hook in the end of the gaff, instead of jaws. Others travel up and down an iron groove or railway, fitted to the lower mast (using no trysail-mast). Others again use a wooden batten nailed to the mast; some an iron jackstay, and some a rope one. *The try-sail masts are preferable, in a gale of wind.*

179.—GETTING UP A GAFF.

Pass the jaw rope; man the throat and peak-halliards, the former best, and sway the gaff up; when high enough, rack the halliards with spun-yarn to their own parts aloft, and the halliards can be hauled up, and coiled in the top out of the way. Steady the gaff amidships, by the vangs.

Note.—All gaffs should be peaked, or elevated to an angle parallel with the mizen-topmast stay.

180.—LOWER STUDDING-SAIL OR SWINGING-BOOMS

The lower swinging-booms have goose-necks fitted on one end, which in line-of-battle ships and frigates, hook to the foremost part of the fore chains, to iron straps fitted for the purpose. They are got in their places when brought alongside, with a burton from the foremost shroud, and another on the after backstay. One-third from the outer end, an iron band is fitted, to which the rigging is hooked. When secured for sea, they are got close into the side and lashed to a bolt for the purpose. When in harbor, in large ships, they are sometimes hooked to eye-bolts in the bends, which bringing them lower down, cause the boats, when moored, to ride easier. A small Jacob's-ladder is fitted to the fore chains, and sets up to the boom close into the side; also one or two seized on the boom some distance out, for the men to get into their boats with.

The fore guy is hooked to the boom, the other end taken forward and rove through a single block strapped in a bolt in the bowsprit cap, and led in on the forecastle. It is sometimes rove through a block on the spritsail-yard, and is of great use in getting the boom from the side; if no spritsail-yard, blocks can be fitted round the outriggers, or whiskers.

The after guy is hooked to the boom, and the other end led in through a sheave in the side; in large ships, on the main deck, close before the gangway port; in flush-deck vessels through the bulwarks. In large vessels they are rove double.

The topping lift is hooked to the boom the same as the guys.

The topping lift block.—Take a single block, large enough for the rope to be rove in; seize it into a single strap, wormed and served, leaving a small eye beyond the seizing, to take several parts of small rope. Seize this block on to the second shroud (if only one swifter forward), half-way between the futtock-stave, and seizing of the eye, passing sufficient turns to secure it well. When seized in this way there will be more space between the shrouds, than if seized closer up, which will allow the topping lift to work clearer, and cause no chafing. I have seen this block seized to the eye of a shroud well up, but prefer the former.

The lizard.—On the topping lift put a large-sized thimble; round this thimble splice a piece of rope about five fathoms long; for a large ship a piece of three-inch rope would be large enough. Reeve the topping lift between the first and second futtock shrouds, through the block, and send the end between the shrouds on deck.

A luff-tackle purchase is often fitted to the topping lift, half-way up the fore rigging.

Hoist up ship and key the boom; put on single blocks for forward and after guys, reeve, hook, and haul taut the topping lift.

Note.—Several ships in the service have span blocks fitted across their fore cap, and a clump block, or bull's-eye, fitted on each fore yard-arm, abaft the lift block. The topping lift is rove through the block on the cap, then through the one on the yard-arm, to the boom; which does away with the lizard, and when the boom is alongside, at sea, the topping lift can be unhooked from the boom, and triced up with the rest of the studding sail gear, under the fore yard. ***This method is much approved of in large ships.***

181.—LOWER STUDDING SAIL OUTHAUL, BLOCK, &c., &c. &c.

Seize a single block into a double strap, leaving an eye to fit the boom end, wormed and served. Then take a piece of six-thread stuff, and pass several turns round the strap and the bolt, and hitch it round all parts.

Topmast studding-sail tack-block.—Take a single block the required size, strap it with a good piece of rope, leaving a tail long enough to clove-hitch round the boom, and seize to the bolt in the end. This block is often strapped round the boom, and kept in its place with a bolt in the end of the boom, or a hole bored for the purpose. Sheaves are sometimes cut, but they are bad, as the least slue in the boom takes away whatever purchase the sheave would give.

Lower studding-sail halliard block, &c., &c.—Seize a single block into a single strap, leaving an eye to fit the boom taut. A small cleat should be nailed on the boom, to prevent the block slipping in, or the strap secured with a bolt. When the halliards are rove, a single block is hooked to the burton pendant, or lashed. The pendant is sometimes fitted with a block spliced in one end, and secured to the mast-head, over the rigging, with a lashing passed through an eye spliced in the other, and round the mast-head. This is quite unnecessary, as the block lashed or hooked to the pendant, answers the same purpose.

Reeving the halliards.—Reeve through the block to the pendant, before the rigging, then through the block on the boom.

Send the hauling part through lubber's hole on deck, and through a leading block.

The boom brace is spliced round the boom between the blocks. A single block is spliced in the end, half-way between the boom; when the yard is square, reeve a fall. The standing part, when the sail is set, is clove-hitched round the foremost shroud of the main rigging; the other end through a leading tail block to the same place. Small ships are not allowed boom braces.

For inner halliards, use the fore clew-jigger, hooked to the forward part of the top. When the sail is not set, and the boom rigged in, the inner halliards are also used to trice the gear up; it is then stopped with yarns snugly to the jackstay, and the ends of the gear coiled inside the futtock-shrouds, being previously stopped together.

182.—TOPMAST STUDDING-SAIL SPAN BLOCKS, HALLIARDS, &c.

Seize two single blocks into each bight of a strap, long enough to go across the topmast cap; allowing the blocks to hang clear on each side. Take a piece of small rope, and pass a lashing round the strap, over both blocks, under the cap, and then seize the blocks to eye-bolts in the cap.

To make the strap, take a piece of rope of sufficient size and length; worm and serve it, splice both ends together, and secure the blocks in their places with round seizings. Through these blocks reeve the halliards; first through the span blocks down; take the upper end and reeve it down on the foreside of the topsail yard, through the block on the neck of the boom-iron; the other end is sent down abaft the foremost crosstrees, before the topmast rigging, through lubber's hole on deck, and through a leading block. When not in use at sea, the bending end is hitched round the clew of the topsail, and the hauling part hauled up in the top. In harbor they are generally unrove, and the span-blocks taken down.

The downhaul is bent to the sail and made up in it.

Sheets are also bent to the sail and made up.

183.—TOPGALLANT STUDDING-SAIL BOOMS, &c.

Tricing lines—Are single. A single block is seized on to a shroud, close up, and a fall rove through it; one end is bent to the boom, the other sent into the top. When in harbor, a thimble should be fitted a few feet above the topsail yard, on the foremost shroud, and the tricing line rove through it. As everything is generally done in a hurry, trying who will be first, the booms are hardly ever properly secured, if lowered, after loosing to dry, and the men running out on the yards with the booms swinging about, frequently occasion accidents.

Topmast studding-sail boom.—When no boom brace is allowed and no lower studding-sail set, carrying the topmast studding-sail, blowing fresh, a brace can be put on, without rigging the boom in, as follows:—Take a belaying-pin, or anything that will answer for a toggle, and secure it to the lower studding-sail halliards, with a clove-hitch round the toggle, hauling the parts well taut; haul the toggle close to the block on the boom, and belay; and it will answer equally as well as a brace. The inner end of the halliards should not be let go, for in case the lower studding-sail requires to be set, the end can be hauled in, the toggle taken out, and the halliards overhauled for bending.

Note.—Should the boom *top up* much, and require a martingale more than a brace, toggle the halliards the same way, and bouse it well taut through a leading-block, perpendicular to the boom.

184.—GETTING STUDDING-SAIL BOOMS UP.

All studding-sail booms have two holes in the inner end, for a heel-lashing, and strap for the in-and-out-jigger, and sometimes a sheave in the other end for the tack. Take a piece of rope long enough for the heel-lashing; make a knot (a wall and crowned), in one end; reeve it through the hole in the boom end, haul through to the knot, and whip the other end; with the latter take two half-hitches, a little inside the sheaves, or outer end, and seize the end to the boom. Take a tail-block and half-hitch it half-way out the fore or main topsail yard, according to the boom required to be got up. Through this block, reeve a rope as a whip, (if a heavy boom, it should be a double one,) bend one end to the span, made with the heel-lashing, so as to balance the boom; the other reeve through a leading block on deck. Stop the hoisting part to the boom end by the sheave, and sway away. When high enough, cut the stops at the boom-end, and the boom will hang in the whip, on a line with the yard; point it through the boom-iron,—cast off the whip and span, and secure the heel-lashing, rigging boom out to square mark.

185.—TOPGALLANT STUDDING-SAIL GEAR.

If blocks in the topgallant rigging, the halliards are rove through them; one end is led into the top, abaft all, the other through the jewel-block on the yard-arm. Jewel blocks are single blocks, seized into single straps, having an eye to go over the bolt in the topgallant yard-arm. A small toggle is secured to the strap with a knittle lanyard. The eye in the strap is put over the bolt, and the toggle put in—the upper end of the halliards are rove through this block, on the foreside of the topgallant yard. When the sail is not bent, the studding-sail halliards are overhauled down, and hitched to the foremost shroud ready for bending. The jewel-blocks are always taken off, when getting ready to send the yards down, and an overhaul knot made on the end of the halliards, to prevent them from unreeving from the blocks. Whenever the order is given to "unbend the topgallant gear," the jewel-blocks must be taken off.

Tacks.—Sheaves are sometimes cut in the boom ends, but as they hardly ever answer well, and generally cause delay, and likewise require more men to get the tack out, blocks are decidedly preferable. Tail-blocks are best, as they can be so easily taken off and put on. Clove-hitching round the boom, and the end secured to the eye-bolt, is preferable to having a hole bored in the boom for the tail to reeve through, as it only weakens it, and is not necessary. The tack is rove through this block, and when the sail is to be set, the inner end is bent to the clew of the sail; the outer end led to the after part of the top, where it is hauled out, and generally belayed to a shroud or cleat.

Note.—Belaying either the halliards or tack to the rigging is bad, as they are constantly coming up. Cleats should be nailed on the after part of the top for the tacks. Two small tail-blocks, one on each side, secured to the after futtock-plate, for leading blocks, are of great use in getting the tacks out.

186—STOWING-HOLD AND SPIRIT-ROOM. (BALLAST AND TANKS).

See that the limbers are clear from chips or dirt, and place the limber boards. Clean, sweep, and white-wash the hold; place hoop-poles athwart-ships for dunnage, as near to each other as possible, so that each pig of iron will rest at least on two of them. The rust should be well beaten off the ballast, and each pig white-washed. As the stowing of a ship's hold and ballast, depends so much on her build, it is not possible to lay down any precise rule; it is, however, recommended to preserve a strict line of *level* in the position of the tanks. To effect this, and to produce the desired uniformity of surface, the stower must commence the stowage from the midship stanchions in the hold, and work *outwards* regularly towards the direction of the wings. The slightest irregularity of surface in the tops of the tanks may be the means of throwing out the general stowage, and ultimately causing a considérable deficit in the quantity of water which the hold is calculated to contain.

A short, though rather a rough way of calculating the weight of ballast required, is to allow one ton of ballast, for ten of tonage, for each class of vessels.*

Winging the ballast tends to make a vessel roll, and building up a-midships to keep her steady. Without ventūring on details, it may be remarked that the plan of keeping the ballast in the body of the ship, and clear of the extremities, seems to be most generally approved of; while at the same time care should be taken to keep her on, or parallel to *the line of flotation*, designated by the builder. The ballast in the spirit-room, should be a continuation of that in the hold. Make a draft of the ballast, indicating the exact number of pigs, the position they occupy, and their exact weight.

Previous to getting on board the water tanks, a plan of stowing them may be easily arranged by means of rough models of them in wood, which a carpenter can easily make. In getting the tanks from the store, attention should be directed to the lid-sockets, which if not properly lined with fearnought, will allow much of their contents to escape in rolling; as also to the obtaining the proper quantity of keys, and see that they are short enough to work between the deck and tanks, if the vessel is a small one. White-washing tanks inside, is found by experience to be highly useful in keeping the water pure. The screws for letting off the water require very careful treatment; for they are apt, if once started, never to be so tight again; and after being

* The weight of chain cables and water tanks, are considered in this calculation. also half of the shot. Also a consultation with the builder.

three or four years in use, the nuts decay, rendering the keys useless. If the water cannot be turned off from the tanks by the proper mode, there seems to be no other way of getting rid of it, in a case of necessity, but by forcing a hole in the bottom with a crowbar.

The tanks should be stowed during the time the ship is rigging.

Note.—By a late order, the valve in the bottom of all water tanks is stopped up, and the screw taken out. Those that are now made new, have no screw. There is also an alteration in the lids for the better.

187.—STOWING CASKS.

Strike down their beds, place and whitewash them; then commence stowing the casks at the after bulk-head in the hold, observing to have the largest casks in the kelson tier, and the gauges of the cask on each side of the kelson, to correspond. Be careful that the bung-holes are all up, the bilge free, and head clear.

After completing the first tier, go on with the second, placing hanging beds between the casks, and stowing barked wood in all the breakages. As the tiers approach the wings, let the size of the cask diminish.

188.—STOWAGE OF PROVISIONS, NAVAL STORES, &c.

Stow the beef on the larboard side, and the pork, starboard side; with the flour, rice, and beans in the wings; chocking all fore and aft with wood. The casks in the spirit-room are stowed in the same manner, with the exception that the stowage is commenced forward, instead of aft. Whiskey, molasses, and vinegar are always stowed in casks. The liquors of the medical department, and purser's stores, are generally stowed in the spirit-room. Dry provisions should not be stowed under the wet, and should be placed in such a manner, that when required, they may be got at without disturbing all the hold.

Make a draft of the lower, and riding tiers, and spirit-room, with the guages of all the casks on the draft; the number of barrels, boxes, &c.,with the kind of provisions they contain.

The shot and wads may also be got on board, and stowed in their respective lockers.

189.—STOWING CHAIN CABLES.

The chain cables are got on board through the hawse-holes,* and paid down the main hatchway, into their respective lockers. They are from *ninety to one hundred and eighty* fathoms in length, and are slip-shackled, or lashed to the kelson.

Note.—See table of allowance of chain cable for class, &c.

190.—TO GET ON BOARD AND STOW THE HEMP CABLES.

Hemp-cables are one hundred and twenty fathoms in length; two are now allowed to all vessels, from a ship of the line, to a third class sloop of war, inclusive. The cables are taken from the rope-walk, and coiled upon a car having a large hole in its bottom, and after being transported to the vessel, or lighter at the wharf, the upper end of the coil is passed down through all the flakes, and through the hole in the bottom of the car, then coiled away again in the lighter. By dipping the end in this manner, grinds or kinks are prevented, and the cable is got into the lighter, with only one turn in it.

The lighter being towed off to the ship, haul under the bows; place mats in the sides and sills of one of the forward ports; get the cables in on deck, and French-flake them fore and aft. They are now with the same number of turns in them, as when they left the rope-walk. See that the tiers are clear, and that the gratings are properly placed for the cable to lay on. Pass the end of the spare one below, and coil away with the sun, on the starboard side of the tier; make the coil as large as possible, taking care not to have too many flakes in a sheave, as the inside strands of the inner ones would be injured, by breaking in.

Pass the ends of the starboard one on the larboard side, and the larboard on the starboard side. Clinch them around the main-mast, or to the beams, coil them away with the sun, letting the ends remain out, to be pointed or tailed if necessary. Join the pointed ends with a short splice, worming the tails along the cable. The upper ends are crowned in the following manner, viz.: clap a seizing round the cable about two fathoms from the end, and unlay it to the seizing. With the three inner strands form an artificial eye; cut off the three next ones and woold

---

* If the vessel is alongside of the wharf, the chain-cables may be got in by a *shoot*, through the *port*, or over the *rail*.

their ends; with the three outer ones, form a crown, worm the ends along the cable, and clap on seizings in proportion.

The stream cable and messenger are coiled away in the tier of the spare cable. The hawsers, if possible, should be stowed in such a manner, that the end of every *one* could be passed up together if required.

191.—CATHEAD STOPPERS.

When not fitted with the slip, or patent stoppers, a good piece of rope, in proportion to the size of the anchor, has a stopper-knot in one end, then rove through the cathead, and hauled taut. It should be well wormed, parceled, and served in the way of the cat-heads, and sufficiently far towards the end, to take the ring of the anchor. The end should have a becket put in, and pointed over. Take a piece of small rope, and splice it into the inside yarns of the stopper, the same as a tail, or knot the yarns together; then marl down, and point over. The becket should be made large enough to take a good hauling-line, for the purpose of hauling the end of the stopper in-board, after being rove through the ring of the anchor.

192.—SHANK PAINTER.

A piece of chain is secured to the side; a large thimble, well parceled, is put into the last link; round this thimble splice the piece of rope intended to make the tail of the shank-painter; it is the same sized rope as the cathead stopper. The other end is pointed, with a becket in.

Note.—The patent iron slip or trick-stopper, is now generally used in the service, by those who can procure them. They are not allowed by the regulation, but quite a number of ships have them fitted.

193.—FISH-DAVIT GEAR.

The davit is stept into a shoe in the fore-chains, for the purpose. A double block is seized into a double strap, leaving an eye to fit the davit-head; both parts of the strap are marled together. Another double block is seized into a double strap, having a large hook* and thimble, to take the arm of the anchor. Take a large single block, seize it into a single strap, leaving an eye to fit the davit-head; it will lay the opposite way to the double one, and allow the hauling part of the fall to lead fore and aft along the gangway; or up aloft through a leader to the fore pendants.

Back rope.—To the back of the hook, clove-hitch and seize the end down, of a piece of rope, long enough to lead to the fore chains, or into the head, when the fish-fall is overhauled. This is taken forward when hooking the fish. Cat-back is used for the same purpose—*i. e., hooking the cat.*

Guys, bolts, rigging, &c.—In the fore and after side of the davit, bolts are driven. The fore-guy is a piece of stout rope, long enough to reach from the davit, when stepped, to the after side of the cat-head, leaving room for lashing. The after-guy is another piece of rope, long enough to reach the after part of the fore-chains, and both fitted as follows:—splice a hook and thimble in one end, into the other splice an eye, and into this eye splice a lashing.

Get a jigger on the foremost swifter, and hoist the davit into the step or shoe. Hook the guys to the bolts in the davit-head, and set them up to the cat-head, and after part of the fore-chains. Put over the double block, then the single, and reeve the fish-fall. Take two tackles, clap a good strap round the foremast, hook the double block to this strap, and the others to selvagee-straps round the davit-head. The strap round the foremast should be in a direct line whith the davit-head when perpendicular. These tackles will answer for topping-lifts, and will be found much better than the old-fashioned topping-lifts for stowing anchors.

Note.—I would recommend the iron davit, in preference to the wooden one, on account of its being more durable, much neater, more convenient for stowage and also requires less gear.

---

* Properly called a fish-hook.

194.—GETTING ON BOARD, AND STOWING ANCHORS.

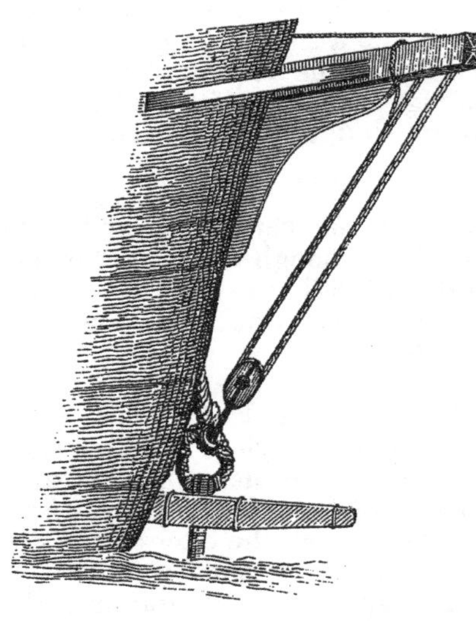

The fish-davits being rigged, reeve and overhaul the cat and fish-falls, get the anchors into a lighter, and tow them under the bows; pass up the stream-cable, and clench it to the ring of the bower-anchor; hook the cat, and run the anchor up to the cat-head. Pass the stopper, hook the fish, and pass the shank-painter. Unbend the stream-cable, and bend it to the waist-anchor, then drop the lighter aft, and secure her under the berth of the anchor. Brace the fore yard in, and the main yard up as much as possible; top them up a little, hook a stout tackle to act as a rolling-tackle, and bouse the lifts and trusses well taut. Pass a lashing round the slings of the yard, to ease the trusses. Hook both top-burtons to the yard-arm, and set well up the opposite breast-backstays. Pass a strap round the topmast, just above the lower cap. Hook the double block of a stout pendant-tackle to this strap, and the single one is hooked just without the place where the bull's-eye for the pendant is to be lashed; haul well taut the lifts, burtons, and pendant-tackles alike—reeve whips, and get up the triatic-stays. The bull's-eyes for the pendants are lashed sufficiently far out on the yards, to allow the anchor to clear the ship's side. Reeve the pendant up through it, and clench the end to the lower mast-head; have a thimble in the lower end, to which the purchases are hooked. Have a thwartship-tackle in readiness, to bouse the anchor to the gunwale; lash the lower block of the main-purchases, to the crown of the anchor, having guys from each fluke to keep it steady. The fore purchase-block is lashed to the ring.

Rack the topsail-tye aloft, and hook the lower block of the fore-topsail halliards to a stout strap, passed round the shank of the anchor amidships, then lashed above the middle of the upper arm of the stock. "Sway away;" when high enough, haul over on the stay and thwart-ship tackles, and get the bill of the anchor upon the gunwale. A cleat is nailed on the lower part of the stock, a lashing passed under it, and round the timber-head in the after part of the forecastle-bulwark for the purpose; another lashing from the same place to the upper arm of the stock, and frap all together. A shore is fitted from the side,

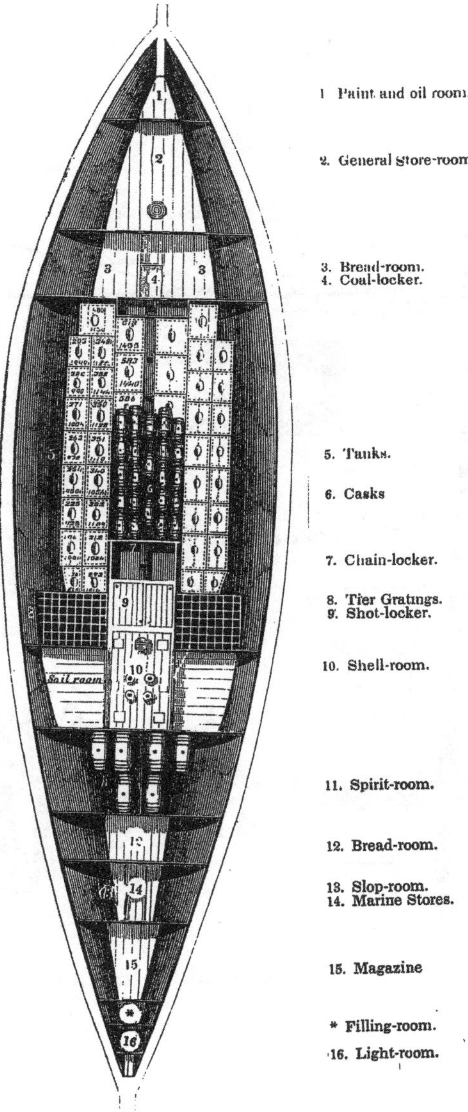

A Represen tation of the Internal Arrangements and Stowage of the Hold of a First-Class Sloop-of-War, U. S. N.

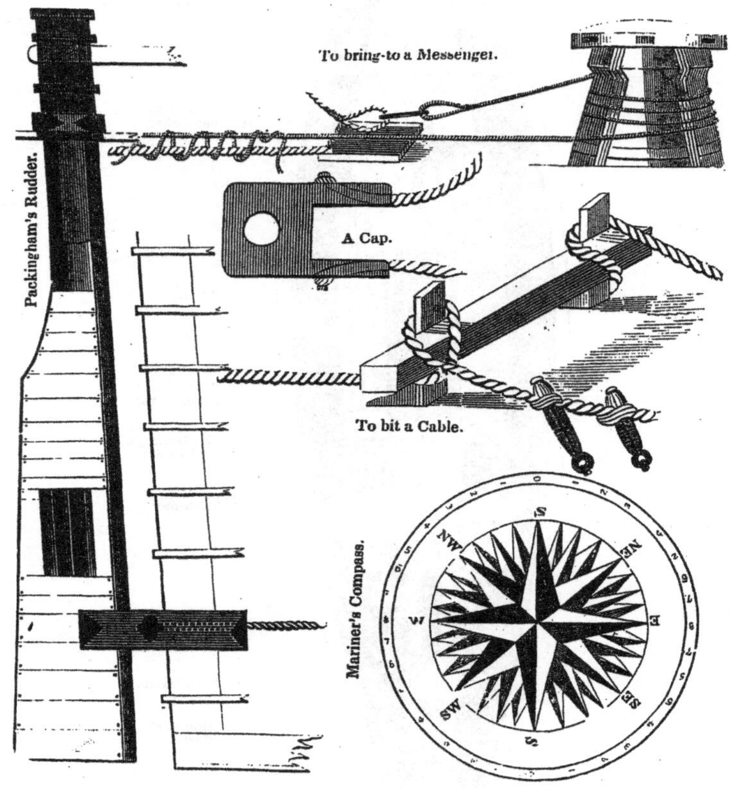

Packingham's Rudder, &c., &c.

on which the anchor rests, and a lashing passed round the shank through a span-shackle bolt in the side for the purpose; the inside fluke rests on a bill-board on the fore end of the chess-tree, or after part of the fore chains. Some ships stow their anchors further forward than others. The anchor being secured, unbend the stream cable, and unlash purchases.

Drop the lighter round on the other side of the ship—shift over the purchases, secure the yards, and get up the other bower and waist-anchors in the same manner. When done, pass the stream-cable below, and coil it down in the tier.

Note.—Belaying cat-head stopper. After being boused well taut with a jigger, take as many turns as the rope will allow, over the timber-head on the forecastle bulwarks, and seize it well to its own part with spun-yarn. The shank-painter is set taut and belayed in the same manner.

195.—BENDING THE CABLES

A rope is rove through the ring of the anchor, the end led in through the hawse-hole, and bent to the cable with a timber-hitch, three or four fathoms from the end, and stopt along to the end of the cable. Haul out on the ring-rope, and when there is sufficient of the end through the ring, cut the stops, unbend the ring-rope, and form an inside clinch, having it smaller than the ring of the anchor. The bends are put on opposite to each other, and a small bend put on near the end to secure it. Render the cables as far as possible through the clinch, and stop them together to prevent chafes, &c.

Note.—The chain cables are shackled to the rings of the anchors; then bend the buoys and buoy-ropes.

196.—TO RANGE AND STOPPER THE CABLES.

Before ranging the cables, they should be bitted, which is done as follows:—When the cables are bent, haul up sufficient slack to form a bight abaft the bitts; throw the bight which is thus formed, over the head of the bitts (and in case it is to be weather bitted, take another *turn* round the cavil). In ranging, get a tail-block over the hatchway, through which reeve a rope; overhaul down, and hitch to the cable. Take the running part close out to the side, bouse on the rope, and flake the cable fore and aft the deck. Clap on deck and bitt-stoppers, before and abaft the bitts; put on rounding at the range, if hemp, which is intended to veer, and also have cable mats in readiness, to be used as may be required. If a hemp-cable, a small range forward of the part bitted; if chain-cable it merely requires bitting; ranging is unnecessary.

Note.—When the anchor is let go, veer from the locker through the compressor—(*i. e.*, supposing it to be a chain.)

197.—STOPPERS, &c., &c.

The trip-stoppers.—Both ends are made fast to eye-bolts under the after part of the fore-channels. The score in the end of the waist-anchor stock rests in the bight, and is used to trip the anchor clear of the ship's side, when let go.

Deck-stoppers are hooked to bolts in the deck. They have a knot worked in the end, with a lanyard fast to it. The lanyard is passed round both the stopper and cable, abaft the knot, and then wormed along the cable, forward of it. (*See claw-stopper*).

Ring-stoppers are ropes middled; the bights are passed through the deck-bolts, the ends rove through the bight, and dogged along the cable.

Bitt-stoppers are tailed and rove through the sampson-knee forward of the bitts, then taken over the cable abaft the bitts, under again, and wormed along the cable forward. A tackle may be hooked to this, and used for veering.

Dog-stoppers are very long, and are used in the tiers. One end is clenched round the main-mast, and the other wormed along the cable.

The wing-stoppers are similar, but are clenched around the orlop-deck beams in the wings.

198.—COMPRESSORS, OR COMBING-STOPPERS.

For hemp-cables they are very long, and are tailed. Two holes are bored through the deck, abaft the after beam of the hatch; one end of the stopper is rove downwards through one of the holes, passed under the cable, and rove up again, through the other hole. Both ends are then dogged round the cable taut, so as to nip it against the beam.

The compressor for chain-cables is an iron elbow, one end of which is bolted to the forward beam of the hatch underneath, and intended to work on the bolt. The elbow goes round the cable, having an eye in the other end, to which a luff-tackle is hooked; which being hauled on, stoppers the cable effectually.

199.—PUTTING ON NIPPERS.

Nippers should be from three to five fathoms in length, and made of the best rope-yarns. They are used when heaving up the anchor, and are passed as follows:—Lay the messenger on the cable, and begin two or three fathoms abaft the hawse-hole; two round turns are first taken with the end of the nipper, round the messenger, and held by a boy, then round both. The other end is wormed round the cable, as the first was round the messenger. When the strain becomes heavy, racking, and even round turns may be used, having also small heavers, and selvagees to secure the ends; taking care to have dry ones to use when the anchor is up and down.

Note.—Some ships have done away with the nippers altogether, and use nothing but the selvagee and heaver.. Each nipper-man provides two selvagees, and one heaver; also an iron pin of proper size to put through the links of the chain-cable, to prevent the muddy chain from slipping through the strap.

200.—IRON CLAW-STOPPERS, AND CLEAR-HAWSE SHACKLES.

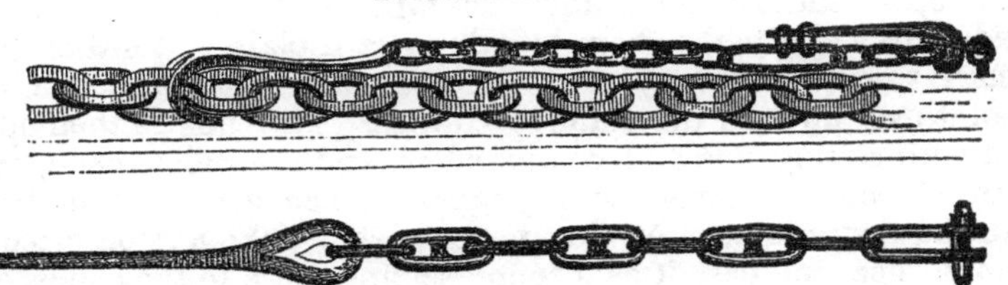

These are used for chain-cables, instead of rope-stoppers, and are found very convenient, and more durable than rope. They are allowed to every ship in the service by the new regulation, and are fitted as follows:—A piece of chain four feet long, is fitted with a devil's-claw in one end, and a slip-hook in the other; a slip-ring also in the long link in the chain, for the end of the slip-hook.

201.—TO CUT, AND PASS A MESSENGER.

The length should be equal to twice the distance from the after part of the capstan, to the roller in the manger, and add four times the circumference of the capstan-band; this is suffi cient for splicing in the eyes and taking turns. The messenger is passed with three round turns, and then the eyes lashed with the lanyard, figure-of-eight fashion. The part which is brought to the cable is undermost.

Note.—Some messengers are fitted with a strap and toggle instead of a lashing; this plan is much quicker than the old way. The size of the strap, ought to be one half the size of the messenger; in length it should be once the circumference of the capstan on the bight. Instead of splicing the two ends of the strap together, make a spritsail-sheet knot with the six strands, reeve one bight of the strap through one eye of the messenger, the other bight through the other eye, and toggle them together.

To dip a messenger.—Cast off the lashing, slack up the turns, and pass the eye up or down, as necessary, between the turns and capstan. Render the turns through each other, and pass the lashing again.

202.—SPLICING ROPE-CABLES.

Cut off the ropemaker's fag-end, and unlay the cable sufficiently far for splicing. Take the inside yarns and lay them up into three strands, equal to the piece of rope intended for the tails, and splice these small strands and tails together. Take the outside yarns and make them into three-yarn plaits or knittles, then marl the remaining yarn down over the splice and tail, and point over all with the plaits or knittles. The cable is then opened with setting fids and commanders, and the splice made, each strand boused through with jiggers; the ends are put in twice on the tier, and once on the anchor part. Take a good piece of small-rope, and pass it as a round-seizing, close to the splice, and cross it on all sides. When finished it will look square; and pass another, with smaller stuff, close to the ends. Worm the ends into the lay of the cable, and pass three or four spun-yarn seizings, at equal distances round them and the cable, to keep them in the lay—make the seizings, and whip the ends of the tails. The size of the seizing, and number of turns, depend on the size of the cable.

Bends.—The small rope used as seizings in clinching, are so called. The end of the cable for clinching to the anchor should be wormed with good strands, and backed with good spun-yarn, and the end capped. The worming should be long enough to form the clinch, and the cable well tarred before and after its being done. The lay of the cable opens in clinching, and being wormed, it prevents the wet getting into the heart of the rope, or lodging. To pass the bends, have a good piece of rope of the length and size required; bring both parts together, leaving one end a third longer than the other; then pass it round both parts of the cable, and put both ends through the bight. Pass the under turns with the short end, the upper or riding-turns with the long one. Stop both ends well with spun-yarn to their next parts, and cross the whole seizing or bend, with sennit; pass the sennit on the bight, and secure both together with a reef-knot.

203.—TO SHIP, AND UNSHIP A RUDDER.

Have the rudder brought under the stern, hung to a scow. Bore a hole through the beam or carling over the rudder case—drive an eyebolt up through it, and fit a washer and forelock. Strap a large single block* with hook and thimble, and hook it to the eye-bolt; reeve a top-pendant through the single block, down through the rudder-case, and hitch it to an eye bolt, which is temporarily fitted into the rudder-head. Clap a deck-tackle on to the other end of the pendant; have heel-ropes leading forward on each side, after being rove through their respective holes in the rudder. Man the deck-tackle fall, and hoist away. When the rudder is high enough, guy it fair with the heel-ropes; see the pintles fair for entering the gudgeons,—lower away, and fit in the wood-lock. Come up the pendant, unreeve the heel-ropes—take the bolt from the rudder-head, also the one from the beam or carling above—ship the tiller, and reeve the wheel-ropes.

To unship it.—Fit the bolts, single block, pendant and deck-tackle as before, unreeve the wheel-ropes, unship the tiller, knock out the wood-lock, and "sway away." When the pintles are clear of the gudgeons, lower away, and secure it to the scow or lighter—tow it on shore, and parbuckle, or hoist it out of the water or scow.

---

* If a top-block can be procured, it will answer best, as the neck of the hook being shorter, it will give more hoist.

204.—GETTING THE GUNS ON BOARD.

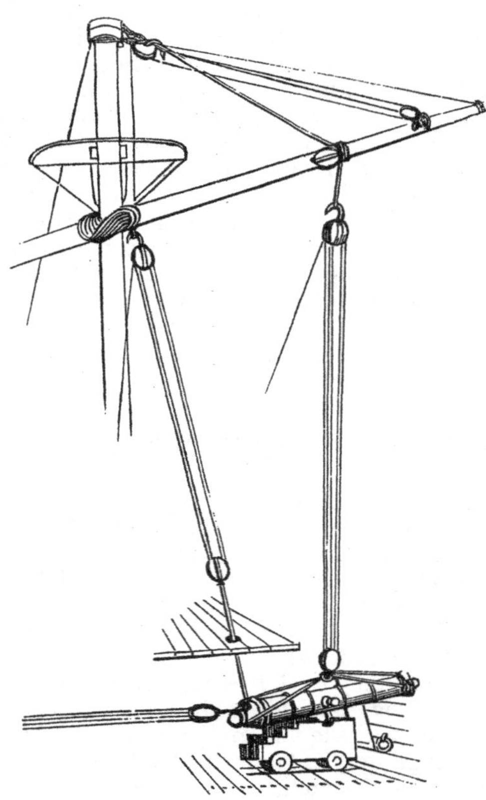

The gun-carriages and all the equipments belonging to the guns are brought alongside in lighters, and hoisted in with the yard & stay. Get them on their respective decks, and reeve the purchase for getting the guns on board.

Securing the main-yard.—To the bolts in the lower cap, hook the double blocks of two burtons. The single ones are hooked to selvagee - straps, round the yard, close to the lifts, and the falls sent on deck, through leading - blocks. Bouse well taut the main-lifts and burtons together, and belay. Then pass a good lashing round the main-yard in the slings, and main-mast, to keep the yard steady, and support the trusses, they being previously boused well taut.

Take the top tackle-pendant, and reeve it through a top-block, secured well to the yard with a good lashing, passed round the hook, on the outside quarter; take the pointed end over the cap, pass it between the head of the mast and heel of the topmast, take two half-hitches on its own part, or that from the yard, and secure the end with a round-seizing of spun-yarn. Get a single whip upon the main-yard, close to the lashing, bend one end to the hook of the top-tackle fall-block; hoist the block up and hook it to the thimble in the pendant. Through this and the other top-tackle fall-block, reeve a fall; clench one end (the standing part), round the main yard close to the block; the other end, when rove full, through a leading block on deck, by the bitts.

The garnet-purchase is a pendant, with a thimble in the upper end, which is hooked to the main-pendant-tackle; the other end is rove down through holes bored in the deck for the purpose, and a stout hook and thimble spliced or turned into the end. The garnet should be long enough to go on the lower-deck, and the holes bored perpendicular to the centre of the port through which the guns are to be got on board. The slings are made of breaching-stuff, twice the length of the gun, the ends spliced together, and the strands put in twice each way; seize an eye on the bight, large enough to go over the breach of the gun; put over the eye, and put the slings along the upper part of the gun, lashing them with a piece of rope round all, just forward of the trunnion; put the other end over the muzzle, and in toggle. Lash the purchase-block to the bight of the slings, and also bend on a hawser to weigh the gun, in the event of parting the purchase. "Sway away;" drop the lighter from under the gun, and when the breach is as high as the port, hook the garnet and also an a-thwartship-tackle to the breech-ring; haul on the tackle and bring the gun in through the port—run a carriage under—lower away; place the trunnions fair, and clamp them; come up the purchases, and transport the gun to its port. The lower and main-deck guns are got in in the same way. The cannonades are taken over the rail; a toggle is put in the muzzle, one bight of the slings over the cascable, the other over the muzzle, and back-lashed to the toggle; the stay or purchase-block is lashed on midships of the slings, and the stay or pendant-tackle to the same place; consequently the gun will come in square. Have the bed and slide ready, place it fair, and drive in the naval-bolt. Ship the screws, beds, and coins; reeve the breeching, hook side and train-tackles; see the guns square in the ports, and secure them.

The main-deck guns might be taken in over the rail, and struck down the main-hatch; but I prefer their being taken in through the port, if plenty of men.

Note.—The reason for having additional security on the main-yard is, because in getting in the guns, the strain is altogether on the yard; while in getting up the anchors, the strain is divided between two yards. The burtons are sometimes frapped in with the main-lift, between the yard and cap; but I prefer their not being done so, as they will all render fairer, when the strain comes on them. It is customary to top the main-yard up; but I saw a line-of-battle ship's guns got in without it, and as it brings a greater strain on the slings and trusses, it should not be done to so great an extent as is the practice.

Caution.—When the garnet-purchase is raising the breech to the level required to place the gun in its carriage, care must be taken that the main-purchase be *not* lowered by a turn, but that the men on the fall "walk back" with a steady step.

When the gun is lodged in its carriage, it is removed to its proper port, and another carriage is rolled to the receiving port, ready for the reception of the next gun, and so on.

205.—FITTING SHACKLE-BREECHINGS.

If it be required to fit the breechings on this recently improved plan, it will be necessary to taper and point both ends of the rope preparatory to splicing or turning-in a shackle on each extremity. The shackle should be turned-in and secured to each end of the breeching by two separate seizings, one close to the shackle, and the other towards the pointed end of the rope. They are frequently spliced into a thimble and then shackled, which I think is much neater.*

By this simple and serviceable method, the breeching may be shifted in a few seconds, it being no longer necessary to reeve it through the ring at the breech. An opening is now made in the cascable, which admits the introduction of the breeching on the bight; and the cascable fitted with a hinge or snatch, and sometimes a bolt going through the cascable, confines the breeching, and prevents it jumping out on the recoil of the gun.

206.—TRIATIC STAYS.

A double block is strapped into a pendant, a hook and thimble spliced into one end; a single block is strapped with a hook and thimble, a fall is rove, the standing-part bent into a becket in the strap of the single block; sometimes the double block is strapped, and the pendant spliced in over the seizing. A good strap with a thimble seized into it, is fitted to the strap of the lower block. A piece of rope is spliced round the strap of the fore-stay block, and the other end, when cut to the required length, spliced round the strap of the main-stay block, and seized. This is called the span, and is generally the length between the fore and main-

---

* This last improvement was introduced by FRANCIS GRICE, *Esq.*, chief Naval Constructor. *U. S. N.*

hatchways. The main-stay hooks to a strap with a thimble in it, from round the main-mast-head on the fore side; the fore from one abaft, fitted in the same manner. The main one generally comes down alongside the slings, the fore one between the trestle-trees, abaft. The pendant and tackle are sometimes fitted separate, to hook, and are easier stowed away.

Note.—In case of emergency, these pendants may be taken round the mast-head, and hooked to their own parts. I have known some ships to use them this way altogether.

207.—HOISTING IN SPARS.

Overhaul down the fore and main-yard tackles, fore and main-stays, and lead their falls to the opposite side of the deck the spars come in at. Hook burtons to the lower caps (double blocks), single ones to selvagees round the lower yard-arm, close inside the lifts. Send the falls on deck, and pull up the lifts and burtons together, and trusses; brace the fore-yard in, and hook on to the spars. They should be always hoisted in as stowed.*

If the spars are too long to come in abreast, between the fore and main-masts, such as topmasts, hook the main-stay to the strap round the foremost end, and fore-stay to the after one; then hook the yards to separate straps made of pieces of stout rope knotted together, or good selvagees, according to the weight of the spar. Man the yards and walk them up; when clear of hammock-nettings, haul on the main-stay, ease the fore and main-yards, keeping the spar square, and get the foremost end inside the rigging; then ease the main-stay, and get the spar in its place on the booms. Small spars can be got in with the main-yard, a double whip on main-stay, or single guy if required.

208.—STOWING BOOMS.

The spars on the starboard side are stowed as follows, viz.: Main-topmast, head aft; main-topgallant, (mast-fishes) half-yard, main topmast studding-sail booms, and jib-boom. On the lar-

* The spars intended to be stowed underneath, should be hoisted in first; such as topmasts, half-yards, and jib-boom, for the lower tier, and round off with the smaller spars on the top.

board side—fore-topmast, head forward; fore-topgallant-mast, mast-fish, half-yard, fore topmast studding-sail booms, flying-jib-boom, &c.

There are several small spars which are equally divided, to make the booms as snug and neat as possible. A great deal of room can be gained by stowing them amidships in one pile, and the boats on each side. As the spars are stowed, they should be *numbered on each end*, also a list taken, and painted on the fore-side of the boom-boards; by so doing it will save much time and trouble to find any spar that may be required; as I have seen all the booms unlashed before a spar was found.

The booms are lashed to span-shackles in the deck for the purpose. A few small spars should be kept out, to drive under the lashing, to set all taut. When stowed they are covered with tarpaulins, or matting made for the purpose. When the spars are all in, square the yards.

Note.—It is becoming the general practice, to stow both topmasts with their heads forward. Many ships stow all their spars amidships in one pile, with the exception of the fore and main-topmasts, which are stowed outside of the boats; spare main-topsail yard on the larboard-quarter, the fore on the starboard-quarter, in the chains, and spare jib-boom across the stern, secured underneath the stern-davits.*

* Some ships stow topmasts and all amidships; but this is a bad plan, as it would be necessary to take out all, to get a topmast if required, it being underneath.

PART III.

REEVING RUNNING RIGGING.

209.—FORE BOWLINES.

The fore bowlines have an eye in one end, to go over the toggle, and are rove through a single block, seized into a single strap, and secured to the fore-stay collar with a seizing passed through an eye left in the strap, and the other end led in on the forecastle.

The fore and main clue-garnets are hitched to the yards, then rove through a block lashed in the clews of the sail, up through a block on the quarter of the yard, down to the fife-rail.

210.—FORE-TOPSAIL CLEWLINES.

Topsail clewlines are fitted the same as clew-garnets, and sometimes with a whip; they come on deck through lubber's hole.

When fitted with a whip, a piece of rope nearly equal to the double clewline, is rove through the quarter-block, and an eye spliced in one end, which is secured with a seizing round the clew, when the sail is bent. In the other end, splice a single block, and reeve a fall through it; one end splice into a bolt in the deck, and the other reeve through a leading-block, well apart from the standing-part.

Note.—The disadvantage of double clewlines, is, the points getting in the clew-blocks when clewing up, or sheeting home.

211.—TOPSAIL BUNTLINES

Are toggled to the foot of the sails, and rove through single blocks at the mast-head, underneath the rigging, and through lubber's hole on deck. Cheeks or sheaves set in the foremost end of the trestle-trees are best, as they keep the buntlines clear of the belly of the sails. Blocks in bolts will do equally as well, but do not look so neat. I would recommend fitting a shoe-block underneath the eyes of the rigging, on each side, in preference.

Buntline-spans are short pieces of rope, with a thimble in one end, and the other end whipped; the buntlines are rove through these thimbles, before being bent to the sail, or rove at the mast-head. At sea these spans are knotted together, abaft the tye-blocks on the yard, and stopped to them. When in harbor, they are let go, to allow the sails being triced well-up to furl, or hauled out to dry, by the bowlines, when toggled to the foot of the sail.

212.—FORETOP BOWLINES

Have an eye spliced in one end to go over the toggle on the bridle; the other is rove through a block at the bowsprit-cap, strapped into a bolt, or a sheave cut in the after end of the bees and led in on the forecastle.

213.—MAIN BUNTLINES.

There are two on each quarter, and reeve on the bights. Reeve first through the large sheave in a shoe-block, then reeve both ends, from forward, through the double block under the fore part of the main-top, and bend or clinch both ends to the holes in the foot of the sail for the purpose. Sometimes toggles are fitted into the holes, with double straps, and an eye spliced into each end of the buntlines. If no shoe-block is to be got, seize two single ones into one strap. Through the other sheave of shoe-block, reeve a fall; clinch one end to the main-stay by the foremast, or splice an eye and seize it round it. The other end reeve through a leading block, seized into a single strap, leaving an eye to seize it to the stay, or through a sheave or leading block in the fore-bitts.

214.—FORE BUNTLINES

Generally toggle to the foot of the sail, and are sometimes clinched; then rove through a double block under the fore part of the fore-top, and through fair leading sheaves in the racks to the bulwarks The buntline should be long enough to allow the sail to belly. The outside leg of the buntline is sometimes rove through a thimble strapped into the foot of the sail, and clenched into a cringle put into the bolt-rope, a few feet above the clew.

215.—MAIN BOWLINE

Is a runner and tackle, and is rove and unrove as required. It is rove through the thimble seized on the bowline bridle; the end of the runner is secured round the fore-bitts, or to a cleat. The lower block of the gun-tackle purchase is fitted with a hook. and hooked to a strap close to the end of the runner, for the purpose. I have seen the main-bowline boused up to the weather-forecastle bulwarks, which I think preferable, not seeing any very great advantage from its being hauled amidships; particularly when it is considered that the main-topsail yard, on a wind, is braced abaft the main-yard.

216.—TOPGALLANT SHEETS

Are rove through the sheave in the topsail-yard, then through the after sheave in the double block in the quarter of the topsail-yard, and through a leading sheave or block on deck. The upper end is bent to the clew of the topgallant-sail; sometimes a long-eye is spliced, which goes over a toggle in the clew of the sail. They are also fitted with sister-hooks, which is the latest and most improved plan.

217.—TOPGALLANT CLEWLINES

Are bent through the clew of the sail, and secured with a sheet-bend; it is then rove through the foremost sheave on the quarter-block on the yard, and sent down through lubber's hole on deck.

218.—FORE TOPGALLANT BOWLINES

Are toggled to the bridle of the sail. The fore one is rove through a single block at the jib-boom end, one on each side, and led in on the forecastle through fair leaders. These blocks are strapped like span-blocks, and lashed together on the upper side with two lashing-eyes; they are sometimes strapped singly, and go over the boom-end, or seized to the guys. Double blocks are also sometimes put in these straps, and the two inner sheaves used as jib-brail-leaders.

219.—MAIN TOPGALLANT BOWLINES

Are toggled to the bridle of the sail, then rove through sheaves cut in the after part of the fore-topmast-crosstrees, and through lubber's hole, through fair leading sheaves on deck. Single tail-blocks are sometimes used, clove-hitched round the after shroud in the fore-topmast rigging, close up to the futtock-stave, or seized.

220.—MIZEN TOPGALLANT BOWLINES

Are toggled to the bridle of the sail, and rove through single blocks on each side of the main-mast head, and through fair leading blocks on deck. A double block is often used instead of two single ones on each side, one sheave for the brace, the other for the bowline. They should be led from lubber's hole abaft all, between the cat-harpen legs, or futtock-shrouds.

221.—TOPGALLANT BUNTLINES

Are seldom used in light weather, although very necessary in taking in sail, when blowing fresh, as they save much time, and in some instances a man's life. On a wind it spills the sail, and prevents its getting over the lee yard-arm; and going free enables the men to furl it much easier. A strong proof of their utility may be inferred from the fact that merchant vessels, who have as little rope rove as possible, and are generally weak-handed, have their sails fitted with buntlines.

They are fitted as follows:—A piece of rope with a thimble on it, is spliced into two eyelet-holes, worked in the foot of the sail, about a third from each clew.* Splice the end of the buntline round the thimble; reeve the other end through a single block, seized into a single strap, and secured round the topgallant mast-head by a lashing passed over all; send the end of the buntline through lubber's hole, on deck before all to the fife-rail.

222.—ROYAL BOWLINES.

The fore royal-bowline is rove through a block at the flying-jib-boom end, and led in on the forecastle, through a fair leader, the same as the topgallant-bowline, and the main-royal bowlines through the chock at fore-topmast head.

223.—REEF-TACKLES

Are sometimes double, and also fitted with a whip, as clew-lines, or pendant and burton. When double, a single block is seized into a single strap, having a thimble in it, and the seizing passed between the block and thimble. This block goes on the bridle, or cringle, in the leech of the topsails. One end of the reef-tackle is clinched round the neck of the boom-iron, the other rove through the block, up through the sheave in the yard-arm, and through the upper sheave in the sister-block, through lubber's hole, and through a leading block or sheave on deck.

---

* This piece of rope is called a span.

When single, an eye is spliced in the end of the pendant, to go over a toggle fitted to a bridle, as above; the other end rove through the yard and sister-block, a single block spliced into the end, and a whip rove, as on the clewline.

Note.—The generality of naval ships use their top-burtons with short hide-pendants; some object to this, as the top-burtons may be wanted, when they are in use as reef-tackles.

224.—LEECH-LINES.

The forward leech-lines are rove through the upper sheave-hole of a shoe-block; both parts are then rove through a double block, hooked with a pendant to the lower cap, then through two single blocks seized to the jackstays on the yards, and are clinched to the leeches of the courses, forward of the sail.

The lower legs are rove through the other sheave-hole in the shoe-block, and the standing-part made fast to the fife-rail; the other end being used to haul up the sails.

The after leech-lines are rove through blocks on the underneath part of the yard, and clinched to the courses abaft the sail, to the same places as the forward ones.

Note.—Shoe-blocks are now pretty much out of fashion—when they are not used, both parts of the leech-lines are led on deck, and the whip-purchase dispensed with.

225.—SLAB-LINES

Are bent to the middle of a span at the foot of the sail, led up abaft, and rove through a block lashed to the grommet or span, around the straps of the quarter-blocks of the lower yards, and down on deck. These are very necessary in light weather, and in rough weather, may be converted into spilling-lines.

226.—ROYAL CLEW-LINES

Are bent to the clews of the sail, rove through the quarter-blocks on the yard, and led either in the tops, or on deck.

Brig-of-War, under full sail.

Scale-draft of a First-Class Frigate.

227.—FITTING TACKS AND SHEETS, BUMKIN-GEAR, &c.

A single block is seized into a single strap, leaving an eye to fit the bumkin; this block is made with a shoulder, which lays on the bumkin when the block is on.

Bumkin-braces are now generally chain; one is hooked to the bow, and two to the cutwater; and set up with a lanyard rove through span-shackles in their ends, and others on the bumkin, or with a turnbuckle.

Reeving the tack.—Clinch the large end round the oumkin, outside the block, having been well wormed, parceled, and served, far enough towards the small end to take the block on the bumkin, when the sail is reefed. Reeve the small end through the block in the sail, then through that on the bumkin, and in on the forecastle through a hole in the bulwarks, for the purpose.

Fore sheet.—The large end is served the same as the tack, and is hooked into a bolt in the side for the purpose; the small end is rove through the block in the sail, and through a sheave in the side, or gangway bulwarks. Large ships generally work the fore-sheet in the waist (main-deck), but it is often worked on the gangway, (spar-deck).

228.—YARD TACKLE TRICING-LINES.

If no cheek on the yard, take the pendants taut along from the yard-arm, and then secure a single tail-block. On the foremost shroud, well up, seize another single block, fitted with a single strap, leaving room when seized-in, for the seizing with which it is secured to the shroud. Round the fiddle-block in the pendant, between both sheaves, secure the tricing-line with a running-eye; then reeve the other end through the cheek, or tail-block, and then through the single block on the shroud, and on deck.

229.—TO REEVE AND TOGGLE ROYAL-HALLIARDS.

Take a round-turn with the yard-rope, well up round the strap of the block, with the long-eye; reeve the bight through the eye and put the toggle in it; then bring the end up from the block seized to the eye of the shroud, and reeve it through the one on the yard-rope, send the end on deck, and reeve it through a leading block.

When half-hitched, the lower block is fitted as described, and secured; the upper one is strapped with a thimble in the strap—reeve the yard-rope through the thimble, and then through the lower block, up through the upper one, and on deck through a leader.

230.—FORE STORM-STAYSAIL GEAR.

To fit the stay.—Take a piece of good rope of proportionable size to the sail; fit one end with two legs as a stay, and lash them abaft the foremast-head, the legs being placed underneath those of the standing-stay. Take a piece of rope the round of the bowsprit, inside the fore-stay collar; splice an eye in each end, and seize a thimble in the bight—splice a lashing in one eye, and secure the strap round the bowsprit, by passing it through both eyes, until sufficient turns are taken to secure it. Reeve the end of this stay through the hanks for the sail, then reeve it through the thimble in the strap, and set it well up with a luff-purchase; the double block hooked to a strap well up the stay, the single one to another strap on the end; then pass a round-seizing round both parts, close to the thimble—come up the luff, and pass another seizing between it and the end, but not at too great a distance, as it will prevent the sail from coming close down.

Halliards.—Have a good strap to go round the foremast-head, close to the stay. It can be fitted with two lashing-eyes, and when so fitted can be easier taken off, and put on. When the sail is to be set, hook the double block of a luff-tackle to this strap, and the single one to the head of the sail; the hauling-part being sent down abaft the fore-yard, and through a leading block on deck.

Downhaul.—A single block is secured to the parts of the strap round the bowsprit—the downhaul is spliced to the head of the sail, then rove through the hanks, through the single block, and led in on the forecastle. When a stay is fitted, the downhaul block is seized to the strap round the bowsprit.

The downhaul is often double; if so, a single block is secured to the head of the sail, the standing-part of the downhaul secured to the strap on the bowsprit, and the hauling-part led in as before.

Sheets.—Deck-tackles are generally used, one on each side; they are hooked to the clew of the sail, and the hooks well moused. When the sheet is aft, the weather one is overhauled. The after blocks are hooked to eye or ring-bolts, as convenient, and should not be too high or too low; if too much up and down, they slack the foot of the sail; if too high, the after leech. The falls are rove through leading blocks, and the all hooks should be well moused.

Note.—These stays when set up, may be secured cutter-stay-fashion, instead of seizing the end up, which will allow the sail to haul close down on the bowsprit.

231.—MAIN STAYSAIL GEAR.

The stay is fitted the same as the fore, and sets up round the cross-piece in the fore bitts, after being rove through the hanks.

The halliards are fitted the same as the fore.

The downhaul is rove through a block strapped round the bitts for the purpose. If rove double they are fitted in the same manner.

Instead of iron hanks, I have seen grommets used, made of pieces of rope, with a wall-knot worked on one end, and an eye spliced in the other; these are long enough to go round the stay and becket. They are secured to eyelet-holes in the sail with a seizing, and are always kept to it. I have seen the sails set on the spring-stays, when fitted in this way, but prefer separate stays.

There are also other ways of setting storm-staysails, but those I have mentioned are in most general use. When a main-trysail can be got, mizen-staysails should never be drawn, as a ship will keep much better to windward with trysails and fore-staysail, than under the staysails alone.

232.—MIZEN-STAYSAIL GEAR.

The halliards are hitched to the collar of the staysail-stay, rove through a block in the head of the sail, then through a leader, and led down on deck.

The downhaul is clinched to the head of the sail. and rove

through the hanks down the mizen-stay. The mizen staysail sheet is a runner, leading through a snatch-block and thimble. A gun-tackle purchase is most commonly used, which answers all purposes.

233.—TOPMAST STAYSAILS, &c., &c.

Fore.—The standing part of the halliards is seized or hitched to the fore topmast spring-stay, then rove through a block in the head of the sail, up through a leading block under the eyes of the topmast rigging, then down on the larboard side of the deck abaft the foremast. The downhaul is hitched to the head of the sail, rove through the hanks, then through a block seized to the tack of the sail, and led in on the forecastle, through a fair leader. The tack is a simple lashing.

The fore topmast staysail and jib-sheets are pendants lashed to the clew of the sail, with a block in the end, through which the sheets are rove; the standing part is hooked to an eyebolt in the bows, and the running part is led in on the forecastle.

Main.—The standing part of the halliards is hitched to the collar of the main-topmast spring-stay, reeving through a block at the head of the sail, then through a block at the main-topmast head, and led down on deck. The downhaul is fitted the same as the fore, and led down by the fore-mast. The tack is rove through a block in the weather fore-rigging, or top.

The main topmast staysail-brails are seized to the leech of the sail, led up through the hanks to a block seized to the upper hank, and can also be used as a downhaul.

The middle, lower, and upper topgallant-staysails and jackstays, may be fitted in one. In this case a double block is turned in, and lashed to the after part of the fore-topmast crosstrees, or mast-head; the lower part is set up in the fore-top, and the upper part at the fore-topgallant mast-head.

The middle staysail-stays are rove through a single block, strapped to the topmast, down on the cap.

The lower and upper topgallant staysail-stays, are rove through blocks fitted to traverse the jackstay, with lock-thimbles, the former being rove through the other sheave of the double block at the topmast cross-trees; the latter through a block at the fore-topgallant mast-head, and both led on deck.

The downhaul blocks are single, and are seized to the straps of the tricing-line blocks. The halliards are whips hitched to the collars of the stays, rove through blocks in the head of the sail, through leading blocks at the mast-head, and down on deck. The tacks are single and led in the fore-top; the sheets are also single, leading in the gangways.

Note.—The principle object to be attended to, in reeving running-rigging, is to avoid the ropes being too much crowded in one place, crossing or chafing each other, or any part of the standing rigging, as it not only destroys it, but also decreases the desired purchase to be obtained by their running clear of each other.

234.—SETTING UP RIGGING FOR A FULL-DUE.

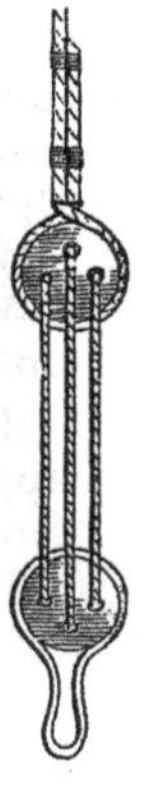

Have all the luffs on deck; fore, main, and mizen pendant-tackles hooked, and tackle-falls laid along for pulling up; new lanyards ready for reeving, seizings, marling-spikes, levers, mallets, grease, small spars for ratling-down, triangles rigged ready for hoisting up the mast, to secure the futtock-shrouds and cat-harpen legs, (if used;) burton-falls sent on deck and rove—all the temporary ratlines cast-off—spars got up underneath the bowsprit with the gratings for the men to work on—topgallant-masts and flying jib-boom housed; and also men stationed at the dead-eyes to turn in if required. Let everything go abaft the masts, commence turning in the dead-eyes, and reeve the lanyards—set up the bowsprit-rigging and secure it. Then man the pendant-tackles, set taut the after-swifters—(if wedges in) get the mast well forward in its place, and secure the stays. Cast off the cat-harpen legs (if fitted), and futtock-shrouds.* Set up the rigging for a full-due, observing the same precautions as when it was first set up.

The lanyard is now rove full, and when racked, take the end and form a clove-hitch above the dead-eye, then rack the surplus-end to the inside parts of the lanyard, until the end is expended. The hitch is formed between the dead-eye and shroud, around both parts, in the space left by stretching—some use a half-hitch taken over all round the shroud, hove well back, the lanyard expended, and the end seized. The ends of the shrouds are then cut square and capped, and the mats laced on.

Rigging-mats are made with small rope, three-quarter-inch,

* Vessels having their futtock-rigging set up to bands round the mast, use no cat-harpen legs, and have therefore no occasion of coming up either of the above.

and are called sword-mats. They are generally the breadth of the dead-eye, and long enough to take in both—the lanyards are laced inside. They are hardly ever used on topmast rigging; they look heavy, and are of no use, except on the forward shrouds and backstays.

235.—STAYING MASTS.

The practice of "staying masts with the wedges in," has been already denounced as contrary to every received system of seamanship. The stays may be set taut with the wedges in, but the masts should be always free in the partners, whenever there is occasion to alter the position of their *standing;* because it is impossible but that the precise situation of the mast must be altered a little, rendering necessary corresponding alterations in the wedges. When these are made and the wedges firmly fixed, there can be no inequalities of play or pressure—the whole becomes a solid mass, yielding naturally and uniformly to the motion of the ship. Whereas, if in setting up the rigging the wedges be kept fast, the mast pressing unequally against them, having too much play in one part, and too little in another, it must inevitably get crippled.

In preparing to set up the rigging, though the stays may not appear to require a pull, it is well to have the luffs and tackle ready; for after lifting the wedges, there is great probability of its being found necessary.

236.—BLACKING RIGGING.

The most convenient method of blacking rigging, is with the topgallant masts on deck, but royal and topgallant rigging placed at the mast-heads; for then men who ride down and black the topmast-stays, can then at the same time easily black the topgallant and royal-stays; or, what is handier still—let the men at the mast-head haul over and black these small stays, and pay them down forward when done. The men also who black down the topmast-backstays, can carry on at the same time with the topgallant and royal-backstays. By this method the masts are kept clean.

If, on the other hand, topgallant-masts be kept up when blacking, the small stays and backstays must be let go, in order that they may be got at by the men on the topmast-stays and backstays; consequently the masts must be adrift, are likely to be daubed over with blacking, and if it should come on to blow fresh, so as to render it necessary to get the topgallant-masts on deck, much injury must result to the blacking.

The topsail and lower lifts should be blackened first, the men having to stand on the yards to do them.

Previous to commencing, the decks should be well sanded, and the paint-work and head covered with old canvass. The quarter-tackle should be clapped on one side of the main-yard, and also a burton hooked, ready for clearing boats.

The finer and warmer the day, the better—the blacking will lay on so much the smoother and thinner; but commencement should be delayed until the dew is well dried off. A dry calm day is the best; for the blacking will not take effect, unless the surface it is laid upon be dry.

237.—STATIONING THE CREW.

In dividing the crew into watches, care should be taken that the physical force is as equally distributed as possible, and that there be as many seamen, ordinary seamen, boys, and marines, in one watch as in another.

Petty officers should be chosen from among the seamen, and those selected who have been long in the service, and have proved faithful. Forecastle men should be middle-aged seamen, with a few ordinary seamen and landsmen. Young active seamen should be selected for topmen, also a few ordinary seamen, landsmen and boys. After-guard, a few elderly seamen, with ordinary seamen and landsmen. Waisters are chiefly landsmen, with a few ordinary seamen; in single-decked vessels, where there are no waisters, more men should be stationed on the forecastle and in the after-guard, in proportion to the number of the crew of the different classes of vessels. Idlers are excused from keeping watch—they are officers' servants, cooks, &c., &c.

Divide each watch into first and second parts, and appoint a captain to each part; number the men belonging to the forecastle, having all the larboard watch even, as two, four, six, and the starboard odd; have the numbers painted on canvass, and let each man sew it on his bag and hammock; having also for greater distinction, the larboard painted red, and the starboard black. The men should be below alternately, so that when one watch is below, there should be an equal number of the other watch on deck.

238.—STATIONING THE CREW AT QUARTERS.

Captains of the guns should be chosen from among the seamen who have been long accustomed to them, steady, with good sight, and quick motion. The largest and stoutest men should be chosen to man the long guns, the others the cannonades. The boarders should be stout men—the firemen and sail-trimmers, active young men. Be particular to station them as near where they are accustomed to do their duty as possible, in order to prevent confusion. Let all the first part of the gun's crew be in one watch, and the second part in the other, so that in the event of going to quarters in the night, the watch on deck can clear away the guns, while the watch below will clear away the hammocks.

To a twelve-pounder cannonade are stationed four men and one boy. All the men stationed at the long guns of a double-decked ship, should be armed with cutlasses, and called "boarders"—the first of the gun's crew to be called second boarders, and *vice versa.* They are only to be called on when required to "board," or in a case of great emergency to "repel boarders," and then every man will repair to the upper-deck, except the firemen, quarter-gunners, and powder boys, who will remain below to protect the ports, or to assist in extinguishing a fire.

All the men stationed at the cannonades should be boarders and sail-trimmers. As boarders, the first part should be armed with pikes; the second part with small-arms, who are to repel the boarders, but not to quit the ship.

In a single-decked ship, all the men stationed are boarders; the first part to be armed with cutlasses, and the second with pikes.

The battery being manned, distribute the rest of the crew as follows:—have a quarter-master at the signals, when in a squadron—topmen and marines in the tops, to repair damages, and act as small-arm-men—a quarter-master and two men at the relieving tackles—men stationed at the passages, to pass full and empty boxes; also others at the shot-lockers. Mastmen to see the rigging clear—cook, and armorer at the galley—the carpenter and his mates at the pumps and wings—the master-at-arms, and ship's corporal in the light-room—the gunner, his mates, quarter-gunners, and cooper, in the magazine, and the surgeon and assistants in the cock-pit.

239.—STATIONING THE CREW FOR MOORING AND UNMOORING.

In stationing the men, place the same number of men, of each watch, to perform a piece of duty. When in a squadron, have quarter-masters at the signals, and also in the chains—men at the wheel—quarter-gunners to overhaul the fish, and grapple the buoys—men to overhaul and hook the cat, and attend the backropes; also others at the mast, to see the rigging clear. Boatswain's mates in the gangways; carpenter's mates to ship and unship the capstan bars, and attend the stanchions, with the music at the capstan—some fore-topmen to put on nippers, or selvagees, some main-topmen to take them off, and boys to carry them forward. Hands to rouse up and veer away the cable, to attend the stoppers, and light forward the messenger. The yeoman in the store-room—master-at-arms, and ship's corporal on the berth-deck, and cook at the galley—tierces in each tier, or chain-locker, and the remainder of the men at the capstan.

240.—LOOSING AND FURLING.

Take the same number of men from each watch, and station them at the same rope, &c. The topmen are to man their respective yards—hands are to attend the boom-jiggers and tricing-lines—forecastle men to attend head-sails, trysail and foresail—main-yard men to look out for the main-sail—after-guard, for the spanker and main-trysail—for the main-topmast staysail, the fore-top-men—for the main-staysail, the gunner's crew—hand stationed to sheet home, and hoist the topsails, and when coming to an anchor, the same men to man the clew-lines, bunt-lines, and weather-braces; and when loosing sails to dry, to man bowlines, or buntlines. In furling, the captains are to be in the bunt, in reefing, at the earings.

241.—STATIONING THE CREW FOR TACKING AND VEERING.

Station the men from the "watch bill"—have hands at the jib-boom end, to overhaul the jib-brails, and light over flying-jib sheets. On the bowsprit end to light over jib-pendants—hands on the bumkins, and in the chains, to overhaul tacks and sheets, and backstay-falls. On deck, at the wheel, spritsail-braces, jib-sheets, jib-brails, braces, bow-lines, clew-garnets, tacks and sheets, backstay-falls, lifts, trusses, spanker-sheets, guys, vangs, and topping-lifts. Aloft, to overhaul lifts and trusses—attend outriggers, and bear the backstays abaft and abreast—the mast-men to see the rigging clear, &c., &c.

For reefing.—The men are stationed as in furling, with the exception of the captains, who are stationed at the earings. When the yards are down, the men from the clew-lines and bunt-lines will haul out the reef-tackles.

242.—GETTING READY TO BEND SAILS.

It is customary to bend the light sails first, such as jibs, spankers, and trysails. Overhaul the jib and flying-jib stay, and halliards, in on the forecastle. Have the lashing spliced into the sheets ready for passing, and seizings to the hanks.

Overhaul down into the top the reef-tackles, and stop the blocks to the foremost shrouds, (or the end if single.) Overhaul the topsail-sheets from the yard-arm, and half-hitch them round a dead-eye, or foremost futtock-plate. Bunt-lines into the top, and stop them to the foremost shroud, above the topsail-yard, or to the tye-blocks—clew-lines into the top, and stop them to the eye of a shroud, and get the harbor-gaskets on the yards. A rope-yarn stop will be quite sufficient for all these purposes. Both burtons should be overhauled on deck before all.

Overhaul down the leech-lines, slab-lines, bunt-lines and clew-garnets, and stop them so as to prevent their flying about.

Take two selvagee-straps, put them round the neck of the boom-irons, and to them hook the double-block of a long jigger;

United States' Ship-of-the-Line Columbus, at Anchor. 80 guns

U. S. Frigate UNITED STATES, under full sail. *50 guns*

the single one overhaul down, and hook to a ring or eye-bolt in the bulwarks, and the fall led through a leading block a-midships.

Lower down the gaffs—overhaul the brails, and have seizings of two-yarn spun-yarn ready, to secure them to the sails. If hoops, seizings should also be put on them, with both ends rove through the bight.

Topgallant yards should be got out of the rigging, and laid on deck out of the way, ready for bending the sails. Top-burtons overhauled down forward of all, for the topsails.

Note.—When the preparations above stated are made, it is intended to bend all the sails together.

243.—BENDING SAILS.

Call all hands to bend sails—get the courses, jib, topsails, and spanker, on deck. Open them out, and see that they are whole and complete; with the bowline-bridles, head and reef-earings, rope-bands, reef-points, sheet, clew-line, and reef-tackle blocks all in their proper places. Bight the topsails down in their respective places forward of the masts, with the clews out. Hook the lower block of the burton to the slings passed round the centre of the sail, and mouse the hook—reeve the fall through a snatch-block or leader, and keep the sail clear of the top as it goes up.

Overhaul the courses athwart the deck, shackle on the sheet, and also the tack, and clew-garnet blocks—reeve and bend the gear—stop the head of the sail to the bunt-lines, use the clew-jiggers for yard-ropes, hooking to the first reef-cringle, and stop the head earings to the block.

The end of the jib-stay having been brought in on the forecastle, reeve in the hanks, and stop the luff of the jib—hook on the halliards—reeve the downhauls—fit the brail-block and reeve the brails—hook on the sheet-blocks, or pendants, and reeve the sheets.

Lower the spanker-gaff—pass the throat and peak-earings, and lace the head to the gaff—seize on the brails, and reeve them and the outhauler. All being ready,

To man the gear.—First, man the top-burtons and sway the topsails clear of the deck—man the jib-halliards and downhaul—yard-ropes, clew-garnets, clew-lines, bunt-lines, reef-tackles, and gaff-halliards: at the word run out the jib, reeve and set up the stay, and seize the tack. Sway the topsails and courses up to the yards, where some hands are ready to receive them. Bend the gear and haul out; then take a turn with the earings—ride down the heads and pass the earings exactly; make fast the rope-bands, fit the leech-line block of the courses—seize on and reeve the leech line. In the mean-time some hands are employed in seizing on the hoops of the trysails and spanker, as they go aloft. After the sails are all bent, it would be well to let them fall, to see that all the gear is bent clear, if so, clew up and furl the courses and topsails, and stow the jib, spanker and trysails.

The topgallant-sails, royals, and studding-sails are bent on deck.

Send the staysails into the tops, fit the jackstays and tricing-line blocks, seize the head of the luff; reeve the halliards, down-hauls, and brails, bend the tacks and sheets; stow the staysails and haul all taut.

Note.—The staysails are not *all* allowed by the new Book of Allowances.

244.—BENDING SMALL SAILS.

By small sails are meant topgallant-sails, royals, flying-jib, studding-sails and staysails.

It is only in ships in good order where the men go through this manœuvre with smartness and method, after being exercised, and having become familiar with the ship and their stations.

First, all the yards, topgallant, royal, and studding-sail, should be got out of the rigging, and down on deck at the same time. Next, a proportion of hands should be sent to each sail, and all bent together, including flying-jib and staysails.

When the topgallant-sails, royals, and studding-sails, are all bent, they should be swayed into the rigging all together, and not one after another.

If the topgallant-yards happen to be across, the best plan, if circumstances will permit, is to bend all the other small sails first, except the flying-jib, and then to wait until the yards are sent down at sunset, to bend topgallant-sails and flying-jib.

Topgallant sails ought not to be bent while the yards are across, because the earings must then be hauled out, and passed *over* the lifts and braces, which precludes the possibility of un-rigging the yard afterwards, without unbending the sail. Sometimes one of the two sets of topgallant-yards are appropriated in harbor to exercise, (sending up and down) while the other is kept below, with the sail bent, ready for crossing.

In bending topgallant-sails, the earings are passed the same as the topsail, and the sail seized to the jackstay, the yard-rope bent, the sails furled, and the yard got into the lower rigging. In furling, bring the leeches taut along the yard, and keep the clews in the bunt, then roll the sail up from the yard-arm, and pass the gaskets. Put the grommet over the yard-arm, man the yard-rope and sway the yard up and down; put the lower yard-arm into the snotter, over the foremost dead-eye; secure the upper yard-arm with a lanyard spliced round the shroud for the purpose; it is called a stop. The lizard should be singled, ready for going aloft, by reeving it once through the thimble on the yard-arm, and half-hitch round the yard-rope with the bight.

Trysails and storm-staysails should be bent at this time, if they are to be bent at all before leaving harbor.

Note.—Good rope-yarns answer very well for robins for topgallant-sails and royals. You are never at a loss for them in bending, and in unbending they are easily cut.

245.—BENDING A SPANKER.

Overhaul the brails well, and pass the sail through their bights. Haul the earing in the jaws out first; then the outer one. Splice the lacing into the outer eyelet-hole, lacing, and secure the lacing in the jaws. Bring the after-leech taut, along the gaff, and within a few inches of the blocks; mark the place for the throat-brails, also for the peak, opposite their respective cheeks on the gaff, and seize the brails to the leech-rope, by passing the seizing between the strands and round the brails. Eyelet-holes, worked close to the leech-rope, are far preferable for seizing the brails to.

The throat-earing is generally passed through an eye-bolt in the lower part of the jaws; but this never brings the sail close to the mast, and looks very bad. In preference, I would recommend having a score cut under the leather in the jaws, and the earing passed from the cringle through this score, and an eye-bolt on the upper side of the jaws, back through the cringle, and so on, until sufficient turns are taken to secure the sail. Large staples also are fitted to the jaws for the purpose, and keys on top, which answer better, and are more secure; also bending battens, instead of lacing round the gaff.

The outer earing is passed round a cleat on the upper side of the gaff, for the purpose. Take the earing from the cringle, pass it round outside the cleat, back through the cringle, and round the cleat, until sufficient turns are taken: then take several inner turns round the gaff and cringle; frap all the outer turns together with the remaining part of the earing, to bring the parts close, and prevent any chance of their slipping over the cleat; take two half-hitches, expend, and seize the end.

To haul out this earing, and stretch the head of the sail well, use a small jigger; secure the double block to an eye-bolt in the end of the gaff, pass three turns of the earing, cat's-paw the end, to which hook the other block, and pull the earing well out. I have frequently seen only one earing used; but would prefer two, as all inner turns, when much strain is on them, should have a separate earing. If a new sail, and requires much stretching, it is hauled well out before passing the earing, by hooking the inner block of the jigger to the cringle. Man the throat and peak-halliards, hoist the sail up gradually, seize the hoops, and reeve the lacing.

Note.—Trysails are bent in the same manner. Some fit them to haul *in* and *out* on the gaff, with hoops.

246.—FITTING SEA-GASKETS.

Gaskets are made with foxes, or small spun-yarn, and platted, like making sennit. The spun-yarn is middled over the bolt, and platted together, the bight forming the eye; sometimes a piece is platted for the eye, then all worked together; if not, the eye is served over afterwards. Sea-gaskets are long enough to have only two on each yard-arm, and to furl the sail over booms and all, when close-reefed, as there will be no more sail on the yard-arms than at any other time. They are secured round the jackstay, by reeving the end through the eye; sometimes round the yard.

247.—FITTING HARBOR-GASKETS.

In making, the eye is left large enough to take a small thimble, then platted broader in the centre, and tapered to a small end. The broad part should be long enough to make the sail in when furled with two reefs. They may be (to look well) about two-and-a-half inches wide, but this is quite a matter of taste. When put on the yard, the thimble is put underneath the jackstay from forward, and secured to it by a seizing passed round the neck of the gasket and jackstay, close to the thimble, and when the sail is ready for their being passed, it is taken up and rove through the thimble, and the sail tossed well up; the end then shoved underneath between the sail and gasket, once or twice. These always look better than any other, are easier passed and secured, and keep the sail well up. There is generally one harbor-gasket to every other seam.

248.—BUNT-GASKETS.

These are always, as to fitting, a matter of taste, but at present they are generally made of wove mat, two or three inches wide, with the two legs crossed, and an eye in each end. I have seen them made of rope, in the following manner:—Take the distance between the two quarter blocks, and measure it off on deck; drive a nail slightly into the deck at each end; then measure from the centre the height the bunt is intended to be, and there drive another nail. Take a piece of rope, from two and a half to three-inch, and measure off sufficient to go over these nails, forming a triangle; splice both ends together, and seize a thimble in each corner; put these thimbles over the nails again, and fill the space in diamonds or squares, according to fancy. The thimbles in each end are secured by the quarter-blocks to the jack-stay, and also in the centre. It is not necessary to have thimbles in each end, as an eye will answer every purpose. A long sennit-gasket is middled and seized by the upper thimble; it should be sufficiently long to go round the mast, when the gasket is boused up, to secure it and the bunt well into the mast.

249.—HAMMOCK GIRTLINES.

Whips are rove at the yard-arms. If rope is not used on purpose for girtlines, the studding-sail halliards will answer; they are rove as follows:—A tail block is put on each side of the jib-boom end, and another on the spanker-boom. Overhaul down the whips, and bend them round the girtlines with a bowline knot, allowing room for their rendering through. Belay the foremost ends of the girtlines and trice up; haul upon the after-part, and get all taut. A man lays out on each yard-arm, and marks the girtline with rope-yarns where the tricing line, or a whip, should be bent; then lower away, cast off the bowline knot, and bend the tricing lines round the girtlines with a rolling hitch.

The whips are led from the lower yards to the lower caps, through blocks hooked to the bolts, and on deck. The lower end of the tricing-line is often bent to the girt-line as an inhaul or downhaul; but it is best to have them separate, as it prevents walking the hammocks up, and laying across the deck; and there are plenty of other ropes' ends which will answer the same purpose.

When one girt-line of a side is not enough, others are rove inside in the same manner. The generality of ships reeve them inside of the lower rigging, as they are much easier got down, and the hammocks are not so likely to get dirty, or overboard.

250.—STOPPING ON HAMMOCKS.

Every man should be obliged to have three knittle-stops at the head, and two at the foot of his hammock. When stopping on, they should overlay at each side about two or three inches, and be stopped together at the foot—numbers up and in.

The forecastle-men should stop their hammocks on forward, next foretop-men, next maintop-men, next mizentop-men, next after-guard, idlers, and boys. Boatswain's mates abreast of each hatchway.

251.—FURLING OR STOWING THE BUNT OF A SAIL.

When the sail is nearly rolled up, hook the bunt-jigger, bouse it well up, lower the buntlines, and *shove* the sail well into the skin, taking pains to keep the bunt square; pass and secure the bunt-gasket—take off the jigger—lower and square the studding-sail booms, and pass the heel-lashings.

252.—FURLING COURSES.

The leeches are handed in along the yard, then the sail rolled up snug, with the ends of the points passed in towards the bunt, to give the sail a gradual increase in that direction. Pass the gaskets, lower the booms, and, if required, stop up the gear.

Bowlines are stopped to the slings close down, and hauled taut on the forecastle.

The bowline-bridles of all sails, in furling, are laid with the toggle towards the bunt, and bridles taut along the yard.

When a sail is neatly furled, it appears neither above nor below the yard—earings well slewed up—sail smooth under the gaskets, bunt square, and a *taut* skin. The heels of the booms should be square, and every thing necessary completed, previous to *squaring* the yards.

253.—MAKING UP SAILS.

In making up a course, stretch the head of the sail well taut along the deck or loft; bring up to the head the belly-band, then the foot, leaving the clew-blocks out at each end; also the bowline-bridles, and roll taut up; pass the head-earing round the sail close inside the bolt-rope, and put a stop of good spun-yarn to every seam. The reef earings are made up in the sail.

In making up a topsail, stretch the head of the sail taut along; bring the second reef up to the head, and lay all the points and earings snugly along; then bring up the belly-band, and then the foot. The clew-blocks, bowline-bridles, reef-tackles, and toggles or span, should be left out, so that when the sail is sent aloft for bending, the sheets can be rove, reef-tackles and bowlines toggled, without loosing the sail, which will be found of great advantage when blowing fresh. Roll well up, stop with spun-yarn at each seam, and expend the head-earings round the ends of the sail.

Topgallant-sails are made up with the clews out, and bowline-bridles, (if wished,) but they are always bent to the yards on deck; so the neater, they can be made up the better.

Note.—The reef-earings of the topsails should be secured to the cringles, before rolling up; bowline-hitch the end of the first reef-earing to the head, second to the first, third to the second, and fourth to the third reef cringles; as there is sometimes much trouble in getting hold of an earing when it is not secured as above.

All spare sails should be *tallied*, before being stowed in the sail-room, as it will prevent all mistakes; but if a sail is properly stowed, and the *master* and *sailmaker* take a list when they are stowing, there never can be any difficulty in finding what may be wanted.

Royals are made up the same as topgallant-sails.

254.—TO MAKE UP A TOPMAST STUDDING-SAIL.

Stretch the sail taut along, and overhaul the downhaul through the thimble and block, and bight it along the whole length of the leech. Then roll up towards the inner leech, lay the sheets along the whole length of the sail, roll up over all, and stop the sail well up with spun-yarn or foxes. The earings are expended round the head of the sail when bent to the yard.

Note.—The topgallant studding-sail is also made up in the same manner.

255.—FURLING FORE AND AFT SAILS, (WITH CLOTHS OR COVERS.)

The jib is hauled close down, and the sea-gasket passed round it. The cloth is then placed over, and the stops tied. Eyelet-holes are made in each edge for the stops. Jib-sheets and halliards stopped, and hauled taut.

Furling Spanker.—It is also furled best with a cover; it can be furled in the two after cloths, the same as a jib, but it never looks so well, takes time, and in most instances has to be loosed two or three times before it gives satisfaction.

In furling with a cover, the sail is brailed close up, and the cover stopped round, commencing from the end of the gaff, and working in to the mast, and down on deck.

Trysails are stowed in the same manner as spankers.

The fore-topmast staysail is stowed as a jib, in the netting.*

Note.—Stowing fore and aft sails requires more handy-work than seamanship, the principal thing being to furl them in the smallest compass, and in the after cloths, as it brings the seams up and down. I have seen staysails admired for their neatness from the deck, when the greater part of the sails were lying loose in the top. This should be avoided as much as possible, as something should be sacrificed in appearance, to preserve a sail from injury. Taking a little trouble will get all the sail in the skin; and although it may be larger, it can be made to look neat.

Jibs require more pains taken in stowing, than any of the other fore and aft sails. There is no necessity of stowing them in their own cloths, when furling cloths are allowed. (*See allowance*).

---

* Canvass bottoms are used instead of nettings, for staysails.

256.—REEFING COURSES TO JACKSTAYS.

When this plan is adopted there is only one point requisite, and that on the fore side of the sail; some use two, but it is unnecessary.

Reeve the point through the eyelet-hole from the after side, the points being made with eyes. Through the eyes reeve a small sized rope; this is called the jack-line. Between every four eyelet-holes, stitch the rope well to the sail, on each yard-arm, leaving three points out. Take a piece of small rope, splice one end to the eyelet-hole in the head of the sail, reeve it through that left in the reef, and splice the other end into the same eyelet hole in the head, leaving about two feet slack. This will be found of much use in gathering the sail up for reefing—it is called a *grab-rope*, or *reef-line.*

257.—REEF-EARINGS

Are fitted the same as the head—an eyelet-hole is worked below the cringle, large enough to take the earing; through this put the earing, reeve the end through the long-eye, and haul it taut through. The earings are sometimes put in the cringles, but the cringle cannot be so well hauled up on the yard, and consequently will not be so well secured for carrying sail; and it not only puts more strain on the yard-arm points, but also injures the sail. They are also fitted on the bight, and passed on both ends; one end for the outer turns, and the other the inner turns.

To pass a reef-earing.—For the first, second, and third reef, take it from the sail, on the foreside of the yard, round the cleat for the purpose, through the cringle, round the yard and through the cringle, until three or four outer turns are passed; then reeve the bight through the cringle from aft forward—take a round turn in the cringle; then take the end from the latter under the yard up abaft over, and through the bight; then back over the yard on the foreside, through the cringle, from underneath the yard; slew the cringle well up, and leech off the sail, and pass sufficient turns to secure; then expend the end round the yard and half-hitch round all, or a clove-hitch to the lift.

A close reef-earing is passed the same way, but hauled out on the after side of the yard. Being hauled out abaft, it covers all the other reefs, and there being so much sail on the fore-side, it would never keep up.

In passing the outer turns for each reef, take two for the first; three for the second and third, and four for the fourth. For the inner turns, expend the earing, except your earings are fitted on the bight.

258.—BENDING STUDDING-SAILS.

All are bent to the yard alike, and the same precautions used as in other sails, keeping the rope next the yard. The earings are rove through the holes in the yard-arms, and cringle in the head of the sails; two or three outer turns are taken, and the earing nearly expended in inner turns, then frap the outer turns together with the end, and half-hitch, if the sail is laced to the yard—the lacing is spliced into one eyelet-hole, rove through the other, and passed round the yard.

They are sometimes bent by half-hitching the lacing, which plan keeps the sail up, and much closer to the yard. A round turn is also used, by being passed round the yard-arm and through the eyelet-hole twice, and from the latter through the next eyelet-hole, round the yard. They are then made up—the topmast studding-sail to the foremost shrouds of fore and main rigging; topgallant, in foremost part of the topmast rigging; and lower, on the booms. The topmast studding-sail is also sometimes kept on the booms, and tarpaulin covers fitted for them.

These sails are sometimes bent with long rope-bands, and unbent when taken in and stowed away, if dry.

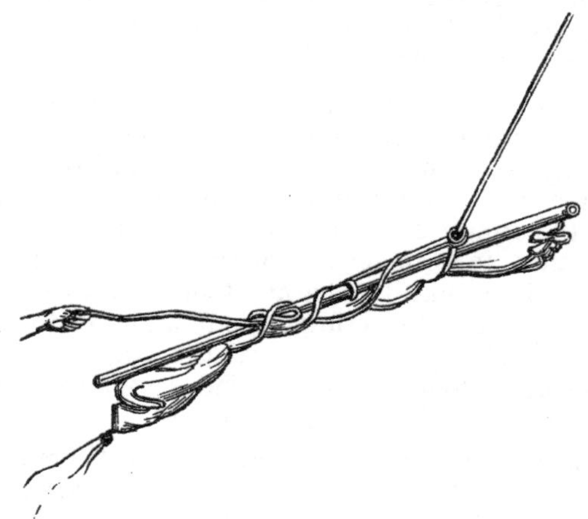

In making up a topmast studding-sail, when bent, overhaul the down-haul the length of the luff or outer leech; then take the foot up to the yard, and place the tack block out. Bight the down-haul along the yard, also the sheets; roll the sail snugly up, and stop it with yarns.

Lower studding-sails are bent and made up in the same manner as topmast studding-sails, with the sheet in.

I have seen these sails when placed in the rigging ready for setting, with the sheets and downhaul left out and stopped to the yards; the tack stopped from the lower yard, up and down the foremost shroud and bent to the sail. This was done with the idea that the sail could be set much quicker; but it was found that the sail on the opposite side (which was set in the general way), was set with less trouble, and in less time. There will be plenty of time to bend the tack and halliards (when the order is given to get ready), while getting burtons up, jiggers on topsail-lift, weather-braces taut, and rigging the booms out.

Note.—The topgallant studding-sail tack is generally kept bent, and slacked when bracing the yards up.

It has frequently occurred to me, when I have heard the order from the quarter-deck, in the event of setting studding-sails, "to rig out and hoist away;" how can it be possible to rig out the fore-topmast studding-sail booms, when probably there may be fifty men clapped on the lower studding-sail halliards, hauling the booms in, and seldom more than six or eight men at the most, on the in-and-out jigger, trying to get the boom out.

I should recommend to rig-out and secure first, then hoist away.

259.—PREPARATIONS FOR LEAVING THE WHARF AND HAULING OUT IN THE STREAM.

To haul off and moor ship.—Before hauling off, all the spare spars should be hoisted in and secured, boat's chocks placed, all the stores, provisions, and water got on board; it would be also well to see that there is a sufficient quantity of brooms, bath-brick for cleaning bright-work, lime and size for whitewash, and everything that is allowed and requisite for the ship. The complement of men from the receiving ship should be got on board, and the boats provided with crews, oars, and sails. When everything necessary is completed, make preparations for hauling off. Get up kedges and hawsers ready for instant service; have the ends of the hawsers pointed up each hatchway, ready for handing out if wanted. Run out a kedge, and drop it where the first, or weather-anchor is to be planted; have lines from the ship to the shore—single the fasts—hang over fenders and out-riggers—man the hawser, cast off the fasts, and warp off; checking her as may be necessary by the lines. When warped out to the kedge, run it up to the bows, and let go the weather anchor; veer as fast as she will take it, assisting her in going astern by the mizen-topsail, if necessary. If to shoot her to either side, use the helm, jib, or spanker, and in case there is no wind, use kedges and hawsers.

When a double scope is out, stopper the cable, and let go the second anchor—furl the mizen-topsail—bring-to on the weather cable, and heave in to the moorings; moor a little taut, to allow for veering. If a hemp-cable, clap on the service, and veer to the hawse-hole.

260.—CARRYING OUT AN ANCHOR WITH A BOAT.

Hang the anchor to the stern of the boat by good stoppers, and have the buoy and buoy-rope attached to it; pass the end of the cable or hawser out through the hawse-hole, and coil away enough of it in the bows of the boat, to reach the bottom. Now capsize the coil in the stern sheets, and then the end will be uppermost; bend on to the anchor. There should also be a sufficient length of the hawser coiled away in the boat to reach the place destined for the anchor. When in the right place, heave over the buoy, and see that the buoy-rope is clear—stand clear of the cable, and slip the stoppers. In case of making a guess-warp, *vice versa.*

261.—MARKING THE LEAD-LINE.

At two fathoms, two strips of leather; at three fathoms, three strips of leather; at five fathoms, a white rag; at seven fathoms, a red rag; at ten fathoms, a piece of leather with a hole in it; at thirteen, the same as three; at fifteen, the same as five; at seventeen, the same as seven; at twenty fathoms, two knots.

Deep-sea lead-lines are marked the same, as far as twenty fathoms, then add one knot for every ten fathoms, and a strip of leather for every five fathoms.

262.—HEAVING THE LEAD

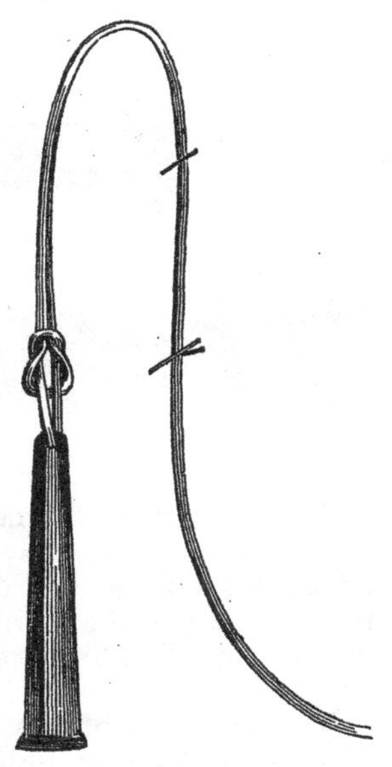

A hole is made in the upper part of the lead, a piece of rope rove through it, and both ends spliced together;* an eye is spliced in the end of the line, put through this strap, the lead shoved through the bight, and hauled taut.

Breast ropes are fitted in the chains, for the men to lean against when heaving the lead. They are made as sword-mats, tapered at each end, and secured to two shrouds, with seizings passed round them, and through the eyes in each.

Heaving the lead is generally performed by a man who stands in the main chains to windward. Having the line all ready to run out, without interruption, he holds it at a distance of nearly a fathom from the lead, and having swung it backwards and forwards three or four times, in order to acquire a greater velocity with the swing, he then swings it over his head, and thence as far forward as is necessary; so that by the lead sinking whilst the ship advances, the line may be almost perpendicular when it reaches the bottom. The person sounding then proclaims the depth of water, in a kind of *singing manner*. Thus: if the mark of five fathoms is close to the surface of the water, he *sings out*, "by the mark 5!" and, as there are no marks at 4, 6, 8, &c., he estimates those numbers, and sings, "by the deep 4!" &c. If he considers it to be a quarter, or a half, more than any particular number, he sings out, "and a quarter 5!" "and a half 4!" &c. If he conceives the depth to be three quarters more than a particular number, he calls it a quarter less than the next; thus, at four fathoms and three-quarters, he calls, "a quarter less 5!" and so on, according to the depth of the water.

---

* A leather becket may be used for light leads, insead of a rope strap.

263.—MARKING A LOG-LINE.

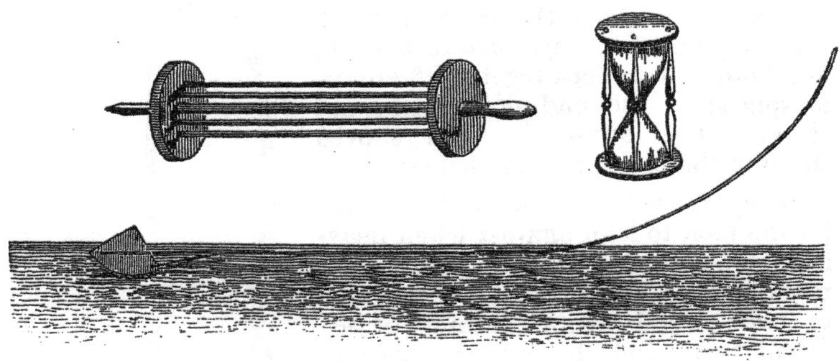

Allow twelve fathoms for stray line, where stick in a white rag; then at every forty-seven feet and six-tenths, mark the line as follows, viz.: at one, one leather; at two, two knots; at three, three knots; and also having a mark at every half-knot. The glasses should be proved with a good watch, having a second-hand.

The principle of the log-line is, that a knot is the same part of a sea-mile, that half-a-minute is of an hour; therefore the length of a knot should be one-hundred-and-twentieth the length of a sea mile, or fifty-one feet; but as it is more convenient to have the knot divided into eight parts, of six feet each, the proportional reduction is necessary in the glass. Therefore as 51 feet : 30 seconds : : 48 feet : 28, 4.17 seconds; but as the fraction can be more easily allowed in the line than the glass, another proportion is necessary, viz., as 28, 4.17 seconds : 48 feet : : 28 seconds to 47.6 feet, or the length of a knot.

Note.—Log-lines are kept on reels for the purpose.

The length of the stray-line is regulated by the size of the ship.

264.—GETTING READY FOR SEA.

Observe and note the exact line of flotation. See that all the rigging is properly up, alow and aloft. See that the preventer-gear is on, as well as breast-ropes for leadsmen, and leads and lines in the chains. If requisite, grease the masts, jib and stay-sail-stays, lifts and trusses, and reef-pendants—sheet-anchor stowed—guns secured—boats hoisted in and secured. Care should be taken that the harness-casks are lashed—chests and tables properly cleated, and binnacles secured. Let the armorer examine the slip-stoppers, and see that they are oiled, and in proper condition—get the swinging-booms fore and aft—awnings below, and awning ridge-ropes down—down jack-staff—see that the tiller-ropes are all clear, and that the tiller moves freely; also that the relieving-tackles and spare tiller-ropes are at hand.

Cross topgallant yards, bend the gear; take the covers off the jibs, staysail, spanker, and trysails, and coil every rope down clear, for running—have the studding-sails stopped, ready for going aloft, and the royal-halliards down on the weather side. Cat and fish overhauled down. Timenoguys in their respective places. Life-buoys in order. Accommodation-ladder unshipped and stowed away. Pendants and ladders taken off the swinging-booms—head-cranes unshipped—chafing-gear on its respective places. It would also be well to see that there is a sufficiency of sand on board.

265.—CLEAR HAWSE.

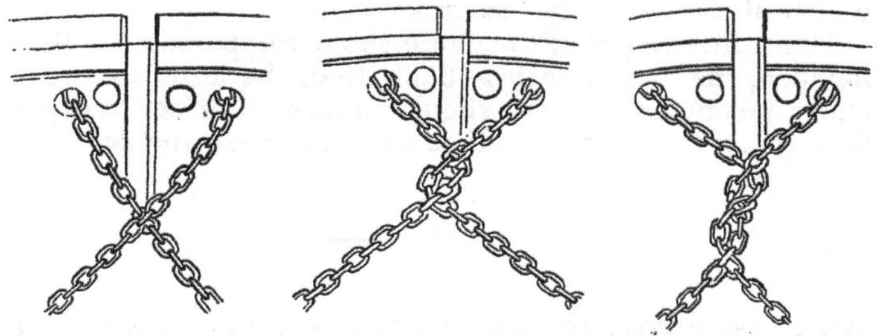

Call all hands to "clear hawse." Lash a stout single-block to the bowsprit, through which reeve the clear hawse-pendant; haul the launch under the bows, or if there is too much sea on, or she is not out, send a hand down in a bowline, and hook the pendant to the riding-cable, below the turn; bouse them up clear of the water, after which pass a stout lashing round both cables.

If there should be a heavy sea on, or the wind flawey and variable, it would be well to pass the end of a hawser out of the hawse-hole, and hitch it to the cable,* to relieve the lashing. Reeve ropes through blocks on each side of the bowsprit end, for bow-lines, and pass them in at the hawse-hole, so as to take out an elbow; for instance—suppose the starboard was the clearing cable, take the larboard bow-line down under the cable, up into the starboard hawse-hole, and the starboard one over to the larboard side of the cable; then follow the lead of the larboard bow-line, bend on several fathoms inside, and stop along to the hawse-

* See clear hawse-shackle and pendant.

hole; draw the splice, or unshackle, bend on the hawse-rope, off-stoppers, and run out; hang the bights to the bowsprit (if hemp-cable), with slip-ropes, and send in the bow-lines again, the same way as before. When the end is out, "cast off," dip it fair, and bend on again to the cable; rouse in, slack down the slip-ropes, and splice or shackle the cable; haul it taut with a deck-tackle, and bitt, and stopper as before. Cast off the hawser, unlash the cable, unreeve the clear hawse-pendant, unlash the block from the bowsprit end, and clear up the deck.

Note.—If there is a round turn and an elbow in the hawse after rousing the cable, repeat the operation as before; it is always well to prevent confusion, by taking out one elbow at a time. A cross, is when the cables lay across each other, or when the ship has *swung foul once;* an elbow is two crosses, and a round turn is three crosses; a round turn and elbow is five crosses. It can readily be seen thus, in clearing hawse with a round turn, a cross will be left in the cables.

The anchor is fouled in the very operation of *letting it go;* the weight of the chain-cable causing the running out part to fall over and foul the stock. To avoid this, some officers pursue the practice of "letting go" the anchor with the cable *bitted,* which plan is strongly recommended.

From the weight of the chain-cable, compared with that of the hempen, the former is less liable than the latter to foul the anchor; but no speculation should induce an officer to depart from that practice which can alone ensure a clear anchor.

266.—WEIGHING AN ANCHOR WITH THE LAUNCH.

This may be done by under-running, when the ship has slipped the cable, or weighing by the buoy-rope, when the anchor is lying in too shoal water for the ship to be hove up to it.

Ship the roller on the stern of the launch, have strong tackles with a jigger also, and some good rope for stoppers. Get the end of the cable over the roller; pass a strap round it, to which hook the double block of the tackle, and the single one to a bolt in the bows; man the fall, and as the cable comes in, French-flake it along the thwarts; when the tackle comes two blocks, "stopper and fleet;" when the cable is "up and down," clap the jigger on the fall of the tackle, and heave the boat's stern well down in the water, and stopper securely. Send all the men in the bows of the boat; jump the boat and break the anchor out of the ground; then man the fall again, off stopper, and heave up; when the ring of the anchor is above water, pass a short ring-stopper, haul the buoy on board, and bring the boat to the ship;

when alongside, hook the cat, and cat the anchor. Get the end of the cable unclinched, passed into the hawse, and the remainder hauled out of the launch. (If chain-cable, unshackle.)

267.—WEIGHING AN ANCHOR WITH A BUOY-ROPE.

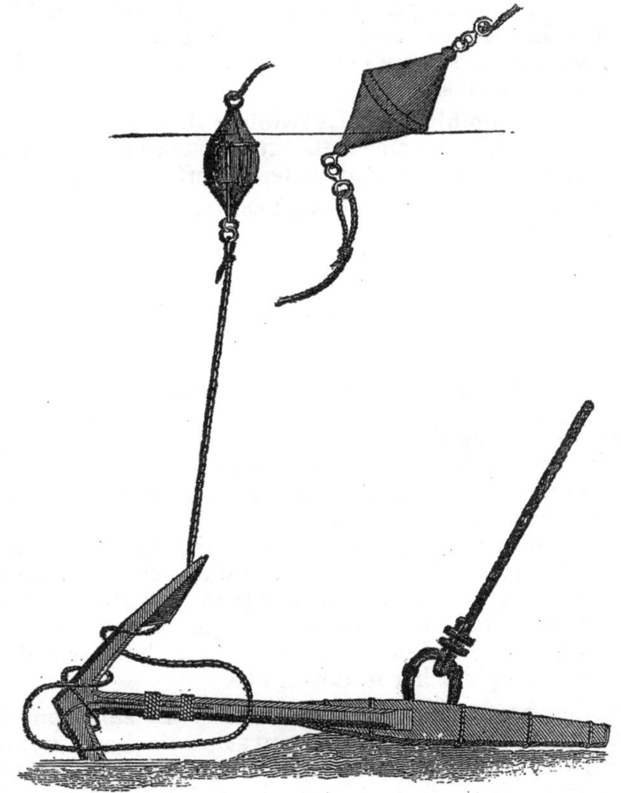

Get the buoy-rope over the roller, clap on a tackle, and weigh the anchor as before. When it is secured, man the capstan, heave the launch in under the bows, and cat the anchor.

Anchors are generally weighed with the buoy-rope when the cable has parted, and the end cannot be grappled; when this is the case, the anchor may be weighed with launch, brought under the bows and catted, and the cable unclinched and hove in; or the ship might be warped over the buoy, and the cat-fall taken to the buoy-rope.

268.—BOATING AN ANCHOR.

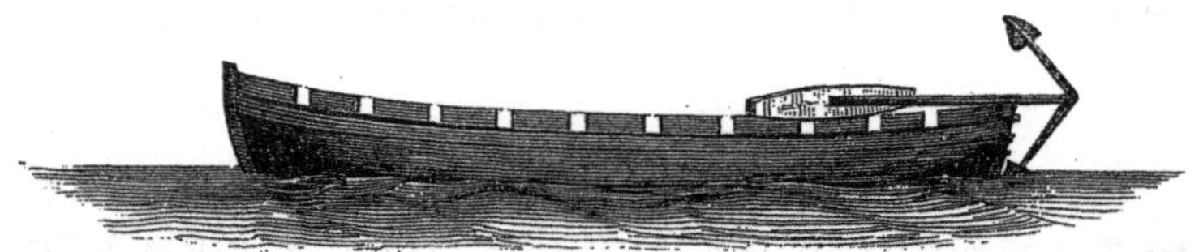

Place the flukes perpendicularly over the stern, and the stock a-thwart-ships in the stern sheets, resting horizontally upon a loose thwart, placed there previously for the purpose, and steady all by one or two lashings.

In letting go, nothing more is required than to cant the anchor over the quarter, by means of the thwart, taking care previously that the buoy, buoy-rope, and cable, be perfectly clear.

Light anchors should be boated contrary to this, *i. e.*, flukes inboard, and stock out.

269.—TAKING IN A LAUNCH.

Brace and secure the yards the same as when getting up the anchors, and also rig the same purchases; place the chocks, pass everything out of the launch, and hook the purchases to spans; have a few hands in the boat to keep her clear of the ship's side. Man the yard tackle falls; have some hands to take in the slack of the stay fall; "walk away;" when the boat leaves the water, take out the plug. When high enough to clear the waist anchor stock, haul over on the main stay, easing away the fore and main yards; when the stern is over the deck, haul over the fore stay, lower, and place her in the chocks.

The other boats may be got on board by the same purchases. The launch is stowed on the larboard side; the first cutter on the starboard side;* the second cutter, inside the launch, and the third cutter inside the first. When all are in, unrig the purchases, square the yards, and set up the gripes.

The quarter and stern boats are hoisted up to their davits, and secured to them by stoppers, and the gripes set up.

---

* *i. e.*, if the ship be a frigate or larger. Single-deck ships have but one nest of boats.

270.—TAKING IN BOATS BOTH SIDES AT ONCE.

The yards are kept square, and secured on both sides by the lifts, burtons, and quarter lifts. Use the winding and stay tackles for the heaviest boats, and the yard tackles for the lightest ones; the topsail halliards forward, and the main pendant tackle aft, acting as stays to bring them on board. It may be necessary to come up the forward backstays, as they would be likely to interfere with the bows of the boats; after which proceed as before.

Taking in a boat at sea.—Back the main-topsail, get the boat to leeward, secure the lower yards as before directed, and hoist her in. The boat coming in to leeward, tackles will be necessary to get her to windward sufficiently to lower away.

When before the wind, a boat might be got in by securing the yards as before, and taking a hawser from aft to the stern of the boat, to keep her from sending or pitching forward when leaving the water, and thereby endangering the yards.

Note.—Some of our large vessels have two sets of yard and stay tackles, for the purpose of taking in boats both sides at once; but the above mentioned gear will answer all purposes in any case of emergency, where the manœuvre is not considered as exercising.

PART IV.

271.—GETTING UNDER-WEIGH.

See that the hawse is clear; overhaul a range of the weather cable—get up nippers—pass the messenger—knock up the stanchions—ship the gratings—ship, and swifter-in the capstan bars—rig the fish-davit—overhaul cat and fish; and call "all hands unmoor ship."

When the cable grows with the angle of the main-stay, the ship is said to ride at a "long stay;" when it grows with the angle of the fore-stay, the ship is said to be at a "short-stay." When perpendicular, the phrase is "up and down." From one or other of the two last mentioned positions, sail is generally made in getting under-weigh.

If from the nature of the ground, or strength of the wind, there should be any probability of dragging the anchor, sail is generally made from a "short stay." In such a case, particular attention ought to be paid that the head yards be not braced too sharp a-box; for the object being to cant the ship with the least possible sternway, the sooner the head sails lift or fill the better. The jibs are hoisted the instant they will take. If, after all, the ship drags her anchor, you can pall the capstan—stopper over all. brace round the head yards, and force her a-head by the sails, as far as may be necessary; then back the head yards, lay-to, and get the anchor up.

If there should be so much wind and sea, as to make it a matter of difficulty to get the anchor, but plenty of sea-room, brace the yards a-box, according to the tack you wish to go upon, and get the anchor up and secured before making sail. In moderate weather, and ordinary circumstances, sail is generally made when the cable is "up and down." Sometimes a stern-board is necessary, with the anchor dragging on the ground; at other times, a tack must be made in that position.

If riding by the starboard cable, and no impediment to port, it will be the most eligible method, to cast her on the starboard tack, as the cable will then be clear of the cutwater, and the ship being to leeward of the anchor, it can be more easily catted and fished. If there should be much sea on, this would be the best plan.

Having determined to cast on the starboard tack, overhaul the lifts, trusses, and backstay-falls. The fore-topsail being put aback, by the starboard braces ; the main and mizen by the wind, with larboard after braces, heaving around briskly, and before breaking ground, give her a shear with the starboard helm ; when up, hoist the jib, keeping the helm a-starboard, until the stern-board exceeds the velocity of the tide, when shift it, grapple the buoy, and cat the anchor. When she has fallen off, so as to fill the after sails, let flow the jib-sheet, haul out the spanker, set topgallant sails and courses, and trim the yards and sails properly.

To cast off on the larboard tack, put the helm a-port, and brace the yards the contrary way.

272.—WHEN THE MESSENGER STRANDS, OR IS LIKELY TO PART.

If the messenger is likely to part, from the great strain upon it, stopper immediately, and either pass a new one, or reeve a viol purchase, assisting it with the cat-fall. Lash the viol block to the cable near the hawse-hole ; clinch one end of the hawser to the main-mast, snatch the bite in the block, and take the other end to the capstan. To assist the viol, pass a strap round the cable, close down to the water, to which hook the cat-fall, and heave up on both purchases.

If the messenger should strand, stopper immediately, cut it, and then knot or splice it.

273.—TO GET UNDER-WEIGH AND STAND BEFORE THE WIND.

Make all preparations for getting under-weigh, heave-in, and make sail as before. Lay the main and mizen topsails square aback; the fore one sharp aback, according to the side it is intended to cast—heave-in, cant her the right way with the helm before tripping, and as soon as the velocity of the stern-board is greater than that of the tide, shift the helm, grapple the buoy, run up the jib as soon as it will take, and haul aft the weather-sheet. While falling off, cat and fish the anchor; as she gathers head-way, shift the helm; when before the wind, right it—square the head yards, and brail up the jib—set topgallant sails, royals, and foresail—haul taut the lifts, trusses, backstay-falls, and if necessary, set the studding-sails.

274.—IN GETTING UNDER-WEIGH, TO BACK ASTERN AND AVOID DANGER.

Make all preparations as before. If required to cast on the starboard tack, sheer her with the starboard helm; to bring the wind on the starboard bow, brace the yards aback, about half-way up with the larboard braces; haul out the spanker and keep the boom nearly amid-ships. Heave up briskly, grapple the buoy, and as soon as the anchor is up, put the helm hard a-weather to keep her to—cat and fish the anchor. Having made sufficient stern-board, shift the helm, brace the after yards, ease off the spanker sheet, and run up the jib. When full aft, brace up the head yards, and as she gathers headway, right the helm and make sail. To cast on the larboard tack, sheer her with the port helm, brace all sharp aback, and proceed as before.

275.—GETTING UNDER-WEIGH—A SHOAL ON EACH BEAM.

It becomes necessary to proceed to sea, and is impossible to weather either of those a-beam; but there is just room to pass between a shoal astern, and either of those a-beam, with the wind *blowing fresh.*

Pass the stream cable out of one of the quarter ports; bend on one end to the cable, and secure the other to the topsail sheet-bitts; draw the splice* of the cable, bend a slip-buoy to it, and heave it overboard. See the stoppers clear for slipping; stop the topsails to the yards with spun-yarn, casting off the gaskets. Loose the courses, jib, and spanker—mast-head the topsail-yards—man the jib-halliards—sheer her from the cable with the helm—slip and run up the jib—keep fast the stream-cable, and let her swing round. When she heads for the passage, slip the stream-cable, right the helm, sheet home the topsails, set the courses, and other sails if necessary; then stand through the passage.

276.—GETTING UNDER-WEIGH IN A NARROW CHANNEL.

At anchor in a narrow channel, riding to a strong leeward tide, and blowing fresh; a ship astern, and also one on each quarter, so near that there is not room to wear, for casting; it is necessary to put to sea, and to do so a passage must be effected between the two ships.

Make all preparations for getting under-weigh, and heave-in as described before. Loose the topsails; if riding by the star-board cable, give her a *rank sheer* with the starboard helm; set up the starboard back-stays, and bear aft the larboard ones; overhaul lifts and trusses; haul out the spanker, and get the boom over on the larboard quarter; lead along the main tack and sheet; run up the jib, and haul aft the weather sheet; "Heave round cheerily;" run the anchor up, grapple the buoy, and as soon as she fills, meet her with the helm; board the main tack to catch her; trim the jib and spanker sheets, set the foresail, and trim sharp; haul taut the bowlines; stand on as far as may be necessary.

Note.—A good deal of uncertainty attends this manœuvre; if there is room, it would be the best plan to lay the yards aback. It is confidently asserted by old experienced seamen, that the above method is perfectly practicable.

---

* If chain cable, unshackle.

277.—HEAD TO WIND, CAST ON STARBOARD TACK.

Everything having been previously prepared, heave in and make sail as before. Sheer her with a starboard helm; brace the head yards sharp up with the starboard braces, and counter brace the after ones; haul out the spanker, and get the boom on the larboard quarter; heave in, and up anchor; up jib as soon as it will take; and when the stern-board exceeds the velocity of the tide, shift the helm. When the after sails are full, trim the spanker, let flow the jib sheet, cat and fish the anchor, haul aft the jib sheet, brace round the head-yards, and make sail.

278.—WINDWARD TIDE—GET UNDER-WEIGH AND STAND BEFORE THE WIND.

Make all preparation for getting under-weigh, heave in, loose jib, up anchor, grapple the buoy, run up the jib, cat and fish the anchor, and make sail with expedition.

If it is necessary to have the ship under greater command, as might be the case in a narrow channel, or crowded harbor, it would be better to proceed as follows :—

Heave in to a "short stay," loose the courses, topsails, jib and spanker. If riding by the starboard cable, sheer her with the starboard helm, and bring the wind on the larboard quarter, brace the yards to, by the larboard braces, and keep them shivering by the helm. "Heave up;" fill the after yards, and square the head ones; haul aft jib sheet on starboard tack; cat and fish the anchor; up helm; fill the head yards, shiver the after ones, get her before the wind, and make sail.

279.—TO GET UNDER-WEIGH, AND STAND OUT ON A WIND.

Make all preparations—commence heaving in; loose jib and spanker; top up and bear over the boom on the right quarter, and the helm to the side which it is intended to cast; "heave up;" get the buoy; haul out on the spanker as soon as it will take. When the wind gets abeam, run up the jib, and meet her with the helm; cat and fish the anchor; loose, sheet home. and hoist the topsails, brace up, bring by and make sail.

A Schooner-of-War getting under weigh

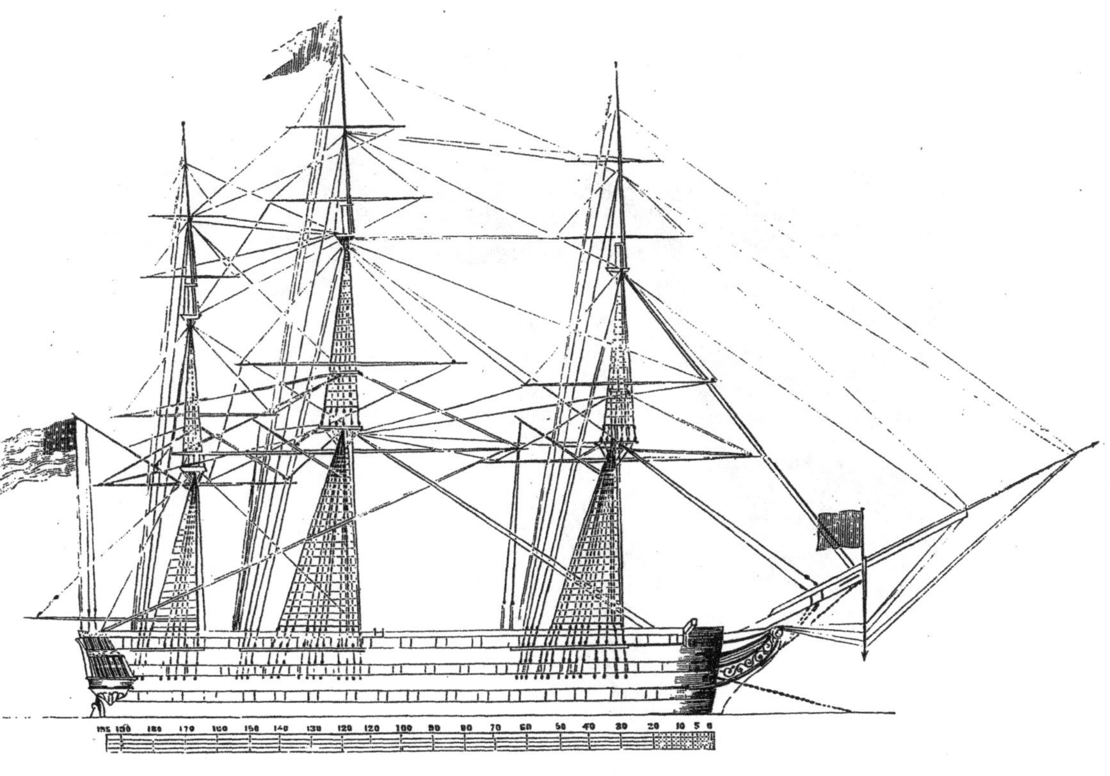

Scale-draft of a First Class Ship-of-the-Line, two decks.

280.—RIDING HEAD TO TIDE, WIND ON THE STARBOARD QUARTER, TO GET UNDER-WEIGH ON THE STARBOARD TACK.

Make all preparations, heave short, loose sails, sheet home and hoist the topsails, bracing them to with the starboard braces; keep them *shivering*, by the assistance of the topsails and helm, —"heave round,"—break ground—put the helm a-starboard—brace full the head yards—run up the jib, and let her pay round to port; heave up the anchor, and grapple the buoy. Haul out the spanker as soon as it will take—shift over the head sheets, and square the head yards—trim aft the jib-sheet, and meet her with the helm. Cat and fish the anchor, and make sail as necessary.

281.—GETTING UNDER-WEIGH—WIND ACROSS THE TIDE.

In getting under-weigh, say ebb-tide, make all preparations, loose, sheet home, and hoist the topsails; brace up the fore and mizen topsails, and lay the main yard to the mast. Give her a spoke or two of the lee wheel, so as to take the main-topsail well aback. "Heave up," cat and fish the anchor, and grapple the buoy; at the same time, set the jib and spanker—fill the main yard, stand on to a convenient place, and then tack or veer.

The evolution is determined by the circumstance of there being more room to windward or to leeward.

Flood-Tide.—Proceed as before, until the anchor is catted and fished; then hoist the jib, haul out the spanker, fill the main-topsail, and stand out, making whatever sail may be judged necessary.

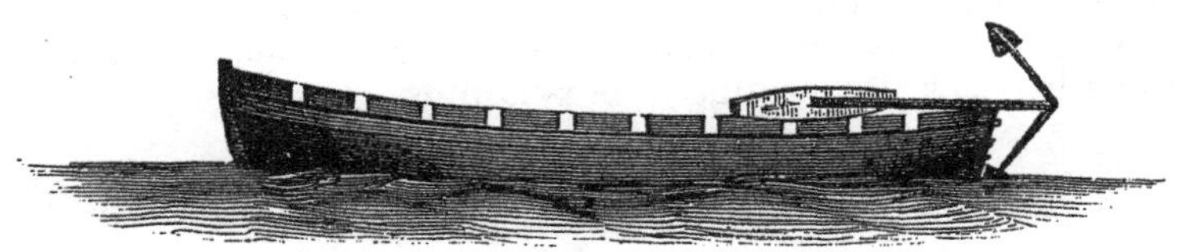

282.—TO BACK AND FILL IN A TIDE-WAY.

This manœuvre is only executed when a ship is to proceed up or down a rapid river against the wind, which is supposed to be light, and may be done by two methods, viz., driving before the wind, or broadside to it. When the channel is broad enough, the latter method is preferable, as the ship will be more under the command of her helm.

283.—DRIVING BEFORE THE WIND.

This is only done in a very narrow channel. Heave up the anchor, and get her before the wind, with just sail enough to keep her so. Suppose her under topsails, and as she drops with the tide, it becomes necessary for her to remain stationary, to allow a ship to pass her stern,—set topgallant-sails, and if required to shoot ahead, drop the foresail. If to avoid a rock, or ship astern, put the helm up or down—haul out the spanker—brace up, and haul aft the jib-sheet, as she comes too; shoot across until clear of danger, when put the helm up, brail up the spanker, shiver the after yards, and when before the wind, brail up the jib. If in standing across, she should get too near the shore—get her on the other tack, by wearing or box-hauling.

284.—DRIVING BROADSIDE-TO

Get under-weigh, and bring her by the wind under the jib, topsails, and spanker; shiver the topsails; when filled, stand on to the middle of the channel; brail up the jib and spanker, and let her *drift* in this situation until she falls off, which she will soon do, owing to her greater immersion aft than forward, which will drift her stern farther to windward. Haul out the spanker, and if this is insufficient, back the mizen-topsail; if she still falls off, back the main also, both square aback, and if she should get a stern-board, put the helm hard a-weather; should she come-to again, shiver the topsails, and brail up the spanker, letting her drift as before.

285.—SECURING THE SHIP FOR SEA.

Take the departure, give the course, and make sail. Beat to quarters—examine the magazine—load, shot, and secure the guns—see that all the gear of the guns is ready for service, and secured. Fill the shot-boxes, rack, and wad-nets—get the anchors on the bows, and lash them—unbend the cable and buoy-ropes; if clean and dry, pay them below; also the messenger, hawsers, stoppers and nippers, and cable-mats, put in the buckles—unreeve, cat and fish, and coil them away below. Get chafing-mats on the yards and rigging—see the booms and boats secured, pumps in good order, and the gratings and tarpaulins ready for putting on. Overhaul the storm-staysail gear, see everything ready for service, and stow it below again.

286.—STOWING THE ANCHORS FOR SEA.

The anchors being catted and fished, clap a stout tackle on them and cat-head stoppers; pass a good lashing through the ring and over the cat-head—expend the stopper in the same way. Hook the pendant-tackle to a strap around the shank—weigh the crown, and bouse the fluke into the bill-port by a thwartship tackle; having another tackle clapt on the end of the anchor-stock which is uppermost, getting it as close to the side as the stock will permit; pass stout shank-lashings also around the stock and cat-head. *Unbend the cable and buoy-rope.*

Note.—The waist-anchors are securely stowed when they are first got on board. Some ships use preventer lashings and jumpers in bad weather, when the ship is lurching in a heavy sea, or when liable to ship *seas* in the waist.

287.—SETTING TOPGALLANT SAILS—BLOWING FRESH.

Point the yards to the wind, and loose the sails; sheet home first to leeward, and then to windward—having a hand to leeward to light the foot over the topmast stay; hoist away, trim the yards, and haul taut the bow-lines.

Note.—In setting topgallant sails over single-reefed topsails, see that the sheets are out square alike.

288.—SETTING COURSES.

Moderate weather.—Man the fore and main-tacks and sheets, attend the rigging—have hands on the lower yards to overhaul it—haul aboard—check the top bow-lines, weather lower lifts, and a little of the lee-main-brace—avast the sheets; get the tacks close down, and then haul aft the sheets—haul taut the main-brace, lifts, trusses, and bowlines.

Blowing fresh.—Man well the sheets, overhaul the leech-lines and lee-bunt-lines; ease down the lee-clew-garnet, slack top bowlines, lower lifts, and lee-main-braces, until the tacks are down; then haul aft the sheets, haul taut the lee-main-brace, weather lifts and bow-lines, and, if necessary, hook and haul taut the rolling-tackle, to ease the trusses.

289.—SETTING THE SPANKER.

Top-up the boom, overhaul lee-topping-lifts, attend the sheets and weather-guy; haul over the lee-guy, and trim the boom—man the outhaul and attend the brails and vangs—let go the brails, haul out and steady the gaff by the vangs.

Note.—The weather-vang should never be hauled, or boused too taut, as it may be the means of carrying away the gaff, especially when using trysails as storm-sails.

290.—SETTING THE JIB.

Cant the spritsail-yard to steady the boom; man the halliards and sheet—see the down-haul and brails clear, take in the slack of the sheet to steady the sail; "hoist away;" and as the sail goes up, ease off the sheet—when taut up, haul aft the sheet.

291.—SETTING LOWER STUDDING-SAILS.

When the boom is out or a-thwartships, and trimmed with the fore yard, the outer halliards and outhauler are to be well manned, taking in the slack of the inner halliards, as the sail goes over the gunwale, and ultimately reaches its destined height. In running away with the lower halliards, care must be taken that the yard be not brought up with a *jerk*, against the topmast studding-sail boom; by this sudden jerk booms are liable to be sprung.

292.—SHIFTING A COURSE AT SEA.

Moderate weather.—In shifting a course at sea, with the watch, and with time to prepare everything for a smart and pretty evolution—get the spare sail up from below, and first of all stretched across the deck. Then, the course being set, stop per the (tack and sheet) clews, and unbend tacks, sheets, clew-garnets, and leech-lines, bending them forthwith to the spare sail; and, when done, untoggle the bowlines, and send the hands aloft—trice up, lay out, cast off robins and earings, and make the two midship robins fast to the bunt-lines—ease in the earings together, and make them also fast to the buntlines a-midships. Lower the sail by the bunt-lines, and gather it in by hand. Unbend the bunt-lines, bend them to the spare sail, and take out the yard-ropes.

Divide the watch to the yard-ropes, bunt-lines and clew-garnets, and haul taut; haul out and up all together—hands aloft bring-to, and when brought-to, haul on board.

Blowing fresh.—First haul the sail up and furl it; then proceed to make fast the midship robins and earings (when cast off) to the bunt-lines, and to lower the sail down by the clew-garnets, as well as buntlines.

Note.—In this case the weather-tack and sheet is of much use in hauling the sail in as it comes down.

293.—TAKING IN A COURSE IN A GALE OF WIND.

Steady the yard as securely as possible, man the clew-garnets, bunt-lines, and leech-lines; ease away the tack and bow-line—haul up to windward, ease off the sheet, haul up, get the sail close to the yard, and furl it.

It is a common practice in clewing-up a course, to *let go* the bowline upon starting the tack. Neither the tack nor the bowline should be let go, but each eased off handsomely by hand. By the adoption of this plan, the sail will bag less to leeward, and the weather-clew can be hauled up with greater ease; but both buntlines should be well manned, and even *better manned*, than the weather clew-garnet. When the latter gear is well up, walk away with the clew-garnet, easing steadily the sheet. But all these precautions will be of little avail, unless there be a good preventer-brace upon the lower yard; or else the yard tackle be hooked to act as such, and brought sufficiently *aft* to prevent the tackle bringing too great a strain in an up-and-down position upon the upper yard-arms.

294.—TAKING IN A TOPSAIL IN A GALE OF WIND.

Steady well the topsail and lower yards, rounding in the weather topsail brace as much as possible. Man the clewlines and buntlines; attend the sheets and bowlines; clew up the lee-sheet, and haul up the buntline. If to save the yard, haul up to leeward first, point the yard to the wind, and steady it again; lay out and furl the sail.

There appears to be still a dispute among seamen as to the preferable method of effecting this service.

When the mast is not considered in danger, and the object be to save the sail, or to ease the ship, the weather clew may be first lifted. But before *starting* the weather sheet, it would be well to ease first a few feet of the *lee*-sheet, in order to lessen the labor of rounding in the weather brace. So soon as the lee-sheet be sufficiently eased to admit of the yard coming in with the weather brace, and both buntlines be as well manned as the weather clewline. the weather sheet may be then eased off, and the weather clewline hauled up, with every prospect of saving the sail.

If there be plenty of sea room, and the ship can be kept away, some officers recommend the practice of bringing the wind abaft the beam, and then hauling up the *lee-clewline first*—taking the precaution to have both buntlines well manned. When this operation is effected, the weather clewline may be hauled up, rounding the brace in, as the ship is again gradually brought to the wind. It will require particular attention to the helm when hauling up the weather clewline, though with judicious management, the helm alone is sufficient to *spill* the sail.

295.—TAKING IN TOP-GALLANT SAILS.

Man the topgallant clewlines; lay aloft, and stand by to furl the sail; attend the braces, bowlines, sheets, and halliards; round in the weather braces, ease away the lee-sheet and halliards; "lower away;" ease away the weather sheet, clew up, haul up the buntlines; steady the yard, lay out and furl the sail.

296.—TAKING IN A SPANKER.

Have the brails and weather vang well manned; attend the outhaul and lee vang; ease away the outhaul; haul over on the weather vang; brail up to leeward; ease off the sheet; haul taut the weather brails; pass the foot gaskets; steady the gaff, and crutch the boom.

297.—SETTING A CLOSE-REEFED TOPSAIL.

Point the yard to the wind, and brace the lower yard a little *sharper* than the topsail yard. Man the sheets, attend the buntlines, and loose the sail; overhaul the lee-buntline, ease down the lee-clewlines, and haul home the lee-sheet; ease off the weather buntline; at the same time slack down the weather clewline, and haul home the weather sheet. Hoist the yard up clear of the cap; brace up, and haul the bowline; steady the lower and topsail yards with the braces and rolling-tackles.

Note.—It must be remembered that a close reefed topsail will not sheet close home, as the yard is to hoist clear of the cap.

298.—A CLOSE-REEFED TOPSAIL SPLITS.

Clew up the sail and steady the yard; cast off some of the rope-bands, so as to pass stops around the sail to secure it. Unbend the sheets, bowlines, and lee-buntlines; unreeve lee-clewline and reef-tackle; bend the weather buntline round the sail, and make the lee-earing fast to the buntline; hook a burton to a strap round the sail, cast off all the rope-bands, and lower away; ease away the weather earing and lower the sail on deck. Stretch along the new sail, overhaul it, then reef the sail at the foot, commencing at the close reef, and taking in each of the three lower reefs separately; then bight it down, and send it aloft, as described before, observing to use the burtons before all. Reeve and bend the gear, stopping the head of the sail to the buntlines; have yard-jiggers hooked to bring the sail to the yard—pass the earings and rope-bands, in the same manner; bring the first reef to the yard, cast out the other reef, haul up the sail; then bring the reefs to the yard alternately, after which set the sail as before.

299.—A JIB SPLITS.

Mind the weather helm, haul the sail down, and hoist the fore-topmast-staysail. Hitch the downhaul around the body of the sail, and also pass stops around it—take the end of a rope from the forcastle, and bend it on to haul in by. Turn out the jib-stays, bend a line on to the end and unreeve it—haul taut the halliards—ease off the downhaul, and haul in. Get up, and overhaul the spare sails; seize on the sheet, bend the halliards and downhaul—stop the sail, and haul out by the downhaul and halliards—reeve the jib-stay, turn it in, and set it up; pass the tack-lashings, reeve the brails, set the jib, and haul down the staysail.

300.—TO WEAR SHIP UNDER CLOSE-REEFED MAIN-TOPSAIL AND STORM-STAYSAILS.

Call all hands "wearship," and station them; have lifts, trusses, and rolling-tackles attended, so the yard and topmast may be well supported in the heavy rolling which they are likely to experience. Haul down the mizen storm-staysail, and when she falls off, up helm; ease off the main storm-staysail sheet, and brace in the main and cross-jack yards; at the same time taking care to keep the maintopsail full, to preserve the head-way, and to keep her a-head of the sea; also to keep it from splitting. When the wind is on the quarter, haul down the main storm-staysail, and shift over the sheet; when before the wind, right the helm, and square the head yards; shift over the fore storm-staysail sheet; watch for a smooth time to bring-her-to; then ease down the helm, hoist the mizen storm-staysail, and when the wind is on the quarter, brace up the yards, hoist the main storm-staysail, haul aft the fore storm-staysail sheet, meet her with the helm, trim the sails, and haul the maintop-bowline.

301.—WEARING UNDER A MAINSAIL.

Make fast a hawser to the slings of the main yard, take it down forward of the sail, haul it well taut, and belay it to the topsail sheet bitts. Call all hands and station them as in the last case; take advantage of her falling off to put the helm up. Ease off the main sheet, and gather in the lee tack, using the yards as in ordinary cases. Should she not go off, send down the cross-jack yard, and mizentopsail yard; house the topmast, and get a drag over the lee quarter, after which proceed as before in bracing the yards, and bring by the wind.

302.—WEARING UNDER BARE POLES.

Send down the after yards and mizen topmast, and bend a hawser to it in-board. Send men in the weather fore rigging with tarpaulins; up helm, and make use of the yards as usual. If she should not go off, it will be necessary, as a last resort, to cut away the mizen mast, veer away the hawser, and use the mizen topmast as a drag to assist in wearing.

303.—CUTTING AWAY THE MASTS.

Clear away all the running rigging attached to the mast, cut away the lanyards of the lee rigging; then the lanyards of the stays and weather rigging.

304.—LAYING-TO UNDER LOWER STAYSAILS, WEAR SHIP.

If it does not blow too fresh, the close-reefed mainsail may be set, as some lofty sail is necessary, to prevent the ship from being pooped; then proceed as in veering under bare poles. If she should not go off, clap a lashing round the bunt of the foresail, and set the weather goose-wing. Should she still not go off, send down the after yards and mizen topmast, making a drag of them. If they have no effect, cut away the mizen mast.

PART V.

305.—PRECAUTIONS FOR SCUDDING.

When scudding in a heavy gale of wind, care should be taken that sufficient of lofty sail be carried on the vessel, to keep her freely and fairly *before* the sea. A ship will scud better with the sea right aft, than quartering. With a heavy sea, the danger to be apprehended is, that the wave traveling faster than the ship, may overtake and break over her. To avoid this, and diminish its danger, some such sail as a close-reefed topsail or foresail is generally kept set as long as possible; but there are times when the foresail is not the best suited, nor the safest for scudding. Some ships that steer badly, and manifest an inclination to *yaw*, will be more steadily steered, and easier managed when scudding under the fore-topsail and fore-staysail. Should the ship happen to broach-to, the foresail, in such a perilous situation, is an unwieldy and unmanageable sail to clew up; and when the sea strikes the ship on the quarter, and causes her head to round-to in the direction ot the wind, the main-topsail tends to assist the sea in producing this dangerous movement; whereas, the fore-staysail, together with the fore-topsail, produces the contrary effect.

It is deeply laden ships that are most liable to get pooped; in which circumstance, a skilful foresight must be exercised in lightening them.

Relieving-tackles should be hooked, and hands stationed to attend them; spare tiller and rudder-chocks at hand, and perfectly ready for use; for, if the ship should get pooped with a heavy sea, the tiller is likely to get snapped, the ship to broach-to, and the rudder, if not quickly secured, to be *unhung*, and after damaging the stern, to be lost. Wreck then almost immediately follows.

When using the foresail, a tackle hooked to the lee fore-tack would be of service in filling the sail.

306.—SCUDDING.—A SHIP BROACHES-TO.

Meet her with the helm, and lee head braces, if necessary; shiver the after yards; should she still come-to, and the sails are taken aback, brace about the head yards, and if necessary, use the helm. If she should get too much stern-board in falling off, haul up the foresail, and pay her off with the fore storm-staysail; fill the after yards as soon as possible, to gather headway, and when she has fallen off sufficiently, brace about the head yards, and trim as before.

Note.—As in scudding, the safety of the ship depends entirely upon the steering, the greatest care should be taken that a steady and expert helmsman is stationed at the wheel, and that when his "trick" is out, and his "relief" arrives to take his place, that he resigns not his hand at the helm, until his successor is in full possession of the easiest method of steering the ship. The officer of the deck should also direct a compass to be placed in the gun-room, and be cautious that a competent seaman is there to attend the relieving tackles, and watch closely the steerage of the ship by the compass-card.

In frigates, and particularly flushed-decked vessels, whose binnacle-lights are liable to be extinguished by the wind, precaution should be taken that lighted lanterns are kept in readiness to supply the place of the blown-out lights. On dark and starless nights, when the steersman has no other guide to govern his steerage than the compass-card, it is of the utmost importance that attention should be paid to this particular; as in a number of instances the accident of *broaching-to* may be traced to the "blowing out" of the binnacle lights, and carelessness of the helmsman. It requires a quick, small *helm* to steer a ship when scudding.

307.—SCUDDING.—BROUGHT BY THE LEE.

A ship is said to be "brought by the lee" when struck aback by a change of wind. If she has headway, which will probably be the case, put the helm a-weather, but if she has sternway, the contrary. Brace round the after yards, and when they are full, the head ones. This is the principle of tacking, but it is not thought as well when scudding in a gale, as the ship might get too rapid sternway, which would be dangerous in a heavy sea. As the object is to preserve the headway, the yards are braced round as soon as possible. If scudding under the main-topsail, and it becomes necessary to reduce sail, take in the fore-topsail, for the main being nearer the centre of gravity, has less tendency to bury the ship, and she is consequently more easily steered.

When scudding under the main-topsail and foresail, the ship is to be brought by the wind, and she should have a tendency to gripe, keep the foresail on her; but if otherwise, take in the foresail, and set the fore storm-staysail; brace up the head yards, then the after ones. Watch for a smooth time, and ease down the helm, taking care to meet her in due time.

The reason for bracing up the head yards before luffing, is, in scudding the ship has a rapid headway, and will mind the helm very quickly; moreover, the sea acting with violence on the quarter, will throw her up into the wind, and unless the head yards are braced up so as to prevent that, she will be in the same situation as if she had broached-to.

308.—HEAVING-TO.

Having determined from the known quality of the ship, what sail would be best to heave-to under; bring by the wind as in the previous subject. If intending to lay-to under a main-topsail, when by the wind, haul up and furl the foresail, down foretop-mast-staysail; if under lower-staysails, hoist them; at the same time taking in the foresail and main-topsail.

The helm is kept a-lee while laying-to, but not lashed down, it being considered best to have a little steerage-way on.

Note.—It is best to bring by the wind under the square-sails, as the ship is more under command than she would be if they were furled.

309.—TAKING IN A LOWER STUDDING-SAIL—BLOWING FRESH.

This is a much nicer operation than young officers generally are inclined to admit, and unless executed with caution and skill on the part of the officer "carrying on the duty" on deck, the probability is, the topmast studding-sail boom will *snap* short in the iron, and the sail, swinging-boom gear and all, will have to be recorded in the log as "expended." When not sailing in a squadron, and the *yawing* of the ship be a matter of minor importance, the officer of the watch is recommended to proceed as follows:—

Place a steady helmsman at the wheel, and stand close to him; man well the sheet, and lead it well aft along the deck; also see that steady hands attend the tack and guys. When perfectly prepared, direct the helmsman with a "small helm," to bring the wind gradually on the opposite quarter, and the moment the body of the sail begins to lose the breeze, and the canvass inclines to shiver, *lower* the outer halliards, ease the tack, and haul in on the sheet as rapidly as possible, lowering the inner halliards at the same time.

Note.—More booms are sprung, and even snapped short in the iron, from the sudden jerk produced by lowering the lower halliards, when the sail is straining and bellying to the breeze, than by even carrying a powerful press of canvass. And here it may be well to impress upon the mind of the young seaman, that a judicious management of the helm, in almost every situation in which it can be placed, will not only aid the physical strength employed, but also greatly facilitate the service sought.

310.—TO UNBEND A TOPSAIL IN A GALE OF WIND.

Those who know the value of *minutes* to men perched aloft in a perilous position, will adopt that method which will eventually cost the least time and trouble. The sail should be *first* furled, then detached from the yard, and sent down on deck (slung amidships) by the long tackle* hooked at the topmast-head, and steadied forward clear of the top-rim by the weather or lee bowline, according to the side on which the sail is to be sent down. (See 298).

Should the ship be rolling or pitching to any extent, and it is not deemed prudent to lower the furled sail "before all," the sail may be sent down through lubber's hole. This method will depend entirely upon the motion of the ship.

311.—SECURING IN A GALE.

See that the yards which have sails set upon them are not unnecessarily sharp up; that the yards whose sails are furled are hoisted clear of the caps; that the runners and tackles are up in good time; that all unnecessary strain is taken off the rigging; and that mats are carefully placed wherever a chafe is likely to occur, such as at the bunts of the furled sails, and at the lee quarters of the yards, which are braced up against the rigging.

See also that the fore and main sheets, if set, be checked a

---

* Generally called the top-burton.

little; the weather lifts and trusses well up and taut; jiggers on topsail lifts, and studding-sails out of the rigging; anchors and guns properly secured; and in a small vessel, the hatches battened down, extra on boats, spare spars, &c., &c.

312.—PREPARATIONS FOR A HURRICANE AT SEA.

Endeavor to get sea room; if you have it, run before the wind. The captain and first officer to cunn the ship; two or three of the best men to steer; the master to keep the time, and the courses steered, and have the ship's place kept worked up.

Previous to its coming on, have a life-line set up on each side of the deck. Furl all sails, and secure them with studding-sail tacks as well as long gaskets; batten down the hatches, and have the relieving tackles on the tiller; down topgallant-yards, and send topgallant-masts on deck, and flying jib-boom in. Clear the tops; gaffs down; rudder-chocks and spare tiller at hand; axes and hawsers at hand; scuppers clear; pumps ready. Let each man wear a belt to secure himself if required to the most convenient place; keep the after yards square; head yards thrown forward, and have the fore-staysail set with double sheets.

313.—PREPARATIONS FOR A HURRICANE AT AN ANCHOR, (*with notes on the Barometer.*)

The ship should be moored with a whole cable each way if in harbor, or if in an open roadstead, veer to a hundred fathoms on each anchor.

The more your berth is out of the way of other ships, the better, as vessels driving, or getting adrift, occasion much damage to those who might otherwise have held on.

If moored, the sheet cable to be bent and ranged, and the anchor let go, and veer on the bowers to the clinches.

All the ground tackle you have should be used. Have a *shackle* abaft the foremost stopper on each cable, ready for slipping if absolutely necessary, to prevent swamping, or from other causes.

Batter down fore and aft.

Down topgallant yards and masts.

If time, unbend sails (topsails and courses, I mean).

Strike lower-yards and topmasts.

Get yards as much fore and aft as possible.

Jib-boom eased in.

Keep try-sails and fore stay-sail bent, and the former reefed. Unreeve the running rigging, that nothing may be aloft to hold the wind.

Clear the tops.

No boats to be above the gunwale.

Axes and hawsers up ready.

If anchors drag, cut away lower masts—the rigging being first cut and cleared. Remember the stays.

Notes and remarks on the Barometer.

SCALE OF BAROMETER AT PRESENT.		As the force of the wind is what is required for service at sea, the following would be better understood.	
Inches.		Inches.	
31.0	- - - - - Very dry.		
30.5	- - - - - Set fair.	30.5	- - - - - Very settled.
30.0	- - - - - Fair.	30.0	- - - - - Fine weather.
		29.7	- - - - - Unsettled.
29.5	- - - - - Changeable.	29.5	- - - - - Gale.
		29.2	- - - - - Storm.
29.0	- - - - - Rain.	29.0	- - - - - Violent storm.
28.5	- - - - - Much rain.	28.5	- - - - - Tempest.
28.0	- - - - - Stormy.		

When the mercury *falls* in the Barometer, it announces rain, or wind, or in general what is called bad weather; and, on the contrary, when it *rises*, it announces fair weather.

When the mercury falls in frosty weather, either snow, or a thaw may be expected; but if it rises in the winter with a north or east wind, it generally forebodes a frost.

If the mercury sinks slowly, we may expect rain, which will probably be of some continuance; but if it rises gradually, we may expect fine weather that will be lasting.

When the Barometer is fluctuating, rising and falling suddenly, the weather may be expected to be like it—changeable.

.When the mercury falls very low, there will be much rain; but if its fall is low and sudden, a high wind frequently follows.

When an extraordinary fall of the mercury happens, without any remarkable change near at hand, there is some probability of a storm at a distance.

In very warm weather the fall of the mercury indicates thunder.

The Barometer will descend sometimes as an indication of wind only, and sometimes rise when the wind is to the north or east.

A north-east wind generally causes the Barometer to rise, and it is generally low with a south-west wind.

An extraordinary fall of the mercury will sometimes take place in summer previous to heavy showers, attended with thunder; but in spring, autumn, and winter, it indicates violent winds.

The mercury is higher in cold than in warm weather, and lower at noon and midnight than at any other period of the day.

The mercury generally falls at the approach of new and full moon, and rises at the quadratures.

Before high tides, there is almost always a great fall of the mercury; this takes place oftener at the full than at the new moon.

The greatest changes of the Barometer commonly take place during clear weather with a north wind, and the smallest risings during cloudy, rainy, or windy weather, with a south or nearly south wind.

The words generally engraved on the plate of the Barometer, rather serve to *mislead*, than to inform; for the changes of weather depend rather on the rising and falling of the mercury, than on its standing at any particular height.

When the mercury is as high as "fair," and the surface of it is *concave*, (which is the case when it begins to descend,) it very often rains; and on the contrary, when the mercury is opposite "rain," and the surface of it is *convex*, (which is the case when it begins to ascend,) fair weather may be expected. These circumstances not being duly attended to, is the principal cause that many people have not a proper confidence in this instrument.

For sea-service, it would be as well to read the Barometer off three times a day at least—at 8 A. M., noon, and 8 P. M.—and oftener if bad weather.

In Europe, if the alteration in the quicksilver should be in as great a proportion as six-tenths of an inch to twenty-four hours, sudden but not lasting changes of weather may be expected.

If the alteration should be gradual, probably in the proportion of two or three-tenths to twenty-four hours, the weather indicated will be likely to last.

One-fifth of the variation of the Barometer, in any climate, in twenty-four hours, may be considered as an indication of sudden change.

If wind should follow rain, the wind may be expected to increase.

Rain following wind is likely to lull it, and the wind may be expected to abate.

314.—THE FOREMAST IS CARRIED AWAY.

Hard up the helm, brace in the after yards, hoist the main-staysail, take in after sail, and endeavor to get before the wind; if successful, keep her so, by veering a range of cable over the stern, and lashing it amidships; if not, which is most likely to be the case, and should carry away the main-topmast also, lay her to under the main-staysail. If the main-topmast should stand, clew-up the main-topsail immediately, get the breast back-stays over the topsail-yard, and set them up as far forward as possible, by means of tackles. Bend hawsers on the wreck, clear it away, *especially the lanyards of the lee-rigging*, so as to preserve the channels and chain-bolts, and endeavor to haul it aboard. Send down the after yards and spars, and save as much of the wreck as possible. Rig a jury-foremast, fitting spars and sails to the best advantage; when the jury-mast is rigged, reeve a main-topmast stay, of a hawser, and take the breast-backstays aft again, after which cut clear of the wreck, if not required.

315.—TO RIG A JURY-MAST.

Take a spare spar, the largest on board, a main-topmast for instance, and launch the head over the night-heads, the heel resting against the stump of the old mast; put on the cross-trees and bolsters, fit the rigging and stays from hawsers, and hook a couple of tackles from the jury-mast head—which take to the sides and haul taut; hook another, which take well aft; lash the heel of the stump to prevent slipping, and raise the mast with the after purchase, tending the stays and pendant-tackles; when up, reeve the lanyards, set up the rigging and stays. Cleet and lash the heel securely. Ship the cap, send up a topgallant-mast for a topmast, fit a topsail yard for a lower yard, and a topgallant yard for a topsail yard, and so on.

316.—ACCIDENTS TO TILLER.

In the event of losing a mast.

Should the tiller break in the rudder head, the rudder must immediately be chocked, that its stump may be taken out and the spare tiller fitted, which, together with the chock, should *always* be placed in readiness for immediate use. While the rudder is useless, the ship must be hove-to till it is repaired, or some contrivance prepared to supply its place.

317.—THE MAIN-MAST IS CARRIED AWAY.

Hard-up the helm, secure the mizen topmast if it still stands, clear the wreck, save as much as possible, and rig a jury main-mast, as above.

318.—THE BOWSPRIT IS CARRIED AWAY.

Hard-up the helm, shiver the after yards, take in after sail, and get the ship before the wind; take the fore-topmast breast-backstays forward over the top-sail yard, hook the pendant tackles and set them up to the cat-heads; unreeve the main-topmast and spring-stays, and set them up to the foretopsail sheet bitts; hitch a hawser to the foretopmast head, take this in through one of the hawse-holes, and set it up on the gun-deck. While this is performing, let some hands be reducing sail, sending down top-gallant yards and masts if they are aloft, and clearing the wreck; rig a jury-bowsprit of a spare main-topmast or a jib-boom.

319.—A TOPMAST IS CARRIED AWAY.

Get the ship before the wind immediately, and reduce sail; hook the top-blocks and reeve hawsers through them; bend the lee one to the topsail-yard, which is probably hanging to leeward of the topmast, with the wreck. Clew up the topsail if practicable, and cut the parrel if it can be got at. The yard now hangs clear of the topmast; bend the weather hawser to the wreck of the topmast; have guys from the weather side of the deck—clear away the lanyards of the rigging and stays, also the rigging leading to the topmast head, and send it down on deck; hook the yard-tackles, slack the braces and trusses, bouse the lower yards forward, and send down the stump; get the topsail-yard down in the lee-gangway, and repair its damages while the spare topmast is got aloft and secured by the old rigging; send aloft the yard, set the topsails, and bring her to her course again.

320.—THE JIB-BOOM IS CARRIED AWAY.

Mind the weather helm, hoist the foretopmast-staysail, and get in the wreck by the fore pendant-tackles, hooked to the fore-stay; reeve a heel-rope and get in the stump; point another boom, and rig it with the old rigging, if sound, if not, with spare ropes or hawsers.

321.—THE FOREMAST IS SPRUNG NEAR THE HOUNDS OR BIBBS.

Get the ship before the wind immediately, reduce sail, and get all the strain off the foremast; secure the main-topmast.

Send down topgallant yards and masts; hook the jeers, and settle the fore yard; hook top-blocks, reeve top-pendants and house topmasts, allowing the heel to come considerably below the defect; fish the foremast with side fishes, and the heel of the topmast, wedging the lashings. Clap a lashing around the doublings of the mast-head, having chocks between; keep the pendant-tackles rove, turn in the rigging afresh, and set it up; wedge the topmast in the cap, and sway the fore yard close up to the heel of the topmast; reef the head sails to diminish the strain if required.

322.—THE FOREMAST AND BOWSPRIT CARRIED AWAY.

Proceed as in 314, the remarks being applied to the present case; lay-to under the main-staysail, to leeward of the wreck, and repair damages on board, in the best possible manner; rig a jury foremast and bowsprit, and then cut clear, having saved as many spars and sails, and as much rigging as possible; if the ship lays easily by the wreck, it would probably be well to ride by it, until the gale abates. If it is absolutely necessary to veer, it might be done as before mentioned, with the assistance of the mainsail, making use of the wreck as a drag, by taking the hawser as a spring to the quarter.

323.—THE BOWSPRIT IS SPRUNG.

Up helm, shiver the after yards, take in after sail, and get the ship before the wind; haul down the head sails, come up the main topmast stays, and set them up on deck; get the fore-topmast breast-backstays forward, hook the fore pendant tackles, and set them up to the cat-head; come up all the head stays, and rig in the head booms; send down upper yards and masts, take the fore-topmast stays through the hawse-hole, and set them up.

Note.—All strain now being off the bowsprit, fish it with the regular fishes; if there are none on board, use the jib-boom; if thought sufficiently strong to bear the strain of the head stays, get them in their proper places, but if not, get stays out merely to make sail.

324.—A TOPMAST IS SPRUNG NEAR THE LOWER CAP.

Get the ship before the wind and reduce sail; if a spare topmast is not to be had, the old one may be housed far enough to allow the spring to come some feet below the cap, setting the lower yard as in the last case; fit a larger chock between the topmast and lowermast head, and clap stout lashings around, above, and below the defect part, wedging them well; reef the foresail so that it can be set with the yard in its present place, and also the topsail, to lessen the strain on the weak spar.

Note.—Sheep-shank the rigging, if required, before setting up.

325.—TO SEND ALOFT A TOPMAST, AND A HEAVY SEA ON.

After the topmast is pointed and rigged, hook the burtons to stout strops, at the rim of the top on each side; hitch hawsers to the mast-head, leading one through a larger block at the fore-topmast head, and another aft through one at the mizen; haul the burtons and hawsers taut; sway aloft the topmast, slacking up as it goes aloft; when fidded, steady the topmast until the rigging and stays are set up.

326.—THE GAMMONING CARRIED AWAY.

Proceed as in 323, until all strain is off the bowsprit; put a stout chock on the bowsprit, and pass the end of the messenger out of a hawse-hole, over the chock, in through the other hawse-hole, and bitt it; take the other end to the capstan, and get the bowsprit well down in its bed by the messenger and bob-stays; come up the old gammoning, and pass a new one.

Note.—Iron gammonings are used for all vessels, by new regulation. (*See **Rigging Table.***)

327.—A LOWER CAP SPLITS.

Take all sail off the mast, pass a stout lashing around the topmast and lower mast-head, which wedge; after which woold and wedge the cap.

328.—THE TRESTLE-TREES ARE SPRUNG.

Get the ship before the wind, take all sail off the mast, send down topgallant yards and masts, housing the others; hook the top-blocks, reeve top-pendants, hook top-tackles, and bouse them well taut, taking all strain off the fid; pass several stout lashings around the heel of the topmast and lower mast-head, cleating them to prevent their slipping; make sail as the mast will bear.

329.—A LOWER YARD IS CARRIED AWAY IN THE SLINGS.

If the fore-yard, get the ship before the wind, haul up the foresail, clew up the topsail, take in all sail on the mizen-mast, unreeve the foretopsail sheets and board them on deck; bring her on your course again, and haul the bowlines.

If a main-yard, keep on the course, haul up the mainsail, clew up the topsail, unreeve the sheets, board them on deck, and haul the bowlines well out; having proceeded thus far, get stout strops around the inner quarter of the yard, and hook the pendant-tackles to bolts in the lower cap, and these strops; if the pendant-tackles are not at hand, use the burtons.

Lash the jear-blocks, reeve the jears, and send the yard down by the jears, lifts, and pendant-tackles; fish the lower yards immediately, if it can be done; if it cannot, rig a topsail yard for a lower yard.

330.—A TOPSAIL YARD IS CARRIED AWAY.

If it is the fore, reduce after sail; mind the weather helm, and keep the ship on her course. If it is the main, stand on, clew up the sail, unbend it, and get it into the top the best manner possible. Get a strop around the topmast-head, above the eyes of the rigging, to which hook a large single block, and reeve a hawser through it. If the yard is completely broken off, bend the hawser which is not secured by the parrel, bend on guys, and send it down; then send down the other piece. If it still remains together, bend on the slings, stop out to leeward, have a tripping line and rolling ropes, and get it fore and aft on deck; take off all the old rigging, which put on to the spare yard in the chains; then bend on the hawser, sway aloft, and cross it as in fitting the ship out, have rolling ropes around it as it goes aloft; bend the topsail, and set it.

331.—THE SHIP LEAKS FASTER THAN THE PUMPS CAN FREE HER.

Find out where the leak is; thrum an old sail very thickly, and have stout ropes attached to each leech; make it up, take it under the bowsprit, and get the ropes on their respective sides; heave the ship too; when her headway eases, drop the sail overboard; after it has sunk beneath the keel, break the stops, haul aft on the ropes attached to each clew; when the body of the sail is over the leak, haul well taut all the ropes attached to the leeches and the head, which will prevent the sail from going aft when going ahead; make sail, and continue pumping.

332.—THE PUMPS ARE CHOKED.

Hoist them out, and clear them.

333.—A SHOT GETS LOOSE IN A GUN SECURED FOR A GALE.

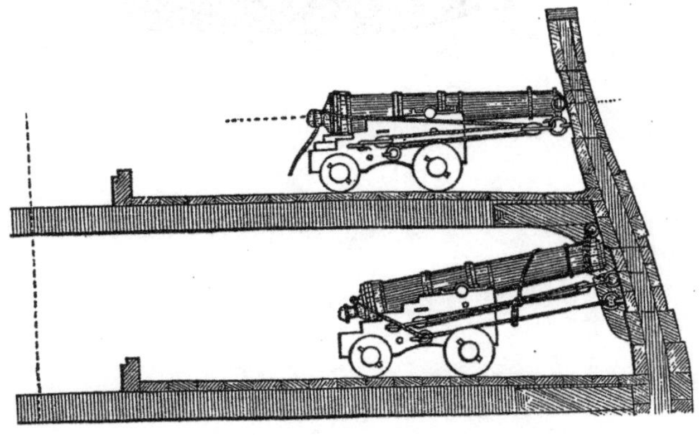

Prick the cartridge well down, and pour vinegar enough in the touch-hole to drown it.

334.—TO THROW A LOWER DECK GUN OVERBOARD.

Fit a chock in the port-sill, and over the pomelion of the gun, to which, from the housing-bolt, hook a stout tackle; unlash the muzzle, heave up the breech, and put in the bed and coin; unreeve the breeching, throw back the cap squares, and place capstan bars under the breech to ease it, and prevent the gun from slipping back into the carriage again; man the side and port tackles, watch the roll, trice up the port briskly, run out, and throw the gun clear of the carriage, by the breech-tackles and capstan-bars; shut in the port immediately.

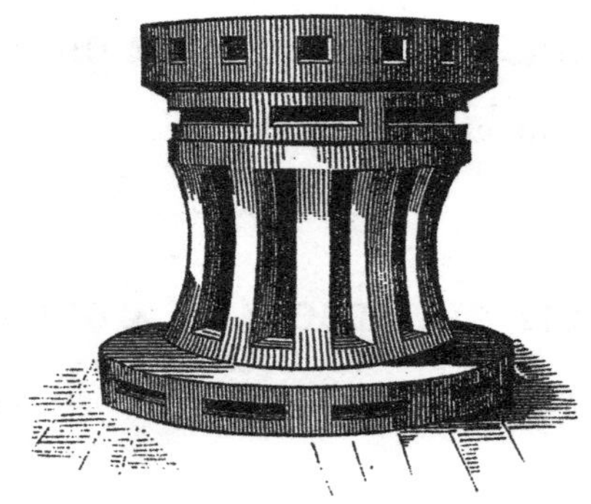

PART VI.

335.—TO TURN REEFS OUT OF THE TOPSAILS AND COURSES.

Haul taut the reef-pendants, and set taut the lower lifts; ease off the bowlines; ease a little of the tacks and sheets of the courses, and settle a few feet of the topsail halliards; haul taut the reef tackles and buntlines, round in a little of the weather braces, to clear the points of the lee-rigging; commence casting off the points of the bunt, taking care to leave none tied, and turning one reef out at a time; ease away both earings together; overhaul the rigging, get the tacks on board; sheet home, hoist the topsails up to a taut leech, out bowlines and make sail.

336.—THE RUDDER IS CARRIED AWAY—TO FIT ANOTHER.

Man the braces immediatly; take in after sails, and let the ship run a little free; rouse up a cable, clove-hitch a hawser over the cable, and then pay it overboard; veer away about twenty fathoms, and lash it amidships on the taffrail; lead the ends of the hawsers through large blocks, lashed to the quarters, and clap tackles on them; steer the ship by this contrivance, until a rudder can be constructed. (*See Plate.*)

Take a spare topmast, cut it the length of the rudder, enlarge the fid-hole to receive the tiller, if not already large enough; take a spare cap and cut away the after part, so as to fit the stern post at the waters' edge, or a little below; pass the topmast through the round hole in the cap; take a spare jib-boom and cut it in two; the pieces are to be bolted on abaft the topmast, after squaring the edges which will come in contact with each other, and cutting a score in the forward part of the jib-boom, next to the topmast, to allow the cap to have room to play in; plank the whole over with stout oak plank, and bolt in a fish abaft all; drive an eye-bolt into the heel of the topmast (now the head of the rudder), and have kentledge attached to the other end to sink it; take an anchor-stock and square two of the edges; cut away a circular score in each, for them to join together around the topmast, below the squares, and thus serve as an upper gudgeon; drive the anchor-stock hoops on the rudder-head, to prevent splitting.

Place the rudder on a stage, near the taffrail; pass a couple of hawsers aft through the hawse-holes, and secure them to the heel of the rudder; have tackles on their inner ends; have two more hawsers or parts of hawsers passed from forward aft, under everything, one each side, and clinch them to the quarter eye-bolts in the cap; have a pendant round as described in another place; launch overboard and rouse up on the head rope; heave in upon the hawsers, and bring the rudder to the stern post, perpendicularly; secure the cap to the stern post and the anchor-stock, around the rudder head; ship the tiller, reeve the wheel-ropes, and rouse in the cable. The kentledge may remain to keep the rudder perpendicular, or may be taken off, as the case may require.

Note.—See improved sketch or plan of temporary rudder.

337.—A SHIP ON FIRE AT SEA.

Hard up the helm, haul up the courses, up spanker, get the ship before the wind, and reduce sail to topsails; beat to quarters, close all the ports, muster the men at their stations, call away the firemen, under charge of their proper officers; let a part fill the engine and wet the sails, while the other part finds out where the fire is, and endeavor to extinguish it if possible—for which purpose use bedding; putting over the gratings and tarpaulins. The gunner and his mates should be in the magazine, ready to drown the powder at a moment's notice; let the carpenters rig and fetch the pumps, and the spar-deck divison clear away the boats, equip them, and get them ready for hoisting out; in the above case, the fire is supposed to be below, and the helm is put up, because wind is less felt; the ports are shut in, and the tarpaulins put on, as they would afford air to the fire; and the courses hauled up, because they strike a current of air down the hatchways, and are also liable to catch. If the fire is on deck, and forward, keep before the wind; if aft, haul close on a wind.

338.—A SHIP ON HER BEAM ENDS.

When the severity of the squall is felt, hard up the helm and let fly everything; but if she goes on her beam ends before she can be got off sufficiently to diminish the effects of the wind, the best way will be to cut away the mizen-mast before the headway ceases, which falling over the lee quarter, will act as a drag, to pay her off; should she not right when before the wind, if there be an anchorage, and the cable is bent, get the drag to the lee-bow, by means of a spring, and rouse in; the wind acting on the flat deck, and under side of the sails, will probably right her. As a last resort, cut away the masts—great decision and rapidity of execution is necessary, as the ship must go down a short time after she goes over.

339.—WIND FREE, ALL SAIL SET, STRUCK BY A SQUALL.

Up helm, let fly the main-sheets, spanker-outhaul, staysail-sheets and halliards, royal and topgallant studding-sail-halliards, royal and topgallant-sheets, and halliards; haul up the mainsail, brail up the spanker, down staysails, and order the topmen to haul in the studding-sails and stow them. When before the wind, right the helm, clew down the topsails, haul up the buntlines, and out reef-tackles, and reef if necessary; clear up the decks as fast as possible.

Note.—In ordinary cases, sheets and tacks should be eased off, for if they should get foul when running through their blocks fast, spars might be endangered; but when struck by a severe squall, the effect of the sails must be diminished as soon as possible, to save the masts, and prevent her from going over.

340.—STRUCK BY A SQUALL ON A LEE SHORE.

If sail cannot be reduced, luff-too and shake her; fill away again, gather headway, and luff again.

341.—STRUCK BY A SQUALL UNDER WHOLE TOPSAILS AND COURSERS.

Up helm, let fly the topsail halliards, main-sheet, spanker outhaul, and lee-topsail sheets; haul up the mainsail, brail up the spanker, clew up the topsails to leeward, then to windward; right the helm, and reef if necessary.

342.—ON A WIND, UNDER WHOLE TOPSAILS—PART THE WEATHER MAIN-TOPSAIL BRACE.

Haul up the mainsail, let go the lee main-brace, haul forward on the lee-maintop-bowline, and aft on the weather main-brace; luff-too, and when the main-topsail shivers, clew it down, haul up the buntlines, out reef tackles, and steady the yard by the bowline, until a new brace can be rove; a burton might be hooked to steady the yard.

343.—THE JIB-DOWNHAUL PARTS.

Untoggle the fore-topgallant-bowlines, and knot them together, above the first hank, between the stay and jib-halliards, which use for a downhaul, until you reeve a new one.

344.—TO CHASE.

A vessel that chases another should have the advantage in point of sailing, because if the ship chased is as good a sailer as the chaser, the latter can never come up to her, if she manœuvred equally as well.

In order to determine whether your ship sails faster than your adversary, get upon the same tack, under the same sail, and keep upon the same course with her; set her exactly with a compass, and if your ship sails best, the sail will soon draw a point more aft; if she has the advantage she will in a short time draw more forward, and if both sail equally well, she will remain at the same point.

345.—TO CHASE TO WINDWARD.

To chase to windward, run upon the same course with the enemy, until he is brought perpendicularly to the same course; when tack and continue the second board, until he is again brought perpendicularly to the same course; always continue this manœuvre by tacking every time the chase is a-beam, on either board, and she will come in the shortest method by your superiority of sailing. Should the chase pass the point, when the chase bears a-beam, he must go about with all dispatch.

Note.—The chase goes about as soon as the chase is exactly a-beam, because at that time, the distance between them is the least possible upon the different boards they hold.

346.—OBSERVATIONS FOR A SHIP TO WINDWARD, WHICH IS CHASED.

The weather ship will always be joined, since it is granted that she does not sail as well as the pursuer, it will be then to her advantage to keep constantly on the same tack, without losing time to heave about, for tacking cannot be so favorable to her as to her adversary, whose sailing is superior.

If the chaser mistakingly stands on and tacks in the wake of the chase, the best course for the latter to pursue is to heave about and pass to windward of him on the other tack, unless you suppose your vessel would have a superiority in going large; for if the chaser persists in tacking in the wake of the other ship, the chase will be much prolonged.

347.—TO CHASE TO LEEWARD.

If the chaser keeps away to cut the chase off, and keeps continually on that course, they will eventually come together where the two courses intersect. This will be exactly executed by the ship in chase, if in the course she has taken, she keeps the chase continually upon the same degree of the compass as at the beginning of the pursuit. This principle applies equally to all the courses which the retreating ship pursues, for if overtaken, it can only be accomplished by keeping in a straight line, if the chase takes another course than that which keeps the two ships upon the same point. These are the only considerations to be made, and they may be corrected, by observing the bearings by an azimuth compass.

348.—TO WINDWARD OF AN ENEMY, WITHIN PISTOL SHOT.—*The weather main rigging is shot away—both ships with main topsails to the mast.*

Up helm, fill away, and run the enemy on board, before she gets headway to prevent it.

349.—WIND ON THE QUARTER, ALL SAIL SET—BRING BY UNDER DOUBLE-REEFED TOPSAILS.

Reduce sail regularly, and clew down the topsails; luff enough to reef, hoist the topsails, and haul close on a wind.

350.—WIND ON THE QUARTER, ALL SAIL SET—BRING-TO ON THE OTHER TACK, UNDER DOUBLE REEFED TOPSAILS.

Reduce sail to topsails, station the crew forward, with one watch of topmen aloft to reef; brail up the spanker, up helm, brace in, and when before the wind, clew down the topsails, haul out reef-tackles, and up buntlines; let the men lay out and reef; wind on the quarter, brace up cross-jack yard, and haul out the spanker; as she comes-too, brace up the fore yard, and meet her with the helm and jib-sheet; when coming-too, a good opportunity will be offered for reefing; when reefed, hoist away the topsails, letting the main go a-back, the others fill.

Note.—Having a dismasted ship in tow, heave-to, make fast the stream cable to the mainmast of the ship, and take it in at the weather gangway, clinching it around the mainmast; then make fast a stout hawser as a spring, and snatch it to a block lashed amidships on the taffrail, so that the ship may either ride on the weather quarter, or be roused astern. In case of veering, rouse in upon the spring, and the manœuvre will be performed with more certainty. After it is executed, the tow-rope must be shifted to the opposite gangway, by means of a spring, &c.

351.—HOW TO GET THE ANCHORS OFF THE BOWS.

Hook the fore pendant-tackle; single the shank-painters, and set them taut with the pendant-tackles; come up the shank-lashings, put the shoes between the bills and bows, by capstan-bars, and then by the shank-painters as far as necessary.

Single and set taut cat-head stoppers, and then unlash the rings.

352.—TO ANCHOR HEAD TO WIND—WIND FREE.

See that the officers and men are at their stations, and the strictest silence preserved, as the ship nears her berth; take in all the studding sails, get the burtons off the yards, and the jiggers off the topgallant yards; send the booms and sails down from aloft; man the fore clew-garnets, buntlines and leechlines; the mainsail is hauled up as the ship is going free; topgallant and royal clewlines; lay aloft and stand by to furl the sails snug, and square the yards by the lifts and braces; have hands by the fore tack and sheet, topgallant and royal sheets, halliards, weather braces, and bowlines; up foresail, in topgallant-sails and royals; furl the sails snug, and square the yards by the lifts and braces, hauling taut the halliards. Man the topsail-clewlines and buntlines, weather braces, jib-downhaul, and spanker-outhaul; attend the sheets, halliards, and spanker-brails, ease down the helm, haul down the jib, haul out the spanker, and when the topsail lifts, clear away the sheets, and clew them up; then let go the halliards, clew down, and square away the yards immediately; haul aft the spanker-sheet, and when the headway ceases, stream the buoy, stand clear of the cable; when she begins to go astern, let go the anchor, brail up the spanker, crotch the boom, haul taut the guys, light-to the cable, as fast as she will take it, until a sufficient scope is out, when stopper. Furl sails, haul taut and stop in the rigging, send the boats' crews aft, to lower the boats down. Let the boatswain go ahead to square the yards—clear up the decks.

Note.—If in going to moor, veer out double the mooring scope, and then let go the anchor; then furl sails and heave in.

353.—TO ANCHOR ON A LEE SHORE.

The ship being on a lee shore, and no room to veer, recourse must be had to letting go all the anchors. For this purpose all the cables are bent and ranged, and all the anchors got ready for letting go; the weather sheet is bitted to the forward bitts. and the weather bower to the after bitts, to windward; the lee bower to the forward bitts, and the lee sheet to the after ones to leeward; no buoy rope is bent except to the weather sheet; the weather sheet is backed by the stream, and the other anchors with kedges; see all the tiers clear, get the ship under storm-staysails, and furl all the square sails; hook the yard tackles; get the lower yards forward, and house topmast; when all is ready, keep her a little off, to get headway. Let go the weather sheet and stream anchors and veer away, then the weather bower and kedge; down helm; haul down fore and main storm stay-sails, and the drift to leeward will carry her to the berth of the last anchor, which let go; haul down the mizen storm stay-sail, and veer away an equal scope on all four cables; observe that they will bear an equal strain, and veer to a long scope, reserving sufficient to freshen the nip with;* see that the cables are well rounded, and watch them carefully. If she should drag, sling the guns with the stoutest spare rigging on board, having a round turn around all these cables, and heave them over; if she should still drag, cut away the masts, and if there be no possibility of preventing her from going on shore, take a stout spring to one of the quarters, slip the cables, let her veer round and go on shore end on.†

Note—In weighing these anchors, bring-to first on the cable which has got the least scope out, taking in the slack of the others with deck-tackles.

354.—SCUDDING UNDER A FORESAIL—TO COME TO AN ANCHOR.

Get both bowers ready for letting go; haul up the foresail, making a due allowance for headway, and run in under bare poles; when near the berth, down helm, out with the spanker, and haul aft mizen storm stay-sail sheet; when by the wind, let go the weather anchor and veer away briskly; when head to wind, let go the lee anchor, and haul down the staysail; veer-to, and bring equal strain on both cables. If necessary, let go more anchors.

355.—TO MAKE A FLYING MOOR.

Make all necessary preparations for coming-to; overhaul and bitt a double range of the weather cable, and bitt the lee one at the range to which she is to be moored. When approaching the anchorage, reduce sail to topsails, jib and spanker, if moderate, but if fresh, to jib and spanker only; when near the berth of the first anchor, luff-to, stream the buoy, and when the headway has

---

* If they are hemp cables; if chain, it is unnecessary.

† See wrecked in a gale.

nearly ceased, let go the weather anchor, up helm, stand on and veer away roundly, to prevent the range from checking her; when the full range is nearly out, hard down the helm, down jib, clew up the topsails, out spanker, and let her lay the range out taut; when taut, let go the lee anchor, *furl sails*, bring-to on the weather-cable, reeving away on the lee one, and heave into the moorings. Moor taut, to allow for veering; clap on service, and veer it; if hemp cable, square the yards, stop in the rigging, and clear up the decks.

356.—TO MOOR WITH A LONG SCOPE OF CHAIN.

Shackle the ends of both chains together, and veer away nearly the whole of the two cables; then let go the other anchor, bring-to on the first cable, heave in, veering away on the other; when into the mooring mark or shackle, stopper and bitt, unshackle the chains, and secure all; clear up the decks, and pay the chain below. (*See Unmooring and Mooring.*)

357.—BLOWING FRESH—IN PORT.

Range the cables, see the anchor clear, and an anchor watch set; have leads-men in the chains—send down the upper yards, if not already down; house top-gallant masts, and point the yards to the wind.

358.—SEND DOWN LOWER YARDS.

Send aloft the jeer-blocks, lash them, and reeve the jeers; see the gear of the courses clear, trusses unrove, and lifts clear for unreeving; hook the yard-tackles and take them forward, heave taut the jeers, unreeve the lanyard of the slings, attend the braces and yard-tackles, lower away by the jeers and lifts. When down make all fast.

359.—TO HOUSE TOPMASTS.

Hook top-blocks, reeve pendants and falls, see the rigging clear that leads to the topmast heads, man the top tackle-falls, slack the lanyards of the rigging, stays and backstays; sway up, out fid, lower away, and haul down on the rigging; when low enough, pass heel-lashings around the lower masts, having canvass in the wake; set taut the rigging and stays. Sheep-shank the backstays, haul taut the running-rigging, and make all snug.

Note.—The topmasts may be housed with the lower yards aloft, by taking the yard-tackles forward and bousing upon them, slacking the braces and trusses at the same time (if not patent trusses). The patent truss has been so improved that the mast can be housed by unclamping one side and bracing sharp up.

360.—TO BACK A BOWER BY A STREAM.

Bend a stream-cable to the flukes of the bower-anchor, observing to let go the stream first; and when the cable is taut, let go the bower. If the bower is already down and dragging, form a clinch with the stream, around the cable, and let her drag until she brings the stream ahead.

361.—TO SWEEP FOR AN ANCHOR.

Make use of long stout running-rigging; middle it, and attach some sinker to the middle, also along the bight, to confine it to the bottom. Coil it away in two boats, and pull to windward of where the anohor is supposed to lie; then pull in an opposite direction, veering away on the bight from both boats; now pull in the direction of the anchor, and when the bight catches, cross the boats, and get a round turn with the rope; make a running bowline on the end of a hawser around the rope, and slip it down; when fast, weigh with the launch.

Note.—A section of small sized chain, with a rope bent to each end, is the best means that can be used to sweep for an anchor. Cross and bring both parts together, after which put on a shackle on both parts, and let it run down to the anchor; then heave up on both parts.

362.—PREPARATIONS FOR LEAVING HARBOR.

Inspect the tiller-ropes, shift hard over the helm, once or twice each way, in order to see that the tiller is not obstructed in its sweep in the gun-room. Place lead-lines in both channels. Point the ends of the hawsers up the hatchways, ready for paying out in any direction. Range both bower cables; see stoppers placed in readiness (bitt and ring). Examine cat-head stoppers, and shank-painters of both bower-anchors.

Should the shank-painters be fitted slip-shackle fashion, care should be taken to place men by them who are acquainted with the method of disengaging the anchors, &c.

363.—WEIGHING ANCHOR IN A HEAD-SEA.

In weighing anchor with a head-sea, precaution should be taken to have previously prepared a good deck-tackle or other purchase, which affix to the messenger (if required), to assist the action of the capstan. There should also be had in readiness an ample quantity of nippers. (*See Passing Nippers.*)

364.—CASTING, OR CUTTING THE CABLE.

When at single anchor in a roadstead, and if it be apprehended that from the direction of the wind, and the local position of the ship with the shore, it may be necessary to have recourse to cutting the cable, and that casting the wrong way would endanger the safety of the vessel, timely precaution should be taken to ensure the ships casting in the right direction.

To effect this purpose, the stream cable should be bent to that of the riding bower, brought through the after part, and taken round the capstan, in readiness to act as a spring, to cant the ship previously to cutting. Axes should be placed abaft in the vicinity of the stream cable, for the purpose of cutting it, after the bower has been severed, and the ship's head cast the desired way.

Note.—A slip or buoy-rope should be brought over "head," so that when the cable is cut, a buoy may be left in the roadstead to denote the position of the anchor.

365.—CLINCHING CABLES.

Whatever be the number of hemp cables which are bent to the anchors, the officer in charge is particularly cautioned to clap on a clinch rounding, towards the inner extremity of each cable, keeping three sheaves in the tier; upon receiving the cables on board, and clinching their respective ends, the officer may proceed as given in the note below.

Chain-cables should never be clinched in a manner which will not admit of their ends being immediately disengaged, in the event of it becoming necessary to slip, or extricate the ship from her anchors; it may be said, that the cable may be unshackled on deck, but it may so happen, that the last shackle is without the hawse—a circumstance which will preclude the possibility of having recourse to this expedient.

Note.—Pay down three sheaves into the tier, and then clap on a racking lashing to the fore beam, previously worming and parceling in the wake of the lashing; measure then, allowing the cable bitted, and clap on a rounding in the wake, where the cable would bring up in the hawse, and chafe in the cutwater. This method leaves room to freshen hawse, in the event of having to veer to the clinch. Few ships adopt the precaution of clapping upon their cables a clinch service; when too late, the necessity of the practice is discovered.

366.—FITTING BUOY-ROPES.

Buoy-ropes are always proportioned to the depth of water. One end is unlaid, and a buoy rope-knot made; it is then laid up again, and whipped. A clove hitch is made, one half of the hitch being on each side of the crown. The end with the knot is seized on the shank, one seizing put on close to the crown, and one close to the end. The other is bent to the buoy. Some prefer the running eye. Put over one arm, and a half-hitch over the other arm, and seized in the cross.

367.—JIB-HALLIARDS WITH A WHIP.

A piece of rope, nearly equal to the double halliards, is rove through the block at the mast-head, and hooked to the head of the jib, a hook being spliced in the end; in the other a single block is spliced high enough from the deck to allow the jib being hauled close down. Through this block reeve a fall, and send both ends down through lubber's-hole ; splice a hook in one end, and hook into a bolt ; reeve the other through a leading-block. Objections have been made to whips, but if the standing part is put a good distance from the hauling, it is impossible that it can take turns in—they can lead abaft the top if necessary. I should recommend their being brought down immediately forward of topsail halliards.

368.—JIB SHEETS, DOUBLE.

Two single blocks are seized into one strap, as span blocks, and the strap secured to the clew* of the sail, with a lashing passed through it, and an eye formed in the strap by crossing both parts together, and passing a throat seizing. One end of the sheet is clinched or spliced into an eye-bolt in the bulwarks, the other end rove through the block in the sail, from out, in and through a fair-leader or sheave in the bulwarks.

With pendants, a piece of rope of sufficient size and length is middled, crossed, and a throat seizing passed round both parts, having an eye in the bight large enough to take a lashing. In each of these pendants, splice a single block ; reeve a whip the same as in the double sheets. The pendants should be long enough to allow the weather one to hang slack on the fore-top-mast stay, when the sheet is aft. (*See Sail Table for iron clews.*)

369.—WRECKED IN A GALE.

When this sad fate appears inevitable, it would be well to make choice (if choice can be made), of what appears the best part of the coast, and the clearest from rocks, for beaching her.

The manner in which the boatmen beach their boats, is by laying them, with the assistance of the helm, half-broadside on, or rather bow and quarter on, having previously given the vessel a *heel, or list in shore.* This may be done either by trimming, or by the sallying of the crew, before the time that the vessel takes the ground. Such a position will offer the best means of saving the crew, who may also be materially assisted by cutting

---

* Iron clews being fitted to all sails, the strap would be likely to chafe. I would recommend snug clump sister-hooks, or shackles, fitted to the clews.

away the masts, so as to fall towards the shore, which may be the means of assisting those on board to reach the shore.

In establishing a communication with the shore, if it be by a boat, the end of the deep sea-lead line should be taken in her, or if it be by some good swimmer, with a cork jacket on, the end of the log line will serve the same purpose; by either of these, hawsers, or other large ropes may afterwards be got on shore.

The means of getting on shore from a wreck are by life boats, rafts, parts of the wreck, or life preservers.

A canvass cot, with large holes at the bottom, to admit the water to pass through freely, and having cross bars of thick rope, should also be kept in readiness for such an occasion.

Raw-hide rope will be the best for traveling grommets. Some other expedients might be mentioned, which are for the consideration of officers in charge of vessels.

370.—SETTING UP RIGGING AT SEA.

Whenever it is required to set up the lower shrouds, at sea, the topmast shrouds should be all let go; this practice is recommended upon the presumption that the lower rigging will not be cast loose, or set up on the occasion of a swell, or that the ship be rolling or pitching. It has been well observed, that by letting go two topmast shrouds at a time, an uneven strain has been brought upon the futtock;* which prevents the shrouds of the lower rigging being equally drawn down.

Upon all occasions of setting up the lower rigging at sea, it is always advisable to have ready prepared as many luffs as possible, so that the shrouds may be set up at a time, and that there may be no delay in shifting the tackles from shroud to shroud. When the lower rigging is up, the futtock plates should be beaten down to the top, and the shrouds set tautly up by means of tackles, ready hooked to there respective lanyards. The method of employing the Spanish windlass, for the purpose of setting up these shrouds, is not to be recommended. It occupies too much time, and often creates unnecessary delay before the topmast rigging can be set up. In staying the topmasts, the boatswain is not recommended to bouse too far forward the heads of the mast, and he should recollect that the angle formed by the main topmast stay, with the fore top, is considerably greater than that of the fore topmast with the bowsprit; and consequently that the lever of the former is more powerful than that of the latter.

* This is only applicable to vessels having their futtock-rigging set up to their lower rigging.

Note.—Vessels not having catharpen legs, need not come up the topmast rigging for the purpose of setting up lower rigging, as the futtock-shrouds set up to the mast.

371.—SLACKING THE JIB-STAY, IN BAD WEATHER.

The jib-stay is always set up as taut as a bar of iron; consequently, when it comes to a blow, both the spray of the sea and the rain tend to tauten it more; in pitching, too, it must assist to spring the boom, work the bowsprit, and cause unnecessary strain upon the rope itself. Whenever it blows so fresh that the jib is not likely to be set, the jib-stay should be slacked. If it be required subsequently to setting the sail, nothing can be easier than to set the stay up, while the jib is loosing. (*Bear this in mind.*)

372.—STOPPING OUT TOPGALLANT YARD ROPES.

The practice of permitting the topmen to stop the topgallant yard ropes out at their own convenience, and consequently at unstated periods, is at variance with that order and regularity which should ever characterize the duties and discipline of a vessel of war.

In well regulated ships, the officer of the watch, following the movements of the senior officers, directs the boatswain or his mates to pipe "out yard ropes;" if tripping-lines are tolerated, the yard rope and tripping-line men should lay out together: by pursuing this system the yards will be kept square, and will not (as is of constant occurrence), be seen for an hour and a half before sunset, topping in different directions. The same rule should be observed when placing on whips for hammock-girtlines, or clothes-lines.

373.—PREVENTER BRACES.

It is desirable to establish a general rule, that when the topsails are treble-reefed, the preventer braces are to be placed on the yards, and that the relieving tackles in the gun room be placed at hand ready for use.

374.—KEEPING A CLEAR ANCHOR.

That part of seamanship which relates to the method of tending a ship to the tide, or in other words of keeping the cable clear of the anchor, may not be inaptly termed the blind branch of the mariner's art—the buoy floating on the surface being the only possible guide that the seaman possesses to point to the position of the anchor hidden under water.

From being little understood, and by young officers it is seldom put in practice, the art of keeping a clear anchor is by many considered a difficult task; but, were officers to give more attention to the matter, and to place less dependence on the master or pilot, they would soon attain every necessary knowledge to meet the most difficult tide case.

375.—ANCHOR TURNING IN THE GROUND.

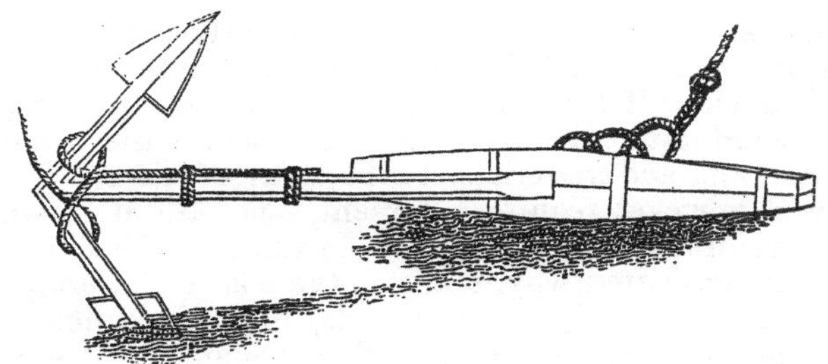

In order to ensure the certainty of an anchor turning in the ground, with the tending or swinging of the ship, it is recommended (whenever it is possible), to resort to this practice: To shoot the ship on the same side of her anchor, at each change of tide; for if the anchor should not turn in the ground, the cable will get foul, either about the stock or upper fluke, and trip it out of ground. (Remember this).

376.—TO TEND TO A WEATHER-TIDE.

Let it be supposed that a ship is riding at single anchor, upon a lee-tide, with the wind in the same direction as the tide, and that it be required, upon the tide setting to windward, to tend the ship clear of the anchor. To effect this, as soon as the ship begins to feel the turn of the weather-tide, and that the vessel brings the wind broad on the weather-bow, the head sails should be hoisted, and the lee-sheets hauled aft, in order to shoot the ship from her anchor, on a taut cable. The helm must be put "a-lee," and kept in that position until the tide sets the ship over to windward of her cable, and the buoy appears on the same side with the helm. If from light winds the buoy bears nearly a-beam, her head sails may be hauled down; but if the breeze be strong, and it causes the ship to shoot in a direction nearly end-on with that of the cable, bringing the buoy on her quarter, it will be necessary to keep the fore-topmast-staysail set, in order to check the vessel, should she be disposed to break her shear against the action of her helm, or be inclined to drop to windward and "go over" her anchor, in a broadside or lateral direction.

377.—A MAN OVERBOARD, AT SEA.

If the ship be going free, and particularly if fast through the water, it is recommended to bring-to with the head-yards a-back, for it is obvious if the main-yard be left square, the ship will be longer coming-to, will shoot farther, increase the distance from the man, and add materially to the delay of succor.

It will however require judgment, especially if blowing fresh, to be careful and right the helm in time, or the ship will fly-to too much, gain sternway, and risk the boat in lowering down.

The best authority recommends, that if possible, the ship should not only be hove a-back when a man falls overboard, but she ought to be brought around on the other tack; of course sail ought to be shortened in stays, and the main-yard kept square. This implies the ship being on a wind, or from the position of having the wind not above two points abaft the beam.

The great merit of such a method of proceeding, is, that if the evolution succeeds, the ship when round will drift towards the man, and although there may be some small risk in lowering the boat in stays from the ship, having at one period sternway, there will in fact be little time lost, if the boat be not lowered until the ship be well round, and the sternway at an end. There is more mischief done generally, by lowering the boat too soon, than by waiting until the fittest moment arrives for doing it coolly. It cannot be too often repeated, that almost the whole depends upon the self-possession of the officer of the deck.

378.—JIB AND STAYSAIL-HALLIARD.

(*Blocks at mast-head.*)

For various reasons it is advisable to dispense with the cheek-blocks, which are usually fitted to the fore topmast-head, for the purpose of reeving the above two ropes, together with the fore topmast staysail-halliards. In the first place, if the fore-topmast be sprung, or carried away in chase, and it be required to shift the mast with all possible speed, considerable time is taken up in removing and replacing cheek-blocks at the mast-head. (*See allowance-table, Blocks.*)

Note.—In some ships the jib and fore-topmast staysail-halliards are rove through gins fitted for the purpose. Gins, however, are not supplied in all ships, but you can always fit fiddle-blocks under the eyes of your rigging; your jib and staysail-halliards reeve in the upper sheaves, and the topsail-buntlines in the lower ones. Cheek-blocks answer well on the trestle-trees.

379.—TO KEEP THE HAWSE CLEAR WHEN MOORED.

When it is nearly slack water, cant her with the helm the right way, and if necessary, make use of jib, spanker, and yards.

380.—TO TEND TO WINDWARD—SINGLE ANCHOR.

When the tide slacks, sheer her with the helm, run up the jib and fore-topmast staysail, with weather-sheets aft; when canted the right way, the lee-sheets may be hauled aft, and and the yards filled, thus setting her abreast to a taut cable; when the buoy is on the lee-quarter, brace the head-yards to the wind, and fill the after ones; when the tide swings her head around so as to shake the sails, haul down and stow them.

381.—TO TEND TO LEEWARD.

As the tide slackens, sheer her to the same side of the buoy on which she came to windward, and fill the yards, which will set her end-on over the cable; she will now by the effect of the wind, bring her stern over the cable, and bring the buoy on her weather-quarter; put the helm "a-weather," and she will shoot ahead, tautening the cable, by sheering her head from the wind. When the wind gets a little aft the beam, hoist the jib, to prevent the cable from drawing her head to wind.

Let her lay in this position until she falls off; when the head-sails shake, haul down and stow them.

382.—TO BACK SHIP—(AT ANCHOR).

As the tide slacks, sheer her to windward, sheet-home and set the mizen-topsail; thus she will back round to leeward as soon as the tide sets up; clew up and furl the mizen-topsail.

383.—TO BREAK THE SHEAR.

When tending to the tide, and the ship comes over her anchor, she may break her shear by canting her stern the wrong way; when this is the case put the helm "a-weather," run the jib up, fill the head-yards, and the after-yards kept-to. Everything is now arranged to bring her round again, when she must be managed as before mentioned.

384.—ON GETTING TO SEA.

Unship the man-ropes, stow them away, secure the gangways, pay down the messenger, and secure anchors and boats. The anchors ought to be secured with preventer stoppers, and painters, particularly where they work with a slip-shackle or tricker, which a rope catching, may drag or drive out. In fact the jib-sheet is apt to do this if not looked to.

Wash and dry the nippers, then stow them away; wash down the anchors and buoys, and black them as soon as possible; when clear of the land, unbend cables, buoys, and buoy-ropes, and ship the blind-buckles, unless prevented by peculiar circumstances.

Take off the harbor-gaskets and have them repaired and blackened afresh, when convenient. If the bunt-gaskets, however, are retained on the yards, roll them up snug and secure them. Put the sea-gaskets on, make them up in cheises, and keep them before the yards.

Place bunt-line spans to their respective yards.

Have the boats' sails and awnings dried and put below.

Quarter-boats clear for lowering.

Besides these, the watch on deck, when not employed in more pressing duties, may be occupied to much advantage as follows, viz.:

1*st*. Exercising small-arms, cutlasses and guns;

2*d*. Pointing all ropes requiring it;

3*d*. Working up a sufficient quantity of junk, into seizing-stuff, mats, swabs, foxes, thumb-lines, knittles, gaskets, reef-points, nippers, salvagees, straps, &c., &c.

385.—ON FIRE REGULATIONS IN THE MERCHANT-SERVICE.

We now come to the most important of all the regulations in a ship, namely, those which operate against the fatal and shocking effects of fire. Whatever good results from stationing people in ordinary cases, cannot be put in competition with this, which provides against the most dreadful catastrophe incident to a ship. From the number of unfortunate accidents of this nature we surely ought to be prepared to our utmost for such an event,

First, by internal precautions; and

Secondly, by the means to be used against the danger.

Let there be great attention in the use of fire and lights.—The regulations on these subjects which exist in men of war are still more required in merchant vessels.

Fires should be put out at eight P. M., and all lights at nine P. M., except those required for the binnacle, and on deck.

The officer of the last dog-watch ought to report the fire extinguished to the captain.

As each man is relieved from the wheel, he should examine below, and report "all well" to the officer of the watch.

No naked light whatever ought to be permitted; let either lanterns or lamps be used.

Spirits should be drawn off by day; a naked light should on no account be permitted near a spirit cask.

Smoking should not be allowed below. I have known more than one ship set on fire by a man's pipe; and by segars, I have no doubt many have been burnt.

In stowing a hold, do not allow naked lights to be used, nor any person to smoke there when so employed.

On receiving cotton as a cargo, both those who ship as well as those who receive it, ought to ascertain that it is in a safe state before it be put on board. I have known instances of its being sold and moved away, when, in a few hours, if it had not been moved, it would have ignited.

I am acquainted with the particulars of a ship that was burnt some years since, where oil had been stowed in the hold with cotton over it, with what was considered safe and secure dunnage between. The cotton, notwithstanding, absorbed a quantity of oil, became heated, and ignited. The crew with difficulty saved themselves in the boats before the flames burst forth, and the vessel was entirely consumed.

Chests containing bottles of inflammable substances, such as vitriol, &c., cannot be too well secured. A medicine chest upset in a gale may set fire to a ship.

Friction matches should never be allowed on board a ship.

The coals in steamers have frequently taken fire, and in many cases with the most fatal consequences. Too much care cannot be taken in the selection of coals; a strict examination ought to be made as to their state when received and stowed, and no suspicious circumstances should be then overlooked. When receiving coals, avoid throwing the fresh ones on the old, which ought to be kept uppermost, and *first* for use. When once they become ignited, I can hardly offer a remedy for the evil.

When coals take fire, some people throw water upon them, and smother the fire by wet beds. Hot water, or steam, if they can be used, are more expeditious than cold water in extinguishing fire, I believe. To attempt to discharge the coals, would allow the air freer access, and would be certain to increase the power of the fire.

A few canvass buckets, with long lanyards, should be always prepared and ready on deck for drawing water.

When a fire is first discovered, shorten all low sails directly, courses up, stay-sails and wind-sails down, boat-covers taken off.

If the sails should take fire from lightning, or any other cause, cutting away the mast appears the most likely method of saving the ship.

At first, endeavor if possible, to stifle the fire; which may be best done by shutting off any draught of air, and smothering it with wet bedding, small sails, &c., until a good supply of water can be applied.

If the fire is forward, put before the wind until it is necessary to "out boats," then bring-to.

If the fire is aft, or a-midships, keep to the wind.

386.—STATION BILL FOR FIRE, IN THE MERCHANT SERVICE.*

Coolness and steadiness in any misfortune by fire are essential to arrest it

If a fire break out below, the hatchways should be immediately covered, to prevent a draught of air.

Ring the ship's bell to call the men to their stations.

MEN'S NAMES.	DUTIES.
A very steady man	To the helm.
The carpenter, and one man.	First, to cover hatchways with gratings and tarpaulins. Secondly, to rig pumps and lead hoses; and Thirdly, get the tools ready for cutting away, if required.
The chief mate, boatswain, and ship's cook.	To attend where the fire is, and pass water to it, &c.
A man of each watch or more.	To the pumps, and to draw water as for washing decks.
A boy.	To collect all the buckets to the part where the water is being drawn.
Remainder of starboard watch.	First duty to haul up courses, brail up trysails and spanker. Second duty, draw and pass water with the fire buckets; then for third duty see below.
Remainder of larboard watch.	First duty, to haul up courses, brail up trysails and spanker. Second duty, to soak small sails and bedding to throw over and smother the fire; then for third duty see below.
Cabin steward, and cabin boy.	If any powder or other combustibles are on board, to throw them overboard if possible, or drown them.
Second mate to direct fire hose, and the supply of water from deck.	If the fresh water is in tanks, turn the waste-valves† of two of them for a first supply for the pump, and then go to direct fire hose, &c.
The crew.	Third duties of the crew, the yard and stay-tackles to be got up ready for getting out boats.

* This bill ought to be written out or printed, and hung up for every one's inspection.

† The mate ought to have the key of the valves of the water tanks in his own keeping.

MEN'S NAMES.	DUTIES.
The crew.	Fourth duties of the crew, if the fire appears to increase, out boats, and lower down the quarter boats; let them lay off in a string to windward, with a man and a boy as keepers, ready for the rest of the crew if required.
The captain - - - - -	To attend at all the stations as he deems best.

If the ship cannot be saved, the passengers and crew are the first objects, with some fresh water and biscuit; a compass, quadrant and Bowditch. Unless there is sufficient time, and it can be done without endangering the sea-worthiness of the boats, nothing should be taken that is not essential to the mere preservation of life, and necessary for navigating the boats.

387.—TAKING TO THE BOATS.

The captain should in his own mind, and by a private memorandum, station the passengers and crew to the boats on board, and likewise make the persons here specified be responsible for having the following articles put into the boats.

Captain.	Compass, Maury on Navigation, sextant, spy-glass, Nautical Almanac, pencils and writing paper, general chart, pocket watch, pair of compasses, &c.
First mate.	Oars, masts, sails, boat-hooks, bolt of canvass, boat's compass, Bowditch's chart, ensign.
Second mate.	Two or three bags of biscuits, some breakers of water, quadrant, pencils and writing paper, half-gill measure, a musket, box of cartridges, and flints or caps.
Surgeon - - - - - - -	Pocket instruments.
Carpenter.	Hammer, nails, sheet-lead, grease, fearnought, oakum, saw, chisel, turn-screw, cold chisel, a vial of sweet oil, any small iron rod.
Third mate, or boat-swain.	Coil of inch rope, long reel, deep-sea reel, painted canvass, marling-spikes, spun-yarn, &c.
Sail maker.	Palm, needles, twine, fishing-lines, hooks, painted canvass, boat's awning.
Cook, and steward.	Tinder-box, flints and tinder, small box, lantern and candles, cheese, cabin biscuit, chocolate.

Each person. { A tin pot, a pocket knife, a change of flannels and stockings.

With a scarcity of food, savages attempt to lessen the cravings of hunger by tightening a belt around the waist; and by sucking a pebble they in some degree alleviate thirst. Chewing tobacco may also be serviceable under such circumstances. In such emergencies all must fare alike.

388.—LOSING A RUDDER AT A CRITICAL MOMENT, (*such as crossing a Bar, &c.*)

A ship might lose her rudder at a critical moment in crossing the bar of a river, when a few minutes more might run her aground, if she were unmanageable; and in this case, what temporary rudder is best becomes a question for which a few moments only are given to decide. The plan of steering by the stream-cable payed out astern, or by the stern-boat lowered instantly, with the plug out, and towed astern by a hawser, with guys leading up to each quarter, would perhaps then be adopted; while a ship losing her rudder at sea would have leisure to adopt any other plan.

It might be an advantage, if every vessel would take some opportunity of trying how she could steer with a stern-boat in the manner described, and what length of tow-line was required to enable her to steer the most easily, so as to avoid wild yawing. The experiment might be made in moderate weather with the wind on the quarter, and also right aft, under top-sails, top-gallant-sails and fore-sail, running five or six knots. Nothing gives confidence so much as practice.

389.—STEAMERS GETTING AGROUND.

As steamers would probably do so with very fresh way on, they ought at once to stop their engines, but on *no account* to attempt to reverse them, until the extent of the injury be ascertained; otherwise they may go down in deep water. Their first duty is to out boats, and place the passengers in safety in them; the crew might then ascertain the state of the vessel; if she is likely to float, and can be got off, the attempt to do so should be made; but if not, the crew can take to the boats.

390.—ON THE DUTY OF REMAINING BY A DAMAGED VESSEL

When two vessels have run foul of each other, the one which is the least injured is bound, by every sense of justice and humanity, to stay by the other to render every assistance in her power; a contrary proceeding ought to make the guilty party liable to some punishment. If one appears likely to sink, the the boat lashings should be cut, that the boat or boats may be got out or float off.

When freshly blows the northern gales,
Then under courses snug we fly;
When lighter breezes swell the sails,
Then royals proudly sweep the sky.

United States' Sloop-of-War Albany under Sail.

United States' Razee or Frigate Independence, at Anchor.

PART VII.

MISCELLANEOUS SUBJECTS.

391.—ON SQUARING YARDS.

Simple as may seem the process of squaring yards, it is nevertheless a piece of duty which requires considerable precision, and this precision can never be obtained without a knowledge of the principle upon which the yards should be squared. A boatswain, ignorant of this principle, will generally proceed thus: he first bouses taut the lower trusses, squares the yards by the braces, and, quite regardless of the distance of the topsail-yards from their respective caps, or looking to see if the yards are a-midships, directs the chief boatswain's mate to take his station on the end of the jib-boom, whilst he himself proceeds in the boat ahead of the ship to square the yards by the lifts. Should the fore-yard be required to be topped to starboard, the boatswain will top away upon the yard-arm until, *by chance*, he discovers he has topped it too high; to remedy this eye sore, he sings out "*Fore-yard to port*," and tops until he raises the larboard arm as high as the starboard; producing by this system of topping, and never settling, a most unsightly bow in the yard. He then squares the fore-topsail yard by the bowed fore-yard, and of course treats the fore-topsail yard to a bit of a bend likewise. He then takes the main yard in hand, which, though probably square by the lifts, can no longer look so in his eye, because the yard arms are not made to cock up like those of the fore yard. "*Main yard to starboard*," he sings out, with an audible voice; the lift is topped several feet to starboard, and then to port, until the yard assumes the desired cock the boatswain has in his eye in squaring the loftier yards by the lifts. Boatswains seldom take the precaution to place hands to tend the top-gallant braces. It should be remembered that the topping of the lifts alter and disturb the square position of the yards by the braces. These may appear minute matters, but unless they be strictly observed, yards never can be properly squared.

In squaring yards by the lifts, the lanyards should always be unrove to two or three turns, the jigger hooked to them and hauled taut; and when topping on one lift always ease the opposite lanyard with the jigger; if not, the lanyard will render with jerks, and the yard will probably have to be topped the opposite way. The lanyards should be rocked when sufficiently up, the plan of nipping with hands being a lazy, bad practice; and after much time spent in getting the yards nicely squared, the lanyards have come up in securing. The ropes should be all hauled taut before the boat comes on board; all the ropes coiled neatly and low in the tops; nothing allowed to hang over the bows, which should be kept quite clear; and everything done to make the ship appear in every respect what a man-of-war ought to be.

Being particular in one part and not in another, has almost a worse appearance than slovenly altogether. As the ship is considered a would-be *man-of-war*, and is the cause of many remarks, which, if heard by the commanding officer, would not be at all complimentary to his nautical knowledge, if anything should be studied more than another, it is the standing rigging and position of the masts and yards, &c., &c.

Note.—Before squaring the yards, the boatswain is recommended to see that the masts, and particularly the lofty spars, are upright and all in one. It frequently happens that after the boatswain has squared all the yards, fore and aft, he detects an awkward inclination in one of the topgallant-masts; he nevertheless returns on board, and reports to the senior lieutenant, yards squared and ropes taut, but afterwards desires the captain of the top to get a pull on the starboard or larboard top-gallant breast-backstay, forgetting that this very pull affects the top-gallant lifts, and consequently alters the position of the yards. The first thing after the masts are all in one, or upright, as you choose to term it, is to get your yards exactly amidships by rolling-tackles; then get them snugly trussed to the mast, and square them by the braces, before proceeding ahead of the ship.

392.—UP TOP-GALLANT MASTS AND YARDS—

(*The Masts, &c. being on deck.*)

One watch of topmen aloft, to get jack or tail blocks on, for yard ropes, as also for *flying jib and staysail halliards;* if the sails are about to be loosed, have jiggers on the topgallant stays, ready for setting up, and burtons overhauled, ready for clapping on the mast ropes; in fidding, the other watch see everything clear, and get tackles on the backstays, ready for setting up the instant the mast is stayed.

WORDS OF COMMAND.

"*All hands, up topgallant-masts and yards,*"—and loose sails if requisite.

"*Sway away,*"—let the masts wait for each other, after placing the topgallant rigging, so that they may afterwards ascend uniformly, and be fidded together. Instantly the fids are in, *stay topgallant-masts*, and set up the quarter, or standing backstays; then without waiting for more of the rigging, proceed to cross topgallant-yards alone, along with the loosing of the sails, as may be requisite, and as is described in 394.

Remarks.—The mast-heads and eyes of the rigging, or funnels, should be greased.

If topgallant-sails are unbent, and royal yard-ropes good, it will make the work of crossing topgallant-yards all the easier, to use *royal* in place of topgallant-yard ropes.

If there be no capshore, the topmast cap is apt to droop forward, and by *catching* and *jaming* the topgallant-masts, to interfere materially in the attempt to send them up smartly; the caps ought therefore to be well looked after. If the topgallant, royal, and skysail masts, be all in one, it is generally found necessary to let fall the bunts of the topsails, in order to get the masts up; at sea the yards must be braced up, the topsails lowered two-thirds down, and the mast sent up to windward.

393.—DOWN TOPGALLANT-MASTS AND YARDS.

One watch, or part of a watch of topmen, aloft, to clear away the topgallant rigging, unreeve flying-jib and staysail-halliards, get jack or tail-blocks on, for royal and topgallant yard-ropes, and burtons on the mast-ropes.

The other watch of topmen on deck, unlace the backstay-mats, and slack the backstay lanyards.

When ready, "*sway away,*" two hands at the mast-head looking out for the fids, the lanyards of which they should be cautioned to see fast; and two on topsail-yard to bear the heel clear, and make fast heel-rope.

When the fids are out, hang the backstays to the tops, lower all the masts together, and get heel-ropes on, which should be in readiness, from the deck to the fid-holes.

If the rigging does not start easily, sway and surge without delay; clap on the lizard through the royal-halliard sheave-hole, as soon as it can be got at; then lower the masts on deck, either placing them fore and aft, or up and down the lower masts.

Haul the rigging and backstays taut down from the mast-heads, and stop them down along the topmast rigging, coiling away the slack bights snug in the tops; also haul taut the stays and all the small ropes.

See that the trucks are fairly placed, so that the signal-halliards may traverse freely.

If the masts are only housed, haul the topgallant rigging and backstays taut, as above, but stay the royal-masts, and sheep-shank and set up the royal backstays and shrouds, if there be any, or what is preferable, stop the slack part in bights, and then set up; also steady the heels of the topgallant-masts to the topmast by a heel-rope.

Remarks.—The yards, according to circumstances, may be either sent down at the moment you begin to lower the masts, or at that when you begin to sway the masts, in order to take out the fid. The former has the best effect, but in that case it is essential to have picked hands to lower, and not to commence lowering until the lower yard-arm is unrigged.

394.—CROSSING TOPGALLANT AND ROYAL-YARDS, AND LOOSING SAIL.

That all the squadron may be prepared to cross yards and loose sail at *eight*, or for any other manœuvre, deemed proper at the hoisting of the colors, the flag ship sometimes makes it a rule to designate seven bells, that is 7 H. 30 M., by giving the preparatory signal. The squadron have then an opportunity of regulating their time by the Commodore's, and making such preparations for eight as may be necessary.

If this be done, and another very proper rule enforced, viz.: the allowing no one, on any account, to be aloft between five minutes before eight, and the time of making the signal, every ship will be upon an equal footing in the keen competition which immediately ensues.

PREPARATIONS.

Send the hands aloft to overhaul the lifts and braces; prepare studding-sail-booms for tricing up, bend the top bowlines to the buntline toggles, overhaul the gear of the courses, coiling it snug down on the lower yards, and take the cloths and half the gaskets off the fore and aft sail; also stretch along and reeve the yard-ropes.

WORDS OF COMMAND.

"All hands, cross yards and loose sails;"

"Aloft, topmen;"

"Aloft, sail loosers;"

Sway out of the chains—viz.: upper topgallant yard-arms clear of top-rims, or lubber's-hole; royal yard-arms clear of cross-trees.

"Sway away;" trice up, lay out.

"Sway across—let fall,"—the men at the same time hoisting jibs and staysails, hauling out the bowlines, getting down the squaring-marks of topgallant and royal lifts and braces, and hoisting ensign, jack, and pendant.

A boat should then be manned without delay, for the boatswain to go ahead, look at the yards, see the head-sails taut up, the bowline properly out, and everything ready for shortening sail.

If the bowlines are not to be hauled out, and, in consequence, the jibs and staysails not hoisted, nor the sheets of trysail and spanker hauled aft, proceed as follows, viz.:—

Keep fast the topsail clewlines, and haul up the buntlines; throw the jibs out off the booms without touching the halliards, and slack off the trysail and spanker-brails; overhaul the brails on one side and haul them up—on the other loose the small sails enough for the wind to blow through, which will prevent their heating, and even should it rain slightly, will avert much harm.

Remark.—The frequent loosing of the sails is essential, to prevent them from *mildewing*, particularly when new, and before the gum has been shaken out.

395.—TOPMAST CARRIED AWAY.

I would recommend vessels to use curb-chain, for parrels for topsail-yards; let it be wormed, parceled and covered with leather; the seizings must be frequently examined. Carrying away a parrel may occasion a serious loss of life, should there happen to be any men on the yard at the time, and even if there are not, this accident is very likely to carry away the topmast.

The funnels used for top-gallant rigging, are frequently used for topmast rigging; they are also very serviceable, and if a topmast is carried away, the funnel is then invaluable, as the topmast may be shifted so much more quickly, the rigging remaining properly placed.

396.—CLEARING THE WRECK OF A TOPMAST.

Watch on deck to secure the wreck, and prevent its doing injury—watch below to shorten sail. Hook top-blocks, reeve in them two hawsers; the stoutest to leeward, for passing round and securing the wreck, in order to get the rigging &c. in-board.

Hook luff-tackles in the lower pendants—let the other topgallant yards be sent down, and the topgallant masts housed until the topmast is shifted. If it be a fore-topmast that is carried away, ease in the jib-boom—cut the lanyards of the topmast rigging, securing the dead-eyes by studding-sail-halliards.

The weather-hawser may be employed to unfid the stump.

397.—CARRYING AWAY A JIB-BOOM.

Send down the fore-topgallant-yard, and house the fore-topgallant-mast; use the fore-topmast staysail-halliards, and lee-fore-bowline, for securing and getting in the wreck.

398.—TO FISH A LOWER YARD IN THE SHORTEST TIME.

Incalculable are the evils which may result to a vessel from the springing or snapping of a lower yard, especially the fore one.

If the yard be severed, get both pieces down on deck, and place them together, to assume, as near as possible, their original position. Hollow out, so as to fit the cylindrical surface of the yard, two spare anchor-stock pieces, (or two proper fishes always fitted, and to be kept as spare stores), in doing which, a depth of two or three inches will suffice; place one piece on the top, and the other secured to the under part of the yard, towards the extremities; dub down the superfluous wood, and round the edges, ready to receive the requisite wooldings.

Previous to boring holes for the bolts, set close-to the anchor-stock pieces, with wedge upon wedge; introduce then eight bolts, of three-quarter inch diameter, which must be severally clinched. Cut scores for eight wooldings, and woold away with *well-stretched rope*, of two-and-a-half inch. The yard may then be replaced aloft. There will be found no necessity for studding-sail booms, or other spare spars.

399.—EXPECTATION OF LOSING A LOWER MAST.

Every vessel should have a spare lower cap on board; it should be in two parts (for the convenience of stowing), with bolts for securing it together.

In the event of losing a lower mast, the cap put on the spare topmasts, and then raised on the stump of the lower mast (having been previously fitted for it), at once enables a jury mast to be stopped and secured; clap on a good heel lashing.

Those vessels which have lower dead-eyes secured to the side, are enabled to get clear of the wreck of a lower mast more readily than those with the old channels and chain plates. Those which are fitted in the last mentioned manner, when likely to lose a lower mast, should reeve a hawser through the lanyards of the rigging on each side, and have it well secured; they will then be enabled to disengage the lanyards from the channels, and get clear of the wreck, whose thumping might otherwise injure either the ship's bottom or rudder.

400.—LYING-TO IN A GALE, AFTER THE LOSS OF MASTS.

Put a stout span on a spare topmast or other large spar, and veer a long scope on a hawser, or stream chain-cable, from the bow, by a spring on it from aft; it may be used for wearing. The wreck of a mast would answer well for lying-to with, and when the weather became fine, the spars and rigging would materially assist in refitting jury masts.

401.—SPARS TO CONVERT IN CASE OF NEED.

Officers will do well to consider what spars they have on board which can be the most readily and efficiently converted, so as to supply the place of any which may be lost.

A spare topmast, or if in a brig, a main-boom, are the spars that could be the most quickly converted into a jury lower mast, or bowsprit; a mizen-mast would be still better, if the weather would permit its being shifted.

A topmast studding-sail boom, with the sail as a lug, makes a sufficiently good mizen.

If the bowsprit is sprung, let the jib-boom be eased in nearly to the bulwark. When a vessel is lying-to, and there is a heavy sea running, it would be prudent to have tackles up for steadying the foremast, as in the event of the bowsprit being struck, and either sprung or carried away, the mast would be saved.

A jib-boom will answer well for making a topsail yard.

Note.—It is surprising how well vessels answer when jury rigged, and in many cases will sail nearly as fast as when they have there proper masts, yards, and sails.

Sails may be reduced by taking out midship cloths, and by the head for depth.

When vessels take the ground, from a falling tide, or any other cause, they ought to be prepared with three shores on a side, the lower ends a little off.

The first abreast the foremast;

The second amidships;

The third abaft the main-sheet sheave.

A measure should be previously taken of the exact depth from the bulwark to the ground. The lower end of the shores require some weight, and a flat piece for a shoe secured on each, if the ground is soft. On the upper end of each shore there should be a cleat on the fore side and after side, for securing the lashing to the bulwark.

For small vessels, two shores on each side would be sufficient; one might be under the fore, and one under the main channel. The preparation of shores will be found to be a very useful one; many vessels fall over on the water leaving them, and then run considerable risk of filling, or not righting again.

402.—GETTING AGROUND.

If a vessel gets aground (the weather being moderate), first get over the spare topmasts on one side, and the jib-boom on the other, as shores abreast of the mainmast, or a little before it; secure some weight to the heel of each; a few shot, or a light pig of ballast will do for that purpose, and if the ground is soft, nail on a piece of plank as a shoe. Furl sails, out all boats, down topgallant yards, and send topgallant masts on deck; start water, and pump it out; lay out a bower anchor; be sure that it is so laid that the ship does not ground on it.

Every officer should make himself well acquainted with the readiest mode of hanging and carrying out a bower anchor, as far as relates to the weight of those belonging to his own vessel, and the description of boats he has to use. If he cannot heave off, he must then endeavor to lighten the vessel by discharging part of the cargo.

Before heaving off, an examination ought to be made, so as to ascertain, as near as possible, the extent of the injury which the vessel has received since aground, if the shore be rocky, that it may be remedied before heaving off, if possible; if the vessel has run on with much way, it is possible that she may not float, even if she were got off. In this case the lives of the passengers and crew become the first consideration.

403.—THE BALLAST SHIFTING AT SEA.

This frequently occasions losses at sea. To prevent its occurrence, when iron ballast is stowed, let a few oak battens be nailed from the sides athwart ships, to secure it; or when shingle ballast is used, place a light flooring over it, secured by a few battens athwart ships. This would most probably prevent such a calamity, which usually occurs when a vessel is struck by a heavy sea, or when hove on her beam ends, and prevents the possibility of her righting again; when the ballast is stowed, it ought to be secured at the same time from shifting; this is of great moment, and a few strong battens will do it. Also have shifting boards amidships, nailed to the stanchions.

404.—VESSELS SURPRISED ON OPPOSITE TACKS.

In cases of surprise and danger, from the accidental meeting of two ships on opposite tacks, in the night, it too often happens that officers are more apt to give orders to *the stranger*, than to take any measure of precaution themselves; such as hailing to put the helm up or down, and to clear them, when they may be as much in fault, and possess the same means of extricating themselves from the difficulty. In situations of this sort, it is much better that both parties should put their *helms down* rather than *up;* the ships will approach each other for a time, but will diminish in velocity, and afterwards separate.

Obstinacy, or a want of judgment in the directing parties, frequently leads both vessels to bear up at the same instant; consequently causing immediate collision. It is a universal rule with seamen, that where there is doubt, the vessel on the *larboard tack* is to bear up or to heave about, for the vessel on the *starboard tack;* were this prudent *regulation* strictly adhered to, and never violated by the obstinacy of parties, accidents would seldom occur; but it sometimes happens that incidental circumstances induce both parties to risk "a trial of skill," by one endeavoring to weather the other. In these cases doubt and hesitation generally prevail, and *disaster* is sure to follow.

405.—MEETING AT SEA.

Bend on the ensign and pendant, if a private ship

Hoist the ensign and pendant, when sufficiently near, if the vessel you are meeting be a ship of war.

In hailing, the ordinary questions commence thus;

"What ship is that?"

"Whence come you?"

"Where are you bound?" &c., &c.

406.—A HINT ON RUNNING TOO LONG.

Vessels ought not to run too long, when the sea is high and breaking, but bring-to in time, and do so by daylight if possible.

407.—A HINT ON ROUNDING-TO IN A GALE.

An experienced seaman remarks, that when he wished to bring-to in a hard gale, when running before a heavy sea, he always watched for a heavy sea breaking abaft the main chains, and immediately after, he eased the helm down, and rounded-to at once, being previously prepared for doing so. In managing this way, he found he could avoid shipping a sea.

408.—ON MAKING YOUR PORT.

Never run for your port in very heavy gales, or thick weather, unless sure of the ship's position.

Note.—There are some ports, that may be entered with safety at night by sailing vessels, but there are many more where it cannot be attempted, without great risk of getting aground, or being wrecked.

I do not know anything to compensate for running that risk, except an urgent necessity; as, when anchored, nothing can be done until morning. Lay-to in preference, and carry a light at the main-stay at night. Gales do not last long, and finer wea ther follows.

While lying-to in gales, always keep the ship steering with the helm nearly "amidships,"—*never* let it be kept "*a lee*," as the ship will not be under command without steerage-way, or be safe and easy.

409.—LYING OFF, AND ON, TO ENTER A PORT.

I have known so many vessels wrecked while lying-to with a topsail to the mast, with their head in shore, that I recommend (if it is moderate weather), to make short tacks, under easy sail, as then the ship's place can always be kept worked up; whereas her drift while lying-to is uncertain. Let the tacks in shore be shorter than the ones off, to give the coast a good berth. It is better to be a mile further out than to get aground.

410.—TO ANCHOR AND VEER A LONG SCOPE OF CABLE.

Whenever, and wherever you anchor, veer a long scope of cable *at once*,—never lay short unless when getting underweigh. No ship ought to lay at single anchor for more than a few hours. Moor with a whole cable each way, as soon as possible. All vessels ought to have *swivels*, and moor with one, to keep a clear hawse.

Bend the sheet-cable, and see the anchor clear for letting go as soon as you have moored. In the winter, be prepared for striking lower yards and topmasts, if necessary.

411.—PREPARATIONS FOR GOING INTO HARBOR.

The paint work outside should be scrubbed, and, if the weather permit, freshen up where most wanted—for instance, under the bows. The masts should be scraped and properly stayed, the tips of studding-sail booms painted, and the rigging slightly touched with blacking, when brown or worn. The good order of the ratlines should be attended to, swinging-boom ladders and pendants got ready, and all the chafing-gear taken off. The boats' sails and awnings should be clean and ready for use, the masts and oars scraped, scrubbed, or painted, as required; the smokesail clean, also the wind-sails. Clean hammocks may be slung, and neatly stowed. The cables (including the *sheet*, if it blows hard), should be bent in plenty of time, &c. &c. The ship's company clean and in uniform—the accommodation ladder got ready, and in good order for shipping when at anchor.

412.—CAUTIONS AT NIGHT—(LOOKOUTS).

A good lookout should be kept at night. As soon as it is dark, every vessel should carry a light under the fore-top; this should be a rule, and not even left optional. If this light were carried in a lantern with green glass, the distinguishing light of a sailing vessel would be known. Steamers on the coast, bays, or harbors, usually carry wheel-house lights, as well as a masthead one.

The sea-going steamers mostly carry two horizontal lights—they are therefore easily distinguished. Sailing vessels on the coast ought always to have a light kept on deck (in a tub or bucket, for shading it), ready to be shown, as steamers sometimes come up astern.

A musket loaded with blank cartridge is useful as a signal to call attention, and should be kept ready at hand.

A vessel on the starboard tack should show a light at the lee-cathead. A vessel on the larboard tack should show a light on the weather cathead.

413.—WHEN TWO VESSELS ARE IN COLLISION.

If in a tide's way, and in less than ten fathoms, the headmost one should anchor either with a stream or bower, as most convenient.

If on *soundings* from thirty to ten fathoms, the headmost vessel should drop a kedge-anchor.

If vessels get foul of each other in deep water (should the weather be sufficiently moderate), get a boat ahead of the headmost and another astern of the sternmost, and *two* apart in opposite ways.

If a vessel anchor too close in another's hawse, the one next ahead of her should send her a tow-line, with which she might pass a hawser on board to enable her to warp clear.

414.—SQUALLS—(CAUTION).

They usually give some notice by gathering up black in the horizon. If the darkness rises up and thins away at the bottom, it will not be strong; but if it still continues thick in the horizon, expect wind. Shorten sail before it comes. Clouds high, with hard edges, denote dry and strong winds. A large halo around the moon betokens high wind. Be guarded when clouds pass overhead—the strength of the wind is then very often most felt.

415.—WATER SPOUTS—(CAUTION).

A water-spout appears like a speaking-trumpet, with the small ends downwards. (It is said the concussion caused by firing guns is likely to disperse it.) If one should be near, and likely to break on board, clew-up and furl all (see the topsail clew-lines are afterwards belayed) batten the hatches, have scupper clear and pumps ready, and spar-deck ports out.

416.—PRESSURE OF WATER AT DIFFERENT DEPTHS.

If a ship has the flattest part of her bottom lying sixteen feet deep (which is often the case), the water then presses sixteen times as much upwards against this flat part, as it does upon any part of the same ship about the waters' edge; and so on any other part, according to the depth. For example, suppose this ship to have four leaks, or plug holes of equal size, that could be driven out occasionally—the first at one foot under water, the second at four feet, the third at nine feet, and the lowest at sixteen feet, in the flat part of her bilge; that hole at four feet deep would leak or let in as much water again, in the same time, as that at one foot; and that at nine feet, three times as much; and that at sixteen feet, four times as much, though it run into the ship upwards; and so on in proportion to the square root of the height of the water above the leak or plug hole. Therefore leaks in ships are more or less dangerous, according to their depth under water.

Note.—On first springing a leak, it will rush in faster until the water inside is as high as the place where the leak is; and will pour in less the higher it gets inside.

417.—ON STOPPING LEAKS.

If we reflect on the present mode, so constantly practiced, of watering, by means of a canvass hose from the shore, through the salt-water into the boat, we can have little doubt of the retentive power of canvass. When it can be at all ascertained where a leak is situated (provided it be not too near the keel, or too much in the run), if it be in any part where you can bring a sail in contact with it, so as to cover it, remember that a canvass hose, when once saturated, becomes *tolerably* water-tight. If part of a sail of No. 1 canvass be doubled and brought by ropes to cover the leak, though it may not stop it, there can be no doubt it will materially assist in reducing it.

This canvass must be well and strongly roped and stitched

together, and it had better not be too large; the smaller it is, (provided the purpose be answered), the better; as it will be less likely to be torn away. In placing it, the rope ought to be outwards. This double canvass may be placed in its position by ropes under the keel or out of the hawse-hole. A sail might be used for this purpose.

418.—EXAMINATION OF CHAIN CABLES.

The cables must be got on deck, pins and bolts driven out of the shackles, and well cleaned and white leaded; every link sounded with a hammer by the armorer, and some of the lengths transposed. Splicing pieces and spare shackles should be remembered at the same time, and treated in the same way.

Note.—Wooden pins are frequently used in connecting the shackles, not being liable to rust, and can always be taken out easy. Hickory is the best wood to make them of.

419.—MINUTE GUNS.

If more than one ship be present, minute guns are not usually fired by all at the same time, as in a common salute, but one ship follows another, taking up the firing in succession.

The interval between the firing of each two guns must of course be determined by the number of guns to be fired, and the time through which they are to be prolonged—a point which is optional, and sometimes extended through the day.

420.—HOISTING ON BOARD MONEY OR PLATE.

In hoisting on board money, plate, or other valuables, a buoy and buoy-rope, corresponding to the depth of water, ought always to be attached thereto, that in case of anything giving way, or the money or plate going to the bottom, there may be a ready means of recovery at hand. For boxes of treasure, strong nets, in place of slings, are most useful and most safe.

Note.—Money nets are made like a common wad-net, excepting that the meshes are made smaller and the stuff larger, say of a two-inch rope.

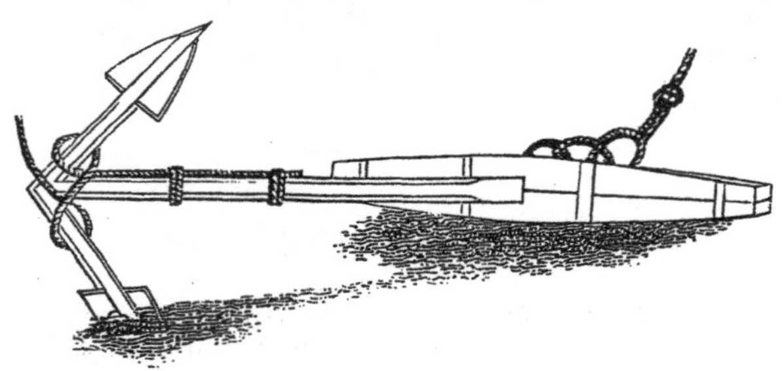

A Sloop-of-War hove-to, for a Pilot.

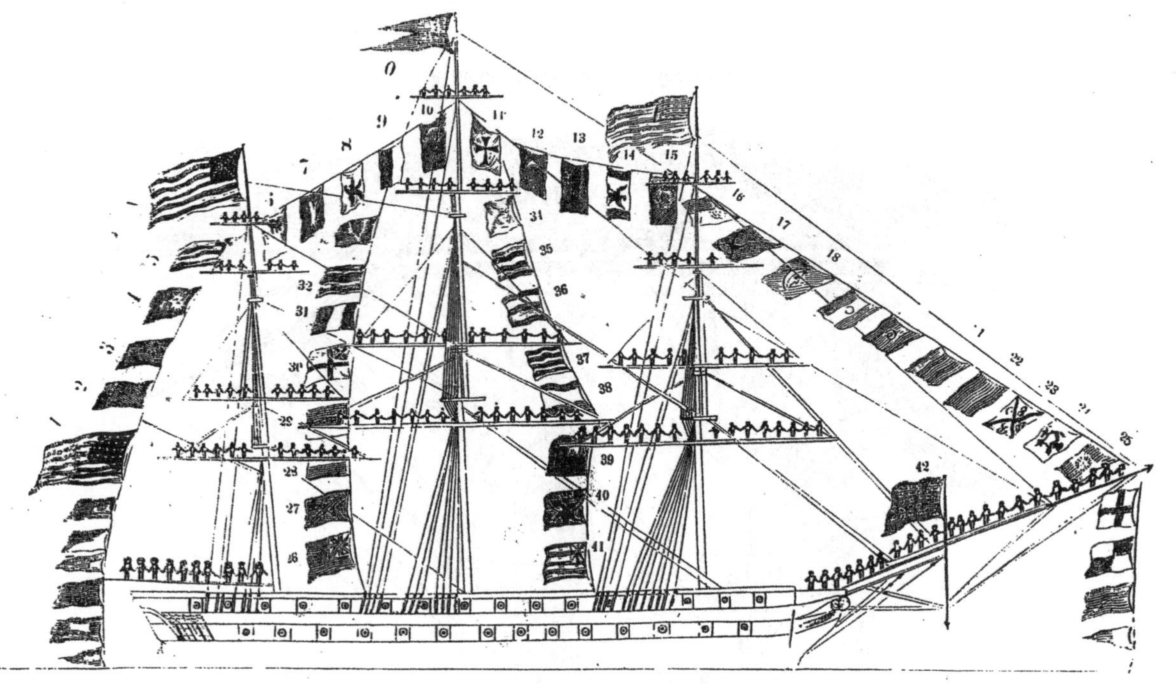

Representation of a Ship-of-war, dressed with Flags, and Yards manned.

1 American Ensign. 2 Ottoman-Greek. 3 Norden. 4. Stralsund. 5 Greek. 6 Brandenburg. 7 Hanover. 8 Prussia. 9 Saxony. 10 E, Morocco. 11 Maltese. 12 Arabia. 13 Columbia. 14 Mexican. 15 Brazil. 16 Hayti. 17 Japan. 18 Mogul. 19 Buenos Ayes. 20 Spanish. 21 Tunis. 22 St. Domingo. 23 Old Sardinia. 24 Majorca. 25 Peru. 26 English (blue). 27 Venezula. 28 Chili. 29 Normandy. 30 English (white). 31 French 32 Tripoli. 33 Salee. 34 Old Portugal. 35 Algiers. 36 Senegal. 37 Oporto. 38 Central America. 39 English (red). 40 E. Russia. 41 Sandwich Islands. 42 American Jack. 0 Commodore's Broad Pendant. *Note.*—Those which have no numbers affixed are the ship's signals, or, rather, the telegraphic numbers.

PART VIII.

421.—STOWING HAMMOCKS.

Nothing adds more to the smart and favorable appearance of a vessel of war than a neat stowage of hammocks. The superintendants of this necessary duty are often at fault, forgetting that negligence in the performance of this service is seldom permitted to pass unnoticed.

In the stowage of hammocks, the officer should stand on the opposite side of the deck, a position which will enable him to preserve a symmetrical line, and guide and direct the stower in his progress fore and aft the netting; they are also enjoined to be careful that the hammocks of the men be properly lashed up. Defaulters in this particular should be reported to the First Lieutenant. Seven turns at equal distances, is the required number of turns with a hammock-lashing.

Note.—In piping-down hammocks, the officers are cautioned not to permit the men to throw them on the deck.

LASHING UP HAMMOCKS.

422.—COCKBILLING YARDS—(*Mourning*).

The most appropriate time for cockbilling yards seems to be daylight, and dark the most proper time for squaring them again; the day then looks as if it were issued in and closed with mourning.

At 8, or the hour of hoisting the colors half-mast, sway up the top-gallant yards, slip the lizard, parrel the yards, and cockbill them with the others previously reversed.

To allow the lower yards to top up properly, the trusses must be slacked; and if the topsail sheets are of chain and go with a whip, one of them must be unshackled from the clew, and to assist the lift in topping, a burton is required.

To allow the topsail yards to top up properly, they must be hoisted two feet or so off the caps, the parrels and braces must be slacked, and paunch mats taken out; if there are jaws on, slack the jaw-rope. Trysail and spanker gaff should be lowered well down, and swinging booms dropped into the water.

The way of topping the yards ought to be governed by the side on which the top-gallant yards are sent up: for instance, if the main-top-gallant yard be sent up on the starboard side, the main and main-topsail yards should be topped to port. The squaring them, when topped, should be done with reference to lower yards; which, in the first place, are topped as high as the top rims will allow; then being squared by the braces, the topsail and top-gallant yards have only to be parallel.

423.—DRESSING SHIP WITH FLAGS.

Though in some particulars the following remarks on dressing with flags refer peculiarly to ships in general, they are applicable to all classes of vessels; so much so indeed, that but little variation will be found necessary in applying them to line-of-battle ships, and so on down to a schooner.

One mode of dressing a ship with flags is to make an arch of them from the flying-jib-boom to the spanker-boom-end; another is to trice the flags up by the signal halliards, stopping them out to the yard-arms: but the best way, perhaps, is to combine these two modes, if there be flags enough. Hoisted to the trucks ought to be the ensign, jack, or the flags of the nation in whose port the ship is lying, or whom it is wished particularly to honor; and to give these room to display themselves, the rest of the flags should only be triced as high as the top-gallant mast-head.

If it be determined to combine the two modes of dressing, as mentioned above, that is, with up and down flags, as well as with an arch, it will prevent confusion and superabundance, and produce an equally good effect to have up and down flags at the main only; and to hoist them, whips or halliards should be placed for the purpose, through the top-gallant studding-sail halliard blocks, and taken *outside* the brace blocks.

The flying-jib halliards will hoist the foremost part of the arch, viz.: that which extends from the flying-boom-end to the fore-top-gallant mast-head. To the mizen-top-gallant mast-head it must be hoisted by a whip placed for the purpose, and hauled out to the gaff-end by a whip.

From the gaff-end the flags composing the arch drop to the water, being stopped out to the boom-end, and distended under it, as well as under the flying-boom, by small hand-leads: there ought also to be downhauls on the arch; also whips with downhauls between top-gallant mast-heads. Care and taste are necessary in sorting and placing the flags. The ensigns should be in corresponding places—for instance at the lower yard-arms. The square flags should all be together; also cornets, pendants, &c., or else a square flag and cornet alternately, and so on.

Bad feeling is sometimes occasioned, when foreign ships-of-war are assembled, by placing national colors injudiciously, in dressing ship. This ought to be studiously avoided. This fact has given rise to the practice, on "gala days," of hoisting nothing but the national flags at each mast-head, or, if in honor of another nation, the flag of that nation at the fore.

One principal beauty, however, of the manœuvre in question, is to have everything so prepared and foreseen, that immediately the yards are crossed, and decently squared, and the mast-head flags broke, all the others may be triced up so as to find their places readily and without confusion, hands previously prepared, laying-out together at the same time to each yard-arm, stopping the up and down flag-halliards there: and then at the "word," laying-in *together*.

At sunset, the best way, perhaps, is to haul the flags down just before sending down the top-gallant yards.

424.—KEEPING THE COPPER CLEAN.

The good or bad condition of the copper on a ship's bottom above the water line, has a wonderful effect upon her appearance. If daubed over with blacking, or otherwise neglected, when possible to attend to it, a slovenly appearance is communicated to the outside look which a ship of war ought to be exempt from.

One way of managing is to scrub off all spots, and rub it occasionally with an oily cloth, when there is leisure; and if this is constantly attended to, perhaps it is the best and simplest plan, although I have heard yachts find river mud better.

Another way is to paint it with red ochre and oil, mixed to the color of new copper. When well and effectually done, this will preserve a good appearance for a long time; but the finest and calmest weather must be taken advantage of to lay it on, as the least ripple will wash all off in its way when wet.

To clean the copper under the water line, seize on to a handy spar of sufficient length, half-a-dozen strong, coarse deck clamps, and apply them against the ship's bottom from a stage, if it can be got; if not, from the largest boat, previously keeling the ship, by running the guns in on one side, and out on the other. The copper of a small vessel may be completely cleaned in this way.

If the copper on the trysail mast, and fore and main-masts of brigs and schooners be attended to and kept clean, it tends very much to the appearance of the vessel. The most common obstacle to this is grease, which generates verdigris excessively, but may be easily prevented by attention.

425.—FURLING FROM A BOWLINE.

The stress of the work here being on the bunt-lines and clew-ropes, but few hands are required on the topsail clew-lines.

Words of Command.

Call—"All hands furl sails."

Man the bunt-lines and clew-lines (including the clew-ropes and head downhauls).

"Aloft, top-men;"—stand by to furl sails.

"Aloft, lower yard-men;"—haul taut—shorten sail—lay-out.

Furl-away, gather up, and pass the gaskets;—lay in off the yards;—stand by the booms. Down booms—rig them out to the mark;—square the heels. Square yards, stopping up gear at the same time. When the yards are squared by the braces, the boatswain ought to hurry ahead, to square them by the lifts. At the same time haul taut the bow-lines, jib and staysail-halliards, and see all the clew-lines close up.

When the yards are squared by the lifts, haul taut topsail and top-gallant sheets, and reef-tackles, as well as all other slack ropes, (heels of the studding-sail square, &c. &c.)

Note.—The topsail and top-gallant sheets and reef-tackles ought not previously to be hauled taut, because they then interfere with squaring the yards by the lifts.

Remarks.—The tacks and sheets are generally kept unrove in harbor, and the courses hauled up by the clew-ropes one bunt-

Representation of a Frigate with her Sails loose to dry.

line and leech-line of a side; the topsails by the bunt-lines only, led through a lizard at the clews, or clew jiggers. The hauling down of the headsails is much facilitated by having the halliards racked and overhauled at the mast-head, and a hand there ready to cut the racking, when the word is given to shorten sail.

426.—HIGH AND LOW BUNTS.

Low, or rolling bunts, require bunt-gaskets, and are tedious in stowing and securing snug—high, or French bunts, require no gaskets, but secure to the topsail-tye by a becket and stopped. Being larger, and more open abaft, the slack sail is more easily stowed in them than in low bunts; neither is any time or labor lost about bunt-gaskets, a circumstance not to be overlooked, in competing with other vessels.

The look is a matter of taste; in general, however, topsail-yards are thought neatest, with first or second-reefed earings hauled partly out, but neither reef-points tied, nor bunt-gaskets on; the bunt described is a French bunt, being secured to the tye by a midship-becket in the first reef band, and the sail furled in the skin of the first reef and back-cloths.

Note.—The proper place for the furling-glutt, is two-thirds of the depth of first reef.

427.—TO CLEAR MAST-HEADS.

Clear mast-heads form a distinguishing mark of a ship-of-war. To make them so, the eyes of the rigging ought to be carefully placed, boused down a-midships by the mast, and beat down at the mast-head with a commander, and the shrouds set up in their places with care. The eyes of the stays, and the slings of the lower yards, ought also to be sent down over all, and nothing more should be on the lower mast-heads, observable to the eye.

Over topmast-heads the ginn-blocks ought to go first, with a span lashing to the pendants, so as to take them close up to the trestle-trees; rigging and stays, same as lower mast-heads—standing parts of ties, through a score in the heel of topgallant-mast, inside of the trestle-trees, and taken abaft the mast-head and lashed together close down on top of the stays. It would be well to put a quarter-seizing on each side, around both stay and tye. This does away with the not uncommon, but slovenly practice, of hitching the standing part of the topsail-tye over the rigging, and expending the end, by heaping it up with five or six turns half-way to the cap.

Opinions are divided as to whether mast-heads painted white, or black, look the best. This is a matter of taste; but it is a matter of certainty, that black shades and conceals, while white tends to display, what a seaman is proud of, the neatness and good order of his rigging, which should not be concealed by a white canvass mast-coat.

The neatest mast-heads I ever saw were painted white, with the upper half of the top-rims and lower-half of the caps of the same color; the lower half of the top rims, and the upper half of the caps, being black; thus the large space of white was terminated and relieved above and below, by a neat, small, but distinct line of black. The topmast cross-trees, topmast-heads, and lower halves of topmast-caps were also white; upper half of caps black. Topmasts scraped close up to the cross-trees, the eyes of the top-gallant and royal rigging covered with canvass, in place of service, and painted black—no paint above topmast-head caps, nor outside of the bowsprit-cap. With clear mast-heads, ought to be combined neat tops, wherein the ropes are flemished, and kept low and snug.

428.—PLACING BELAYING-CLEATS IN TOPS.

If the belaying-cleats for studding-sail tacks and halliards, top-gallant and royal lifts, and royal sheets, are placed on the cross-pieces, or carlines of tops, and not on the shrouds or mast-heads, the rigging there will look much neater.

429.—MAKING SWABS.

Old rope, called junk, is unlaid into yarns. Make a grommet with a good strand; then take some of the yarns of the junk, take the twist or lay well out, and middle them in the grommet, and continue to fill up (to the size required), close to the grommet; clap on a good seizing of spun-yarn, and then, if wished, *snake it;* sometimes the handle, or grommet, is made by splicing both ends together, the splice laying in the head of the swab. In making the grommet, the ends of the strands should not be cut off, but seized-in with the rest of the swab.

430.—STOWAGE OF SWABS.

Swabs in the head are an eye-sore; attention should be directed to the contrivance of some other stow-hole for them, to which they should be rigorously confined, except when in use.

431.—JUNK.

Junk is supplied for the purpose of working up into various uses—such as into swabs, spun-yarn, knittle-stuff, lacings, seizings, earings, gaskets, &c., &c.,—all of which the supply in proper kind is generally inadequate. Good junk is got out of such materials as condemned cables—they having been necessarily made of the best stuff, and condemned before being much injured. Old messengers, old rigging, &c., make bad junk, not being condemned generally until much worn.

Of the worst junk swabs and spun-yarn should be made; of the best, knittle and seizing-stuff, lacings, earings, &c. The seizing-stuff is intended for blocks, ratlines, &c.; the knittle stuff for making mats, as well as lacings and earings, for studding-sails, boats' sails, &c., and the spun-yarn for fitting and refitting. A surplus stock of all these ought constantly to be at hand, in store, for the purpose of refitting or replacing anything that may happen to be carried away, without loss of time. In order to effect this, the watch on deck, or part of them, ought to be constantly at work about the junk, when circumstances permit, drawing, knotting, and balling of yarns, and assisting the ropemaker in laying up the above mentioned small stuff, either till the junk is exhausted, or till there is an ample stock on hand.

Large junk, such as lengths of cables, should be unlaid before being put below, that it may admit of being snugly stowed.

432.—MAKING MATS, AND CHAFING GEAR.

The breadth of mats for lanyards of rigging, is determined by the size of the dead-eye, which the mat ought nearly to cover; the length by the distance from the upper to the lower dead-eye. For lacing, small beckets should be worked in each corner and side. The mats on the foremost swifters of the lower rigging and backstays, should be longer than the others, on account of the foot and clew of the courses, when reefed and hauled aft, grinding against them high up; or shifting mats for that especial purpose should be kept, to put on at sea and take off in harbor. Thrum-mats are required for the paunch of lower topsail and topgallant yards, to prevent chafing. Those that follow are only required at sea; so that for neatness and economy, they may always be taken off when going into harbor.

To take the chafe off the rigging, when the lower yards are braced up, a large square hanging mat is required, thrummed on each side of the futtock-shrouds. This has a lanyard in each corner, and is clapped on thereby, with the upper half on the foremost futtock-shrouds, the lower half on the foremost swifters; the middle part being in a line with the catharpens.

On each side of the bunts of the courses, before all, a thrum-mat is requisite, to prevent the head of the sail chafing against the stay where they come in contact, when the yards are braced up. A breeches-mat is also required on the stay itself, for the same purpose. Small, square, neat mats, in the way of leech-lines, on each side, are also necessary, to prevent chafing.

To prevent the topsail yards, when braced up, from chafing the foremost shrouds of the topmast rigging, a quarter mat abaft the yards on each side, is required.

A thrum-mat is necessary on the horn of each foremast cross-tree, to prevent their wearing holes in the topgallant sails.

For the backstays, in the wake of the lower yards, when braced up, mats or platting, or some such substitute, is necessary as a protection. Merchant vessels use *Scotsmen* [slips of wood so called]; but for ships of war, I think leather, snugly stitched and kept on in harbor, as well as at sea, is the best.

In a brig, the boom-mainsail will sometimes have a hole fretted in it, by chafing against the quarter boat's stanchions, or the belaying cleats there; these ought therefore to be protected by mats.

433.—GASKETS.

There is a great risk of gaskets marking and spoiling the looks of the sails, if not thoroughly dried before being used.

The number of sea-gaskets must depend upon the size of the ship; the smallest, however, such as a schooner or brig, requiring four for each side of lower yards, and the same for topsail yards. For topgallant and royal yards, half the number is enough; for boom mainsail, six; for jib and flying-jib, five each.

Harbor-gaskets answer best with one end tapered and the other worked with an eye. By reeving and unreeving the tapered end through the eye, and round the jackstay, they are then easily put on or taken off. Their length ought to be sufficient for a round turn round the sail and yard, with enough of end to tack in and secure between the sail and round turn abaft, or rather, on upper quarter abaft. Their breadth is a matter of fancy, but broad ones are generally preferred. They should be carefully placed upon the yards, as nearly as possible, at equal distances.

Note.—If any long gaskets are used, half the number is sufficient.

434.—SCRAPING AND GREASING MASTS.

When the blacking of the rigging is dry, the masts ought to be scraped and cleaned, then greased. For the men to stand upon when scraping the lower masts, rig triangles of capstan bars, with whips to the mast-heads; for hoisting and lowering, with the topmasts, handspikes answer instead of capstan bars, and the royal and topgallant masts may be managed from a bowline in the end of a girt-line, or a span from shroud to shroud.

To prevent spotting the deck, the deck-cloths ought to be spread, and some hands kept constantly sweeping up the shavings.

The topgallant and royal yard-arms should not be neglected· The studding-sail booms, except when new, ought to have the least possible shaving taken off them by a carpenter, and then varnished. This does not injure them more than scraping, and keeps them infinitely smoother.

Before laying on the grease, the captains of the tops, &c., should report that everything is scraped and ready, and the boatswain should examine.

Note.—It is customary in some ships first to scrape masts, then tar down the rigging, and lastly paint; but there is objections to this, as the men are liable to daub the masts when tarring down, and they would have to be done over again.

Studding-sail booms should never be greased, as they are liable to daub the sail.

435.—MANNING YARDS.

If previously aware that the yards are to be manned in the course of the day, clap on life-lines instantly; the topgallant and royal yards are crossed in the morning, the hands laying out and in together; then square yards.

Fewer men being required for manning yards than furling sails, those required for the former may be easily sized and *selected* from among the latter, keeping them always on their respective yards—the tallest outside.

The yard-arm men extend their outside arms straight, holding on by the studding-sail halliards, whilst they clap their inner arms over the life-lines, holding it fast under the arm-pit; the next man in the same way extends his outer arm, and grapples the shoulder of the yard-arm man; then passes his inner arm over the life-line, clasping it under his arm-pit, and so on to the bunt.

The appearance of the boat, at whatever distance it may be, is the customary signal for manning yards; yet it would be at times a preferable rule to endeavor to judge of the distance, and act so that the men may not be more than ten minutes or a quarter of an hour aloft.

The men on the yards ought to face the boat; that is, when the boat is abaft the beam, they ought to face aft; when before the beam, forward: but in a ship, when the commodore* ascends the side, the hand on the cross-jack and mizen-topsail yards ought to face forward—all others as before, aft.

436.—MAN ROPES—(SIDE).

If side or man-ropes be covered with canvass or baize, the stitches should be taken through the strands of the rope, to prevent the covering getting out of its place, and puckering; and to take the chafe or nip in the wake of the eye-bolt, through which they reeve, a small bit of leather should be neatly stitched on.

The handsomest and most durable man-ropes are those entirely pointed over with neat, small line. The job is a tedious one, but worth the expense and trouble.

437.—SPARE DEAD-EYES.

A good plan for spare dead-eyes of rigging is to have them in two pieces, and with small bolts fixing them together, so that in the event of carrying one away, it can be easily replaced, without having to take chain, plate and all to a smiths' shop.

---

* Or the personage whom it is intended to honor.

438.—HIDE ROPE.

Where there is much and continued friction, or a short nip, hide rope is found to have great advantage over hemp; some say thirty per cent. Thus it is good for wheel-ropes, whip for hatchway, topsail-ties, trusses, topgallant and royal sheets and yard ropes, parrels, jib-pendants, lacings, reef-pendants and lash ing, studding-sail tacks and halliards.

For preservation above deck, hide rope should have a coating of two parts of grease and one of tar; below deck, a coat of neats' foot oil. When not wanted, such as wheel-ropes in harbor, it should be kept under cover.

Note.—Hide rope is now allowed by regulation for tailing all sheets, also for ties, truss, pendants, &c., &c. (*See rigging table.*)

439.—HAWSE-HOLE WINDSAIL.

A windsail to carry the great draught of the hawse-holes down into the holds, &c., is a very useful thing, though not common.

440.—FIGHTING LADDERS.

Some ships have fighting ladders of rope always set up, ready, and the wooden ones for common use placed against them.

Note.—Iron Jacob's-ladders fitted amidships in hatchways are very useful in the morning when washing decks, or at quarters, when the wooden ladders are unshipped.

441.—HAWSE BUCKLERS.

Bucklers are of two sorts; half-bucklers, shipped when the cables are bent, and blind-bucklers when they are unbent. The object of the first is to prevent shipping water through the hawse-holes, while the cables are bent, and are put on, after filling with shakings the hawse-hole through which the cable runs; they are secured by upright, iron bars, slipping on and off upon grooves above and below.

Blind-bucklers are put on after a plug (called hawse-plug, of the size of the hawse-hole) has been thrust in. They are secured the same way as the half-bucklers.

When the cables are ordered to be clear for running, the half-bucklers should be unshipped.

Note.—Half-bucklers are made with a score to fit the cable.

442.—MAKING FAST A WARP TO A VESSEL.

The best place for making a warp fast to, is the bitts, after passing through the spare hawse-hole: *there* it will not interfere with the side or paint work; is perfectly clear, quite secure, and ready to let go in an instant. If made fast to the cables, which is next best, it is more difficult to let go.

443.—FITTING QUARTER BOATS' GRIPES.

Boats' gripes are made with spun-yarn or small rope, as a sword-mat: one end is secured round the davit-head, the other, when the boat is up, passed under her bottom, and secured in the *chains* with a lashing.

444.—FITTING GIGS' SLINGS.

Gigs' slings are made as sword mats. When sufficient is made to take the boat's bottom and clear the gunwales, the spun-yarn, or rope between each part, is fitted as a stopper or selvagee, parceled and served over, and a thimble seized in the bight, which the tackles hook to. The stretches, made of wood, are put between both parts of the slings, long enough to keep them two or three inches off the gunwale.

For the span, measure the length from the after ring-bolts to the slings; when in their place, leave six inches for splicing, and cut the rope; measure from the after-slings to the fore ones, leaving about six inches and cut; measure from the fore-slings to the ring-bolt in the stern and cut; splice a hook and thimble in the ends, the other ends splice together, forming two cut splices, large enough to go over the thimbles in the slings, and seize them in their place.

Note.—Some prefer artificial eyes worked in the ends of the slings, to go over the end of the stretcher ; this is not so safe.

445.—SCRUBBING A BOAT'S BOTTOM, ON LEAVING HARBOR.

It frequently happens in preparing for sea, a large boat's bottom, such as a launch, or any other boom boat, requires cleaning, and there happens to be no place at hand to haul her up on shore, in preference to hoisting her up and doing it aboard, and causing a great *muss* on deck; hoist her out of the water by the cat, and another tackle to the bowsprit, and scrub her bottom from another boat (or catamaran).

446.—CARRYING LIGHT BOATS ON LAND.

The best way to cary a boat, is to upset her, and let the men, with their jackets on their shoulders, (or some such protection against the sharp pressure of the gunwale,) stand under and take the gunwales on each side on their shoulders; some hands may also be advantageously placed in amidships under the thwarts.

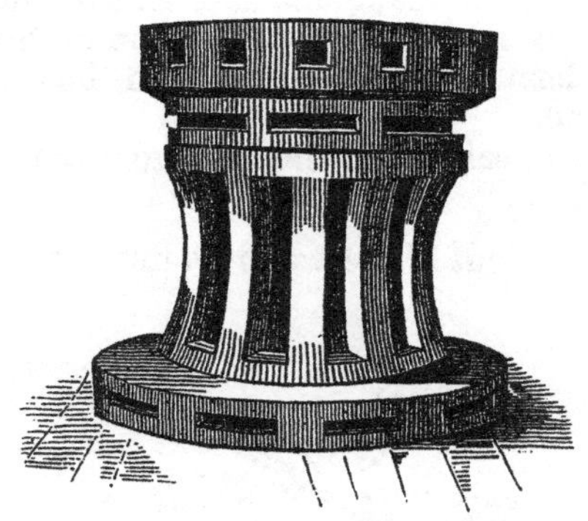

447.—MISCELLANEOUS NOTES ON WORKING BOATS.

If a boat be crank, or if it be wished in working to windward to accelerate speed, all hands should sit down in the bottom of the boat. If in haste, working to windward, pull the weather oars.

A boat with only one sail, such as a lug, should never attempt beating to windward, except when necessary to give the crew a spell.

Let no one ever sit on the gunwale, but accustom the crew to sit in their places, and to make and shorten sail without stirring from their seats. Besides the due execution of this manœuvre, the safety of the boat is much implicated in the degree of attention paid to this rule.

In taking in a lug sail, lower the halliards and haul down on the weather-leach.

Note.—Keep boats out of the water as much as possible.

448.—DUTIES OF BOATS' CREWS.

A SHIP OF WAR'S LAUNCH.

Nothing sooner indicates the order and discipline of a vessel of war, than the clean state and efficient condition of the boats, together with the personal appearance of their crews. In this particular, sufficient care is not always observed in the service; in well regulated ships, the coxswains are compelled to report to the senior lieutenant the state of their respective boats, and in the morning to ascertain from the officer of the boat, the manner he may require the crews to be dressed for the day &c., &c.

449.—BOATS GOING ON DISTANT SERVICE.

Memoranda of articles required for distant service—viz.: spy-glass, compass, pencil and paper, chart, watch, lead and line, tinder-box, grapnel and rope, stern-fast, hammer, nails, spike for guns, spare rope, (size of boat's gear,) spare tiller, spare oars, blue-lights, lanterns and candles, casks or kegs for water, arm-chest, flints, turn-screw, towing-nets, pea-coats, muffling for oars, fishing-lines, iron pot, fuel, each man a knife, an axe, a maul, a crow-bar, needles, twine, colors, rations for the boat's crew at discretion.

450.—BOATS UNDER SAIL.

A SHIP OF WAR'S CUTTER.

Care should be taken that the halliards be coiled up clear for running, that the sheets be not belayed, and that the crew, in shortening sail to a squall, do not shift their seats, or, as is too common a custom, stand upon the thwarts to gather in the shaking sail; in lowering a lug, or lateen sail, haul down alone on the luff, (the fore-leech;) the after one better be left untouched.

Coxswains should also be cautioned of the danger of letting go the helm. This is often inadvertently done wrong—sometimes to secure the heel of the bumkin, or to get a pull of the main or mizen-sheet. By this thoughtless practice, boats are liable to fly up in the wind, the sails to be taken aback, be difficult to lower, and eventually to cant over and capsize to windward.

451.—GIVING A ROPE TO A BOAT.

When a boat from a lee-tide, or running-sea, requires from the ship the aid of a rope, care must be taken that the tow-line be passed as far forward as possible. The position of the fore-channels is too far aft, and causes too short a scope. The tow-line should be passed from the cat-head, with a slip-rope to the crown of the spare or sheet-anchor, which, if slacked when the bowman secures the tow-line, the boat will ride with a good scope, and with comparative ease.

Caution.—The tow-line should never be made fast to the ring in the bow of the boat; it should be passed through the ring by way of a fair-leader, and eventually secured to the bottom of the boat or thwart.

Mooring boats.—Boats are best moored at the guess-swarp-boom. In this position they ride under the eye of the officer of the deck, and are less liable to be damaged than when secured alongside, or moored astern.

Boat-keepers, unless especially called to assist in the execution of urgent or heavy service, should never be permitted to leave their boats.

452.—CROSSING A BAR WITH SURF, IN BOATS.

As a boat will not rise over surf as over an unbroken wave, but on the contrary, the surf boils over and into the boat, the less surface there is presented, and the higher it is out of the water, the better. For this reason a boat ought to be kept stem on, or right before it, when the heaviest waves approach, waiting till they are past, to pursue her way edgeways across the bar.

Stem on is the safest, the smallest surface and the strongest and highest part of the boat being in that way presented to the surf, while the rudder and oars possess sufficient power to maintain the position assumed. Right before it has the disadvantage of lowness of stern, which makes pooping more likely than taking water over the bows—protracted exposure to the wave, (for you must go along with it,) and the tendency to gripe and broach-to, which from the rudder being lifted and left out of the water, and rendered useless as soon as the broken wave passes it, is often irresistible and fatal, and can only be counteracted by the skill and steadiness of the crew, in steering the boat by their oars until the rudder comes again into play. If a boat broaches-to in these circumstances, she will most likely fill, and instantly upset, in which case, I believe the best plan is to cling to the boat (or some of her gear), and endeavor to right her again, if possible.

453.—HAULING UP BOATS.

A gig's crew may haul up their boat, but for all other boats, it requires at least double the number of their crews, assisted by rollers and tackles.

A line-of-battle-ship's launch may be hauled up by five-and-forty hands, in the following manner: run her bow on to the beach, and let a few hands on each quarter keep her in that position, by setting their oars against the ground; next sweep her with a hawser, and guy it up at the stern to a proper height by several turns of the painter; to this hawser hook on the double block of a long tackle, the other end, or single block being overhauled to a proper length, and made fast as most convenient.

Pass the bight of another hawser round the stern post, and having guyed it up on each side to the main thwart, there hook on, on each side, a quarter tackle also, overhauled to a proper length, and hooked on at the other end, as most convenient; man these with the remaining hands: then having placed rollers in succession to take the boat's fore-foot and keel, proceed to haul away. When up, the loose thwarts set against the ground and wash streak will keep her upright. Smaller boats do not require quarter tackles; a few hands on the quarters to keep them upright, answer the purpose. Heavy boats especially should not be turned bottom up, it strains them so much. The loose thwarts might be placed for the rollers to roll on, if the ground is soft.

454.—LOWERING BOATS.

On lowering boats from the quarter or stern, care must be taken that the moment the boat touches the water, the *after* tackles be quickly unhooked from the slings or ring bolts. If in a tide's way the precaution be not observed, the probability is, the boat will immediately fill, and the men in the boat be exposed to imminent peril.

455.—TURNING UP THE HANDS.

In calling up the hands, or calling the crew to the performance of their duties, the boatswain too often indulges in piercing pipes, and drawling tones of superfluous length. Boatswains have a singular propensity to demonstrate the soundness of their lungs, by an endless protraction of a note on their piercing pipes. They should not be so fond of supplying the place of sea birds. This is not the worst feature in their taste; for when at last they utter the required summons, they give it forth in tones so drawling, that the first words are often forgotten before the last are out.

Note.—A-l-l h-a-n-d-s a-b-o-u-t-s-h-i-p.—This lengthy summons, and a longer-winded whistle, and each pipe and phrase three times repeated by the boatswain and his mates, the ship may be ashore before the leader of the band is convinced how *dearly he has paid for his whistle.*

456.—INSPECTION OF RIGGING—MORNING AND EVENING.

In the morning the boatswain will be required to inspect as early as possible the state and condition of the standing and running rigging, and to report the result of his examination to the officer of the morning watch. He should be particularly careful to see that the ratlines of the rigging are properly secure; that the topsail sheet service is not chafed, and that all the quarter and paunch mats are properly placed.

Evening.—The boatswain should inspect at evening quarters all the rigging, stoppers and necessary gear required upon the occasion of clearing for action; so that in the event of being surprised by an enemy at night, such gear may be placed at hand for immediate use. He should also see that the toggles fitted to the lower and topsail braces, be securely seized to their respective parts.

457.—INSPECTION OF STOWED ANCHORS—(AT SEA).

In boisterous weather, and particularly if the ship be laboring or lurching heavily, the boatswain should inspect the several anchors, and see that they are securely stowed. In small vessels, where anchors, in a heavy sea, are constantly buried under water, it is necessary to take the precaution of passing preventer stocks and shank lashings. The quarter boats should also be inspected, and the boatswain should report to the officer of the watch the result of such inspection.

458.—INSPECTION OF BOATS—(AT SEA).

Every evening after sunset, the boatswain will be required to inspect the boats on the booms, to see that they be perfectly clear, and that their sling-spans be severally hooked for hoisting out. In tropical climates it is strongly recommended to uncover the boats after the sun has set, in order that they may benefit by the dew and air. Each cover should be made up and placed in the bow of the boat.

459.—GAMMONING THE BOWSPRIT.

The better way to gammon the bowsprit in a large ship, is to get a caulker's stage under the bows, fore and aft, under the bowsprit; secure one end snug to the stern, then get a stout tackle from the extreme end of the bowsprit; overhaul down and sling the outer end of the stage; hook on your tackle to the slings, lead your fall down on the stage; send the men down, and bouse well taut, so as to get the weight of the stage as much as possible on the bowsprit. Now your stage being secured, you can proceed to gammon your bowsprit.

Get two stout luff-tackles on the stage and voil block; then get a span around the inner end of the stage to hook your voil block to; having your voil hooked, clinch your gammoning round your bowsprit with a running clinch or a running eye; jam your turn well round the bowsprit, then reeve down through the gammoning hole up over the bowsprit, then pass your end down through the scuttle on to the stage; reeve it through the voil blocks on the stage; clap on your luffs, and bouse away, leading your fall fore and aft the stage.

Note.—Leading your fall in this way has a tendency to lift up the inner end of the stage, and of course your pulling down, and the weight of the stage on the gammoning, must certainly bring the bowsprit snug down in its bed, and set your gammoning up very taut. Having got your first turn taut, rack it well; pass another, and so on until you fill up your gammoning hole, jamming your last turn under all parts of the gammoning on the opposite side of the bowsprit from the way you have passed your gammoning.

When you are setting up your gammoning, two men ought to attend with commanders, to beat it solid round the bowsprit.

When they are setting up, some people use a great deal of tar and slush on gammoning, but the less the better. A piece of good leather under your gammoning is much better than tarred parceling; and when your gammoning is passed, turn your leather over aft and nail it down to the bowsprit. Your gammoning ought to be strapped with large strands in the room of rope, it being much softer and better to the gammoning, and all well covered to protect it from the weather. If you use parceling, let it be dry and new, with a coat of tar over all when completed.

460.—PRECAUTION IN REEVING RUNNING-RIGGING.

In reeving running-rigging, the boatswain is recommended not to cut and reeve, but on the contrary, to reeve and cut.

However correct the rigging list may appear, there will be always found a difference of a few fathoms in rope; and it so happens that the difference is *invariably* on the wrong side, the allowance being said to be shorter than the measurement per rope.

Note.—It were much to be desired that the running-rigging, previous to reeving, should be stretched to the capstan. The old practice of taking the end through the coil will in some measure relieve the rope of many of its kinks, but taking the mere turns out of a rope is not sufficient to facilitate its run through the blocks. Such ropes as topsail-sheets, topgallant-sheets and braces, and jib and staysail-halliards, should be all stretched before they are rove in their respective blocks. Moreover, if there be any time more than another that a vessel will require her ropes to run freely, it is upon the occasion of her first leaving port, with a green and undisciplined crew.

461.—TOPSAIL TYES.

Topsail tyes are now rove in some ships sufficiently long to send the yards down with, and when not wanted for that purpose, the surplus ends pertaining to the standing parts secured to the mast-head.

In some ships a strop and thimble are fitted under the rigging, or a score cut in the heel of the topgallant-mast for the purpose of reeving through the standing part of the tye, which is secured breeching-fashion with two strong seizings, and then stopped down the topmast rigging.

In shifting yards, this method will be found to save much time and trouble; the surplus end will also answer to sling the topsail-yard with, when going into action.

462.—PRECAUTION IN BLACKING THE RIGGING.

In blacking the rigging, the first precaution that should be taken by the boatswain, is to cover with old canvass, or hammocks, the lower mast-heads, and particularly the caps. The blacking should be put on hot. Thin tar, with a certain portion of lamp-black, hot salt-water, whisky, and a little litharge mixed together, make an admirable mixture for blacking the rigging.

It is not recommended to blacken the royal and topgallant rigging aloft; this rigging may be previously blackened and triced up to dry.

463.—FORE AND MAIN BUNTLINES.

The buntlines of the courses are frequently found to jam aloft, and when rove on the bight, and led forward, constantly to become cable-laid. Buntlines will be found to lead fairer, and to haul the sails higher up, by fitting them after the following method.

In the fore part of the top between the trestle-trees, cut two holes; into these holes insert leaden pipes, backstay-fall fashion; hook to the foremost bolt, on each side of the lower cap, a block, through which each buntline-leg is to be rove; take each through the holes cut in the top, and pass them down before all, and toggle them to the foot of the sail, the hauling part to lead aft through the lubber's hole, and a block turned in at a proper distance, to allow the after leg to act the part of a pendant.

Through this block a whip purchase is rove; by this method the buntlines will be always kept clear, and they will be found, on letting go the whips, to overhaul themselves. In port, when the ship is moored, the buntline-blocks, with the ropes rove, may be unhooked from the bolts in the cap, and placed in the top, immediately over the holes through which the foremost legs are rove in, and can be hooked in a moment, when wanted.

464.—TOPGALLANT MAST ROPES.

For expedition the mast-rope rove upon the bight, with lizards taken through the royal sheave, must be preferred to the old method of fidding masts, by the double operation of two mast ropes, namely the long and the short. If delay is desired, or in other words, people prefer going the longest way to work, the short mast-rope must be put in requisition. The mast rope, how-

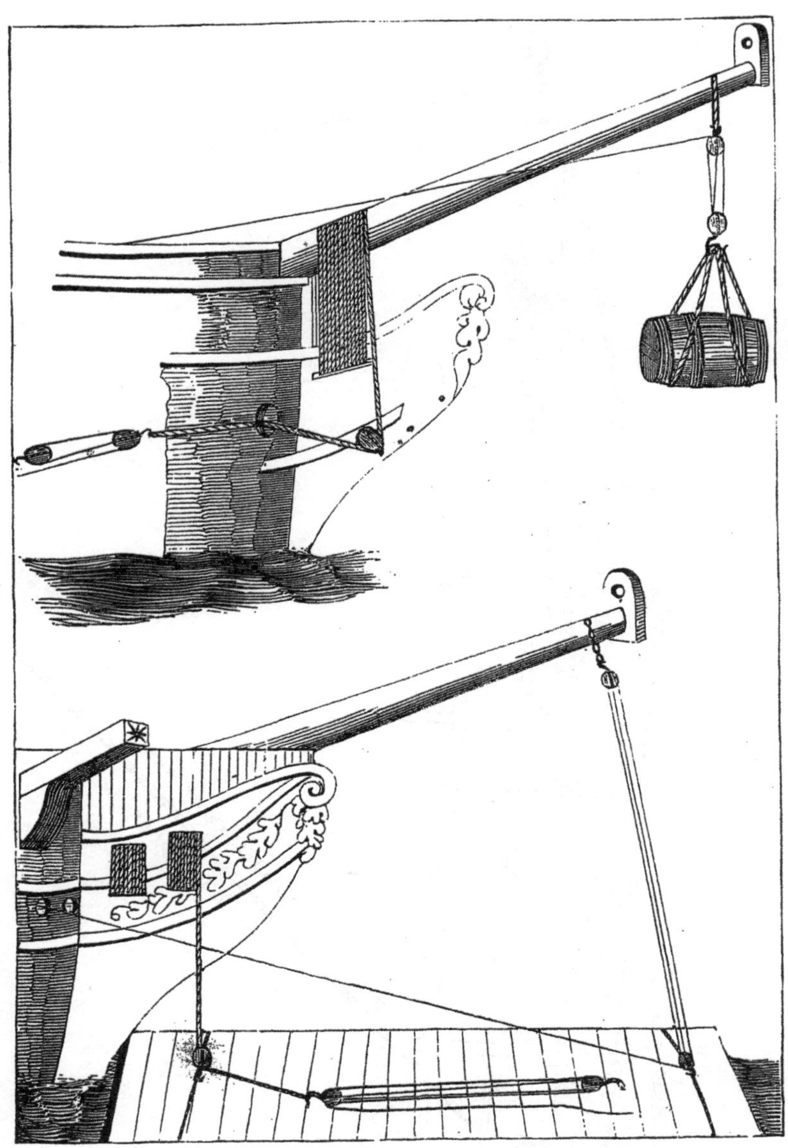

Gammoning the Bowsprit.

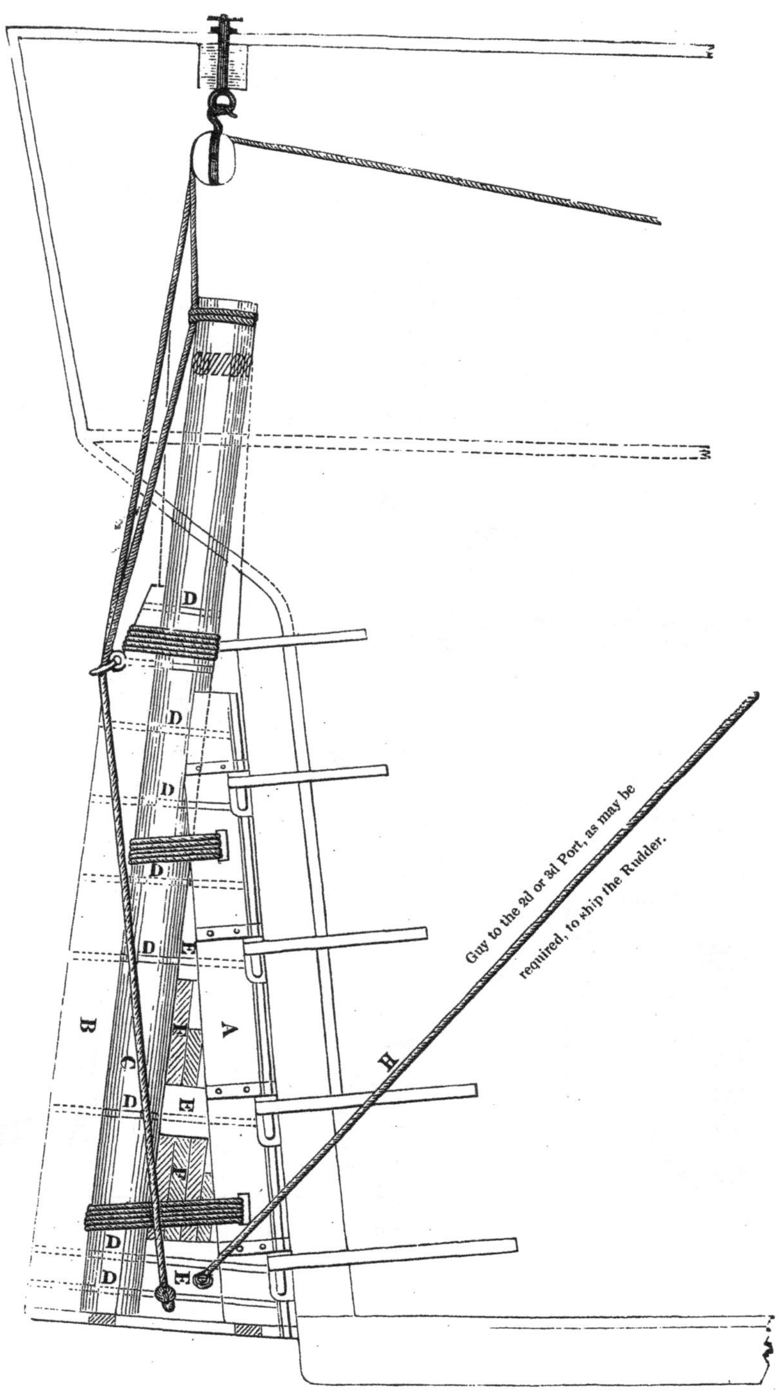

Representation of a Temporary Rudder. (see page 255)

ever, rove upon the bight with lizards, is better calculated for harbor practice than for sea service. The mast rope which is here recommended is applicable to every purpose, may be fitted as follows: The rope is rove as usual, stopped to the topgallant mast-head, and royal sheave-hole, leaving a long end over the upper stop to hitch to the bolt in the cap before cutting the stops.

To prevent the ropes from slipping, rack both parts together above the sheave-hole in the heel of the mast.

465.—FUTTOCK SHROUDS.

In all vessels of war, futtock shrouds are too long. Ships whose lower yards are slung high, and braced sharply up, have their futtock shrouds considerably shorter than the established length.

466.—TOPS AND HALF TOPS.

Many seamen affect to disapprove of half tops, asserting that two halves can never be so well secured as the whole. This is mere prejudice; for practical purposes a half top must be always preferred, especially in large ships.

467.—STRIKING OR HOUSING TOPMASTS.

The absence of forethought, or a little practical precaution on the part of the boatswain and petty officers, is sometimes the cause of this operation being one of no little labor. When the hands are turned up, strike topmasts. The lanyards of the after rigging, back-stays and topmast-rigging should be severally slacked, whilst the jib-stay, fore-topmast-staysail-halliards, topsail-halliards, topsail lifts, reef-tackles and topgallant-sheets ought to be well overhauled. Steady hands should be placed to attend the spring and standing-stays.

When blowing hard, head-to-wind, topmasts constantly bend in the cap, from the circumstance of letting go and overhauling too much of the stays.

Should there be any unusual strain on the top-tackle-pendants, it is well to "stand-fast" the falls for a few seconds, in order that the people aloft may examine the vicinity of the trestle-trees; and the mast may produce sufficient strain to carry away the top-tackle-falls, if not the pendants. This precaution is most particularly directed during periods of striking topmasts in the dark.

When the masts are struck, they should be kept on the right slue, and their heels securely lashed, in the event of the ship parting, or it becomes necessary to set close-reefed-topsails, with the mast down. The practice of sheep-shanking back-stays is not recommended; the back-stays may be set up through the medium of good luff-tackles, and by such means the mast may be rendered sufficiently secure to support the strain of a close-reefed-topsail.

468.—SWAYING UP TOPMASTS.

In performing this heavy operation, every care should be taken to overhaul well, and to see that such of the standing and running-rigging are perfectly clear, which are calculated to impede the ascent of the masts.

The topsail-lifts, topsail-tyes, reef-tackles, jib and staysail-halliards should be well overhauled below and aloft, and the lanyards of the topmast-rigging and back-stays be got ready for setting up, the moment the mast is fidded and stayed. The forecastle men should have luffs led along the bowsprit, and tackles up and down the foremast ready for staying the fore and main-topmasts. No topmast should be fidded by a single top-tackle-pendant. It is true that small vessels are not allowed a second pendant, but such ships should reeve a hawser through the dead sheave for the purpose of acting the part of a preventer, in the event of the top-tackle-fall parting. The same precaution should be taken with respect to the position of the cross-trees overhead as has been already mentioned under the head of rigging topmasts.

Note.—Such ships should be prepared with stoppers, with two tails and a toggle, so as to clap on the top-tackle pendants about a foot abaft, and under the top-block hooked to the cap.

Topmasts ascend comparatively easy until the fid-hole comes within six inches of the trestle-trees; then a heavy strain is brought upon the pendants, particularly upon the falls.

469.—UNMOORING.

It frequently occurs in unmooring vessels of war that the veering-cable is not sufficiently veered. In weighing the first anchor, a considerable strain has been felt at the capstan, in consequence of the ship not being permitted to bring the cable up and down. It is recommended to veer three or four fathoms after the cable is said to be up and down. This can do no harm; it will put the whole strain of the ship on the anchor; that is, in weighing, and thereby facilitate tripping it.

470.—REEF LINES TO THE TOPSAILS.

Few ships in the service are fitted with these lines. In some ships they are attached. In reefing topsails, when blowing fresh and particularly when steering a course, or going large, reef-lines assist materially to spill the sail and enable the men on the yards to get hold of the points, which are difficult to reach when the canvass is bellying to the breeze.

Reef-lines are thus fitted:—Take a piece of small rope, splice one end into an eyelet-hole in the head of the sail, seize it around the neck of one of the first reef-points, on the foreside of the sail, in a straight line with the eyelet-hole, leaving enough slack to prevent the sail girting; then seize it under to the second, then the third reef; splice an eye in the end and seize it to the neck of a close-reef point. In large ships there should be three reef-lines on each yard-arm; in small vessels two will be sufficient.

471.—REEFING COURSES.

To execute this service with security as well as with celerity, the reef-earings should be formed of rope sufficiently strong to bear being boused out by the boom-jiggers; by this method the inner turns of small rope may be passed with facility.

The outer earing should be led through a block or cheek, fitted for the purpose; this earing, it must be remembered, is not to be considered as a substitute for the reef-pendant; it should also be hooked and hauled out by a separate tackle. It is the general custom now, to fit all reef-earings on the bight, and pass on both ends.

472.—TOPGALLANT-MASTS STRUCK.

When topgallant-masts are struck, care should be taken that a small mat be placed between the topmast and the heel of the topgallant-mast; proper heel lashings should also be fitted for the purpose of securing the latter.

473.—HAILING ALOFT.

Hailing aloft, in well regulated ships, is much repressed by the boatswain; for bluster is a general indication of but little work, or the truth of the adage, "*All noise and no work.*"

474.—PROPORTIONS FOR CABLES—(*Hemp*).

The sheet and bower-cable, one inch in circumference for every two feet of beam. The stream-cable and messenger, two-thirds of the sheet or bower chain-cables, which are used for bowers; an allowance is made of one eighth of an inch for the diameter of the wire of the links, for every inch of circumference of the hemp-cables. The same rule applies in all cases where iron rigging is substituted for hemp.

Note.—Cable-yarns are spun two-fifths longer than the cable for which they are intended. The yarns for one hundred and twenty fathoms of cable, must be two hundred fathoms long; for a shroud-laid rope the yarns are one-third longer—*i. e.*, ninety for sixty fathoms. (*See table of cables.*)

475.—PROPORTIONS FOR ANCHORS.

For the sheet and bower-anchors, take two-thirds the number of feet which the ship draws with all her stores, &c., on board, and add it to the breadth of beam, allowing one hundred-weight for every foot. The stream-anchor one third of the sheet or bower.

For ships smaller than frigates, an allowance of five hundred weight for every hundred tons burthen, should be made for sheet and bower-anchors.

In stocking an anchor, add together the length of the shank, and half the round of the ring, for the length of the stock. The stock is as many inches in thickness in the middle, as the shank is long in feet, and is tapered to half the size at the end. In puddening an anchor ring, cut the lengths three times the round of the ring.

Note.—This anchor is for hemp-cables; if for chain-cables, the length of shank may be reduced one fourth, but not in weight. (*See allowance table.*)

476.—WHAT LENGTH IS NECESSARY TO FORM A CLINCH.

In bending cables, the length of rope necessary to form a clinch, is equal to the length of the shank of the anchor.

477.—REFERENCES TO SKETCH OF TEMPORARY RUDDER. *(facing page 251)*

A. A piece of oak fitted with iron pintles, before launching or while in dock, and supplied to the ship when going to sea;

B. A piece for the back, and provided for the same;

C. A spare topmast, cut off clear of the sheave-hole; a jib-boom might do, of the *new regulation.*

D. Iron bolts;

E. Chocks;

F. Iron-pig ballast (if necessary);

G. Eye-bolt in quarter-deck beam, to be put in when required;

H. Rope-guys (through the heel-chock E), to assist in hanging the rudder. (*See sketch of temporary rudder.*)

478.—TO SPLICE AN OLD CABLE TO A NEW ONE.

Take the old one to a rope-walk, unlay the strands, and splice them to the strands of the new one with long splices, after which lay up the latter. It can be done in another way, but it requires a good and neat *marlingspike-sailor* to do it.

479.—STRIP SHIP

Begin aloft, and go down regularly, sending down by a reverse operation. Commence with the topgallant and royal-rigging, and rig in the flying-jib-boom: next send down topsail and lower yards, topmast-caps; unrig the topmasts, get in the jib-boom and spritsail-yards; get off lower caps, tops and rigging; unrig the bowsprit, and unrig all gaffs, booms and davits.

Note.—Tally and strop-up rigging as fast as unrove and sent down.

480.—PROPORTIONS OF SPARS FOR MERCHANT SHIPS, LENGTH OF SPARS, &c., &c.

Main-mast equal to two-and-a-half times the ship's beam.

Fore-mast equal to eight-ninths the main-mast.

Mizen-mast equal to five-sixths of the main-mast.

Bowsprit two-thirds of the main-mast, one-third of which ought to be in-board.

Main-topmast three-fifths of the main-mast.

Main-topgallant-mast one-half of the main-topmast, exclusive of the pole, which is generally one-half the length of the topgallant-mast or a little longer.

Fore-topmast three-fifths of the foremast.

Fore-topgallant-mast one-half the length of the fore-topmast, exclusive of the pole, which is half the length of the topgallant mast.

Mizen-topmast three-fifths of the mizen-mast.

Mizen-topgallant-mast one-half the length of the mizen-topmast, and the pole one half the length of the topgallant-mast.

Jib-boom the length of the bowsprit, two-thirds of which length is rigged without the bowsprit-cap.

Main-yard twice the ship's extreme breadth.

Main-topsail-yard two-thirds of main-yard.

Main-topgallant-yard two-thirds of main-topsail-yard.

Fore-yard seven-eighths of main-yard.

Fore-topsail-yard two-thirds of fore-yard.

Fore-topgallant-yard two-thirds of the fore-topsail-yard.

Royal-yards two-thirds the length of the respective topgallant yards.

Cross-jack-yard same length of main-topsail-yard.

Mizen-topsail-yards the same length of the main-topgallant-yard.

Mizen-topgallant-yard two-thirds of mizen-topsail-yard.

Spritsail-yards five-sixths of the fore-topsail-yard.

Remark.—Some have the spritsail-yard the length of the fore-topsail-yard, or nearly so; if it should be much shorter, the jib-sheets will chafe against the spritsail-braces.

Spanker boom the length of the main-topsail-yard; it is however made sometimes longer, and sometimes shorter, according to fancy. Mizen-gaff two-thirds of the spanker-boom—liable to the same variation. Topsail yard-arms to be long enough to haul out close-reef-earing.

481.—THICKNESS OF SPARS—MASTS.

It has been customary to allow for every three feet of the main-mast's length, one inch of the diameter in the partners; nine-tenths of an inch in diameter in the middle, between the partners and the extremity of the head, and two-thirds under the hounds, and all other masts in the same proportion; and with these proportions masts have been usually made: I am however of opinion that one-quarter of an inch to the foot is much better.

482.—YARDS.

For every four feet of their length, allow one inch of diameter in the slings, and half that diameter within the squares at the yard-arm.

483.—DISTANCE FOR PLACING LOWER MASTS, *in vessels of two masts.*

Foremasts one-seventh the length of spar-deck from forward. Main two and five-sevenths as far from the foremast.

Note.—The above rule is not to be considered proper for all vessels; their places must be governed by the form of the vessel.

484.—RULE FOR PLACING MASTS IN A SHIP.

Take the ship's length from the after part of the stem to the fore part of the stern-post, and divide it into sevenths. Place the foremast one-seventh of this length from the stem, the main-mast three-sevenths from the fore-mast, the mizen and stern-post.

This rule is for a full-built ship; it must therefore be varied when applied to vessels that are sharp, and the stem and stern posts of which rake; the foremast must accordingly be placed farther aft, the mizen-mast farther forward, and the distance between the masts proportionably regulated.

485.—RAISING SHEARS ON A WHARF.

The following sketch will show the plan of raising a pair of shears on *a dock, or wharf*, the shears being 91 feet in length, and 29 inches in diameter, and connected together at the top by heavy trestle-trees. They are used for masting ships, and raising heavy boilers of steam-vessels, &c.

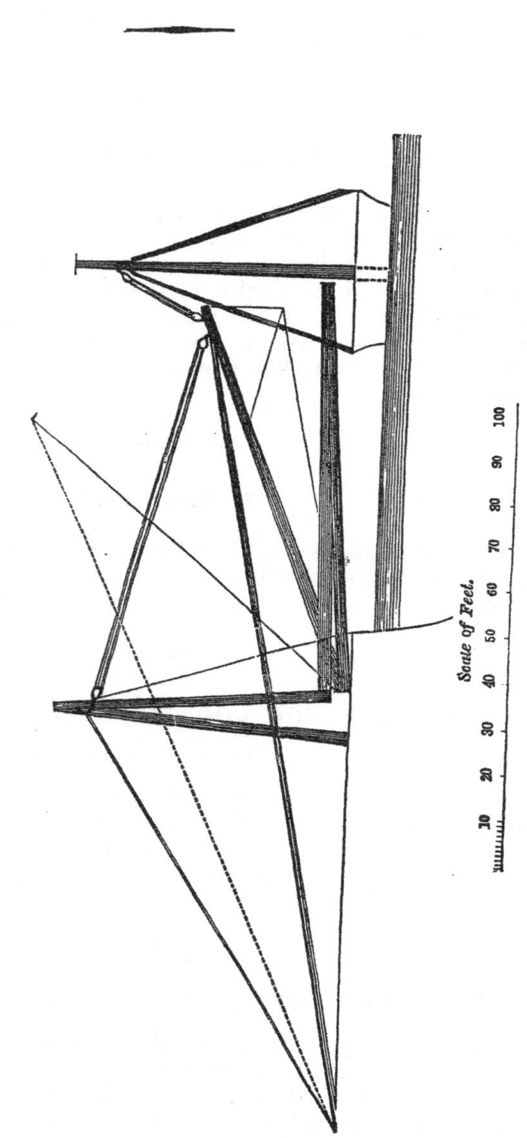

486.—TO FIND THE TONNAGE OF A VESSEL, BY THE UNITED STATES' MEASUREMENT.

The length is taken from the fore part of the main stern, to the after part of the stern-post. The beam is measured at the extreme breadth to the outside of the bends; three-fifths this beam is taken off the length, before the calculation is made. For a double-decked vessel, half the breadth of beam, is called the depth of hold, and for a single-deck it is the same, except that the hold is measured at the fore part of the hatchway, from the deck down to the ceiling alongside the keelson.

To proceed on in this calculation, after all the allowances have been made, the length must be multiplied by the breadth, and the product by the depth of the hold; then divide the last product by 95, and the quotient will give the tonnage required.

Formerly the British divided by 94, both for merchant vessels, and ships of war; but I have been informed they now divide by 100, which is the reason that they make our ships' tonnage less than we do.

Notes on the tonnage of a vessel.—The ship-carpenters' tonnage in Philadelphia differs from the United States' measurement.

A rule staff is laid under the keel, projecting; a line is plumbed from the upper part of the stern to the rule staff; the keel is measured from its after part to the plumb line, and including the rule staff, this is called the length of keel straight rabbit. The beam is measured from skin to skin, on the inside; three-fifths of the beam is taken off the keel straight rabbit, for the length, and the calculation, in other respects, is the same as in the United States' measurement; so that the carpenters' tonnage in Philadelphia will be less, according to the rake of the stern-post, &c.

The dead rise of a vessel is found by having a staff half the beam from skin to skin, at the extreme breadth, which staff is laid even across on the ceiling of the fore part of the main hatchway. One of the timber boards being taken up, a line is let fall from the staff to the skin alongside the keelson, and what it measures is the vessels dead rise; so that in order to know how sharp a vessel is, it is customary to ask how much dead-rise she has.

487.—STEPPING AND RAKING LOWER MASTS.

Foremasts of all ships should be stepped plumb, or perpendicular, to a water-line. All mainmasts should rake one inch to every four feet above deck, and all mizen-masts should rake one inch to every three feet above deck. All bowsprits should be stepped in a direct line, drawn from the step of the mainmast to the lower part of the bowsprit bed; this line answers for the lower part of the bowsprit.

It has been the opinion of many sea-officers, that a mast, by raking, will aid a ship in sailing; but it has been satisfactorily proved, that it has the contrary effect: for instance, a ship that has her masts perpendicular only, has to bear them in two positions; the one on the step, and the other on the side of support; her yards hang free, brace easy, and bear no strain against them; whereas a ship with her masts raking, has to bear them in three positions—the one on the step, one on the side of support, and the other, which is very great, on the fore and aft stays; her yards also hang very heavy against the mast, which adds also to the fore support. This must cause a great check in the progressive movements in the ship. A sharp vessel or ship, with a lean harping, by raking her masts, frequently eases her in pitching, but never adds to her sailing, the wind having less power on her sails, and the principal reason why a ship's main and mizen masts, should rake a little from her foremast is, that by separating the masts in this way, the wind has a better chance of effecting its full power on all the sails, and of striking that part of them, which otherwise would be of little or no advantage to the ship.

488.—MOORING.

It has been argued and proved, that if ships have room to lay at single anchor with chain-cables, they are more safe than when moored. The following example is given as an illustration.

Let A be moored with 75 fathoms S. E. and N. W. and B be at single anchor, with the same scope of chain; a gale commences from the S. W.; the strain on each of A's cables is double the strain on B's.

It blows harder, and B lets go her other bower, and veers 150 fathoms on the first, and 75 on the second cable. A also veers 150 fathoms on both cables, but B still keeps her advantage, the strain being only as 88 to 100; it is clear, therefore, that if either ship parts her cable, it must be A that will part first.

If A had her mooring swivel on, she could not veer with any advantage, as the strain on that part of the cable between the swivel and anchor must remain constant; for this reason, it is obvious that moorings should *not* be laid down across the prevailing winds.

The above may be shown practically by stretching a small line between two points, and suspending a weight in the middle; see what weight it will bear, and afterwards try what the same line will bear vertically; the latter will be the ship at single anchor, the former the one moored.

PART IX.

489.—PREPARATIONS FOR HEAVING DOWN.

CLEARING THE SHIP.

The ship should be stripped to lower-masts and lower-rigging, cleared of everything excepting the spars and running-gear, which will be required for lashings; top and gear-tackles, runners, luffs, pendant-tackles, and in fact all the tackles of every size. The hammock-nettings should be taken off, the loose bulk-heads removed, and everything that is not applicable to the operation to be performed, as it is desirable to have the ship as light as possible. The lower yards should be kept aloft till the outriggers are placed.

CHOICE AND POSITION OF THE OUTRIGGERS AND SHORES.

If left to your own resources, and large, rough spars are not to be obtained, the following may be used for outriggers, three of which will be required for each mast; *i. e.*, fore and main.

Main-mast.	*Fore-mast.*
1 Main-topmast.	1 Fore-topmast.
1 Main-topsail-yard.	1 Fore-topsail-yard.
1 Half-yard (rough).	1 Cross-jack-yard.

Note.—If you can get other spars, the yards should not be used.

The spars should be placed in the main-deck-ports before and abaft the masts. When they are placed, the lower-yards, caps, tops and cross-trees may be sent down and landed.

The shores should then be placed with their heels resting in shoes or the spare fishes, close out to the water-ways, and their heads between the trestle-trees before and abaft the mast-heads.

MAST-HEAD SHORES.

Main-mast.	*Fore-mast.*
1 Main-topmast.	1 Fore-topmast.
1 Spanker-boom.	1 Jib-boom.

In preference to using belly-shores, I would recommend to fish the main-mast with the two mizen-topmasts, and the foremast with fore and main-topgallant-masts; if no other spars are to be had, the topgallant-studdingsail-booms must be cut up for shores for the decks and outriggers.

CARPENTERS' WORK.

In the mean time the carpenters should be employed in shoring the outriggers and decks under the beams, on which the mast-head-shores rest: good stages should also be prepared, the spare-shackle or gammoning-bolts got ready; the copper should be stripped where they are to be driven, viz.: before, abaft, and between the outriggers, as low as convenient for driving, and fore-locking them on the inside, or as the water-line will allow.

Note.—The holes should be bored slanting upwards, so that the martingales will rather tend to set them in than draw them out; the shackles or rings of the gammoning-bolts should then be well parceled.

SECURING THE OUTRIGGERS.

In the meantime a party of riggers or seamen should be employed to fit the martingales and outrigger-shrouds, and to strap the purchase-blocks.

MARTINGALES.

The size of the martingales must depend upon the angle which you are able to give them, as their size must increase as their angle becomes less. If the bolts are near the water-line, three parts of eight-inch for each outrigger will be found sufficient. The main outriggers should be cleated about eighteen feet from the side, for the rigging. The heels should be well shored down and securely lashed; they should also be securely lashed down or gammoned to the breeching-bolts or scupper-holes, and shored by diagonal shores in the angles of the port-sills, that the spars in rising may bring an equal pressure on all parts; otherwise it would probably strain the top sides: the outriggers should also have a stout lashing to the train-bolts amidships. If the topsail-yards are used (which is not advisable when other spars can be obtained), the inner yard-arms must not be allowed to butt the ship's side, or water-ways; they should have chain-snotters, and must be shored in all directions. The fore-outriggers should be cleated about fifteen feet from the ship's side, and secured inboard as the main. In addition to the martingale, the three outriggers for each mast may be connected by luffs boused well taut, and the stay-tackles may be used for fore and after-guys, which will bring all to a fair strain. Any farther security that may suggest itself at the time, according to circumstances, should not be omitted, as you will never err by being on the safe side.

STRAPS FOR PURCHASE-BLOCKS.

I would also recommend the straps for the purchase-blocks should be warped of new, three-inch rope, selvagee-fashion, instead of the large rope-strap. The upper one will take about two coils, which will give about twenty-eight parts in the strap. The strap being middled, and the block seized in, the eyes or legs should pass round the mast-head, and lash on the same side as the block, and above it, which will give four times twenty-eight parts of three-inch rope in the neck of the strap.

PIT-BLOCKS.

The length of the lower strap must vary according to the pit you heave down to. It should contain at least thirty parts of three-inch, and also have four parts of the strap in the neck. If the pit is deep, it will be better to warp two separate straps of half the length for the lower blocks. The same way for the foremast, which may be securely lashed as most convenient, but neither of the blocks should be lashed at the mast-head until the outrigger-shrouds are over, set up hand-taut, and matted over all.

Note.—A second or preventer-purchase is required to each mast.

PREVENTIVE SHROUDS.*

For the main-mast, two lengths of the stream-cable (well parceled) may next be put over the main-mast-head; these may be set up through the lower-deck-ports, and kept clear of the channels by short outriggers of hard wood, with grooves in the outer end to receive the cable resting in the channels, butting against the ship's side, and cleated round the heel, to form a step; the outrigger-shrouds for each mast may then go over. They should be about eleven-inch-rope; they must be well parceled: dead-eyes or blocks may be used to set them up, as convenient.

---

* Small sized chain-cable may be used to a good advantage if it can be obtained.

For further security, the following purchases may be used.

FOR THE MAIN-MAST,

Two main-top-tackles lashed at the mast-head; one set up at the main-tack-bolts, the other to the after-quarter-deck-port; two mast-head-runners to assist the main-stay; two belly-stays of eleven-inch,* lashed one-third down the mast, and set up on the *weather-side;* two main-yard tackles lashed one-third down; one set up in the main-tack-bolts, the other, after-quarter-deck-port.

FOR THE FORE-MAST.

To assist the lower rigging, two threefold purchases lashed to the spare chain-plate-bolts; two launches' purchases lashed to the mast-head, and set up, one to the cat-head, and the other to the after part of the fore-chains; two runners lashed at the mast-head; one set up to the cat-head, one to the chess-tree-bolts; two belly-stays of eleven inch, one-third way down the mast, and set up half-way in on the bowsprit; two fore-top-tackles one-third down the mast; one to the cat-head, one to the chess-tree-water-ways, or scupper-holes, as most convenient.

THE BOWSPRIT

May be secured by the two fore-yard-tackles, hooked on the weather-side.

THE MIZEN-MAST

May be shored with one shore at the mast-head, and the mizen-pendant-tackles and burtons may be used to assist the rigging, if considered necessary.

SETTING UP THE RIGGING.

The wedges being taken out, and the masts drawn over to the opposite partners, the shores may be cleated and lashed above the rigging, and below the trestle-trees with good worn rope of three or three-and-a-half-inch; the lashing should be passed on both, with racking turns, hove taut by a Spanish windlass, the ends frapped round all parts, and secured; the heels should also be lashed to the side, so that they can have no play forward or aft. The outriggers' and martingales being well set up to the span-shackle bolts, and secured otherwise as before mentioned, the lower rigging and outrigger-shrouds may be set up to a fair and equal strain, respectively; the outrigger-shrouds may be a little tauter than the rigging, because they have a longer drift, and are less strained when offering the same support; in proportion, the additional purchases may then be set up.

---

* *i. e.*, Supposing the vessel to be one of the largest class of frigates.

There is one point in the foregoing arrangements that merits peculiar attention; having once measured the distance between the mast-heads, and the same between your lower blocks, you must be careful to preserve the same distance between the mast-heads whenever you may have occasion to set up afresh; if you neglect this, your mast spreads apart as the ship comes down, and the stays and rigging are unfairly strained.

The slack of the opposite rigging should then be taken in, and a swifter should be rove to keep it from hanging in a bight as the ship goes down.

When the masts are thus secured, the purchase-blocks may be lashed, and the shores wedged under the heels until they have taken part of the strain off the rigging. Care should be taken that the shore-heads are clear of the trestle-trees; the strain should not be wholly upon the shores and deck, but each shroud and purchase must bear its proportion.

PURCHASE FALLS.

Eleven-inch fall tailed with eight inch, is sufficient for the heaviest ship in the service. If you have only your own resources, use the large hawsers tailed with the smaller, or whatever rope is convenient in the store-room, which may suit the purpose.

Note.—In reeving, use a small line for that purpose; you will also save time and trouble by using the capstan* in reeving and overhauling the falls, which is a work of considerable time.

Two-and-a-half-inch stuff is a good size for a reeving line.

MAST-HEAD STOPPERS.

Two good stoppers of eleven-inch rope should be fitted to each mast; they may go with a clove-hitch round the mast-head, the ends being long enough to reeve through the strap of the lower purchase-blocks, to hitch and seize back; a small jigger, and two balls of spun-yarn should be ready for each purchase; the leading block should also be lashed alongside of its respective pit-block with a long lashing, to allow the leader to rise high enough to clear the fall of the edge of the pit; and stoppers must also be fitted for each leader-crab or capstan.

The greatest attention is required to the leading of the falls, as the slightest chafe or rub, with so great a strain, might prove of serious consequence; a sharp axe should be ready at each pit.

---

* If at the wharf or navy-yard, cattle might be clapped on to reeve the fall with greater facility.

THE PIT.

The formation of the pit, or sleeper, in which your lower block is secured, must vary so much in locality, that no general rule can be given.

ANCHORS AND CABLES.

The bowers may be landed, or used to moor the ship with, head and stern; the sheet-anchors may next be laid out a-beam as tripping-anchors, at such a distance according to the depth of the water, as may ensure their holding; one should be abreast of the foremast, the other opposite the main-mast; a stout hawser should be bent to the ring of each, and brought in at the second lower-deck port, abaft the main-mast, and first port abaft the foremast, on the same side as the anchors are laid out.

The chains to these tripping-anchors should be tailed with a stream-cable, which is to pass under the ship's bottom and in at the quarter-deck port, abaft the main channels and second port on the forecastle; these ports should be well lined, and stoppers fitted ready for fleeting; a three-fold purchase stretched across the deck, may be here applied, so that when you have tripped the ship off by the hawsers you may bouse the cables in taut, stopper and rack to the breeching-bolts.

In tripping off, you must be careful to keep the ship parallel to the pits, or you may chance to bring one anchor home.

CAULKING, &C.

While the foregoing preparations are being made, the pumps should be shortened, to work on the lower deck. The caulkers and carpenters should be employed upon the side that is to be hove down, stopping the air-holes on all the decks, and thoroughly caulking every seam or hole that will either be immersed, or exposed to the action of the water that may find admittance, particularly in the wake of the hammock-nettings that have been removed, and round the quarter-galleries.

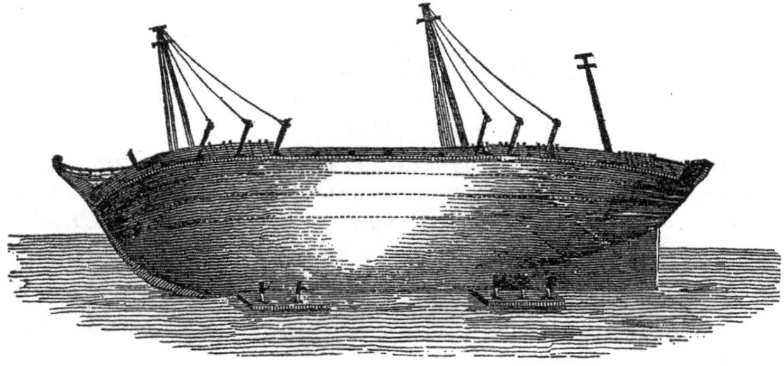

Representation of a Frigate, hove down to a dock or Wharf.

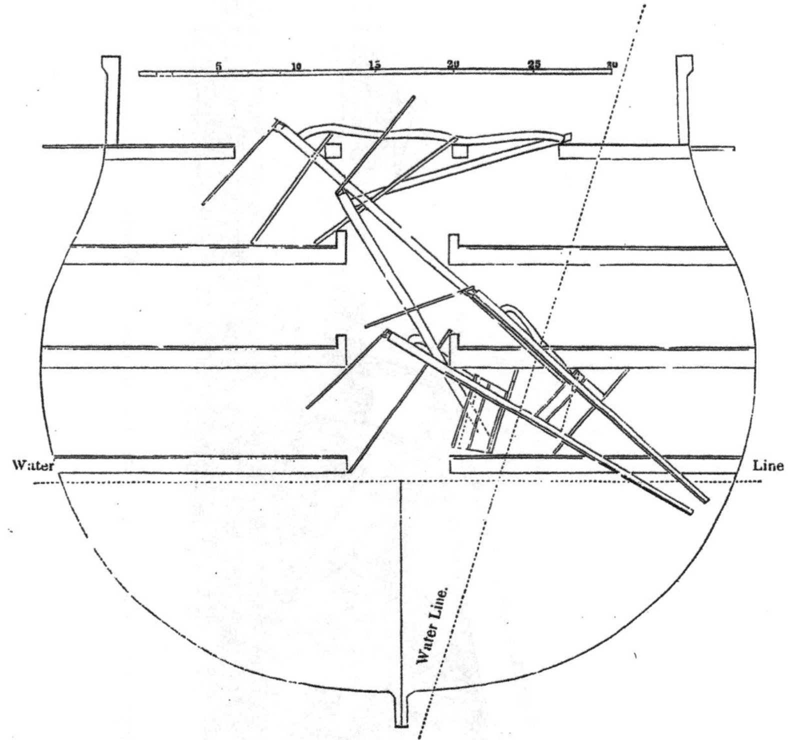

Arrangement of the Pumps in heaving down.

The caulking should be considered a very important point; the smallest hole that can admit water must be carefully stopped.

The main-deck ports must be filled up in the centre with plank, well caulked, and covered with tarred canvass; the lower deck ports and scuttles thoroughly caulked in; the holes for the port-pendants plugged, cross-caulked, and payed over, and the scuppers made tight in the same manner; and it must be remembered that want of attention to these particulars may cost you hours at the pumps, or perhaps oblige you to right the ship at a moment when you might advantageously continue the repair; the hawse-holes and stern-ports need not be stopped, for they will not be near the water when the ship is keel out

LADDERS, &c.

Battens four inches deep, should be nailed fore and aft on each deck; knotted ropes and Jacob's-ladders should be placed at convenient distances, to secure ready access to every part of the ship, which is more difficult when she is down than would be imagined.

Note.—The hatchway ladders should all be lashed.

ARRANGEMENT OF THE PUMPS.

If the water must be raised more than thirty feet, two sets of pumps will be required; the lower ones must throw the water into tubs or tanks placed on the lower deck—the upper ones must be placed in these vessels, and raise it from them to the upper deck; for this purpose nine or ten pumps will be required; they may be built square, of plank caulked in the seams, well parceled and woolded, or if timber can be had, may be formed by sawing straight spars in half lengthwise, and rejoining them after they are hollowed; then parceling, tarring, and woolding all over.

The number required being completed, the lower and orlop-decks must be scuttled, to allow the pumps to be placed at the required angle, so that their ends may rest a little below the orlop-wing gratings; the main and upper deck pumps may be sufficiently sloped in the hatchways with their heels in the vessels, which are raised on platforms inclined at an angle, to preserve their level when the ship is down.

The pumps should have large holes in their nozzles, and troughs should be made to carry the water over the skids to leeward on the upper deck.

Substantial platforms must be secured at the same angle, at convenient positions, for the men to work the pumps.

The pumps should be tried before you heave down, to see that they are tight, and also when in position to see that the brakes work clear of the beams and comings.

Any fire engines that can be procured, should be worked in the hold on similar platforms, with their hoses led on deck.

WEIGHT FOR HEELING AND TRIPPING SHIP.

The rigging being set up, the purchase falls rove, the pumps rigged and all the foregoing preparations made, fifteen or twenty tons of water in casks may be placed on the side to be hove down, and lashed to the breeching-bolts, &c., on the quarter-deck and fore-castle.

PREPARATIONS FOR HEAVING.

The ship may then be hove off by the tripping-hawsers to the distance of seventy or eighty feet from the pits, and the tripping-cables boused well taut.

The men required to work the pumps and engines, should be on board, with a proportion of carpenters to stop small leaks, clear the pumps, attend the masts in the partners, &c.; the hand-pumps should be used as long as they will act, so as to keep the ship perfectly dry; the 'men' should be to leeward on the upper deck, to assist with their weight the purchases; at *slack water* you may commence heaving; the ship will incline 15° before the slack of the falls is through, and will continue to close the pits until she is down to 35°; she will then begin to go off. It must be remembered that the main-mast is to heave the ship down; the fore purchase is only an assistant, and must not be unfairly hove upon; avoid surging as much as possible; the moment the pumps will draw they must begin to work. When the ship is down the falls must be stoppered and racked, the mast-head stoppers passed, boused taut and secured; you may then walk back and reverse the falls upon the capstans, taking a turn round the bitts with the running part, which is to be hove off by the capstans as you ease up, and will cause less surging.

STAGES.

Substantial floating stages having been previously made by the carpenters, should now be ready to haul in; a large boat containing tool-chests and the stores necessary for stopping the leak, should be in attendance; when the ship is down, not a single second should be lost; let your men sing out *cheer* at the pumps, and forego that part of your discipline for a short time, which might be a hindrance to your immediate object. Watch narrowly the purchases and be ready to ease-up at a moment's warning, if they slacken or any of the gear carries away. In easing-up, when the main-deck scuppers are out of water, hold on, take the lead or canvass off that secured them, and let the water escape from the deck; you may get rid of several tons thus without much labor.

The carpenters must be careful in clearing the injured part, not to increase the leak by undertaking more than they are able to perform; as a general rule, make all as tight as possible before you think of easing-up for the night.

490.—A DERRICK.

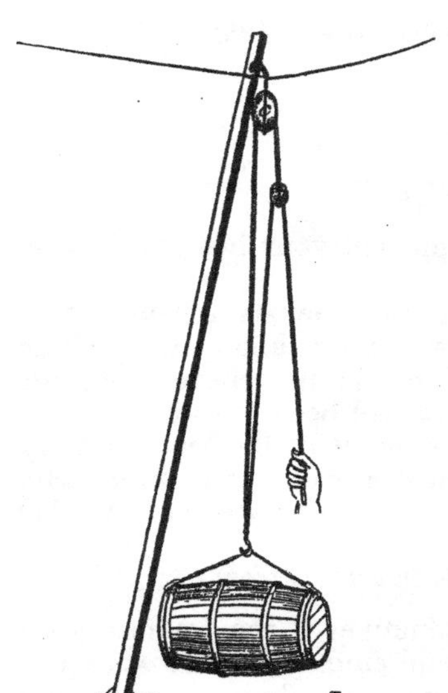

What is termed a derrick, is a single spar rounded off at the heel to set in a shoe, (similar to a shear-leg;) the upper end is made with shoulders or cleats, to stop the purchase-block from working down, also the guys; the derrick may be used for many purposes instead of shears to great advantage, especially on board of merchant ships when discharging, it being so easily swung from a perpendicular position to rake over the ship's side, the heel resting in its shoe, and the head canted in any position by the guys; any kind of a purchase may be used at a derrick-head, but the most general, is the single and double-burton.

On the subject of providing means—few ships go to sea without a spare topmast or a spar to make one, which spar is in every way calculated for a derrick, if it will make a topmast.

The rigging, (that is the various guys and ropes necessary to sustain it in its position,) and the purchase-blocks for lifting the weight, may be secured to the spar any height above the deck to suit the particular purpose in hand, without either cutting the spar, or nailing on cleats—as by a well managed arrangement of lashings, all slipping or shifting of position may certainly be prevented.

Note.—The more a derrick approaches a perpendicular position, the less will be the strain upon the guys.

GENERAL CAUTIONS.

In any very intricate Navigation,

Anchor at night or when in doubt.
Take frequent and short departures.
Pay particular attention that the proper course is steered.
Hand in the chains, and lead kept going.
Good look out.
Anchors ready, and cables clear.
Canvass well regulated and be ready for bringing up.
Boats ready, tackles at hand.
Stream cable and hawsers ready.
Top-gallant-mast-ropes rove.

Taken in a Squall.

A vigilant look out, will usually prevent your being taken by a squall in an unprepared state.

If taken in a squall with the wind on the beam, before it, or close hauled, keep your luff, and lower away, and clew up all as fast as you can. In doing so the ship will be relieved, and the canvass got in better than if the helm had been put up.

But if taken in a squall with the wind abaft the beam, putting the helm up, and running away from it, as well as shortening sail, will then be the readiest mode of easing a ship. (Remember this.)

On Good Order—(Merchant Service).

In a man-of-war, discipline is productive of the greatest good—the energies of all are called for, and employed as most required; but even without martial law good regulations might, and ought to be established in every ship, at all times, and in all places.

The greatest assistance to the promotion of good order, would be SOBRIETY in seamen. The few shades in the sterling qualities which belong to them, many of their irregularities and acts of insubordination, may be traced to intemperance. They might abstain, perhaps, but they cannot refrain. If owners would give $1 a month in lieu of spirits, and have a mutual agreement respecting its use abroad, with a stipulated penalty for drunkenness, ships might be managed much more safely, and with greater ease and economy than at present; half the work of discipline would then be effected.

Where the men are sober, have entire confidence in their officers, and are well treated, not harrassed unnecessarily, and see that the comforts they ought to have are properly attended to—I think it would be found in most instances, that effective good order would establish itself. Where it does exist, the vessel's services are rendered in every way more effective and beneficial to her employers, as well as more agreeable to the officers, crew, and passengers, if any, and her chances of casualties considerably lessened.

The remedy, too, is in a great measure in the hands of ship-owners and captains themselves; for if they required certificates of sobriety before they would ship men, drunken ones would either remain unemployed or become sober,—for even a sober landsman, is more useful than a drunken sailor.

On Cleanliness, as regards the Preservation of Life in Vessels.

Nothing is toc trifling for an officer's attention, that tends to the health and benefit of those dependent on his care and fore-thought.

Every vessel should be pumped out *morning* and *evening*.

A clean, sweet, and dry hold is essential to the health of the crew.

Nothing can be more injurious than for men to sleep over bilge-water, which must be the case if any water is left in the hold at night.

The hold ought to be cleared often, and when it is, it should be white-washed; and also the between-decks frequently white-washed.

On Painting.

In tropical climates, avoid painting as much as possible, particularly in-board.

On the Health of Men, in the Merchant Service.

In port, in tropical climates, give the men a little coffee before they go to work in the morning.

The inconsiderate indulgence in new rum, has been one great means of increasing the numbers attacked with yellow fever.

Do not allow the men to lay about in night dews; and particularly not to wait about at wharfs.

Allow the men the use of fresh water whenever it can be spared, for washing clothes, and also for themselves.

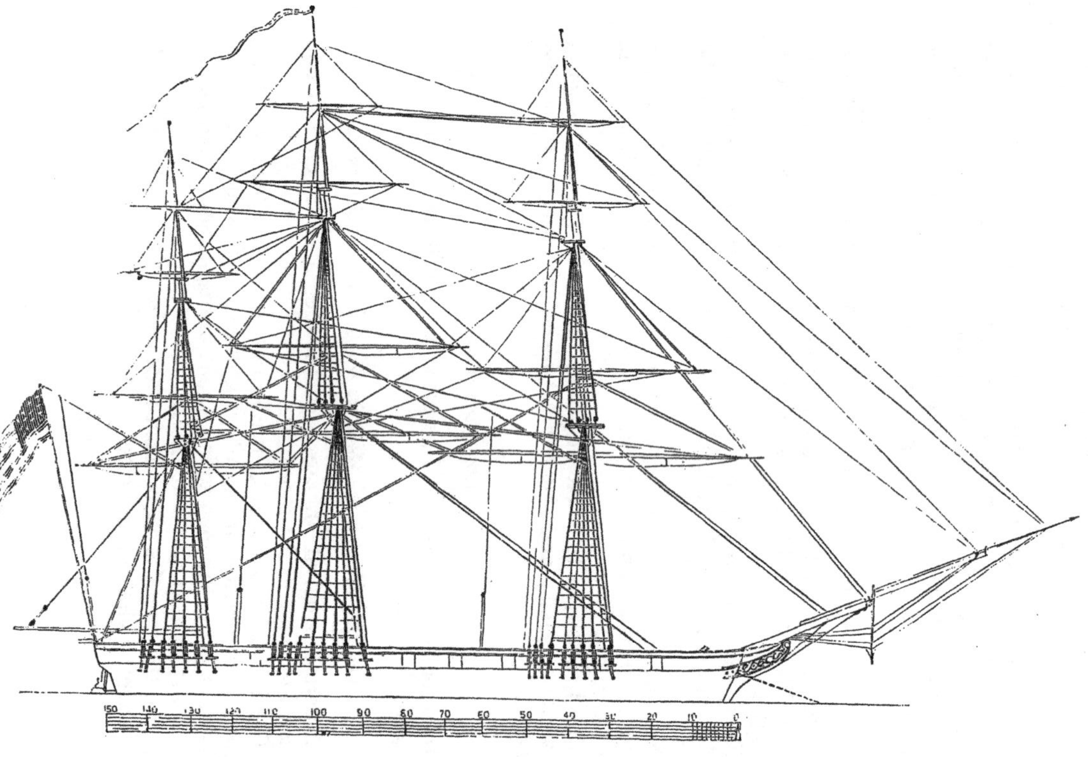

Scale-draft of the United States' Sloop-of-War ALBANY.

PART X.

491.—EXPLANATION OF SEA TERMS.

Aback. A sail is aback when its forward surface is acted upon by the wind.

Abaft. The hinder part of the ship. Behind, thus abaft the foremast, means anything nearer to the stern than the foremast.

Aboard. In the ship; as the cargo is aboard. A ship is said to fall aboard when she runs foul of another. To get aboard the main-tack is to bring the clew of the mainsail down to the chess-tree.

About. A ship is said to be going about, when in the act of backing; the order for which is "*ready about there.*"

Abreast. Opposite to.

Adrift. Broken loose from the moorings.

Afloat. Swimming; not touching the bottom.

Afore. That part of the ship nearest to the stem or head.

Aft. Behind; as stand farther aft—stand nearer to the stern.

After. Hinder, as the after ports—those ports nearest the stern—after sails, after hatchway, &c., &c.

Aground. Not having water enough to float the ship, which rests on the ground.

Ahead. Before the ship.

A-lee. The helm is a-lee when the tiller is put to the lee-side.—"Hard-a-lee," when it is put as far as it will go.

All in the wind. When the wind blows on the leeches or outward extremities of the sails, and causes them to shake.

All hands, ahoy. This word given by the boatswain and his mates at the hatchway to assemble the ship's company.

Aloft. Up above; in the rigging; on the yards; at the mast-head, &c.

Alongside. Close to the ship's side.

Amidships. In the middle of the ship. The helm is amidships when the tiller is not put over, either to one side or the other.

To anchor. To let the anchor fall overboard, that it may hold the ship.

To foul the anchor. To let the cable be twisted round the upper fluke, &c.

To drag the anchor. When the ship pulls it with her, from the violence of the wind.

Anchorage. Ground fit to anchor in.

The anchor is a cock bill. It is hanging by the stopper at the cat-head.

The anchor is a-peak. Near to the ship. Thus at different distances it is called a long peak, a stay peak, a short peak.

The anchor is a-weigh or a-trip. Loosened from the ground by heaving in the cable.

The anchor is backed. Another anchor is placed at a certain distance before it, and attached to it by the cable of the former being fastened to it, which fixes it firmly in the ground.

The anchor is catted. Drawn up to the cat-head.

The anchor is fished. Its inner arm is drawn up by the fish-pendant.

To weigh the anchor. To heave it up by the capstan or windlass.

The sheet-anchor, is of the same size and weight of the two bower anchors, and the spare anchor; it is a resource and dependence should either of the bowers part, for which purpose the cable is always kept ready bent with a long range, that it may be let go on an emergency.

Best bower or small bower anchors, are the two anchors which are stowed the farthest forward, or near the bows.

The stream-anchor, is used to bring the ship up with occasionally, or to steady the ship when she comes to a temporary mooring.

The kedge-anchor. The smallest of the anchors, to which a hawser or cable is generally bent, and used for warping ship.

An end. Any spar or mast placed perpendicularly. The topmasts are an end; they are swayed up and fidded above the lower masts.

All an end. All the masts are up in their proper stations.

A-peak. (See Anchor.)

Ashore. On land; aground.

Astern. Behind the ship.

Athwart. Across. Athwart hawse, across the stem; athwart ships, anything lying in a direction across the ship; athwart the fore-foot, a shot fired by another ship across the bows.

Atrip. (See Anchor.)

Avast. To cease hauling; to stop.

Aweigh. (See Anchor.)

Aweather. The helm is said to be aweather, when the tiller is put over to the windward side of the ship; hard aweather, when it it is put over as far as it will go.

Awning. A canvass canopy, placed over the deck when the sun is powerful.

To back the sails. To expose their forward surfaces to the wind, by hauling in the weather braces.

Back-stays. Ropes fixed at the topmast and topgallant-mast heads, and extended to the chains on the ship's sides.

To bag-pipe the mizen. To bring the sheet over to the weather-mizen-shrouds, in order to lay it aback.

To balance the mizen. Rolling up a portion of it at the peak.

Ballast. A quantity of iron, stone, gravel, &c., placed in the hold to give a ship proper stability when she has no cargo, or but a small quantity of goods, &c.

Bands. Pieces of canvass sewn across the sail, called reef-bands—also a piece stuck on the middle of the sail, to strengthen it when half-worn.

Bar. A shoal running across the mouth of a harbor.

Capstan bars. Pieces of timber put into the holes in the drum-head of the capstan, (where they are secured with iron pins,) to heave up the anchor, &c.

Bare poles. Having no sail up.

Battens. Slips of wood nailed on the slings of the yard, which are eight square—also over the tarpaulings of a hatchway to keep the water out in stormy weather.

Bays. In men-of-war, the starboard and larboard sides between decks, before the bitts; in small vessels, amidships.

Beams. Strong pieces of timber across the ship, under the decks, bound to the side by knees. They support and keep the ship together.

On the beam. When the wind blows at a right angle with the keel.

Before the beam. When the wind or object bears on some point less than a right angle, or ninety degrees from the ship's head.

Abaft the beam. When the wind or object bears on some point which is more than a right angle of ninety degrees from the ship's course.

Bearing. The point of the compass on which any object appears; it is also applied to an object which lies opposite to any part of the ship; thus the buoy, &c., bears on the beam, the bow, the quarter, &c.

Beating to windward. Tacking, and endeavoring to get to windward of some head land.

Becalmed. Having no wind to fill the sails. The ship being deprived of the power of the wind, by the intervention of high land, a large ship, &c.

Beckets. Short straps, having an eye in one end and a double walled knot on the other—for suspending a yard, &c., till wanted; such as the beckets for the royal-yards, for the bights of the sheets, &c.

To belay. To make fast.

Bend. A kind of knot—as a sheet-bend, &c., or a seizing, such as the bends of the cable.

To bend. To make fast—as to bend the sails, the cable, &c.

Bends. The streaks of thick stuff, or strongest planks in the ship's sides, on the broadest part; these are also called the wales.

Between decks. Any part of the ship below, betwen two decks.

Bight. Any part of a rope between the ends, also a collar or eye formed by a rope.

Bilge. The flat part of a ship's bottom. Bilge water, that which rests in the bilge, either from rain, shipping water, &c.

Binnacle. The frame or box which contains the compass.

Berth. A place of anchorage; a cabin or apartment.

Bitts. Large, upright pins of timber, with a cross piece, over which the bight of the cable is put, also smaller ones to belay ropes, such as topsail-sheets, &c.

To bitt. To place a bight of the cable over the bitts.

Blocks. Instruments with sheaves or pulleys, used to increase the power of ropes.

Block and block. When the two blocks of a tackle are drawn so close together that there is no more of the fall left to haul upon; it is also termed chock-a-block.

To make a board. To tack.

To make a stern board. To drive a ship stern foremost, by laying the sails aback.

Boarding. Entering an enemy's ship by force; the men are called boarders.

Boarding netting. Net work triced round the ship to prevent the boarders from entering.

Boats. Small vessels. Those belonging to ships are the long boat, the launch, the cutter, the yawl, and the jolly-boat.

Boatswain. The officer who has charge of the cordage, boats, rigging, &c.

Bobstays. Ropes rove through the cutwater, and set up with dead-eyes under the bowsprit, to act against the power of the fore stays. Sometimes one of these is taken to the end of the bowsprit to act against the fore-topmast stays.

Bolsters. Pieces of wood or canvass stuffed, placed on the lower trestle-trees to keep the rigging from chafing.

Bolts. Iron fastenings by which the ship is secured in her hull.

Bolt-ropes. Ropes sewn round the edges of the sails.

Booms. Large poles, used to extend the studding-sails, spanker, jibs, &c.

Boom-irons. Iron caps fixed on the yard-arms for the studding-sail-booms to rest in.

Bows. The round part of the ship, forward.

To bouse. To haul upon.

Bower. (See Anchor.)

Bowlines. Ropes made fast to the leeches, or sides of the sails, to pull them forward.

Bowsprit. A mast projecting over the stem.

Box-hauling. A method of waring or turning a ship from the wind.

Boxing-off. Turning the ship's head from the wind by backing the head sails.

Braces. Ropes fastened to the yard-arms to brace them about, also a security to the rudder, fixed to the stern-post.

Brails. Ropes applied to the after leeches of the mizen, and some of the staysails to draw them up.

To break bulk. To begin to unload.

To break the sheer. To swerve from the proper direction in which a ship should be when at anchor.

Breaming. Burning the stuff which is collected on the ship's bottom during a long voyage.

Breast-hooks. Pieces of timber placed across the bows of a ship to keep them together.

Breast-work. Railing on the fore part of the quarter deck, where ropes are belayed.

Breeching. A stout rope fixed to the cascable of a gun, fastened to the ship's side to prevent its running in.

Bridles. The upper part of the moorings laid in harbors for men-of-war; also ropes attached from the leeches of the square sails to the bowlines.

To bring up. To come to an anchor.

To bring to. To make a ship stationary, stopping her way by bracing some of the sails aback, and keeping others full, so as to counterpoise each other.

To bring by the lee. When a ship is sailing with the wind very large, and flies off from it so as to bring it on the other side, the sails catching aback, she is then said to be brought by the lee; this is a dangerous position in a high sea.

To broach-to. Flying up in the wind, so as to bring it on the other side when blowing fresh.

Bulk-heads. Partitions in the ship.

Bull's-eye. A wooden thimble.

Bumkin, or boomkin. A short boom fitted to the bows of a ship for the purpose of hauling down the fore tack to; it is supported on each side by a shroud.

Bunt. The middle part of a square-sail, also the fore leech of a quadrangular staysail.

Buntlines. Ropes attached to the foot of a square-sail, to haul it up.

Burton pendants. The first piece of rigging which goes over the topmast-head, to which is hooked a tackle to set up the topmast-shrouds.

Bush. Metal in the sheaves of blocks which have iron pins.

Butt-end. The end of a plank in a ship's side.

Buttock. That part of a ship's hull under the stern, between the water-line and wing-transom.

By the board. Over the side. A mast is said to go by the board when it is carried or shot away just above the deck.

By the head. When a ship is deeper in the water forward than aft.

By the stern. The reverse of by the head.

By the wind. When a ship is as near to the wind as her head can lie, with the sails filled.

Cabin. A room or apartment; also a bed place.

Cable. A large rope by which the ship is secured to the anchor. Cables take their names from the anchor to which they belong; as the sheet-cable, the best bower-cable, &c. They are generally 120 fathoms in length.

To bitt the cable. (See Bitts.)

To heave in the cable. To pull it into the ship by the windlass or capstan.

To pay out the cable. To pass it out of the hawse-hole.

To veer away the cable. To slacken it so that it may run out, as in paying out.

To serve the cable. To wrap it round with rope, plait, or horse-hide, to keep it from chafing.

To slip the cable. To let it run clear out.

Cable tier. That part of the orlop-deck where the cables are coiled.

To coil the cable. To lay it on the deck in a circular form.

Caboose. The place where the victuals are dressed in merchantmen.

Call. A silver pipe or whistle used by the boatswain and his mates, by the sounding of which they call up the hands, direct them to haul, to veer, to belay, &c., &c.

Canted. Anything turned from its square position.

Canvass. Strong cloth, of which the sails are made.

Cap. A block of wood which secures the topmast to the lower mast.

Capsize. To turn over.

Capstan. A machine for drawing up the anchor by the messenger, which is taken round it and applied to the cable by the nippers.

Careening. Heaving a vessel down on one side, to clean or repair her bottom.

Carrick bend. A kind of knot.

Cast. To pay a ship's head off by backing the head sails when heaving up the anchor, so as to bring the wind on the side required.

Cat-block. A large, double or threefold block, used for drawing the anchor up to the cat head.

Cat-head. A large piece of timber or crane, projecting over the bow, for drawing up the anchor clear from the ship's side.

Cat-harpings. Short legs of rope seized to the upper part of the lower shrouds and futtock-staves, to keep them from bulging out by the strain of the futtock-shrouds, and to permit the bracing up of the lower yards.

Cat's-paw. A light air, perceived by its effect upon the water, but not durable; also a twist made on the bight of a rope.

To Caulk. To drive oakum into the seams of the sides, decks, &c.

Chains. Links of iron bolted to the ship's sides, having dead-eyes in the upper ends, to which the shrouds are connected by the lanyards.

Channels. Strong, broad planks, bolted to the sides to keep the dead-eyes in the chains from the side, to spread the rigging farther out.

Chapeling. A ship is said to build a chapel, when by neglect in light winds she turns round so as to bring the wind on the same part it was before she moved.

Chase. A ship pursued by another.

Bow-chase. A gun in the fore part of the ship.

Stern-chase. A gun pointing astern in the after part of the ship.

To chase. To pursue; to follow.

To cheer. To huzza. What cheer-ho! a salutation.

Chock-a-block. (See block and block.)

To clap on. To make fast; as, clap on the stoppers, &c.

To claw off. To beat to windward from a lee-shore

Cleats. Pieces of wood to fasten ropes to.

Close-hauled. As anigh the wind as a ship can lie.

Club-hauling. Tacking by means of an anchor.

Clues or Clews. The lower corners of the square sails.

Coamings. The borders of the hatchways which are raised above the deck.

Coiling. Laying a rope down in a circular form.

Companion. A wooden covering over the cabin hatchway.

Course. The point of the compass on which the ship sails; the mainsail, foresail and mizen are also called courses.

Crab. A small capstan.

To cun the ship. To direct the helmsman how to steer.

Cutwater. The knee of the head.

Davit. A crane of timber used for fishing the anchors.

Dead-eye. A block with three holes in, to receive the lanyard of a shroud or stay.

Dog-vane. A small vane made of cork and feathers, and placed on the weather side of the quarter deck.

Dolphin. A wreath of rope placed round a mast. (See Pudding.)

To Douse. To let fly the halliards of a topsail; to lower away briskly, &c.

Downhauler. A rope to pull down the staysails, topmast, studdingsails, &c.

Drift. Driving to leeward; driving with the tide. Drifts are also those parts where the rails are cut off an end with scrolls.

Driver. A large sail suspended to the mizen-gaff.

Dunnage. Wood, &c. laid at the bottom of a ship to keep the cargo dry.

Earings. Small ropes to make fast the upper corners of square-sails, &c.

Ease-off. To slacken.

End-for-end. To let a rope or cable run quite out.

End-on. When a ship's bows and head sails are only seen.

Ensign. A national flag worn by ships at their gaff-ends.

Fag-end. The end of a rope which is untwisted.

Fake. One circle of a coil of rope.

Falling-off. When a ship moves from the wind farther than she ought.

Fid. A tapered piece of wood, or iron, to splice ropes with; also a piece of wood which supports one mast upon the trestle-trees of another.

To Fill. To brace the yards so that the wind may strike the sails on their after surfaces.

Flukes. The broad parts or palms of the anchors. (See Anchor.)

Fore. That part of the ship nearest to the head.

Fore and aft. The lengthway of the ship; or in the direction of the keel.

Fore-castle. A short deck in the fore part of the ship.

Forging-a-head. Forced a-head by the wind.

Foul hawse. When the cables are twisted.

To founder. To sink.

Full and by. (See close-hauled.)

Furling. Making fast the sails to the yards by the gaskets.

Gaff The spar or yard, to which the mizen of a ship, or the mainsail of a brig or cutter is bent.

Gang-way. A deck reaching from the quarter-deck to the fore-castle; also the place where persons enter the ship.

Gasket. A piece of plat to fasten the sails to the yard.

Girt. A ship is girted when her cables are too tight, which prevents her swinging.

Goose-neck. An iron hook at the end of a boom.

Goose-wings. The outer extremities of a main or foresail, when loose, the rest of it being furled.

Goring. Cutting a sail obliquely.

Gripe. A piece of timber that joins the keel and the cut-water.

Griping. When a ship carries her helm much to windward.

Gunnel. The upper part of a ship's side.

Guy. A rope to steady a boom.

Gybing. When (by the wind being large), it is necessary to shift the boom of a fore and aft sail.

Halliards. Tackles or ropes to hoist up the sails.

To Hand. (The same as to furl.)

Hatchway. A square hole in the deck, which communicates with the hold, or another deck.

To Haul. To pull.

To Hail. To call out to another ship.

A clear Hawse. When the cables are not twisted.

A foul Hawse. When the cables lie across, or are twisted.

Hawse-holes. The holes through which the cables pass.

Hawser. A small cable.

To Heel. To incline to one side.

Helm. A wooden bar put through the head of a rudder; also called a tiller.

To Hitch. To make fast.

The Hold. The lower apartment of a ship, where the provisions and goods are stowed.

To haul Home. To pull the clew of a sail, &c. as far as it will go.

Horse. A rope made fast to the yard, on which the men stand.

Hull. The body of a ship.

Jewel-blocks. Blocks at the topsail-yard-arms for the topmast-studding-sail halliards.

Jigger. A purchase used in merchant ships to hold on the cable.

Junk. Pieces of old cable, out of which mats, gaskets, &c. are made. (See article on Junk.)

Jury-masts. Temporary masts, when the others are carried or shot away.

Keckling. Old rope passed round the cable at short distances.

Kink. A twist or turn in a rope.

To Labor. To pitch and roll heavily.

Land-fall. Discovering the land.

Larboard. The left side.

Launch-ho. To let go the top rope when the topmast is fidded.

Leeward. That point which the wind blows.

Lee-lurch. When the ship rolls to leeward.

Lee-tide. When the wind and tide are the same way.

Lizard. A small piece of rope with a thimble spliced into a larger one.

Looming. The appearance of a distant object; such as a ship, the land, &c.

Lubber. A sailor who does not know his duty.

Luff. A direction to the steersman to put the helm to leeward.

Luff-tackle. A large tackle consisting of a double and single block.

Lying-to. (See To bring-to.)

To man the yards. To send men upon them.

To moor. To secure a ship by more than one cable.

Moorings. The place where a vessel is moored; also anchors with chains and bridles, laid in rivers for men-of-war to ride by.

Neap-tides. Those tides which happen when the moon is in her quarters, and are not so high as the Spring-tides.

Neaped. A ship is said to be neaped, when she is left on shore by these tides, and must wait for the next Spring-tides.

To Near the land. To approach the shore.

To Near. A direction to the helmsman to put the helm little "a-weather;" to keep the sails full; to let her come no nearer to the wind.

Nippers. Plaiting or selvagees, to bind the cable to the messenger.

Off-and-on. Coming near the land on one tack, and leaving it on another.

Offing. Out to sea from the land.

Orlop-deck. The lowest deck in the ship, lying on the beams of the hold. The place where the cables are coiled, and where other stores are kept.

Overboard. Out of the ship.

Overhauling. To haul a fall of rope through a block till it is slack—also examining a ship.

Painter. A rope by which a boat is made fast.

To Pass. To hand anything from one to another, or to place a rope or lashing round the yard, &c.

Pay. To rub tar, pitch, or anything, with a brush.

To pay off. To make a ship's head recede from the wind, by backing the head-sails.

To Peak up. To raise the after end of a gaff.

Plying. Turning to windward.

Pooping. A ship is said to be pooped when she is struck by a heavy sea, on the stern or quarter.

Port. To the left side. This term is used for the helmsman to put the helm to the left, instead of the word *Larboard*, to make a distinction from the affinity of sound in the word *Starboard*.

Preventer. Anything for temporary security, as a preventer-brace, &c.

Pendant, or Pennant. A sort of long, narrow banner.

Pendant (*broad*). A sort of flag terminating in two points.

Pendant. The name of a piece of rope applied to different objects on ship-board; *i. e.*, fish-pendants, rudder-pendants, &c.

Quarter. That part of a ship's side between the main-chains and the stern.

Racking a Fall. Seizing the parts of a tackle-fall together by cross-turns.

Rake. The projection of a ship at the stem and stern, beyond the extent of the keel—also the inclination of a ship's masts, either forward or aft from a perpendicular line.

Range of Cable. A sufficient length hauled up to permit the anchor to drop to the bottom.

To Rattle down the Shrouds. To fix the ratlings on them.

To Reef. To reduce a sail by tying it round the yard with points.

To Reeve. To put a rope through a block, &c.

To Ride. To be held by the cable; to ride easy, is when a ship does not labor much; to ride hard, is when a ship pitches with violence.

To Rig. To fit the rigging to the mast.

To Right. A ship is said to right when she rises to her upright position, after being laid down by a violent squall.

To Right the Helm. To put it a-midships, or in its fore and aft position parallel to the keel.

To Round-in. To haul in a brace, &c., which is not very tight.

To Rouse-in. To haul in the slack part of the cable.

To Run down. When one ship sinks another by running over her.

To Scud. To sail before the wind in a storm.

To Scuttle a Ship. To make holes in her bottom to sink her.

To Serve. To wind anything around a cable or rope, to prevent its being chafed.

To Seize. To make fast or bind.

To Sheer. To go in and out, and not in a direct course.

To Ship. To put anything on board; to ship a sea, when a sea breaks into a ship.

To Shiver. To make the sails shake.

The Slack of a Rope, &c. That part which hangs loose.

To Slip a Cable. To let it run out to the end.

To Slue. To turn anything about.

To Sound. To find the bottom by a leaden plummet.

To take a Spell. To be in turn on duty at the lead, the pump, &c.

To Spill. To take the wind out of the sails by the braces, &c., in order ro reef or to hand them.

To Splice. To join two ropes together, by uniting the strands.

Spoon-drift. A continued flying of the spray and waves over the surface of the sea.

To Spring a Mast. To crack or split it.

A Spring. A rope made fast to the cable at the bow and taken in abaft, in order to expose the ship's side in any direction.

Spring-tides. The highest tides at the full and change of the moon.

To Stand-on. To keep in the course.

To Stand-by. To be ready.

Starboard. The right side.

To Steer. To manage a ship by the movement of the helm.

To Stopper the Cable. To keep it from running out by fastening short ropes to it, called stoppers.

Strand. One of the divisions of a rope.

Stranded When one of the divisions of a rope is broken—also when a ship is run on shore. so that she cannot be got off, she is said to be stranded.

To Stretch. To stand on different tacks, under a press of sail.

To Strike. To beat against the bottom—also to lower the flag in token of submission. Lowering the topmasts, is commonly termed striking them.

To Surge the Messenger. To slack it suddenly.

To Sway. To hoist up the yards and topmasts.

To Swing. To turn a ship from one side of her anchor to another, at the change of the tide.

To Tack. To turn a ship by the sails and rudder against the wind.

Taut. A corruption of *tight.*

Taunt. Long, lofty.

Tending. The movement of a vessel in swinging at anchor.

Tier. The place where cables are coiled.

Traverse. To sail on different courses. When a rope runs freely through a thimble, &c., it is said to traverse.

Trying. Laying-to in a gale of wind under a small sail.

Turning to Windward. Tacking.

Twice-laid stuff Rope made from the yarns of a cable, &c., which has been half-worn.

To Veer and Haul. To pull a rope, and then slacken it.

To Unbend. To cast loose.

To Unmoor. To reduce a ship to a single anchor, after riding by two.

To Unreeve. To pull a rope out of a block.

To Unrig. To deprive a ship of her rigging.

To Unship. To take anything from the place in which it was fixed.

Waist of a Ship. The part between the main and fore-drifts; also a term sometimes used for the spare or waist-anchor, from its being stowed near the fore-drift, or fore part of the waist.

Wake. The track left by the ship on the water which she has passed over.

Wales. (*See Bends*).

To Wear. To turn a ship round from the wind.

To Warp. To move a ship by hawsers.

Watch. A division of the ship's company, who keep the deck for a certain time. One is called starboard, and the other the larboard watch.

Water-logged. The state of a leaky ship, when she is so full of water as to be heavy and unmanageable.

Way of a Ship. Her progress through the water.

To Weather a Ship. To get to windward of her.

A Weather Tide. A tide or stream which runs to windward.

Weather-Beaten. Anything worn or damaged by bad weather.

To Weigh. To heave the anchor out of the ground.

To Whip. To bind the end of a rope with yarn to prevent its untwisting; also to hoist anything by a rope which is rove through a single block.

Wind's-eye. That point from which the wind blows in a direct line.

Between Wind and Water. That part of the ship's bottom which is just at the surface of the water, or what is called the water-line.

To Wind a Boat, &c. To turn it round from its original position.

Wind-Rode. When a ship is kept astern, &c., of her anchor, solely by the wind.

To Windward. Towards that point from which the wind blows.

To Work to Windward. To make progress against the wind by tacking.

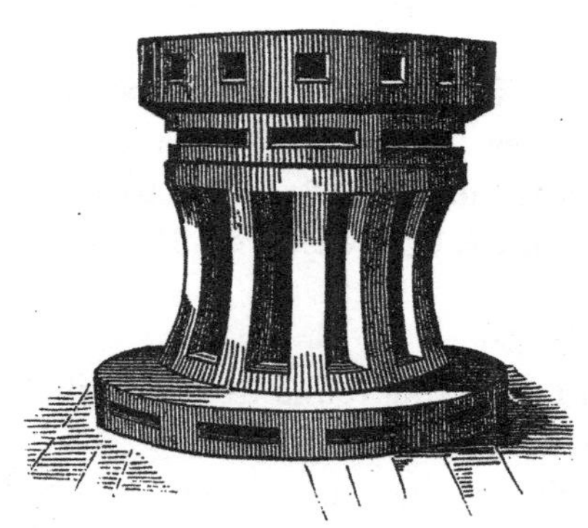

PART XI.

TABLES

RELATING TO

RIGGING, BLOCKS, SPARS, ANCHORS, CABLES, &c.

492.—A Table showing the Weight of Cables and Anchors, used in Ships and Vessels of War, U. S. N.

Names of Ships.	Rate in Guns.	Hemp Cables.			Chain Cables.			Total Weight	Anchors.				Total Weight
		Sheet.	Stream.	Weight.	Bower.	Sheet.	Weight.	of Hemp and Chain Cables.	Sheet.	Bower.	Stream.	Weight.	of Anchors and Cables.
				tons. cwt. qrs. lbs.			tons. cwt. qrs. lbs.	tons. cwt. qrs. lbs.				tons. cwt. qrs. lbs.	tons. cwt. qrs. lbs.
Pennsylvania - - - -	120	2	1	19 7 2 22	2	1	44 2 1 16	63 10 0 13	2	2	1	21 10 0 0	85 0 0 13
Delaware - - - -	80	2	1	17 9 3 7	2	1	44 2 1 16	61 12 0 23	2	2	1	19 8 0 0	81 0 0 23
Franklin - - - -	74	2	1	16 2 2 4	2	1	30 4 1 9	46 6 3 13	2	2	1	18 4 0 0	64 10 3 13
Independence - - -	68	2	1	13 14 2 24	2	1	30 4 1 9	43 19 0 8	2	2	1	17 0 0 0	60 19 0 8
Brandywine - - -	44	2	1	13 1 0 11	2	1	23 7 3 2	36 8 3 13	2	2	1	14 16 0 0	51 4 3 13
Constellation - - -	36	2	1	11 13 0 8	2	1	19 3 1 15	30 16 1 23	2	2	1	11 13 0 0	42 9 1 23
Sloops, 1st Class - -	24	2	1	8 19 2 12	2	1	13 18 1 21	22 18 0 8	2	2	1	8 2 0 0	31 0 0 8
Sloops, 2d Class - -	22	2	1	7 17 1 16	2	1	12 19 3 14	20 17 1 5	2	2	1	7 1 0 0	27 18 1 5
Sloops, 3d Class - -	16	2	1	6 16 2 23	2	1	10 16 1 5	17 13 0 3	2	2	1	6 0 0 0	23 13 0 3
Brig Truxton - - -	12	–	1	0 16 0 20	2	1	6 15 1 22	7 11 2 17	1	2	1	2 11 0 0	10 2 2 17
Schooners - - - -	10	–	1	0 12 0 0	2	1	5 6 0 12	5 18 0 12	1	2	1	2 7 0 0	8 5 0 12
Steamers, 1st Class -	–	–	1	1 18 3 18	2	1	17 8 2 2	19 7 1 20	1	2	1	9 1 0 0	28 8 1 20
Steamers. 2d Class -	–	–	1	1 11 0 10	2	1	13 18 1 21	15 9 2 6	1	2	1	6 4 0 0	21 13 2 6

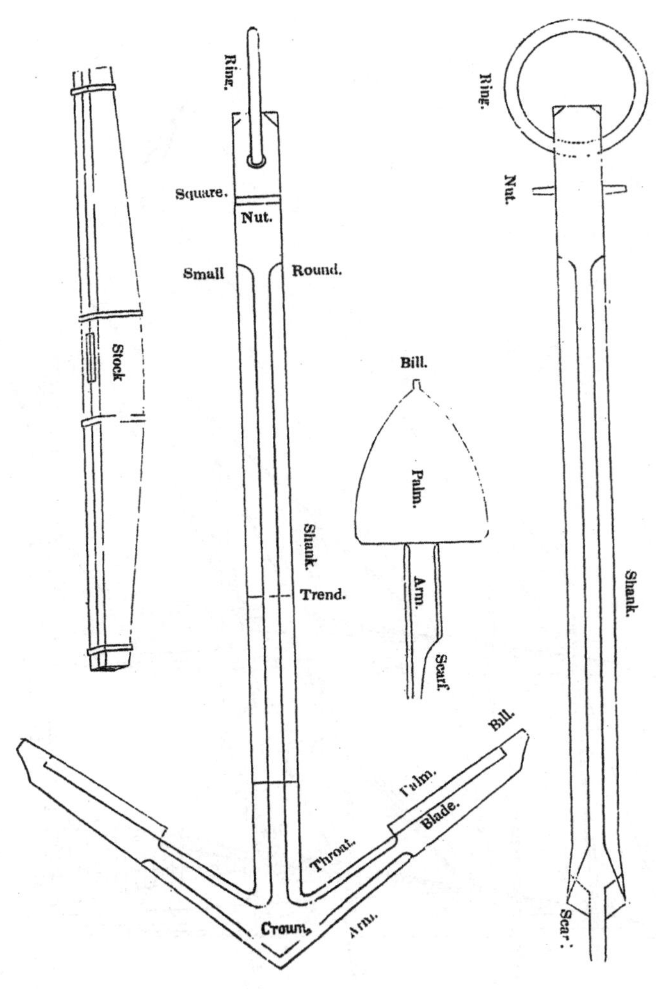

A Sketch showing the Names of the different parts of an Anchor.

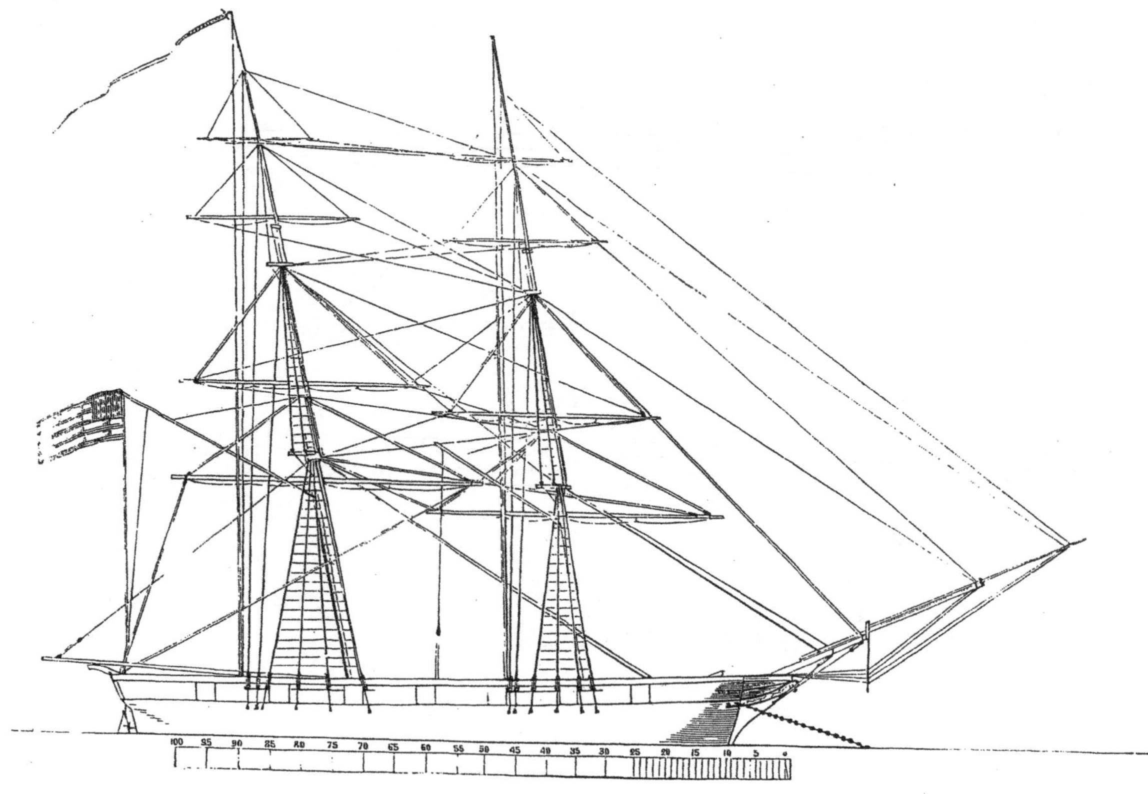

Scale-draft of a Brig-of-War.

493.—A Table Showing the Weight, Size and Length of Guns and Carriages, U. S. Navy.

SIZE OF GUNS.	WEIGHT OF GUN.			WEIGHT OF CARRIAGE.			LENGTH OF GUN.		TOTAL.		
	cwt.	qrs.	lbs.	cwt.	qrs.	lbs.	ft.	in.	cwt.	qrs.	lbs.
42 Pounder, Long Gun, -	70	0	0		–		9	1			
32 " - - - - - -	61	0	0		–		9	2			
32 " - - - - - -	51	0	0	8	2	0	8	4	59	2	0
32 " - - - - - -	60	0	0		–		9	2			
32 " - - - - - -	50	0	0		–		8	4			
32 " - - - - - -	42	2	0	8	1	0	8	2	50	3	0
32 " - - - - - -	61	2	0	9	1	0	9	2	70	3	0
32 " - - - - - -	41	0	0		–		8	0			
32 " - - - - - -	41	0	0	8	0	0	7	0	49	0	0
32 " - - - - - -	32	0	0		–		6	7			
32 " - - - - - -	51	0	0		–		9	0			
32 " - - - - - -	43	0	0		–		8	0			
24 " Long Medium,	49	0	0	6	3	0	9	4½	55	3	0
24 " - - - - - -	49	0	0		–		8	4½			
24 " - - - - - -	49	0	0	6	3	0	8	4	55	3	0
24 " - - - - - -	32	0	0		–		6	7			
18 " - - - - - -	38	0	0	5	2	0	8	0	43	2	0
18 " - - - - - -	40	0	0	5	2	0	9	2	45	2	0
18 " - - - - - -	36	0	0		–		7	7½			
12 " - - - - - -	23	0	0	4	3	0	6	8½	27	3	0
9 " - - - - - -	18	0	0		–		6	1			
9 " - - - - - -	18	0	0	3	3	0	5	11	21	3	0
12 inch Peace Maker, - -	150	0	0								
10 inch Shell Gun, - - -	136	3	9								
8 " " - - -	63	0	0		–		8	10			
8 " " - - -	68	2	0		–		9	1			
8 " " - - -	64	0	0		–		8	10			
8 " " - - -	53	0	0		–		8	4			
CARRONADES.											
42 Pounder, - - - - - -	27	0	0	7	2	0	4	3	34	2	0
32 " - - - - - -	20	0	0		–		4	1			
32 " - - - - - -	21	0	0		–		4	2			
32 " - - - - - -	19	0	0	6	2	14	–		25	2	14
24 " - - - - - -	13	0	0	5	2	0	3	7	18	2	0
24 " - - - - - -	15	0	0	6	0	0	3	9	21	0	0

494.—A Table showing the Weight of Chain Cable.

				Pounds.
150 Fathoms	of $2\frac{1}{4}$	inch weighs	- - - - - -	45 249
150	" $2\frac{1}{8}$	"	- - - - - -	37 400
150	" 2	"	- - - - - -	37 372
150	" $1\frac{15}{16}$	"	- - - - - -	34 125
150	" $1\frac{7}{8}$	"	- - - - - -	32 225
150	" $1\frac{3}{4}$	"	- - - - - -	27 192
150	" $1\frac{11}{16}$	"	- - - - - -	25 350
150	" $1\frac{5}{8}$	"	- - - - - -	23 934
150	" $1\frac{3}{8}$	"	- - - - - -	17 204
150	" $1\frac{1}{4}$	"	- - - - - -	14 384
150	" $1\frac{1}{8}$	"	- - - - - -	11 921

495.—A Table showing how many Fathoms make 112 Pounds of 4-strand shroud-laid Rope.

fath.	feet	in.	of (inches)	in size.
486 fath.	0 feet	0 in.	of 1	inch in size.
313 "	3 "	0 "	$1\frac{1}{4}$	" "
216 "	3 "	0 "	$1\frac{1}{2}$	" "
159 "	3 "	0 "	$1\frac{3}{4}$	" "
124 "	3 "	0 "	2	" "
96 "	2 "	0 "	$2\frac{1}{4}$	" "
77 "	3 "	0 "	$2\frac{1}{2}$	" "
65 "	4 "	0 "	$2\frac{3}{4}$	" "
54 "	0 "	0 "	3	" "
45 "	5 "	2 "	$3\frac{1}{4}$	" "
39 "	3 "	0 "	$3\frac{1}{2}$	" "
34 "	3 "	9 "	$3\frac{3}{4}$	" "
30 "	1 "	6 "	4	" "
26 "	5 "	0 "	$4\frac{1}{4}$	" "
24 "	0 "	0 "	$4\frac{1}{2}$	" "
21 "	3 "	0 "	$4\frac{3}{4}$	" "
19 "	3 "	0 "	5	" "
17 "	4 "	0 "	$5\frac{1}{4}$	" "
16 "	1 "	0 "	$5\frac{1}{2}$	" "
14 "	4 "	0 "	$5\frac{3}{4}$	" "
13 "	3 "	0 "	6	" "
12 "	2 "	0 "	$6\frac{1}{4}$	" "
11 "	3 "	0 "	$6\frac{1}{2}$	" "
10 "	4 "	0 "	$6\frac{3}{4}$	" "
9 "	5 "	0 "	7	" "
9 "	1 "	0 "	$7\frac{1}{4}$	" "
8 "	4 "	0 "	$7\frac{1}{2}$	" "
8 fath.	3 feet	6 in.	of $7\frac{3}{4}$	inches in size.
7 "	3 "	6 "	8	" "
7 "	0 "	8 "	$8\frac{1}{4}$	" "
6 "	4 "	3 "	$8\frac{1}{2}$	" "
6 "	2 "	1 "	$8\frac{3}{4}$	" "
6 "	0 "	0 "	9	" "
5 "	4 "	0 "	$9\frac{1}{4}$	" "
5 "	2 "	0 "	$9\frac{1}{2}$	" "
5 "	0 "	0 "	$9\frac{3}{4}$	" "
4 "	5 "	0 "	10	" "
4 "	4 "	1 "	$10\frac{1}{4}$	" "
4 "	2 "	1 "	$10\frac{1}{2}$	" "
4 "	1 "	0 "	$10\frac{3}{4}$	" "
4 "	0 "	3 "	11	" "
3 "	5 "	7 "	$11\frac{1}{4}$	" "
3 "	4 "	1 "	$11\frac{1}{2}$	" "
3 "	3 "	3 "	$11\frac{3}{4}$	" "
3 "	2 "	3 "	12	" "
3 "	2 "	1 "	$12\frac{1}{4}$	" "
3 "	2 "	0 "	$12\frac{1}{2}$	" "
3 "	1 "	8 "	$12\frac{3}{4}$	" "
2 "	5 "	3 "	13	" "
2 "	4 "	9 "	$13\frac{1}{4}$	" "
2 "	4 "	0 "	$13\frac{1}{2}$	" "
2 "	3 "	6 "	$13\frac{3}{4}$	" "
2 "	2 "	4 "	14	" "

496.—Weight of one Foot of Bar Iron of the following forms.

THICKNESS.	SQUARE.	OCTAGONAL.	ROUND.	THICKNESS.	SQUARE.	OCTAGONAL.	ROUND.
Inches.	Pounds.	Pounds.	Pounds.	Inches.	Pounds.	Pounds.	Pounds.
3	29.45	24.27	23.14	1¼	5.11	4.14	4.02
2½	20.45	16.85	16.07	1⅛	4.14	3.41	3.25
2¼	16.56	13.65	13.02	1	3.27	2.70	2.57
2	13.09	10.79	10.29	⅞	2.51	2.06	1.97
1⅞	11.50	9.48	9.04	¾	1.84	1.52	1.45
1¾	10.02	8.26	7.87	⅝	1.28	1.05	1.00
1⅝	8.64	7.12	6.79	½	.81	.67	.64
1½	7.36	6.07	5.78	⅜	.46	.38	.36
1⅜	6.19	5.10	4.86	¼	.17	.17	.16

NOTE.—The above Table shows pounds and hundredths of pounds.

497.—A Table showing the Weight of 100 Fathoms of Cable-laid Rope, from 2 to 26 inches.

ALSO A COMPARATIVE SIZE OF CHAIN.

SIZE.	THREADS.	WEIGHT.	CHAIN EQUAL.	SIZE.	THREADS.	WEIGHT.	CHAIN EQUAL.
		cwt. qrs. lbs.				cwt. qrs. lbs.	
2	27	3 26		14½	1098	40 1 12	1⅜
2½	36	1 1 8		15	1170	43 0 1	
3	54	1 3 25		15½	1251	45 3 26	1½
3½	72	2 2 16		16	1332	48 3 24	
4	99	3 1 6	⅝	16½	1413	51 3 21	
4½	108	3 3 24		17	1503	55 1 0	1⅝
5	135	4 3 23		17½	1593	58 2 6	
5½	162	5 3 22		18	1683	61 3 13	1¾
6	189	6 3 21		18½	1782	65 2 1	
6½	216	7 3 21		19	1881	69 0 17	1⅞
7	252	9 1 1		19½	1980	72 3 4	
7½	288	10 2 9		20	2088	76 3 1	
8	336	12 0 26	¾	20½	2187	80 1 16	
8½	378	13 3 15		21	2295	84 1 14	2
9	423	15 2 25		21½	2403	88 1 10	
9½	468	17 0 22	⅞	22	2520	92 2 16	
10	522	19 0 21	1	22½	2646	97 1 3	
10½	576	21 0 19	1	23	2763	101 2 8	2⅛
11	630	23 0 18		23½	2880	105 3 14	
11½	684	25 0 15	1⅛	24	3006	110 2 1	2⅛
12	747	27 1 23	1⅛	24½	3132	115 0 16	
12½	810	29 3 3		25	3235	119 3 2	2⅛
13	882	32 1 19		25½	3393	124 2 16	
13½	954	35 0 7	1¼	26	3528	129 2 22	2⅛
14	1026	37 2 24					

NOTE.—The Size Chain are set down opposite their respective Hemp Cables, as near as can be calculated, within a fraction.

498.—A Table for showing the Strength of Hemp Cables; their Weight, Size, and Number of Yarns in each.

Size in Inches	Number of Yarns.	Weight of 100 Fathoms in lbs.	Breaking Strain in Tons. Maximum.	Breaking Strain in Tons. Minimum.	Mean.
26	3528	14112	122.2	105.9	111.6
25½	3393	13572	117.5	101.9	107.3
25	3267	13068	113.	98.	103.2
24½	3122	12488	114.4	94.4	102.5
24	3006	12024	115.7	91.	101.9
23½	2880	11520	117.	87.6	101.3
23	2763	11052	118.3	84.2	100.7
22½	2646	10584	119.5	81.	100.1
22	2529	10116	111.4	77.9	95.
21½	2412	9648	103.5	74.9	90.1
21	2304	9216	95.8	72.	85.3
20½	2196	8784	88.3	69.2	80.6
20	2088	8352	81.	66.5	76.1
19½	1980	7920	76.7	62.1	71.3
19	1881	7524	72.6	57.9	66.6
18½	1782	7128	68.6	53.8	62.1
18	1692	6768	64.7	49.8	57.7
17½	1597	6388	61.	46.	53.4
17	1512	6048	57.3	44.9	51.
16½	1422	5688	53.9	43.8	48.7
16	1332	5328	50.5	42.8	46.5
15½	1251	5004	47.3	41.9	44.3
15	1179	4716	44.2	41.	42.3
14½	1098	4392	41.6	38.4	39.9
14	1026	4104	39.1	36.	37.6
13½	954	3816	36.7	33.6	35.4
13	882	3528	34.4	31.3	33.3
12½	810	3240	32.2	29.2	31.3
12	756	3024	29.8	26.6	28.6
11½	693	2772	27.6	24.2	26.1
11	630	2520	25.5	21.8	23.7
10½	576	2304	23.4	19.6	21.4
10	522	2088	21.5	17.5	19.2
9½	468	1872	19.	15.7	17.1
9	432	1728	16.7	14.	15.2
8½	396	1584	14.6	12.4	13.4
8	315	1260	12.6	10.9	11.7
7½	288	1152	10.7	9.5	10.2
7	252	1008	9.3	8.2	8.8
6½	216	864	8.1	7.	7.5
6	189	756	7.	5.8	6.3
5½	162	648	5.9	4.8	5.3
5	135	540	5.	3.9	4.3
4½	108	432	4.	3.1	3.4
4	90	360	3.2	2.5	2.7
3½	69	276	2.4	1.9	2.1
3	54	216	1.8	1.4	1.5

NOTE.—The above Table shows tons and hundredths of tons.

499.—A Table showing the Strength of Plain-laid Rope of three Strands.

Size.	Number of Yarns in Rope.	Weight of 100 Fathoms in lbs.	Breaking Strain in Tons.		Mean.
			Maximum.	Minimum.	
12	1173	2940	45.5	35.	40.
11½	1077	–	41.7	32.	36.7
11	987	–	38.2	29.3	33.6
10½	900	–	34.9	26.7	30.7
10	816	2136	31.7	24.2	27.9
9½	738	–	28.6	21.8	25.2
9	660	1712	25.7	19.6	22.6
8½	591	–	23.	17.5	20.2
8	522	1379	20.4	15.5	18.
7½	459	–	18.	13.6	15.8
7	399	–	15.8	11.8	13.8
6½	345	–	13.7	10.2	12.
6	294	834	11.75	8.7	10.3
5½	249	712	9.8	7.3	8.7
5	204	–	8.2	6.1	7.2
4½	168	413	6.7	5.	5.9
4	132	–	5.3	4.	4.7
3½	102	–	4.1	3.2	3.7
3	75	203	3.1	2.4	2.8
2¼	54	–	2.2	1.8	2.1
2	33	–	1.5	1.3	1.4
1¾	27	–	1.28	1.13	1.23
1½	21	–	.90	.86	.88
1¼	15	–	.60	.53	.56
1	12	–	.58	.46	.51
¾	9	–	.51	.42	.46
½	6	–	.28	.28	.28

NOTE.—The above Table shows tons and hundredths of tons.

500.—A Table for showing the Strength of Chain Cable, as tested in Fifteen Fathom Lengths.

Size.	Required Testing Strain in Tons.	Weight of 100 Fathoms in lbs.	Breaking Strain in Tons.		Mean.
			Maximum.	Minimum.	
2¼	91⅛	27216	130.3	121.8	125.9
2⅛	81¼	24276	116.2	108.6	112.3
2	72	21504	103.	96.25	99.5
1⅞	63¼	18900	99.	88.	92.8
1¾	55⅛	16464	85.25	65.	74.1
1⅝	47½	14196	75.	59.5	66.5
1½	40½	12096	65.5	54.5	59.5
1⅜	34	10164	53.6	44.4	48.5
1¼	28½	8400	42.8	35.3	38.5
1⅛	22¾	6804	33.	27.	29.5
1	18	5376	27.25	22.	24.3
⅞	13¾	4116	22.5	20.3	21.1
¾	10⅛	3024	15.	12.5	13.5
11/16	8½	2541	12.3	10.8	11.4
⅝	7	2100	9.87	9.37	9.5
9/16	5½	1701			
½	4½	1344	6.3	5.9	6.

Note.—The above Table shows tons and hundredths of tons.

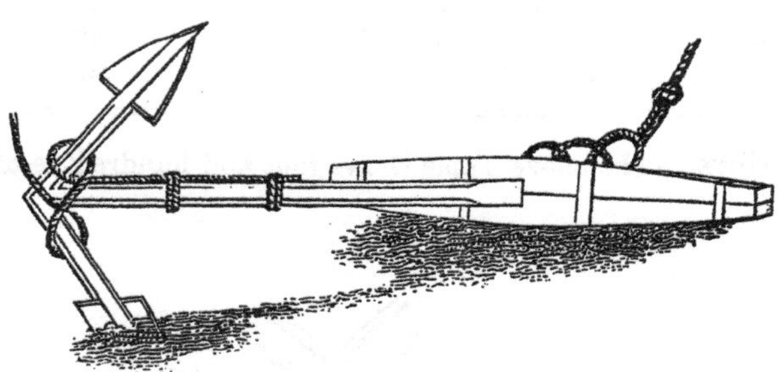

501.—A Table showing the Strength of Short Round-linked Bobstay, Bowsprit-shroud or Crane Chain, without Studs, such as is used for Rigging, &c.

Size.	Weight of 100 Fathoms in lbs.	BREAKING STRAIN IN TONS.		Mean.	Required Test of Strength.
		Maximum.	Minimum.		
$1\frac{5}{8}$	15569	75.	68.	73.	31.6
$1\frac{1}{2}$	–	64.	58.2	62.3	27.
$1\frac{7}{16}$	–	59.	53.8	57.4	24.7
$1\frac{3}{8}$	–	54.2	49.6	52.8	22.6
$1\frac{5}{16}$	–	49.7	45.5	48.4	20.6
$1\frac{1}{4}$	–	45.3	41.7	44.1	18.8
$1\frac{3}{16}$	–	41.2	38.	40.1	17.
$1\frac{1}{8}$	7481	37.3	34.5	36.3	15.3
$1\frac{1}{16}$	–	33.6	31.2	32.7	13.6
1	6490	30.1	28.1	29.3	12.
$\frac{15}{16}$	5600	26.8	25.2	26.1	10.5
$\frac{7}{8}$	4500	23.7	22.5	23.1	9.1
$\frac{13}{16}$	4000	20.9	20.	20.4	7.9
$\frac{3}{4}$	3449	17.8	16.6	17.3	6.8
$\frac{11}{16}$	2900	14.9	13.5	14.6	5.6
$\frac{5}{8}$	2538	12.3	10.8	12.	4.6
$\frac{9}{16}$	2001	10.	8.7	9.7	3.8
$\frac{1}{2}$	1583	7.9	6.9	7.7	3.
$\frac{7}{16}$	1060	6.	5.2	5.9	2.3
$\frac{3}{8}$	827	4.4	3.8	4.3	1.6
$\frac{5}{16}$	581	3.	2.7	3.	1.1
$\frac{1}{4}$	392	1.9	1.7	1.9	.75
$\frac{3}{16}$	–	1.1	.97	1.	.42

NOTE.—The above Table shows tons and hundredths of tons.

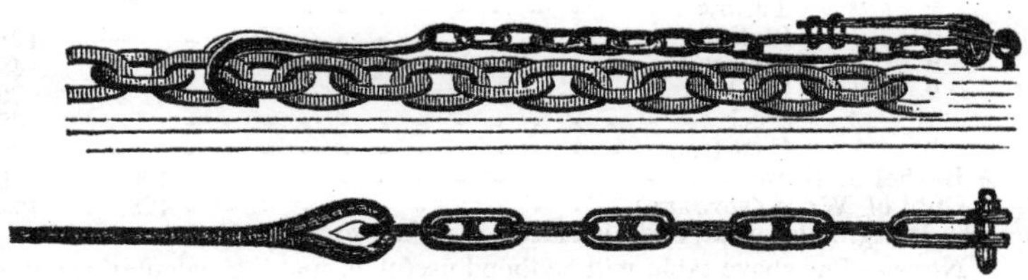

502.—Weight of Timber in a green and seasoned State.

Description of Timber.	Weight of Cubic Foot.			
	Green.		Seasoned.	
	lbs.	oz.	lbs.	oz.
Live Oak	76	10	70	8
White Oak	59	14	54	0
Red Oak	63	12	60	10
Hickory	58	14	52	15
Locust	60	12	56	4
Cypress	48	3	36	0
Cedar	32	0	30	4
Maple	45	0	34	4
Yellow Pine	48	12	35	8
White Pine	36	12	30	11
Spruce	43	15	28	14
Elm	56	8	37	5
Beech	60	0	53	6
White Ash	58	3	50	0

NOTE.—The average weight of the different species of timber, used in building and equipping ships-of-war in the United States' Navy, may be reckoned about 50 lbs. to the cubic foot.

503.—A Table of Measures and Weights of different Substances.

A ton of water (net weight), 250 gallons.	Cub. in.	lbs. oz.
A cubic foot of Water (specific gravity)	—	62 9
" " Sea-water	—	64 2
" " New York Harbor-water	—	63 14
" " Cork	—	15 0
" " Tallow	—	59 0
" " Platina	—	1218.75
" " Copper	—	486.75
" " Lead	—	709.05
" " Steel	—	489.08
" " Cast Iron	–	450.45
A Bushel of Beans	100.	63.
A Cord of Wood (stowage)	128.	1700.

The Weight of a Man and his Effects is from 2 to 2½ cwt.

NOTE.—The above table will be found useful in making calculations of stowage, and also in keeping the ship properly trimmed.

504.—A Table of Weight of Tarred Cordage.

CABLES.

				cwt.	qr.	lbs.
1	Fathom of	24	inch weighs	1	1	4
1	"	22	"	1	0	9
1	"	20	"	0	3	16
1	"	19	"	0	3	6
1	"	17	"	0	2	16
1	"	16	"	0	2	8
1	"	15	"	0	1	27
100	"	14	"	41	2	20
100	"	13½	"	38	3	1
100	"	13	"	35	3	9
100	"	12½	"	32	3	17
100	"	11½	"	30	1	10
100	"	11	"	26	1	19
100	"	10½	"	23	1	17
100	"	10	"	21	0	3

HAWSERS OF 130 FATAOMS.

				cwt.	qr.	lbs.
130	Fathoms of	6½	inch weighs	13	1	11
130	"	6	"	11	1	13
130	"	5½	"	9	2	2
130	"	5	"	7	3	19
130	"	4½	"	6	1	22
130	"	4	"	5	0	14
130	"	3½	"	3	3	7
130	Fathoms of	3	inch weighs	2	3	20
130	"	2½	"	2	0	5
130	"	2	"	1	1	6
130	"	1½	"	0	3	13
130	"	1	"	0	1	20
130	"	¾	"	0	1	4

HAWSERS OF 120 FATHOMS.

				cwt.	qr.	lbs.
120	Fathoms of	9½	inch weighs	22	2	9
120	"	9	"	20	1	17
120	"	8½	"	18	0	26
120	"	8	"	16	0	6
120	"	7½	"	13	3	16
120	"	7	"	12	0	18
120	"	6½	"	10	1	19
120	"	6	"	9	0	12
120	"	5½	"	7	3	7
120	"	5	"	6	2	1
120	"	4½	"	5	0	23
120	"	4	"	4	0	18
120	"	3½	"	3	1	22
120	"	3	"	2	2	11
120	"	2½	"	1	3	0
120	"	2	"	1	1	4

505.—A Table showing the comparative Strength between Iron Chains and Hemp Cables.

Also the Size required agreeably to Tonnage, with the Weight equal to Cable.

SIZE OF CHAIN.	Vessel's Tonnage.	Size of Rope.	Weight of Anchor.	Proof required.	Weight per Fathom.
Five-sixteenths of an inch - - -	–	2½	–	¾ ton.	5½
Three-eighths " - - -	–	3¼	–	1½	8
Seven-sixteenths " - - -	–	4	–	2½	11
One-half " - - -	20	4¾	1½ cwt.	3	14
Nine-sixteenth " - - -	30	5½	2	4½	18
Five-eighths " - - -	40	6¼	2½	6	24
Eleven-sixteenths " - - -	50	7	3	7½	28
Three-quarters " - - -	60	7¾	4	9	32
Thirteen-sixteenths " - - -	75	8½	4½	11	38
Seven-eighths " - - -	95	9¼	5½	13	44
Fifteen-sixteenths " - - -	120	10	6½	15	50
One inch - - - - - - - - -	150	10¾	8	17	56
One and one-sixteenth inch - -	180	11½	9	19	62
One and one-eighth inch - - -	210	12	10½	21½	70
One and three-sixteenths inch -	240	12¾	12	24	78
One and one-quarter inch - - -	280	13½	13½	27	86
One and five-sixteenths inch - -	320	14¼	15	30	96
One and three-eighths inch - -	360	15	16½	33	108
One and seven-sixteenths inch -	400	15½	18	36	115
One and one-half inch - - - -	450	16	20	40	125

506.—A Table showing the Length, Breadth and Strength of Flax and Cotton Canvass, as used in U. S. N.

Together with the Number, Length and Breadth of Strips cut crosswise and lengthwise, used in the test of Strength, and the average weight required of them, before received for use.

NUMBER OF CANVASS.	Number of yards in Bolt.	Weight of Bolt.	Breadth of Canvass.	Distance of blue thread fm selvagee	Number of Strips cut for a test.	Breadth of Strips, cut crosswise.	Length of Strips, cut crosswise.	Breadth of Strips, cut lengthwise.	Length of Strips, cut lengthwise.	Average weight required to be borne by 3 strips separately, cut crosswise.	Average weight required to be borne by 3 strips separately, cut lengthwise.
	Yards.	lbs. oz.	Inches.	Inches.	Number.	Inches.	Inches.	Inches.	Inches.	lbs.	lbs.
Flax Canvass, No. 1,	40	42.	20	1¾	6	1	20	1	24	470	316
" " No. 2,	40	38.	20	1¾	6	1	20	1	24	420	280
" " No. 3,	40	35.	20	1⅝	6	1	20	1	24	370	250
" " No. 4,	40	32.	20	1⅝	6	1	20	1	24	340	230
" " No. 5,	40	29.	20	1⅝	6	1	20	1	24	320	216
" " No. 6,	40	26.	20	1⅜	6	1	20	1	24	300	200
" " No. 7,	40	23.	20	1¼	6	1	20	1	24	280	193
" " No. 8,	40	20.	20	1¼	6	1¼	20	1¼	24	300	213
" " No. 9,	40	18.6	20	1¼	6	1¼	20	1¼	24	298	210
Cotton Canvass, No. 1,	50	42.	20	1⅞	Used for the purpose of making Tarpaulins, &c.						
" " No. 2,	50	42.	20	1⅞							
" " No. 3,	50	40.	20	1⅝	Used for Hammock-cloths, Awnings, Boom-covers, &c.						
" " No. 4,	50	38.	20	1⅝							
" " No. 5,	50	36.	20	1⅜	Used for making Studding-sail and Fore and Aft Sail Covers, &c.						
" " No. 6,	50	34.	20	1⅜							
" " No. 7,	50	32.	20	1⅛	Used for Boats' Awnings, Awning Curtains, &c.						
" " No. 8,	50	30.	20	1⅛							
" " No. 9,	50	28.	20	⅞	Used for Gigs' Sails, Side-screens, &c.						
" " No. 10,	50	26.	20	⅞							
Hammock and Bag Stuff, No. 1,	50	105.	42	1⅝	Used for making Hammocks.						
" " " No. 4,	50	75.	42	1⅝	Used for making Clothes-bags.						

Note.—There is no test required for strength for Cotton Canvass, it not being used for making sails in the Navy.

507.—Cordage Table, showing the Weight of one Fathom Rope, from 1 inch to 24 inches inclusive, plain laid 3-strand, such as used for running rigging, &c.

Size Rope.	lbs. oz.	Size Rope.	lbs. oz.
1 inch weighs - - - -	.3¾	9 inch weighs - - - -	18.10⅜
1¼ " " - - - - -	.5¾	9¼ " " - - - - -	19.11⅜
1½ " " - - - - -	.8¼	9½ " " - - - - -	20.13⅜
1¾ " " - - - - -	.11¼	9¾ " " - - - - -	21.14⅔
2 " " - - - - -	.14¾	10 " " - - - - -	23.1½
2¼ " " - - - - -	1.2⅔	10¼ " " - - - - -	24.3½
2½ " " - - - - -	1.7	10½ " " - - - - -	25.7
2¾ " " - - - - -	1.11⅞	10¾ " " - - - - -	26.11⅜
3 " " - - - - -	2.1⅕	11 " " - - - - -	27.14½
3¼ " " - - - - -	2.7	11¼ " " - - - - -	29.1¼
3½ " " - - - - -	2.13⅕	11½ " " - - - - -	30.9
3¾ " " - - - - -	3.2⅜	11¾ " " - - - - -	31.14
4 " " - - - - -	3.11	12 " " - - - - -	33.3
4¼ " " - - - - -	4.1⅜	12¼ " " - - - - -	34.9½
4½ " " - - - - -	4.10⅔	12½ " " - - - - -	36.
4¾ " " - - - - -	5.3⅜	12¾ " " - - - - -	37.8
5 " " - - - - -	5.12¼	13 " " - - - - -	38.15
5¼ " " - - - - -	6.5⅔	13¼ " " - - - - -	40.8¼
5½ " " - - - - -	7.	13½ " " - - - - -	42.
5¾ " " - - - - -	7.9⅞	13¾ " " - - - - -	43.9¼
6 " " - - - - -	8.4¾	14 " " - - - - -	45.4¾
6¼ " " - - - - -	9.	15 " " - - - - -	52.0⅓
6½ " " - - - - -	9.11¾	16 " " - - - - -	59.5
6¾ " " - - - - -	10.8	17 " " - - - - -	66.10
7 " " - - - - -	11.4⅔	18 " " - - - - -	74.10
7¼ " " - - - - -	12.2	19 " " - - - - -	83.2
7½ " " - - - - -	13.0⅜	20 " " - - - - -	92.11
7¾ " " - - - - -	13.13⅔	21 " " - - - - -	102.1
8 " " - - - - -	14.12⅓	22 " " - - - - -	112.
8¼ " " - - - - -	15.11½	23 " " - - - - -	122.3
8½ " " - - - - -	16.10½	24 " " - - - - -	134.6
8¾ " " - - - - -	17.10½		

Rule to find the weight of any sized Rope.—A rope of 1 inch circumference requires 486 fathoms to make one hundred weight. The superficial part of all circles being in proportion to the square of their diameters, consequently the square of their circumference. Therefore, a rope of 1 inch in circumference, whose square is one, has 486 fathoms to a cwt.; and, therefore, 486 being divided by the square of the circumference of any rope, the quotient will give the number of fathoms. For instance,

9×9 = 81)486(6. The number of fathoms in a cwt.
486
—

Rule to find the weight of 120 fathoms of any sized Cable.—Multiply the circumference by the circumference, and divide the product by 4, and the quotient will be the number of cwts. in 120 fathoms.

508.—A Table showing the Length of the First Warp of Standing Rigging.

Number of Guns.	Fore.					Main.					Mizen.				
	Shrouds.	T. M. Shrouds.	T. M. Backstay	T. G. Shrouds.	T. G. Backstay	Shrouds.	T. M. Shrouds.	T. M. Backstay	T. G. Shrouds.	T. G. Backstay	Shrouds.	T. M. Shrouds.	T. M. Backstay	T. G. Shrouds.	T. G. Backstay
	Ft. In.	Ft. In.	Ft. In.	Ft. In.	Ft. In	Ft. In.	Ft. In.	Ft. In.	Ft. In.	Ft. In.	Ft. In.	Ft. In.	Ft. In.	Ft. In.	Ft. In.
SHIPS OF THE LINE.															
One hundred	62.0	55.6	116.0	82.0	140.0	71.0	60.0	128.0	88.0	150.0	55.0	43.0	95.0	63.0	114.0
Ninety-eight	61.0	52.0	109.0	76.0	132.0	68.0	58.0	122.0	85.0	148.9	51.0	41.0	88.0	59.0	106.0
Eighty	55.0	50.0	105.0	73.10	126.0	62.0	56.0	114.0	82.0	139.0	48.0	40.0	82.0	57.0	105.0
Eighty	66.0	60.0	123.0	86.0	150.0	69.0	65.0	132.0	95.6	160.6	59.6	42.0	96.0	60.0	117.0
Seventy-four	65.0	55.6	118.0	80.0	143.0	74.0	59.0	129.0	87.0	158.0	60.0	42.0	97.0	60.0	117.0
FRIGATES.															
Sixty-four	55.0	47.0	101.0	70.0	127.0	61.0	52.0	113.0	76.0	137.0	50.0	38.0	85.6	54.0	99.0
Fifty	50.0	44.6	93.0	64.0	114.0	57.0	48.0	102.0	73.0	126.0	45.0	36.0	78.0	48.0	93.0
Forty-four	46.0	41.0	89.0	60.0	108.0	54.0	46.6	100.0	69.0	123.0	43.0	36.0	78.0	48.0	87.0
Thirty-eight	54.0	40.6	92.0	62.0	109.0	58.0	46.3	102.3	68.0	123.0	50.0	36.0	78.3	47.0	95.0
Thirty-six	53.0	42.0	93.0	62.0	110.0	60.0	49.6	102.0	72.0	126.0	47.0	37.6	79.6	55.0	96.0
Thirty-two	48.0	39.0	85.6	58.0	104.0	55.0	45.0	96.9	66.0	118.0	46.6	34.6	75.0	47.6	93.0
Twenty-eight	45.0	38.0	82.6	56.0	100.0	52.9	43.0	92.0	63.0	122.0	44.6	32.0	72.0	45.0	90.0
SLOOPS.															
Twenty-four	42.0	36.0	78.0	53.0	96.0	47.0	39.6	86.0	60.0	105.0	43.0	30.0	69.0	42.0	87.0
Twenty	40.0	35.0	75.0	51.0	89.0	45.0	38.6	81.0	57.0	98.0	40.0	27.0	66.0	39.0	81.0
Sixteen	38.0	30.0	66.0	44.0	80.0	42.0	33.6	72.0	49.0	87.6	35.6	24.0	57.0		
BRIGS.															
Ten	31.6	26.6	56.6	42.0	72.0	37.6	29.6	66.0	45.0	84.0					

509.—A Table of Foreign Ordnance.

Pounders.	Long Guns.			Iron.		Brass.		French.		Spanish.		Dutch.		Portuguese.		Russian.	
	Calibre.	Diameter of Shot.	Weight of Lead.	Length.	Weight.	Length.	Weight.	Diameter of Shot.	Weight of Shot.	Diameter.	Weight.	Diameter.	Weight.	Diameter.	Weight.	Diameter.	Weight.
Sixty-eight Pounder	8.0080	7.848	103.2														
Forty-two Pounder	6.8208	6.6844	63.88	9.6	67.0.0	16.6	66.0.0	–	–	–	–	–	–	7.49	59.09	6.86	45.4
Thirty-two Pounder	6.2297	6.1051	48.65	9.6	55.0.0	10.0	55.2.0	6.3496	36.	6.84	45.	6.4	36.87	6.8	35.12	6.47	38.08
Twenty-four Pounder	5.6601	5.5469	36.44	9.0	47.2.0	9.6	53.0.9	5.808	27.55	6.03	30.84	5.92	29.18	5.93	29.32	6.	30.38
Eighteen Pounder	5.1425	5.0397	27.43	9.0	40.0.0	5.9	18.0.0	5.074	18.37	5.52	23.65	5.45	22.77	5.4	22.14	5.45	22.77
Twelve Pounder	4.4924	4.4026	18.25	9.0	32.0.0	9.0	31.2.8	4.61	13.78	4.8	15.55	4.76	15.16	4.7	14.6	4.76	15.16
Nine Pounder	4.0816	4.	13.71	7.0	23.0.0	6.6	18.0.0	4.027	9.18	4.2	10.42	4.13	9.9	4.3	11.18	4.17	10.20
Six Pounder	3.5656	3.4943	9.109	8.0	22.0.0	6.0	8.3.27	–	–	–	–	3.78	7.6	3.75	7.42	3.78	7.60
Nondescript	–	–	–	6.0	16.2.0												
Four Pounder	3.1149	3.0526	6.08	6.0	22.1.0	–	–	3.196	4.59								
Three Pounder	2.8301	2.7734	4.552	4.6	7.1.0	3.6	2.2.27										
Two Pounder	2.4723	2.4228	3.037	–	–	–	3.1.0										
One Pounder	1.9622	1.923	1.517														
MORTARS.			Filled.														
Thirteen Inches	13.	12.783	349.19	5.3	82.1.0	5.3	82.0.8										
Land-piece	13.	12.783	349.19	3.7½	36.2.12	3.7½	25.0.10										
Ten Inches	10.	9.833	158.958	4.8	41.0.0	4.8	33.0.0		Non-	des-	cript.	–	–	–	–	–	–
Land-piece	–	–	–	2.9	16.0.6	2.9	10.1.25										
Eight Inches	8.	7.867	81.407	2.1¼	8.0.10	2.1¾	4.1.8										
Six and a-half Inches	5.8	5.703	31.009														

510.—A Table showing the Quantity of Provisions, Slop Clothing and Small Stores, for 200 men, for four months, in the U. S. Navy.

SMALL STORES.	
Tobacco (plugs)	1,000
Soap (bars)	800
Mustard (bottles)	100
Pepper (bottles)	100
Knives (1 each)	200
Spoons (1 each)	200
Fine Combs (1 each)	200
Coarse Combs (1 each)	200
Tin Pots (1 each)	200
Tin Pans (1 each)	200
Scrubbing Brushes (1 each)	200
Ribbon (pieces)	100
Tape (pieces)	100
Needles (papers)	100
White Thread (pounds)	50
Blue Thread (pounds)	50
Thimbles (1 each)	200
Beeswax (cakes)	100
Blacking (boxes)	200
Scissors (1 pair each)	200
Shoe Brushes (1 pair each)	200
Mittens (1 pair each)	200
Cotton Handkerchiefs	50
SLOP CLOTHING.	
Mattresses (1 each)	200
Blankets (2 each)	400
Pea-jackets	100
Trowsers (1 pair each)	200
Duck Frocks (1 each)	200
Duck Trowsers (2 pairs each)	400
White Flannel Shirts (2 each)	400
Blue Flannel Shirts (2 each)	400
Drawers (2 pairs each)	400
Hats (1 each)	200
Shoes (1 pair each)	200
Stockings (2 pairs each)	400
Black Handkerchiefs (1 each)	200
Boots (1 pair each)	200
PROVISIONS.	
Bread (pounds)	22,320
Beef (pounds)	14,652
Pork (pounds)	10,914
Flour (pounds)	1,819
Raisins (pounds)	910
Tea (pounds)	400
Sugar (pounds)	3,210
Rice (pounds)	3,636
Beans (pounds)	5,460
Pickles (pounds)	1,819
Vinegar (gallons)	228
Spirits (gallons)	750

Allowing per centage for waste.

N. B.—All recruits, when received on board of receiving-ships of the U. S. Navy, are required to have an outfit in slop clothing, &c., of one blue cloth jacket, one pair of blue cloth trowsers, 2 duck frocks, one pair of duck trowsers, two blue flannel shirts, one pair of drawers, one hat, one pair of shoes, two pairs of stockings, one black silk handkerchief, two pounds of tobacco, two pounds of soap, one knife, one tin pot, pan and spoon; the greater part of which they have when transferred to vessels for sea-service. This being the case, there is no necessity for having the full amount, as above stated, in slops and small stores in the purser's department, for issue in the course of four months.

QUANTITY OF WATER FOR EACH CLASS.

Ships of the Line—Three Decks, 110,000 gallons; Two Decks—1st Class, 82,000 gals.; 2d Class, 78,000 gals.; *Razees*, 55,000 gals.; *Frigates*—32 Pounder, 48,000 gals.; 24 Pounder, 43,000 gals.; 18 Pounder, 34,900 gals.; *Sloops*—32 Pounder, 21,000 gals.; 24 Pounder, 19,000 gals.; Sixteen 32 lb. Carronades, 15,000 gals.; *Brigs*, 8,000 gals.; *Brigantines* and *Schooners* 7,900 gals.; *Steamers*—1st Class, 23,500 gals.; 2d Class, 10,000 gals.; 3d Class, 5,000 gals.; *Receiving Vessels*—Ships of the Line, 14,600 gals.

511.—Exhibit of the Navy Ration,

Showing the component parts for each day of the week, and the value at which they are to be computed, under the 2d, 4th and 5th Sections of the Act of Congress, " To establish and regulate the Navy Ration," approved 29th August, 1842.

Days of the Week.	Pounds.						Ounces.							Pints.			
	Beef.	Pork.	Flour.	Rice.	Raisins or dried fruits.	Pickles or Cranberries	Biscuit.	Sugar.	Tea. (Either)	Coffee. (Either)	Cocoa. (Either)	Butter.	Cheese.	Beans.	Molasses.	Vinegar.	Spirits.
Sunday - - - - - - - -	1	—	½	—	¼	—	14	2	¼	1	1	—	—	—	—	—	¼
Monday - - - - - - - -	—	1	—	—	—	—	14	2	¼	1	1	—	—	½	—	—	¼
Tuesday - - - - - - - -	1	—	—	½	—	—	14	2	¼	1	1	2	2	—	—	—	¼
Wednesday - - - - - -	—	1	—	—	—	¼	14	2	¼	1	1	—	—	½	—	—	¼
Thursday - - - - - - -	1	—	½	—	¼	—	14	2	¼	1	1	—	—	—	—	—	¼
Friday - - - - - - - -	1	—	—	½	—	—	14	2	¼	1	1	2	2	—	½	—	¼
Saturday - - - - - - - -	—	1	—	—	—	¼	14	2	¼	1	1	—	—	½	—	½	¼
Weekly Quantity - - -	4	3	1	1	½	½	98	14	1¾	7	7	4	4	1½	½	½	1¾

VALUATION OF THE WEEKLY QUANTITY, &c.

3	pounds of	Pork - - -	7½	cents per	pound, - - -	22½	cents.
4	"	Beef - - -	6	"	" - - -	24	"
1	"	Flour - - -	4	"	" - - -	4	"
1	"	Rice - - -	3	"	" - - -	3	"
½	"	Raisins, &c. - -	13	"	" - - -	6½	"
½	"	Pickles, &c. - -	12½	"	" - - -	6¼	"
98	ounces of	Bread - - -	4	"	" - - -	24½	"
14	"	Sugar - - -	8	"	" - - -	7	"
1¾	"	Tea } of same val.					
7	"	Coffee } of same val.	80	"	" - - -	8¾	"
7	"	Cocoa } of same val.					
4	"	Butter - - -	23	"	" - - -	5¾	"
4	"	Cheese - - -	16	"	" - - -	4	"
1½	pints of	Beans - - -	24	"	gallon - - -	4½	"
½	"	Molasses - -	64	"	" - - -	4	"
½	"	Vinegar - - -	20	"	" - - -	1¼	"
1¾	"	Spirits - - -	64	"	" - - -	14	"
		Averaging 20 cents per day, or weekly - - -				$1.40	

The foregoing exhibit of the component parts, &c., of the Navy Ration, has been compiled in pursuance of the act of Congress, and will be strictly observed by commanders of vessels and by pursers, as a regulation of this Department, prescribing the daily issue of provisions, and the valuation at which they are to be commuted. All persons "attached to vessels for sea-service," are entitled individually to one ration per day.

Every commissioned or warrant-officer, of, or over, twenty-one years of age, may, at his option, commute the entire ration, or only the spirit portion of it: provided the commutation, in either case, be made for not less than three consecutive months. And every other person, of the above-named age, entitled to a ration, may commute the spirit component, under the limitation of time, unless sooner detached, or entitled to a discharge.

No officer or other person, under twenty-one years of age, shall be permitted to draw the spirit part of his ration. Its value in money, as estimated by the foregoing table, will be credited to him by the purser, and paid whenever the commander of the vessel, to which such officer or person may belong, shall direct.

The messes of a ship's crew may, with the sanction of the commanding officer, commute, daily or weekly, one or more entire rations, for not less than three months (unless sooner detached, or entitled to a discharge); the commutation to be paid by the purser, at such times as the said commanding officer shall deem fit.

Pursers having the delivery of rations, will make out and transmit, monthly and otherwise, by the earliest opportunities, to the Bureau of Provisions and Clothing of this Department, abstracts of provisions, agreeably to such forms as may be furnished to them from that bureau, approved by the Second Comptroller of the Treasury; their provision accounts, as heretofore, will be rendered to the Fourth Auditor's office.

A. P. UPSHUR, *Secretary of the Navy.*

AN ACT TO ESTABLISH AND REGULATE THE NAVY RATION.

SEC. 1. *Be it enacted by the Senate and House of Representatives of the United States of America, in Congress assembled,* That the navy ration shall consist of the following daily allowance of provisions for each person:—One pound of salted pork, with half a pint of peas or beans; or one pound of salted beef, with half a pound of flour, and a quarter of a pound of raisins, dried apples, or other dried fruits; or one pound of salt beef, with half a pound of rice, two ounces of butter, and two ounces of cheese; together with fourteen ounces of biscuit, one quarter of an ounce of tea, or one ounce of coffee, or one ounce of cocoa, two ounces of sugar, and one gill of spirits; and of a weekly allowance of half a pound of pickles or cranberries, half a pint of molasses, and half a pint of vinegar.

SEC. 2. *And be it further enacted,* That fresh meat may be substituted for salt beef or pork, and vegetables or sauer-kraut for other articles usually issued with the salted meats, allowing one and a quarter pounds of fresh meat for one pound of salted beef or pork, and regulating the quantity of vegetables or sauer-kraut, so as to equal the value of those articles for which they may be substituted.

SEC. 3. *And be it further enacted,* That, should it be necessary to vary the above described daily allowance, it shall be lawful to substitute one pound of soft bread, or one pound of flour, or half a pound of rice, for fourteen ounces of biscuit; half a pint of wine for a gill of spirits; half a pound of rice for half a pint of peas or beans; half a pint of beans or peas for half a pound of rice. When it may be deemed expedient by the President of the United States, Secretary of the Navy, commander of a fleet or squadron, or a single ship, when not acting under the authority of another officer on foreign service, the articles of butter, cheese, raisins, dried apples (or other dried fruits), pickles and molasses may be substituted for each other and for spirits; *provided* the article substituted shall not exceed in value the article for which it may be issued, according to the scale of prices which is or may be established for the same.

SEC. 4. *And be it further enacted*, That in cases of necessity the daily allowance of provisions may be diminished or varied, by the discretion of the senior officer present in command; but payment shall be made to the persons whose allowance shall be thus diminished, according to the scale of prices which is or may be established for the same; but a commander, who shall thus make a diminution or variation, shall report to his commanding officer, or to the Navy Department, the necessity for the same, and give to the purser written orders, specifying particularly the diminution or reduction which is to be made.

SEC. 5. *And be it further enacted*, That no commissioned officer, or midshipman, or any person under twenty-one years of age, shall be allowed to draw the spirit part of the daily ration; and all other persons shall be permitted to relinquish that part of their ration, under such restrictions as the President of the United States may authorize; and to every person who, by this section, is prohibited from drawing, or who may relinquish, the spirit part of his ration, there shall be paid, in lieu thereof, the value of the same in money, according to the prices which are or may be established for the same.

SEC. 6. *And be it further enacted*, That the provisions of this act shall go into effect, in the United States, on the first day of the succeeding quarter after it becomes a law; and in vessels abroad, on the first day of the succeeding quarter after its official receipt, and any acts, or parts of acts, which may be contrary to, or inconsistent with, the provisions of this act, shall be and are hereby repealed.

512.—TABLE

For finding the Distance of an Object by two Bearings, and the Distance run between them.

Difference between Course and Second Bearing in Points.	DIFFERENCE BETWEEN THE COURSE AND FIRST BEARING IN POINTS OF THE COMPASS.																
	2	2½	3	3½	4	4½	5	5½	6	6½	7	7½	8	8½	9	9½	10
3½	1																
4	1.00																
4½	0.81	1.23															
5	0.69	1.00	1.45														
5½	0.60	0.85	1.17	1.66													
6	0.54	0.74	1.00	1.35	1.85												
6½	0.49	0.67	0.88	1.14	1.50	2.02											
7	0.46	0.61	0.79	1.00	1.27	1.64	2.17										
7½	0.43	0.57	0.72	0.90	1.11	1.39	1.77	2.30									
8	0.41	0.53	0.67	0.82	1.00	1.22	1.50	1.87	2.41								
8½	0.40	0.51	0.63	0.76	0.92	1.09	1.31	1.58	1.96	2.50							
9	0.39	0.49	0.60	0.72	0.85	1.00	1.18	1.39	1.66	2.03	2.56						
9½	0.38	0.48	0.58	0.69	0.80	0.93	1.08	1.25	1.46	1.72	2.08	2.60					
10	0.38	0.47	0.57	0.66	0.76	0.88	1.00	1.14	1.31	1.51	1.76	2.11	2.61				
10½	0.38	0.47	0.56	0.65	0.74	0.84	0.94	1.06	1.19	1.35	1.55	1.79	2.12	2.60			
11	0.39	0.47	0.56	0.64	0.72	0.81	0.90	1.00	1.11	1.24	1.39	1.57	1.80	2.11	2.56		
11½	0.40	0.48	0.56	0.63	0.71	0.79	0.87	0.95	1.05	1.15	1.27	1.41	1.58	1.79	2.08	2.50	
12	0.41	0.49	0.57	0.64	0.71	0.78	0.85	0.92	1.00	1,08	1.18	1.29	1.41	1.57	1.76	2.03	2.41
12½	0.43	0.51	0.58	0.65	0.71	0.77	0.83	0.90	0.97	1.03	1.11	1.20	1.29	1.41	1.55	1.72	1.96

The Table is to be entered with the number of points contained between the ships head and the *first* bearing of the object, at the top, and with the number of points, reckoned the same way, between the ship's head and the *second* bearing, at the side; the number in the table at the intersection of the two columns being multiplied by the distance run, is the distance from the object at the time the *last* bearing was taken.

Example.—A Light-house bears N. W., and after running W. by S. 8 miles, it bears N. N. E.; the number of points between W. by S. and N. W. is 5, and that between W. by S. and N. N. E. is 11; then under 5 points at the top, and abreast of 11 points at the side, stands the number 0.9, which being multiplied by 8 gives 7.2 miles, the distance at the time of the last (N. N. E.) bearing.

If the bearings are observed to quarter points, the numbers may be taken out accordingly; this needs no example.

513.—Dimensions of the Masts and Spars of the U. S. Steam-ship Princeton.

Above Deck.				
49 ft. 2 in.	Fore-mast, 70 ft.	Head, 12 ft.		Diameter, 24½ in.
53 ft.	Main-mast, 74 ft.	" 12 ft.		" 25 in.
46 ft. 8 in.	Mizen-mast, 54 ft. 6 in.	" 10 ft.		" 18½ in.
Fore and Main Top-mast, 42 ft.		" 7 ft. 6 in.		Cap, 14¼ in.
Do. Top-gallant M., 22 ft.		Hoist, 14 ft. 6 in.	Royal 9 ft.	Pole-cap, 8½ in.
Mizen Top-mast, 33 ft.		Head, 5 ft. 6 in.		Cap, 11 in.
" Top-gallant Mast, 18 ft.		Hoist, 12 ft.	Royal, 7 ft.	Pole, 6¾ in.

	Ft. In.			Ft. In.		Inch.
Fore and Main Yard - - -	68.	- - - -	Arms,	4.	Sling,	15½
" " Top Yard, - -	54.	- - - -	"	4.6	"	13
" " Top-gal't Yard,	37.	- - - -	"	2.6	"	7¾
" " Royal Yard, -	25.6	- - - -	"	1.3	"	5½
Mizen Yard, - - - - - - -	54.	- - - -	"	4.6	"	13
" Top Yard, - - - -	39.	- - - -	"	3.6	"	9
" Top-gallant Yard, - -	26.6	- - - -	"	1.9	"	6¼
" Royal Yard, - - - -	19.	- - - -	"	1.	"	4
Bowsprit (Outboard), - - -	25.6	- - - -		–	Bed,	25
Jib-boom " - - -	24.	Inb'd, 20 ft.	Head,	3.	Cap,	13½
Flying " " - - -	19.	- - - -	"	5.	"	8
Spanker-boom, - - - - -	47.6	- - - -	"	2.	Slings,	9
Spanker-gaff, - - - - - - -	39.	- - - -	"	8.	"	7
Swinging-booms - - - - -	45.6	- - - - - - - -			"	8
Top-mast Steering-sail Booms,	35.	- - - - - - - -			"	7
T. G. M. " "	28.	- - - - - - - -			"	5½
Royal " "	19.	- - - - - - - -			"	3¾
Lower " Yards,	17.	- - - - - - - -			"	5
Top-mast " "	21.	- - - - - - - -			"	5
T. G. M. " "	16.	- - - - - - - -			"	4
Royal " "	10.	- - - - - - - -			"	3
Mizen Try-sail Mast, - - -	38.	- - - - - - - -			"	7½

	Ft.	In.
The Fore-mast from top of deck to top of kelson is buried, -	20.	4
The Main-mast " " " " " -	20.	7
The Mizen-mast " " " " " -	7.	10
Which leaves the Fore-mast just - - - - -	69.	8
And the Main-mast, - - - - - - - -	73.	7
Length between perpendiculars, - - - - - - .	156,	
Length of Spar-deck, - - - - - - - -	165.	2
Length of Keel, - - - - - - - -	142.	9
Extreme breadth of Beam, - - - - - - - -	30.	
Depth of Hold to Spar-deck, - - - - - - -	21.	8
Dead rise at half breadth, - - - - - - - -	2.	3½

514.—A Table of the Size of Short-link Chain, when used as Rigging.

NAMES OF CHAIN.	SHIPS OF THE LINE.		1ST CLASS FRIGATES.		1ST CLASS SLOOPS.		BRIGS.	
Bobstay	1¼ in.		1⅛ in.		1 in.		⅞ in.	
Bowsprit Shrouds to clear the chain cable	1⅛		1		⅞		¾	
Gammoning (if chains are used)	1		⅞		¾		⅝	
Martingale Stays	⅞		⅞		¾		⅝	
" Guys or Back-rope	¾		¾		⅝		½	
Bumkin Braces	1⅛		1		¾		⅝	
Shank Painter	1		1		⅞		⅝	
Cat-Stoppers	1⅛		1		⅞		¾	
Slings for Fore and Main Yards	Single Part. 1½ in.	Doub. Part. 1⅛ in.						
" Cross-Jack Yard	1⅛	⅞						
" Top-sail Tyes		⅞						
Slings for Top-sail Sheets	Outer Half. ⅞ in.	Inner Half. ¾ in.	Outer Half. ¾ in.	Inner Half. ⅝ in.	Outer Half. ⅝ in.	Inner Half. ½ in.	Outer Half. ½ in.	Inner Half. ⅜ in.
Preventer Slings for Yards	Fore & Main. 1¼ in.	Cr. Jack. ⅞ in.	Fore & Main. 1⅛ in.	Cr. Jack. ¾ in.	Fore & Main. 1 in.	Cr. Jack. ⅝ in.	Fore and Main. ¾ in.	
Guys for Quarter-boat's Davits		⅝		½		⅜	¼	
Topping-lifts to Quarter Davits*		¾		⅝		½	⅜	

* If the Topping-lifts are fitted with a span, a reduction of one-third in the size of the chain for span will be necessary.

A Table of the Size of Short-link Chain, when used as Rigging—*Concluded.*

NAMES OF CHAIN.	SHIPS OF THE LINE.	1ST CLASS FRIGATES.	1ST CLASS SLOOPS.	BRIGS.
Riding Stoppers - - - - - - - - - - -	1 in	$\frac{7}{8}$ in.	$\frac{3}{4}$ in.	$\frac{5}{8}$ in.
Tyes or Preventer Tyes for Gaffs, - - - - - - -	$1\frac{1}{8}$	1	$\frac{7}{8}$	$\frac{3}{4}$
Sheet Cable, snaps of three tails in tapering lengths of - -	[Triang. Ring & Shack.] 6 feet each.	[Triang. Ring & Shack.] 6 feet each.	[Triang. Ring & Shack.] 6 feet each.	[Triang. Ring & Shack.] 6 feet each.
" " " " in diameter - - - - -	$1\frac{1}{4}$ in., $1\frac{1}{8}$, 1, $\frac{1}{2}$	$2\frac{1}{8}$ in., $1\frac{1}{8}$, 1, $\frac{3}{4}$	1 in., $\frac{5}{8}$, $\frac{1}{2}$, $\frac{3}{8}$	$\frac{7}{8}$ in., $\frac{1}{2}$ $\frac{3}{4}$, $\frac{1}{4}$
Stream Cable, snaps, in tapering lengths of - - - - -	6 feet each.	6 feet each.		
" " in diameter, - - - - - - -	$1\frac{3}{4}$ in., 1, $\frac{3}{4}$, $\frac{1}{2}$	$1\frac{1}{2}$ in., $\frac{3}{4}$, $\frac{5}{8}$, $\frac{3}{8}$		
Fifteen Fathoms of Chain Cable, to connect the snaps and Sheet Cable - - - - - - - - - - - - -	$2\frac{1}{4}$ in.	$2\frac{1}{8}$ in.	1 in.	$\frac{7}{8}$ in.
Ten Fathoms of Chain Cable, to shackle round the Mast - -	2	$1\frac{3}{4}$	1	$\frac{7}{8}$
Fifteen Fathoms of Chain Cable, to connect the snaps and Stream Cable - - - - - - - - - - - - -	$1\frac{3}{4}$	$1\frac{1}{2}$	$1\frac{1}{8}$	$\frac{3}{4}$
Ten Fathoms of Chain Cable, to shackle round the Mast - -	$1\frac{1}{2}$	$1\frac{1}{4}$	$1\frac{1}{8}$	1
Messengers, when chain - - - - - - - - - -	$1\frac{1}{2}$	$1\frac{1}{4}$	$1\frac{1}{8}$	1
Main Rigging, to come down, to clear the heat from the chimney	First Class Steamers. 1 in.	Second Class Steamers. $\frac{3}{4}$ in.		
Mizen " " " " " " " (if necessary) - - - - - - - - - - - -	$\frac{3}{4}$	$\frac{5}{8}$		

NOTE.—One-eighth of an inch of Iron in diameter is more than equal to an inch of Hemp Rope in circumference.

 515.—A Table showing the Dimensions of the Masts

FRENCH SHIPS AS PUBLISHED, AND

	Three-deck Ships.						Two-deck Ships.			
							First Class.			
	AMERICAN.		ENGLISH.		FRENCH.		AMERICAN.		ENGLISH.	
	Length.	Diamet.	Length.	Diamet.	Length.	Diamet.	Length.	Diamet.	Length.	Diamet.
	Ft. In.	Inch.	Ft. In.	Inch	Ft. In.	Inch	Ft. In.	Inch.	Ft. In.	Inch
Length of Lower-deck - -	–	–	205.	–	206.6	–	–	–	193.10	–
Breadth Extreme - - - -	–	–	54.6	–	59.6	–	–	–	51.5	–
Main Mast to the hound -	132.	41.	106.7	41	109.8	41½	124.6	40.	101.7	39¾
Main Mast head - - - -	22.	–	20.7	–	18.1	–	20.	–	19.8	–
Main Top-mast to the hound	70.	21.5	64.11	22	68.5	23⅝	70.	21.5	59.8	20¾
Main Top-mast head - -	12.	–	10.1	–	9.4	–	12.	–	9.7	–
Main Top-gallant Mast to the hound - - - - -	41.	12.	33.	12⅛	35.2	12¾	41.	12.	30.5	11½
Main Top-gallant Mast pole - - - - - - - -	24.	9.5	23.	–	19.2	–	24.	9.5	21.6	–
Fore Mast to the hound -	120.	37.	98.11	38	102.2	39⅝	115.	36.5	92.6	37
Fore Mast head - - . -	20.	–	19.1	–	17.	–	18.	–	18.6	–
Fore Top-mast to the hound	63.	21.5	52.2	22	62.10	23⅝	63.	21.5	53.10	20⅜
Fore Top-Mast head - -	10.6	–	9.2	–	8.6	–	10.6	–	8.8	
Fore Top-gallant Mast to the hound - - - - -	37.6	12.	30.1	11	30.11	11¼	37.6	12.	26.4	10
Fore Top-gallant Mast pole - - - - - - - -	22.	8.7½	21.	–	17.	–	22.	8.7½	20.	–
Mizen Mast to the hound -	110.	27.	73.4	25	76.7	27⅛	105.	26.5	71.2	25⅝
Mizen Mast head - - -	17.	–	12.9	–	11.8	–	16.	–	12.10	–
Mizen Top mast to the hound	55.	16.5	46.6	14½	48.	14⅝	55.	16.5	43.9	14
Mizen Top-mast head - -	9.	–	7.4	–	6.4	–	9.	–	7.	–
Mizen Top-gallant Mast to the hound - - - - -	33.6	9.5	22.	8⅝	27.11	9¼	33.6	9.5	21.7	8½
Mizen Top-gallant Mast pole - - - - - - - -	20.	7.	15.	–	14.11	–	20.	7.	17.6	–
Main Yard - - - - -	110.	24.	109.3	26	117.	27⅝	107.6	23.5	103.3	24¾
Fore Yard - - - - - - -	100.	23.	95.	22⅜	106.6	25½	96.	21.5	89.9	21½
Cross-Jack Yard - - - -	80.	16.	78.8	16⅞	92.	19⅛	80.	16.	74.3	16
Main Top-sail Yard - -	82.	18.	78.8	16⅞	82.4	17	78.	17.5	74.3	16
Fore Top-sail Yard - - -	75.	16.	69.	14⅜	78.6	17	71.	16.	64.8	13⅞
Mizen Top-sail Yard - -	52.	11.	52.6	11	60.8	13⅞	52.	11.	49.	10⅛
Main Top-gallant Yard -	52.	10.	51.10	10½	54.4	10⅛	52.	10.5	46.	9⅜
Fore Top-gallant Yard -	48.	9.5	46.3	9½	48.11	9	46.	9.5	38.10	8
Mizen Top-gallant Yard -	33.	6.	36.3	7½	42.7	8½	33.	6.5	34.	7
Bowsprit - - - - - - -	81.	–	75.1	37	74.6	40⅜	78.	–	71.11	36
Sprit-sail Yard - - - -	52.	11.	69.	14⅜	72.5	16½	52.	11.	64.8	13⅞
Spanker Boom - - - -	60.	13.	74.4	14⅜	–	–	60.	13.	70.2	13⅞
Gaff - - - - - - - - -	38.	9.	55.9	12½	–	–	38.	9.	43.	7¾
Jib-Boom - - - - - - -	60.	Cap 16.5	46.3	9½	63.11	17	60.	Cap. 16.5	50.	14½

REDUCED TO ENGLISH MEASURE.

Two-deck Ships.								Frigates.							
1st Class.		2d Class.						AMERICAN.				ENGLISH.		FRENCH.	
FRENCH.		AMERICAN		ENGLISH.		FRENCH.		1st Class.		2d Class.					
Length.	Diamet.	Length.	Diamet.	Length.	Diamet.	Length.	Diamet.	Length.	Diamet.	Length.	Diamet.	Length.	Diamet.	Length.	Diamet.
Ft. In.	Inch	Ft. In.	Inch.	Ft. In.	Inch	Ft. In.	Inch	Ft. In.	Inch.	Ft. In	Inch.	Ft. In.	Inch	Ft. In.	Inch
191.8	–	–	–	176.	–	179.11	–	–	–	–	–	151.5	–	151.2	
50.	–	–	–	47.6	–	47.	–	–	–	–	–	40.1	–	38.4	
105.5	38½	117.	36.5	93.	36	95.8	36⅜	105.	34.6	95.	31.5	77.6	28	81.2	29½
17.	–	20.	–	18.	–	15.11	–	18.	–	16.	–	15.	–	13.1	
65.5	21¾	70.	21.5	56.2	19½	60.2	20¼	63.	19.3	56.	17.	46.10	16⅛	52.10	17½
9.	–	10.	–	9.1	–	9.	–	9.7	–	9.6	–	7.6	–	7.11	
34.2	11¾	41.	12.	29.0½	11	33.	11¼	37.6	11.	33.6	10.	23.8	9	30.11	10⅝
18.1	–	24.	9.5	21.	–	13.	–	22.	8.8	20.	6.6	19.	–	17.	
95.11	36¾	105.	33.	84.9	–	88.5	36½	95.	31.5	86.	28.	71.1	25	72.1	26½
15.11	–	18.	–	16.6	–	14.11	–	16.	–	14.6	–	13.9	–	12.1	
59.11	21¾	63.	21.5	50.	–	57.11	20¼	56.	19.3	51.	17.	41.6	16⅛	48.1	17½
8.2	–	10.6	–	8.	–	7.	–	9.6	–	8.4	–	6.8	–	7.2	
29.10	10⅛	37.6	12.	25.3½	9⅝	29.10	11⅛	33.6	11.	30.	10.	20.5	7¾	27.8	10⅜
15.11	–	22.	8.7½	19.6	–	10.7	–	20.	7.5	18.	6.6	17.6	–	14.11	
67.11	24½	98.	26.	66.7	23⅜	57.	19	84.	24.	76.	20.	57.	19	57.6	19½
10.7	–	16.	–	11.1	–	9.11	–	12.4	–	11.	–	9.11	–	9.6	
46.5	13¾	53.	16.	41.4	13	45.10	13¾	46.4	13.5	41.	12.	35.6¾	11⅞	38.5	12¾
5.11	–	5.9	–	6.8	–	5.4	–	6.8	–	6.	–	5.8¾	–	6.4	
29.10	7⅞	33.6	9.5	21.0½	8	29.7	7⅝	24.6	8.5	21.	6.5	17.11½	6⅞	21.4	7⅝
10.7	–	20.	7.	17.	–	9.6	–	16.6	–	14.	4.6	15.6	–	10.7	
106.6	26⅝	105.	23.5	96.8	22⅝	97.11	27¾	95.	20.	86.6	19.	81.9	18⅞	85.2	20¾
96.6	24⅜	90.	21.	84.8	19⅝	89.5	24⅜	84.	18.5	76.	18.	71.5	16⅜	74.6	17½
96.9	18⅛	80.	16.	70.6	14⅝	89.5	15⅞	66.	14.	65.1	13.	59.	12¼	58.6	12⅛
79.10	17	77.	17.	70.6	14⅝	74.6	15⅜	71.6	16.	65.	15.	59.	12¼	61.9	12½
62.11	15⅞	67.	15.	61.6	12¾	66.	14⅞	62.	14.7	57.	13.	53.4	11½	54.4	11¼
55.4	9½	49.	11.3	46.1	19⅝	66.	13¾	45.	10.	40.	9.	40.8	8¼	47.11	8¼
50.	8½	51.	10.5	45.10	9¼	47.9	7¾	45.	9.5	40.	8.	37.6	7½	40.5	7⅝
44.8	7½	45.	9.4	40.	8½	42.7	7⅜	41.	9.	38.	7.5	32.11	6½	35.4	6⅞
38.4	6⅝	32.	7.	32.	6⅝	36.6	6¼	30.	6.	26.	5.2	28.	5½	30.10	6⅞
69.2	37½	72.	–	61.6	12¾	66.	24⅜	66.	–	60.	–	53.4	11½	55.4	27¾
71.4	16½	49.	10.5	61.6	12¾	64.11	14⅞	44.6	10.	40.	9.	53.4	11½	58.6	11¾
48.11	6⅜	60.	13.	66.	12¾	47.11	5¾	50.	11.	45.	10.	55.8	11		
–	–	38.	9.	50.2	11⅞	–	–	32.	8.	30.	7.	42.5	10		
56.5	13¾	54.	Cap 16.3	40.	8½	53.2	13¼	50.	Cap. 14.3	45.	Cap. 13.	–	–	58.6	12⅜

516.—A Table showing the Complement of Officers and Crew allowed to Vessels of each Class, U. S. N.

Rank or Ratings.	Ships of the Line. 3 Decks.	Ships of the Line. 2 Decks. 1st Class.	Ships of the Line. 2 Decks. 2d Class.	Razees.	Frigates. 32 Pounder.	Frigates. 24 Pounder.	Frigates. 18 Pounder.	Sloops. 32 Pounder.	Sloops. 24 Pounder.	Sloops. 16, 32 lb. Carronades.	Brigs.	Brigantines & Schooners.	Steamers. 1st Class.	Steamers. 2d Class.	Steamers. 3d Class.	Receiving Vessels. Ships of the Line.	Receiving Vessels. Frigates.	Receiving Vessels. Smaller.	Pay per Month.	Remarks.
Captain	1	1	1	1	1	1	1	1 or	–	–	–	–	1	–	–	1			As regulated by law.	(a) To act as Watch Officers if necessary.
Commander	1	1	1	–	–	–	–	1	1	1	1	1	–	1						
Lieutenants	9	6	6	6	5	4	4	3	3	3	2	2	3	2	–	4				
Master	1	1	1	1	1	1	1	*a*1	*a*1	*a*1	*a*1	*a*1	*a*1	*a*1	–	1				
Surgeon	1	1	1	1	1	1	1	1	1	1	–	–	1	–	–	1				
Purser	1	1	1	1	1	1	1	1	1	1	1	1	1	1	–	1				
Chaplain*	1	1	1													1				
Professor of Mathematics	1	1	1	1	1	1	1	1	–	–	–	–	1	–	–	1				
Passed or other Assistant Surgeons	4	3	3	2	2	2	2	1	1	1	1 p'd	1 p'd	1	1 p'd	1	1				
Passed and other Midshipmen	21	18	18	12	12	12	12	8	7	6	3	3	7	5	4	6				
Boatswains	1	1	1	1	1	1	1	1	1	1	–	–	1	–	–	1				
Gunner	1	1	1	1	1	1	1	1	1	1	–	–	1	1	–	1				
Carpenter	1	1	1	1	1	1	1	1	1	1	–	–	1	1	–	1				
Sail-maker	1	1	1	1	1	1	1	1	1	1	–	–	1	–	–	1				
Clerk to Captain or Commanding Officer	1	1	1	1	1	1	1	1	1	1	1	1	1	1	1	1	By special order.	By special order.		
Clerk to Commander	1	1	1																	
Clerk to Purser	1	1	1	1	1	1	1													
Yeoman	1	1	1	1	1	1	1	1	1	1	1	1	1	1	1	1				YEOMEN. $40 in Ships of the Line; 35 in Frigates; 25 in Sloops; 18 in smaller.
Armorer	1	1	1	1	1	1	1	1	1	1	–	–	1	1	–	1				
Ship's Steward	1	1	1	1	1	1	1	1	1	1	1	1	1	1	1	1			$18	
Master at Arms	1	1	1	1	1	1	1	1	1	1	–	–	1	1	–	1			19	ARMORER. $25 in Ships of the Line; 20 in Frigates; 15 in Sloops.
Boatswain's Mates	8	6	6	4	4	4	3	3	2	2	2	2	3	2	1	2	–	–	19	
Gunner's Mates	6	4	4	2	2	2	2	1	1	1	1	1	1	–	1	–	–	–	19	
Amount carried forward	66	55	55	41	40	39	38	30	27	26	15	15	29	20	10	28				

* Razees and Frigates having the Commander of a Squadron on board, are also entitled to a Chaplain.

A Table showing the Complement of Officers and Crew allowed to Vessels of each Class, U. S. N.—*Cont'd.*

Rank or Ratings.	Ships of the Line.			Razees.	Frigates.			Sloops.			Brigs.	Brigantines & Schooners.	Steamers.			Receiving Vessels.			Pay per Month.	Remarks.
	3 Decks.	2 Decks 1st Class.	2 Decks 2d Class.		32 Pounder.	24 Pounder.	18 Pounder.	32 Pounder.	24 Pounder.	16, 32 lb. Carronades.			1st Class.	2d Class.	3d Class.	Ships of the Line.	Frigates.	Smaller.		
Amount brought forward	66	55	55	41	40	39	38	30	27	26	15	15	29	20	10	28				
Carpenter's Mates	4	3	3	2	2	2	2	1	1	1	1	1	1	–	1	–	–	–	$19	
Sail-maker's Mates	2	2	2	1	1	1	1	1	1	1	1	1	1	1	–	–	–	–	15	
Ship's Cook	1	1	1	1	1	1	1	1	1	1	1	1	1	1	–	1	–	–	18	
Coxswain	–	–	–	–	–	–	–	–	–	–	–	–	–	–	–	–	–	–	18	
Quarter-Masters	12	10	10	8	8	8	6	4	4	4	3	3	4	3	2	–	–	–	18	
Quarter-Gunners	24	18	18	12	12	10	8	4	4	4	2	2	4	2	–	–	–	–	15	
Captains of Forecastle	4	4	4	4	4	4	3	2	2	2	1	1	2	2	–	–			18	
Captains of Tops	8	8	8	6	6	6	6	6	4	4	2	1	4	–	–	–			15	
Captains of Afterguard	2	2	2	2	2	2	2	2	2	2	1	1	2	–	–	–			15	
Captains of Hold	2	2	2	2	2	2	2	1	1	1	1	1	1	1	–	1	By special order.	By special order.	15	
Cooper	1	1	1	1	1	1	1	1	1	1	1	1	1	1	–	–			15	
Painter	1	1	1	1	1	1	1	–	–	–	–	–	–	–	–	–			15	
Armorer's Mate	1	1	1	–	–	–	–	–	–	–	1	1	–	–	–	–			15	
Surgeon's Steward	1	1	1	1	1	1	1	1	1	1	1	1	1	1	–	1			18	
Ship's Corporal	3	3	3	2	2	2	2	1	1	1	1	1	1	–	1	1	–	–	15	
Master of Band	1	1	1	1	1	1	1	–	–	–	–	–	–	–	–	–	–	–	18	
Cabin Steward	1	1	1	1	1	1	1	1	1	1	1	1	1	1	1	1	–	–	18	
Cabin Cook	1	1	1	1	1	1	1	1	1	1	1	1	1	1	1	1	–	–	15	
Ward-room-Steward	1	1	1	1	1	1	1	1	1	1	–	–	1	1	1	1	–	–	18	
Ward-room Cook	1	1	1	1	1	1	1	1	1	1	–	–	1	1	1	1	–	–	15	
Seamen	250	200	180	125	110	100	80	42	40	26	15	15	40	10	8	10	–	–	12	
Ordinary Seamen	250	200	180	125	110	100	80	42	40	26	15	15	40	10	8	20	–	–	10	
Landsmen and Boys	374	226	226	151	112	85	52	41	30	19	16	16	30	12	8	40	–	–	9	For landsmen, and $8 to $6 for boys.
Amount carried forward	1011	743	703	490	420	370	291	184	164	124	80	79	166	68	42	106				

A Table showing the Complement of Officers and Crew allowed to Vessels of each Class, U. S. N.—*Cont'd.*

Rank or Ratings.	Ships of the Line.			Razees.	Frigates.			Sloops.			Brigs.	Brigantines & Schooners.	Steamers.			Receiving Vessels.			Pay per month.	Remarks.
	3 decks.	2 decks 1st Class.	2 decks 2d Class.		32 Pounder.	24 Pounder.	18 Pounder.	32 Pounder.	24 Pounder.	16, 32 lb. Carronades.			1st Class.	2d Class.	3d Class.	Ships of the Line.	Frigates.	Smaller.		
Amount brought forward	1011	743	703	490	420	370	291	184	164	124	80	79	166	68	42	106				
Musicians, First Class	8	6	6	6	6	6	5	–	–	–	–	–	–	–	–	–	–	–	$12	
Musicians, Second Class	6	5	5	4	4	4	4	–	–	–	–	–	–	–	–	–	–	–	10	
Chief Engineer	–	–	–	–	–	–	–	–	–	–	–	–	1	1	–	–	–	–		
First Assistant Engineer	–	–	–	–	–	–	–	–	–	–	–	–	2	1	1	–	–	–		
Second Assistant Engineer	–	–	–	–	–	–	–	–	–	–	–	–	2	2	1	–	–	–		
Third Assistant Engineer	–	–	–	–	–	–	–	–	–	–	–	–	2	1	1	–	–	–		
Firemen	–	–	–	–	–	–	–	–	–	–	–	–	18	8	2	–	–	–		
Coal Heavers	–	–	–	–	–	–	–	–	–	–	–	–	18	4	3	–				
Total, excepting Marines	1025	754	714	500	430	380	300	184	164	124	80	79	209	85	50	106	By special order.	By special order.	As regulated by law.	
MARINES.																				
Captains	1	1	1																	
Lieutenants	2	2	2	1	1	1	1	–	–	–	–	–	–	–	–	1	–	–		
Sergeants	4	3	3	3	3	3	3	2	2	2	–	–	2	1	–	3	–	–		
Corporals	4	4	4	4	4	4	3	2	2	2	–	–	2	2	–	3	–	–		
Drummers	2	2	2	1	1	1	1	1	1	1	–	–	1	–	–	1	–	–		
Fifers	2	2	2	1	1	1	1	1	1	1	–	–	1	–	–	1	–	–		
Privates	60	52	52	40	40	40	40	20	20	20	–	–	20	12	–	31	–	–		*Note.*—Special complements will be designated by the Department, for vessels which do not fall under any regular class.
Total Marines	75	66	66	50	50	50	49	26	26	26	–	–	26	15	–	40				
Total complements	1100	820	780	550	480	430	349	210	190	150	80	79	235	100	50	146				

NOTE.—Vessels in which the Commander of a Squadron is embarked, may bear, as supernumeraries in addition to her complement, by order of such commander, one Lieutenant, one Clerk, one Coxswain, one Cabin Cook, one Cabin Steward, one Seaman, and two Ordinary Seamen.

The number allowed, is not to be exceeded in any rating, without the authority of the Secretary of the Navy, unless to make good deficiencies in some superior rating. And vessels, when otherwise ready for sea, are not to be detained on account of deficiencies in their complements, if the whole number of Petty Officers and persons of inferior rating, shall be equal to nine-tenths of the whole number allotted as their complements. The total number is not to be exceeded without the direction or sanction of the Secretary of the Navy.

COMMODORE	C. MORRIS,	*Chief*	*of Bureau,*	*Const., Equip. and Repairs.*
"	L. WARRINGTON,	"	"	*Docks and Yards.*
"	W. M. CRANE,	"	"	*Ordnance and Hydrography.*
"	W. B. SHUBRICK,	"	"	*Provision and Clothing.*
SURGEON	THOMAS HARRIS,	"	"	*Medicine and Surgery.*

The foregoing Table of Complements of Officers and Crews for U. S. Vessels of War, is approved, and will be hereafter regarded as the guide, by which Vessels of War of all classes are to be prepared for sea; excepting that, when there shall be in a Squadron a Frigate, or Vessel of larger class, a Captain of Marines shall be detailed for duty as Commanding Officer of the *Marine Guard* on board said Ship.

J. Y. MASON, *Secretary of the Navy.*

Names of the different Spars.	Ships of the Line.									Razees.		
	THREE DECKS.			TWO DECKS.								
				1st Class.			2d Class.					
	Length.	Diameter.	Masthead.	Length.	Diameter.	Masthead.	Length.	Diameter.	Masthead.	Length.	Diameter.	Masthead.
	Ft. In.	Inch.	Ft. In.	Ft. In.	Inch.	Ft. In.	Ft. In.	Inch.	Ft. In.	Ft. In.	Inch.	Ft. In.
Main Mast - - -	132.	42.7	22.	124.6	40.2	20.	117.	36.8	20.	113.	36.8	20.
Main Top-mast - -	70.	21.5	12.	70.	21.5	12.	70.	21.5	12.	70.	21.5	12.
Main Top-gallant Mast - - - -	35.	12.	–	35.	12.	–	35.	12.	–	35.	12.	–
Main Royal Mast -	23.6	–	–	23.6	–	–	23.6	–	–	23.6	–	–
Main Flag Pole -	9.¾	4.	–	9.¾	4.	–	9.¾	4.	–	9.¾	4.	–
Fore mast - - -	120.	38.8	20.	115.	36.8	8.	105.	34.	18.	101.	34.	18.
Fore Top-mast - -	63.	21.5	10.6	63.	21.5	10.6	63.	21.5	10.6	63.	21.5	10.6
Fore Top-gallant Mast - - - -	32.	12.	–	32.	12.	–	32.	12.	–	32.	12.	–
Fore Royal Mast -	21.4	–	–	21.4	–	–	21.4	–	–	21.4	–	–
Fore Flag Pole - -	8.6	4.	–	8.6	4.	–	8.6	4.	–	8.6	4.	–
Mizen Mast - - -	110.	27.5	17.	105.	26.5	16.	98.	26.	16.	94.	26.	16.
Mizen Top-mast -	55.	15.8	9.	55.	15.8	9.	53.	15.3	9.	53.	15.3	9.
Mizen Top-gallant Mast - - - -	29.	9.8	–	29.	9.8	–	29.	9.8	–	29.	9.8	–
Mizen Royal Mast	19.4	–	–	19.4	–	–	19.4	–	–	19.4	–	–
Mizen Flag Pole -	7.9	3.7	–	7.9	3.7	–	7.9	3.7	–	7.9	3.7	–
			Yard Arm.			Yard Arm.			Yard Arm.			Yard Arm.
Main Yard - - -	110.	26.4	5.	107.6	25.7	5.	105.	25.3	5.	105.	25.3	5.
Main Top-sail Yard	82.	20.5	7.	78.	19.5	6.6	77.	19.2	6.6	77.	19.2	6.6
Main Top-gallant Yard - - - -	52.	11.8	2.	52.	11.8	2.	49.	11.2	2.	49.	11.2	2.
Main Royal Yard -	36.	7.2	1.6	36.	7.2	1.6	35.1	7.	1.6	35.1	7.	1.6
Fore Yard - - -	100.	24.	5.	96.	23.	5.	90.	21.6	4.	90.	21.6	4.
Fore Top-sail Yard	75.	18.8	6.6	71.	17.8	6.	67.	16.8	5.6	67.	16.8	5.6
Fore Top-gallant Yard - - - -	48.	10.9	2.	46.	10.7	2.	45.	10.5	2.	45.	10.5	2.
Fore Royal Yard -	33.	6.6	1.6	33.	6.6	1.6	30.5	6.1	1.3	30.5	6.1	1.3
Cross-jack Yard -	80.	16.	7.6	80.	16.	7.6	76.	15.2	7.6	76.	15.2	7.6
Mizen Top-sail Yard	53.	11.1	4.6	53.	11.1	4.6	49.6	10.2	4.	49.6	10.2	4.
Mizen Top-gallant Yard - - - -	33.	6.6	1.6	33.	6.6	1.6	32.	6.4	1.6	32.	6.4	1.6
Mizen Royal Yard	23.	4.6	1.	23.	4.6	1.	21.	4.2	.11	21.	4.2	.11
Sprit-sail Yard - -												
Bow-sprit - - - -	80.	–	–	78.	–	–	72.	–	–	72.	–	–
Jib-boom - - - -	60.	17.8	–	60.	17.8	–	54.	16.	–	54.	16.	–
Flying Jib-boom -	61.	12.	–	61.	12.	–	56.	11.	–	56.	11.	–
Pole - - - - -	9.	–	–	9.	–	–	9.	–	–	9.	–	–

Frigates.						Sloops.								
1st Class.			2d Class.			1st Class.			2d Class.			3d Class.		
Length.	Diameter.	Masthead.	Length.	Diameter.	Masthead.	Length.	Diameter.	Masthead.	Length.	Diameter.	Masthead.	Length.	Diameter.	Masthead.
Ft. In.	Inch.	Ft. In.	Ft. In.	Inch.	Ft. In.	Ft. In.	Inch.	Ft. In.	Ft. In.	Inch	Ft. In.	Ft. In.	Inch.	Ft. In.
105.	34.	18.	95.	30.8	16.	80.	25.8	14.	75.	24.2	12.	72.	24.2	12.
63.	19.3	9.7	56.	17.4	9.6	47.	14.8	7.	45.	14.5	6.9	45.	14.5	6.9
32.	11.	–	29.	10.	–	24.	8.	–	22.	7.5	–	22.	7.5	–
21.8	–	–	19.4	–	–	16.	–	–	14.8	–	–	14.8	–	–
8.8	4.	–	7.9	3.5	–	6.5	3.5	–	6.	3.	–	6.	3.	–
95.	30.8	16.	86.	27.9	14.6	72.	23.3	12.	67.6	21.8	11.	64.6	21.8	11.
56.	19.3	9.6	51.	17.4	8.4	43.	14.6	6.9	42.	14.5	6.4	42.	14.5	6.4
29.	11.	–	25.8	10.	–	23.	8.3	–	21.	7.	–	21.	7.	–
19.4	–	–	17.1	–	–	15.4	–	–	14.	–	–	14.	–	–
7.9	4.	–	6.10	3.5	–	6.	3.5	–	5.7	3.	–	5.7	3.	–
87.	24.8	12.4	79.	21.	11.	66.	18.	10.	63.9	16.	10.	60.9	16.	10.
46.4	13.3	6.8	41.	11.8	6.	37.	11.	6.	32.	9.9	5.	32.	9.9	5.
24.6	8.	–	21.	7.	–	20.	6.5	–	16.	5.3	–	16.	5.3	–
16.4	–	–	14.	–	–	13.4	–	–	10.8	–	–	10.8	–	–
6.6	3.6	–	5.7	3.3	–	5.2	3.3	–	4.3	2.8	–	4.3	2.8	–
		Yard Arm.			Yard Arm.			Yard Arm.			Yard Arm.			Yard Arm.
95.	22.6	4.9	86.6	20.	4.4	75.	17.5	3.9	67.6	15.9	4.	67.6	15.9	4.
71.6	17.8	6.	65.	15.5	5.5	56.	13.4	5.	52.2	12.6	5.	52.2	12.6	5.
44.	10.2	2.	40.	9.	2.	37.	8.4	2.	34.	7.6	2.	34.	7.6	2.
30.	6.	1.6	27.	5.4	1.3	25.	5.	1.	22.9	4.5	.9	22.9	4.5	.9
84.	20.2	4.6	76.	17.9	4.	65.	15.2	3.3	60.9	14.1	3.8	60.9	14.1	3.8
62.	15.5	5.3	57.	13.6	5.	49.	11.5	4.8	46.	11.1	5.	46.	11.1	5.
41.	9.3	2.	38.	8.5	2.	32.	7.3	1.9	30.6	6.8	1.9	30.6	6.8	1.9
27.	5.4	1.3	25.	5.	1.	22.	4.4	.9	20.6	4.1	.8	20.6	4.1	.8
66.	13.2	7.	64.	12.8	7.	53.	10.6	4.9	51.10	10.4	4.	51.10	10.4	4.
46.	9.5	4.	41.	8.5	4.	36.6	7.6	3.6	34.8	7.3	3.3	34.8	7.3	3.3
30.	6.	1.6	26.	5.2	1.4	22.6	4.5	1.4	22.	4.4	1.3	22.	4.4	1.3
19.	3.8	.9	16.	3.2	.8	15.	3.	.6	14.	2.8	.6	14.	2.8	.6
66.	–	–	60.	–	–	50.	–	–	48.	–	–	46.	–	–
50.	14.8	–	45.	13.5	–	38.	11.2	–	34.6	10.	–	34.6	10.	–
54.	10.8	–	45.	9.	–	40.	8.	–	38.9	7.8	–	38.9	7.8	–
8.8	–	–	7.9	–	–	6.5	–	–	6.	–	–	6.	–	–

Names of the different Spars.	Ships of the Line.									Razees.		
	THREE DECKS.			TWO DECKS.								
				1st Class.			2d Class.					
	Length.	Diameter.	Length of Pole.	Length.	Diameter.	Length of Pole.	Length.	Diameter.	Length of Pole.	Length.	Diameter.	Length of Pole.
	Ft. In.	Inch.	Ft. In.	Ft. In.	Inch.	Ft. In.	Ft. In.	Inch.	Ft. In.	Ft. In.	Inch.	Ft. In.
Main Gaff - - -	33.	8.2	–	33.	8.2	–	30.	7.4	–	30.	7.4	–
M'n Top-mast Studding-sail Boom -	55.	11.5	–	53.9	11.	–	52.6	11.	–	52.6	11.	–
Yard for Main Top-mast Studding-sail - - - - -	24.	4.8	–	24.	4.8	–	23.6	4.7	–	23.6	4.7	–
Main Top-gallant Studd'g-sail Boom	41.	8.6	–	39.	8.2	–	38.	6.8	–	38.	6.8	–
Yard for Main Top-gallant Studding-sail - - - - -	24.	4.8	–	24.	4.8	–	23.6	4.7	–	23.6	4.7	–
Fore Gaff - - - -	37.	9.2	–	37.	9.2	–	36.	8.8	–	36.	8.8	–
Lower Swinging Boom - - - -	65.	13.	–	60.	12.	–	58.	11.6	–	58.	11.6	–
Yard for Lower Studding-sail - - -	32.6	6.5	–	30.	6.	–	29.	5.8	–	29.	5.8	–
Fore Top-mast Studding-sail Boom -	50.	10.5	–	48.	10.	–	45.	9.4	–	45.	9.4	–
Yard for Fore Top-mast Studding-sail - - - - -	31.	6.2	–	29.9	6.	–	28.	5.6	–	28.	5.6	–
Fore Top-gall't Studding-sail Boom -	37.6	7.8	–	35.	7.4	–	33.6	7.	–	33.6	7.	–
Yard for Fore Top-gallant Studding-sail - - - - -	22.	4.4	–	21.	4.2	–	20.6	4.	–	20.6	4.	–
Spanker Boom - -	60.	12.5	–	60.	12.5	–	57.	11.8	–	57.	11.8	–
Ring-tail Boom - -	30.	6.	–	30.	6.	–	28.6	5.7	–	28.6	5.7	–
Mizen Gaff - - -	38.	9.4	5.	38.	9.4	5.	35.	8.6	5.	35.	8.6	5.
Square-sail Boom -	–	–	–	–	–	–	–	–	–	–	–	–
Yard for Square-sail - - - - -	–	–	–	–	–	–	–	–	–	–	–	–
Jack Gaff - - - -	17.	6.	–	16.	5.5	–	16.	5.5	–	16.	5.5	–
Dolphin Striker - -	22.	9.	3.	20.	8.5	3.	20.	8.5	3.	20.	8.5	3.

Frigates.						Sloops.								
1st Class.			2d Class.			1st Class.			2d Class.			3d Class.		
Length.	Diameter.	Length of Pole.	Length.	Diameter.	Length of Pole.	Length.	Diameter.	Length of Pole.	Length.	Diameter.	Length of Pole.	Length.	Diameter.	Length of Pole.
Ft. In.	Inch.	Ft. In.	Ft. In.	Inch.	Ft. In.	Ft. In.	Inch.	Ft. In.	Ft. In.	Inch	Ft. In.	Ft. In.	Inch.	Ft. In.
28.6	7.1	–	27.	6.8	–	19.5	5.	–	17.	4.4	–	17.	4.4	–
47.6	9.9	–	43.3	9.	–	37.6	7.8	–	33.9	7.	–	33.9	7.	–
20.	4.	–	18.	3.6	–	16.6	3.3	–	15.	3.	–	15.	3.	–
35.9	7.4	–	32.6	6.8	–	28.	5.8	–	26.	5.4	–	26.	5.4	–
20.	4.	–	18.	3.6	–	16.6	3.3	–	15.	3.	–	15.	3.	–
33.6	8.3	–	33.	8.2	–	26.	6.4	–	25.	6.2	–	25.	6.2	–
51.3	10.2	–	46.3	9.2	–	42.	8.4	–	40.9	8.2	–	40.9	8.2	–
25.6	5.	–	23.	4.6	–	21.	4.2	–	20.4	4.	–	20.4	4.	–
42.	8.8	–	38.	8.	–	32.6	6.8	–	30.3	6.4	–	30.3	6.4	–
25.9	5.2	–	23.6	4.7	–	19.10	4.	–	18.	3.6	–	18.	3.6	–
31.	6.5	–	28.6	6.	–	24.6	5.2	–	23.	4.9	–	23.	4.9	–
18.6	3.7	–	17.	3.4	–	14.	3.3	–	13.6	2.7	–	13.6	2.7	–
50.	10.5	–	45.	9.5	–	35.	7.7	–	34.	7.4	–	34.	7.4	–
25.	5.	–	22.6	4.5	–	17.6	3.5	–	17.	3.4	–	17.	3.4	–
32.	7.8	4.6	30.	7.4	4.6	28.	6.8	4.	26.	6.4	4.	26.	6.4	4.
–	–	–	–	–	–	–	–	–	–	–	–	–	–	–
–	–	–	–	–	–	–	–	–	–	–	–	–	–	–
14.	4.2	–	14.	4.2	–	13.	3.7	–	11.	3.2	–	11.	3.2	–
18.	7.5	2.	18.	7.5	2.	15.	7.	2.	14.	6.3	1.8	14.	6.3	1.8

Names of the different Spars.	Brigs.			Brigantines.			Schooners.			Remarks.
	Length.	Diameter.	Masthead.	Length.	Diameter.	Masthead.	Length.	Diameter.	Masthead.	
	Ft. In.	Inch.	Ft. In.	Ft. In.	Inch.	Ft. In.	Ft. In.	Inch.	Ft. In.	
Main Mast - - -	72.2	22.6	12.2	76.	20.	8.	78.8	20.3	8.	
Main Top-mast - -	40.6	12 6	6.9	21.	6.3	–	26.2	7.5		
Main Top-gallant Mast - - - -	20.3	7.2	–	14.	5.2	–	13.1	5.		
Main Royal Mast -	13.4	–	–	6.6						
Main Flag Pole -	5.4	2.5	–	5.4	–	–	6.	2.5	–	Diameter at the Truck.
Fore Mast - - -	64.8	22.	11.3	55.	18.7	9.2	75.8	21.3	8.	
Fore Top-mast - -	40.6	12.6	6.9	32.6	10.4	5.6	26.2	7.5		
Fore Top-gall't Mast	20.3	7.2	–	18.3	6.8	–	13.1	5.		
Fore Royal Mast -	13.6	–	–	12.						
Fore Flag Pole - -	5.4	2.5	–	5.	–	–	6.	2.5	–	Diameter at the Truck.
Mizen Flag Pole -	–	–	–	–	–	–	–	–	–	Diameter at the Truck.
			Yard Arm.			Yard Arm.			Yard Arm.	
Main Yard - - -	59.6	14.	3.	35.6	8.	2.9				
Main Top-sail Yard	44.7	10.6	3.8	24.6	5.5	1.4				
Main Top-gal't Yard	28.4	6.5	1.4	16.3	3.2	.9				
Main Royal Yard -	18.11	3.6	.9							
Fore Yard - - -	59.6	14.	3.	45.	10.1	2.9	50.	11.3	2.6	
Fore Top-sail Yard	44.7	10.7	3.8	33.6	7.7	3.	33.4	7.4	2.6	
Fore Top-gall't Yard	28.4	6.5	1 4	22.	4.5	1.6	22.2	4.5	1.	
Fore Royal Yard -	18.11	4.	.9	14.9	3.	.9				
Sprit-sail Yard - -										
Bow-sprit - - - -	42.	–	–	17.6	Out	b'rd.	29.1	18.		
Jib-boom - - - -	32.5	9.5	–	14.	Out	b'rd.	37.	11.		
Flying Jib-boom -	34.5	6.8	–	12.	Out	b'rd.				
Pole - - - - - -	5.4	–	–	3.4						
			L'gth Pole.			L'gth Pole.			L'gth Pole.	
Main Gaff - - -	39.8	9.8	5.	25.	8.5	5.	25.	8.5	5.	Poles to the M'n Gaffs of Brigs, Brigantines and Sch'ners are not included in the lengths given.
M'n Top-mast Studding-sail Boom -	29.	6.								
Yard for Main Top-mast Studding-sail	12.10	2.6								
Main Top-gallant Studd'g-sail Boom	22.3	4.6								
Yard for Main Top-gal't Studding-sail	12.10	2.6								
Fore Gaff - - - -	25.	6.2	–	24.	8.	–	25.	8.		
Lower Swinging Boom - - - -	31.6	6.4	–	22.	4.6	–	22.	4.6		
Yard for Lower Studding-sail - - -	15.3	3.	–	11.	2.6	–	11.	2.6		
Fore Top-mast Studding-sail Boom -	29.9	6.2	–	22.6	4.8	–	25.	5.3		
Yard for Fore Top-mast Studding-sail	18.7	3.8	–	13.9	3.	–	14.2	3.		
Fore Top-gall't Studding-sail Boom -	22.3	4.7	–	16.9	3.6	–	16.8	3.6		
Yard for Fore Top-gall'nt Studd'g-sail	12.10	2.6	–	9.6	2.	–	10.1	2.2		
Spanker Boom - -	59.6	13.	–	50.	11.	–	50.	11.		
Square-sail Boom -	–	–	–	–	–	–	45.	9.7		
Yard for Square-sail	–	–	–	–	–	–	22.8	5.		
Jack Gaff - - - -	9.	3.	–	9.	3.	–	9.	3.		
Dolphin Striker - -	–	–	–	–	–	–	–	–	–	Length for Brigs and Schooners gov'd by Steeve of Bowsprit.

A Cordage Table of Feet and Fathoms.

Feet.	Fath.	Feet.	Fath.	Feet.	Fath.	Feet.	Fath.	Feet.	Fath.	Feet.	Fath.	Feet.	Fath.
30	5 0	155	25 5	280	46 4	405	67 3	530	88 2	655	109 1	780	130 0
35	5 5	160	26 4	285	47 3	410	68 2	535	89 1	660	110 0	785	130 5
40	6 4	165	27 3	290	48 2	415	69 1	540	90 0	665	110 5	790	131 4
45	7 3	170	28 2	295	49 1	420	70 0	545	90 5	670	111 4	795	132 3
50	8 2	175	29 1	300	50 0	425	70 5	550	91 4	675	112 3	800	133 2
55	9 1	180	30 0	305	50 5	430	71 4	555	92 3	680	113 2	805	134 1
60	10 0	185	30 5	310	51 4	435	72 3	560	93 2	685	114 1	810	135 0
65	10 5	190	31 4	315	52 3	440	73 2	565	94 1	690	115 0	815	135 5
70	11 4	195	32 3	320	53 2	445	74 1	570	95 0	695	115 5	820	136 4
75	12 3	200	33 2	325	54 1	450	75 0	575	95 5	700	116 4	825	137 3
80	13 2	205	34 1	330	55 0	455	75 5	580	96 4	705	117 3	830	138 2
85	14 1	210	35 0	335	55 5	460	76 4	585	97 3	310	118 2	835	139 1
90	15 0	215	35 5	340	56 4	465	77 3	590	98 2	715	119 1	840	140 0
95	15 5	220	36 4	345	57 3	470	78 2	595	99 1	720	120 0	845	140 5
100	16 4	225	37 3	350	58 2	475	79 1	600	100 0	725	120 5	850	141 4
105	17 3	230	38 2	355	59 1	480	80 0	605	100 5	730	121 4	855	142 3
110	18 2	235	39 1	360	60 0	485	80 5	610	101 4	735	122 3	860	143 2
115	19 1	240	40 0	365	60 5	490	81 4	615	102 3	740	123 2	865	144 1
120	20 0	245	40 5	370	61 4	495	82 3	620	103 2	745	124 1	870	145 0
125	20 5	250	41 4	375	62 3	500	83 2	625	104 1	750	125 0	875	145 5
130	21 4	255	42 3	380	63 2	505	84 1	630	105 0	755	125 5	880	146 4
135	22 3	260	43 2	385	64 1	510	85 0	635	105 5	760	126 4	885	147 3
140	23 2	265	44 1	390	65 0	515	85 5	640	106 4	765	127 3	890	148 2
145	24 1	270	45 0	395	65 5	520	86 4	645	107 3	770	128 2	895	149 1
150	25 0	275	45 5	400	66 4	525	87 3	650	108 2	775	129 1	900	150 0

Weight of Cables of 120 fathoms from 3 to 25 inches.

Three inch cable weighs 252 pounds; 3½ inch, 336 pounds; 4, 448; 4½, 560; 5, 700; 5½, 840; 6, 1008; 6½, 1176; 7, 1340; 7½, 1568; 8, 1792; 8½, 2016; 9, 2268; 9½, 2520; 10, 2800; 10½, 3080; 11, 3388; 11½, 3696; 12, 4032; 12½, 4368; 13, 4732; 13½, 5056; 14, 5480; 14½, 5880; 15, 6328; 15½, 6720; 16, 7168; 16½, 7616; 17, 8092; 17½, 8568; 18, 9072; 18½, 9520; 19, 10108; 19½, 10640; 20, 11200; 20½, 11760; 21, 12348; 21½, 12936; 22, 13452; 22½, 14168; 23, 14840; 23½, 15456; 24, 16128; 25, 17500.

518.—A Table showing the Dimensions of Materials, used in constructing Tops, Trestle-trees, Cross-trees, and Caps, U. S. N.

Dimensions of Tops.	Ships of the Line.						Frigates.						Sloops.						Brigs.		
	Fore and Main Top.			Mizen Top.			Fore and Main Top.			Mizen Top.			Fore and Main Top.			Mizen Top.			Fore and Main Top.		
	Breadth, Inches.	Thickness, Inches.	Tapered to Inches.	Breadth, Inches.	Thickness, Inches.	Tapered to Inches.	Breadth, Inches.	Thickness, Inches.	Tapered to Inches.	Breadth, Inches.	Thickness, Inches.	Tapered to Inches.	Breadth, Inches.	Thickness, Inches.	Tapered to Inches.	Breadth, Inches.	Thickness, Inches.	Tapered to Inches.	Breadth, Inches.	Thickness, Inches.	Tapered to Inches.
Plank in two thicknesses (if White Pine) - - - - - -	–	$1\frac{1}{2}$	–	–	$1\frac{1}{5}$	–	–	$1\frac{1}{4}$	–	–	1	–	–	1	–	–	$\frac{7}{8}$	–	–	$\frac{7}{8}$	–
Plank in two thicknesses (if Yellow Pine) - - - - - -	–	$1\frac{1}{4}$	–	–	1	–	–	$1\frac{1}{8}$	–	–	$\frac{7}{8}$	–	–	$\frac{7}{8}$	–	–	$\frac{3}{4}$	–	–	$\frac{3}{4}$	–
Rim of White Oak - - - -	13	$2\frac{1}{2}$	–	10	$1\frac{3}{4}$	–	11	2	–	8	$1\frac{1}{4}$	–	9	$1\frac{1}{2}$	–	6	1	–	7	$1\frac{1}{4}$	–
Lubber-board of White Oak -	9	3	–	8	$2\frac{1}{2}$	–	8	$2\frac{3}{4}$	–	7	$1\frac{3}{4}$	–	7	2	–	5	$1\frac{1}{4}$	–	6	$1\frac{3}{4}$	–
Battons of White Oak - - -	$3\frac{1}{2}$	$3\frac{1}{2}$	$2\frac{1}{2}$	3	$2\frac{3}{4}$	2	3	3	2	$2\frac{1}{2}$	$2\frac{1}{2}$	$1\frac{1}{2}$	$2\frac{1}{2}$	$2\frac{1}{2}$	$1\frac{1}{2}$	2	2	$1\frac{1}{4}$	2	2	$1\frac{1}{4}$
Iron Plates - - - - - -	5	$\frac{1}{2}$	–	$4\frac{1}{2}$	$\frac{7}{16}$	–	$4\frac{1}{2}$	$\frac{7}{16}$	–	4	$\frac{3}{8}$	–	4	$\frac{3}{8}$	–	$3\frac{1}{2}$	$\frac{5}{16}$	–	$3\frac{1}{2}$	$\frac{5}{16}$	–
Upper Cross-trees - - - -	–	$6\frac{1}{4}$	4	–	5	$3\frac{1}{2}$	–	$5\frac{1}{2}$	$3\frac{1}{2}$	–	4	3	–	$4\frac{1}{2}$	3	–	$3\frac{1}{2}$	$2\frac{1}{2}$	–	4	$2\frac{1}{2}$

NOTE.—The Breadth of Upper Cross-trees, same as lower.

NOTE.—These Cross-trees to be fayed down over the Battons, and secured to the Lower Cross-trees by bolts at each end, and by four Staples and Toggles, so that they may be readily removed when it is necessary to lift the top. The Strap and Eye-bolts for the lower lifts to be placed on the caps, abreast of the middle of the Top-mast hole.

PROPORTIONS FOR TOPS, TRESTLE-TREES, CROSS-TREES AND CAPS.

MAIN TOP.—*Breadth.* One-half the moulded breadth of beam.

FORE TOP.—Nine-tenths of Main Top.

MIZEN TOP.—Four-fifths of Fore Top.

All Tops must be in length two-thirds of their breadth, and must be made light, with upper Cross-trees upon the Top over the lower ones, fayed down on the Battons and keyed together.

LOWER TRESTLE-TREES.—*Length.* The length of their respective Tops.
Depth. Three-fifths of their respective masts at the partners.
Breadth or Thickness. One-half their depth.

LOWER CROSS-TREES.—*Length.* Breadth of their respective Tops.
Breadth. Breadth of their respective Trestle-trees.
Depth or Thickness. Two-thirds of their breadth.

TOPMAST TRESTLE-TREES.—*Length.* To be governed by the Cross-trees and Chocks.
Breadth. Seven-twelfths of Lower Trestle-trees of their respective masts.
Depth. Seven-twelfths of Lower Trestle-trees of their respective masts.

TOPMAST CROSS-TREES.—*Length after Horn.* Four-sixths of the Lower After Cross-trees of their respective masts.
Length forward Horn. Five-sixths of after one.
Breadth. Breadth of their respective Trestle-trees.
Depth or Thickness. Four-fifths of Breadth. The Horns to sweep nine inches in sixteen feet.

BOWSPRIT CAP.—*Length.* Four times the diameter of the Jib-boom.
Breadth. One diameter and a-half of the Jib-boom.
Thickness. One-half the Breadth.

LOWER CAP.—*Length.* Four times the diameter of the Top-mast.
Breadth. One diameter and four-sixths of the Top-mast.
Thickness. One-half the Breadth.

TOPMAST CAP.—*Length.* To be governed by the Cross-trees, Chocks, and Masts.
Breadth. One diameter and four-sixteenths of the Top-gallant Mast.
Thickness. One-half the Breadth.

519.—A Table showing the Complement and Quality of Boats allowed to each Class of Vessels, U. S. N.

Names of Boats.	Ships of the Line.									Razees.			Frigates.						Sloops.		
	THREE DECKS.			TWO DECKS. First Class.			TWO DECKS. Second Class.						First Class.			Second Class.			First Class.		
	Length.	Depth.	Breadth.	Length.	Depth.	Breadth.	Length.	Depth.	Breadth.	Length.	Depth.	Breadth.	Length.	Depth.	Breadth.	Length.	Depth.	Breadth.	Length.	Depth.	Breadth.
	Ft In.	Ft. In.	Ft. In.	Ft. In.	Ft. In.	Ft. In.	Ft. In.	Ft. In.	Ft. In.	Ft. In.	Ft. In.	Ft. In.	Ft. In.	Ft. In.	Ft. In.	Ft. In.	Ft. In.	Ft. In.	Ft. In.	Ft. In.	Ft. In.
1st Launch - -	40.	4.6	10.8	38.	4.5	10.1	36.	4.4	9.7	36.	4.4	10.1	34.	4.2	9.6	32.	4.	9.	30.	3.10	8.5
2d Launch - -	40.	4.6	10.8	38.	4.5	10.1	36.	4.4	9.7	33.	4.	9.	31.	3.10	8.5	29.	3.7	7.10	–	–	–
1st Cutter - - -	36.	3.6	9.6	34.	3.5	9.	33.	3.2	8.9	30.	3.	7.11	28.	2.10	7.5	26.6	2.8	7.	27.6	2.10	7.5
2d Cutter - - -	36.	3.6	9.6	34.	3.5	9.	33.	3.2	8.9	27.6	2.9	7.2	25.6	2.7	6.8	24.	2.4	6.3	25.	2.6	6.8
3d Cutter - - -	33.	3.2	8.5	28.	2.6	7.	28.	2.6	7.	27.	2.6	6.9	27.	2.6	6.9	–	–	–	26.	2.4	6.6
4th Cutter - -	33.	3.2	8.5	28.	2.6	7.	28.	2.6	7.	–	–	–	–	–	–	–	–	–	26.	2.4	6.6
5th Cutter - -	30.	2.7	7.6	–	–	–	–	–	–	–	–	–	–	–	–	–	–	–	25.	2.3	6.
6th Cutter - -	30.	2.7	7.6																		
1st Whale-boat -	30.	2.9	7.8	29.	2.8	7.5	29.	2.8	7.5	28.	2.5	7.2	28.	2.5	7.2	28.	2.5	7.2			
2d Whale-boat -	30.	2.9	7.8	29.	2.8	7.5	29.	2.8	7.5												
Barge - - - -	38.	2.8	7.2	35.6	2.7	6.9	34.	2.6	6.6	34.	2.6	6.6	28.	2.4	6.	28.	2.4	6.			
Gig - - - - -	38.	2.	5.6	36.	1.11	5.4	34.	1.10	5.2	34.	1.10	5.2	28.	1.8	5.	28.	1.8	5.			

All boat's bottoms are to be boarded with cypress and to be copper-fastened; their stem and stern plates are also to be made of copper.

Gigs, Barges, Waist and Quarter-boats are to have copper knees.

Launches, First and Second Cutters, for three-deck ships, are to be fitted without knees; the clamps are to be made sufficiently strong for the athwart bolts to pass through them and forelock; the ends of the athwarts are to be fitted with iron plates.

Launches and First Cutters for Ships of the Line of two decks, Razees, Frigates, and first-class Sloops of War, and Launches for second and third class Sloops, Steamers, Brigs and Brigantines, are to be fitted as the Launches for three-deck ships.

All Launches are to be coppered.

Barges, Gigs, Whale-boats and Cutters are to be fitted with composition row-locks.

Schooners' Launches will be of the size allowed to Brigs, when the breadth of beam and deck arrangements will permit.

A Table showing the Complement and Quality of Boats allowed to each Class of Vessels, U. S. N.—*Conc'd.*

Names of Boats.	Sloops.						Brigs.			Brigantines.			Schooners.			Steamers.					
	Second Class.			Third Class.												First Class.			Second Class.		
	Length.	Depth.	Breadth.	Length.	Depth.	Breadth.	Length.	Depth.	Breadth.	Length.	Depth.	Breadth.	Length.	Depth.	Breadth.	Length.	Depth.	Breadth.	Length.	Depth.	Breadth.
	Ft. In.	Ft. In.	Ft. In.	Ft. In.	Ft. In.	Ft. In.	Ft. In.	Ft. In.	Ft. In.	Ft. In.	Ft. In.	Ft. In.	Ft. In.	Ft. In.	Ft. In.	Ft. In.	Ft. In.	Ft. In.	Ft. In.	Ft. In.	Ft. In.
1st Launch - -	29.	3.8	8.3	26.	3.4	7.4	24.	3.	6.10	24.	3.	6.10	–	–	–	34.	4.1	9.6	30.	3.10	8.5
2d Launch - -	–	–	–	–	–	–	–	–	–	–	–	–	–	–	–	31.	3.10	8.5			
1st Cutter - - -	26.6	2.9	7.2	24.	2.8	6.6	22.	2.6	6.	22.	2.6	6.	22.	2.6	6.	30.	2.7	7.6	27.6	2.10	7.5
2d Cutter - - -	26.	2.4	6.6	25.	2.3	6.	22.	2.2	5.6	22.	2.1	5.6	22.	1.11	5.3	27.	2.6	6.9	26.	2.4	6.3
3d Cutter - - -	26.	2.4	6.6	25.	2.3	6.	22.	2.2	5.6	22.	2.1	5.6	22.	1.11	5.3	27.	2.6	6.9	26.	2.4	6.3
4th Cutter - -	25.	2.2	6.	24.	2.2	5.10	–	–	–	–	–	–	–	–	–	–	–	–	25.	2.3	6.
1st Whale-boat -	–	–	–	–	–	–	–	–	–	–	–	–	–	–	–	29.	2.8	7.5			
Gig - - - - -	–	–	–	–	–	–	–	–	–	–	–	–	–	–	–	32.	1.9	5.1			

Second class Steamers' Launches and First Cutters will be of the size allowed to second class Sloops of War, when these will stow to better advantage than those designated.

In fitting the dead wood and aprons of boats that stow in nests, boat-builders will see that no unnecessary wood is used about them, and that the keels are reduced forward and aft, to make the bottom of keel convex, so that the boats may be stowed as low as possible.

All boats are to have two ring-bolts through their stem and stern posts; the lower bolts to be from nine to twelve inches below the upper ones, with an oblong ring to be of the same height as the upper ones when they are both turned up; and all Launches are to be fitted with a ring-bolt one-fifth from each end, and another amid-ships down through the keel, to be well clinched on the outside.

Rollers forward and aft in all First Launches, are to be of length sufficient to take the chain of their respective ships; the rollers of Second Launches are to be five inches in length.

The timbers of Second Launches are to be one-third larger than those of First Cutters of the old class, and the rest of the materials are to be in like proportion to make a light Launch.

All Launches are to be fitted with wells and self-fleeting windlasses amid-ships,.for weighing anchors.

All Whale-boats are to be lap-streaked, or clinker-built.

520.—A Table showing the Weight, Size, Length, and Quantity of Anchors, Cables, Hawsers, &c., &c., allowed to the different Classes of Vessels, U. S. N.

Names of Articles.	Ships of the Line.						Razees.		Frigates.				Sloops.	
	THREE DECKS.		TWO DECKS. First Class.		TWO DECKS. Second Class.				First Class.		Second Class.		First Class.	
	No.	Weight.	No.	Weight.	No.	Weight.	No.	Weight.	No.	Weight.	No.	Weight.	No.	Weight.
ANCHORS, &c.														
Sheets	2	10,000	2	9,000	2	8,500	2	8,000	2	7,000	2	5,500	2	3,800
Bowers	2	} 10,000	2	} 9,000	2	} 8,500	2	} 8,000	2	} 7,000	2	} 5,500	2	3,800
Spare	1		1		1		1		1		1		—	—
Stream	1	3,000	1	2,800	1	2,400	1	2,000	1	1,600	1	1,300	1	1,000
Kedges	5	1 of 1,400 1 of 1,300 1 of 1,100 1 of 900 1 of 700	4	1 of 1,200 1 of 900 1 of 700 1 of 500	4	1 of 1,100 1 of 900 1 of 700 1 of 500	4	1 of 1,000 1 of 800 1 of 600 1 of 500	4	1 of 900 1 of 700 1 of 600 1 of 400	4	1 of 800 1 of 700 1 of 600 1 of 400	3	1 of 600 1 of 450 1 of 300
BOAT ANCHORS.														
1st Launch,	1	300	1	220	1	200	1	200	1	180	1	150	1	130
2d Launch	1	200	1	180	1	160	1	150	1	120	1	100	1	80
1st Cutter	1	150	1	100	1	100	1	100	1	80	1	60	1	50
2d Cutter	1	100	1	100	1	80	1	80	1	60	1	50		
3d Cutter	1	75	1	70	1	60								
4th Cutter	1	50	1	50	1									
Grapnels	2	1 of 150 1 of 80	2	1 of 150 1 of 80	2	1 of 150 1 of 80	2	1 of 150 1 of 80	2	1 of 100 1 of 60	2	1 of 100 1 of 50	2	1 of 80 1 of 40

A Table showing the Weight, Size, Length, and Quantity of Anchors, Cables, Hawsers, &c., &c., allowed to the different Classes of Vessels, U. S. N.—*Cont'd.*

Names of Articles.	Ships of the Line.									Razeès.			Frigates.						Sloops.		
	THREE DECKS.			TWO DECKS.									First Class.			Second Class.			First Class.		
				First Class.			Second Class.														
	No.	Inch.	Fathoms each.	No.	Inch.	Fathoms each.	No.	Inch.	Fathoms each.	No.	Inch.	Fathoms each.	No.	Inch.	Fathoms each.	No.	Inch.	Fathoms each.	No.	Inch.	Fathoms each.
CABLES.																					
Sheets (hemp) - - -	2	25	120	2	24	120	2	23	120	2	$22\frac{1}{2}$	120	1	22	120	1	21	120	1	17	120
Sheets (chain) - - -	1	$2\frac{1}{4}$	180	1	$2\frac{1}{4}$	180	1	$2\frac{1}{8}$	180	1	$2\frac{1}{8}$	165	1	$1\frac{15}{16}$	165	1	$1\frac{13}{16}$	165	1	$1\frac{11}{16}$	150
Bowers (chain) - - -	2	$2\frac{1}{4}$	180	2	$2\frac{1}{4}$	180	2	$2\frac{1}{8}$	180	2	$2\frac{1}{8}$	165	2	$1\frac{15}{16}$	165	2	$1\frac{13}{16}$	165	2	$1\frac{11}{16}$	150
Stream (hemp) - - -	1	16	120	1	15	120	1	14	120	1	13	120	1	$13\frac{1}{2}$	120	1	12	120	1	11	120
Hawsers (hemp) - -	6	2 of 7 in. 2 of 9 in. 2 of 11 in.		6	2 of 6 in. 2 of 8 in. 2 of 10 in.		6	2 of 6 in. 2 of 8 in. 2 of 10 in.		6	2 of 6 in. 2 of 8 in. 2 of 10 in.		5	1 of 6 in 2 of 7 in 2 of 9 in		5	2 of 6 in 2 of 8 in 1 of 9 in		4	2 of 6 in 1 of 7 in 1 of 8 in	
Messengers (hemp) -	1	16 inches.		1	15 inches.		1	14 inches.		1	$13\frac{1}{2}$ inches.		1	13 inches.		1	12 inches.		1	11 inches.	
Towlines (Manilla) -	5	5 inch. each.		4	5 inch. each.		4	5 inch. each.		4	5 inch. each.		3	1 of 4 in 2 of 5 in		2	1 of $4\frac{1}{2}$ 1 of 4 in		2	1 of $4\frac{1}{2}$ 1 of 4 in	
Chain for Launch - -	1	$\frac{3}{8}$ in. 50 fath.		1	$\frac{3}{8}$ in. 50 fath.		1	$\frac{5}{16}$ in. 50 fa.		1	$\frac{5}{16}$ in. 50 fa.		1	$\frac{5}{16}$ in. 45 f.		1	$\frac{1}{4}$ in. 45 fa.		1	$\frac{1}{4}$ in. 40 fa.	

A Table showing the Weight, Size, Length, and Quantity of Anchors, Cables, Hawsers, &c., &c., allowed to the different Classes of Vessels, U. S. N.—*Cont'd.*

Names of Articles.	Sloops.				Brigs.		Brigantines.		Schooners.		Steamers.				Remarks.
	Second Class.		Third Class.								First Class.		Second Class.		
	No.	Weight.	No.	Weight.	No.	Weight.	No.	Weight.	No.	Weight.	No.	Weight.	No.	Weight.	
ANCHORS, &c.															
Sheets - - - -	2	3,300	2	2,800	1	1,500	1	1,400	1	1,400	1	5,500	1	3,800	
Bowers - - -	2	3,300	2	2,800	2	1,500	2	1,400	2	1,400	2	5,500	2	3,800	
Stream - - -	1	900	1	800	1	600	1	500	1	500	1	1,600	1	1,000	
Kedges - - -	3	1 of 500 1 of 400 1 of 300	3	1 of 500 1 of 400 1 of 300	2	1 of 500 1 of 300	2	1 of 450 1 of 300	2	1 of 400 1 of 250	3	1 of 800 1 of 600 1 of 400	3	1 of 600 1 of 400 1 of 300	Waist anchors for all classes of Sloops of War, and all anchors for vessels up to a Brig, inclusive, together with all stream anchors and kedges, are to be iron-stocked.
BOAT ANCHORS.															
1st Launch, -	1	100	1	90	1	80	1	80	1	80	1	150	1	130	
2d Launch -	1	60	1	50	1	40	1	40	1	40	1	100	1	80	
1st Cutter - -	1	40	1	40	–	–	–	–	–	–	1	60	1	50	
2d Cutter - -	–	–	–	–	–	–	–	–	–	–	1	50	–	–	
Grapnels - -	2	1 of 60 1 of 40	2	1 of 60 1 of 30	2	1 of 50 1 of 20	2	1 of 50 1 of 20	2	1 of 50 1 of 20	2	1 of 100 1 of 50	2	1 of 80 1 of 40	

A Table showing the Weight, Size, Length, and Quantity of Anchors, Cables, Hawsers, &c., &c., allowed to the different Classes of Vessels, U. S. N.—*Cont'd.*

Names of Articles.	Sloops.						Brigs.			Brigantines.			Schooners.			Steamers.						Remarks.
	Second Class.			Third Class.												First Class.			Second Class.			
	No.	Inch.	Fathoms each.	No.	Inch.	Fathoms each.	No.	Inch.	Fathoms each.	No.	Inch	Fathoms each.	No.	Inch.	Fathoms each.	No.	Inch.	Fathoms each.	No.	Inch.	Fathoms each.	
CABLES.																						
Sheets (hemp) -	1	16	120	1	15	120	–	–	–	–	–	–	–	–	–	–	–	–	–	–	–	One hemp cable allowed to all small vessels, at the discretion of the commander.
Sheets (chain) -	1	$1\frac{10}{16}$	120	1	$1\frac{8}{16}$	120	1	$1\frac{4}{16}$	105	1	$1\frac{2}{16}$	105	1	$1\frac{1}{16}$	105	1	$1\frac{13}{16}$	150	1	$1\frac{11}{16}$	150	
Bowers (chain) -	2	$1\frac{10}{16}$	150	2	$1\frac{8}{16}$	150	2	$1\frac{4}{16}$	120	2	$1\frac{2}{16}$	120	2	$1\frac{1}{16}$	120	2	$1\frac{13}{16}$	150	2	$1\frac{11}{16}$	150	
Stream (hemp) -	1	10	120	1	9	120	1	8	120	1	7	120	1	7	120	1	13	120	1	11	120	
Hawsers (hemp)	3	1 of 5 in 1 of 6 in 1 of 7 in		3	1 of 5 in 1 of 6 in 1 of 7 in		2	1 of 5 in 1 of 6 in		2	1 of 5 in 1 of 6 in		2	1 of 5 in 1 of $4\frac{1}{2}$		4	1 of 6 in 2 of 8 in 1 of 9 in		4	2 of 6 in 1 of 7 in 1 of 8 in		In Ships of the Line, and Frigates, two of these hawsers may be of Manilla, and in smaller vessels, one.
Messengers (h'mp)	1	10 inches.		1	9 inches.		–	–		–	–		–	–		1	12 inches.		1	11 inches.		
Towlines (Manilla)	2	1 of $4\frac{1}{2}$ 1 of 4 in		2	1 of $4\frac{1}{2}$ 1 of 4 in		2	4 in. each.		2	4 in. each.		2	4 in. each.		2	1 of 4 in 1 of 5 in		2	1 of $4\frac{1}{2}$ 1 of 4 in		
Chain for Launch	1	$\frac{1}{4}$ in. 40 fa.		1	$\frac{3}{16}$ in. 40 f.		1	$\frac{3}{16}$ in. 35 f.		1	$\frac{3}{16}$ in. 30 f.		1	$\frac{3}{16}$ in. 30 f.		1	$\frac{1}{4}$ in. 45 fa.		1	$\frac{1}{4}$ in. 40 fa.		

521.—A Table showing the Size, Quantity, Quality and Number of Sails allowed to each Class of Vessels, U. S. N.

Names of Sails.	Ships of the Line.						Razees.						Frigates. First Class.						Frigates. Second Class.						Sloops. First Class.						Sloops. Second Class.					
	No. of Sails.	No. Canvas.	Size Rope. Head.	Foot.	Leech.	Hoist.	No. of Sails.	No. Canvas.	Size Rope. Head.	Foot.	Leech.	Hoist.	No. of Sails.	No. Canvas.	Size Rope. Head.	Foot.	Leech.	Hoist.	No. of Sails.	No. Canvas.	Size Rope. Head.	Foot.	Leech.	Hoist.	No. of Sails.	No. Canvas.	Size Rope. Head.	Foot.	Leech.	Hoist.	No. of Sails.	No. Canvas.	Size Rope. Head.	Foot.	Leech.	Hoist.
Fore Sails - - -	2	1	3¼	6	6	–	2	1	3	5¾	5¾	–	2	1	3	5½	5½	–	2	1	2¾	5¼	5¼	–	2	2	2½	4½	4½	–	2	2	2¼	4¼	4¼	
Fore Top Sails - -	2	1	3¼	6	4½	–	2	1	3	5¾	4¼	–	2	1	3	5½	4¼	–	2	1	2¾	5¼	4	–	2	2	2½	4½	3½	–	2	2	2¼	4¼	3¼	
Fore Top-gallant Sails - - - -	2	4	2	4	2¾	–	2	4	2	3¾	2¾	–	2	5	2	3½	2½	–	2	5	1¾	3¼	2¼	–	2	6	1¾	3	2¼	–	2	6	1½	2¾	2¼	
Fore Royals - - -	2	7	1½	2¾	2	–	2	7	1½	2½	2	–	2	7	1½	2½	2	–	2	7	1½	2¼	2	–	2	8	1½	2¼	1¾	–	2	8	1¼	2	1¾	
Main Sails - - -	2	1	3¼	5½	5½	–	2	2	3	5¼	5¼	–	2	2	3	5	5	–	2	2	2¾	4¾	4¾	–	2	2	2½	4	4	–	2	2	2¼	3¾	3¾	
Main Top Sails -	3	1	3¼	6	4¾	–	3	1	3	5¾	4½	–	3	1	3	5¾	4½	–	3	1	2¾	5½	4¼	–	3	2	2½	4½	3¾	–	3	2	2¼	4¼	3½	
Main Top-gallant Sails - - - - -	2	4	2	4	2¾	–	2	4	2	3¾	2¾	–	2	5	2	3½	2½	–	2	5	1¾	3¼	2¼	–	2	6	1¾	3	2¼	–	2	6	1½	2¾	2¼	
Main Royals - - -	2	7	1½	2¾	2	–	2	7	1½	2½	1¾	–	2	7	1½	2½	2	–	2	7	1½	2¼	2	–	2	8	1½	2¼	1¾	–	2	8	1¼	2	1¾	
Mizen Top-sails -	2	2	2¾	5	3¾	–	2	2	2¾	4¾	3½	–	2	3	2½	4½	3¼	–	2	3	2¼	4¼	3	–	2	3	2	4	3	–	2	3	2	3¾	2¾	
Mizen Top-gallant Sails - - - - -	2	5	1¾	2¾	2¼	–	2	5	1¾	2½	2	–	2	6	1½	2½	2	–	2	6	1¼	2¼	2	–	2	7	1½	2¼	1¾	–	2	7	1½	2	1¾	
Mizen Royals - -	2	8	1½	2	1¾	–	2	8	1½	2	1¾	–	2	8	1¼	2	1½	–	2	8	1¼	1¾	1½	–	2	8	1¼	2	1½	–	2	8	1	1¾	1½	
Lower Studding-sail	2	6	2¾	2¾	2¾	–	2	6	2¾	2¾	2¾	–	2	6	2½	2½	2½	–	2	6	2¼	2¼	2¼	–	2	7	2¼	2¼	2¼	–	2	7	2	2	2	
Fore Top-mast Studding-sails - - -	2	5	2	2¾	2¾	–	2	5	2	2¾	2¾	–	2	5	1¾	2½	2½	–	2	5	1¾	2¼	2¼	–	2	6	1¾	2¼	2¼	–	2	6	1½	2	2	

A Table showing the Size, Quantity, Quality and Number of Sails allowed to each Class of Vessels, U. S. N.

Names of Sails.	Ships of the Line.						Razees.					
			Size Rope.						Size Rope.			
	No. of Sails.	No. Canvas.	Head.	Foot.	Leech.	Hoist.	No. of Sails.	No. Canvas.	Head.	Foot.	Leech.	Hoist.
Fore Top-gallant Studding-sails -	2	7	1½	2¼	2¼	–	2	7	1½	2¼	2¼	–
Main T'p-mast Studding-sails - - -	2	5	1½	2¾	2¾	–	2	5	2	2¾	2¾	–
Main Top-gallant Studding-sails -	2	7	1½	2¼	2¼	–	2	7	1½	2¼	2¼	–
Flying-Jibs - - -	2	6	–	2¾	2¾	3	2	6	–	2½	2½	3
Standing-Jibs - -	2	3	–	3¼	3¼	3¾	2	3	–	3	3¼	3½
Fore Try-sails - -	1	1	2¼	3¾	3¾	3¾	1	1	2¼	3½	3½	3½
Main Try-sails - -	1	1	2¼	3½	3½	3½	1	1	2¼	3¼	3¼	3¼
Storm Mizen - - -	1	1	2	3	3	3	1	1	2	3	3	3
Spankers - - - -	2	3	2¼	2¾	3¼	3¼	2	3	2¼	2½	3	3
Fore Storm Stay-sail	1	1	–	3½	3½	4¼	1	1	–	3½	3½	4¼
Main Storm Stay-sail	1	1	–	3¾	3¾	4¼	1	1	–	3¾	3¾	4¼
Miz. Storm Stay-sail	1	1	–	3½	3½	3¾	1	1	–	3¾	3¼	3¾
Fore Top-mast Stay-sails - - - - -	2	1	–	3½	3½	3½	1	1	–	3¼	3¼	3¼

Names of Sails.	Frigates. First Class.						Frigates. Second Class.					
			Size Rope.						Size Rope.			
	No. of Sails.	No. Canvas.	Head.	Foot.	Leech.	Hoist.	No. of Sails.	No. Canvas.	Head.	Foot.	Leech.	Hoist.
Fore Top-gallant Studding-sails -	2	7	1½	2	2	–	2	7	1½	2	2	–
Main T'p-mast Studding-sails - - -	2	5	1¾	2½	2½	–	2	5	1¾	2¼	2¼	–
Main Top-gallant Studding-sails -	2	7	1½	2	2	–	2	7	1½	2	2	–
Flying-Jibs - - -	2	6	–	2¼	2¼	2¾	2	6	–	2	2	2½
Standing-Jibs - -	2	4	–	2¾	3	3½	2	4	–	2½	2¾	3¼
Fore Try-sails - -	1	1	2	3¼	3¼	3¼	1	1	2	3	3	3
Main Try-sails - -	1	1	2	3	3	3	1	1	2	2¾	2¾	2¾
Storm Mizen - - -	1	1	2	2¾	2¾	2¾	1	1	2	2½	2½	2½
Spankers - - - -	2	4	2	2¼	3	3	2	4	1¾	2	2¾	2¾
Fore Storm Stay-sail	1	1	–	3¼	3¼	3¾	1	1	–	3	3	3½
Main Storm Stay-sail	1	1	–	3½	3½	4	1	1	–	3¼	3¼	3¾
Miz. Storm Stay-sail	1	1	–	3¼	3¼	3½	1	1	–	3¼	3¼	3½
Fore Top-mast Stay-sails - - - - -	2	1	–	3¼	3¼	3¼	2	1	–	3¼	3¼	3¼

Names of Sails.	Sloops. First Class.						Sloops. Second Class.					
			Size Rope.						Size Rope.			
	No. of Sails.	No. Canvas	Head.	Foot.	Leech.	Hoist.	No. of Sails.	No. Canvas	Head.	Foot.	Leech.	Hoist.
Fore Top-gallant Studding-sails -	2	8	1¼	1¾	1¾	–	2	8	1¼	1¾	1¾	–
Main T'p-mast Studding-sails - - -	2	6	1¾	2¼	2¼	–	2	6	1½	2	2	–
Main Top-gallant Studding-sails -	2	8	1¼	1¾	1¾	–	2	8	1¼	1¾	1¾	–
Flying-Jibs - - -	2	7	–	2	2	2½	2	7	–	2	2	2
Standing-Jibs - -	2	4	–	2½	2¾	3	2	4	–	2¼	2¼	3
Fore Try-sails - -	1	2	1¾	3	3	3	1	2	1¾	2¾	2¾	2¾
Main Try-sails - -	1	2	1¾	2¾	2¾	2¾	1	2	1½	2½	2½	2½
Storm Mizen - - -	1	2	1¾	2½	2½	2½	1	2	1½	2¼	2¼	2¼
Spankers - - - -	2	4	1¾	2	2¾	2¾	2	4	1¾	2	2½	2½
Fore Storm Stay-sail	1	1	–	3	3	3½	1	2	–	3	3	3
Main Storm Stay-sail	1	1	–	3¼	3¼	3¾	1	2	–	3	3	3½
Miz. Storm Stay-sail	1	1	–	3	3	3¼	1	2	–	2¾	2¾	3
Fore Top-mast Stay-sails - - - - -	2	2	–	3	3	3	2	2	–	3	3	3

A Table showing the Size, Quantity, Quality and Number of Sails allowed to each Class of Vessels, U. S. N.—*Continued.*

Names of Sails.	Sloops. THIRD CLASS.						Brigs.						Brigantines.						Schooners.						Steamers.						Remarks.
			Size Rope.						Size Rope.						Size Rope.						Size Rope.						Size Rope.				
	No. of Sails.	No. Canvas.	Head.	Foot.	Leech.	Hoist.	No. of Sails.	No. Canvas.	Head.	Foot.	Leech.	Hoist.	No. of Sails.	No. Canvas.	Head.	Foot.	Leech.	Hoist.	No. of Sails.	No. Canvas.	Head.	Foot.	Leech.	Hoist.	No. of Sails.	No. Canvas.	Head.	Foot.	Leech.	Hoist.	
Fore Sails - - -	2	2	2	4	4	–	2	3	2	4	4	–	2	3	2	3½	3½	–	2	1	1¾	3	3¼	3½	2	2	2¾	5	5		
Fore Top-sails - -	2	2	2	4	3	–	2	3	2	4	3	–	2	3	2	3½	2¾	–	2	5	1½	2¾	2¼	–	2	2	2¾	5	3¾		All fore and aft sails, as well as Courses, Top-sails and Top-gallant Sails, to be finished with Iron Clews.
Fore Top-gallant Sails - - - -	2	6	1½	2½	2	–	2	7	1½	2½	2	–	2	7	1¼	2¼	2	–	2	8	1¼	2	1¾	–	2	6	1¾	3¼	2¼		
Fore Royals - - -	2	8	1	2	1½	–	2	8	1¼	2	1½	–	2	8	1¼	2	1½	–	1	8	1	1½	1	–	2	3	2¾	4½	4½		
Main Sails - - -	2	2	2¼	3¾	3¾	–	2	3	2	3½	3½	–	2	2	1¾	3	3¼	3½	2	2	1¾	3	3¼	3½	3	2	2¾	5¼	4		
Main Top-sails -	3	2	2¼	4¼	3¼	–	2	3	2	4	3	–	2	6	1¾	2½	2	–	1	7	1½	2¼	2	–	2	6	1¾	3¼	2¼		
Main Top-gallant Sails - - - - -	2	6	1½	2½	2	–	2	7	1½	2½	2	–	2	8	1¼	1¾	1¾	–	1	8	1¼	2	1½								
Main Royals - - -	2	8	1¼	2	1½	–	2	8	1¼	2	1½																				
Mizen Top-sails -	2	4	1¾	3½	2¾																										
Mizen Top-gallant Sails - - - - -	2	7	1½	2	1¾																										
Mizen Royals - -	2	8	1	1¾	1½																										
Lower Studding-sails	2	7	2	2	2	–	2	8	2	2	2	–	2	8	2	2	2	–	2	8	2	2	2	–	2	6	2½	2½	2½		
Fore Top-mast Studding-sails - - -	2	6	1½	2	2	–	2	7	1½	2	2	–	2	8	1½	2	2	–	2	8	1¼	1¾	1¾	–	2	5	1¾	2½	2½		

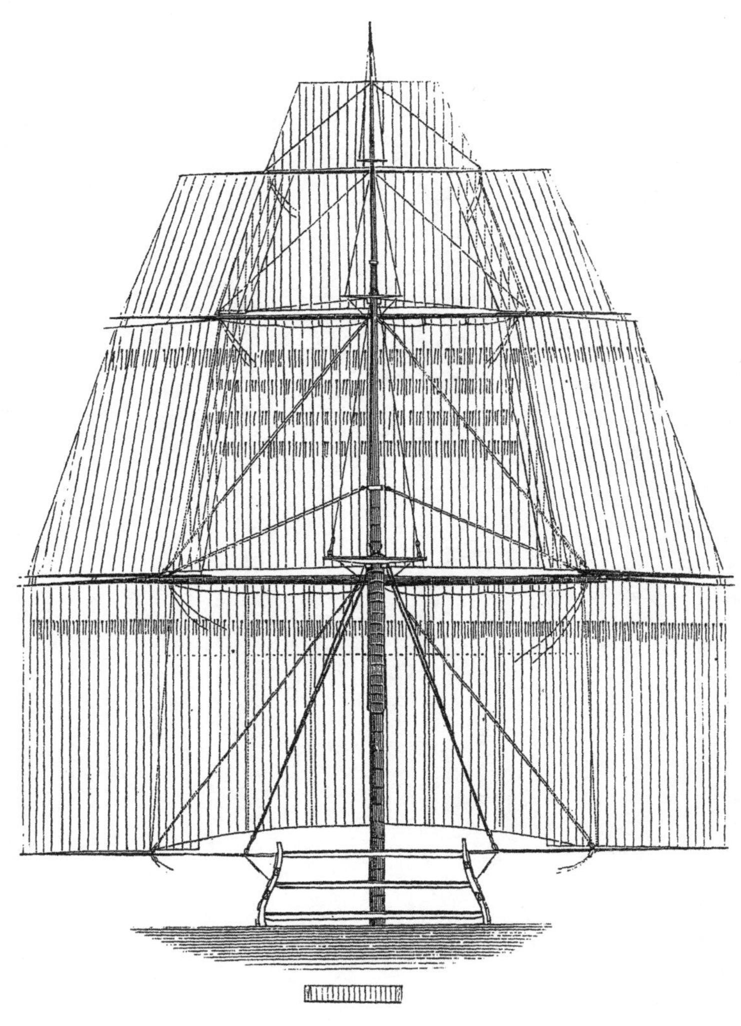

Scale of 16 feet.

Representation of masts, Yards, Sails, &c.

A Table showing the Size, Quantity, Quality and Number of Sails allowed to each Class of Vessels, U. S. N.—*Concluded.*

Names of Sails.	Sloops. Third Class.						Brigs.						Brigantines.						Schooners.						Steamers.						Remarks.
			Size Rope.						Size Rope.						Size Rope.						Size Rope.						Size Rope.				
	No. of Sails.	No. Canvas.	Head.	Foot.	Leech.	Hoist.	No. of Sails.	No. Canvas.	Head.	Foot.	Leech.	Hoist.	No. of Sails.	No. Canvas.	Head.	Foot.	Leech.	Hoist.	No. of Sails.	No. Canvas	Head.	Foot.	Leech.	Hoist.	No. of Sails.	No. Canvas	Head.	Foot.	Leech.	Hoist.	
Fore Top-gallant Studding-sails -	2	8	1¼	1¾	1¾	–	2	8	1¼	1¾	1¾	–	2	8	1¼	1½	1½	–	2	8	1	1¼	1¼	–	2	8	1¼	1¾	1¾		
Main T'p-mast Studding-sails - - -	2	6	1½	2	2	–	2	7	1½	2	2	–	–	–	–	–	–	–	–	–	–	–	–	–	2	5	1¾	2½	2½		
Main Top-gallant Studding-sails -	2	8	1¼	1¾	1¾	–	2	8	1¼	1¾	1¾	–	–	–	–	–	–	–	–	–	–	–	–	–	2	8	1¼	1¾	1¾		
Flying-Jibs - - -	2	7	–	2	2	2	2	7	–	2	2	2¼	2	8	–	2	2	2¼	2	6	–	2¾	2¾	3	2	6	–	2¼	2¼	2¾	
Standing-Jibs - -	2	5	–	2	2½	2¾	2	5	–	2¼	2¼	2¾	2	6	–	2¼	2¼	2½	2	1	–	3¼	3¾	3¾	2	4	–	2½	2¾	3¼	
Fore Try-sails - -	1	2	1¾	2½	2½	2½	1	3	1½	2¼	2¼	2¾	1	3	1½	2½	2½	2½	–	–	–	–	–	–	1	1	2	3¼	3¼	3¼	
Main Try-sails - -	1	2	1½	2¼	2¼	2¼	2	3	2	2¼	3¼	3½	–	–	–	–	–	–	–	–	–	–	–	–	1	1	2	3	3	3	
Storm Mizen - - -	1	2	1½	2	2	2	–	–	–	–	–	–	–	–	–	–	–	–	–	–	–	–	–	–	1	2	1¾	2½	2½	2½	
Spankers - - - -	2	5	1¾	2	2¼	2¼	–	–	–	–	–	–	–	–	–	–	–	–	–	–	–	–	–	–	2	3	1¾	2	2¾	2¾	
Fore Storm Stay-sail	1	2	–	3	3	3	1	2	–	2¾	2¾	3¼	1	2	–	2½	2½	3	–	–	–	–	–	–	1	1	–	3¼	3¼	3¾	
Main Storm Stay-sail	1	2	–	3	3	3	1	2	–	3	3	3½																			
Miz. Storm Stay-sail	1	2	–	2¾	2¾	3																									
Fore Top-mast Stay-sails - - - -	2	2	–	3	3	3	2	2	–	2¾	2¾	2¾	2	3	–	2½	2½	2½	–	–	–	–	–	–	2	2	–	3	3	3	
Square Sail - - -	–	–	–	–	–	–	–	–	–	–	–	–	–	–	–	–	–	–	1	7	1¾	2¼	2¼								

522.—A Table showing the Quantity of Canvass, Rope, &c., allowed for one Suit of Sails for each Class of Vessels, U. S. N.

Names of the different Sails	Ships of the Line.																	
	THREE DECKS.						TWO DECKS. First Class.						TWO DECKS. Second Class.					
	Body of Sail, yards.	Lining of Sail, yards.	Fath. Bolt-rope. Head.	Foot.	Leech.	Hoist.	Body of Sail, yards.	Lining of Sail, yards.	Fath. Bolt-rope. Head.	Foot.	Leech.	Hoist.	Body of Sail, yards.	Lining of Sail, yards.	Fath. Bolt-rope. Head.	Foot.	Leech.	Hoist.
Fore Course -	900	234	14⅓	14½	16⅔	–	847	227	13	13½	16	–	758	218	12¾	13	15⅓	–
Fore Top-sail	848	340	9¾	14½	19	–	818	333	9¼	13½	19	–	777	319	8½	13	18	–
Fore Top-gallant Sail -	361½	80	7	10	12⅓	–	335	77	6⅓	9⅔	13⅓	–	311	60	6¼	9	11	–
Fore Royal -	162	11	4⅔	7	8⅓	–	153	10	4½	6⅔	8⅓	–	149	9	4¼	6½	8	–
Main Course -	1200	278	15½	18	20	–	1172	271	15¼	17½	19⅓	–	1110	259	15	17¼	18⅔	–
Main Top-sail	1040	400	10½	16	21	–	997	380	10	15½	21	–	984	360	9¾	15¼	21	–
Main Top-gallant Sail -	426	89	7⅔	11¼	12½	–	406	83	7⅔	10½	12½	–	399	80	7½	10⅓	12½	–
Main Royal -	195	12	5	8	8½	–	195	11	5	8	8½	–	190	10	4¾	7⅔	8½	–
Mizen Top-sail	581	190	6½	10½	16½	–	581	190	6½	10½	16½	–	413	180	6⅓	9½	14	–
Mizen Top-gallant Sail -	216	49	4½	7¼	10½	–	216	49	4½	7¼	10½	–	198	45	4⅓	7	10½	–
Mizen Royal -	98	6	3	5	8	–	98	6	3	5	8	–	94	5	2¾	4¾	8	–
Flying-Jib - -	382	–	–	6¾	13¾	18	367	–	–	6	13	17	332	–	–	5¾	12½	16½
Jib - - - -	664	–	–	9⅓	17	21⅓	650	–	–	9	16½	20	600	–	–	8⅔	16	19⅓
Fore Top-mast Stay-sail -	310	–	–	6	12	15	290	–	–	5¾	11	14	260	–	–	5½	10½	13⅓

Names of the different Sails	Razees.						Frigates. First Class.						Frigates. Second Class.					
	Body of Sail, yards.	Lining of Sail, yards.	Fath. Bolt-rope. Head.	Foot.	Leech.	Hoist.	Body of Sail, yards.	Lining of Sail, yards.	Fath. Bolt-rope. Head.	Foot.	Leech.	Hoist.	Body of Sail, yards.	Lining of Sail, yards.	Fath. Bolt-rope. Head.	Foot.	Leech.	Hoist.
Fore Course -	758	218	12¾	13	15⅓	–	600	145	12	12½	14	–	531	135	10⅔	11	13	
Fore Top-sail	777	319	8½	13	18	–	596	230	8¼	12½	16	–	510	196	7¼	11	15	
Fore Top-gallant Sail -	311	60	6¼	9	11	–	269	50	6	8½	10½	–	210	40	5¼	7¾	9½	
Fore Royal -	149	9	4¼	6½	8	–	123	7	4	6⅓	7¾	–	101¾	6	3½	5½	7	
Main Course -	1110	259	15	17¼	18⅔	–	844	200	14	16	17	–	770	185	12⅓	14⅓	16	
Main Top-sail	984	360	9¾	15¼	21	–	800	250	9½	14½	19½	–	661	210	8½	13	17	
Main Top-gallant Sail -	399	80	7½	10⅓	12½	–	337	58	6½	10	12¼	–	257	45	5½	9	11	
Main Royal -	190	10	4¾	7⅔	8½	–	150	8	4¼	7	8	–	116½	8	3¾	5¾	7¼	
Mizen Top-sail	413	180	6⅓	9½	14	–	360	115	5¾	9¼	13½	–	321	90	5	8½	12½	
Mizen Top-gallant Sail -	198	45	4⅓	7	10⅓	–	152	36	4	6	9	–	114½	25	3½	5½	8	
Mizen Royal -	94	5	2¾	4¾	8	–	67	5	2½	4⅓	6½	–	48	4	2¼	4	5½	
Flying-Jib - -	332	–	–	5¾	12½	16½	292	–	–	5½	12½	15	247	–	–	5¼	11	14
Jib - - - -	600	–	–	8⅔	16	19⅓	500	–	–	7½	13½	17	404	–	–	7¼	12¼	16
Fore Top-mast Stay-sail -	260	–	–	5½	10½	13⅓	223	–	–	5	10½	12	196	–	–	4¾	9⅝	11⅓

Note.—Iron clews are fitted to all sails (new regulation) as per pattern.

A Table showing the Quantity of Canvass, Rope, &c., allowed for one Suit of Sails for each Class of Vessels, U. S. N.—*Continued.*

Names of the different Sails	Ships of the Line.																	
	THREE DECKS.						TWO DECKS.											
							First Class.						Second Class.					
	Body of Sail, yards.	Lining of Sail, yards.	Fath. Bolt-rope.				Body of Sail, yards.	Lining of Sail, yards.	Fath. Bolt-rope.				Body of Sail, yards.	Lining of Sail, yards.	Fath. Bolt-rope.			
			Head.	Foot.	Leech.	Hoist.			Head.	Foot.	Leech.	Hoist.			Head.	Foot.	Leech.	Hoist.
Fore Storm Stay-sail -	276	–	–	8	7¼	10⅔	242	–	–	7¾	7	9¼	220	–	–	7½	6¾	9
Main Storm Stay-sail -	430	–	–	10⅔	8⅔	14⅔	397	–	–	10	8½	14½	355	–	–	9½	8¼	14
Mizen Storm Stay-sail -	245	–	–	7⅔	7¼	11	237	–	–	7½	7	11	230	–	–	7¼	6¾	10½
Storm Mizen -	270	–	4	6	8½	6½	260	–	4	5½	8½	6½	250	–	–	5¼	8¼	6¼
Fore Try-sail -	549	–	6	9¼	11⅓	8	545	–	6	9	11⅓	8	500	–	5¾	8⅔	11	7¾
Main Try-sail	504	–	5⅓	7¾	10⅔	8¼	499	–	5⅓	7½	10⅔	8¼	450	–	4¾	7¼	10	8
Spanker - -	568	–	6	9½	10⅓	7⅓	542	–	6	9½	10⅓	7⅓	500	–	6	9½	10	6½
Lower Studding-sail -	749	–	10½	10½	18¼	–	686	–	9⅔	9⅔	18	–	590	–	9⅓	9⅓	17½	–
Fore Top-mast Studding-sail	426	–	4½	7¼	19⅓	–	424	–	4½	7	19⅓	–	356	–	4	6	19	–
Fore Top-gall't Studding-sail	173	–	3	5	12½	–	173	–	3	5	12½	–	161	–	2¾	4¾	12	–
Main Top-mast Studding-sail	512	–	5	7½	21½	–	512	–	5	7½	21½	–	483	–	4¾	7	21½	–
Main Top-gal't Studding-sail	209	–	3⅓	5½	14½	–	209	–	3⅓	5½	14½	–	208	–	3⅓	5½	14½	–
Tot. of Canvass and Bolt-rope	13,960		844				13,406		816				12,423		783			

Names of the different Sails	Razees.						Frigates.											
							First Class.						Second Class.					
	Body of Sail, yards.	Lining of Sail, yards.	Fath. Bolt-rope.				Body of Sail, yards.	Lining of Sail, yards.	Fath. Bolt-rope.				Body of Sail, yards.	Lining of Sail, yards.	Fath. Bolt-rope.			
			Head.	Foot.	Leech.	Hoist.			Head.	Foot.	Leech.	Hoist.			Head.	Foot.	Leech.	Hoist.
Fore Storm Stay-sail -	220	–	–	7½	6¾	9	170	–	–	7	6½	8½	152	–	–	6¼	5½	8
Main Storm Stay-sail -	355	–	–	9½	8¼	14	307	–	–	7½	8	12	261	–	–	6	7⅔	11¼
Mizen Storm Stay-sail -	230	–	–	7¼	6¾	10½	179	–	–	6¼	6½	9	153	–	–	5½	6⅓	8⅔
Storm Mizen -	250	–	–	5¼	8¼	6¼	230	–	3½	5	8½	6	203	–	3¼	4½	7½	5½
Fore Try-sail -	500	–	5¾	8⅔	11	7¾	410	–	5½	7½	9	6	337	–	5¼	7¼	8½	5½
Main Try-sail	450	–	4¾	7¼	10	8	360	–	4¾	6½	9	7	309	–	4¼	6	8⅓	6¼
Spanker - -	500	–	6	9½	10	6½	410	–	5½	8	8	6	322	–	5	7¼	7½	5½
Lower Studding-sail -	590	–	9⅓	9⅓	17½	–	440	–	8¼	8¼	15	–	420	–	7¼	7¼	14⅓	
Fore Top-mast Studding-sail	356	–	4	6	19	–	315	–	3½	6	17	–	241	–	3¼	5¼	15½	
Fore Top-gall't Studding-sail	161	–	2¾	4¾	12	–	140	–	2¾	4½	11¼	–	121	–	2½	4	10	
Main Top-mast Studding-sail	483	–	4¾	7	21½	–	360	–	4¼	7	20	–	323	–	4	6	18	
Main Top-gal't Studding-sail	208	–	3⅓	5½	14½	–	170	–	3¼	5¼	12¼	–	144	–	3	5	11½	
Tot. of Canvass and Bolt-rope	12,423		783				10,112		719				8,418		655			

A Table showing the Quantity of Canvass, Rope, &c., allowed for one Suit of Sails for each Class of Vessels, U. S. N.—*Continued.*

Names of the different Sails	Sloops.																	
	First Class.						Second Class.						Third Class.					
	Body of Sail, yards.	Lining of Sail, yards.	Fath. Bolt-rope. Head.	Foot.	Leech.	Hoist.	Body of Sail, yards.	Lining of Sail, yards.	Fa. Bolt-rope. Head.	Foot.	Leech.	Hoist.	Body of Sail, yards.	Lining of Sail, yards.	Fa. Bolt-rope. Head.	Foot.	Leech.	Hoist.
Fore Course -	428	73½	9	9½	12	–	376	65	8½	9	11	–	363	65	8½	9	10⅜	–
Fore Top-sail	383	130	6¼	9½	13⅜	–	340	120	5½	9	13	–	340	120	5½	9	12¾	–
Fore Top-gallant Sail -	165	30	4⅓	6⅜	8⅓	–	135	25	4	6	8	–	135	25	4	6	8	–
Fore Royal -	74	4	3¼	4⅜	5⅜	–	62	3	3	4¼	5¼	–	62	3	3	4¼	5¼	–
Main Course -	595	86	10½	11⅜	14	–	497	76	9½	10⅜	13	–	486	76	9¼	10½	12¾	–
Main Top-sail	486	151	7¼	11	15	–	418	140	6¾	10½	14½	–	418	140	6¾	10½	14¼	–
Main Top-gallant Sail -	200	40	5¼	7½	9	–	167¾	35	5	7	8¾	–	167¾	35	5	7	8¾	–
Main Royal -	92	5	3⅜	5½	6⅓	–	75¾	4	3¼	5¼	6¼	–	75¾	4	3¼	5¼	6¼	–
Mizen Top-sail	244	85	4½	7	11⅜	–	206	75	4¼	6¾	11¼	–	206	75	4¼	6¾	11¼	–
Mizen Top-gallant Sail -	106	20	3¼	5	7½	–	80	16	3	4¾	7¼	–	80	16	3	4¾	7¼	–
Mizen Royal -	45	3	2¼	3½	5	–	36	3	2	3¼	4¾	–	36	3	2	3¼	4¾	–
Flying-Jib - -	164	–	–	4⅜	9	11⅜	150	–	–	4¼	8¾	11¼	146	–	–	4¼	8½	11
Jib - - - -	276	–	–	6	10⅓	13⅓	265	–	–	5¾	10	13	259	–	–	5¾	9¾	12¾
Fore Topmast Stay-sail -	138	–	–	3⅜	7⅜	9	120	–	–	3¼	7¼	9¾	117	–	–	3¼	7	9⅓

Names of the different Sails	Brigs.					Brigantines.					Schooners.					Steamers.					
	Body of Sail, yards.	Fa. Bolt-rope. Head.	Foot.	Leech.	Hoist.	Body of Sail, yards.	Fa. Bolt-rope. Head.	Foot.	Leech.	Hoist.	Body of Sail, yards.	Fa. Bolt-rope. Head.	Foot.	Leech.	Hoist.	Body of Sail, yards.	Lining of Sail, yards.	Fa. Bolt-rope. Head.	Foot.	Leech.	Hoist.
Fore Course -	300	7½	8	9⅜	–	261	6⅓	6⅜	9	–	420	4	7⅓	10	8⅓	755	137	12⅜	13	16	
Fore Top-sail	290	5	8	10	–	232	4¼	6⅜	9⅓	–	240	4¼	7⅓	10	–	734	206	8⅓	13	19⅓	
Fore Top-gallant Sail -	97	3½	5⅓	6⅓	–	96	3	4½	7⅓	–	73	3	4⅜	5⅓	–	342	40	5½	8⅜	13½	
Fore Royal -	47	2¾	3¾	4⅓	–	42	2	3⅓	5	–											
Main Course -	367	8¼	9½	11¾	–	445	4	8	9½	8⅜	452	4	8	10	8½	785	142	12⅜	14	16⅓	
Main Top-sail	330	6	9¼	11⅓	–	146	3½	5	7½	–	Gaff. 106	–	4	7⅜	10½	734	206	8⅓	14	19½	
Main Top-gallant Sail -	112	4¼	6½	6⅔	–	54½	2⅓	3⅜	5⅓	–	Sq. sl. 471	7	8	16⅜	–	342	40	5½	8⅜	13⅓	
Main Royal -	57	3	4⅜	4⅜	–																
Mizen Top-sail																					
Mizen Top-gallant Sail -																					
Mizen Royal -																					
Flying-Jib - -	110	–	3¾	7½	10½	106	–	3⅓	7¼	9⅜	135	–	4⅜	10	12⅜						
Jib - - - -	175	–	5¼	8¾	11¾	145	–	3¾	10⅜	11⅓	195	–	6	8	9	573	–	–	8	16	20
Fore Topmast Stay-sail -	82	–	3	6½	9	63	–	2½	6	7	–	–	–	–	–	253	–	–	5	11	13

A Table showing the Quantity of Canvass, Rope, &c., allowed for one Suit of Sails for each Class of Vessels, U. S. N.—*Concluded.*

Names of the different Sails	Sloops. First Class. Body of Sail, yards.	Lining of Sail, yards.	Fath. Bolt-rope. Head.	Foot.	Leech.	Hoist.	Second Class. Body of Sail, yards.	Lining of Sail, yards.	Fa. Bolt-rope. Head.	Foot.	Leech.	Hoist.	Third Class. Body of Sail, yards.	Lining of Sail, yards.	Fa. Bolt-rope. Head.	Foot.	Leech.	Hoist.
Fore Storm Stay-sail -	124	–	–	5	5¼	6⅔	115	–	–	4¾	5	6¼	113	–	–	4¾	4¾	6
Main Storm Stay-sail -	204	–	–	7	6	9⅔	190	–	–	6¾	5¾	9¼	185	–	–	6¾	5½	9
Mizen Storm Stay-sail -	90	–	–	3⅔	5	6⅔	85	–	–	3¼	4¾	6¼	83	–	–	3¼	4½	6
Storm Mizen -	180	–	2¾	4¼	5¼	5	160	–	2¼	4	5½	4¾	157	–	2½	4	5¼	4½
Fore Try-sail -	256	–	4	6	7	5⅓	230	–	3¾	5¾	6¾	5	224	–	3¾	5¾	6½	4¾
Main Try-sail	190	–	3	4	6⅓	5⅔	175	–	2¾	3¾	6	5½	170	–	2¾	3¾	5¾	5¼
Spanker - -	242	–	4⅓	5⅔	6½	5⅔	230	–	4	5¼	6¼	5½	224	–	4	5¼	6	5¼
Lower Studding-sail -	325	–	5½	7	13⅓	–	260	–	5¼	6¾	13	–	250	–	5¼	6¾	12½	–
Fore Top-mast Studding-sail	174	–	3	5	14	–	164	–	2¾	4¾	13½	–	164	–	2¾	4¾	13	–
Fore Top-gall't Studding-sail	82	–	2¼	4	9	–	77	–	2	3¾	8¾	–	77	–	2	3¾	8½	–
Main Top-mast Studding-sail	217	–	3¼	6	16	–	207	–	3	5¾	15½	–	207	–	3	5¾	15¼	–
Main Top-gal't Studding-sail	94	–	2½	5	9½	–	89	–	2¼	4¾	9¼	–	89	–	2¼	4¾	9	–
Tot. of Canvass and Bolt-rope	6,301		565				5,472		537				5,296		526			

Names of the different Sails	Brigs. Body of Sail, yards.	Fa. Bolt-rope. Head.	Foot.	Leech.	Hoist.	Brigantines. Body of Sail, yards.	Fa. Bolt-rope. Head.	Foot.	Leech.	Hoist.	Schooners. Body of Sail, yards.	Fa. Bolt-rope. Head.	Foot.	Leech.	Hoist.	Steamers. Body of Sail, yards.	Lining of Sail, yards.	Fa. Bolt-rope Head.	Foot.	Leech.	Hoist.
Fore Storm Stay-sail -	80	–	4½	4¼	5½	61	–	3	5	6¼	–	–	–	–	–	310	–	–	8⅔	7	11
Main Storm Stay-sail -																					
Mizen Storm Stay-sail -																					
Storm Mizen -																					
Fore Try-sail -	152	3½	5½	6¼	4¼	200	3½	5	6	4½	–	–	–	–	–	570	–	6	9¼	10⅔	7
Main Try-sail	350	5⅓	8¾	6⅓	5½	–	–	–	–	–	–	–	–	–	–	360	–	4½	6⅓	9	7
Spanker - -	–	–	–	–	–	–	–	–	–	–	–	–	–	–	–	412	–	5½	7¼	9	6⅝
Lower Studding-sail -	180	4¾	4¾	11½	–	149	4	4½	9½	–	216	3⅓	4	16⅔	–	463	–	7½	7½	16	
Fore Top-mast Studding-sail	100	2½	4⅓	12⅓	–	95	2⅓	4¼	12¼	–	79	2	3	10	–	346	–	4	6	19¼	
Fore Top-gall't Studding-sail	45	1¾	3⅓	7¾	–	40	1¾	3¼	7½	–	27	1	2¼	5⅓	–	155	–	3	5¼	12	
Main Top-mast Studding-sail	–	–	–	–	–	–	–	–	–	–	–	–	–	–	–	346	–	4	6	19¼	
Main Top-gal't Studding-sail	53	2	4⅓	8½	–	–	–	–	–	–	–	–	–	–	–	155	–	3	5¼	12	
Tot. of Canvass and Bolt-rope	2927	353				2135	268				2414	247				8,406		542			

 523.—A Table showing the Length and Size of Stand-

Names of Rigging.	Ships of the Line.									Razees.			Frigates.		
	3 decks.			2 decks.									1st Class.		
				1st Class.			2d Class.								
	No.	Size.	Length.	No.	Size.	Length.	No.	Size.	Length.	No.	Size.	Length.	No.	Size.	Length.
BOWSPRIT GEAR.															
Gammoning (Iron for all classes of vessels															
Shrouds (pairs) - -	2	9	38	2	9	34	2	9	32	2	8½	32	2	8	30
Collars for Shrouds -	2	9	8	2	9	7	2	9	7	2	8½	7	2	8	7
Lanyards for Shrouds (four-stranded) - -	4	4	32	4	4	32	4	4	32	4	4	32	4	3¾	34
Bobstays (pairs) - -	2	10½	36	2	10½	32	2	10	31	2	10	31	2	10	26
Collars for Bobstays	2	10½	7	2	10½	6½	2	10	6½	2	10	6½	2	10	6½
Lanyards for Bobstays (four-stranded) - -	2	5¼	17	2	5¼	17	2	5	17	2	5	17	2	5	18
Cap Bobstay - - -	1	7	20	1	7	17	1	7	17	1	7	17	1	6½	15
Collar for Cap Bobstay	1	7	3½	1	7	3½	1	7	3	1	7	3	1	6½	2½
Lanyard for Cap Bobstay (four-stranded)	1	3½	8½	1	3½	8½	1	3½	8½	1	3½	8½	1	3¼	8½
Manropes - - - -	2	4½	18	2	4½	18	2	4½	18	2	4½	17	2	4¼	16
Bumkin Braces (Iron for all vessels - -															
SPRIT-SAIL YARD GEAR.															
Parrel - - - - - -	1	5	10	1	5	10	1	5	9	1	5	7	1	4	7
Tye - - - - - - -	1	4½	2	1	4½	2	1	4½	2	1	4½	2	1	4	2
Foot Ropes - - - -	2	3½	16	2	3½	16	2	3½	16	2	3½	15	2	3¼	12
Lifts - - - - - -	2	4½	31	2	4½	30	2	4½	30	2	4½	28	2	4¼	26
Braces - - - - - -	2	3¼	108	2	3¼	106	2	3¼	103	2	3¼	103	2	3	86
JIB-BOOM GEAR.															
Jib Stay - - - - -	1	8	45	1	8	44	1	8	43	1	8	42	1	7½	39
Jib Guys (pairs) - -	2	6	75	2	6	72	2	6	72	2	6	68	2	5½	68
Jib Falls - - - -	4	3	40	4	3	40	4	3	40	4	3	40	4	2¾	40
Foot Ropes - - - -	2	4	18	2	4	18	2	4	18	2	4	17	2	3¾	16
Martingale Stay - -	1	8	10	1	8	9	1	8	8	1	8	8	1	7½	7½
Martingale Backropes (pair) - - - - -	1	5½	20	1	5½	17	1	5½	17	1	5½	17	1	5	16
Martingale Falls - -	2	3	16	2	3	16	2	3	16	2	3	16	2	2¾	16
Halliards - - - -	1	3¾	70	1	3¾	70	1	3½	64	1	3¼	67	1	3¼	62
Downhaul - - - -	1	3	42	1	3	40	1	2¾	35	1	2½	36	1	2½	35
Sheets - - - - -	2	4½	80	2	4½	70	2	4½	62	2	3¾	62	2	3½	68
Pendants - - - -	2	6	8	2	6	8	2	6	7	2	5¾	7	2	5¾	6½
Brails - - - - -	2	2¾	68	2	2¾	60	2	2¾	57	2	2¾	58	2	2½	56
FLYING JIB-BOOM GEAR.															
Flying-Jib Stay - -	1	5	52	1	5	50	1	5	47	1	4½	48	1	4½	43
Flying-Jib Guys - -	2	4	52	2	4	50	2	4	44	2	3¾	44	2	3¾	40
Flying-Jib Falls - -	2	3	24	2	3	24	2	3	24	2	2¾	24	2	2¾	20
Foot Ropes - - - -	2	3	11	2	3	10	2	3	10	2	3	10	2	3	9
Martingale Stay - -	1	5	24	1	5	20	1	5	20	1	4½	20	1	4½	18
Halliards - - - -	1	3½	60	1	3½	58	1	3½	53	1	3	54	1	3	51
Downhaul - - - -	1	2¾	46	1	2¾	46	1	2¾	39	1	2½	40	1	2½	36
Sheets - - - - -	2	5¾	52	2	3¾	50	2	3¾	46	2	3¼	48	2	3¼	40
Heel-rope - - - -	1	3	34	1	3	32	1	3	30	1	3	30	1	2¾	30

NOTE.—The Lanyards for all Standing Rigging should be four-stranded rope.

Frigates. 2d Class.			Sloops. 1st Class.			Sloops. 2d Class.			Sloops. 3d Class.			Brigs.			Brigantines			Schooners.			Steamers		
No.	Size.	Length.	No.	Size.	Length.	No.	Size.	Length.	No.	Size.	Length.	No.	Size.	Length.	No.	Size.	Length.	No.	Size.	Length.	No.	Size.	Length.
2	7½	24	1	7	12	1	6½	11	1	6	10	1	5½	7	1	5½	8	1	5½	8	2	7½	2
2	7½	6	1	7	3	1	6½	2½	1	6	2½	1	5	2½	1	4¾	2½	1	4¾	2	2	7½	6
4	3½	34	2	3	12	2	3	12	2	3	12	2	2½	14	2	2¼	10	2	2¼	8	4	3½	28
2	9	25	2	8	20	2	7½	18	2	7½	18	2	6	14	2	6	14	1	6	7	2	9	28
2	9	6	2	8	5	2	7½	5	2	7½	5	2	6	5	2	6	5	1	6	2	2	9	6
2	4½	18	2	4	14	2	3¾	12	2	3¾	12	2	3	14	2	3	14	1	3	7	2	4½	14
1	6	14	1	5½	12	1	5½	11	1	5	11	—	—	—	—	—	—	—	—	—	1	6	15
1	6	2½	1	5½	2½	1	5½	2	1	5	2	—	—	—	—	—	—	—	—	—	1	6	2
1	3	8½	1	2¾	7	1	2¾	6	1	2½	6	—	—	—	—	—	—	—	—	—	1	3	7
2	4	15	2	3½	12	2	3½	12	2	3¼	11	2	3	8	2	3	8	—	—	—	2	4	14
1	4	6	1	3½	5	1	3	5	1	3	5	—	—	—	—	—	—	—	—	—	1	4	6
1	3½	2	1	3½	2	1	3¼	2	1	3¼	2	—	—	—	—	—	—	—	—	—	1	3½	2
2	3	10	2	2¾	8	2	2¾	7	2	2½	6	—	—	—	—	—	—	—	—	—	2	3	10
2	4	22	2	3¼	18	2	3¼	16	2	3	15	—	—	—	—	—	—	—	—	—	2	4	22
2	3	72	2	3	62	2	2¾	58	2	2½	54	—	—	—	—	—	—	—	—	—	2	3	72
1	7	34	1	6	28	1	6	28	1	5¼	26	1	5	27	1	5	24	1	5	23	1	5¾	37
2	5¼	64	2	5	48	2	4¾	44	2	4½	42	1	5	18	1	5	16	1	5	16	2	5¼	62
4	2¾	40	4	2½	36	4	2½	32	4	2¼	30	2	2½	18	—	—	—	—	—	—	4	2¾	40
2	3½	14	2	3¼	12	2	3¼	10	2	3	9	2	2¾	9	2	2¾	8	2	2½	9	2	3½	14
1	7½	7½	1	6½	6½	1	6	6½	1	5½	6	1	5½	5	1	5½	4½	1	5½	4½	1	7½	7
1	4½	15	1	4¼	14	1	4	13	1	3½	12	1	3½	9	1	3½	9	1	3½	8	1	4½	15
2	2½	16	2	2¼	14	2	2¼	12	2	2	12	—	—	—	—	—	—	—	—	—	2	2½	16
1	3	55	1	2¾	46	1	2¾	44	1	2½	42	1	2½	45	1	2½	42	1	2¾	26	1	3	66
1	2½	32	1	2¼	28	1	2¼	26	1	2	24	1	2	22	1	2	20	1	2	21	1	2½	34
2	3¼	60	2	3¼	56	2	3	50	2	3	44	2	2¾	43	2	2¾	42	2	2¾	40	2	3¼	60
2	5½	6	2	5¼	5	2	5	5	2	5	5	2	4½	5	2	4½	5	2	4½	6	2	5½	6
2	2¼	52	2	2	46	2	2	44	2	2	42	2	2	40	2	2	36	—	—	—	2	2¼	54
1	4¼	38	1	4	34	1	3¾	32	1	3½	30	1	3¼	30	1	3¼	27	1	3½	27	1	4¼	38
2	3¾	34	2	3½	30	2	3¼	30	2	3¼	28	2	3	32	2	3	20	2	2¾	24	2	3¾	34
2	2½	20	2	2¼	16	2	2	14	2	2	14	—	—	—	—	—	—	—	—	—	2	2½	20
2	3	8	2	2¾	7	2	2¾	7	2	2½	7	2	2½	7	2	2½	6	2	2¼	6	2	3	8
1	4¼	17	1	4	15	1	4	13	1	3¾	12	1	3½	11	1	3½	10½	1	3¾	10	1	4¼	17
1	2¾	45	1	2½	39	1	2¼	37	1	2¼	37	1	2	37	1	2	34	1	2	33	1	2¾	46
1	2¼	34	1	2	30	1	1¾	30	1	1¾	26	1	1¾	26	1	1¾	22	1	1¾	26	1	2¼	34
2	3	38	2	2½	30	2	2½	30	2	2½	28	2	2¼	26	2	2¼	24	2	2	24	2	3	38
1	2¾	26	1	2½	20	1	2¼	20	1	2	19	1	1¾	18	1	1½	15	1	1½	14	1	2¾	26

Names of Rigging.	Ships of the Line.									Razees.			Frigates.		
	3 Decks.			2 Decks.									1st Class.		
				1st Class.			2d Class.								
	No.	Size.	Length.	No.	Size.	Length.	No.	Size.	Length.	No.	Size.	Length.	No.	Size.	Length.
FORE-MAST AND YARD GEAR.															
Pendants (pairs) -	2	10½	10	2	10½	10	2	10	10	2	10	10	2	10	10
Shrouds (pairs)* - -	10	10½	124 / 134	10	10½	120 / 134	10	10	114 / 119	10	10	123 / 128	9	10	92 / 116
Lanyards for Shrouds (four-stranded) - -	20	5¼	200	20	5¼	160	20	5	160	20	5	160	18	5	153
Stays - - - - -	2	15	40	2	15	40	2	14½	38	2	14½	39	2	14	46
Collars for Stays - -	2	9	19	2	9	18	2	9	18	2	8½	18			
Futtock Shrouds - -	12	6½	30	12	6½	30	12	6¼	30	12	6	30	10	5¾	25
Slings Proper (to go over Cap)—Chain for all vessels - -															
Slings, Preventer -	1	12	11	1	12	10	1	11	10	1	10½	10	1	10	9
Lanyard for Slings -	1	5	21	1	5	21	1	4¾	21	1	4¾	21	1	4¾	21
Pendant Tackle Falls	2	4	118	2	4	114	2	4	94	2	3¾	98	2	3¾	98
Runner - - - - -	1	8	14	1	8	14	1	8	14	1	7	14	1	7	14
Falls for Runner - -	1	4	45	1	4	45	1	4	39	1	3¾	39	1	3¾	42
Jeer Falls - - - -	2	5¾	130	2	5¾	130	2	5½	108	2	5¼	112	2	5	104
Jackstays (bending) Iron - - - - -															
Jackstays (reefing) -	2	3½	17	2	3½	16	2	3¼	16	2	3¼	16	2	3	14
Foot Ropes - - - -	2	5	18	2	5	17	2	4¾	17	2	4¾	17	2	4¾	15
Stirrups - - - - -	8	3¼	8	8	3¼	8	6	3	6	6	3	6	6	3	6
Truss Pendants (hide)	2	7	22	2	7	20	2	6½	19	2	6½	19	2	6¼	18
Falls for Truss Pendants - - - - -	2	3¼	52	2	3¼	50	2	3	48	2	3	50	2	3	48
Lifts - - - - - -	2	5¼	90	2	5¼	80	2	5	78	2	5	80	2	4¾	70
Braces - - - - -	2	4¾	154	2	4½	150	2	4½	154	2	4½	156	2	4¼	148
Tacks (tapered) - -	2	6½	80	2	6½	80	2	6½	68	2	6½	70	2	6	66
Sheets (tapered) - -	2	6½	84	2	6½	84	2	6½	72	2	6½	74	2	6	68
Clew Garnets - - -	2	4	84	2	4	80	2	3¾	74	2	3¾	78	2	3½	64
Bowlines - - - -	2	4	64	2	4	62	2	3¾	60	2	3¾	60	2	3½	56
Reef Pendants - -	2	4½	11	2	4½	10	2	4¼	10	2	4¼	10	2	4¼	9
Bunt-lines (pairs) -	2	3¼	54	2	3¼	52	2	3	48	2	3	50	2	3	40
Bunt-line Whips -	2	3	52	2	3	48	2	2¾	44	2	2¾	46	2	2¾	40
Leech-lines - - -	4	3	110	4	3	110	4	2¾	105	4	2¾	108	4	2½	104
After Leech-lines -	4	3	100	4	3	100	4	2¾	84	4	2¾	88	4	2½	80
Slab-lines - - - -	1	2½	22	1	2½	22	1	2½	21	1	2¼	22	1	2¼	20
Clew Jiggers - - -	2	2¾	86	2	2¾	80	2	2½	70	2	2½	72	2	2½	70
Lift Jiggers - - -	2	3¼	36	2	3¼	36	2	3	36	2	3	36	2	3	30
Boom Jiggers - - -	2	2¾	42	2	2¾	40	2	2½	34	2	2½	36	2	2¼	34
Boom Jiggers (in and out) - - - - -	2	3	66	2	3	60	2	3	58	2	3	60	2	2¾	56
Bunt Whip - - -	1	2½	23	1	2½	23	1	2½	21	1	2½	22	1	2¼	20
Fore Storm Stay Sail Stay - - - - -	1	9	15	1	9	14	1	8½	13	1	8½	14	1	8	13
Halliards - - - -	1	3¾	39	1	3¾	36	1	3½	34	1	3½	36	1	3¼	33
Downhaul - - - -	1	2¾	21	1	2¾	20	1	2¾	18	1	2¾	18	1	2½	18
Lower Studding-sail Halliards - - -	2	4	98	2	4	96	2	4	84	2	3¾	88	2	3¾	92
Lower Studding-sail Inner Halliards -	2	3	60	2	3	54	2	3	50	2	3	52	2	2¾	52

* It will be remembered that the specific lengths given in these Tables are

Frigates.			Sloops.									Brigs.			Brig-antines			Schoon-ers.			Steamers.		
2d Class.			1st Class.			2d Class.			3d Class.														
No.	Size.	Length.	No.	Size.	Length.	No.	Size.	Length.	No.	Size.	Length.	No.	Size.	Length.	No.	Size.	Length.	No.	Size.	Length.	No.	Size.	Length.
2	9	9	2	8	8	2	7½	8	2	7½	8	2	6	7	2	6	7	1	6	4	2	9	9
8	9	{79 82	6	8	104	6	7½	102	5	7½	80	5	6	74	5	6	73	4	6	88	8	9	{92 95
16	4½	136	12	4	96	12	3¾	90	10	3¾	75	10	3	70	–	–	–	–	–	–	16	4½	136
2	12½	44	2	10½	38	2	10	34	2	9½	32	2	8	34	2	7½	32	1	10½	19	2	12½	52
10	5½	25	–	Iron	–	–	Iron	–	–	I'n	–	–	I'n	–	–	I'n	–	–	Iron	–	10	5½	28
1	9	9	1	8	8	1	7½	7	1	7½	7	1	6	7	1	6	7	–	–	–	1	9	9
1	4½	20	1	4	16	1	3½	15	1	3½	15	1	3	14	1	3	14	–	–	–	1	4½	18
2	3½	88	2	3¼	78	2	3¼	72	2	3¼	70	2	3	66	2	3	58	2	2¾	90	2	3½	94
1	7	13	–	–	–	–	–	–	–	–	–	–	–	–	–	–	–	–	–	–	1	7	13
1	3¾	36	–	–	–	–	–	–	–	–	–	–	–	–	–	–	–	–	–	–	1	3¾	36
2	5	84	–	–	–	–	–	–	–	–	–	–	–	–	–	–	–	–	–	–	2	5	100
2	3	13	2	2¾	11	2	2½	10	2	2½	10	2	2¼	10	2	2½	9	–	–	–	2	3	13
2	4¼	14	2	4	12	2	3¾	11	2	3½	11	2	3¼	11	2	3¼	10	2	3	11	2	4¼	14
6	2¾	6	4	2¾	4	4	2½	4	4	2½	4	4	2¼	4	4	2¼	4	4	2	4	6	2¾	6
–	Pat.	–	–	Pat.	–	–	Pat.	–	–	P't	–	–	P't	–	–	P't	–	–	Pat.	–	–	Pat.	–
2	5¼	54	2	4½	42	2	4¼	38	2	5¼	36	2	4½	32	2	4½	28	2	4	36	2	5¼	62
2	4	145	2	3¾	108	2	3½	100	2	3½	90	2	3	85	2	3	85	2	2¾	90	2	4	126
2	5½	62	2	5	48	2	4¾	44	2	4½	42	2	4	42	2	4	42	2	3½	30	2	5½	80
2	5½	64	2	5	50	2	4¾	46	2	4½	44	2	4	44	2	4	44	2	2¾	20	2	5½	80
2	3¼	54	2	3	52	2	3	42	2	3	42	2	2½	46	2	2½	46	–	–	–	2	3¼	78
2	3¼	52	2	3	46	2	3	44	2	3	40	2	2¾	38	2	2¾	36	–	–	–	2	3¼	58
																		Ya	rd R	'pe			
2	4	9	2	3¾	8	2	3½	8	2	3½	8	2	3¼	8	2	3¼	8	2	3¼	58	2	4	9
2	2¾	36	2	2½	32	2	2¼	31	2	2	30	4	2	72	2	2	60	–	–	–	2	2¾	48
2	2¼	36	2	2¼	34	2	2	30	2	2	30	–	–	–	–	–	–	–	–	–	2	2¼	42
4	2¼	88	4	2	72	4	2	72	4	2	72	2	2	36	2	2	36	–	–	–	4	2¼	104
4	2¼	72	4	2	60	4	2	56	4	2	54	2	2	34	2	2	28	–	–	–	4	2¼	88
1	2	18	1	2	15	1	2	14	1	2	13	1	2	17	1	2	14	–	–	–	1	2	22
2	2¼	62	2	2	50	2	2	50	2	2	50	2	2	48	2	2	48	–	–	–	2	2¼	76
2	2¾	26	2	2½	24	2	2½	24	2	2½	24	2	2	20	2	2	20	2	2	20	2	2¾	26
2	2¼	30	2	2	24	2	2	24	2	2	24	2	1¾	24	2	1¾	18	–	–	–	2	2¼	32
2	2½	52	2	2¼	46	2	2	40	2	2	38	2	1¾	36	2	1¾	34	–	–	–	2	2½	58
1	2	18	1	2	14	1	2	14	1	2	14	1	1¾	12	1	1¾	12	–	–	–	1	2	20
1	7	11	1	6½	9	1	6½	9	1	6	8½	1	6	10	1	6	10	1	7½	14	1	7	14
1	3¼	29	1	3	25	1	3	24	1	2¾	24	1	2¾	28	1	2¾	26	1	3	33	1	3¼	37
1	2¼	16	1	2¼	14	1	2	13	1	2	12	1	2	12	1	2	12	1	2¾	15	1	2¼	18
2	3½	82	2	3¼	66	2	3	64	2	3	62	2	2¾	60	2	2¾	56	2	2¾	58	2	3½	82
2	2½	48	2	2¼	40	2	2¼	34	2	2	32	2	2	36	2	2	34	–	–	–	2	2½	52

full pattern lengths for each gang of Standing Rigging.

Names of Rigging.	Ships of the Line.									Razees.			Frigates.		
	3 DECKS.			2 DECKS.									1st Class.		
				1st Class.			2d Class.								
	No.	Size.	Length.	No.	Size.	Length.	No.	Size.	Length.	No.	Size.	Length.	No.	Size.	Length.
FORE-MAST AND YARD GEAR. *Con.*															
Lower Studding-sail Sheets - - - -	2	4¼	32	2	4¼	32	2	4	30	2	3¾	30	2	3¼	30
Lower Studding-sail Outhaul - - - -	2	4	58	2	4	56	2	4	50	2	3¾	50	2	3¾	52
Swinging-boom Topping-lifts - - - -	2	5½	44	2	5½	40	2	5¼	38	2	5	40	2	4½	38
Falls and Lizard for Topping-lifts - -	2	3½	108	2	3½	104	2	3¼	100	2	3¼	100	2	3	94
After Guys - - - -	2	3¾	76	2	3¾	70	2	3¾	66	2	3½	66	2	3½	60
Forward Guys - -	2	3¾	128	2	3¾	120	2	3¾	108	2	3½	108	2	3½	106
Gear Tricing-lines -	2	3	44	2	3	42	2	3	42	2	3	42	2	2¾	40
FORE TOP-MAST & YARD GEAR.															
Shrouds and Pendants (pairs) - - - -	6	7	123	6	7	123	6	7	123	6	6½	123	[illegible]	[illegible]	86
Lanyards for Shrouds and Pendants - -	12	3½	84	12	3½	84	12	3½	84	12	3¼	84	10	3	70
Stays - - - - - -	2	9½	70	2	9½	65	2	9½	64	2	9½	65	2	9	62
Breast Backstays(prs)	2	8	82	2	8	80	2	7½	78	2	7½	81	2	7	72
Falls for Breast Backstays - - - - -	4	3¾	52	4	3¾	52	4	3¾	52	4	3¾	52	4	3½	52
Standing Backstays (pairs) - - - -	2	10	88	2	10	86	2	10	84	2	10	86	2	9½	78
Lanyards for Standing Backstays - - -	4	5	40	4	5	40	4	5	40	4	5	40	4	4¾	40
Cat-Harpen Legs -	2	4½	4	2	4½	4	2	4¼	4	2	4¼	4	2	4¼	4
Top-Burtons - - -	2	3½	176	2	3½	170	2	3½	158	2	3½	162	2	3¼	150
Runners - - - -	2	4½	8	2	4½	8	2	4½	8	2	4½	8	2	4	7
Top Tackle Pendants	2	9	53	2	9	52	2	9	45	2	9	47	2	8½	44
Top Tackle Falls -	2	5	160	2	5	150	2	5	130	2	4¾	135	2	4½	130
Jackstays (bending) Iron - - - - - -															
Foot Ropes - - - -	2	4	15	2	4	15	2	4	12	2	4	12	2	3¾	13
Stirrups - - - - -	6	3	6	6	3	6	6	3	6	6	3	6	6	2¾	6
Flemish Horses - -	2	3	6	2	3	6	2	3	6	2	3	6	2	3	5
Parrel - - - - - -	1	7	6	1	7	6	1	7	6	1	7	6	1	6½	5
Top-sail Ties (all hide) - - - - - -	2	7	38	2	7	36	2	7	36	2	7	36	2	6½	31
Halliards for Top-sail Tyes - - - - - -	2	4	120	2	4	116	2	4	98	2	4	106	2	3¾	106
Rolling Tackle - -	1	3	18	1	3	18	1	3	18	1	3	18	1	3	16
Lifts - - - - - - -	2	7	36	2	7	34	2	7	34	2	6½	34	2	6	31
Braces - - - - - -	2	4½	118	2	4½	116	2	4½	113	2	4¼	113	2	4	104
Stay-sail Halliards -	1	3	68	1	3	68	1	3	68	1	3	70	1	2¾	66
Stay-sail Downhaul -	1	2½	40	1	2½	40	1	2½	40	1	2½	42	1	2½	38
Stay-sail Sheets - -	2	3	60	2	3	60	2	3	60	2	3	62	2	3	58
Sheets - - - - - -	2	6½	82	2	6½	80	2	6½	71	2	6¼	72	2	6	68
Clew-lines - - - - -	2	3¾	96	2	3¾	95	2	3¾	88	2	3½	90	2	3½	80
Bow-lines - - - - -	2	3½	72	2	3½	70	2	3½	64	2	3½	64	2	3½	60
Bunt-lines - - - - -	2	3¾	71	2	3¾	70	2	3¾	65	2	3½	67	2	3½	62
Reef Pend'ts (all hide)	2	4¾	15	2	4¾	14	2	4¾	14	2	4¾	14	2	4½	12

Frigates.			Sloops.									Brigs.			Brigantines.			Schooners.			Steamers.		
2d Class.			1st Class.			2d Class.			3d Class.														
No.	Size.	Length.	No.	Size.	Length.	No.	Size.	Length.	No.	Size.	Length.	No.	Size.	Length.	No.	Size.	Length.	No.	Size.	Length.	No.	Size.	Length.
2	3	28	2	3	26	2	2¾	26	2	2¾	24	2	2½	18	2	2½	18	2	2½	12	2	3	30
2	3½	48	2	3¼	34	2	3	32	2	3	31	2	2¾	30	2	2¾	30	2	2¾	36	2	3½	46
2	4¼	36	2	4	32	2	3¾	30	2	3¾	30	2	3½	28	2	3½	26	2	3½	36	2	4¼	42
2	2¾	90	2	2½	76	2	2¼	74	2	2¼	73	2	2	68	2	2	66	2	2¼	30	2	2¾	90
2	3¼	54	2	3	50	2	2¾	44	2	2¾	42	2	2½	40	2	2½	38	2	3	36	2	3¼	64
2	3¼	94	2	3	78	2	2¾	72	2	2¾	70	2	2½	64	2	2½	62	2	3	36	2	3¼	100
2	2½	36	2	2¼	30	2	2	28	2	2	27	2	1¾	26	2	1¾	26	–	–	–	2	2½	42
5	5½	82	4	4½	58	4	4¼	57	3	4¼	45	3	4	39	3	4	39	2	3¾	24	5	5½	106
10	2¾	70	8	2¼	56	8	2¼	56	6	2¼	42	–	–	–	–	–	–	–	–	–	10	2¾	70
2	8½	54	2	7½	45	2	7	44	2	7	43	2	5½	42	2	5½	42	1	4½	24	2	8½	64
2	7	64	1	7	28	1	6½	27	1	6	26	1	5½	25	1	5½	23	–	–	–	2	7	80
4	3¼	52	2	3¼	24	2	3	22	2	3	21	2	2¾	16	2	2¾	16	–	–	–	4	3¼	52
2	9	68	2	8	60	2	7½	58	2	7½	56	1	6½	28	1	6½	26	1	4½	28	2	9	84
4	4½	40	4	4	36	4	3¾	36	4	3¾	36	–	–	–	–	–	–	–	–	–	4	4½	40
2	4	3	2	3½	3	2	3¼	3	2	3¼	3	2	3	3	2	3	3	2	2½	2	2	4	3
2	3¼	134	2	3	112	2	3	104	2	2¾	100	2	2½	98	2	2½	90	–	–	–	2	3¼	160
2	4	7	2	3¾	6	2	3¾	6	2	3¾	6	2	3½	6	2	3½	5	–	–	–	2	4	7
2	8	40	2	6½	35	2	6½	32	1	6½	18	1	5	18	1	5	16	Lg 1	m'st 4	r'p 34	2	8	46
2	4	116	–	–	–	–	–	–	–	–	–	–	–	–	–	–	–	–	–	–	2	4	134
2	3½	11	2	3¼	9	2	3¼	9	2	3	9	2	2¾	8	2	2¾	8	2	2½	8	2	3½	12
6	2½	6	4	2¼	4	4	2	4	4	2	4	4	2	4	4	2	4	2	2	4	6	2½	6
2	3	5	2	2½	4	2	2½	4	2	2½	4	2	2	4	2	2	4	2	2	3	2	3	5
1	6½	4½	1	6	4½	1	5½	4	1	5½	4	1	5	4	1	5	4	1	3½	3	1	6½	5
2	6½	30	2	6	23	2	5½	22	2	5½	22	1	5½	9	1	5½	8	1	4½	7	2	6½	41
2	3½	90	2	3¼	82	2	3¼	70	2	3	68	1	3	30	1	3	30	1	2¾	41	2	3½	100
1	2¾	15	1	2½	14	1	2½	13	1	2½	12	1	2	12	1	2	12	1	2	5	1	2¾	15
2	5½	29	2	5	26	2	5	25	2	5	24	2	4½	21	2	4½	21	2	4	20	2	5½	35
2	3½	94	2	3¼	78	2	3¼	74	2	3	72	2	2¾	60	2	2¾	64	2	2½	64	2	3½	124
1	2¾	65	1	2½	60	1	2½	60	1	2½	56	1	2¼	48	1	2¼	48	–	–	–	1	2¾	60
1	2¼	36	1	2	34	1	2	32	1	2	32	1	2	30	1	1¾	30	–	–	–	1	2	34
2	2¾	56	2	2½	52	2	2½	50	2	2½	50	2	2¼	48	2	2¼	48	–	–	–	2	2½	50
2	5¾	64	2	5¼	54	2	5	48	2	5	46	2	4	46	2	4	46	2	3¾	46	2	5¾	71
2	3¼	74	2	3	62	2	3	60	2	2¾	59	2	2½	58	2	2½	56	2	2¼	56	2	3¼	86
2	3¼	50	2	3	48	2	3	44	2	2¾	42	2	2½	40	2	2¼	40	2	2	52	2	3¼	60
2	3¼	54	2	3	50	2	3	46	2	2¾	45	2	2½	42	2	2½	42	2	2¼	44	2	3¼	66
2	4¼	11	2	4	10	2	4	10	2	3¾	10	2	3½	7	2	3¼	7	2	3	7	2	4¼	12

Names of Rigging.	Ships of the Line.									Razees.			Frigates.		
	3 Decks.			2 Decks.									1st Class.		
				1st Class.			2d Class.								
	No.	Size.	Length.	No.	Size.	Length.	No.	Size.	Length.	No.	Size.	Length.	No.	Size.	Length.
FORE TOP-MAST & YARD GEAR. *Con.*															
Whips for Reef Pendants	2	3¼	79	2	3¼	78	2	3¼	74	2	3¼	74	2	3¼	66
Clew Jiggers	2	2½	102	2	2½	96	2	2½	92	2	2½	94	2	2¼	86
Lift Jiggers	2	3	24	2	3	24	2	3	24	2	3	24	2	2¾	24
Bunt-runner	1	4	11	1	4	10	1	4	10	1	4	10	1	4	8
Jigger for Bunt-runner	1	3	30	1	3	30	1	3	30	1	3	30	1	2¾	25
Boom Tricing-lines	2	2½	30	2	2½	26	2	2	26	2	2	26	2	2	22
Studding-s'l Halliards	2	4	104	2	4	100	2	4	96	2	3¾	100	2	3¾	92
Studding-sail Tacks	2	3½	94	2	3½	86	2	3½	80	2	3½	84	2	3¼	84
Studding-sail Sheets	2	3¼	56	2	3¼	48	2	3¼	45	2	3¼	47	2	3¼	46
Studding-sail Downhauls	2	3	70	2	3	68	2	2¾	60	2	2¾	62	2	2½	60
Studding-sail Boom Brace	2	3½	60	2	3½	60	2	3½	60	2	3½	60	2	3¼	50
Studding-sail Topping-lifts	2	4	40	2	4	40	2	4	40	2	4	40	2	3½	35
FORE TOP-GAL'NT M'ST & YARD GEAR															
Shrouds (pairs)	2	5	66	2	5	64	2	5	63	2	5	63	2	4½	56
Stay	1	5	46	1	5	45	1	5	41	1	5	42	1	4½	39
Breast Backstays (prs)	1	5	52	1	5	51	1	5	49	1	5	50	1	4¼	46
Falls for Breast Backstays	2	2¾	24	2	2¾	24	2	2½	24	2	2½	24	2	2¼	20
Standing Backstays (pairs)	1	6	56	1	6	54	1	6	51	1	6	53	1	5½	48
Long Yard, or Mast Rope	1	6½	58	1	6½	58	1	6	52	1	5¾	54	1	5½	49
Short Mast Rope	1	5¾	12	1	5¾	12	1	5½	12	1	5½	12	1	5¼	10½
Jackstays (Iron)															
Foot Ropes	2	3	9	2	3	9	2	3	8½	2	2¾	8½	2	2½	8
Stirrups	2	2½	2	2	2½	2	2	2¼	2	2	2¼	2	2	2	2
Parrel	1	4	3	1	4	3	1	4	3	1	4	3	1	3½	3
Lifts	2	3¾	52	2	3¾	50	2	3½	50	2	3½	50	2	3¼	44
Braces	2	2¾	128	2	2¾	120	2	2½	116	2	2½	118	2	2¼	112
Halliards	1	3¼	57	1	3¼	56	1	3	52	1	3	53	1	2¾	48
Sheets	2	4½	66	2	4½	65	2	4¼	60	2	4¼	62	2	3¾	56
Clew-lines	2	2½	90	2	2½	84	2	2¼	81	2	2¼	83	2	2	78
Bow-lines	2	2¼	96	2	2¾	94	2	2	88	2	2	88	2	2	84
Bunt-lines	2	2¾	48	2	2¾	48	2	2½	44	2	2½	44	2	2¼	40
Lift Jiggers	2	2½	24	2	2½	24	2	2¼	24	2	2¼	24	2	2	20
Bunt Jiggers	1	2¾	22	1	2¾	21	1	2½	20	1	2½	20	1	2¼	18
Tripping-line	1	2¾	29	1	2¾	26	1	2½	24	1	2½	25	1	2¼	24
Studding-sail Hall'rds	2	3	94	2	3	88	2	3	84	2	3	86	2	2¾	84
Studding-sail Sheets	2	3½	32	2	3½	28	2	3¼	27	2	3¼	27	2	3	24
Studding-sail Tacks	2	2¾	64	2	2¾	58	2	2¾	54	2	2½	54	2	2¼	54
F'RE ROYAL MAST AND YARD GEAR.															
Shrouds (pair)	1	4	38	1	4	38	1	4	37	1	4	37	1	3½	32
Falls for Shrouds	2	2	10	2	2	10	2	2	10	2	2	10	2	2	8
Stay	1	3¼	58	1	3¼	57	1	3¼	52	1	3	53	1	3	46

Frigates.			Sloops.									Brigs.			Brig-antines			Schoon-ers.			Steamers.		
2d Class.			1st Class.			2d Class.			3d Class.														
No.	Size	Length.	No	Size.	Length.	No.	Size.	Length.	No.	Size.	Length.	No.	Size.	Length.	No.	Size.	Length.	No.	Size.	Length.	No.	Size.	Length.
2	3	60	2	2¾	56	2	2½	50	2	2½	48	2	2¼	46	2	2	46	2	2	50	2	3	76
2	2¼	80	2	2	66	2	2	62	2	2	60	2	1¾	60	2	1¾	60	2	1½	46	2	2¼	94
2	2¾	24	2	2½	22	2	2½	20	2	2½	18	2	2¼	16	2	2¼	16	2	2¼	12	2	2¾	24
1	3½	8	1	3	7	1	3	6	1	3	6	1	3	6	1	3	6	–	–	–	1	3½	10
1	2½	22	1	2	18	1	2	16	1	2	16	1	2	12	1	2	12	–	–	–	1	2½	32
2	2	20	2	1½	20	2	1½	20	2	1½	20	2	1¼	18	2	1¼	18	2	1¼	14	2	2	30
2	3½	82	2	3¼	68	2	3	64	2	3	63	2	2¾	62	2	2¾	60	2	2½	66	2	3½	98
2	3	79	2	3	62	2	2¾	56	2	2¾	54	2	2½	50	2	2½	48	2	2¼	72	2	3	98
2	3	42	2	3	40	2	2¾	38	2	2¾	37	2	2¾	30	2	2¾	30	2	2½	32	2	3	44
2	2¼	54	2	2¼	42	2	2	41	2	2	40	2	1¾	36	2	1¾	36	2	1½	40	2	2¼	58
2	3¼	50	2	3	40	2	3	40	2	3	40	–	–	–	–	–	–	–	–	–	2	3¼	60
2	3½	35	2	3½	30	2	3¼	30	2	3¼	30	–	–	–	–	–	–	–	–	–	2	3½	40
2	4	52	2	3½	44	2	3½	42	2	3	41	2	2¾	36	2	2¾	36	1	2½	15	2	3¾	68
1	4	35	1	3½	31	1	3¼	30	1	3	29	1	2¾	27	1	2¾	26	1	2½	28	1	4	40
1	4	42	1	3½	37	1	3¼	35	1	3	33	1	2¾	31	1	2¾	29	–	–	–	1	4	53
2	2	20	2	2	16	2	2	14	2	2	14	2	1½	14	2	1½	14	–	–	–	2	2	20
1	5	44	1	4½	39	1	4	37	1	4	36	1	3½	33	1	3½	30	1	3	34	1	5	54
1	5¼	44	1	4½	41	1	4¼	36	1	4¼	35	1	3¾	34	1	3¾	34	1	3	35	1	5¼	55
1	4¾	9½	1	4	8½	1	3¾	8	1	3¾	8	1	3½	7	1	3½	7	–	–	–	1	4¾	12
2	2½	8	2	2¼	7	2	2¼	7	2	2¼	7	2	2	6	2	2	6	2	2	6	2	2½	8
2	2	2	2	2	2	2	2	2	2	2	2	–	–	–	–	–	–	–	–	–	2	2	2
1	3¼	3	1	3	2½	1	3	2	1	3	2	1	2½	2	1	2½	2	1	2	2	1	3½	3
2	3	42	2	2¾	36	2	2½	34	2	2½	33	2	2¼	30	2	2¼	30	2	2	28	2	3	45
2	2¼	102	2	2	80	2	2	75	2	2	74	2	2¼	48	2	2¼	48	2	2	52	2	2¼	132
1	2¾	45	1	2½	35	1	2¼	32	1	2	30	1	2	25	1	2	25	–	–	–	1	2¾	54
2	3½	50	2	3¼	46	2	3	42	2	3	41	2	2¾	40	2	2¾	38	2	2	44	2	3½	60
2	2	74	2	1¾	60	2	1½	56	2	1½	54	2	1½	42	2	1½	42	2	1¼	48	2	2	80
2	2	74	2	1¾	62	2	1½	58	2	1½	54	2	1¼	53	2	1¼	52	2	1¼	54	2	2	84
2	2¼	36	1	2¼	17	1	2	15	1	2	14	1	1¾	14	1	1¾	14	–	–	–	2	2¼	46
2	2	20	2	1¾	16	2	1½	15	2	1½	14	2	1¼	12	2	1¼	12	–	–	–	2	2	20
1	2	17	1	1¾	16	1	1½	15	1	1½	15	1	1¼	13	1	1¼	13	–	–	–	1	2	22
1	2¼	22	1	2	20	1	1¾	19	1	1¾	18	1	1½	17	1	1½	17	1	1½	18	1	2¼	26
2	2½	74	2	2¼	62	2	2¼	58	2	2¼	56	2	2¼	54	2	2¼	52	2	2	70	2	2½	92
2	2¾	22	2	2½	20	2	2¼	20	2	2¼	20	2	2	16	2	2	16	2	2	36	2	2¾	28
2	2¼	46	2	2	38	2	2	37	2	2	36	2	1¾	32	2	1¾	32	2	1¾	32	2	2¼	46
1	3¼	30	1	3	28	1	3	26	1	2½	24	1	2½	22	1	2½	21						
2	2	8	2	1½	8	2	1½	8	2	1¼	8	2	1¼	7	2	1¼	7						
1	2¾	40	1	2¾	34	1	2½	34	1	2½	33	1	2¼	32	1	2	30						

Names of Rigging.	Ships of the Line.									Razees.			Frigates.		
	3 DECKS.			2 DECKS.									1st Class.		
				1st Class.			2d Class.								
	No.	Size.	Length.	No.	Size.	Length.	No.	Size.	Length.	No.	Size.	Length.	No.	Size.	Length.
F'RE ROYAL MAST & YARD GEAR. *Con.*															
Backstays (pair) - -	1	4	62	1	4	60	1	4	57	1	4	60	1	3½	54
Yardrope - - - - -	1	3¾	62	1	3¾	60	1	3½	58	1	3½	60	1	3¼	54
Jackstays (Iron) - -															
Foot Ropes - - - -	2	2¾	7	2	2¾	7	2	2¾	7	2	2¾	7	2	2½	6
Parrel - - - - - -	1	1½	2	1	1½	2	1	1½	2	1	1½	2	1	1½	2
Lifts - - - - - - -	2	3	58	2	3	56	2	3	52	2	2½	52	2	2½	48
Braces - - - - - -	2	2¾	104	2	2¾	106	2	2¾	86	2	2½	86	2	2½	78
Halliards - - - - -	1	2½	37	1	2½	33	1	2¼	32	1	2¼	33	1	2	30
Sheets - - - - - -	2	3	44	2	3	40	2	3	40	2	3	40	2	2¾	38
Clew-lines - - - - -	2	2½	48	2	2½	46	2	2¼	46	2	2¼	46	2	2	42
Bow-lines - - - - -	2	2¼	114	2	2¼	110	2	2¼	101	2	2	103	2	2	100
Bunt-line - - - - -	1	2½	27	1	2½	25	1	2¼	24	1	2¼	24	1	2	22
Tripping-line - - -	1	2	30	1	2	30	1	2	28	1	2	29	1	2	26
FORE TRY-SAIL M'ST & GAFF G'AR.															
Peak Halliards - -	1	3¾	63	1	3¾	60	1	3¾	53	1	3½	56	1	3½	58
Throat Halliards -	1	3¼	45	1	3¼	45	1	3¼	39	1	3¼	42	1	3¼	38
Vangs - - - - - -	2	3	68	2	2½	60	2	3	56	2	3	58	2	2½	56
Peak Brails (pairs of)	2	2	88	2	2	80	2	2	78	2	2	78	2	2	74
Throat Brails (p'rs of)	1	3½	44	1	3½	42	1	3½	40	1	3½	40	1	3¼	38
Middle Brails (p'rs of)	1	3	38	1	3	36	1	2¾	36	1	2¾	36	1	2½	32
Foot Brails (pairs of)	1	3	44	1	3	40	1	3	40	1	2¾	40	1	2½	34
Sheets - - - - - -	2	4	91	2	4	90	2	3½	85	2	3½	85	2	3½	78
MAIN-MAST AND YARD GEAR.															
Pendants (pairs) - -	2	10½	11	2	10½	10½	2	10	10	2	10	10	2	10	10
Shrouds (pairs) - -	11	10½	Warps. {111, 113, 88}	10	10½	{142, 147}	10	10	{127, 133}	10	10	{135, 141}	10	10	{122, 132}
Lanyards for Shrouds	22	5¼	220	20	5¼	200	20	5	170	20	5	170	20	5	170
Stays - - - - - -	2	15	55	2	15	54	2	14½	50	2	14½	51	2	14	51
Futtock Shrouds - -	12	6½	39	12	6½	36	12	6	30	12	6	30	10	5¾	25
Slings Proper (to go over Cap)—Chain for all vessels - -															
Slings, Preventer -	1	12	12	1	12	11	1	11½	10	1	11½	10	1	10	9½
Lanyard for Slings (four-stranded) - -	1	5	22	1	5	22	1	4¾	21	1	4¾	21	1	4¾	20
Pendant Tackle Falls*	2	4	120	2	4	114	2	4	108	2	3¾	112	2	3¾	104
Runner - - - - - -	1	8	24	1	8	23	1	8	22	1	7	22	1	7	18
Falls for Runner - -	1	4	59	1	4	59	1	4	59	1	3¾	59	1	3¾	44
Jeer Falls - - - - -	2	5¾	140	2	5¾	136	2	5½	130	2	5¼	134	2	5	110
Jackstays (bending) Iron - - - - -															
Jackstays (reefing) -	2	3½	18	2	3½	18	2	3½	18	2	3½	18	2	3¼	15
Foot Ropes - - - -	2	5¼	20	2	5¼	19	2	5	19	2	5	19	2	4¾	16

* **All small vessels which are not allowed Jeers and Top Tackle Falls, the Pendant Tackle Falls**

Frigates. 2d Class.			Sloops. 1st Class.			Sloops. 2d Class.			Sloops. 3d Class.			Brigs.			Brig-antines			Schoon-ers.			Steamers.		
No.	Size.	Length.	No.	Size.	Length.	No.	Size.	Length.	No.	Size.	Length.	No.	Size.	Length.	No.	Size.	Length.	No.	Size.	Length.	No.	Size.	Length.
1	3¼	50	1	3	42	1	3	41	1	2½	40	1	2½	36	1	2½	34						
1	3	48	1	2¾	43	1	2½	40	1	2½	38	1	2½	36	1	2½	34						
2	2½	6	2	2½	5	2	2¼	5	2	2¼	5	2	2	5	2	2	5						
1	1½	2	1	1¼	2	1	1¼	2	1	1¼	2	1	1¼	1½	1	1¼	1½						
2	2½	44	2	2¼	40	2	2	36	2	2	35	2	2	32	2	2	32						
2	2¼	68	2	2	56	2	2	52	2	2	50	2	2	48	2	2	46						
1	1¾	28																					
2	2½	34	2	2¼	28	2	2	27	2	2	26	2	2	26	2	2	26						
2	2	40	2	1½	32	2	1½	30	2	1½	30	2	1¼	29	2	1¼	29						
2	1¾	82	2	1¼	72	2	1¼	72	2	1¼	68	2	1	66	2	1	60						
1	2	20																					
1	1¾	24	1	1¼	22	1	1¼	21	1	1¼	20	1	1	19	1	1	18						
1	3¼	45	1	3	31	1	3	30	1	3	29	1	2¾	28	1	2¾	27	1	3¼	55	1	3¼	55
1	3	34	1	2¾	30	1	2¾	28	1	2¾	26	1	2½	25	1	2½	25	1	3¼	40	1	3	43
2	2¼	52	2	2¼	46	2	2	44	2	2	43	2	2	42	2	2	40	2	2¾	58	2	2¼	60
2	2	64	1	2	31	1	1½	30	1	1½	28	1	1¼	28	1	1¼	28	2	1¼	80	2	2	76
1	3	36	1	2¾	34	1	2¾	28	1	2¾	28	1	2½	28	1	2½	28	pen. 1 w'ip 2	3½ 2¾	16 40	1	3	38
1	2¼	30	1	2	28	1	2	26	1	2	26	1	1¾	25	1	1¾	25	1	2¼	28	1	2¼	34
1	2¼	32	1	2	28	1	2	26	1	2	26	1	2	25	1	2	25	1	2½	36	1	2¼	36
2	3½	66	2	3	54	2	3	50	2	3	46	2	3	36	2	2¾	36	2	4¼	54	2	3½	78
2	9	9	2	8	9	2	7½	8	2	7½	8	2	6	7	1	6	4	1	6	4	2	9	9
9	9	86 113	7	8	140	7	7½	129	6	7½	108	5	6	82	3	6	67	3	6	66	9	9	90 120
18	4½	153	14	4	112	14	3¾	112	12	3¾	96	10	3	70	–	–	–	–	–	–	18	4½	153
2	12½	44	2	10½	40	2	10	36	2	9½	34	2	8	34	2	6½	30	2	6½	30	2	12½	58
10	5½	25	–	Iron	–	–	Iron	–	–	I'n	–	–	I'n	–	–	I'n	–	–	I'n	–	12	5½	30
1	10	9	1	8	8	1	7½	8	1	7½	8	1	6	7	–	–	–	–	–	–	1	10	9
1	4¾	18	1	4	16	1	3½	15	1	3½	15	1	3	14	–	–	–	–	–	–	1	4¾	18
2	3½	90	2	3¼	84	2	3¼	80	2	3¼	74	2	3	70	2	3	90	2	2¾	90	2	3½	94
1	7	16	–	–	–	–	–	–	–	–	–	–	–	–	–	–	–	–	–	–	1	7	20
1	3¾	40	–	–	–	–	–	–	–	–	–	–	–	–	–	–	–	–	–	–	1	3¾	64
2	5	90	–	–	–	–	–	–	–	–	–	–	–	–	–	–	–	–	–	–	2	5	100
2	3	14	2	2¾	13	2	2½	11	2	2½	11	2	2½	10	–	–	–	–	–	–	2	3	13
2	4½	15½	2	4¼	14	2	4	13	2	3¾	13	2	3½	11	2	3¼	9	2	3¼	9	2	4½	14

may be increased in size one-fourth in addition to the specified size in the foregoing Table.

Names of Rigging.	Ships of the Line.									Razees.			Frigates.		
	3 Decks.			2 Decks.									1st Class.		
				1st Class.			2d Class.								
	No.	Size.	Length.	No.	Size.	Length.	No.	Size.	Length.	No.	Size.	Length.	No.	Size.	Length.
MAIN-MAST AND YARD GEAR. *Con.*															
Stirrups - - - - -	8	3¼	8	8	3¼	8	6	3	6	6	3	6	6	3	6
Truss Pendants (hide)	2	7	23	2	7	22	2	6½	21	2	6½	21	2	6½	18
Falls for Truss Pendants - - - - -	2	3½	53	2	3½	52	2	3	50	2	3	52	2	3	54
Lifts - - - - - -	2	5½	102	2	5½	86	2	5¼	80	2	5¼	82	2	5	78
Braces - - - - -	2	4¾	180	2	4½	180	2	4½	180	2	4½	180	2	4½	168
Tacks (tapered) - -	2	6½	90	2	6½	82	2	6½	70	2	6½	72	2	6	70
Sheets (tapered) - -	2	6½	94	2	6½	86	2	6½	74	2	6½	76	2	6	74
Clew Garnets - - -	2	4	90	2	4	84	2	3¾	80	2	3¾	84	2	3½	74
Runner (for Main Bow-line) - - -	1	4½	8	1	4½	7	1	4½	7	1	4½	7	1	4	6
Whip for Runner -	1	3¼	18	1	3	15	1	3	15	1	3	15	1	3	15
Reef Pendants - -	2	4½	12	2	4½	12	2	4¼	12	2	4¼	12	2	4¼	10
Bunt-lines (pairs) -	2	3¼	68	2	3¼	68	2	3	60	2	3	62	2	3	60
Bunt-line Whips -	2	3	72	2	3	62	2	2¾	62	2	2¾	62	2	2¾	62
Leech-lines - - -	4	3	128	4	3	116	4	2¾	112	4	2¾	116	4	2½	108
After Leech-lines -	4	3	108	4	3	106	4	2¾	98	4	2¾	100	4	2½	84
Slab-line - - - -	1	2½	23	1	2½	23	1	2¼	23	1	2¼	23	1	2¼	21
Clew Jiggers - - -	2	3	98	2	3	96	2	2¾	88	2	2¾	92	2	2¾	80
Lift Jiggers - - -	2	3¼	36	2	3¼	36	2	3	36	2	3	36	2	3	34
Boom Jiggers - - -	2	2¾	52	2	2¾	50	2	2½	42	2	2½	44	2	2¼	40
Boom Jiggers (in and out) - - - - -	2	3	74	2	3	66	2	3	62	2	3	64	2	2¾	60
Bunt Whip - - -	1	2½	28	1	2½	27	1	2½	26	1	2½	27	1	2¼	22
MAIN TOP-MAST & YARD GEAR.															
Shrouds and Pendants (pairs) - - - -	6	7	135	6	7	130	6	7	131	6	6½	131	5	6	100
Lanyards for Pendants - - - - -	12	3½	96	12	3½	84	12	3½	84	12	3¼	84	10	3	70
Stays - - - - -	2	9½	69	2	9½	64	2	9½	62	2	9½	63	2	9	61
Breast Backstays (prs)	2	8	92	2	8	88	2	7½	86	2	7½	88	2	7	80
Falls for Breast Backstays - - - - -	4	3¾	52	4	3¾	52	4	3½	52	4	3½	52	4	3¼	52
Standing Backstays (pairs) - - - -	2	10	96	2	10	96	2	10	92	2	10	94	2	9½	86
Lanyards for Standing Backstays - - -	4	5	40	4	5	40	4	5	40	4	5	40	4	4¾	40
Cat-Harpen Legs -	2	4½	4	2	4½	4	2	4¼	4	2	4¼	4	2	4¼	4
Top-Burtons - - -	2	3½	192	2	3½	180	2	3½	174	2	3½	178	2	3¼	162
Runners - - - -	2	4½	8	2	4½	8	2	4½	8	2	4½	8	2	4	7
Top Tackle Pendants	2	9	58	2	9	55	2	9	47	2	9	50	2	8½	48
Top Tackle Falls -	2	5	170	2	5	160	2	5	145	2	4¾	150	2	4½	142
Jackstays (Iron) - -															
Foot Ropes - - - -	2	4	17	2	4	16	2	4	15	2	4	15	2	3¾	14
Stirrups - - - - -	6	3	6	6	3	6	6	3	6	6	3	6	6	2¾	6
Flemish Horses - -	2	3	7	2	3	6	2	3	6	2	3	6	2	3	6
Parrel - - - - - -	1	7	6	1	7	6	1	7	6	1	7	6	1	6¾	5
Top-sail Ties (all hide) - - - - -	2	7	42	2	7	40	2	7	40	2	7	40	2	6¾	36

Frigates.			Sloops.									Brigs.			Brig-antines			Schoon-ers.			Steamers.		
2d Class.			1st Class.			2d Class.			3d Class.														
No.	Size.	Length.	No	Size.	Length.	No.	Size.	Length.	No.	Size.	Length.	No.	Size.	Length.	No.	Size.	Length.	No.	Size.	Length.	No.	Size.	Length.
6	2¾	6	4	2¾	4	4	2½	4	4	2½	4	4	2¼	4	4	2¼	4	4	2	4	6	2¾	6
–	Pat.	–	–	Pat.	–	–	Pat.	–	–	P't	–	–	P't	–	–	P't	–	–	P't	–	–	Pat.	
–	Pat.																						
2	5½	58	2	4½	48	2	4½	46	2	5½	44	2	4¾	38	2	4	36	2	3	34	2	5½	62
2	4	150	2	3¾	100	2	3½	100	2	3¼	92	2	3	84	2	2½	60	2	2½	66	2	4	160
2	5½	58	2	5	50	2	4¾	44	2	4¼	44	2	4	42	–	–	–	–	–	–	2	5½	80
2	5½	62	2	5	54	2	4¾	46	2	4¼	46	2	4	46	–	–	–	–	–	–	2	5½	84
2	3¼	64	2	3	58	2	3	52	2	3	52	2	2½	50	–	–	–	–	–	–	2	3¼	78
1	4	6	1	3½	6	1	3½	5	1	3½	5	1	3	5	–	–	–	–	–	–	1	4	7
1	3	14	1	2½	14	1	2½	13	1	2½	13	1	2	10	–	–	–	–	–	–	1	3	18
2	4	9½	2	3¾	9	2	3½	9	2	3½	9	2	3¼	8	2	5	13	2	5	13	2	4	9
2	2¾	52	2	2½	46	2	2¼	44	2	2	43	2	2	40	–	–	–	–	–	–	2	2¾	48
2	2½	58	2	2½	50	2	2	48	2	2	46	2	2	38	–	–	–	–	–	–	2	2¼	42
4	2½	96	4	2	88	4	2	80	4	2	79	2	2	40	–	–	–	–	–	–	4	2½	105
4	2¼	80	4	2	68	4	2	64	4	2	62	2	2	36	–	–	–	–	–	–	4	2¼	88
1	2	20	1	2	17	1	2	16	1	2	15	1	2	18	–	–	–	–	–	–	1	2	22
2	2½	72	2	2¼	60	2	2¼	56	2	2	56	2	2	60	–	–	–	–	–	–	2	2½	76
2	2¾	30	2	2½	24	2	2½	23	2	2½	23	2	2	30	–	–	–	–	–	–	2	2¾	26
2	2½	32	2	2	28	2	2	27	2	2	27	2	1¾	27	–	–	–	–	–	–	2	2¼	32
2	2½	56	2	2¼	50	2	2	44	2	2	43	2	1¾	46	–	–	–	–	–	–	2	2½	58
1	2	18	1	2	16	1	2	15	1	2	15	1	1¾	13	–	–	–	–	–	–	1	2	20
5	5½	88	4	4½	62	4	4¼	60	3	4½	47	3	4	42	2	3	24	2	3	24	5	5½	106
10	2¾	70	8	2¼	56	8	2¼	56	6	2¼	42	–	–	–	–	–	–	–	–	–	10	2¾	70
2	8½	53	2	7½	39	2	7	37	2	7	36	1	6¼	20	1	3	14	1	3	10	2	8½	72
2	7	72	1	7	31	1	6½	30	1	6	29	1	5½	28	–	–	–	–	–	–	2	7	80
4	3½	52	2	3½	24	2	3¼	22	2	3	22	2	2¾	16	–	–	–	–	–	–	4	3¼	52
2	9	76	2	8	67	2	7½	64	2	7½	63	1	6¼	29	1	3½	28	1	3	30	2	9	84
4	4½	40	4	4	36	4	3¾	36	4	3¾	36	–	–	–	–	–	–	–	–	–	4	4½	40
2	4	3½	2	3½	3	2	3¼	3	2	3¼	3	2	3	3	2	3	3	2	2½	2	2	4	3
2	3¼	146	2	3	128	2	3	120	2	2¾	112	2	2½	104	–	–	–	–	–	–	2	3¼	160
2	4	7	2	3¾	6	2	3¾	6	2	3¾	6	2	3½	6	–	–	–	–	–	–	2	4	7
2	8	41	2	6½	38	2	6½	34	1	6½	20	1	5	20	Lg 1	ms 4	rope 34	Lg 1	ms 4	rope 34	2	8	46
2	4	122	–	–	–	–	–	–	–	–	–	–	–	–	–	–	–	–	–	–	2	4	134
2	3½	12	2	3½	11	2	3¼	10	2	3	10	2	2¾	8	2	2¾	7	2	2¾	7	2	3½	12
6	2½	6	4	2¼	4	4	2	4	4	2	4	4	2	4	2	2	2	2	2	2	6	2½	6
2	3	5	2	2½	4	2	2½	4	2	2½	4	2	2	4	2	2	4	2	2	4	2	3	5
1	6½	4½	1	6	4	1	6	4	1	6	4	1	5	4	1	4	3	1	4	3	1	6½	5
2	6½	32	2	6	25	2	5½	24	2	5½	23	1	5½	9	1	5	8	1	4½	7	2	6½	41

Names of Rigging.	Ships of the Line.									Razees.			Frigates.		
	3 decks.			2 decks.									1st Class.		
				1st Class.			2d Class.								
	No.	Size.	Length.	No	Size.	Length.	No.	Size.	Length.	No.	Size.	Length.	No.	Size.	Length.
MAIN TOP-MAST & YARD GEAR. *Con.*															
Halliards for Top-sail Tyes - - - - -	2	4	134	2	4	130	2	4	120	2	4	124	2	3¾	122
Rolling Tackle - -	1	3	20	1	3	20	1	3	20	1	3	20	1	3	18
Lifts - - - - - - -	2	7	38	2	7	36	2	7	34	2	6½	34	2	6	31
Braces - - - - - -	2	4½	120	2	4½	120	2	4½	120	2	4¼	122	2	4	100
Sheets - - - - - -	2	6½	88	2	6½	82	2	6½	79	2	6¼	81	2	6	78
Clew-lines - - - - -	2	3¾	106	2	3¾	104	2	3¾	99	2	3¼	102	2	3½	90
Bow-lines - - - - -	2	3½	78	2	3½	76	2	3½	70	2	3½	70	2	3½	64
Bunt-lines - - - - -	2	3¾	82	2	3¾	74	2	3¾	72	2	3¾	74	2	3½	68
Reef Pend'ts (all hide)	2	4¾	16	2	4¾	15	2	4¾	15	2	4¾	15	2	4½	13
Whips for Reef Pendants - - - - - -	2	3½	88	2	3½	80	2	3½	78	2	3¼	80	2	3¼	76
Clew Jiggers - - -	2	2½	108	2	2½	104	2	2½	100	2	2½	104	2	2¼	96
Lift Jiggers - - -	2	3	24	2	3	24	2	3	24	2	3	24	2	2¾	24
Bunt-runner - - -	1	4	11	1	4	10	1	4	10	1	4	10	1	4	9
Jigger for Bunt-runner	1	3	38	1	3	35	1	3	35	1	3	35	1	2¾	28
Boom Tricing-lines -	2	2½	32	2	2½	28	2	2½	28	2	2½	28	2	2	24
Studding-s'l Halliards	2	4	114	2	4	108	2	4	104	2	4	108	2	3¾	98
Studding-sail Tacks	2	3½	112	2	3½	104	2	3½	98	2	3½	102	2	3¼	94
Studding-sail Sheets	2	3¼	60	2	3¼	50	2	3¼	50	2	3¼	50	2	3¼	48
Studding-sail Downhauls - - - - -	2	3	74	2	3	68	2	2¾	67	2	2¾	68	2	2½	64
MAIN TOP-GAL'NT M'ST & YARD GEAR															
Shrouds (pairs) - -	2	5	73	2	5	68	2	5	67	2	5	67	2	4½	60
Stay - - - - - - -	1	5	29	1	5	27	1	5	26	1	5	26	1	4½	24
Breast Backstays (pr.)	1	5	58	1	5	57	1	5	55	1	4½	56	1	4¼	50
Falls for Breast Backstays - - - - - -	2	2¾	24	2	2¾	20	2	2¾	20	2	2½	20	2	2½	20
Standing Backstays (pair) - - - -	1	6	61	1	6	60	1	6	57	1	6	59	1	5½	53
Long Yard, or Mast Rope - - - - - -	1	6½	64	1	6½	61	1	6	58	1	5¾	60	1	5½	53
Short Mast Rope - -	1	6	14	1	5¾	14	1	5½	13	1	5½	13	1	5¼	12
Jackstays (Iron) - -															
Foot Ropes - - - - -	2	3¼	10	2	3¼	10	2	3	10	2	3	10	2	2¾	9
Stirrups - - - - - -	2	2½	2	2	2½	2	2	2¼	2	2	2¼	2	2	2	2
Parrel - - - - - -	1	4	3	1	4	3	1	4	3	1	4	3	1	3½	3
Lifts - - - - - - -	2	4	58	2	3¾	56	2	3½	56	2	3½	56	2	3¼	50
Braces - - - - - -	2	3¾	118	2	2¾	116	2	2½	104	2	2½	106	2	2¼	100
Halliards - - - - -	1	3¼	61	1	3¼	60	1	3	59	1	3	60	1	2¾	56
Sheets - - - - - -	2	4½	70	2	4½	68	2	4¼	66	2	4¼	68	2	4	64
Clew-lines - - - - -	2	2½	98	2	2½	90	2	2¼	88	2	2½	90	2	2	84
Bow-lines - - - - -	2	2¼	88	2	2¼	85	2	2	82	2	2	83	2	2	78
Bunt-lines - - - - -	2	2¾	50	2	2¾	50	2	2½	46	2	2½	46	2	2½	42
Lift Jiggers - - -	2	2¾	24	2	2¾	24	2	2¼	24	2	2¼	24	2	2	20
Bunt Jigger - - -	1	2¾	24	1	2¾	22	1	2½	22	1	2½	22	1	2¼	21
Tripping-line - - -	1	2¾	31	1	2¾	30	1	2½	27	1	2½	28	1	2¼	26
Studding-sail Halliards - - - - -	2	3½	104	2	3½	98	2	3½	97	2	3¼	98	2	3	92

Frigates.			Sloops.									Brigs.			Brig-antines			Schoon-ers.			Steamers.		
2d Class.			1st Class.			2d Class.			3d Class.														
No.	Size.	Length.	No.	Size.	Length.	No.	Size.	Length.	No.	Size.	Length.	No.	Size.	Length.	No.	Size.	Length.	No.	Size.	Length.	No.	Size.	Length.
2	3½	100	2	3¼	90	2	3¼	80	2	3	76	1	3	34	1	2½	43	1	2½	34	2	3½	100
															Ro	l'g	rope	Ro	l'g	rope			
1	2¾	16	1	2½	14	1	2½	13	1	2½	12	1	2	12	1	2	5	1	2	5	1	2¾	15
2	5½	30	2	5	28	2	5	27	2	5	26	2	4½	22	2	3¾	18	2	3½	18	2	5½	35
2	3½	100	2	3¼	92	2	3¼	90	2	3	88	2	2½	64	2	2½	64	2	2½	64	2	3½	90
2	5¾	70	2	5¼	58	2	5	54	2	5	50	2	4	52	2	3½	46	2	3½	46	2	5¾	71
2	3¼	80	2	3	70	2	3	66	2	3	64	2	2½	60	2	2	52	2	2	52	2	3¼	86
2	3¼	58	2	3	50	2	3	44	2	2¾	43	2	2½	42	2	2	42	2	2	42	2	3¼	74
2	3¼	60	2	3	54	2	3	48	2	3	47	2	2¾	44	1	2	22	1	2	22	2	3¼	66
2	4¼	12	2	4	10	2	4	10	2	3¾	9	2	3½	7	–	–	–	–	–	–	2	4¼	12
2	3	68	2	2¾	60	2	2½	56	2	2½	55	2	2¼	48	–	–	–	–	–	–	2	3	76
2	2¼	82	2	2	76	2	2	64	2	2	60	2	1¾	66	2	1½	46	–	–	–	2	2¼	94
2	2¾	24	2	2½	22	2	2½	21	2	2½	20	2	2¼	16	2	2¼	16	2	2	16	2	2¾	24
1	3½	9	1	3	7	1	3	7	1	3	7	1	3	6	–	–	–	–	–	–	1	3½	10
1	2½	26	1	2	20	1	2	19	1	2	18	1	2	12	–	–	–	–	–	–	1	2½	22
2	2	22	2	1½	20	2	1½	20	2	1½	20	2	1¼	20	–	–	–	–	–	–	2	2	30
2	3½	88	2	3¼	74	2	3	70	2	3	68	2	2¾	64	–	–	–	–	–	–	2	3½	98
2	3	84	2	3	72	2	2¾	64	2	2¾	62	2	2½	60	–	–	–	–	–	–	2	3	98
2	3¼	46	2	3	44	2	3	40	2	3	39	2	2¾	32	–	–	–	–	–	–	2	3¼	44
2	2¼	60	2	2¼	50	2	2	48	2	2	46	2	2	38	–	–	–	–	–	–	2	2¼	58
2	4	56	2	3½	48	2	3½	46	2	3	45	2	2¾	38	1	2¼	15	1	2¼	15	2	3¾	68
1	4¼	22	1	3¾	19	1	3½	18	1	3¼	17	1	3	14	1	2½	16	1	2½	12	1	4¼	31
1	4	46	1	3½	40	1	3¼	38	1	3	36	1	3	32	–	–	–	–	–	–	1	4	53
2	2¼	20	2	2	16	2	2	15	2	2	15	2	1½	14	–	–	–	–	–	–	2	2¼	20
1	5	48	1	4½	42	1	4	39	1	4	38	1	3½	34	1	2¾	34	1	2¾	34	1	5	54
1	5¼	48	1	4½	43	1	4¼	40	1	4¼	39	1	3¾	36	1	2¼	36	–	–	–	1	5¼	55
1	4¾	11	1	4½	9	1	4	9	1	4	9	1	3½	7	–	–	–	–	–	–	1	4¾	12
2	2½	9	2	2¼	8	2	2¼	7	2	2¼	7	2	2	6	2	2	5	–	–	–	2	2½	8
2	2	2	2	2	2	2	2	2	2	2	2	–	–	–	–	–	–	–	–	–	2	2	2
1	3½	3	1	3	2	1	3	2	1	3	2	1	2½	2	1	2½	2	–	–	–	1	3½	3
2	3	46	2	2¾	40	2	2½	38	2	2½	36	2	2¼	31	2	2	24	–	–	–	2	3	45
2	2¼	88	2	2	76	2	2	66	2	2	65	2	2	50	2	2	48	–	–	–	2	2¼	94
1	2½	48	1	2½	40	1	2¼	38	1	2	36	1	2	26	–	–	–	–	–	–	1	2½	54
2	3¾	56	2	3½	50	2	3¼	46	2	3¼	44	2	2¾	41	2	2¼	44	–	–	–	2	3¾	60
2	2	78	2	1¾	66	2	1½	58	2	1½	55	2	1½	44	2	1½	46	–	–	–	2	2	80
2	2	68	2	2	64	2	1¾	56	2	1¾	53	2	1¾	48	–	–	–	–	–	–	2	2	86
2	2¼	38	1	2¼	18	1	2¼	16	1	2¼	16	1	2	30	–	–	–	–	–	–	2	2¼	46
2	2	20	2	1¾	16	2	1½	16	2	1½	15	2	1¼	12	–	–	–	–	–	–	2	2	20
1	2	19	1	1¾	17	1	1½	15	1	1½	15	1	1¼	13	–	–	–	–	–	–	1	2	22
1	2¼	24	1	2	22	1	1¾	20	1	1¾	19	1	1½	19	1	1	18	–	–	–	1	2¼	26
2	2¾	80	2	2¾	70	2	2½	64	2	2½	60	2	2½	58	–	–	–	–	–	–	2	2¾	92

Names of Rigging.	Ships of the Line.									Razees.			Frigates.		
	3 DECKS.			2 DECKS.									1st Class.		
				1st Class.			2d Class.								
	No.	Size.	Length.	No.	Size.	Length.	No.	Size.	Length.	No.	Size.	Length.	No.	Size.	Length.
MAIN TOP-GAL'NT M. & Y'D GEAR. *Con*															
Studding-sail Sheets	2	3½	33	2	3½	30	2	3¼	28	2	3¼	30	2	3	28
Studding-sail Tacks	2	3	70	2	3	64	2	3	64	2	3	64	2	2½	60
MAIN ROYAL M'ST & YARD GEAR.															
Shrouds (pair) - -	1	4	42	1	4	40	1	4	40	1	4	40	1	3½	36
Falls for Shrouds -	2	2	10	2	2	10	2	2	10	2	2	10	2	2	8
Stay - - - - - - -	1	3¼	34	1	3¼	31	1	3¼	30	1	3¼	30	1	3	28
Backstays (pair) - -	1	4	69	1	4	68	1	4	65	1	4	67	1	3¾	60
Yardrope - - - - -	1	3¾	71	1	3¾	70	1	3½	64	1	3½	66	1	3¼	62
Jackstays (Iron) - -															
Foot Ropes - - - - -	2	2¾	8	2	2¾	8	2	2¾	7	2	2¾	7	2	2½	6
Parrel - - - - - -	1	1½	2	1	1½	2	1	1½	2	1	1½	2	1	1½	2
Lifts - - - - - - -	2	3	62	2	3	60	2	3	60	2	2½	60	2	2½	54
Braces - - - - - -	2	2¾	72	2	2¾	70	2	2¾	64	2	2½	64	2	2½	56
Halliards - - - - -	1	2½	43	1	2½	42	1	2¼	37	1	2¼	38	1	2¼	35
Sheets - - - - - -	2	3½	48	2	3¼	46	2	3¼	44	2	3	44	2	3	42
Clew-lines - - - - -	2	2½	53	2	2½	52	2	2½	50	2	2¼	50	2	2¼	48
Bow-lines - - - - -	2	2¼	72	2	2¼	64	2	2¼	58	2	2	64	2	2	60
Bunt-lines - - - - -	1	2½	28	1	2½	27	1	2¼	25	1	2	27	1	2	24
Tripping-line - - -	1	2	34	1	2	33	1	2	31	1	2	32	1	2	29
Main-boom Topping-lifts - - - - -	–	–	–	–	–	–	–	–	–	–	–	–	–	–	–
Falls for Main-boom Topping-lifts - -	–	–	–	–	–	–	–	–	–	–	–	–	–	–	–
MAIN TRY-SAIL M'ST & GAFF G'AR.															
Peak Halliards - -	1	3½	63	1	3½	63	1	3½	59	1	3½	63	1	3¼	48
Throat Halliards -	1	3½	48	1	3½	48	1	3¼	42	1	3¼	46	1	3	43
Vangs - - - - - -	2	3	68	2	3	60	2	3	58	2	3	60	2	2½	56
Peak Brails (pairs) -	1	2½	42	1	2½	38	1	2½	37	1	2½	38	1	2¼	36
Throat Brails (pairs)	1	3½	46	1	3½	43	1	3¼	42	1	3¼	43	1	3	38
Middle Brails (pairs)	1	2¾	38	1	2¾	34	1	2¾	34	1	2½	34	1	2½	32
Foot Brails (pairs) -	1	3	36	1	3	34	1	3	34	1	2¾	34	1	2½	34
Sheets - - - - - -	2	4	62	2	4	60	2	3½	60	2	3½	60	2	3½	54
Outhauler - - - -	–	–	–	–	–	–	–	–	–	–	–	–	–	–	–
Boom Tackle for Outhauler - - - -	–	–	–	–	–	–	–	–	–	–	–	–	–	–	–
Reef Pendants for Outhauler - - - -	–	–	–	–	–	–	–	–	–	–	–	–	–	–	–
Reef Tackle for Outhauler - - - -	–	–	–	–	–	–	–	–	–	–	–	–	–	–	–
MIZEN-MAST & CR. JACK YARD GEAR.															
Shrouds and Pendants (pairs) - - - -	6	8	144	6	8	143	6	7½	136	6	7½	136	6	7	136
Lanyards for Shrouds and Pendants - -	12	4	96	12	4	96	12	3¾	84	12	3¾	84	12	3½	84
Stay - - - - - - -	1	9½	19	1	9½	18	1	9	17	1	9	18	1	9	17

Frigates.			Sloops.									Brigs.			Brig-antines			Schoon-ers.			Steamers.		
2d Class.			1st Class.			2d Class.			3d Class.														
No.	Size.	Length.	No	Size.	Length.	No.	Size.	Length.	No.	Size.	Length.	No.	Size.	Length.	No.	Size.	Length.	No.	Size.	Length.	No.	Size.	Length.
2	2¾	26	2	2½	22	2	2¼	20	2	2¼	20	2	2	18	–	–	–	–	–	–	2	2¾	28
2	2¼	50	2	2	42	2	2	40	2	2	38	2	1¾	33	–	–	–	–	–	–	2	2¼	32
1	3¼	32	1	3	30	1	3	27	1	2¾	26	1	2¾	22									
2	2	8	2	1¾	8	2	1¾	8	2	1½	8	2	1½	7									
1	3	25	1	2¾	23	1	2¾	20	1	2½	19	1	2¼	17									
1	3½	54	1	3¼	48	1	3	42	1	3	42	1	3	37									
1	3	54	1	2¾	46	1	2½	43	1	2½	42	1	2½	39									
2	2½	6	2	2¼	5	2	2¼	5	2	2¼	5	2	2	5									
1	1½	2	1	1¼	2	1	1¼	2	1	1¼	2	1	1¼	1½									
2	2½	50	2	2¼	42	2	2¼	38	2	2	37	2	2	32									
2	2¼	52	2	2	42	2	2	39	2	2	37	2	2	38									
1	2	32																					
2	2¾	38	2	2½	34	2	2¼	32	2	2	30	2	2	28									
2	2	44	2	1½	38	2	1½	36	2	1½	34	2	1¼	30									
2	1¾	52	2	1¼	44	2	1¼	42	2	1¼	42	2	1	38									
1	2	22																					
1	1¾	26	1	1½	23	1	1½	22	1	1½	21	1	1¼	19									
–	–	–	–	–	–	–	–	–	–	–	–	2	4	30	2	5	40	2	5	40			
–	–	–	–	–	–	–	–	–	–	–	–	2	2¾	30	2	3	36	2	3	36			
1	3	40	1	2¾	34	1	2¾	31	1	2¾	30	1	3¼	44	1	3¾	54	1	3¾	54	1	3	41
1	2¾	38	1	2¾	33	1	2½	31	1	2½	30	1	3¼	28	1	3¼	38	1	3¼	38	1	2¾	44
2	2¼	52	2	2	48	2	1¾	46	2	1¾	44	2	2¼	42	2	2½	56	2	2½	30	2	2¼	58
1	2	34	1	2	32	1	1¾	30	1	1¾	28	2	1½	64	1	2	42	1	2	40	1	2	40
1	2¾	36	1	2¾	32	1	2½	30	1	2½	28	1	3¼	34	1	3¼	40	1	3¼	38	1	2¾	36
1	2¼	30	1	2	28	1	1¾	26	1	1¾	24	1	1¾	31	1	2	34	1	2	34	1	2¼	38
1	2½	28	1	2	26	1	2	24	1	2	22	1	2¾	30	1	2½	38	1	2½	36	1	2¼	32
2	3½	44	2	3	34	2	3	32	2	3	31	2	3	60	1	4	35	1	4	35	2	3½	52
–	–	–	–	–	–	–	–	–	–	–	–	1	3¾	22	1	4	25	1	4	25			
–	–	–	–	–	–	–	–	–	–	–	–	2	2½	50	2	2¾	60	2	2¾	60			
–	–	–	–	–	–	–	–	–	–	–	–	2	5½	6	2	5½	6	2	5½	6			
–	–	–	–	–	–	–	–	–	–	–	–	1	3	15	1	3	18	1	3	18			
5	6½	98	5	6	86	5	5½	78	5	5½	76	–	–	–	–	–	–	–	–	–	5	6½	103
10	3¼	70	10	3	70	10	2¾	70	10	2¾	70	–	–	–	–	–	–	–	–	–	10	3¼	80
1	8	16	1	7¾	13	1	7½	13	1	7½	12	–	–	–	–	–	–	–	–	–	1	8	17

Names of Rigging.	Ships of the Line.									Razees.			Frigates.		
	3 DECKS.			2 DECKS.									1st Class.		
				1st Class.			2d Class.								
	No.	Size.	Length.	No.	Size.	Length.	No.	Size.	Length.	No.	Size.	Length.	No.	Size.	Length.
MIZEN-MAST & CR. JACK Y. GEAR. *Con.*															
Futtock Shrouds - -	8	5½	24	8	5½	20	8	5½	20	8	5½	20	8	5¼	20
Slings (Chain for all vessels) - - - -															
Pendant Tackle Falls	2	3¼	110	2	3¼	106	2	3¼	90	2	3¼	94	2	3	92
Foot Ropes - - - -	2	3½	16	2	3½	16	2	3½	14	2	3½	14	2	3¼	12
Stirrups - - - - -	4	3	4	4	3	4	4	3	4	4	3	4	4	3	4
Truss Pendants (all hide) - - - - -	1	6	8	1	6	8	1	6	8	1	6	8	1	5½	7
Fall for Truss Pendants - - - - -	1	3	20	1	3	20	1	3	20	1	3	20	1	2¾	20
Lifts - - - - - -	2	5½	26	2	5½	26	2	5½	22	2	5½	22	2	5	20
Braces - - - - -	2	3	88	2	3	86	2	3	76	2	3	80	2	3	68
MIZEN TOP-M'ST & YARD GEAR.															
Shrouds and Pendants (pairs) - - - -	4	5¼	74	4	5¼	69	4	5¼	69	4	5¼	69	4	5	62
Lanyards for Shrouds and Pendants - -	8	2¾	56	8	2¾	56	8	2¾	56	8	2¾	56	8	2½	56
Stay - - - - - -	1	6	15	1	6	14	1	6	13	1	6	13	1	5½	12
Breast Backstays (pr.)	1	6	38	1	6	38	1	6	35	1	6	36	1	5¾	32
Falls for Breast Backstays - - - - -	2	3	20	2	3	20	2	3	20	2	3	20	2	2¾	20
Standing Backstays (pairs) - - - -	1	7½	39	1	7½	38	1	7½	36	1	7½	38	1	7¼	34
Lanyards for Standing Backstays - - -	2	3¾	20	2	3¾	20	2	3¾	20	2	3¾	20	2	3½	20
Cat-Harpen Legs -	2	3½	3½	2	3½	3½	2	3½	3½	2	3½	3½	2	3	3
Top-Burtons - - -	2	3	150	2	3	150	2	3	132	2	2¾	140	2	2¾	130
Runners - - - -	2	3½	7	2	3½	7	2	3½	7	2	3½	7	2	3	7
Top Tackle Pendants	1	6¼	26	1	6¼	26	1	6¼	23	1	6¼	25	1	6	22
Jackstays (Iron) - -															
Foot Ropes - - - -	2	3¼	11	2	3¼	10	2	3¼	10	2	3¼	10	2	3	9
Stirrups - - - - -	4	2¾	4	4	2¾	4	4	2¾	4	4	2¾	4	4	2½	4
Flemish Horses - -	2	2½	5	2	2½	5	2	2½	5	2	2½	5	2	2	4
Parrel - - - - -	1	5¼	4	1	5¼	4	1	5¼	4	1	5¼	4	1	5	3
Top-sail Tye (all hide) - - - - -	1	5½	15	1	5½	14	1	5½	13	1	5½	13	1	5¼	13
Halliards for Top-sail Tye - - - - -	1	3	56	1	3	55	1	3	50	1	3	52	1	2¾	49
Rolling Tackle - -	1	2¾	15	1	2¾	15	1	2¾	15	1	2¾	15	1	2½	14
Lifts - - - - - -	2	4	31	2	4	30	2	4	29	2	4	29	2	3¾	27
Braces - - - - -	2	2¾	96	2	2¾	96	2	2¾	84	2	2¾	86	2	2½	80
Sheets - - - - -	2	5	52	2	5	50	2	5	46	2	5	48	2	4¾	46
Clew-lines - - - -	2	3	82	2	3	78	2	3	76	2	3	78	2	2¾	72
Bow-lines - - - -	2	2¾	58	2	2¾	52	2	2¾	50	2	2¾	52	2	2½	50
Bunt-lines - - - -	2	3	64	2	3	58	2	3	55	2	3	57	2	2¾	54
Reef Pend'ts (all hide)	2	3¼	12	2	3¼	12	2	3¼	12	2	3¼	12	2	3	10
Whips for Reef Pendants - - - - -	2	2½	68	2	2½	64	2	2½	64	2	2½	64	2	2¼	60
Clew Jiggers - - -	2	2½	88	2	2½	82	2	2½	78	2	2½	80	2	2¼	74
Lift Jiggers - - -	2	2¾	20	2	2¾	20	2	2¾	20	2	2¾	20	2	2½	20

Frigates.			Sloops.									Brigs.			Brig-antines			Schoon-ers.			Steamers.		
2d Class.			1st Class.			2d Class.			3d Class.														
No.	Size.	Length.	No	Size.	Length.	No.	Size.	Length.	No.	Size.	Length.	No.	Size.	Length.	No.	Size.	Length.	No.	Size.	Length.	No.	Size.	Length.
–	Iron	–	–	Iron	–	–	Iron	–	–	I'n	–	–	–	–	–	–	–	–	–	–	–	Iron	
2	3	74	2	2¾	68	2	2¾	62	2	2¾	60	–	–	–	–	–	–	–	–	–	2	3	80
2	3¼	11	2	3	10	2	3	9	2	2¾	9	–	–	–	–	–	–	–	–	–	2	3¼	11
4	3	4	–	–	–	–	–	–	–	–	–	–	–	–	–	–	–	–	–	–	4	3	4
–	Pat.	–	–	Pat.	–	–	Pat.	–	–	P't	–	–	–	–	–	–	–	–	–	–	–	Pat.	
2	4¾	16	2	4¼	15	2	4	15	2	4	15	–	–	–	–	–	–	–	–	–	2	4¾	16
2	2¾	62	2	2¾	54	2	2½	52	2	2½	50	–	–	–	–	–	–	–	–	–	2	2¾	64
4	4½	54	3	4½	38	3	4¼	34	3	4	34	–	–	–	–	–	–	–	–	–	4	4½	36
8	2¼	56	6	2¼	39	6	2¼	36	6	2	36	–	–	–	–	–	–	–	–	–	8	2¼	56
1	5	12	1	4¾	10	1	4½	9	1	4½	9	–	–	–	–	–	–	–	–	–	1	5	13
1	5½	28	1	5¼	25	1	5	23	1	5	22	–	–	–	–	–	–	–	–	–	1	5½	28
2	2½	20	2	2½	16	2	2½	16	2	2½	16	–	–	–	–	–	–	–	–	–	2	2½	24
1	7	30	1	6¾	28	1	6½	26	1	6½	25	–	–	–	–	–	–	–	–	–	1	7	36
2	3½	20	–	–	–	–	–	–	–	–	–	–	–	–	–	–	–	–	–	–	2	3½	20
2	3	3	2	2½	3	2	2½	3	2	2½	3	–	–	–	–	–	–	–	–	–	2	3	3
2	2½	118	2	2¼	98	2	2¼	88	2	2¼	86	–	–	–	–	–	–	–	–	–	2	2½	120
2	3	7	2	3	6	2	3	6	2	3	6	–	–	–	–	–	–	–	–	–	2	3	5
1	5½	19	1	5¼	18	1	5	17	1	5	16	–	–	–	–	–	–	–	–	–	1	5½	20
2	2¾	8	2	2½	7	2	2½	7	2	2½	7	–	–	–	–	–	–	–	–	–	2	2¾	9
4	2¼	4	4	2	4	4	2	4	4	2	4	–	–	–	–	–	–	–	–	–	4	2¼	4
2	2	3	2	2	3	2	2	3	2	2	3	–	–	–	–	–	–	–	–	–	2	2	3
1	4½	3	1	4	3	1	4	3	1	4	3	–	–	–	–	–	–	–	–	–	1	4½	3½
1	5	13	1	5¼	9	1	5¼	8	1	5¼	8	–	–	–	–	–	–	–	–	–	1	5	16
1	2½	40	1	2½	33	1	2¼	30	1	2¼	29	–	–	–	–	–	–	–	–	–	1	2½	45
1	2¼	13	1	2	12	1	2	12	1	2	12	–	–	–	–	–	–	–	–	–	1	2¼	15
2	3½	22	2	3¼	21	2	3	20	2	3	19	–	–	–	–	–	–	–	–	–	2	3½	25
2	2¼	70	2	2	58	2	2	56	2	2	54	–	–	–	–	–	–	–	–	–	2	2¼	90
2	4	40	2	3¾	38	2	3½	36	2	3½	34	–	–	–	–	–	–	–	–	–	2	4	48
2	2½	62	2	2¼	58	2	2¼	52	2	2	48	–	–	–	–	–	–	–	–	–	2	2½	72
2	2¼	44	2	2	38	2	2	36	2	2	36	–	–	–	–	–	–	–	–	–	2	2¼	58
2	2½	46	2	2¼	42	2	2	38	2	2	36	–	–	–	–	–	–	–	–	–	2	2½	50
2	3	9	2	2¾	8	2	2½	8	2	2½	8	–	–	–	–	–	–	–	–	–	2	3	9
2	2¼	52	2	2	50	2	2	48	2	2	46	–	–	–	–	–	–	–	–	–	2	2¼	58
2	2	66	2	2	56	2	2	52	2	2	50	–	–	–	–	–	–	–	–	–	2	2	72
2	2¼	18	2	2	16	2	1¾	14	2	1¾	14	–	–	–	–	–	–	–	–	–	2	2¼	20

Names of Rigging.	Ships of the Line. 3 Decks.			2 Decks. 1st Class.			2 Decks. 2d Class.			Razees.			Frigates. 1st Class.		
	No.	Size.	Length.	No.	Size.	Length.	No.	Size.	Length.	No.	Size.	Length.	No.	Size.	Length.
MIZEN TOP-M'ST & YARD GEAR. *Con.*															
Bunt-runner - - -	1	3¼	10	1	3¼	9	1	3¼	9	1	3¼	9	1	3	8
Jigger-fall for Bunt-runner - - - -	1	2½	17	1	2½	16	1	2½	16	1	2½	16	1	2¼	14
MIZ. TOP-GALL'NT M'ST & YARD GEAR															
Shrouds (pairs) - -	2	3½	58	2	3½	55	2	3¼	53	2	3¼	53	2	3	46
Stay - - - - - - -	1	3½	17	1	3½	15	1	3½	15	1	3½	15	1	3¼	14
Breast Backstays (pr.)	1	3½	47	1	3½	46	1	3¼	43	1	3¼	44	1	3¼	40
Falls for Breast Backstays - - - - - -	2	2	20	2	2	20	2	2	20	2	2	20	2	2	20
Standing Backstays (pair) - - - -	1	4½	49	1	4½	48	1	4¼	45	1	4¼	46	1	4	43
Long Yard, or Mast Rope - - - - -	1	4	53	1	4	52	1	4	47	1	4	48	1	3¾	43
Short Mast Rope - -	1	3¾	12	1	3¾	11	1	3¾	10	1	3¾	10	1	3½	9
Jackstays (Iron) - -															
Foot Ropes - - - - -	2	2½	7	2	2½	7	2	2½	7	2	2½	7	2	2¼	6
Stirrups - - - - - -	2	2¼	2	2	2¼	2	2	2¼	2	2	2¼	2	2	2	2
Parrel - - - - - -	1	3	2	1	3	2	1	3	2	1	3	2	1	2½	2
Lifts - - - - - - -	2	3	48	2	3	44	2	3	44	2	3	44	2	2¾	38
Braces - - - - - -	2	2½	78	2	2½	76	2	2½	72	2	2½	74	2	2¼	68
Halliards - - - - -	1	2¾	48	1	2¾	45	1	2¾	42	1	2¾	43	1	2½	42
Sheets - - - - - -	2	3	56	2	3	54	2	3	49	2	3	50	2	2¾	49
Clew-lines - - - - -	2	2½	66	2	2½	60	2	2½	56	2	2½	58	2	2	50
Bow-lines - - - - -	2	2	78	2	2	76	2	2	72	2	2	74	2	1¾	64
Bunt-lines - - - - -	1	2	22	1	2	21	1	2	19	1	2	19	1	2	18
Lift Jiggers - - -	2	1¾	20	2	1¾	20	2	1¾	20	2	1¾	20	2	1½	20
Bunt Jiggers - - -	1	1¾	20	1	1¾	19	1	1¾	18	1	1¾	18	1	1½	16
Tripping-line - - -	1	1¾	25	1	1¾	24	1	1¾	21	1	1¾	22	1	1½	22
MIZ. ROYAL MAST & YARD GEAR.															
Shrouds (pair) - - -	1	3	35	1	3	34	1	3	32	1	3	32	1	2½	27
Falls for Shrouds -	2	1¾	12	2	1¾	12	2	1¾	12	2	1¾	12	2	1½	8
Stay - - - - - - -	1	2¾	22	1	2¾	21	1	2¾	20	1	2¾	20	1	2½	19
Backstays (pair) - -	1	3	56	1	3	54	1	3	50	1	3	52	1	2½	48
Yardrope - - - - -	1	3	57	1	3	56	1	3	52	1	3	54	1	2¾	50
Jackstays (Iron) - -															
Foot Ropes - - - - -	2	2	5	2	2	5	2	2	5	2	2	5	2	2	5
Parrel - - - - - -	1	1	2	1	1	2	1	1	2	1	1	2	1	1	2
Lifts - - - - - - -	2	2¾	53	2	2¾	52	2	2¾	46	2	2¾	48	2	2½	42
Braces - - - - - -	2	1¾	60	2	1¾	50	2	1¾	46	2	1¾	46	2	1½	46
Halliards - - - - -	1	2	33	1	2	30	1	2	29	1	2	30	1	2	28
Sheets - - - - - -	2	2¼	38	2	2¼	36	2	2¼	36	2	2¼	36	2	2	30
Clew-lines - - - - -	2	1¾	42	2	1¾	40	2	1¾	40	2	1¾	40	2	1½	38
Bow-lines - - - - -	2	1¼	56	2	1¼	48	2	1¼	44	2	1¼	44	2	1	46
Bunt-lines - - - - -	1	1½	23	1	1½	22	1	1½	22	1	1½	22	1	1½	18
Tripping-line - - - -	1	1¼	29	1	1¼	29	1	1¼	26	1	1¼	27	1	1¼	24
SPANKER BOOM AND GAFF GEAR.															
Topping-lifts - - -	2	5½	41	2	5½	40	2	5½	40	2	5½	40	2	5½	38

Frigates.			Sloops.									Brigs.			Brig-antines			Schoon-ers.			Steamers.		
2d Class.			1st Class.			2d Class.			3d Class.														
No.	Size.	Length.	No	Size.	Length.	No.	Size.	Length.	No.	Size.	Length.	No.	Size.	Length.	No.	Size.	Length.	No.	Size.	Length.	No.	Size.	Length.
1	3	7	1	3	6	1	3	6	1	3	6	–	–	–	–	–	–	–	–	–	1	3	7
1	2¼	14	1	2¼	12	1	2¼	12	1	2	12	–	–	–	–	–	–	–	–	–	1	2¼	14
2	3	41	2	2¾	39	2	2½	34	2	2½	33	–	–	–	–	–	–	–	–	–	2	3	46
1	3	13	1	2¾	11	1	2½	10	1	2½	10	–	–	–	–	–	–	–	–	–	1	3	14
1	3	36	1	2¾	32	1	2½	29	1	2½	27	–	–	–	–	–	–	–	–	–	1	3	40
2	2	18	2	1½	14	2	1½	14	2	1¼	14	–	–	–	–	–	–	–	–	–	2	2	18
1	3¾	38	1	3½	34	1	3¼	31	1	3¼	29	–	–	–	–	–	–	–	–	–	1	3¾	44
1	3½	38	1	3¼	33	1	3	32	1	3	30	–	–	–	–	–	–	–	–	–	1	3½	45
1	3¼	8	1	3	7	1	3	7	1	3	7	–	–	–	–	–	–	–	–	–	1	3¼	8
2	2	6	2	2	5	2	2	5	2	2	5	–	–	–	–	–	–	–	–	–	2	2	7
2	2	2	2	2	2	2	2	2	2	2	2	–	–	–	–	–	–	–	–	–	2	2	2
1	2½	2	1	2	2	1	2	2	1	2	2	–	–	–	–	–	–	–	–	–	1	2½	2
2	2½	36	2	2¼	32	2	2	27	2	2	26	–	–	–	–	–	–	–	–	–	2	2½	40
2	2	60	2	1¾	50	2	1¾	46	2	1¾	45	–	–	–	–	–	–	–	–	–	2	2	64
1	2¼	34	1	2	29	1	2	28	1	2	26	–	–	–	–	–	–	–	–	–	1	2¼	40
2	2¾	42	2	2½	38	2	2¼	36	2	2¼	35	–	–	–	–	–	–	–	–	–	2	2¾	45
2	2	46	2	1¾	44	2	1¾	42	2	1¾	40	–	–	–	–	–	–	–	–	–	2	2	45
2	1½	56	2	1¼	50	2	1	48	2	1	48	–	–	–	–	–	–	–	–	–	2	1½	62
1	1¾	16	1	1½	14	1	1¼	12	1	1¼	12	–	–	–	–	–	–	–	–	–	1	1¾	18
2	1¼	18	2	1¼	16	2	1¼	14	2	1¼	14	–	–	–	–	–	–	–	–	–	2	1¼	18
1	1¼	14	1	1	12	1	1	10	1	1	10	–	–	–	–	–	–	–	–	–	1	1¼	15
1	1½	20	1	1	18	1	1	16	1	1	15	–	–	–	–	–	–	–	–	–	1	1½	20
1	2¼	25	1	2¼	24	1	2	19	1	2	19												
2	1¼	8	2	1	8	2	1	8	2	1	8												
1	2¼	17	1	2	14	1	1¾	13	1	1¾	12												
1	2¼	42	1	2¼	38	1	2	34	1	2	31												
1	2½	43	1	2¼	38	1	2¼	34	1	2¼	32												
2	2	4	2	2	4	2	2	4	2	2	4												
1	1	2	1	1	2	1	1	2	1	1	2												
2	2¼	38	2	2	36	2	2	32	2	2	30												
2	1½	42	2	1½	32	2	1¼	30	2	1¼	28												
1	2	25																					
2	1¾	28	2	1¾	24	2	1¾	22	2	1¾	20												
2	1¼	34	2	1	28	2	1	26	2	1	24												
2	1	42	2	1	30	2	1	28	2	1	28												
1	1½	16																					
1	1¼	22	1	1	20	1	1	18	1	1	16												
2	5	32	2	4¾	28	2	4½	27	2	4¼	25	–	–	–	–	–	–	–	–	–	2	5	38

Names of Rigging.	Ships of the Line.									Razees.			Frigates.		
	3 decks.			2 decks.									1st Class.		
				1st Class.			2d Class.								
	No.	Size.	Length.	No.	Size.	Length.	No.	Size.	Length.	No.	Size.	Length.	No.	Size.	Length.
SPANKER BOOM & GAFF GEAR. *Con.*															
Falls for Topping-lifts	2	3	36	2	3	36	2	3	36	2	3	36	2	2¾	34
Foot Ropes - - - -	2	3	11	2	3	11	2	3	10	2	3	10	2	2¾	10
Sheets - - - - - -	2	3¼	74	2	3¼	70	2	3¼	70	2	3¼	70	2	3	58
Outhauler - - - - -	1	4	33	1	4	32	1	4	31	1	4	31	1	3¾	30
Peak Halliards - -	1	3¾	67	1	3¾	66	1	3¾	64	1	3¾	66	1	3½	60
Throat Halliards -	1	3¼	40	1	3¼	39	1	3¼	38	1	3¼	39	1	3	37
Vangs - - - - - -	2	3	60	2	3	56	2	3	55	2	3	56	2	2¾	48
Peak Brails - - -	2	2	82	2	2	80	2	2	78	2	2	79	2	2	76
Throat Brails - - -	1	3¼	45	1	3¼	44	1	3¼	42	1	3¼	43	1	3¼	38
Middle Brails - - -	1	2½	41	1	2½	40	1	2½	40	1	2½	40	1	2¼	34
Foot Brails - - -	1	3	39	1	3	38	1	3	38	1	3	38	1	2½	36
GAFF TOP-SAIL GEAR.															
Halliards - - - - -	–	–	–	–	–	–	–	–	–	–	–	–	–	–	–
Outhauler - - - - -	–	–	–	–	–	–	–	–	–	–	–	–	–	–	–
Sheets - - - - - -	–	–	–	–	–	–	–	–	–	–	–	–	–	–	–
Downhaul - - - - -	–	–	–	–	–	–	–	–	–	–	–	–	–	–	–
MISCELLANEOUS GEAR.															
Braces, Preventer (Lower Yards) - -	2	3¾	116	2	3¾	116	2	3¾	116	2	3½	116	2	3½	112
Braces, Preventer (Top-sail Yards) -	2	3¼	112	2	3¼	112	2	3¼	112	2	3	112	2	3	108
Cleets, Iron, for Tops	36	–	–	36	–	–	36	–	–	36	–	–	36	–	–
Chain Slings for Top-sail Yards - - -	3	–	–	3	–	–	3	–	–	3	–	–	3	–	–
Chain Slings for Gaff	6	–	–	6	–	–	6	–	–	6	–	–	6	–	–
Falls, Cat - - - - -	2	6	130	2	6	130	2	6	125	2	5¾	125	2	5½	120
Falls, Fish—the sizes and lengths given for Sloops, Brigs & Sch. are for Fish Pend'nts	2	4¾	140	2	4¾	140	2	4¾	135	2	4½	135	2	4¼	120
Falls, Stern Boat - -	4	3¼	120	4	3¼	120	4	3¼	120	4	3	116	4	3	112
Falls, Quarter Boats	4	3¾	160	4	3¾	160	4	3¾	160	4	3¾	160	4	3½	150
Falls, Waist Boats -	4	3¾	135	4	3¾	135	4	3¾	135	4	3½	132	4	3½	132
Falls, Deck Tackle -	1	4¼	65	1	4¼	65	1	4¼	65	1	4	62	1	4	62
Falls, Stock and Bill Tackles - - - -	2	3½	60	2	3½	60	2	3½	60	2	3½	58	2	3¼	58
Falls, Luff Tackles -	30	4	300	30	4	300	30	4	300	30	3¾	300	30	3¾	300
Falls, Stay Luff Tack.	4	4	100	4	4	100	4	4	100	4	3¾	100	4	3¾	100
Falls, Jiggers - - -	8	2¾	160	8	2¾	160	8	2¾	160	8	2¾	160	8	2¾	160
Fenders, Boat (Stuffed Leather) — one set for each boat - -															
Futtock Staves (Iron)	18	–	–	18	–	–	18	–	–	18	–	–	18	–	–
Guys, Fish Davit -	4	8	20	4	8	20	4	8	20	4	7½	20	4	7½	20
Guys, Quarter Davit	–	–	chain												
Guys, Waist Davit	–	–	chain												
Gripes, Launch - -	1	6	26	1	6	26	1	5¾	26	1	5¾	25	1	5½	24
Girt-lines, Fore Mast-head - - - - -	2	3¼	96	2	3¼	96	2	3¼	96	2	3¼	96	2	3	90

Frigates.			Sloops.									Brigs.			Brig-antines			Schoon-ers.			Steamers.		
2d Class.			1st Class.			2d Class.			3d Class.														
No.	Size.	Length.	No	Size.	Length.	No.	Size.	Length.	No.	Size.	Length.	No.	Size.	Length.	No.	Size.	Length.	No.	Size.	Length.	No.	Size.	Length.
2	2½	30	2	2½	28	2	2¼	26	2	2¼	26	–	–	–	–	–	–	–	–	–	2	2½	36
2	2½	8	2	2½	7	2	2¼	7	2	2¼	7	–	–	–	–	–	–	–	–	–	2	2½	8
2	2¾	56	2	2¾	52	2	2½	50	2	2½	50	–	–	–	–	–	–	–	–	–	2	2¾	50
1	3½	24	1	3	18	1	3	17	1	2¾	17	–	–	–	–	–	–	–	–	–	1	3½	23
1	3¼	47	1	3	38	1	2¾	36	1	2¾	35	–	–	–	–	–	–	–	–	–	1	3¼	55
1	3	30	1	2¾	27	1	2½	23	1	2½	23	–	–	–	–	–	–	–	–	–	1	3	39
2	2½	46	2	2¼	44	2	2¼	21	2	2¼	21	–	–	–	–	–	–	–	–	–	2	2½	60
2	2	72	2	1¾	64	1	1¾	30	1	1¾	30	–	–	–	–	–	–	–	–	–	2	2	80
1	3	36	1	2¾	32	1	2½	28	1	2½	28	–	–	–	–	–	–	–	–	–	1	3	38
1	2	30	1	2	28	1	1¾	26	1	1¾	24	–	–	–	–	–	–	–	–	–	1	2	32
1	2¼	34	1	2¼	26	1	2	24	1	2	22	–	–	–	–	–	–	–	–	–	1	2¼	34
–	–	–	–	–	–	–	–	–	–	–	–	–	–	–	–	–	–	1	3	34	1	3	37
–	–	–	–	–	–	–	–	–	–	–	–	–	–	–	–	–	–	1	3	26	1	3	29
–	–	–	–	–	–	–	–	–	–	–	–	–	–	–	–	–	–	2	2¾	26	2	2½	28
–	–	–	–	–	–	–	–	–	–	–	–	–	–	–	–	–	–	1	2½	18	1	2	20
2	3¼	108	2	3	106	2	3	100	2	3	100	2	2¾	95	1	2¾	45	1	2½	45	2	3¼	108
2	2¾	108	2	2¾	96	2	2½	90	2	2½	90	2	2½	88	1	2¼	42	1	2¼	42	2	2¾	100
36	–	–	30	–	–	30	–	–	30	–	–	20	–	–	18	–	–	12	–	–	36	–	–
3	–	–	3	–	–	3	–	–	3	–	–	2	–	–	2	–	–	2	–	–	2	–	–
6	–	–	6	–	–	6	–	–	6	–	–	4	–	–	4	–	–	4	–	–	6	–	–
2	5	100	2	4½	95	2	4½	90	2	4¼	90	2	3¾	60	2	3½	56	2	3¼	40	2	5	100
2	4	120	2	6	8	2	5¾	8	2	5¾	8	2	5	7	2	4½	7	2	4	6	2	4	120
2	3	52	2	2¾	48	2	2¾	46	2	2¾	46	2	2½	44	2	2½	40	2	2½	40	2	3	52
4	3¼	140	4	3	135	4	3	130	4	3	130	4	2¾	120	4	2¾	116	4	2¾	112	4	3¼	140
1	3¾	60	1	3¾	58	1	3½	56	1	3½	56	1	3¼	52	1	3¼	52	1	3¼	50	1	3¾	60
2	3¼	56	2	3	52	2	3	48	2	3	48	2	2¾	44	2	2½	44	2	2½	42	2	3¼	56
28	3½	280	24	3¼	240	24	3¼	240	24	3¼	240	12	3	120	12	3	120	12	3	120	28	3½	280
4	3½	100	4	3¼	100	4	3¼	100	4	3¼	100	4	3	100	2	3	50	2	3	50	4	3¼	100
8	2½	160	8	2½	160	8	2½	160	8	2½	160	6	2¼	120	6	2¼	120	6	2¼	120	8	2½	160
18	–	–	18	–	–	18	–	–	18	–	–	12	–	–	10	–	–	8	–	–	18	–	–
4	7	18	–	–	Cr's	Da	vit.	–	–	–	–	–	–	–	–	–	–	–	–	–	4	7	18
1	5¼	23	1	5	22	1	4¾	21	1	4¾	21	1	4½	20	1	4¼	18	1	4¼	18	1	5¼	23
2	3	85	2	2¾	80	2	2¾	76	2	2¾	76	2	2½	74	2	2½	70	2	2½	70	2	3	85

Names of Rigging.	Ships of the Line.									Razees.			Frigates.		
	3 DECKS.			2 DECKS. 1st Class.			2 DECKS. 2d Class.						1st Class.		
	No.	Size.	Length.	No.	Size.	Length.	No.	Size.	Length.	No.	Size.	Length.	No.	Size.	Length.
MISCELLANEOUS GEAR. *Con.*															
Girt-lines, Main Mast-head - - - - -	2	3¼	108	2	3¼	108	2	3¼	108	2	3¼	108	2	3	104
Girt-lines, Miz. Mast-head - - - - -	2	3	88	2	3	88	2	3	88	2	3	88	2	2¾	86
Girt-lines, Hammock	10	3¼	640	10	3¼	640	8	3	512	8	3	512	6	3	360
Hooks, Can (Iron) -	2	2	2	2	2	2	2	2	2	2	2	2	2	2	2
Hawse Pend. & Hook	1	8	18	1	7½	16	1	7½	16	1	7	15	1	6½	14
Hawse R'pe& Shackle	1	12	20	1	11	18	1	11	18	1	10	17	1	10	16
Halliards, Signal (set)	1	–	–	1	–	–	1	–	–	1	–	–	1	–	–
Hooks, Fish (fr anch.)	2	–	–	2	–	–	2	–	–	2	–	–	2	–	–
Jacks, Iron (sets) - -	1	–	–	1	–	–	1	–	–	1	–	–	1	–	–
Lines, Clothes (Manil.)	52	2½	1560	52	2½	1560	50	2½	1500	48	2¼	1440	44	2¼	1230
Lines, Tricing, Ham.	6	3¼	144	6	3¼	144	6	3	144	6	3	144	6	3	132
Nippers (dozens of) -	4	–	–	4	–	–	4	–	–	3	–	–	3	–	–
Rungs for Jacob Ladders (set) - - - -	1	–	–	1	–	–	1	–	–	1	–	–	1	–	–
Ropes, Buoy - - -	2	7	40	2	7	40	2	7	40	2	6½	40	2	6	40
Ropes, Ridge, Awnings (set of) - -	1	–	–	1	–	–	1	–	–	1	–	–	1	–	–
Ropes, Old (for lashings)—as much as may be required -															
Ropes, Back (for Cat-Blocks) - - - -	2	3	30	2	3	30	2	3	30	2	3	25	2	2½	25
Rudder Pendants and Chains—as may be required) - - -															
Stoppers, Cat-head -	2	10	7	2	10	7	2	9½	7	2	9½	6	2	9	6
Stoppers, Ring - -	6	6	18	6	6	18	6	5¾	17	6	5½	17	6	5¼	16
Stoppers, Deck (chain claw) - - - - -	8	–	4 feet.	8	–	4 ft.	8	–	4 ft.	8	–	4 ft.	8	–	4 ft.
Stoppers, Boats - -	4	3½	32	4	3½	32	4	3½	32	4	3¼	32	4	3¼	32
Stoppers, Fighting, doz	3	5	100	3	5	100	3	5	100	3	5	100	3	4¾	100
Stoppers, Bit - - -	4	10	9	4	10	9	4	10	9	4	9½	9	4	9½	9
Strap Selvagees (doz.)	4	–	–	4	–	–	4	–	–	3	–	–	3	–	–
Swabs (dozens) - -	4	–	–	4	–	–	4	–	–	3	–	–	3	–	–
Seines - - - - - -	1	–	80	1	–	80	1	–	80	1	–	70	1	–	60
Shank Painters (a part (Chain) - - - -	2	9	5	2	9	5	2	8½	5	2	8½	4	2	8	4
Spare, Quarter Davit	–	–	chain												
Spare, Waist Davit	–	–	chain												
Travelers, iron, for Top-sail Tyes - -	6	–	–	6	–	–	6	–	–	6	–	–	6	–	–
Topping-lifts fr Quarter Davits - - -	–	–	chain												
Tackle, Fore-yard -	2	4	90	2	4	90	2	4	90	2	4	90	2	3¾	88
Tackle, Pendants -	2	7	8	2	7	8	2	7	8	2	7	8	2	6¾	8
Tackle, Fore-stay* -	1	4	60	1	4	60	1	4	60	1	4	60	1	3¾	55
Tackle, Main-yard -	2	4	108	2	4	108	2	4	108	2	4	108	2	3¾	102
Tackle, Pendants -	2	7	8	2	7	8	2	7	8	2	7	8	2	6¾	8
Tackle, Main-stay* -	1	4	60	1	4	60	1	4	60	1	4	60	1	3¾	55
Triatic Stay - - -	1	8	20	1	8	20	1	8	20	1	7½	20	1	7½	19
Quarter and Stay -	1	4	80	1	4	80	1	4	80	1	4	80	1	3¾	78

* Or Triatic Stay-tackle.

Frigates.			Sloops.									Brigs.			Brig-antines			Schoon-ers.			Steamers.		
2d Class.			1st Class.			2d Class.			3d Class.														
No.	Size.	Length.	No	Size.	Length.	No.	Size.	Length.	No.	Size.	Length.	No.	Size.	Length.	No.	Size.	Length.	No.	Size.	Length.	No.	Size.	Length.
2	3	100	2	2¾	96	2	2¾	92	2	2¾	92	2	2½	92	2	2½	92	2	2½	92	2	3	100
2	2¾	84	2	2½	80	2	2½	78	2	2½	78	–	–	–	–	–	–	–	–	–	2	2¾	84
5	3	325	4	2¾	200	4	2¾	180	4	2¾	180	4	2½	170	3	2½	120	3	2½	120	5	3	325
2	2	2	2	2	2	2	2	2	2	2	2	2	2	2	2	2	2	1	1	1	2	2	2
1	6½	13	1	6	10	1	5½	9	1	5	8	–	–	–	–	–	–	–	–	–	1	6½	13
1	9	15	1	8	11	1	8	10	1	7	9	–	–	–	–	–	–	–	–	–	1	9	15
1	–	–	1	–	–	1	–	–	1	–	–	1	–	–	1	–	–	1	–	–	1	–	–
2	–	–	2	–	–	2	–	–	2	–	–	2	–	–	2	–	–	2	–	–	2	–	–
1	–	–	1	–	–	1	–	–	1	–	–	1	–	–	1	–	–	1	–	–	1	–	–
40	2¼	1100	34	2	900	30	2	750	30	2	750	20	2	500	16	2	400	12	2	300	40	2¼	1100
6	3	125	6	2¾	120	6	2¾	120	6	2¾	120	4	2½	85	4	2½	85	4	2½	85	6	3	125
3	–	–	2	–	–	2	–	–	2	–	–	–	–	–	–	–	–	–	–	–	3	–	–
1	–	–	1	–	–	1	–	–	1	–	–	1	–	–	1	–	–	1	–	–	1	–	–
2	5½	40	2	5	40	2	5	40	2	4½	40	2	4	40	2	4	40	2	4	40	2	5½	40
1	–	–	1	–	–	1	–	–	1	–	–	1	–	–	1	–	–	1	–	–	1	–	–
2	2½	25	2	2	20	2	2	20	2	2	20	2	2	15	2	2	15	–	–	–	2	2½	25
2	6½	6	2	6½	5	2	6	5	2	6	5	2	5½	3	2	5½	3	2	5	3	2	6½	6
4	5	14	4	4¾	12	4	4½	10	2	4½	10	2	4	10	2	3½	8	2	3½	8	4	5	14
6	–	4 ft.	4	–	4 ft	4	–	4 ft	4	–	4 ft	4	–	4 ft	4	–	4 ft	4	–	4 ft	6	–	4 ft.
4	3¼	28	4	3	26	4	3	24	4	3	24	4	2¾	22	4	2¾	20	4	2¾	20	4	3¼	28
3	4½	100	2½	4	80	2½	4	80	2½	4	80	2	3¾	60	2	3¾	60	2	3¾	60	3	4½	100
4	8½	8	3	7½	8	3	7	7	3	7	7	3	6½	7	3	6	7	3	6	7	4	8½	8
3	–	–	2	–	–	2	–	–	2	–	–	2	–	–	2	–	–	2	–	–	3	–	–
3	–	–	2	–	–	2	–	–	2	–	–	2	–	–	2	–	–	2	–	–	3	–	–
1	–	50	1	–	40	1	–	40	1	–	40	1	–	35	1	–	35	1	–	35	1	–	50
2	6	4	2	5¾	3	2	5½	3	2	5½	3	2	5	2	2	5	2	2	4½	2	2	6	4
6	–	–	6	–	–	6	–	–	6	–	–	2	–	–	2	–	–	–	–	–	4	–	–
2	3¾	84	2	3½	76	2	3½	72	2	3½	70	1	3	33	1	3	33	–	–	–	2	3¾	84
2	6½	7½	2	6	6	2	5¾	6	2	5	6	1	5	3	1	5	3	–	–	–	2	6½	7½
1	3¾	54	1	3½	50	1	3½	48	1	3½	46	1	3	40	1	3	40	–	–	–	1	3¾	54
2	3¾	100	2	3½	86	2	3¼	84	2	3¼	84	1	3	40	–	–	–	–	–	–	2	3¾	100
2	6½	7½	2	6	6	2	5¾	6	2	5½	6	1	5	3	–	–	–	–	–	–	2	6½	7½
1	3¾	54	1	3½	50	1	3½	48	1	3½	46	1	3	40	1	3	40	–	–	–	1	3¾	54
1	7	18	1	6½	18	1	6½	18	1	6½	18	1	6	17	1	5	15	–	–	–	1	7	18
1	3¼	70	1	3¼	65	1	3	62	1	3	62	1	3	60	–	–	–	–	–	–	1	3¼	70

Names of Blocks.	Description of Block.	Ships of the Line. 3 Decks. No.	Size.	Swallow.	2 Decks. 1st Class. No.	Size.	Swallow.	2d Class. No.	Size.	Swallow.	Razees. No.	Size.	Swallow.	Frigates. 1st Class. No.	Size.	Swallow.
FLYING JIB-BOOM.																
Downhaul - -	S.	1	7	1.0	1	7	1.0	1	7	1.0	1	7	1.0	1	7	1.0
Royal Bow-lines -	S.	2	6	.8	2	6	.8	2	6	.8	2	6	.8	2	6	.8
Halliards F. T. Gallant-mast-head -	S.	1	7	1.3	1	7	1.3	1	7	1.3	1	7	1.3	1	7	1.3
JIB-BOOM.																
Downhaul - -	S.	1	8	1.3	1	8	1.3	1	8	1.3	1	8	1.3	1	8	1.3
Brails on Stay -	S.	2	6	.9	2	6	.9	2	6	.9	2	6	.9	2	6	.9
Brails leading on Boom-end - -	S.	2	7	.9	2	7	.9	2	7	.9	2	6	.9	2	6	.9
Martingale back-ropes	D.	2	10	1.6	2	10	1.6	2	10	1.6	2	10	1.6	2	9	1.5
Martingale back-ropes	S.	2	10	1.6	2	10	1.6	2	10	1.6	2	10	1.6	2	9	1.5
Top-gallant Bow-lines	S.	2	7	.9	2	7	.9	2	7	.9	2	7	.9	2	6	.8
Guy Tackles - -	D.	4	12	1.2	4	12	1.2	4	12	1.2	4	12	1.2	4	12	1.2
Guy-Tackles - -	S.	4	12	1.2	4	12	1.2	4	12	1.2	4	12	1.2	4	12	1.2
Jib-stay Tackle -	D.	1	12	1.1	1	12	1.1	1	12	1.1	1	12	1.1	1	11	1.1
Jib-stay Tackle -	S.	1	12	1.1	1	12	1.1	1	12	1.1	1	12	1.1	1	11	1.1
Sheets in Clew of Sail	S.	2	13	1.5	2	13	1.5	2	13	1.5	2	12	1.5	2	12	1.4
Hall'rds in head of Sail	S.	1	12	1.4	1	12	1.4	1	12	1.4	1	12	1.4	1	11	1.2
Halliards on top-mast Trestle-trees -	S. Iron b'd.	1	12	1.4	1	12	1.4	1	12	1.4	1	12	1.4	1	12	1.4
SPRIT-SAIL YARD.																
Lifts leading to Bowsprit Cap - -	S.	2	12	1.5	2	12	1.5	2	12	1.5	2	10	1.3	2	10	1.3
Brace on Yard-arm	S.	2	11	1.3	2	11	1.3	2	11	1.3	2	10	1.2	2	10	1.2
Brace on Fore-stay	S.	2	11	1.3	2	11	1.3	2	11	1.3	2	10	1.2	2	10	1.2
Brace on Trestle-trees	S.	2	11	1.3	2	11	1.3	2	11	1.3	2	10	1.2	2	10	1.2
BOWSPRIT.																
Fore-top Bow-lines	S.	2	12	1.5	2	12	1.5	2	12	1.5	2	12	1.5	2	12	1.5
Fore Bow-lines -	S.	2	12	1.5	2	12	1.5	2	12	1.5	2	12	1.5	2	12	1.5
Fore Top-mast Stay-sail Downhaul -	S.	1	8	1.3	1	8	1.3	1	8	1.3	1	8	1.2	1	8	1.2
Fore top-mast Hall'rds in head of Sail -	S.	1	12	1.6	1	12	1.6	1	12	1.6	1	11	1.4	1	11	1.4
F. T. Mast Hall'rds on top-mast trestle trees	S. Iron b'd.	1	12	1.6	1	12	1.6	1	12	1.6	1	11	1.4	1	11	1.4
F. T. Mast Stay-sail sheets in clew of sail	S.	2	12	1.5	2	12	1.5	2	12	1.5	2	12	1.5	2	12	1.5
F. Storm stay-sail stay on Bowsprit -	S. Clump.	1	14	2.8	1	14	2.8	1	14	2.8	1	12	2.4	1	12	2.4
F. Storm Stay-sail Downhaul - -	S.	1	8	1.2	1	8	1.2	1	8	1.2	1	8	1.2	1	8	1.2
F. storm stay-sail halliards in head of sail	S.	1	12	1.4	1	12	1.4	1	12	1.4	1	12	1.4	1	11	1.3
F.S. stay-sail halliards on Trestle-trees -	S.	1	12	1.4	1	12	1.4	1	12	1.4	1	12	1.4	1	11	1.3
Bumkin Blocks, (fore tacks) - -	S. Should'r.	2	15	2.3	2	15	2.3	2	15	2.3	2	14	2.2	2	14	2.2
FOREM'ST & YARD.																
Runner - - - -	S.	1	17	3.0	1	17	3.0	1	17	3.0	1	16	2.8	1	16	2.8

Frigates.			Sloops of War.									Brigs.			Brigantines.			Schooners.			Steamers.		
2d Class.			1st Class.			2d Class.			3d Class.														
No.	Size.	Swallow.	No.	Size.	Swallow.	No.	Size.	Swallow.	No.	Size.	Swallow.	No.	Size.	Swallow.	No.	Size.	Swallow.	No.	Size.	Swallow.	No.	Size.	Swallow.
1	7	1.0	1	6	.9	1	6	.9	1	6	.9	1	6	.9	1	5	.8	1	5	.8	1	7	1.0
2	6	.8	2	6	.8	2	6	.8	2	5	.7	2	5	.7	–	–	–	–	–	–	2	6	.8
1	7	1.3	1	7	1.3	1	6	1.1	1	6	1.1	1	6	1.1	1	6	1.1	1	6	1.1	1	7	1.3
1	8	1.3	1	8	1.3	1	7	1.2	1	7	1.2	1	6	1.0	1	6	1.0	1	6	1.0	1	8	1.3
2	6	.9	2	6	.9	2	6	.9	2	6	.9	2	6	.9	2	5	.8	2	5	.8	2	6	.9
2	6	.9	2	6	.9	2	6	.9	2	6	.9	2	6	.9	2	5	.8	2	5	.8	2	6	.9
2	9	1.5	2	8	1.4	2	8	1.4	2	8	1.4	2	7	1.2	2	7	1.2	2	7	1.2	2	9	1.5
2	9	1.5	2	8	1.4	2	8	1.4	2	8	1.4	2	7	1.2	2	7	1.2	2	7	1.2	2	9	1.5
2	6	.8	2	6	.8	2	6	.8	2	6	.8	2	5	.7	2	5	.7	2	5	.7	2	6	.8
4	10	1.2	4	10	1.2	4	10	1.2	4	10	1.2	4	9	1.1	4	9	1.1	4	8	1.0	4	10	1.2
4	10	1.2	4	10	1.2	4	10	1.2	4	10	1.2	4	9	1.1	4	9	1.1	4	8	1.0	4	10	1.2
1	10	1.1	1	10	1.1	1	10	1.1	1	9	1.1	1	9	1.0	1	9	1.0	1	8	1.0	1	10	1.1
1	10	1.1	1	10	1.1	1	10	1.1	1	9	1.1	1	9	1.0	1	9	1.0	1	8	1.0	1	10	1.1
2	10	1.2	2	9	1.1	2	9	1.1	2	9	1.1	2	8	1.0	2	8	1.0	2	8	1.0	2	10	1.2
1	10	1.2	1	10	1.2	1	9	1.1	1	8	1.1	1	8	1.0	1	8	1.0	1	7	.9	1	10	1.2
1	12	1.2	1	10	1.2	1	10	1.0	1	10	1.0	1	10	1.0	1	10	1.0	1	10	1.0	1	12	1.2
2	10	1.3	2	9	1.2	2	9	1.2	2	8	1.1	–	–	–	–	–	–	–	–	–	2	10	1.3
2	10	1.2	2	9	1.1	2	9	1.1	2	8	1.0	–	–	–	–	–	–	–	–	–	2	10	1.2
2	10	1.2	2	9	1.1	2	9	1.1	2	8	1.0	–	–	–	–	–	–	–	–	–	2	10	1.2
2	10	1.2	2	9	1.1	2	9	1.1	2	8	1.0	–	–	–	–	–	–	–	–	–	2	10	1.2
2	11	1.5	2	10	1.4	2	10	1.4	2	9	1.3	2	8	1.2	2	8	1.2	2	8	1.2	2	11	1.5
2	11	1.5	2	10	1.4	2	10	1.4	2	9	1.3	2	8	1.2	2	8	1.2	–	–	–	2	11	1.5
1	8	1.2	1	7	1.0	1	7	1.0	1	7	1.0	1	6	.9	1	6	.9	–	–	–	1	8	1.2
1	11	1.4	1	10	1.2	1	10	1.2	1	9	1.1	1	8	1.1	1	8	1.0	–	–	–	1	11	1.4
1	11	1.4	1	10	1.2	1	10	1.2	1	9	1.1	1	8	1.1	1	8	1.0	–	–	–	1	11	.4
2	11	1.4	2	10	1.3	2	10	1.3	2	9	1.2	2	8	1.0	2	8	1.0	–	–	–	2	11	1.4
1	12	2.4	1	10	2.0	1	10	2.0	1	9	1.8	1	8	1.6	1	8	1.6	–	–	–	1	12	2.4
1	8	1.2	1	7	1.0	1	7	1.0	1	6	.9	1	6	.9	1	6	.9	–	–	–	1	8	1.2
1	11	1.3	1	10	1.2	1	10	1.2	1	9	1.1	1	8	1.0	1	8	1.0	–	–	–	1	11	1.3
1	11	1.3	1	10	1.2	1	10	1.2	1	9	1.1	1	8	1.0	1	8	1.0	–	–	–	1	11	1.3
2	14	2.2	2	12	2.0	2	12	2.0	2	11	1.8	2	9	1.6	2	9	1.6	–	–	–	2	14	2.2
1	15	2.6	–	–	–	–	–	–	–	–	–	–	–	–	–	–	–	–	–	–	1	15	2.6

Names of Blocks.	Description of Block.	Ships of the Line.									Razees.			Frigates.		
		3 DECKS.			2 DECKS.											
					1st Class.			2d Class.						1st Class.		
		No.	Size.	Swallow.	No.	Size.	Swallow.	No.	Size.	Swallow.	No.	Size.	Swallow.	No.	Size.	Swallow.
FOREM'ST & YARD. *Continued.*																
Tackle for Runner	D.	1	17	1.6	1	17	1.6	1	17	1.6	1	17	1.6	1	17	1.6
Tackle for Runner	S.	1	17	1.6	1	17	1.6	1	17	1.6	1	17	1.6	1	17	1.6
Pendant Tackles -	D.	2	17	1.6	2	17	1.6	2	17	1.6	2	17	1.6	2	16	1.5
Pendant Tackles -	D.	2	17	1.6	2	17	1.6	2	17	1.6	2	17	1.6	2	16	1.5
Truss Tackles - -	D.	2	10	1.3	2	10	1.3	2	10	1.3	2	10	1.3	2	10	1.3
Truss Tackles - -	S.	2	10	1.3	2	10	1.3	2	10	1.3	2	10	1.3	2	10	1.3
Jeers - - - - - -	T.	2	22	2.4	2	22	2.4	2	22	2.4	2	22	2.4	2	20	2.1
Jeers - - - - - -	D.	2	22	2.4	2	22	2.4	2	22	2.4	2	22	2.4	2	20	2.1
Jeer Leaders - -	S.	2	20	2.2	2	20	2.2	2	20	2.2	2	20	2.1	2	20	2.1
Quarter Blocks - -	S. Iron b'd.	2	16	2.3	2	16	2.3	2	16	2.3	2	16	2.3	2	14	2.1
Clew Garnet - -	S. Iron b'd.	2	14	1.7	2	14	1.7	2	14	1.7	2	14	1.7	2	13	1.6
Clews of Sail - -	S.	2	12	1.7	2	12	1.7	2		1.7	2	12	1.7	2	11	1.6
Bunt-lines under Fore Top - - - - -	D.	2	9	1.3	2	9	1.3	2	9	1.3	2	9	1.3	2	9	1.3
Bunt-lines under Fore Top - - - - -	Shoe.	2	18	1.3	2	18	1.3	2	18	1.3	2	18	1.3	2	16	1.2
Leech-lines on Yard	S.	4	8	1.2	4	8	1.2	4	8	1.2	4	8	1.2	4	8	1.2
Leech-lines under Top	D.	2	8	1.4	2	8	1.4	2	8	1.4	2	8	1.2	2	8	1.2
Leech-lines After -	D.	2	8	1.3	2	8	1.3	2	8	1.3	2	8	1.2	2	8	1.2
Leech-lines After -	S.	4	8	1.3	4	8	1.3	4	8	1.3	4	8	1.2	4	8	1.2
Braces on Yard-arms	S.	2	15	1.6	2	15	1.6	2	15	1.6	2	15	1.6	2	15	1.6
Braces leading under Main Trestle-trees	S.	2	15	1.6	2	15	1.6	2	15	1.6	2	15	1.6	2	15	1.6
Lifts on Cap - - -	D.	2	16	2.2	2	16	2.2	2	16	2.2	2	16	2.2	2	16	2.2
Lifts on Yard-arms	S.	2	16	2.2	2	16	2.2	2	16	2.2	2	16	2.2	2	16	2.2
Lift Jiggers - - -	D.	2	10	1.1	2	10	1.1	2	10	1.1	2	10	1.1	2	10	1.1
Lift Jiggers - - -	S.	2	10	1.1	2	10	1.1	2	10	1.1	2	10	1.1	2	10	1.1
Boom Jiggers - -	S.	4	9	1.1	4	9	1.1	4	9	1.1	4	9	1.1	4	8	1.0
Boom Jiggers (in and out) - - - - -	S.	6	9	1.1	6	9	1.1	6	9	1.1	6	9	1.1	6	8	1.0
Clew Jiggers - -	S.	4	8	1.1	4	8	1.1	4	8	1.1	4	8	1.1	4	8	1.1
Bunt Jiggers - -	S.	3	8	1.1	3	8	1.1	3	8	1.1	3	8	1.1	3	8	1.1
Reef Tackles on Yard	S. d'ble sc'e	2	12	1.8	2	12	1.8	2	12	1.8	2	12	1.8	2	12	1.8
Fore Tacks in Clews of Sail - - - -	S.	2	15	2.3	2	15	2.3	2	15	2.3	2	14	2.2	2	14	2.2
Sheets in Clews of Sail - - - - -	S.	2	15	2.3	2	15	2.3	2	15	2.3	2	14	2.2	2	14	2.2
Swinging-boom Topping-lifts, - - -	S. clamp.	2	11	1.5	2	11	1.5	2	11	1.5	2	11	1.5	2	11	1.5
Swinging-boom Topping-whips, - -	D.	2	11	1.1	2	11	1.1	2	11	1.1	2	11	1.1	2	10	1.0
Swinging-boom Topping-whips, - -	S.	2	11	1.1	2	11	1.1	2	11	1.1	2	11	1.1	2	10	1.0
Pendants for outer Halliards, - - -	S.	2	16	1.8	2	16	1.8	2	16	1.8	2	15	1.7	2	14	1.6
Outer Studding-sail Halliards on Boom	S.	2	12	1.8	2	12	1.8	2	12	1.8	2	12	1.8	2	11	1.7
Inner Studding-sail Halliards on Yard	S.	2	9	1.3	2	9	1.3	2	9	1.3	2	9	1.3	2	9	1.3
Inner Studding-sail Halliards on Quarter	S.	2	9	1.3	2	9	1.3	2	9	1.3	2	9	1.3	2	9	1.3
Tripping-line - -	S.	2	9	1.1	2	9	1.1	2	9	1.1	2	9	1.1	2	9	1.1

Frigates.			Sloops of War.									Brigs.			Brigantines.			Schooners.			Steamers.		
2d Class.			1st Class.			2d Class.			3d Class.														
No.	Size.	Swallow.	No.	Size.	Swallow.	No.	Size.	Swallow.	No.	Size.	Swallow.	No.	Size.	Swallow.	No.	Size.	Swallow.	No.	Size.	Swallow.	No.	Size.	Swallow.
1	16	1.6	–	–	–	–	–	–	–	–	–	–	–	–	–	–	–	–	–	–	1	16	1.6
1	16	1.6	–	–	–	–	–	–	–	–	–	–	–	–	–	–	–	–	–	–	1	16	1.6
2	15	1.5	2	14	1.4	2	13	1.4	2	13	1.4	2	12	1.3	2	12	1.3	2	10	1.2	2	15	1.5
2	15	1.5	2	14	1.4	2	13	1.4	2	13	1.4	2	12	1.3	2	12	1.3	2	10	1.2	2	15	1.5
–	p't	–	–	p't	–	–	p't	–	–	p't	–	–	p't	–	–	p't	–	–	p't	–	–	p't	–
2	18	2.0	–	–	–	–	–	–	–	–	–	–	–	–	–	–	–	–	–	–	2	18	2.0
2	18	2.0	–	–	–	–	–	–	–	–	–	–	–	–	–	–	–	–	–	–	2	18	2.0
2	18	2.0	–	–	–	–	–	–	–	–	–	–	–	–	–	–	–	–	–	–	2	18	2.0
2	14	2.1	2	13	2.0	2	13	2.0	2	12	1.8	2	10	1.6	2	10	1.6	2	9	1.4	2	14	2.1
2	13	1.6	2	12	1.5	2	11	1.4	2	11	1.4	2	9	1.2	2	9	1.2	2	8	1.1	2	13	1.6
2	10	1.5	2	10	1.5	2	9	1.4	2	9	1.4	2	8	1.2	2	8	1.2	–	–	–	2	10	1.5
2	9	1.3	2	8	1.2	2	8	1.2	2	8	1.2	2	7	1.0	2	7	1.0	–	–	–	2	9	1.3
2	16	1.2	2	14	1.1	2	14	1.1	2	12	1.0	2	12	1.0	2	12	1.0	–	–	–	2	16	1.2
4	7	1.0	4	7	1.0	4	6	.9	4	6	.9	4	5	.8	4	5	.8	–	–	–	4	7	1.0
2	7	1.0	2	7	1.0	2	6	.9	2	6	.9	2	5	.8	2	5	.8	–	–	–	2	7	1.0
2	7	1.0	2	7	1.0	2	6	.9	2	6	.9	2	5	.8	2	5	.8	–	–	–	2	7	1.0
4	7	1.0	4	7	1.0	4	6	.9	4	6	.9	4	5	.8	4	5	.8	–	–	–	4	7	1.0
2	14	1.5	2	14	1.5	2	13	1.4	2	12	1.3	2	10	1.2	2	10	1.2	2	9	1.1	2	14	1.5
2	14	1.5	2	14	1.5	2	13	1.4	2	12	1.3	2	10	1.2	2	10	1.2	2	9	1.1	2	14	1.5
2s.	14	2.0	2s.	12	1.8	2s.	12	1.8	2s.	11	1.7	2s.	9	1.5	2s.	9	1.5	2s	8	1.2	2s.	14	2.0
2	14	2.0	2	12	1.8	2	12	1.8	2	11	1.7	–	–	–	–	–	–	–	–	–	2	14	2.0
2	9	1.0	2	8	.9	2	8	.9	2	8	.9	2	7	.8	2	7	.8	2	7	.8	2	9	1.0
2	9	1.0	2	8	.9	2	8	.9	2	8	.9	2	7	.8	2	7	.8	2	7	.8	2	9	1.0
4	8	1.0	4	7	.9	4	7	.9	4	7	.9	2	6	.8	2	6	.8	–	–	–	4	8	1.0
6	8	1.0	6	7	.9	6	7	.9	6	7	.9	6	6	.8	6	6	.8	–	–	–	6	8	1.0
4	8	1.1	4	7	1.0	4	7	1.0	4	7	1.0	2	6	.9	2	6	.9	–	–	–	4	8	1.1
3	7	1.0	3	7	1.0	3	6	.9	3	6	.9	1	6	.9	1	6	.9	–	–	–	3	7	1.0
2	11	1.7	2	10	1.6	2	10	1.6	2	10	1.6	2	8	1.4	2	8	1.4	–	–	–	2	11	1.7
2	14	2.2	2	12	2.0	2	12	2.0	2	11	1.8	2	9	1.6	2	9	1.6	–	–	–	2	14	2.2
2	14	2.2	2	12	2.0	2	12	2.0	2	11	1.8	2	9	1.6	2	9	1.6	–	–	–	2	14	2.2
2	10	1.4	2	9	1.3	2	9	1.3	2	9	1.3	2	8	1.2	2	8	1.2	2	8	1.2	2	10	1.4
2	10	1.0	2	9	.9	2	9	.9	2	8	.9	2	7	.8	2	7	.8	2	7	.8	2	10	1.0
2	10	1.0	2	9	.9	2	9	.9	2	8	.9	2	7	.8	2	7	.8	2	7	.8	2	10	1.0
2	14	1.6	2	12	1.4	2	12	1.4	2	11	1.3	2	9	1.1	2	9	1.1	2	9	1.1	2	14	1.6
2	10	1.6	2	9	1.5	2	9	1.5	2	9	1.5	2	7	1.1	2	7	1.1	2	7	1.1	2	10	1.6
2	8	1.2	2	8	1.2	2	8	1.1	2	8	1.1	2	7	.9	2	7	.9	2	7	.9	2	8	1.2
2	8	1.2	2	8	1.2	2	8	1.1	2	8	1.1	2	7	.9	2	7	.9	2	7	.9	2	8	1.2
2	8	1.0	2	8	1.0	2	8	1.0	2	8	1.0	2	7	.8	2	7	.8	2	7	.8	2	8	1.0

Names of Blocks.	Description of Block.	Ships of the Line.									Razees.			Frigates.		
		3 decks.			2 decks.											
					1st Class.			2d Class.						1st Class.		
		No.	Size.	Swallow.	No.	Size.	Swallow.	No.	Size.	Swallow.	No.	Size.	Swallow.	No.	Size.	Swallow.
FOREM'ST & YARD. *Continued.*																
Lower Studding-sail Downhaul - -	S.	2	7	1.0	2	7	1.0	2	7	1.0	2	7	1.0	2	7	1.0
After Guys - - -	S. Iron b'd.	2	11	1.5	2	11	1.5	2	11	1.5	2	10	1.2	2	10	1.2
Forward Guys (Cheek on Bowsprit) - -	S.	2	11	1.5	2	11	1.5	2	11	1.5	2	10	1.2	2	10	1.2
Tacks on Boom-end	S.	2	11	1.6	2	11	1.6	2	11	1.6	2	10	1.2	2	10	1.2
Tricing-lines for Studding-sail Gear -	S.	2	8	1.1	2	8	1.1	2	8	1.1	2	8	1.1	2	8	1.1
FORE TOP MAST AND YARD.																
Top Blocks - - -	S. Iron b'd.	2	22	3.6	2	22	3.6	2	22	3.6	2	20	3.0	2	20	3.0
Top Tackles - -	D.	4	20	2.0	4	20	2.0	4	20	2.0	4	20	2.0	4	19	1.9
Top Leaders - -	S.	2	20	2.0	2	20	2.0	2	20	2.0	2	20	2.0	2	19	1.9
Top Burtons - -	Fiddle.	2	20	1.4	2	20	1.4	2	20	1.4	2	18	1.4	2	18	1.4
Top Burtons - -	S.	2	12	1.4	2	12	1.4	2	12	1.4	2	11	1.4	2	11	1.4
Top Runners - -	S.	2	12	1.7	2	12	1.7	2	12	1.7	2	11	1.5	2	11	1.5
Breast Backstays -	D.	4	15	1.4	4	15	1.4	4	15	1.4	4	14	1.4	4	14	1.4
Breast Backstays -	T. Iron b'd.	4	15	1.4	4	15	1.4	4	15	1.4	4	14	1.4	4	14	1.4
Gin Blocks (To be fitted with band over Trestle Trees -	S.	2	18	2.7	2	18	2.7	2	18	2.7	2	18	2.7	2	17	2.7
Tye Blocks - - -	S. Iron b'd.	2	19	2.5	2	19	2.5	2	19	2.5	2	18	2.5	2	17	2.4
Fly Blocks - - -	D.	2	22	1.6	2	22	1.6	2	22	1.6	2	20	1.6	2	20	1.6
Fly Blocks - - -	S.	2	22	1.6	2	22	1.6	2	22	1.6	2	20	1.6	2	20	1.6
Leaders for Fly Blocks	S.	2	22	1.6	2	22	1.6	2	22	1.6	2	20	1.6	2	20	1.6
Braces on Yard-arms	S.	2	17	1.7	2	17	1.7	2	17	1.7	2	16	1.7	2	16	1.6
Braces on Collar of Main Stay - -	S.	2	14	1.7	2	14	1.7	2	14	1.7	2	12	1.7	2	11	1.6
Braces under Main Trestle Trees -	S.	2	15	1.7	2	15	1.7	2	15	1.7	2	15	1.7	2	14	1.6
Sister - - - - - -	D.	2	20	2.2	2	20	2.2	2	20	2.2	2	20	2.1	2	19	2.0
Leaders for Lifts -	S. Clump.	2	12	2.2	2	12	2.2	2	12	2.2	2	10	2.1	2	10	2.0
Lift Jiggers - - -	D.	2	10	1.0	2	10	1.0	2	10	1.0	2	10	1.0	2	9	1.0
Lift Jiggers - - -	S.	2	10	1.0	2	10	1.0	2	10	1.0	2	10	1.0	2	9	1.0
Quarter Blocks - -	D. Iron b'd.	2	13	1.7	2	13	1.7	2	13	1.7	2	13	1.7	2	13	1.6
Clew-lines in Clews of Top-sail - -	S.	2	12	1.7	2	12	1.7	2	12	1.7	2	11	1.6	2	11	1.6
Rolling Tackle - -	D.	2	11	1.6	2	11	1.6	2	11	1.6	2	11	1.6	2	11	1.6
Rolling Tackle - -	S.	2	11	1.6	2	11	1.6	2	11	1.6	2	11	1.6	2	11	1.6
Bunt-lines at Mast-head - - - - -	S. Iron b'd.	2	12	1.6	2	12	1.6	2	12	1.6	2	12	1.6	2	12	1.6
Reef Tackle Whips	S.	4	12	1.6	4	12	1.6	4	12	1.6	4	12	1.6	4	12	1.6
Sheets in Clews of Top-sail - - -	S.	2	13	2.3	2	13	2.3	2	13	2.3	2	12	2.2	2	12	2.2
Bunt-runner - - -	S.	1	10	1.4	1	10	1.4	1	10	1.4	1	10	1.4	1	9	1.2
Jigger for Bunt-runner	D.	1	8	1.2	1	8	1.2	1	8	1.2	1	8	1.2	1	8	1.2
Jigger for Bunt-runner	S.	1	8	1.2	1	8	1.2	1	8	1.2	1	8	1.2	1	8	1.2
Clew Jiggers - -	S.	4	9	1.2	4	9	1.2	4	9	1.2	4	9	1.2	4	9	1.2
Boom Tricing-lines	S.	2	8	1.0	2	8	1.0	2	8	1.0	2	8	1.0	2	8	1.0
Span for Studding-sail Halliards - - -	S.	2	13	1.7	2	13	1.7	2	13	1.7	2	13	1.7	2	12	1.6
Jewel Blocks - -	S.	2	13	1.7	2	13	1.7	2	13	1.7	2	13	1.7	2	12	1.6

Frigates.			Sloops of War.									Brigs.			Brigantines.			Schooners.			Steamers.		
2d Class.			1st Class.			2d Class.			3d Class.														
No.	Size.	Swallow.	No.	Size.	Swallow.	No.	Size.	Swallow.	No.	Size.	Swallow.	No.	Size.	Swallow.	No.	Size.	Swallow.	No.	Size.	Swallow.	No.	Size.	Swallow.
2	6	1.0	2	6	.9	2	6	.9	2	6	.9	2	6	.9	2	6	.9	–	–	–	2	6	1.0
2	9	1.0	2	9	1.0	2	9	1.0	2	8	1.0	2	8	1.0	2	8	1.0	2	8	1.0	2	10	1.2
2	9	1.0	2	9	1.0	2	9	1.0	2	8	1.0	2	8	1.0	2	8	1.0	2	8	1.0	2	10	1.2
2	9	1.0	2	9	1.0	2	9	1.0	2	8	.9	2	8	.9	2	8	.9	2	8	.9	2	10	1.2
2	7	1.0	2	7	1.0	2	7	1.0	2	6	1.0	2	6	.9	2	6	.9	–	–	–	2	7	1.0
2	20	3.0	2	18	2.5	2	18	2.5	1	16	2.2	1	14	2.0	1	14	2.0	1	10	1.5	2	20	3.0
4	18	1.9	4	16	1.8	4	16	1.8	2	14	1.5	–	–	–	–	–	–	–	–	–	4	18	1.9
2	18	1.9	2	16	1.8	2	16	1.8	1	14	1.5	–	–	–	–	–	–	–	–	–	2	18	1.9
2	16	1.4	2	15	1.4	2	14	1.0	2	14	1.0	2	13	.9	2	13	.9	–	–	–	2	16	1.4
2	10	1.4	2	9	1.0	2	9	1.0	2	9	1.0	2	8	.9	2	8	.9	–	–	–	2	10	1.4
2	10	1.5	2	10	1.5	2	9	1.2	2	9	1.2	2	8	1.2	2	8	1.2	2	8	1.2	2	10	1.5
4	14	1.4	2	12	1.3	2	12	1.2	2	12	1.2	2	10	1.2	2	10	1.2	2	10	1.2	4	14	1.4
4	14	1.4	2	12	1.3	2	12	1.2	2	12	1.2	2	10	1.2	2	10	1.2	2	10	1.2	4	14	1.4
2	16	2.5	2	14	2.4	2	14	2.4	1	12	1.8	–	–	–	–	–	–	–	–	–	2	16	2.3
2	16	2.3	1	14	2.0	1	12	1.8	1	12	1.8	–	–	–	–	–	–	–	–	–	2	16	2.3
2	18	1.5	2	16	1.4	2	14	1.4	1	12	1.4	1	10	1.2	1	10	1.2	1	10	1.2	2	18	1.5
2	18	1.5	2	16	1.4	2	14	1.4	1	12	1.4	1	10	1.2	1	10	1.2	1	10	1.2	2	18	1.5
2	18	1.5	2	16	1.4	2	14	1.4	1	12	1.4	1	10	1.2	1	10	1.2	1	10	1.2	2	18	1.5
2	15	1.6	2	14	1.5	2	13	1.4	2	12	1.4	2	10	1.2	2	10	1.2	2	8	1.0	2	15	1.6
2	10	1.6	2	9	1.5	2	9	1.4	2	8	1.4	2	7	1.2	2	7	1.2	–	–	–	2	10	1.6
2	14	1.6	2	12	1.5	2	12	1.4	2	10	1.4	2	10	1.2	2	10	1.2	2	10	1.2	2	14	1.6
2	18	2.0	2	16	1.9	2	15	1.8	2	14	1.8	2	13	1.7	2	12	1.7	2	10	1.4	2	18	2.0
2	10	2.0	2	10	1.9	2	9	1.8	2	8	1.8	2	8	1.7	2	7	1.7	2	7	1.4	2	10	2.0
2	9	1.0	2	8	.9	2	8	.9	2	8	.9	2	7	.8	2	7	.8	2	7	.8	2	9	1.0
2	9	1.0	2	8	.9	2	8	.9	2	8	.9	2	7	.8	2	7	.8	2	7	.8	2	9	1.0
2	12	1.6	2	11	1.6	2	10	1.5	2	10	1.4	2	9	1.3	2	9	1.3	2	8	1.2	2	12	1.6
2	10	1.5	2	9	1.4	2	9	1.4	2	9	1.4	2	8	1.2	2	8	1.2	2	8	1.2	2	10	1.5
2	10	1.5	2	9	1.4	2	9	1.4	2	9	1.4	2	8	1.2	2	8	1.2	2	8	1.2	2	10	1.5
2	10	1.5	2	9	1.4	2	9	1.4	2	9	1.4	2	8	1.2	2	8	1.2	2	8	1.2	2	10	1.5
2	11	1.6	2	9	1.4	2	9	1.4	2	9	1.4	2	8	1.2	2	8	1.2	2	8	1.2	2	11	1.6
4	11	1.6	4	9	1.4	4	9	1.4	4	9	1.4	2	8	1.2	2	8	1.2	2	8	1.2	4	11	1.6
2	11	2.0	2	10	1.9	2	10	1.9	2	10	1.9	2	–	–	–	–	–	–	–	–	2	11	2.0
1	9	1.2	1	8	1.0	1	8	1.0	1	8	1.0	1	8	.9	1	8	.9	1	6	.9	1	9	1.2
1	7	1.1	1	7	1.0	1	7	1.0	1	7	1.0	1	6	.9	1	6	.9	1	6	.9	1	7	1.1
1	7	1.1	1	7	1.0	1	7	1.0	1	7	1.0	1	6	.9	1	6	.9	1	6	.9	1	7	1.1
4	8	1.1	4	8	1.1	4	8	1.1	4	7	1.0	2	7	1.0	2	7	1.0	2	6	.9	4	8	1.1
2	7	.9	2	7	.9	2	7	.9	2	7	.9	2	6	.8	2	6	.8	–	–	–	2	7	.9
2	12	1.6	2	11	1.6	2	11	1.6	2	10	1.5	2	10	1.5	2	10	1.5	2	9	1.4	2	12	1.6
2	12	1.6	2	11	1.6	2	11	1.6	2	10	1.5	2	10	1.5	2	10	1.5	2	9	1.4	2	12	1.6

Names of Blocks.	Description of Block.	Ships of the Line. 3 DECKS. No.	Size.	Swallow.	2 DECKS. 1st Class. No.	Size.	Swallow.	2d Class. No.	Size.	Swallow.	Razees. No.	Size.	Swallow.	Frigates. 1st Class. No.	Size.	Swallow.
FORE TOP-MAST AND YARD. *Contin.*																
Studding-sail Tacks on Boom ends -	S.	2	8	1.1	2	8	1.1	2	8	1.1	2	8	1.1	2	7	1.1
Studding-sail Down-haul in sails - -	S.	2	8	1.0	2	8	1.0	2	8	1.0	2	8	1.0	2	8	1.0
Leaders for Boom-braces in Main Rigging - - - - -	S.	2	9	1.1	2	9	1.1	2	9	1.1	2	8	1.1	2	7	1.1
F'RE TOP-GAL'NT MAST AND YARD.																
Top Block - - -	S. Iron b'd.	1	14	2.2	1	14	2.2	1	14	2.2	1	14	2.0	1	13	2.0
Breast Backstays -	S.	2	11	1.1	2	11	1.1	2	11	1.1	2	10	1.1	2	10	1.1
Breast Backstays in Channels - - -	D. Iron b'd.	2	11	1.1	2	11	1.1	2	11	1.1	2	10	1.1	2	10	1.1
Halliards - - - -	D.	2	12	1.3	2	12	1.3	2	12	1.3	2	10	1.3	2	10	1.3
Braces on Yard-arms	S.	2	9	1.1	2	9	1.1	2	9	1.1	2	9	1.1	2	9	1.1
Braces on Collar of Main Top-m'st Stay	S.	2	7	1.1	2	7	1.1	2	7	1.1	2	7	1.1	2	7	1.1
Braces on Main Top-mast-head - - -	S.	2	7	1.1	2	7	1.1	2	7	1.1	2	7	1.1	2	7	1.1
Sister - - - - -	S.	2	10	1.6	2	10	1.6	2	10	1.6	2	9	1.5	2	9	1.5
Lifts in Top - - -	S. Clamp.	2	6	1.6	2	6	1.6	2	6	1.6	2	6	1.5	2	6	1.5
Lift Jiggers - - -	D.	2	8	1.0	2	8	1.0	2	8	1.0	2	8	1.0	2	8	1.0
Lift Jiggers - - -	S.	2	8	1.0	2	8	1.0	2	8	1.0	2	8	1.0	2	8	1.0
Quarter Blocks - -	D.	2	10	1.4	2	10	1.4	2	10	1.4	2	10	1.4	2	10	1.4
Bunt-lines - - -	S.	2	8	1.0	2	8	1.0	2	8	1.0	2	8	1.0	2	8	1.0
Span Blocks, Top-gallant Studding-sail Halliards - - -	S.	2	8	1.2	2	8	1.2	2	8	1.2	2	8	1.0	2	8	1.0
Jewel Blocks - -	S.	2	8	1.2	2	8	1.2	2	8	1.2	2	8	1.0	2	8	1.0
Studding-sail Tacks on Boom Ends -	S.	2	7	1.1	2	7	1.1	2	7	1.1	2	7	1.1	2	7	1.1
F'RE ROYAL MAST AND YARD.																
Breast Backstays -	S.	2	8	1.1	2	8	1.1	2	8	1.1	2	7	1.0	2	7	1.0
Breast Backstays in Top - - - - -	D. Iron b'd.	2	8	1.1	2	8	1.1	2	8	1.1	2	7	1.0	2	7	1.0
Royal Braces M'n T'p-gallant Mast-head	S.	2	6	.9	2	6	.9	2	6	.9	2	6	.9	2	6	.9
Quarter Blocks -	S.	2	6	.9	2	6	.9	2	6	.9	2	6	.9	2	6	.9
Bunt-line Blocks -	S.	1	6	.9	1	6	.9	1	6	.9	1	6	.9	1	6	.9
FORE TRY-SAIL MAST & GAFF.																
Peak Halliards - -	D. Iron b'd.	1	12	1.5	1	12	1.5	1	12	1.5	1	12	1.5	1	12	1.5
Peak Halliards - -	S.	2	12	1.5	2	12	1.5	2	12	1.5	2	12	1.5	2	12	1.5
Throat Halliards -	D.	1	12	1.5	1	12	1.5	1	12	1.5	1	12	1.5	1	12	1.5
Throat Halliards -	S. Iron b'd.	1	12	1.5	1	12	1.5	1	12	1.5	1	12	1.5	1	12	1.5
Peak Brails - - -	Cheek.															
Throat Brails - -	S.	2	9	1.2	2	9	1.2	2	9	1.2	2	9	1.2	2	9	1.2
Middle Brails - -	S.	2	10	1.1	2	10	1.1	2	10	1.1	2	9	1.0	2	9	1.0
Foot Brails - - -	S.	2	8	1.1	2	8	1.1	2	8	1.1	2	8	1.1	2	8	1.1
Sheets - - - - -	S.	4	13	1.7	4	13	1.7	4	13	1.7	4	12	1.6	4	12	1.6
Vangs - - - - -	S.	2	8	1.2	2	8	1.2	2	8	1.2	2	8	1.2	2	8	1.2

Frigates.			Sloops of War.									Brigs.			Brigantines.			Schooners.			Steamers.		
2d Class.			1st Class.			2d Class.			3d Class.														
No.	Size.	Swallow.	No.	Size.	Swallow.	No.	Size.	Swallow.	No.	Size.	Swallow.	No.	Size.	Swallow.	No.	Size.	Swallow.	No.	Size.	Swallow.	No.	Size.	Swallow.
2	7	1.1	2	7	1.1	2	6	.9	2	6	.9	2	5	.8	2	5	.8	2	5	.8	2	7	1.1
2	7	.9	2	7	.9	2	7	.9	2	7	.9	2	6	.8	2	6	.8	2	6	.8	2	7	.9
2	7	1.1	2	6	1.0	2	6	1.0	2	6	1.0	2	6	1.0	2	6	1.0	2	6	1.0	2	7	1.1
1	12	2.0	1	11	1.8	1	11	1.8	1	10	1.6	1	9	1.4	1	9	1.4	–	–	–	1	12	2.0
2	9	1.0	2	8	1.0	2	8	1.0	2	8	1.0	2	7	.9	2	7	.9	2	7	.9	2	9	1.0
2	9	1.0	2	8	1.0	2	8	1.0	2	8	1.0	2	7	.9	2	7	.9	2	7	.9	2	9	1.0
2	10	1.2	2	8	1.2	2	8	1.2	2	8	1.2	2	7	1.0	2	7	1.0	2	7	1.0	2	10	1.2
2	8	1.0	2	7	1.0	2	7	1.0	2	7	1.0	–	–	–	–	–	–	–	–	–	2	8	1.0
2	7	1.0	2	6	1.0	2	6	1.0	2	6	1.0	2	5	.9	2	5	.9	–	–	–	2	7	1.0
2	7	1.0	2	6	1.0	2	6	1.0	2	6	1.0	2	5	.9	2	5	.9	2	5	.9	2	7	1.0
2	8	1.4	2	7	1.4	2	7	1.4	2	7	1.4	2	6	1.3	2	6	1.3	2	5	1.2	2	8	1.4
2	6	1.4	2	6	1.4	2	6	1.4	2	6	1.4	2	6	1.4	2	6	1.4	–	–	–	2	6	1.4
2	7	1.0	2	7	1.0	2	6	.9	2	6	.9	2	5	.8	2	5	.8	–	–	–	2	7	1.0
2	7	1.0	2	7	1.0	2	6	.9	2	6	.9	2	5	.8	2	5	.8	–	–	–	2	7	1.0
2	9	1.4	2	8	1.3	2	7	1.2	2	7	1.2	2	6	1.1	2	6	1.1	–	–	–	2	9	1.4
2	7	1.0	2	6	1.0	1	6	.9	1	6	.9	1	6	.9	1	6	.9	–	–	–	2	7	1.0
2	7	1.0	2	6	1.0	2	6	.9	2	6	.9	2	6	.9	2	6	.9	2	6	.9	2	7	1.0
2	7	1.0	2	6	1.0	2	6	.9	2	6	.9	2	6	.9	2	6	.9	2	6	.9	2	7	1.0
2	7	1.0	2	6	1.0	2	6	.9	2	6	.9	2	6	.9	2	6	.9	2	5	.8	2	7	1.0
2	6	.9	2	6	.9	2	6	.9	2	6	.9	2	5	.8	2	5	.8	–	–	–	2	6	.9
2	6	.9	2	6	.9	2	6	.9	2	6	.9	2	5	.8	2	5	.8	–	–	–	2	6	.9
2	6	.9	2	5	.8	2	5	.8	2	5	.8	2	5	.8	2	5	.8	-	–	–	2	6	.9
2	6	.9	2	5	.8	2	5	.8	2	5	.8	2	5	.8	2	5	.8	-	–	–	2	6	.9
1	6	.9	1	5	.8	1	5	.8	1	5	.8	–	–	–	–	–	–	–	–	–	1	6	.9
1	11	1.4	1	10	1.3	1	10	1.3	1	10	1.3	1	8	1.1	1	8	1.1	1	14	1.7	1	11	1.4
2	11	1.4	1	10	1.3	1	10	1.3	1	10	1.3	1	8	1.1	1	8	1.1	2	14	1.7	2	11	1.4
1	11	1.4	1	10	1.3	1	10	1.3	1	10	1.3	1	8	1.1	1	8	1.1	1	14	1.7	1	11	1.4
1	11	1.4	1	10	1.3	1	10	1.3	1	10	1.3	1	8	1.1	1	8	1.1	1	14	1.7	1	11	1.4
2	8	1.1	2	8	1.1	2	8	1.1	2	8	1.1	2	7	1.0	2	7	1.0	2	9	1.2	2	8	1.1
2	8	.9	2	7	.8	2	7	.8	2	7	.8	2	6	.7	2	6	.7	2	7	.9	2	8	.9
2	8	1.1	2	7	1.0	2	7	1.0	2	7	1.0	2	6	.9	2	6	.9	2	9	1.5	2	8	1.1
4	11	1.5	4	10	1.4	4	10	1.4	4	10	1.4	4	8	1.2	4	8	1.2	4	13	1.1	4	11	1.5
2	8	1.2	2	7	1.1	2	7	1.1	2	7	1.1	2	6	1.0	2	6	1.0	2	8	1.2	2	8	1.2

Names of Blocks.	Description of Block.	Ships of the Line. 3 Decks.			Ships of the Line. 2 Decks. 1st Class.			Ships of the Line. 2 Decks. 2d Class.			Razees.			Frigates. 1st Class.		
		No.	Size.	Swallow.	No.	Size.	Swallow.	No.	Size.	Swallow.	No.	Size.	Swallow.	No.	Size.	Swallow.
MAIN MAST AND YARD.																
Runner - - - -	S.	1	17	3.0	1	17	3.0	1	17	3.0	1	16	2.8	1	16	2.8
Tackle for Runner	D.	1	17	1.6	1	17	1.6	1	17	1.6	1	16	1.6	1	16	1.6
Tackle for Runner	S.	1	17	1.6	1	17	1.6	1	17	1.6	1	17	1.6	1	16	1.6
Pendant Taekles -	D.	2	17	1.6	2	17	1.6	2	17	1.6	2	17	1.6	2	16	1.6
Pendant Tackles -	S.	2	17	1.6	2	17	1.6	2	17	1.6	2	16	1.6	2	16	1.6
Truss Tackles - -	D.	2	10	1.3	2	10	1.3	2	10	1.3	2	10	1.3	2	10	1.3
Truss Tackles - -	S.	2	10	1.3	2	10	1.3	2	10	1.3	2	10	1.3	2	10	1.3
Jeers - - - - -	T.	2	22	2.4	2	22	2.4	2	22	2.4	2	22	2.4	2	20	2.4
Jeers - - - - -	D.	2	22	2.4	2	22	2.4	2	22	2.4	2	22	2.4	2	20	2.4
Jeer Leaders - -	S.	2	22	2.4	2	22	2.4	2	22	2.4	2	22	2.4	2	20	2.4
Quarter Blocks - -	S. Iron b'd.	2	17	2.3	2	17	2.3	2	17	2.3	2	16	2.2	2	16	2.2
Clew Garnet - -	S. Iron b'd.	2	15	1.7	2	15	1.7	2	15	1.7	2	14	1.6	2	14	1.6
Clews of Sail - -	S.	2	13	1.7	2	13	1.7	2	13	1.7	2	12	1.6	2	12	1.6
Bunt-lines under M'n Top - - - - -	D.	2	10	1.3	2	10	1.3	2	10	1.3	2	10	1.3	2	10	1.3
Bunt-lines under M'n Top - - - - -	Shoe.	2	18	1.3	2	18	1.3	2	18	1.3	2	18	1.3	2	18	1.3
Leech-lines on Yard	S.	4	8	1.3	4	8	1.3	4	8	1.3	4	8	1.3	4	8	1.3
Leech-lines under Top	D.	2	8	1.3	2	8	1.3	2	8	1.3	2	8	1.3	2	8	1.3
Leech-lines After -	D.	2	8	1.3	2	8	1.3	2	8	1.3	2	8	1.3	2	8	1.3
Leech-lines After -	S.	4	8	1.3	4	8	1.3	4	8	1.3	4	8	1.3	4	8	1.3
Braces on Yard-arms	S.	2	20	2.0	2	20	2.0	2	20	2.0	2	19	2.0	2	19	2.0
Braces on Bumkins	S.	2	20	2.0	2	20	2.0	2	20	2.0	2	19	2.0	2	19	2.0
Lifts on Cap - - -	D.	2	17	2.3	2	17	2.3	2	17	2.3	2	16	2.3	2	16	2.3
Lifts on Yard-arms	S.	2	16	2.3	2	16	2.3	2	16	2.3	2	15	2.3	2	14	2.2
Lift Jiggers - - -	D.	2	10	1.1	2	10	1.1	2	10	1.1	2	10	1.1	2	10	1.1
Lift Jiggers - - -	S.	2	10	1 1	2	10	1.1	2	10	1.1	2	10	1.1	2	10	1.1
Boom Jiggers - -	S.	4	9	1.1	4	9	1.1	4	9	1.1	4	9	1.1	4	8	1.0
Boom Jiggers (in and out) - - - - -	S.	6	9	1.1	6	9	1.1	6	9	1.1	6	9	1.1	6	8	1.0
Clew Jiggers - -	S.	4	9	1.1	4	9	1.1	4	9	1.1	4	9	1.1	4	9	1.1
Bunt Jiggers - -	S.	3	8	1.1	3	8	1.1	3	8	1.1	3	8	1.1	3	8	1.1
Reef Tackles on Yard	S. d'ble sc'e	2	12	1.8	2	12	1.8	2	12	1.8	2	11	1.8	2	11	1.8
Tack Blocks - - -	S.	2	16	2.3	2	16	2.3	2	16	2.3	2	15	2.3	2	15	2.3
Tacks in Clews of Sail - - - - -	S.	2	16	2.3	2	16	2.3	2	16	2.3	2	15	2.3	2	15	2.3
Sheets in Clews of Sail - - - - -	S.	2	16	2.3	2	16	2.3	2	16	2.3	2	15	2.3	2	15	2.3
Runner for Bow-line	S.	2	11	1.3	2	11	1.3	2	11	1.3	2	10	1.3	2	10	1.3
Jigger for Bow-line	S.	2	11	1.3	2	11	1.3	2	11	1.3	2	10	1.3	2	10	1.3
Tricing-lines for Studding-sail Gear -	S.	2	8	1.1	2	8	1.1	2	8	1.1	2	8	1.1	2	8	1.1
MAIN TOP-MAST & YARD.																
Top Blocks - - -	S. Iron b'd.	2	22	3.6	2	22	3.6	2	22	3.6	2	20	3.0	2	20	3.0
Top Tackles - -	D.	4	22	2.6	4	22	2.6	4	22	2.6	4	20	2.6	4	20	2.6
Top Leaders - -	S.	2	20	2.6	2	20	2.6	2	20	2.6	2	20	2.6	2	20	2.6
Top Burtons - -	Fiddle.	2	20	1.4	2	20	1.4	2	20	1.4	2	18	1.4	2	18	1.4
Top Burtons - -	S.	2	12	1.4	2	12	1.4	2	12	1.4	2	11	1.4	2	11	1.4
Top Runners - -	S.	2	12	2.8	2	12	2.8	2	12	2.8	2	11	2.8	2	11	2.8

Frigates.			Sloops of War.									Brigs.			Brigantines.			Schooners.			Steamers.		
2d Class.			1st Class.			2d Class.			3d Class.														
No.	Size.	Swallow.	No.	Size.	Swallow.	No.	Size.	Swallow.	No.	Size.	Swallow.	No.	Size.	Swallow.	No.	Size.	Swallow.	No.	Size.	Swallow.	No.	Size.	Swallow.
1	15	2.6	–	–	–	–	–	–	–	–	–	–	–	–	–	–	–	–	–	–	1	15	2.6
1	15	1.6	–	–	–	–	–	–	–	–	–	–	–	–	–	–	–	–	–	–	1	15	1.6
1	15	1.6	–	–	–	–	–	–	–	–	–	–	–	–	–	–	–	–	–	–	1	15	1.6
2	15	1.6	2	14	1.5	2	13	1.5	2	13	1.5	2	12	1.4	2	12	1.4	2	10	1.3	2	15	1.6
2	15	1.6	2	14	1.5	2	13	1.5	2	13	1.5	2	12	1.4	2	12	1.4	2	10	1.3	2	15	1.6
–	p't	–	–	p't	–	–	p't	–	–	p't	–	–	p't	–	–	p't	–	–	p't	–	–	p't	–
2	19	2.3	–	–	–	–	–	–	–	–	–	–	–	–	–	–	–	–	–	–	2	19	2.3
2	19	2.3	–	–	–	–	–	–	–	–	–	–	–	–	–	–	–	–	–	–	2	19	2.3
2	19	2.3	–	–	–	–	–	–	–	–	–	–	–	–	–	–	–	–	–	–	2	19	2.3
2	15	2.1	2	14	2.0	2	12	1.9	2	12	1.9	2	10	1.6	2	8	1.2	–	–	–	2	15	2.1
2	13	1.5	2	12	1.4	2	11	1.4	2	11	1.4	2	9	1.2	–	–	–	–	–	–	2	13	1.5
2	11	1.5	2	10	1.4	2	9	1.4	2	9	1.4	2	8	1.2	–	–	–	–	–	–	2	11	1.5
2	9	1.2	2	8	1.2	2	8	1.2	2	8	1.2	2	7	1.1	–	–	–	–	–	–	2	9	1.2
2	16	1.3	2	14	1.2	2	14	1.2	2	14	1.2	2	12	1.1	–	–	–	–	–	–	2	16	1.3
4	8	1.3	4	7	1.2	4	7	1.2	4	7	1.2	2	6	1.1	–	–	–	–	–	–	4	8	1.3
2	8	1.3	2	7	1.2	2	7	1.2	2	7	1.2	2	6	1.1	–	–	–	–	–	–	2	8	1.3
2	8	1.3	2	7	1.2	2	7	1.2	2	7	1.2	2	6	1.1	–	–	–	–	–	–	2	8	1.3
4	8	1.3	4	7	1.2	4	7	1.2	4	7	1.2	4	6	1.1	–	–	–	–	–	–	4	8	1.3
2	18	1.9	2	16	1.8	2	15	1.8	2	14	1.7	2	10	1.2	2	8	1.0	2	8	1.0	2	18	1.9
2	18	1.9	2	16	1.8	2	15	1.8	2	14	1.7	–	–	–	–	–	–	–	–	–	2	18	1.9
2s.	15	2.2	2s.	12	2.0	2s.	11	1.9	2s.	11	1.9	2s.	8	1.6	2s.	7	1.2	–	–	–	2s.	15	2.2
2	13	2.1	2	12	2.0	2	10	1.8	–	–	–	–	–	–	–	–	–	–	–	–	2	13	2.1
2	9	1.0	2	8	1.0	2	7	.9	2	7	.9	2	6	.9	–	–	–	–	–	–	2	9	1.0
2	9	1.0	2	8	1.0	2	7	.9	2	7	.9	2	6	.9	–	–	–	–	–	–	2	9	1.0
4	8	1.0	4	7	.9	4	7	.9	4	7	.9	2	6	.8	–	–	–	–	–	–	4	8	1.0
6	8	1.0	6	7	.9	6	7	.9	6	7	.9	6	6	.8	–	–	–	–	–	–	6	8	1.0
4	8	1.0	4	7	.9	4	7	.9	4	7	.9	4	6	.8	–	–	–	–	–	–	4	8	1.0
3	7	1.0	3	7	1.0	3	6	.9	3	6	.9	3	6	.9	–	–	–	–	–	–	3	7	1.0
2	10	1.7	2	9	1.6	2	9	1.6	2	9	1.6	2	8	1.4	–	–	–	–	–	–	2	10	1.7
2	14	2.2	2	12	2.0	2	11	2.0	2	11	2.0	2	8	1.6	–	–	–	–	–	–	2	14	2.2
2	14	2.2	2	12	2.0	2	11	2.0	2	11	2.0	2	8	1.6	–	–	–	–	–	–	2	14	2.2
2	14	2.2	2	12	2.0	2	11	2.0	2	11	2.0	2	10	1.8	–	–	–	–	–	–	2	14	2.2
2	9	1.2	2	8	1.2	2	6	1.2	2	6	1.2	2	5	1.2	–	–	–	–	–	–	2	9	1.2
2	9	1.2	2	8	1.2	2	6	1.2	2	6	1.2	2	5	1.2	–	–	–	–	–	–	2	9	1.2
2	8	1.1	2	7	1.0	2	7	1.0	2	7	1.0	2	6	.9	–	–	–	–	–	–	2	8	1.1
2	20	3.0	2	18	2.5	2	18	2.5	1	16	2.2	1	14	2.0	1	10	2.0	1	10	2.0	2	20	3.0
4	18	2.4	4	16	1.8	4	16	1.8	2	14	1.5	–	–	–	–	–	–	–	–	–	4	18	2.4
2	18	2.4	2	16	1.8	2	16	1.8	1	14	1.5	–	–	–	–	–	–	–	–	–	2	18	2.4
2	17	1.4	2	16	1.4	2	15	1.4	2	15	1.4	2	14	1.0	–	–	–	–	–	–	2	17	1.4
2	10	1.4	2	9	1.4	2	9	1.4	2	8	1.0	2	7	.9	–	–	–	–	–	–	2	10	1.4
2	10	2.6	2	9	2.5	2	8	2.4	2	8	2.4	2	7	2.2	–	–	–	–	–	–	2	10	2.6

Names of Blocks.	Description of Block.	Ships of the Line. 3 Decks.			2 Decks. 1st Class.			2 Decks. 2d Class.			Razees.			Frigates. 1st Class.		
		No.	Size.	Swallow.	No.	Size.	Swallow.	No.	Size.	Swallow.	No.	Size.	Swallow.	No.	Size.	Swallow.
MAIN TOP-MAST & YARD—*Continued.*																
Breast Backstays -	D.	4	15	1.4	4	15	1.4	4	15	1.4	4	14	1.4	4	14	1.4
Breast Backstays -	T. Iron b'd.	4	15	1.4	4	15	1.4	4	15	1.4	4	14	1.4	4	14	1.4
Stay leading in Fore Top - - - - -	S.	1	15	3.6	1	15	3.6	1	15	3.6	1	14	3.6	1	14	3.6
Spring Stay leading in Fore Top - -	S.	1	15	3.6	1	15	3.6	1	15	3.6	1	14	3.6	1	14	3.6
Gin Blocks (To be fitted with band over Trestle Trees -	S.	2	18	2.7	2	18	2.7	2	18	2.7	2	18	2.7	2	17	2.7
Tye Blocks - - -	S. Iron b'd.	2	20	2.7	2	20	2.7	2	20	2.7	2	18	2.6	2	18	2.6
Fly Blocks - - -	D.	2	24	1.6	2	24	1.6	2	24	1.6	2	24	1.6	2	22	1.5
Fly Blocks - - -	S.	2	24	1.6	2	24	1.6	2	24	1.6	2	24	1.6	2	22	1.5
Leaders for Fly Blocks	S.	2	22	1.6	2	22	1.6	2	22	1.6	2	20	1.6	2	20	1.6
Braces on Yard-arms	S.	2	18	1.8	2	18	1.8	2	18	1.8	2	18	1.8	2	16	1.7
Braces on Mizen M'st	S.	2	14	1.8	2	14	1.8	2	14	1.8	2	14	1.8	2	14	1.7
Sister - - - - -	D.	2	20	2.3	2	20	2.3	2	20	2.3	2	20	2.3	2	19	2.2
Leaders for Lifts -	S. Clamp.	2	12	2.3	2	12	2.3	2	12	2.3	2	10	2.3	2	10	2.2
Lift Jiggers - - -	D.	2	10	1.0	2	10	1.0	2	10	1.0	2	10	1.0	2	10	1.0
Lift Jiggers - - -	S.	2	10	1.0	2	10	1.0	2	10	1.0	2	10	1.0	2	10	1.0
Quarter Blocks - -	D. Iron b'd.	2	13	1.7	2	13	1.7	2	13	1.7	2	13	1.7	2	13	1.7
Clew-lines in Clews of sail - - - -	S.	2	12	1.6	2	12	1.6	2	12	1.6	2	12	1.6	2	12	1.6
Rolling Tackle - -	D.	1	11	1.6	1	11	1.6	1	11	1.6	1	11	1.6	1	11	1.6
Rolling Tackle - -	S.	1	11	1.6	1	11	1.6	1	11	1.6	1	11	1.6	1	11	1.6
Bunt-lines - - -	S. Iron b'd.	2	13	1.6	2	13	1.6	2	13	1.6	2	13	1.6	2	12	1.6
Reef Tackle Whips	S.	4	9	1.3	4	9	1.3	4	9	1.3	4	9	1.3	4	9	1.3
Sheets in Clews of Sail - - - - -	S.	2	13	2.3	2	13	2.3	2	13	2.3	2	12	2.2	2	12	2.2
Bunt-runner - - -	S.	1	10	1.2	1	10	1.2	1	10	1.2	1	10	1.2	1	9	1.1
Jigger for Bunt-runner	D.	1	8	1.4	1	8	1.4	1	8	1.4	1	8	1.4	1	8	1.4
Jigger for Bunt-runner	S.	2	7	1.2	2	7	1.2	2	7	1.2	2	7	1.2	2	7	1.1
Clew Jiggers - -	S.	4	9	1.2	4	9	1.2	4	9	1.2	4	9	1.2	4	8	1.1
Boom Tricing-lines	S.	2	8	1.0	2	8	1.0	2	8	1.0	2	8	1.0	2	8	1.0
Bow-lines in Fore Top - - - - -	S.	2	13	1.6	2	13	1.6	2	13	1.1	2	13	1.6	2	12	1.5
Span for Studding-sail Halliards - - -	S.	2	13	1.7	2	13	1.7	2	13	1.7	2	13	1.7	2	12	1.6
Jewel Blocks - -	S.	2	13	1.7	2	13	1.7	2	13	1.7	2	13	1.7	2	12	1.6
Studding-sail Tacks on Boom ends -	S.	2	10	1.6	2	10	1.6	2	10	1.6	2	9	1.5	2	8	1.4
Studding-sail Down-hauler in Sails -	S.	2	8	1.0	2	8	1.0	2	8	1.0	2	8	1.0	2	7	.9
Leaders for Boom-braces on Bumkin	S.	2	9	1.1	2	9	1.1	2	9	1.1	2	8	1.1	2	7	1.1
MAIN TOP-GAL'NT MAST AND YARD.																
Top Block - - -	S. Iron b'd.	1	14	2.2	1	14	2.2	1	14	2.2	1	14	2.2	1	13	2.0
Breast Backstays -	S.	2	11	1.1	2	11	1.1	2	11	1.1	2	10	1.1	2	10	1.1
Breast Backstays in Channels - - -	D. Iron b'd.	2	11	1.1	2	11	1.1	2	11	1.1	2	10	1.1	2	10	1.1
Halliards - - - -	D.	2	12	1.3	2	12	1.3	2	12	1.3	2	12	1.3	2	10	1.2

Frigates.			Sloops of War.									Brigs.			Brigantines.			Schooners.			Steamers.		
2d Class.			1st Class.			2d Class.			3d Class.														
No.	Size.	Swallow.	No.	Size.	Swallow.	No.	Size.	Swallow.	No.	Size.	Swallow.	No.	Size.	Swallow.	No.	Size.	Swallow.	No.	Size.	Swallow.	No.	Size.	Swallow.
4	13	1.4	2	12	1.3	2	11	1.3	2	10	1.2	2	9	1.0	–	–	–	–	–	–	4	13	1.4
4	13	1.4	2	12	1.3	2	11	1.3	2	10	1.2	2	9	1.0	–	–	–	–	–	–	4	13	1.4
1	13	3.4	1	12	3.2	1	12	3.2	1	11	3.0	1	9	2.8	–	–	–	–	–	–	1	13	3.4
1	13	3.4	1	12	3.2	1	12	3.2	1	11	3.0	1	9	2.8	–	–	–	–	–	–	1	13	3.4
2	16	2.5	2	14	2.4	2	14	2.4	2	12	1.8	–	–	–	–	–	–	–	–	–	2	15	2.5
2	16	2.4	1	14	2.2	1	13	2.0	1	12	1.9	1	10	1.8	–	–	–	–	–	–	2	16	2.4
2	22	1.5	2	20	1.4	2	16	1.4	2	16	1.4	2	12	1.3	1	12	1.3	1	12	1.3	2	22	1.5
2	22	1.5	2	20	1.4	2	16	1.4	2	16	1.4	2	12	1.3	1	12	1.3	1	12	1.3	2	22	1.5
2	18	1.5	2	16	1.4	2	14	1.4	2	12	1.4	2	10	1.2	1	10	1.2	1	10	1.2	2	18	1.5
2	15	1.7	2	14	1.6	2	14	1.6	2	13	1.5	2	12	1.4	2	12	1.4	2	10	1.2	2	15	1.7
2	14	1.7	2	14	1.6	2	14	1.6	2	13	1.5	2	12	1.4	2	12	1.4	–	–	–	2	14	1.7
2	18	2.2	2	16	2.0	2	15	1.9	2	14	1.8	2	13	1.5	2	18	1.2	–	–	–	2	18	2.2
2	9	2.2	2	9	2.0	2	8	1.9	2	8	1.8	2	7	1.5	2	7	1.5	–	–	–	2	9	2.2
2	9	1.0	2	9	1.0	2	8	.9	2	8	.9	2	7	.8	2	7	.8	–	–	–	2	9	1.0
2	9	1.0	2	9	1.0	2	8	.9	2	8	.9	2	7	.8	2	7	.8	–	–	–	2	9	1.0
2	12	1.6	2	11	1.5	2	11	1.5	2	10	1.4	2	10	1.4	2	9	1.2	–	–	–	2	12	1.6
2	11	1.5	2	10	1.3	2	10	1.3	2	10	1.3	2	9	1.1	2	9	1.1	–	–	–	2	11	1.5
1	11	1.5	1	10	1.3	1	10	1.3	1	10	1.3	1	9	1.1	–	–	–	–	–	–	1	11	1.5
1	11	1.5	1	10	1.3	1	10	1.3	1	10	1.3	1	9	1.1	–	–	–	–	–	–	1	11	1.5
2	11	1.5	2	10	1.3	2	10	1.3	2	10	1.3	2	9	1.1	2	9	1.1	–	–	–	2	11	1.5
4	8	1.2	4	8	1.2	4	7	1.0	4	7	1.0	2	6	.9	2	6	.9	–	–	–	4	8	1.2
2	11	2.0	2	10	1.8	2	10	1.8	2	9	1.7	2	8	1.6	–	–	–	–	–	–	2	11	2.0
1	9	1.1	1	8	1.0	1	8	1.0	1	8	1.0	1	8	.9	1	8	.9	1	6	.9	1	9	1.1
1	7	1.1	1	7	1.1	1	7	1.1	1	7	1.1	1	6	.9	1	6	.9	1	6	.9	1	7	1.1
2	6	1.1	2	6	1.0	2	6	1.0	2	6	1.0	–	–	–	–	–	–	–	–	–	2	6	1.1
4	8	1.1	4	7	1.0	4	7	1.0	4	6	.9	4	6	.9	4	6	.9	–	–	–	4	8	1.1
2	7	.9	2	7	.9	2	7	.9	2	7	.9	2	6	.8	2	6	.8	–	–	–	2	7	.9
2	12	1.5	2	11	1.4	2	10	1.2	2	10	1.2	2	9	1.1	–	–	–	–	–	–	2	12	1.5
2	12	1.6	2	11	1.5	2	11	1.5	2	10	1.4	2	9	1.2	–	–	–	–	–	–	2	12	1.6
2	12	1.6	2	11	1.5	2	11	1.5	2	10	1.4	2	9	1.2	–	–	–	–	–	–	2	12	1.6
2	8	1.4	2	7	1.3	2	6	1.2	2	5	1.1	2	5	1.1	–	–	–	–	–	–	2	8	1.4
2	7	.9	2	6	.9	2	6	.9	2	6	.9	2	5	.7	–	–	–	–	–	–	2	7	.9
2	7	1.1	2	6	1.0	2	6	1.0	2	6	1.0	2	6	1.0	–	–	–	–	–	–	2	7	1.1
1	12	2.0	1	11	1.8	1	11	1.8	1	10	1.6	1	9	1.4	–	–	–	–	–	–	1	12	2.0
2	9	1.0	2	9	1.0	2	8	1.0	2	8	1.0	2	7	.9	–	–	–	–	–	–	2	9	1.0
2	9	1.0	2	9	1.0	2	8	1.0	2	8	1.0	2	7	.9	–	–	–	–	–	–	2	9	1.0
2	10	1.2	2	8	1.1	2	8	1.1	2	8	1.0	2	7	1.0	–	–	–	–	–	–	2	10	1.2

Names of Blocks.	Description of Block.	Ships of the Line.									Razees.			Frigates.		
		3 DECKS.			2 DECKS.											
					1stClass.			2d Class.						1stClass.		
		No.	Size.	Swallow.	No.	Size.	Swallow.	No.	Size.	Swallow.	No.	Size.	Swallow.	No.	Size.	Swallow.
MAIN TOP-GAL'NT MAST & YARD. *Con.*																
Braces on Yard-arms	S.	2	10	1.1	2	10	1.1	2	10	1.1	2	9	1.0	2	8	1.0
Braces on Collar of Miz. Top-mast Stay	S.	2	7	1.2	2	7	1.2	2	7	1.2	2	7	1.0	2	6	1.0
Braces at Mizen Top-mast-head - - -	S.	2	7	1.2	2	7	1.2	2	7	1.2	2	7	1.0	2	6	1.0
Sister - - - - -	S.	2	10	1.6	2	10	1.6	2	10	1.6	2	9	1.5	2	9	1.5
Lifts in Top - - -	S. Clamp.	2	9	1.6	2	9	1.6	2	9	1.6	2	9	1.5	2	9	1.5
Lift Jiggers - - -	D.	2	9	1.0	2	9	1.0	2	9	1.0	2	9	1.0	2	8	.9
Lift Jiggers - - -	S.	2	9	1.0	2	9	1.0	2	9	1.0	2	9	1.0	2	8	.9
Quarter Blocks - -	D.	2	10	1.4	2	10	1.4	2	10	1.4	2	10	1.4	2	10	1.4
Bunt-lines - - -	S.	2	8	.9	2	8	.9	2	8	.9	2	8	.9	2	7	.8
Span Blocks, Main Top-gallant Studding-sail Halliards	S.	2	8	1.2	2	8	1.2	2	8	1.2	2	8	1.2	2	8	1.2
Jewel Blocks - -	S.	2	8	1.2	2	8	1.2	2	8	1.2	2	8	1.2	2	8	1.2
Studding-sail Tacks on Boom ends -	S.	2	7	1.1	2	7	1.1	2	7	1.1	2	7	1.1	2	6	1.0
MA'N ROYAL MAST AND YARD.																
Breast Backstays -	S.	2	9	1.1	2	9	1.1	2	9	1.1	2	8	1.0	2	8	1.0
Breast Backstays in Top - - - - -	D. Iron b'd.	2	9	1.1	2	9	1.1	2	9	1.1	2	8	1.0	2	8	1.0
Royal Braces Mizen Top-gallant Mast-head - - - -	S.	2	7	1.1	2	7	1.1	2	7	1.1	2	7	1.1	2	7	1.1
Quarter Blocks -	S.	2	7	.9	2	7	.9	2	7	.9	2	6	.8	2	6	.8
Bunt-line - - - -	S.	1	6	.9	1	6	.9	1	6	.9	1	6	.9	1	6	.9
Bow-lines leading to F. T. G. Mast-head	S.	2	6	.8	2	6	.8	2	6	.8	2	6	.8	2	6	.8
MAIN TRY-SAIL MAST & GAFF.																
Peak Halliards - -	D. Iron b'd.	1	12	1.4	1	12	1.4	1	12	1.4	1	12	1.4	1	12	1.4
Peak Halliards - -	S.	1	12	1.4	1	12	1.4	1	12	1.4	1	12	1.4	1	12	1.4
Throat Halliards -	D.	1	12	1.4	1	12	1.4	1	12	1.4	1	12	1.4	1	12	1.4
Throat Halliards -	S. Iron b'd.	1	12	1.4	1	12	1.4	1	12	1.4	1	12	1.4	1	12	1.4
Peak Brails - - -	Cheek.															
Throat Brails - -	S.	2	9	1.2	2	9	1.2	2	9	1.2	2	8	1.2	2	8	1.2
Middle Brails - -	S.	2	9	1.2	2	9	1.2	2	9	1.2	2	8	1.2	2	8	1.2
Foot Brails - - -	S.	2	9	1.2	2	9	1.2	2	9	1.2	2	8	1.2	2	8	1.2
Sheets - - - - -	S.	4	10	1.5	4	10	1.5	4	10	1.5	4	10	1.4	4	10	1.4
Sheets on Booms of two-masted vessels	D.	–	–	–	–	–	–	–	–	–	–	–	–	–	–	–
Vangs - - - - -	S.	2	8	1.2	2	8	1.2	2	8	1.2	2	8	1.2	2	8	1.2
MIZEN MAST AND CROSS-JACK Y'RD.																
Pendant Tackles -	D.	2	14	1.6	2	14	1.6	2	14	1.6	2	13	1.5	2	13	1.5
Pendant Tackles -	S.	2	14	1.6	2	14	1.6	2	14	1.6	2	13	1.5	2	13	1.5
Truss Tackles - -	D.	1	9	1.1	1	9	1.1	1	9	1.1	1	8	1.0	1	8	1.0

Frigates.			Sloops of War.									Brigs.			Brigantines.			Schooners.			Steamers.		
2d Class.			1st Class.			2d Class.			3d Class.														
No.	Size.	Swallow.	No.	Size.	Swallow.	No.	Size.	Swallow.	No.	Size.	Swallow.	No.	Size.	Swallow.	No.	Size.	Swallow.	No.	Size.	Swallow.	No.	Size.	Swallow.
2	8	1.0	2	7	.9	2	6	.9	2	6	.9	–	–	–	–	–	–	–	–	–	2	8	1.0
2	6	1.0	2	5	.9	2	5	.9	2	5	.9	–	–	–	–	–	–	–	–	–	2	6	1.0
2	6	1.0	2	5	.9	2	5	.9	2	5	.9	–	–	–	–	–	–	–	–	–	2	6	1.0
2	8	1.4	2	7	1.3	2	7	1.3	2	6	1.2	2	5	1.1	–	–	–	–	–	–	2	8	1.4
2	8	1.4	2	8	1.4	2	8	1.4	2	8	1.4	–	–	–	–	–	–	–	–	–	2	8	1.4
2	8	.9	2	7	.8	2	7	.8	2	6	.8	2	6	.7	–	–	–	–	–	–	2	8	.9
2	8	.9	2	7	.8	2	7	.8	2	6	.8	2	6	.7	–	–	–	–	–	–	2	8	.9
2	10	1.4	2	9	1.3	2	8	1.2	2	8	1.2	2	8	1.2	2	7	1.0	–	–	–	2	9	1.3
2	7	.8	2	7	.8	1	6	.8	1	6	.7	1	5	.6	–	–	–	–	–	–	2	7	.8
2	7	1.1	2	7	1.1	2	6	1.0	2	6	1.0	2	6	.9	–	–	–	–	–	–	2	7	1.1
2	7	1.1	2	7	1.1	2	6	1.0	2	6	1.0	2	6	.9	–	–	–	–	–	–	2	7	1.1
2	6	1.0	2	5	.9	2	5	.9	2	5	.9	2	5	.8	–	–	–	–	–	–	2	6	1.0
2	7	.9	2	6	.8	2	6	.7	2	6	.7	2	6	.6	–	–	–	–	–	–	2	7	.9
2	7	.9	2	6	.8	2	6	.7	2	6	.7	2	6	.6	–	–	–	–	–	–	2	7	.9
2	6	1.0	2	6	1.0	2	6	1.0	2	6	1.0	2	5	.9	–	–	–	–	–	–	2	6	1.0
2	5	.7	2	5	.7	2	5	.7	2	5	.7	2	4	.6	–	–	–	–	–	–	2	5	.7
1	6	.9	–	–	–	–	–	–	–	–	–	–	–	–	–	–	–	–	–	–	1	6	.9
2	5	.7	2	5	.7	2	5	.7	2	5	.7	2	4	.6	–	–	–	–	–	–	2	5	.7
1	11	1.4	1	10	1.3	1	10	1.3	1	8	1.1	1	8	1.1	1	14	1.6	1	14	1.6	1	11	1.4
1	11	1.4	1	10	1.3	1	10	1.3	1	8	1.1	1	8	1.1	2	14	1.6	2	14	1.6	1	11	1.4
1	11	1.4	1	10	1.3	1	10	1.3	1	8	1.1	1	8	1.1	1	14	1.6	1	14	1.6	1	11	1.4
1	11	1.4	1	10	1.3	1	10	1.3	1	8	1.1	1	8	1.1	1	14	1.6	1	14	1.6	1	11	1.4
2	8	1.2	2	7	1.1	2	7	1.1	2	7	1.1	2	6	1.0	2	8	1.2	2	8	1.2	2	8	1.2
2	8	1.2	2	7	1.1	2	7	1.1	2	7	1.1	2	6	1.0	2	8	1.2	2	8	1.2	2	8	1.2
2	8	1.2	2	7	1.1	2	7	1.1	2	7	1.1	2	6	1.0	2	8	1.2	2	8	1.2	2	8	1.2
4	9	1.4	4	8	1.2	4	8	1.2	4	8	1.2	2	12	1.5	2	12	1.5	2	12	1.5	4	9	1.4
–	–	–	–	–	–	–	–	–	–	–	–	2	12	1.5	2	12	1.5	2	12	1.5			
2	7	1.1	2	7	1.1	2	6	1.0	2	6	1.0	2	6	1.0	2	6	1.0	2	6	1.0	2	7	1.1
2	12	1.4	2	11	1.3	2	11	1.3	2	11	1.3	–	–	–	–	–	–	–	–	–	2	12	1.4
2	12	1.4	2	11	1.3	2	11	1.3	2	11	1.3	–	–	–	–	–	–	–	–	–	2	12	1.4
–	p't	–	–	p't	–	–	p't	–	–	p't	–	–	–	–	–	–	–	–	–	–	–	p t	–

Names of Blocks.	Description of Block.	Ships of the Line. 3 DECKS.			2 DECKS. 1st Class.			2 DECKS. 2d Class.			Razees.			Frigates. 1st Class.		
		No.	Size.	Swallow.	No.	Size.	Swallow.	No.	Size.	Swallow.	No.	Size.	Swallow.	No.	Size.	Swallow.
MIZEN MAST AND CR. JACK Y'RD. *Con.*																
Truss Tackles - -	S.	1	9	1.1	1	9	1.1	1	9	1.1	1	8	1.0	1	8	1.0
Quarter Blocks - -	S. Iron b'd.	2	12	2.0	2	12	2.0	2	12	2.0	2	11	2.0	2	11	2.0
Braces on Yard-arms	S.	2	12	1.4	2	12	1.4	2	12	1.4	2	11	1.4	2	11	1.4
Braces leading under Main Trestle Trees	D.	2	10	1.4	2	10	1.4	2	10	1.4	2	9	1.4	2	9	1.4
Lifts on Cap - - -	S.	2	12	1.8	2	12	1.8	2	12	1.8	2	11	1.8	2	11	1.8
Quarter Davit Topping-lifts - - -	D.	2	10	1.2	2	10	1.2	2	10	1.2	2	9	1.2	2	9	1.2
Quarter Davit Topping-lifts - - -	S.	2	10	1.2	2	10	1.2	2	10	1.2	2	9	1.2	2	9	1.2
MIZEN TOP-MAST AND YARD.																
Top Blocks - - -	S. Iron b'd.	2	17	2.8	2	17	2.8	2	17	2.8	2	16	2.6	1	15	2.4
Top Burtons - -	Fiddle.	2	18	1.1	2	18	1.1	2	18	1.1	2	18	1.1	2	16	1.1
Top Burtons - -	S.	2	10	1.1	2	10	1.1	2	10	1.1	2	10	1.1	2	10	1.1
Top Runners - -	S.	2	10	1.5	2	10	1.5	2	10	1.5	2	10	1.5	2	10	1.4
Breast Backstays -	D.	2	13	1.3	2	13	1.3	2	13	1.3	2	13	1.3	2	13	1.3
Breast Backstays -	T. Iron b'd.	2	13	1.3	2	13	1.3	2	13	1.3	2	13	1.3	2	13	1.3
Stay leading in Main Top - - - - -	S.	1	10	2.5	1	10	2.5	1	10	2.5	1	10	2.5	1	8	2.0
Tye - - - - - -	S. Iron b'd.	1	13	2.5	1	13	2.5	1	13	2.5	1	13	2.5	1	12	2.0
Fly - - - - - - -	D.	1	16	1.4	1	16	1.4	1	16	1.4	1	16	1.4	1	15	1.4
Fly - - - - - - -	S.	1	16	1.4	1	16	1.4	1	16	1.4	1	16	1.4	1	15	1.4
Braces on Yard-arms	S.	2	12	1.3	2	12	1.3	2	12	1.3	2	12	1.3	2	11	1.2
Braces leading at the Main Masthead -	S.	2	12	1.3	2	12	1.3	2	12	1.3	2	12	1.3	2	11	1.2
Sister - - - - - -	D.	2	18	1.7	2	18	1.7	2	18	1.7	2	18	1.7	2	16	1.7
Leaders for Lifts -	S. Clamp.	2	9	1.7	2	9	1.7	2	9	1.7	2	8	1.7	2	8	1.7
Lift Jiggers - - -	D.	2	8	.8	2	8	.8	2	8	.8	2	8	.8	2	8	.8
Lift Jiggers - - -	S.	2	8	.8	2	8	.8	2	8	.8	2	8	.8	2	8	.8
Quarter Blocks -	D. Iron b'd.	2	11	1.4	2	11	1.4	2	11	1.4	2	10	1.4	2	10	1.4
Clew-lines in Clews of sail - - - -	S.	2	9	1.4	2	9	1.4	2	9	1.4	2	8	1.3	2	8	1.3
Rolling Tackle - -	S.	1	8	1.2	1	8	1.2	1	8	1.2	1	8	1.2	1	8	1.2
Rolling Tackle - -	D.	1	8	1.2	1	8	1.2	1	8	1.2	1	8	1.2	1	8	1.2
Bunt-lines - - -	S. Iron b'd.	2	10	1.1	2	10	1.1	2	10	1.1	2	10	1.1	2	10	1.1
Reef Tackle Whips	S.	2	7	1.1	2	7	1.1	2	7	1.1	2	7	1.1	2	7	1.1
Sheets in Clews of Sail - - - - -	S.	2	11	2.0	2	11	2.0	2	11	2.0	2	10	1.9	2	10	1.9
Bunt-runner - - -	S.	1	8	1.0	1	8	1.0	1	8	1.0	1	8	1.0	1	8	1.0
Jigger for Bunt-runner	S.	2	8	1.0	2	8	1.0	2	8	1.0	2	7	1.0	2	7	1.0
Clew Jiggers - -	S.	4	8	1.0	4	8	1.0	4	8	1.0	4	8	1.0	4	8	1.0
Bow-lines in the Main Top - - - - -	S.	2	8	1.0	2	8	1.0	2	8	1.0	2	8	1.0	2	8	1.0
MIZEN TOP-GAL'T MAST & YARD.																
Top Block - - -	S. Iron b'd.	1	12	1.4	1	12	1.4	1	12	1.4	1	11	1.4	1	11	1.4
Breast Backstays -	S.	2	12	1.4	2	12	1.4	2	12	1.4	2	11	1.4	2	11	1.4
Breast Backstays in Channels - - -	D. Iron b'd.	2	12	1.4	2	12	1.4	2	12	1.4	2	11	1.4	2	11	1.4

Frigates.			Sloops of War.									Brigs.			Brigantines.			Schooners.			Steamers.		
2d Class.			1st Class.			2d Class.			3d Class.														
No.	Size.	Swallow.	No.	Size.	Swallow.	No.	Size.	Swallow.	No.	Size.	Swallow.	No.	Size.	Swallow.	No.	Size.	Swallow.	No.	Size.	Swallow.	No.	Size.	Swallow.
–	p't	–	–	p't	–	–	p't	–	–	p't	–	–	–	–	–	–	–	–	–	–	–	p't	–
2	10	1.8	2	9	1.7	2	8	1.6	2	8	1.6	–	–	–	–	–	–	–	–	–	2	10	1.8
2	10	1.3	2	9	1.2	2	9	1.2	2	8	1.1	–	–	–	–	–	–	–	–	–	2	10	1.3
2	8	1.3	2	8	1.2	2	7	1.1	2	7	1.1	–	–	–	–	–	–	–	–	–	2	8	1.3
2	10	1.7	2	8	1.5	2	8	1.5	2	8	1.5	–	–	–	–	–	–	–	–	–	2	10	1.7
2	9	1.2	2	8	1.1	2	8	1.1	2	8	1.1	–	–	–	–	–	–	–	–	–	2	9	1.2
2	9	1.2	2	8	1.1	2	8	1.1	2	8	1.1	–	–	–	–	–	–	–	–	–	2	9	1.2
1	14	2.0	1	14	2.0	1	13	1.8	1	13	1.8	–	–	–	–	–	–	–	–	–	1	14	2.0
2	16	1.0	2	14	1.0	2	14	1.0	2	14	.9	–	–	–	–	–	–	–	–	–	2	16	1.0
2	10	1.0	2	9	1.0	2	9	1.0	2	9	.9	–	–	–	–	–	–	–	–	–	2	10	1.0
2	10	1.4	2	9	1.2	2	9	1.2	2	9	1.2	–	–	–	–	–	–	–	–	–	2	10	1.4
2	12	1.2	2	11	1.2	2	11	1.2	2	11	1.2	–	–	–	–	–	–	–	–	–	2	12	1.2
2	12	1.2	2	11	1.2	2	11	1.2	2	11	1.2	–	–	–	–	–	–	–	–	–	2	12	1.2
1	8	2.0	1	8	2.0	1	8	2.0	1	8	2.0	–	–	–	–	–	–	–	–	–	1	8	2.0
1	14	1.2	1	12	1.1	1	12	1.1	1	11	1.0	–	–	–	–	–	–	–	–	–	1	14	1.2
1	14	1.2	1	12	1.1	1	12	1.1	1	11	1.0	–	–	–	–	–	–	–	–	–	1	14	1.2
2	10	1.1	2	10	1.1	2	9	1.0	2	8	.9	–	–	–	–	–	–	–	–	–	2	10	1.1
2	10	1.1	2	10	1.1	2	9	1.0	2	8	.9	–	–	–	–	–	–	–	–	–	2	10	1.1
2	15	1.5	2	13	1.5	2	13	1.4	2	13	1.4	–	–	–	–	–	–	–	–	–	2	15	1.5
2	8	1.5	2	7	1.5	2	6	1.4	2	6	1.4	–	–	–	–	–	–	–	–	–	2	8	1.5
2	7	.8	2	7	.8	2	6	.7	2	6	.7	–	–	–	–	–	–	–	–	–	2	7	.8
2	7	.8	2	7	.8	2	6	.7	2	6	.7	–	–	–	–	–	–	–	–	–	2	7	.8
2	9	1.3	2	8	1.3	2	8	1.3	2	8	1.3	–	–	–	–	–	–	–	–	–	2	9	1.3
2	8	1.3	2	7	1.2	2	7	1.2	2	6	1.1	–	–	–	–	–	–	–	–	–	2	8	1.3
1	7	1.0	1	7	1.0	1	6	.9	1	6	.9	–	–	–	–	–	–	–	–	–	1	7	1.0
1	7	1.0	1	7	1.0	1	6	.9	1	6	.9	–	–	–	–	–	–	–	–	–	1	7	1.0
2	9	1.1	2	8	1.0	2	8	1.0	2	7	.9	–	–	–	–	–	–	–	–	–	2	9	1.1
2	6	1.0	2	6	1.0	2	6	1.0	2	6	1.0	–	–	–	–	–	–	–	–	–	2	6	1.0
2	9	1.8	2	8	1.7	2	8	1.7	2	8	1.7	–	–	–	–	–	–	–	–	–	2	9	1.8
1	8	1.0	1	7	.9	1	7	.9	1	7	.9	–	–	–	–	–	–	–	–	–	1	8	1.0
2	7	1.0	2	6	.9	2	6	.9	2	6	.9	–	–	–	–	–	–	–	–	–	2	7	1.0
2	7	.8	2	7	.8	2	6	.7	2	6	.7	–	–	–	–	–	–	–	–	–	2	7	.8
2	7	.8	2	7	.8	2	6	.7	2	6	.7	–	–	–	–	–	–	–	–	–	2	7	.8
1	10	1.4	1	9	1.3	1	8	1.3	1	8	1.3	–	–	–	–	–	–	–	–	–	1	10	1.4
2	10	1.4	2	9	1.3	2	8	1.3	2	8	1.3	–	–	–	–	–	–	–	–	–	2	10	1.4
2	10	1.4	2	9	1.3	2	8	1.3	2	8	1.3	–	–	–	–	–	–	–	–	–	2	10	1.4

Names of Blocks.	Description of Block.	Ships of the Line.									Razees.			Frigates.		
		3 DECKS.			2 DECKS.											
					1st Class.			2d Class.						1st Class.		
		No.	Size.	Swallow.	No.	Size.	Swallow.	No.	Size.	Swallow.	No.	Size.	Swallow.	No.	Size.	Swallow.
MIZEN TOP-GAL'T MAST & YARD. *Con.*																
Halliards - - -	D.	1	8	1.2	1	8	1.2	1	8	1.2	1	8	1.2	1	8	1.2
Halliards - - -	S.	1	8	1.2	1	8	1.2	1	8	1.2	1	8	1.2	1	8	1.2
Braces on Yard-arms																
Braces on Main Top-mast Backstays -	D.	2	6	1.0	2	6	1.0	2	6	1.0	2	6	1.0	2	6	1.0
Sister - - - - -	S.	2	8	1.4	2	8	1.4	2	8	1.4	2	7	1.3	2	7	1.3
Lifts in Top (Bull's Eyes) - - - -	S.	2	–	–	2	–	–	2	–	–	2	–	–	2	–	–
Lift Jiggers - - -	D.	2	7	1.0	2	7	1.0	2	7	1.0	2	7	1.0	2	7	1.0
Lift Jiggers - - -	S.	2	7	1.0	2	7	1.0	2	7	1.0	2	7	1.0	2	7	1.0
Quarter Blocks -	D.	2	7	1.2	2	7	1.2	2	7	1.2	2	7	1.2	2	7	1.2
Bunt-line - - - -	S.	1	7	1.2	1	7	1.2	1	7	1.2	1	7	1.2	1	7	1.2
Bow-lines at Main Top-mast head -	D.	2	7	1.2	2	7	1.2	2	7	1.2	2	7	1.2	2	7	1.2
MIZ. ROYAL MAST AND YARD.																
Breast Backstays -	S.	2	7	.8	2	7	.8	2	7	.8	2	6	.8	2	6	.8
Breast Backstays in Top - - - - -	D. Iron b'd.	2	7	.8	2	7	.8	2	7	.8	2	6	.8	2	6	.8
Quarter Blocks - -	S.	2	6	.8	2	6	.8	2	6	.8	2	6	.8	2	6	.8
Braces Main Top-mast-head - - -	S.	2	6	1.0	2	6	1.0	2	6	1.0	2	6	1.0	2	6	1.0
Bow-lines leading to M'n Top-mast head	S.	2	6	1.0	2	6	1.0	2	6	1.0	2	6	1.0	2	6	1.0
Bunt-lines - - -	S.	1	6	1.0	1	6	1.0	1	6	1.0	1	6	1.0	1	6	1.0
SPANKER BOOM AND GAFF.																
Topping-lifts - -	S.	2	13	2.7	2	13	2.7	2	13	2.7	2	13	2.7	2	12	2.5
Tackles for Topping-lifts - - - - -	D.	2	12	1.2	2	12	1.2	2	12	1.2	2	12	1.2	2	11	1.2
Tackles for Topping-lifts - - - - -	S.	2	12	1.2	2	12	1.2	2	12	1.2	2	12	1.2	2	11	1.2
Sheets - - - - -	D.	2	12	1.7	2	12	1.7	2	12	1.7	2	12	1.7	2	11	1.5
Sheets - - - - -	S.	2	12	1.7	2	12	1.7	2	12	1.7	2	12	1.7	2	11	1.5
Peak Halliards - -	D. Iron b'd.	1	14	1.4	1	14	1.4	1	14	1.4	1	13	1.4	1	13	1.4
Peak Halliards - -	S.	2	13	1.4	2	13	1.4	2	13	1.4	2	12	1.4	2	12	1.4
Throat Halliards -	D.	1	14	1.4	1	14	1.4	1	14	1.4	1	13	1.4	1	13	1.4
Throat Halliards -	S. Iron b'd.	1	14	1.4	1	14	1.4	1	14	1.4	1	13	1.4	1	13	1.4
Peak Brails - - -	Cheek.															
Throat Brails - -	S.	2	9	1.2	2	9	1.2	2	9	1.2	2	9	1.2	2	8	1.1
Middle Brails - -	S.	2	8	1.1	2	8	1.1	2	8	1.1	2	8	1.1	2	8	1.0
Foot Brails - - -	S.	2	8	1.1	2	8	1.1	2	8	1.1	2	8	1.1	2	8	1.0
Outhauler - - -	S.	1	13	1.7	1	13	1.7	1	13	1.7	1	13	1.7	1	12	1.5
Vangs - - - - -	S.	2	8	1.2	2	8	1.2	2	8	1.2	2	8	1.2	2	7	1.1
Vangs leading on Quarter - - -	S.	2	8	1.2	2	8	1.2	2	8	1.2	2	8	1.2	2	7	1.1
Dasher Block (Ensign Halliards) -	D.	1	–	–	1	–	–	1	–	–	1	–	–	1	–	–

Frigates. 2d Class.			Sloops of War. 1st Class.			Sloops of War. 2d Class.			Sloops of War. 3d Class.			Brigs.			Brigantines.			Schooners.			Steamers.		
No.	Size.	Swallow.	No.	Size.	Swallow.	No.	Size.	Swallow.	No.	Size.	Swallow.	No.	Size.	Swallow.	No.	Size.	Swallow.	No.	Size.	Swallow.	No.	Size.	Swallow.
1	7	1.0	1	7	1.0	1	6	.9	1	6	.9	–	–	–	–	–	–	–	–	–	1	7	1.0
1	7	1.0	1	7	1.0	1	6	.9	1	6	.9	–	–	–	–	–	–	–	–	–	1	7	1.0
2	5	.9	2	5	.9	2	4	.8	2	5	.9	–	–	–	–	–	–	–	–	–	2	5	.9
2	7	1.3	2	6	1.2	2	6	1.2	2	5	1.0	–	–	–	–	–	–	–	–	–	2	7	1.3
2	–	–	2	–	–	2	–	–	2	–	–	–	–	–	–	–	–	–	–	–	2	–	–
2	6	.9	2	6	.9	2	5	.8	2	5	.8	–	–	–	–	–	–	–	–	–	2	6	.9
2	6	.9	2	6	.9	2	5	.8	2	5	.8	–	–	–	–	–	–	–	–	–	2	6	.9
2	6	1.1	2	6	1.1	2	5	1.0	2	5	1.0	–	–	–	–	–	–	–	–	–	2	6	1.1
1	6	1.1	1	5	1.0	1	5	1.0	1	5	.9	–	–	–	–	–	–	–	–	–	1	6	1.1
2	6	1.1	2	5	1.0	2	5	1.0	2	5	.9	–	–	–	–	–	–	–	–	–	2	6	1.1
2	6	.8	2	5	.8	2	5	.8	2	5	.8	–	–	–	–	–	–	–	–	–	2	6	.8
2	6	.8	2	5	.8	2	5	.8	2	5	.8	–	–	–	–	–	–	–	–	–	2	6	.8
2	6	.8	2	5	.8	2	5	.8	2	5	.8	–	–	–	–	–	–	–	–	–	2	6	.8
2	5	.9	2	5	.9	2	5	.8	2	5	.8	–	–	–	–	–	–	–	–	–	2	5	.9
2	5	.9	2	5	.9	2	5	.8	2	5	.8	–	–	–	–	–	–	–	–	–	2	5	.9
1	5	.9	1	5	.9	1	5	.8	1	5	.8	–	–	–	–	–	–	–	–	–	1	5	.9
2	12	2.5	2	11	2.0	2	11	2.0	2	11	2.0	2	10	1.8	2	10	1.8	2	11	2.0	2	12	2.5
2	10	1.1	2	9	1.0	2	8	.9	2	8	.9	2	8	.9	4	10	1.1	4	11	1.2	2	10	1.1
2	10	1.1	2	9	1.0	2	8	.9	2	8	.9	2	8	.9	2	10	1.1	2	11	1.2	2	10	1.1
2	10	1.4	2	10	1.4	2	10	1.4	2	10	1.4	–	–	–	–	–	–	–	–	–	2	10	1.4
2	10	1.4	2	10	1.4	2	10	1.4	2	10	1.4	–	–	–	–	–	–	–	–	–	2	10	1.4
1	12	1.3	1	11	1.2	1	10	1.1	1	10	1.1	–	–	–	–	–	–	–	–	–	1	12	1.3
2	11	1.3	1	10	1.3	1	10	1.2	1	9	1.1	–	–	–	–	–	–	–	–	–	2	11	1.3
1	12	1.3	1	11	1.2	1	10	1.1	1	10	1.1	–	–	–	–	–	–	–	–	–	1	12	1.3
1	12	1.3	1	11	1.2	1	10	1.1	1	10	1.1	–	–	–	–	–	–	–	–	–	1	12	1.3
2	8	1.1	2	8	1.1	2	7	1.0	2	7	1.0	–	–	–	–	–	–	–	–	–	2	8	1.1
2	8	1.0	2	7	.9	2	7	.9	2	7	.9	–	–	–	–	–	–	–	–	–	2	8	1.0
2	8	1.0	2	7	.9	2	7	.9	2	7	.9	–	–	–	–	–	–	–	–	–	2	8	1.0
1	12	1.5	1	10	1.4	1	9	1.2	1	9	1.2	–	–	–	–	–	–	–	–	–	1	12	1.5
2	7	1.1	2	7	1.1	2	7	1.1	2	6	.9	–	–	–	–	–	–	–	–	–	2	7	1.1
2	7	1.1	2	7	1.1	2	7	1.1	2	6	.9	–	–	–	–	–	–	–	–	–	2	7	1.1
1	–	–	1	–	–	1	–	–	1	–	–	1	–	–	1	–	–	1	–	–	1	–	–

Names of Blocks.	Des. of Bl'ck.	Ships of the Line.									Razees.			Frigates.		
		3 Decks.			2 Decks.											
					1st Class.			2d Class.						1st Class.		
		No.	Size.	Swallow.	No.	Size.	Swallow.	No.	Size.	Swallow.	No.	Size.	Swallow	No.	Size.	Swallow.
MISCELLANEOUS BLOCKS.																
Cat Blocks - - -	T.	2	20	2.6	2	20	2.6	2	20	2.6	2	20	2.5	2	18	2.2
Cat Backropes - -	S.	4	9	1.2	4	9	1.2	4	9	1.2	4	9	1.2	4	8	1.1
Fish Tackle - -	D.	4	20	2.2	4	20	2.2	4	20	2.2	4	20	2.2	4	20	2.0
Fish Leaders - -	S.	3	18	2.2	3	18	2.2	3	18	2.2	3	18	2.2	3	16	1.8
Clear Hawse Pend'nts	S.	1	–	–	1	–	–	1	–	–	1	–	–	1	–	–
Bull's Eyes for clothes-lines - - - - -	–	100	–	–	100	–	–	100	–	–	100	–	–	80	–	–
Cap Bobstay Hearts	L. Vit.	2	–	–	2	–	–	2	–	–	2	–	–	2	–	–
Middle and Inner H'rts	L. Vit.	4	–	–	4	–	–	4	–	–	4	–	–	4	–	–
Bowsprit Shr'ds H'rts	L. Vit.	8	–	–	8	–	–	8	–	–	8	–	–	8	–	–
Iron-strapped Bull's Eyes (in head), size and number as req'd																
Luff Tackle Blocks	S.	60	12	1.4	60	12	1.4	60	12	1.4	60	12	1.4	40	12	1.4
Luff Tackle Blocks for Stays - - - -	D.	16	15	1.8	16	15	1.8	16	15	1.8	16	14	1.6	16	14	1.6
Leading Rigging on Fo'castle and Gangways - - - -	Assort	12	–	–	12	–	–	12	–	–	12	–	–	12	–	–
Fife-rail Leaders -	S. d. sc	56	–	–	56	–	–	56	–	–	56	–	–	56	–	–
Side Leaders - -	–	100	–	–	100	–	–	100	–	–	100	–	–	100	–	–
Snatch Blocks - -	Assort	20	–	–	20	–	–	20	–	–	20	–	–	20	–	–
Hammock Girt-lines	S.	20	12	1.8	20	12	1.8	20	12	1.8	20	12	1.8	16	11	1.5
Ham'ck Tricing-lines	S.	12	10	1.4	12	10	1.4	12	10	1.4	12	10	1.4	12	9	1.0
Relieving Tackles -	D.	2	10	1.4	2	10	1.4	2	10	1.4	2	10	1.4	2	10	1.4
Relieving Tackles -	S.	2	10	1.4	2	10	1.4	2	10	1.4	2	10	1.4	2	10	1.4
Awning Jiggers -	D.	8	10	1.4	8	10	1.4	8	10	1.4	8	10	1.4	8	9	1.2
Lower Yard Whips	S.	4	9	1.1	4	9	1.1	4	9	1.1	4	9	1.1	4	8	1.0
Crow-foot Halliards for Awnings - -	S.	12	7	.9	12	7	.9	12	7	.9	12	7	.9	12	7	.9
Stern, Quarter and Waist Davit Blocks	D. Ir b.	20	10	1.4	20	10	1.4	20	10	1.4	20	10	1.4	12	10	1.4
Leading Trucks -	D.	30	–	–	30	–	–	30	–	–	30	–	–	30	–	–
Leading Trucks -	S.	30	–	–	30	–	–	30	–	–	30	–	–	30	–	–
Fore Yard - - -	Fiddle	2	33	1.7	2	33	1.7	2	33	1.7	2	33	1.7	2	33	1.7
Fore Yard - - -	S.	2	18	1.7	2	18	1.7	2	18	1.7	2	16	1.7	2	16	1.7
Fore Stay - - -	D.	1	17	1.7	1	17	1.7	1	17	1.7	1	16	1.7	1	16	1.7
Fore Stay - - -	S.	1	17	1.7	1	17	1.7	1	17	1.7	1	16	1.7	1	16	1.7
Main Yard - - -	Fiddle	2	33	1.7	2	33	1.7	2	33	1.7	2	33	1.7	2	33	1.7
Main Yard - - -	S.	2	18	1.7	2	18	1.7	2	18	1.7	2	16	1.7	2	16	1.7
Main Stay - - -	D.	1	17	1.7	1	17	1.7	1	17	1.7	1	16	1.7	1	16	1.7
Main Stay - - -	S.	1	17	1.7	1	17	1.7	1	17	1.7	1	16	1.7	1	16	1.7
Quarter and Stay -	S.	4	16	1.6	4	16	1.6	4	16	1.6	4	15	1.6	4	15	1.6
Dead Eyes (set) -	–	1	–	–	1	–	–	1	–	–	1	–	–	1	–	–
Stock and Bill Tackle	D.	2	12	1.6	2	12	1.6	2	12	1.6	2	12	1.6	2	12	1.6
Stock and Bill Tackle	S.	2	12	1.6	2	12	1.6	2	12	1.6	2	12	1.6	2	12	1.6
Trucks for Jaws of Gaff (set) - - -	–	1	–	–	1	–	–	1	–	–	1	–	–	1	–	–
Masthead Trucks(set)	–	1	–	–	1	–	–	1	–	–	1	–	–	1	–	–
F. T. Studding-sail Boom Burtons -	D.	2	10	1.1	2	10	1.1	2	10	1.1	2	10	1.1	2	10	1.1
F. T. Studding-sail Boom Burtons -	S.	2	10	1.1	2	10	1.1	2	10	1.1	2	10	1.1	2	10	1.1

Frigates.			Sloops of War.									Brigs.			Brigantines.			Schooners.			Steamers.		
2d Class.			1st Class.			2d Class.			3d Class.														
No.	Size.	Swallow.	No.	Size.	Swallow.	No.	Size.	Swallow.	No.	Size.	Swallow.	No.	Size.	Swallow.	No.	Size.	Swallow.	No.	Size.	Swallow.	No.	Size.	Swallow.
2	17	2.1	2	16	2.0	2	15	1.9	2	14	1.8	2D	13	1.7	2D	12	1.6	2D	11	1.5	2	17	2.1
4	8	1.1	4	7	1.0	4	7	1.0	4	7	1.0	–	–	–	–	–	–	–	–	–	4	8	1.1
4	18	2.0	–	–	–	–	–	–	–	–	–	–	–	–	–	–	–	–	–	–	4	18	2.0
3	16	1.8	–	–	–	–	–	–	–	–	–	–	–	–	–	–	–	–	–	–	3	16	1.8
1	–	–	1	–	–	1	–	–	1	–	–	1	–	–	1	–	–	1	–	–	1	–	–
60	–	–	40	–	–	40	–	–	40	–	–	20	–	–	20	–	–	20	–	–	60	–	–
2	–	–	2	–	–	2	–	–	2	–	–	2	–	–	2	–	–	2	–	–	2	–	–
4	–	–	4	–	–	4	–	–	4	–	–	2	–	–	2	–	–	2	–	–	4	–	–
8	–	–	4	–	–	4	–	–	4	–	–	4	–	–	4	–	–	4	–	–	8	–	–
40	11	1.4	24	10	1.2	24	10	1.2	24	10	1.2	20	10	1.2	20	9	1.1	20	9	1.1	40	11	1.4
16	13	1.5	8	12	1.4	8	12	1.3	8	11	1.3	8	11	1.3	4	10	1.2	4	10	1.2	16	13	1.5
12	–	–	8	–	–	8	–	–	8	–	–	–	–	–	–	–	–	–	–	–	12	–	–
40	–	–	36	–	–	36	–	–	36	–	–	20	–	–	20	–	–	20	–	–	40	–	–
100	–	–	80	–	–	80	–	–	70	–	–	40	–	–	40	–	–	20	–	–	100	–	–
20	–	–	15	–	–	15	–	–	15	–	–	10	–	–	10	–	–	8	–	–	15	–	–
16	10	1.4	12	10	1.4	12	9	1.2	12	9	1.2	8	9	1.2	8	9	1.2	8	9	1.1	16	10	1.4
12	9	1.0	12	9	1.0	12	8	1.0	12	8	1.0	8	7	.9	8	7	.9	8	7	.9	12	9	1.0
2	10	1.4	2	10	1.4	2	9	1.2	2	9	1.2	2	9	1.2	2	9	1.2	2	9	1.2	2	10	1.4
2	10	1.4	2	10	1.4	2	9	1.2	2	9	1.2	2	9	1.2	2	9	1.2	2	9	1.2	2	10	1.4
8	9	1.2	8	8	1.1	8	8	1.1	8	7	.9	6	7	.9	6	6	.8	6	6	.8	8	9	1.2
4	8	1.0	4	7	1.0	4	7	1.0	4	7	1.0	4	6	.8	4	6	.8	2	6	.8	4	8	1.0
12	6	.8	6	6	.8	6	6	.8	6	6	.8	4	5	.7	4	5	.7	4	5	.7	6	6	.8
12	10	1.2	10	9	1.1	10	9	1.1	10	8	1.0	10	8	1.0	10	8	1.0	10	8	1.0	12	10	1.2
30	–	–	20	–	–	20	–	–	20	–	–	12	–	–	12	–	–	12	–	–	30	–	–
30	–	–	20	–	–	20	–	–	20	–	–	12	–	–	12	–	–	12	–	–	30	–	–
2	30	1.6	2	24	1.5	2	22	1.5	2	22	1.4	1	20	1.4	1	20	1.3	1	20	1.3	2	30	1.6
2	16	1.5	2	14	1.5	2	13	1.3	2	13	1.3	1	12	1.2	1	12	1.2	1	10	1.1	2	16	1.5
1	15	1.6	1	13	1.5	1	13	1.5	1	13	1.5	1	12	1.3	1	10	1.2	–	–	–	1	15	1.6
1	15	1.6	1	13	1.5	1	13	1.5	1	13	1.5	1	12	1.3	1	10	1.2	–	–	–	1	15	1.6
2	30	1.6	2	24	1.5	2	22	1.5	2	22	1.4	1	20	1.4	1	20	1.3	1	20	1.3	2	30	1.6
2	16	1.5	2	14	1.5	2	13	1.3	2	13	1.3	1	12	1.2	1	12	1.2	1	10	1.1	2	16	1.5
1	15	1.6	1	13	1.5	1	13	1.5	1	13	1.5	1	12	1.3	1	10	1.2	–	–	–	1	15	1.6
1	15	1.6	1	13	1.5	1	13	1.5	1	13	1.5	1	12	1.3	1	10	1.2	–	–	–	1	15	1.6
4	14	1.5	4	13	1.5	4	12	1.4	4	12	1.4	4	10	1.1	–	–	–	–	–	–	4	14	1.5
1	–	–	1	–	–	1	–	–	1	–	–	1	–	–	1	–	–	1	–	–	1	–	–
2	11	1.4	2	11	1.4	2	10	1.2	2	10	1.2	–	–	–	–	–	–	–	–	–	2	11	1.4
2	11	1.4	2	11	1.4	2	10	1.2	2	10	1.2	–	–	–	–	–	–	–	–	–	2	11	1.4
1	–	–	1	–	–	1	–	–	1	–	–	1	–	–	1	–	–	1	–	–	1	–	–
1	–	–	1	–	–	1	–	–	1	–	–	1	–	–	1	–	–	1	–	–	1	–	–
2	10	1.1	2	9	1.0	2	9	1.0	2	9	1.0	–	–	–	–	–	–	–	–	–	2	10	1.0
2	10	1.1	2	9	1.0	2	9	1.0	2	9	1.0	–	–	–	–	–	–	–	–	–	2	10	1.0

525.—A Table showing the projective Distances from Spar-deck of U. S. Ship North Carolina.

From Night-head to Bowsprit Cap - - -	53	feet.
" " to Jib-boom - - -	91	"
" " to Flying Jib-boom - - -	109	"
" " to Jib of Jib-Truck - -	128	"
From Spar-deck to Fore Cap - - - - -	77½	"
" " to F. T. M. Cap - - -	122½	"
" " to F. T. Gallant Cap - - -	145½	"
" " to F. Royal Cap - - -	170½	"
" " to F. Sky-sail Truck - - -	187½	"
" " to Main Cap - - -	90	"
" " to M. T. M. Cap - - -	141	"
" " to M. T. Gallant Cap - -	166	"
" " to M. Royal Cap - - -	193½	"
" " to M. Sky-sail Truck - -	211½	"
" " to Mizen Cap - - - - -	75½	"
" " to M. T. M. Cap - - -	116	"
" " to M. T. Gallant Cap - - -	136	"
" " to M. Royal Cap - - -	158	"
" " to M. Sky-sail Truck - - -	173	"
Length on Spar-deck - - - - - -	209	"
Main Gun-deck - - - - - - - - -	207	"
Lower Gun-deck - - - - - - - -	201	"
Extreme length from Night-head to Taffrail -	210	"

	Ft. In.
Breadth of Beam - - - - - - - - -	53.6
Depth from Taffrail to False Keel - - - -	53.4
Height from Water to Port-sill - - - - -	7.6
Height between deck from Spar to Main Gun-deck	7.1
" " " from Main to Lower Gun-deck	7.3
" " " from Lower to Orlop - -	7.3
Size of Spar-deck Beam - - - - - -	10
" of Main Gun-deck Beam - - - - -	1.3
" of Lower Gun-deck Beam - - - - -	1.3
Height from Port-sills to Spar-deck - - - -	.7
" " to Main Gun-deck - -	1.11¾
" " to Lower Gun-deck - -	2.2

				Ft. In.
Distance between Ports No.	1 and 2,	Spar-deck	-	8.1
" " "	2 " 3,	"	-	12.5
" " "	3 " 4,	"	-	7.
" " "	4 " 5,	"	-	6.10
" " "	5 " 6,	"	-	8.
" " "	6 " 7,	"	-	8.
" " "	7 " 8,	"	-	8.
" " "	8 " 9,	"	-	7.9
" " "	9 " 10,	"	-	7.
" " "	10 " 11,	"	-	7.10
" " "	11 " 12,	"	-	5.10
" " "	12 " 13,	"	-	7.
" " "	13 " 14,	"	-	10.3
" " "	14 " 15,	"	-	6.8
" " "	15 " 16,	"	-	10.2
" " "	16 " 17,	"	-	9.9
" " "	17 " 18,	"	-	6.
" "	After Port and Counter		- -	7.6
" "	Bridle Port and No. 1 Main Gun-deck		- - - - - -	11.
" "	All the other Ports		- -	8.
" "	After Port and Counter		- -	12.6

Between Ports on Lower Gun-deck the same.

		Length.	Depth.
Size of Spar-deck Ports	- - - - -	3.1	3.6
" Main Gun-deck do.	- - - - -	3.6	2.11
" Lower Gun-deck do.	- - - -	3.2	2.11

526.—A Table showing the Weight of the Armament, Stores, Outfits and Provisions of the U. S. Sloop of War Albany, fitted out at the Navy Yard, New York.

DATE WHEN PUT ON BOARD.	Ballast.	Tanks.	Casks and Brakers.	Beds & Ch'cks for Tanks and Casks—wood, &c.	Chain Cables and other Chains.	Hemp Cables, H'wsers, Tow-lines and Messengers.	Lower Cross-trees, Trestle-trees, Tops, Lower Masts, Bowsprit Caps and Shores.	Anchors, Kedges and Grapnels.	Guns and Gun Carriages.	Ammunition & Equipment of Guns.	Other Masts and Yards, including Spare Spars.
	ton. cwt. qrs. lbs.	ton. cwt. qrs. lbs.	ton. cwt. qrs. lbs.	ton. cwt. qrs. lbs	ton. cwt. qrs. lbs.	ton. cwt. qrs. lbs.	ton. cwt. qrs. lbs.	ton. cwt. qrs. lbs.	ton. cwt. qrs. lbs.	ton. cwt. qrs. lbs.	ton cwt. qrs. lbs.
First Day - - -	1.13.1.24	5. 8.0.14	–	–	36. 1.3.20						
Second Day - -	–	19. 4.1. 1	1.16.0.22	–	–	–	0. 5.1. 8	4. 5.2.10	–	24. 8.1. 0	
Third Day - -	–	–	–	–	–	–	19.11.3. 0	0.11.0. 8			
Fourth Day - -	9. 0.0.13	–	–	–	–	–	1. 9.0.26	–	–	–	3. 4.2.20
Fifth Day - - -	–		1.11.0.18	3.12.1.16	–	8. 3.0.15	0.11.0. 0	–	–	–	1. 1.3.12
Sixth Day - - -	–		2.11.1.25	–	–	–	–	–	61.11.0.10		
Seventh Day - -	–	44 Tanks.	–	–	–	–	–	–	0. 3.1.22	–	8.16.1. 3
Eighth Day - -	–		–	–	0.11.1. 6	–	–	5. 6.0. 1	–	–	3. 8.1. 6
Ninth Day - - -	–		0. 7.1. 6	–	–	–	–	–	–	5. 9.3.18	
Tenth Day - -	–	–	–	3.12.1.16	–	–	–	–	0. 9.1.24	7.16.2.17	2. 9.3.10
Eleventh Day - -	–	–	0. 3.2. 4	1.16.0.22	–	–	–	–	–	0. 1.2.12	1.15.1.15
Twelfth Day - -	–	–	–	–	–	–	–	–	–	–	1. 3.1.26
Thirteenth Day -	–	–	–	3.12.1.16	–	–	–	0. 7.0.20	–		
Fourteenth Day -	–	–	–	–	–	–	–	–	–	5. 7.0.26	
Fifteenth Day -	–	–	–	3.12.1.16	–	–	–	–	–	4. 7.0. 0	
Total, - -	10.13.2. 9	24.12.1.15	6. 9.2.19	16. 5.3. 2	36.13.0.26	8. 3.0.15	20.17.1. 6	10. 9.3.11	62. 4.0. 0	47.10.2.17	21.19.3. 8

A Table showing the Weight of the Armament, Stores, Outfits and Provisions of the U. S. Sloop of War Albany, fitted out at the Navy Yard, New York.—*Continued.*

DATE WHEN PUT ON BOARD.	Rigg'g, Blocks and Dead Eyes Bolsters.	Boats and their Equipments.	Water.	Whiskey, Vinegar and Molasses.	Galley, Forge, and their Appurtenances—Spare Iron.	Coal, Paints, Paint Oil, and Naval Stores.	Miscellaneous Articles—Plank, &c.	Carpenters' & Joiners' Work, including Furniture & Mess Chest.	Provisions, including Priv'te Stores of Officers.	Sails, Canvass, Spare Hammocks & Bags.	Weight of Officers and Crew, & their effects.
	ton. cwt. qrs. lbs.	ton. cwt. qrs. lbs.	ton. cwt. qrs. lbs.	ton. cwt. qrs. lbs.	ton. cwt. qrs. lbs.	ton. cwt. qrs. lbs.	ton cwt. qrs. lbs.	ton. cwt. qrs. lbs.	ton. cwt. qrs. lbs.	ton. cwt. qrs. lbs.	ton. cwt. qrs. lbs.
First Day - - -	–	–	83.16.1. 4								
Second Day - -	–	–	–	–	–	–	0. 3.0.24				
Third Day - -	0.14.0.10		23,468 Gallons of Water.								
Fourth Day - -	4. 6.0. 8										
Fifth Day - - -	0. 3.0.25										
Sixth Day - - -	1. 4.0. 3	–		–	2. 7.0.21	2.17.3. 3	0. 3.0. 0				
Seventh Day - -	9.14.0.22										
Eighth Day - -	1.15.2.14	2.18.2.18		–	–	–	0. 2.0.16				
Ninth Day - - -	0. 5.3.14	–		–	–	–	0. 1.2. 7	–	20. 4.1.17		
Tenth Day - -	8.13.0.13	–		–	0.16.1.18	–	0. 6.1.11	0. 1.2. 8	11.17.2.10	0. 8.3.20	
Eleventh Day - -	0.10.1.24	2. 1.3.21		7. 0.1. 9	–	3. 8.3. 2	1.14.3. 4	0.16.3.22	9.15.0. 9	3.14.2.26	
Twelfth Day - -	0.19.3.17	0. 8.3. 0	–	–	–	1. 9.1.27	0. 5.2.14	0. 7.3. 6	3.12.3.17	–	3. 3.0. 4
Thirteenth Day -	0.11.0.18	–	–	–	–	–	0.13.1.25	0.13.2.24	2. 2.3. 3	0. 9.1. 4	18. 5.1.19
Fourteenth Day -	0.10.0.23	0. 6.0.27	–	–	–	0. 1.0.10	1. 0.1. 2	–	3. 2.0.11	2.19.1.14	
Fifteenth Day -	–	–	–	0. 2.3.22	–	–	0.14.1. 1	–	3.17.0. 0	1. 6.3. 4	
Total, - -	29. 7.3.23	5.15.2.10	83.16.1. 4	7. 3.1. 3	3. 3.2.11	7.17.0.14	5. 4.2.20	2. 0.0. 4	54.11.3.11	8.19.0.12	21. 8.1.23

A Table showing the Weight of the Armament, Stores, Outfits and Provisions of the U. S. Sloop of War Albany, fitted out at the Navy Yard, New York.—*Concluded.*

DATE WHEN PUT ON BOARD.	Small Arms & Arm-chest.	Purser's Stores	Boatswain's Stores.	Gunner's Stores.	Carpenter's Stores.	Sailmaker's Stores.	Master's Stores.	Hospital Stores.	Aggregate Amount of Weight per day.	Draft of Water forward ending each day.	Draft of Water aft ending each day.
	ton. cwt. qrs. lbs.	ton. cwt. qrs. lbs.	ton. cwt. qrs. lbs.	ton. cwt. qrs. lbs.	ton. cwt. qrs. lbs.	ton. cwt. qrs. lbs.	ton. cwt. qrs. lbs.	ton. cwt. qrs. lbs.	ton. cwt. qrs. lbs.	feet. inches.	feet. inches.
First Day - - -	–	–	–	–	–	–	–	–	126.19.3. 6		
Second Day - -	–	–	–	–	–	–	–	–	50. 2.3. 9		
Third Day - -	–	–	–	–	–	–	–	–	20.17.0.18	12. 7	14. 0
Fourth Day - -	–	–	–	–	–	–	–	–	18. 0.0.11	13. 0	15. 0
Fifth Day - - -	–	–	–	–	–	–	–	–	15. 2.3. 2	13. 2	15. 6
Sixth Day - - -	–	–	–	2. 6.3.24	–	–	–	–	73. 1.2. 2	14. 1	15.10
Seventh Day - -	–	–	–	–	–	–	–	–	18.13.3.19	14. 3	15.11
Eighth Day - -	–	–	–	–	–	–	–	–	14. 2.0. 5	14. 5½	15.10½
Ninth Day - - -	–	–	–	–	–	–	–	–	26. 9.0. 6	14. 6½	15.10
Tenth Day - -	–	–	–	1.17.2. 5	–	–	–	–	38. 9.3.12	14. 8	15.11
Eleventh Day - -	–	–	3.18.2. 5	–	–	0.17.1.23	–	–	37.16.3. 2	15.10	16. 2
Twelfth Day - -	–	–	1.10.0.15	0. 7.3.24	–	–	0. 3.0. 5	1. 3.1.25	14.15.2.12	15.11½	16. 4
Thirteenth Day -	–	–	–	–	1.13.1. 2	–	0.11.2.27	–	29. 0.1.18	16. 2	16. 7½
Fourteenth Day -	0. 7.1.24	8. 3.1.13	–	0. 6.0.27	–	–	–	–	22. 3.2. 9	16. 4	17. 3
Fifteenth Day -	–	3. 4.1.16	0.16.3.12	–	0. 5.2.24	1. 6.3. 4	–	–	19.14.0.15	16. 4	17. 6
Total, - -	0. 7.1.24	11. 7.3. 1	6. 5.2. 4	4.18.2.24	1.18.3.26	2. 4.0.27	0.14.3. 4	1. 3.1.25	525. 9.2. 6		

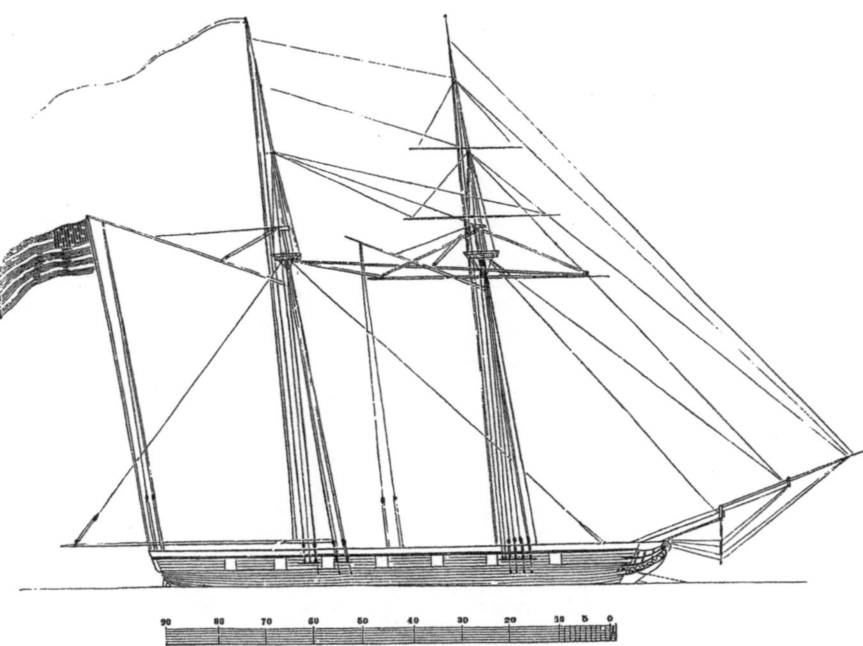

Scale-draft of a Schooner-of-War, twelve guns.

RECIPES.

527.—FOR BLACKING SHIP'S STANDING-RIGGING.

To a half barrel of tar add 6 gallons of whiskey, 4 pounds of litharge, 4 pounds lamp-black, 2 buckets of boiling beef-pickle, or hot salt water out of the coppers, if the other cannot be had conveniently; mix well together and apply immediately.

528.—FOR BLACKING GUNS.

Six pound of beeswax mixed with one gallon of spirits of turpentine, one paper of lamp-black, mixed well together, for twenty 24 pounders.

Note.—The beeswax to be cut fine, and dissolved in spirits of turpentine before being mixed with the lamp-black.

529.—FOR BLACKING HAMMOCK-CLOTHS, YARDS, AND BENDS.

First scrub the cloth well with salt water, and while wet put on the first coat of priming, which should be well-ground paint, with one and-a-half pounds of beeswax added to each gallon of paint; after the first coat is dry, put on second, mixed as follows, viz.: one pound lamp-black mixed for paint, one pound red lead, one gallon paint oil, half pound litharge, and half an ounce of indigo, boiled for half an hour, and stirred at intervals. Care should be taken that the composition boils that length of time. After it has cooled a little, add one pint of spirits of turpentine; apply when warm, and it will dry in a short time with a beautiful gloss, and be perfectly limber. This last mixture has been found very suitable for yards, and also the bends; but it must never be used too warm, particularly on canvass, in which case it will lose its gloss. The priming, or first coat, is not put on cloths that have been blacked before.

530.—FOR MAKING LIQUID-BLACKING.

Four ounces of ivory black, five or six table-spoonsful of molasses, one and a-half ounce oil of vitriol, one and a-half ounce sweet oil, and six gills of vinegar. After mixing the ingredients together well and stirring them frequently, the blacking will be fit for use.

531.—FOR BLACKING GUNS.

Six ounces of lamp-black, three pints of spirits of turpentine, and three ounces of litharge to be put in after the lamp-black and turpentine are well mixed; add one ounce of umber to give it a gloss, and one gallon bright varnish.

532.—COMPOSITION FOR BLACKING GUNS.

Six pounds of beeswax cut up fine, then add seven quarts spirits of turpentine; let it stand until it is well dissolved, then add one pound lamp-black, and mix it well together.

533.—FOR MAKING BLACK-VARNISH, NO. I.

Two pounds of gum shellac, two pounds umber, one gallon linseed oil, and quarter pound of lamp-black; boiled together for four hours over a slow fire.

534.—COMPOSITION FOR BLACKING HAMMOCK CLOTHS, NO. I.

Twenty pounds of beeswax, four pounds rosin, two gallons spirits of turpentine, one gallon paint oil, and six pound of lamp-black. Boil them well together, and keep it warm while putting on.

Note.—To be primed first with lead-colored paint.

535.—COMPOSITION FOR HAMMOCK CLOTHS, NO. II.

Forty-eight pounds of yellow ochre, eight pounds black paint, half pound soap, and three pints of fresh water.

536.—FOR HAMMOCK CLOTHS, NO. III.

Half a pound of black paint, three pounds yellow ochre, half pound of soap, three-quarters of a gill of fresh water.

537.—FOR HAMMOCK CLOTHS, NO. IV.

Eighty pounds black paint well ground, ten gallons linseed oil, ten pounds of beeswax, five pounds litharge, and one gallon of spirits of turpentine. For blacking bends, add two gallons of tar.

538.—FOR MAKING BLACK-VARNISH, NO. II.

One gallon of the spirits of turpentine, one pound and four ounces of rosin, one pound and four ounces lamp-black, and one quart of linseed oil; to be boiled on a slow fire for half-an-hour, then used or laid on when cold.

539.—SOLDER FOR COPPER.

Nothing is necessary here, but good tough borax and brass, well mixed together with water, to the consistence of paste.

540.—SOLDER FOR LEAD.

Take two parts of water-lead, and one part of tin; its goodness is tried by melting it, and pouring the size of a half dollar piece on a table; then if it be good there will arise small, bright stars or beads on it. Apply rosin when you use it.

541.—TO MAKE THE BEST DRYING OIL.

Mix one pound of litharge of gold to every six gallons of oil; boil it over a slow fire, but not too much, least it prove too thick, and be unserviceable.

542.—FOR BLACK STAIN.

Four ounces of copperas; iron rust, or a few pieces of old iron hoop; one gallon of vinegar; half pound lamp-black, and a small quantity of oak shavings.

543.—BLACKING GUNS, SHOT, &c.

Coal tar alone, or mixed with a little salt water, is a good thing for blacking guns and shot. It should be laid on quite warm, and if the day be cold, a hot shot may with advantage be put into the guns to warm the metal, and make it take the blacking better, due attention being previously paid to unloading.

Lay the stuff on as thin as possible, with paint-brushes, using hot loggerheads or bolts to keep it warm.

If well laid on, and wiped afterwards with an oil-cloth occasionally, this process will prevent rust, and preserve the good look of the guns for a length of time, without having recourse to washing with water.

544.—FRENCH RECIPE FOR BLACKING GUNS, &c.

To one gallon of vinegar, put ten ounces of lamp-black, and one pound and a-half of clear sifted iron-rust, and mix them well together.

Lay this on the guns after a good coat of black paint, and rub it occasionally with a soft oil-cloth.

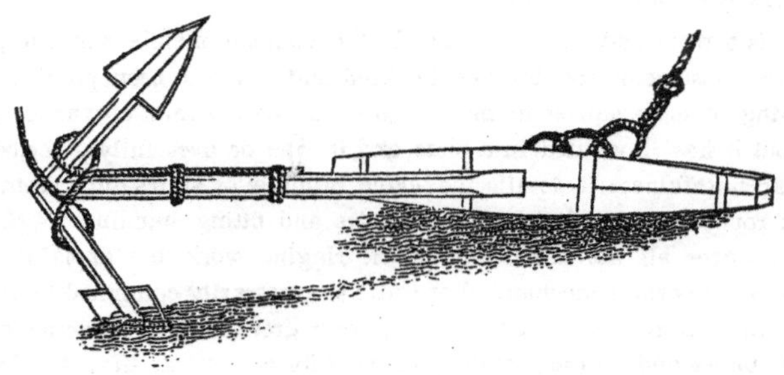

OPINIONS OF THE PRESS.

From the Sailor's Magazine.

THE KEDGE ANCHOR; or, YOUNG SAILOR'S ASSISTANT: *second edition, improved and enlarged with additional matter, illustrated with seventy engravings, and tables, 8vo., pp.* 420. By WILLIAM BRADY, *Sailing Master, U. S. Navy; reviewed by a Master Mariner.*

This is a work very much needed for the younger members of our profession, being the most complete thing of the kind that has ever been published. There is nothing of the smallest moment in use on board a man-of-war, or merchantman, but it has illustrated in a plate, and its use or uses fully described. With singular faithfulness it details the whole minutiæ of ship's duty, from the knotting of ropeyarns to splicing heavy cables and fitting standing rigging. It not only embraces all the particulars of the rigging work, but explains with equal clearness the various mechanical operations necessarily combined to fit out a first class ship. Here the novice may acquire a great deal by practising from the various plates and figures, while preparing for a nautical life; besides, from its fullness on those subjects the most interesting to the young sailor, it will be calculated to lead him to study his Manual, and thereby not entirely lose all relish for study, when first embarking in his ocean life, which has hitherto been so common and so disadvantageous to young men. There is no kind of duty on ship-board but is here explained, and I conceive it the most valuable work not only for novices, but for every grade in our profession. There is a great deal of very useful information for all, however experienced they may be. Every kind of spar is described, with its relative proportions and use—the rules for which few men can carry in their minds. And it is quite important to know, in masting and sparring a ship, what are the principles which govern the usage of the day, even if we alter the proportions afterward to suit our own caprice or fancy.

The author has clearly shown himself to be master of his business; he has described fully all the various parts of the ship's hull and spars—the different pieces of standing and running rigging, with the way to fit the one and how to cut and reeve the other. He teaches how to get the masts and yards on board, aloft, and rigged—he speaks of all with sufficient clearness, and at the same time does not unnecessarily multiply words. After rigging and sparring the ship, he bends the sails, after the most judicious plan in fitting out for sea, or when blown away or split in a storm—and after putting the ship to sea, as it were, he then, in a seamanlike manner, explains all the various evolutions through which a ship may be passed, and supposes almost every extremity to which a ship is liable, giving the modern, and I might add, profitably improved method of doing things;

for it is well known, that during the last 30 years there have been very many and equally great improvements in the method of rigging as well as working sea-going ships.

I observe the author explains, in such places as have been deemed necessary, the different methods in use on board heavy-armed ships and merchantmen, which makes the book the more valuable to both classes of the service. Mr. Brady has some capital and useful remarks on the subject of the barometer, some of which I found entirely new to myself, although having used one for the last twenty years. But I conceive that his tables are very valuable even to shipmasters. Instead of lumbering up this book with what in fact belongs to an epitome of navigation, as has been the practice generally hitherto, he has confined himself, strictly speaking, to only those subjects which would naturally occur to one as coming under the head of seamanship—or, in other words, he has compiled literally "a Sailor's Assistant." I confidently assert, I have never seen the same amount of really useful and practical information in the same space adapted to our profession before. Here we find enumerated for the various classes of vessels, according to their tonnage, the requisite number of anchors, cables, guns, carriages, shot, &c., with their size, weight, and the comparative strength of the cables and rigging both chain and hemp: also a variety of most useful intelligence, and which must have been elicited only after considerable practical experiment—all of the most interesting as well as useful importance, not only to the novice, but the officer—the master—and I would even confidently add, that there is a great deal of information contained in this work which would make it a valuable acquisition to every ship-owner's counting-room. There is nothing put on board the various classes of ships, but is described in the book, first to tell how it is made, and how it is rigged—how it is taken on board (if heavy)—its weight, and the amount allowed according to the length of the cruise. Nothing is omitted. I conceive that every ship-owner would find it an acquisition as a counting-house companion, as well as a "Young Sailor's Assistant." His recipes, which I find at the termination of the book, are not without their value; and although simple in themselves, yet not generally known.

I cannot close without saying a few words in relation to the very judicious remarks he has made under the head of "good order" (merchant service) and cleanliness. It is undeniable that temperance and cleanliness would add much to the health, comfort, and good order of a crew; but it must be allowed that comparatively little has been done for the sailor—much more must be done before he will be made to realize the terrible effects of intemperance and licentiousness upon both body and soul, for time and eternity. It is cheering to see that spirits have been banished from the list of small stores on board of respectable American ships: and we can but hope that, ere long, through the influence of the efforts that are being made, especially for seamen, among several denominations of Christians in this city—by their building handsome churches on shore and afloat—splendid Homes which are made to them homes indeed when they resort to them—by their donations of books and libraries adapted to their characters and profession—that a few years will see them a different and vastly improved class of men. Already do we begin to see the influence of the leaven that has been cast among them, which leads us to the conviction that there is a better time coming for the sailor; and we cannot but hope and trust that all ranks of Christians will be diligent in prayer to God that "the abundance of the sea may be speedily converted unto him." Finally, with the author I also think it entirely unnecessary for him to offer any apology in sending this work abroad to the public. If I may be allowed to offer an opinion on the merits of the composition or its style, I must say I have come to the conclusion, in the absence of any other guide but this book, being an utter stranger to the author, that he is—he *must be*—a seaman—a scholar—and a gentleman. I observe he professes, as his motto, "Hope for his anchor, and Heaven for his guide," and I fervently pray that neither the one nor the other may ever fail him.

From the Literary World.

THE KEDGE ANCHOR; or, YOUNG SAILOR'S ASSISTANT. By WM. BRADY, *Sailing Master, U. S. N.* Published by the Author.

Nowadays, when all science, arts, and callings are delineated in books, and the pen is wielded by members of every profession, it is no marvel that an excellently planned work, upon all things pertaining to seamanship, should be presented to the public by a gentleman of the marline-spike. And albeit the author tells us that that instrument is to him more familiar than the pen, he has, nevertheless, shown himself quite expert with the latter.

"The Kedge Anchor" (a happy title, at least to Jack) has already run through one edition, which, for a purely practical work, is the best evidence of its merits. The present edition is, in many respects, an improvement upon the former, containing additional matter, plates and tables. To a sailor this work is invaluable; indeed, it is by far the best of the sort we ever remember to have seen. Generally, works of this description are loosely and carelessly put together; to use a nautical phrase, they are by no means "ship-shape and Bristol fashion," and, in many cases, are mere servile copies, or abridgments of obsolete books on the same subject. The sailor-poet's (Falconer) Marine Dictionary, published many years ago, has been the source from which most of them have been compiled. But in seamanship, as in everything else, great improvements and changes have, from time to time, been effected, and Mr. Brady's volume contains them all. We cordially commend his book to all the purchasers of Bowditch's Navigation; and we will futhermore guaranty that he who masters both, will be fully qualified to conduct a vessel round the globe with unerring certainty—enter a harbor as unexceptionably and gracefully as ever Brummel did a drawing-room, and cockbill his yards at a symmetrical angle.

Not only to seamen, but to many landsmen, the "Kedge Anchor" cannot fail to be an acceptable volume. Its copious dictionary of sea terms, its excellent illustrations of nautical manœuvres and the information imparted upon all things pertaining to the construction, rig, and appointment of the ships in our navy, make the book truly valuable. From the "gammoning" of a bowsprit, and the staying of a royal-mast, to the taking of a "bowline-in-the-bight," the student in tar will find all the information he can desire.

The book is well got up, contains numerous well-executed cuts, and is alike creditable to author and publisher. We specially commend it to the members of the Yacht Club, as a *vade mecum* for blue water.

From the New York Journal of Commerce.

THE KEDGE ANCHOR; or, YOUNG SAILOR'S ASSISTANT. By WILLIAM BRADY, *S. M., U. S. N.*

This work, as its title imports, is designed as an assistant for the young Sailor, through the various branches of his arduous profession. It contains useful instructions in every department of seamanship, with ample directions, which will impart to the young officer a great deal of valuable information in the duties of his profession, and enable him to act in the most judicious manner in many trying emergencies.

In addition to many suggestions, which will prove valuable to every grade of seamen, it contains more thorough descriptions of the innumerable articles belonging to the various classes of vessels, than any other work ever published in this country; and is embellished with over seventy engravings, in illustration of the subjects treated of in its pages. The work is furnished with over one hundred pages of tables, which are valuable not only to the sea-faring man, but to all who are in any way interested in maritime pursuits. The entire work is contained in a volume of 420 pages, octavo, stereotype edition. It is printed on fine paper, and bound in handsome style. For sale by R. L. Shaw, No. 222 Water street, N. Y.

From the True Sun.

THE KEDGE ANCHOR; or, YOUNG SAILOR'S ASSISTANT.

We have had for several days lying on our table a massive octavo volume of some 420 pages, of which we have given the title. The author of it is William Brady, S. M., U. S. N., and it is on sale at the Sailor's Home, and by most of the nautical stationers. The whole science of seamanship appears to be included in this fine volume, from the coiling of a rope to the dissection of a man-of-war and every nautical appendage thereof. No jot or tittle of a seaman's duty appears to have been overlooked; everything is explained, and the most intricate things illustrated by engravings. The entire typographical execution and material of the volume are excellent; we do not find the price attached to it; but to the seaman —to the young seaman particularly—it must be invaluable.

From the New York Courier & Enquirer.

THE KEDGE ANCHOR; or, YOUNG SAILOR'S ASSISTANT, *&c., &c., illustrated with seventy engravings.* By WM. BRADY, *S. M., U. S. N. 2d edition, enlarged and improved.* New York.

This is a handsome and no doubt a useful handbook for the young sailor or officer, explaining as it does, and illustrating by handsome cuts the various manipulations of the Sailor's craft.

The instruction comprehends the whole of the duties of the sailor, as well as regards the practical evolutions of the vessel, as the various details connected with rigging the vessel.

The volume has already gone through one edition, which is presumptive evidence of its merits—and we dare say there will be ample demand for this second edition.

From the Long Island Star.

THE KEDGE ANCHOR; OR, YOUNG SAILOR'S ASSISTANT.

We have just received the second edition of a very neat work, entitled "The Kedge Anchor," improved and enlarged, with additional matter, plates, and tables, by Mr. William Brady, and dedicated to the United States Navy and Merchant Service.

It is very neatly bound and good print, and is intended to instruct "Young Seamen" in rigging, knotting, splicing, blocks, purchases, and other miscellaneous matter applicable to vessels and ships of war. It is illustrated with seventy engravings, also a great number of Tables useful to seamen. It is also printed on beautiful paper, and it instructs you to build vessels of war.

Published at New York by Mr. Wm. Brady, and sold at R. L. Shaw's Nautical Store, 222 Water street, N. Y.

It is octavo size, 420 pages, and handsomely illustrated with fine wood-cuts, representing many of the most beautifully modeled vessels in the U. S. Navy. It is a work of much labor and expense, and should be in the possession of every seaman, more especially those of the Navy. A copy of the work may be seen at this office.

From the New York Sunday Dispatch.

THE KEDGE ANCHOR; OR, YOUNG SAILOR'S ASSISTANT.

The extraordinary demand for the above meritorious work has, in a very shor time, exhausted the first edition.

The author, William Brady, a sailing master in the United States Navy, has published a second edition, with additional tables and somewhat improved in typographical beauty. It is useless for us to speak of its merits as a text-book for the young officer. It is most emphatically a work of great merit, and one which will commend *itself* to all classes whose "march is o'er the mountain wave." The remarks it contains on that invaluable instrument the Barometer, are correct, and will do much to destroy the unfounded prejudice which some have against it

The volume contains a great number of plates, neatly executed, which serve to illustrate with precision a variety of nautical evolutions. The precautions for scudding are worthy of attention. It is a well-known fact among *sailors* that many a good ship has been boarded by a sea, while scudding under *short sail*, when the disaster might easily have been avoided by showing more canvas. The work contains all the tables necessary for sparring and rigging a ship, and that in so plain and practical a manner that we cannot see how it is possible for any one to make a mistake; on the whole, we are inclined to think, that, though the author modestly calls it a *Kedge Anchor*, there is many an old salt who will look upon it as his *best bower*.

From the New York Express.

THE KEDGE ANCHOR. By WILLIAM BRADY, *U. S. N.*

This is the title of a very handsome volume, professing to give thorough descriptions of the almost innumerable equipments belonging to the various classes of vessels. We are not "old salt" enough to speak as to the accuracy of its teachings, but it seems to be very complete and intelligible; and is illustrated with drawings of more ways of doing things than any but a sailor would ever dream of.

From the New York Tribune.

THE KEDGE ANCHOR; or, YOUNG SAILOR'S ASSISTANT. By WILLIAM BRADY, *S. M., U. S. N.* New York: R. L. Shaw, 222 Water st., 1 vol. 8vo., pp. 420, with numerous engravings.

This work, as its title imports, is designed as an assistant for the young Sailor through the various branches of his arduous profession. It contains useful instructions in every department of seamanship, with ample directions, which will impart to the young officer a great deal of valuable information in the duties of his profession, and enable him to act in the most judicious manner in many trying emergencies.

In addition to many suggestions, which will prove valuable to every grade of seamen, it contains more thorough descriptions of the innumerable articles belonging to the various classes of vessels than any other work ever published in this country; and is embellished with over seventy engravings in illustration of the subjects treated of in its pages. The work is furnished with over one hundred pages of tables, which are valuable not only to the seafaring man but to all who are in any way interested in maritime pursuits. The entire work is contained in a volume of 420 pages, octavo stereotype edition. It is printed on fine paper and bound in handsome style.

From the Brooklyn Daily Advertiser.

THE KEDGE ANCHOR; or, YOUNG SAILOR'S ASSISTANT—is the title of a work just published by William Brady, Sailing Master in the U. S. Navy. Mr. Brady is a thorough seaman and eminently qualified to the task he has here undertaken. Every information is given appertaining to the practical evolutions of modern seamanship-rigging, knotting, splicing, blocks, purchases, running rigging, and other miscellaneous matters, applicable to ships of war and others. Illustrated with several engravings. Also tables of rigging, spars, sails, blocks, canvas, cordage, chain and hemp-cables, hawsers, &c., relative to every class of vessels. To those who are about to become sailors, the Kedge Anchor is invaluable; and those who have followed the sea, no matter how long, may derive information therefrom. It should be on board every vessel and in every library, as much may be found to interest even the landsman. The work meets the approval of the most able commanders in the merchant and naval service. The author is now attached to the Brooklyn Navy Yard, holding the appointment of Sailing Master, and is known as one of the best practiced seamen in the navy.

From the New York Sun.

THE KEDGE ANCHOR; or, YOUNG SAILOR'S ASSISTANT, by WM. BRADY, of the *U. S. Navy*, is the most unique and useful book for young seamen we have any knowledge of. Published by the author.

From the New York Herald.

THE KEDGE ANCHOR; or, YOUNG SAILOR'S ASSISTANT. By WM. BRADY, *S. M., U. S. N.*, second edition. R. L. Shaw, 222 Water street. This is decidedly the best work for the maritime community, and the best adapted to convey perfect instruction to all who desire to learn the profession of seamanship, that we have ever seen. It has reached a second edition, and deserves to reach twenty, as it no doubt will. We shall have more to say respecting this valuable work; and in the mean time it should find a place in every library and on board every ship.

A CATALOG OF SELECTED

DOVER BOOKS

IN ALL FIELDS OF INTEREST

THE BATTLES THAT CHANGED HISTORY, Fletcher Pratt. Historian profiles 16 crucial conflicts, ancient to modern, that changed the course of Western civilization. Gripping accounts of battles led by Alexander the Great, Joan of Arc, Ulysses S. Grant, other commanders. 27 maps. 352pp. 5⅜ x 8½. 0-486-41129-X

BEETHOVEN'S LETTERS, Ludwig van Beethoven. Edited by Dr. A. C. Kalischer. Features 457 letters to fellow musicians, friends, greats, patrons, and literary men. Reveals musical thoughts, quirks of personality, insights, and daily events. Includes 15 plates. 410pp. 5⅜ x 8½. 0-486-22769-3

BERNICE BOBS HER HAIR AND OTHER STORIES, F. Scott Fitzgerald. This brilliant anthology includes 6 of Fitzgerald's most popular stories: "The Diamond as Big as the Ritz," the title tale, "The Offshore Pirate," "The Ice Palace," "The Jelly Bean," and "May Day." 176pp. 5⅜ x 8½. 0-486-47049-0

BESLER'S BOOK OF FLOWERS AND PLANTS: 73 Full-Color Plates from Hortus Eystettensis, 1613, Basilius Besler. Here is a selection of magnificent plates from the *Hortus Eystettensis,* which vividly illustrated and identified the plants, flowers, and trees that thrived in the legendary German garden at Eichstätt. 80pp. 8⅜ x 11. 0-486-46005-3

THE BOOK OF KELLS, Edited by Blanche Cirker. Painstakingly reproduced from a rare facsimile edition, this volume contains full-page decorations, portraits, illustrations, plus a sampling of textual leaves with exquisite calligraphy and ornamentation. 32 full-color illustrations. 32pp. 9⅜ x 12¼. 0-486-24345-1

THE BOOK OF THE CROSSBOW: With an Additional Section on Catapults and Other Siege Engines, Ralph Payne-Gallwey. Fascinating study traces history and use of crossbow as military and sporting weapon, from Middle Ages to modern times. Also covers related weapons: balistas, catapults, Turkish bows, more. Over 240 illustrations. 400pp. 7¼ x 10⅛. 0-486-28720-3

THE BUNGALOW BOOK: Floor Plans and Photos of 112 Houses, 1910, Henry L. Wilson. Here are 112 of the most popular and economic blueprints of the early 20th century — plus an illustration or photograph of each completed house. A wonderful time capsule that still offers a wealth of valuable insights. 160pp. 8⅜ x 11. 0-486-45104-6

THE CALL OF THE WILD, Jack London. A classic novel of adventure, drawn from London's own experiences as a Klondike adventurer, relating the story of a heroic dog caught in the brutal life of the Alaska Gold Rush. Note. 64pp. 5³⁄₁₆ x 8¼. 0-486-26472-6

CANDIDE, Voltaire. Edited by Francois-Marie Arouet. One of the world's great satires since its first publication in 1759. Witty, caustic skewering of romance, science, philosophy, religion, government — nearly all human ideals and institutions. 112pp. 5³⁄₁₆ x 8¼. 0-486-26689-3

CELEBRATED IN THEIR TIME: Photographic Portraits from the George Grantham Bain Collection, Edited by Amy Pastan. With an Introduction by Michael Carlebach. Remarkable portrait gallery features 112 rare images of Albert Einstein, Charlie Chaplin, the Wright Brothers, Henry Ford, and other luminaries from the worlds of politics, art, entertainment, and industry. 128pp. 8⅜ x 11. 0-486-46754-6

CHARIOTS FOR APOLLO: The NASA History of Manned Lunar Spacecraft to 1969, Courtney G. Brooks, James M. Grimwood, and Loyd S. Swenson, Jr. This illustrated history by a trio of experts is the definitive reference on the Apollo spacecraft and lunar modules. It traces the vehicles' design, development, and operation in space. More than 100 photographs and illustrations. 576pp. 6¾ x 9¼. 0-486-46756-2

DOOMED SHIPS: Great Ocean Liner Disasters, William H. Miller, Jr. Nearly 200 photographs, many from private collections, highlight tales of some of the vessels whose pleasure cruises ended in catastrophe: the *Morro Castle, Normandie, Andrea Doria, Europa,* and many others. 128pp. 8⅞ x 11¾. 0-486-45366-9

THE DORÉ BIBLE ILLUSTRATIONS, Gustave Doré. Detailed plates from the Bible: the Creation scenes, Adam and Eve, horrifying visions of the Flood, the battle sequences with their monumental crowds, depictions of the life of Jesus, 241 plates in all. 241pp. 9 x 12. 0-486-23004-X

DRAWING DRAPERY FROM HEAD TO TOE, Cliff Young. Expert guidance on how to draw shirts, pants, skirts, gloves, hats, and coats on the human figure, including folds in relation to the body, pull and crush, action folds, creases, more. Over 200 drawings. 48pp. 8¼ x 11. 0-486-45591-2

DUBLINERS, James Joyce. A fine and accessible introduction to the work of one of the 20th century's most influential writers, this collection features 15 tales, including a masterpiece of the short-story genre, "The Dead." 160pp. 5³⁄₁₆ x 8¼. 0-486-26870-5

EASY-TO-MAKE POP-UPS, Joan Irvine. Illustrated by Barbara Reid. Dozens of wonderful ideas for three-dimensional paper fun — from holiday greeting cards with moving parts to a pop-up menagerie. Easy-to-follow, illustrated instructions for more than 30 projects. 299 black-and-white illustrations. 96pp. 8⅝ x 11. 0-486-44622-0

EASY-TO-MAKE STORYBOOK DOLLS: A "Novel" Approach to Cloth Dollmaking, Sherralyn St. Clair. Favorite fictional characters come alive in this unique beginner's dollmaking guide. Includes patterns for Pollyanna, Dorothy from *The Wonderful Wizard of Oz,* Mary of *The Secret Garden,* plus easy-to-follow instructions, 263 black-and-white illustrations, and an 8-page color insert. 112pp. 8¼ x 11. 0-486-47360-0

EINSTEIN'S ESSAYS IN SCIENCE, Albert Einstein. Speeches and essays in accessible, everyday language profile influential physicists such as Niels Bohr and Isaac Newton. They also explore areas of physics to which the author made major contributions. 128pp. 5 x 8. 0-486-47011-3

EL DORADO: Further Adventures of the Scarlet Pimpernel, Baroness Orczy. A popular sequel to *The Scarlet Pimpernel,* this suspenseful story recounts the Pimpernel's attempts to rescue the Dauphin from imprisonment during the French Revolution. An irresistible blend of intrigue, period detail, and vibrant characterizations. 352pp. 5³⁄₁₆ x 8¼. 0-486-44026-5

ELEGANT SMALL HOMES OF THE TWENTIES: 99 Designs from a Competition, Chicago Tribune. Nearly 100 designs for five- and six-room houses feature New England and Southern colonials, Normandy cottages, stately Italianate dwellings, and other fascinating snapshots of American domestic architecture of the 1920s. 112pp. 9 x 12. 0-486-46910-7

THE ELEMENTS OF STYLE: The Original Edition, William Strunk, Jr. This is the book that generations of writers have relied upon for timeless advice on grammar, diction, syntax, and other essentials. In concise terms, it identifies the principal requirements of proper style and common errors. 64pp. 5⅜ x 8½. 0-486-44798-7

THE ELUSIVE PIMPERNEL, Baroness Orczy. Robespierre's revolutionaries find their wicked schemes thwarted by the heroic Pimpernel — Sir Percival Blakeney. In this thrilling sequel, Chauvelin devises a plot to eliminate the Pimpernel and his wife. 272pp. 5³⁄₁₆ x 8¼. 0-486-45464-9

FIVE ACRES AND INDEPENDENCE, Maurice G. Kains. Great back-to-the-land classic explains basics of self-sufficient farming. The one book to get. 95 illustrations. 397pp. 5⅜ x 8½. 0-486-20974-1

FLAGG'S SMALL HOUSES: Their Economic Design and Construction, 1922, Ernest Flagg. Although most famous for his skyscrapers, Flagg was also a proponent of the well-designed single-family dwelling. His classic treatise features innovations that save space, materials, and cost. 526 illustrations. 160pp. 9⅜ x 12¼. 0-486-45197-6

FLATLAND: A Romance of Many Dimensions, Edwin A. Abbott. Classic of science (and mathematical) fiction — charmingly illustrated by the author — describes the adventures of A. Square, a resident of Flatland, in Spaceland (three dimensions), Lineland (one dimension), and Pointland (no dimensions). 96pp. 5³⁄₁₆ x 8¼. 0-486-27263-X

FRANKENSTEIN, Mary Shelley. The story of Victor Frankenstein's monstrous creation and the havoc it caused has enthralled generations of readers and inspired countless writers of horror and suspense. With the author's own 1831 introduction. 176pp. 5³⁄₁₆ x 8¼. 0-486-28211-2

THE GARGOYLE BOOK: 572 Examples from Gothic Architecture, Lester Burbank Bridaham. Dispelling the conventional wisdom that French Gothic architectural flourishes were born of despair or gloom, Bridaham reveals the whimsical nature of these creations and the ingenious artisans who made them. 572 illustrations. 224pp. 8⅜ x 11. 0-486-44754-5

THE GIFT OF THE MAGI AND OTHER SHORT STORIES, O. Henry. Sixteen captivating stories by one of America's most popular storytellers. Included are such classics as "The Gift of the Magi," "The Last Leaf," and "The Ransom of Red Chief." Publisher's Note. 96pp. 5³⁄₁₆ x 8¼. 0-486-27061-0

THE GOETHE TREASURY: Selected Prose and Poetry, Johann Wolfgang von Goethe. Edited, Selected, and with an Introduction by Thomas Mann. In addition to his lyric poetry, Goethe wrote travel sketches, autobiographical studies, essays, letters, and proverbs in rhyme and prose. This collection presents outstanding examples from each genre. 368pp. 5⅜ x 8½. 0-486-44780-4

GREAT EXPECTATIONS, Charles Dickens. Orphaned Pip is apprenticed to the dirty work of the forge but dreams of becoming a gentleman — and one day finds himself in possession of "great expectations." Dickens' finest novel. 400pp. 5³⁄₁₆ x 8¼. 0-486-41586-4

GREAT WRITERS ON THE ART OF FICTION: From Mark Twain to Joyce Carol Oates, Edited by James Daley. An indispensable source of advice and inspiration, this anthology features essays by Henry James, Kate Chopin, Willa Cather, Sinclair Lewis, Jack London, Raymond Chandler, Raymond Carver, Eudora Welty, and Kurt Vonnegut, Jr. 192pp. 5⅜ x 8½. 0-486-45128-3

HAMLET, William Shakespeare. The quintessential Shakespearean tragedy, whose highly charged confrontations and anguished soliloquies probe depths of human feeling rarely sounded in any art. Reprinted from an authoritative British edition complete with illuminating footnotes. 128pp. 5³⁄₁₆ x 8¼. 0-486-27278-8

THE HAUNTED HOUSE, Charles Dickens. A Yuletide gathering in an eerie country retreat provides the backdrop for Dickens and his friends — including Elizabeth Gaskell and Wilkie Collins — who take turns spinning supernatural yarns. 144pp. 5⅜ x 8½. 0-486-46309-5

THE JUNGLE, Upton Sinclair. 1906 bestseller shockingly reveals intolerable labor practices and working conditions in the Chicago stockyards as it tells the grim story of a Slavic family that emigrates to America full of optimism but soon faces despair. 320pp. 5³⁄₁₆ x 8¼. 0-486-41923-1

THE KINGDOM OF GOD IS WITHIN YOU, Leo Tolstoy. The soul-searching book that inspired Gandhi to embrace the concept of passive resistance, Tolstoy's 1894 polemic clearly outlines a radical, well-reasoned revision of traditional Christian thinking. 352pp. 5³⁄₁₆ x 8¼. 0-486-45138-0

THE LADY OR THE TIGER?: and Other Logic Puzzles, Raymond M. Smullyan. Created by a renowned puzzle master, these whimsically themed challenges involve paradoxes about probability, time, and change; metapuzzles; and self-referentiality. Nineteen chapters advance in difficulty from relatively simple to highly complex. 1982 edition. 240pp. 5⅜ x 8½. 0-486-47027-X

LEAVES OF GRASS: The Original 1855 Edition, Walt Whitman. Whitman's immortal collection includes some of the greatest poems of modern times, including his masterpiece, "Song of Myself." Shattering standard conventions, it stands as an unabashed celebration of body and nature. 128pp. 5³⁄₁₆ x 8¼. 0-486-45676-5

LES MISÉRABLES, Victor Hugo. Translated by Charles E. Wilbour. Abridged by James K. Robinson. A convict's heroic struggle for justice and redemption plays out against a fiery backdrop of the Napoleonic wars. This edition features the excellent original translation and a sensitive abridgment. 304pp. 6⅛ x 9¼. 0-486-45789-3

LILITH: A Romance, George MacDonald. In this novel by the father of fantasy literature, a man travels through time to meet Adam and Eve and to explore humanity's fall from grace and ultimate redemption. 240pp. 5⅜ x 8½. 0-486-46818-6

THE LOST LANGUAGE OF SYMBOLISM, Harold Bayley. This remarkable book reveals the hidden meaning behind familiar images and words, from the origins of Santa Claus to the fleur-de-lys, drawing from mythology, folklore, religious texts, and fairy tales. 1,418 illustrations. 784pp. 5⅜ x 8½. 0-486-44787-1

MACBETH, William Shakespeare. A Scottish nobleman murders the king in order to succeed to the throne. Tortured by his conscience and fearful of discovery, he becomes tangled in a web of treachery and deceit that ultimately spells his doom. 96pp. 5³⁄₁₆ x 8¼. 0-486-27802-6

MAKING AUTHENTIC CRAFTSMAN FURNITURE: Instructions and Plans for 62 Projects, Gustav Stickley. Make authentic reproductions of handsome, functional, durable furniture: tables, chairs, wall cabinets, desks, a hall tree, and more. Construction plans with drawings, schematics, dimensions, and lumber specs reprinted from 1900s *The Craftsman* magazine. 128pp. 8⅛ x 11. 0-486-25000-8

MATHEMATICS FOR THE NONMATHEMATICIAN, Morris Kline. Erudite and entertaining overview follows development of mathematics from ancient Greeks to present. Topics include logic and mathematics, the fundamental concept, differential calculus, probability theory, much more. Exercises and problems. 641pp. 5⅜ x 8½. 0-486-24823-2

MEMOIRS OF AN ARABIAN PRINCESS FROM ZANZIBAR, Emily Ruete. This 19th-century autobiography offers a rare inside look at the society surrounding a sultan's palace. A real-life princess in exile recalls her vanished world of harems, slave trading, and court intrigues. 288pp. 5⅜ x 8½. 0-486-47121-7

THE METAMORPHOSIS AND OTHER STORIES, Franz Kafka. Excellent new English translations of title story (considered by many critics Kafka's most perfect work), plus "The Judgment," "In the Penal Colony," "A Country Doctor," and "A Report to an Academy." Note. 96pp. 5³⁄₁₆ x 8¼. 0-486-29030-1

MICROSCOPIC ART FORMS FROM THE PLANT WORLD, R. Anheisser. From undulating curves to complex geometrics, a world of fascinating images abound in this classic, illustrated survey of microscopic plants. Features 400 detailed illustrations of nature's minute but magnificent handiwork. The accompanying CD-ROM includes all of the images in the book. 128pp. 9 x 9. 0-486-46013-4

A MIDSUMMER NIGHT'S DREAM, William Shakespeare. Among the most popular of Shakespeare's comedies, this enchanting play humorously celebrates the vagaries of love as it focuses upon the intertwined romances of several pairs of lovers. Explanatory footnotes. 80pp. 5³⁄₁₆ x 8¼. 0-486-27067-X

THE MONEY CHANGERS, Upton Sinclair. Originally published in 1908, this cautionary novel from the author of *The Jungle* explores corruption within the American system as a group of power brokers joins forces for personal gain, triggering a crash on Wall Street. 192pp. 5⅜ x 8½. 0-486-46917-4

THE MOST POPULAR HOMES OF THE TWENTIES, William A. Radford. With a New Introduction by Daniel D. Reiff. Based on a rare 1925 catalog, this architectural showcase features floor plans, construction details, and photos of 26 homes, plus articles on entrances, porches, garages, and more. 250 illustrations, 21 color plates. 176pp. 8⅜ x 11. 0-486-47028-8

MY 66 YEARS IN THE BIG LEAGUES, Connie Mack. With a New Introduction by Rich Westcott. A Founding Father of modern baseball, Mack holds the record for most wins — and losses — by a major league manager. Enhanced by 70 photographs, his warmhearted autobiography is populated by many legends of the game. 288pp. 5⅜ x 8½. 0-486-47184-5

NARRATIVE OF THE LIFE OF FREDERICK DOUGLASS, Frederick Douglass. Douglass's graphic depictions of slavery, harrowing escape to freedom, and life as a newspaper editor, eloquent orator, and impassioned abolitionist. 96pp. 5³⁄₁₆ x 8¼. 0-486-28499-9

THE NIGHTLESS CITY: Geisha and Courtesan Life in Old Tokyo, J. E. de Becker. This unsurpassed study from 100 years ago ventured into Tokyo's red-light district to survey geisha and courtesan life and offer meticulous descriptions of training, dress, social hierarchy, and erotic practices. 49 black-and-white illustrations; 2 maps. 496pp. 5⅜ x 8½. 0-486-45563-7

THE ODYSSEY, Homer. Excellent prose translation of ancient epic recounts adventures of the homeward-bound Odysseus. Fantastic cast of gods, giants, cannibals, sirens, other supernatural creatures — true classic of Western literature. 256pp. 5³⁄₁₆ x 8¼. 0-486-40654-7

OEDIPUS REX, Sophocles. Landmark of Western drama concerns the catastrophe that ensues when King Oedipus discovers he has inadvertently killed his father and married his mother. Masterly construction, dramatic irony. Explanatory footnotes. 64pp. 5³⁄₁₆ x 8¼. 0-486-26877-2

ONCE UPON A TIME: The Way America Was, Eric Sloane. Nostalgic text and drawings brim with gentle philosophies and descriptions of how we used to live — self-sufficiently — on the land, in homes, and among the things built by hand. 44 line illustrations. 64pp. 8⅜ x 11. 0-486-44411-2

ONE OF OURS, Willa Cather. The Pulitzer Prize-winning novel about a young Nebraskan looking for something to believe in. Alienated from his parents, rejected by his wife, he finds his destiny on the bloody battlefields of World War I. 352pp. 5³⁄₁₆ x 8¼. 0-486-45599-8

ORIGAMI YOU CAN USE: 27 Practical Projects, Rick Beech. Origami models can be more than decorative, and this unique volume shows how! The 27 practical projects include a CD case, frame, napkin ring, and dish. Easy instructions feature 400 two-color illustrations. 96pp. 8¼ x 11. 0-486-47057-1

OTHELLO, William Shakespeare. Towering tragedy tells the story of a Moorish general who earns the enmity of his ensign Iago when he passes him over for a promotion. Masterly portrait of an archvillain. Explanatory footnotes. 112pp. 5³⁄₁₆ x 8¼. 0-486-29097-2

PARADISE LOST, John Milton. Notes by John A. Himes. First published in 1667, *Paradise Lost* ranks among the greatest of English literature's epic poems. It's a sublime retelling of Adam and Eve's fall from grace and expulsion from Eden. Notes by John A. Himes. 480pp. 5³⁄₁₆ x 8¼. 0-486-44287-X

PASSING, Nella Larsen. Married to a successful physician and prominently ensconced in society, Irene Redfield leads a charmed existence — until a chance encounter with a childhood friend who has been "passing for white." 112pp. 5⅜ x 8½. 0-486-43713-2

PERSPECTIVE DRAWING FOR BEGINNERS, Len A. Doust. Doust carefully explains the roles of lines, boxes, and circles, and shows how visualizing shapes and forms can be used in accurate depictions of perspective. One of the most concise introductions available. 33 illustrations. 64pp. 5⅜ x 8½. 0-486-45149-6

PERSPECTIVE MADE EASY, Ernest R. Norling. Perspective is easy; yet, surprisingly few artists know the simple rules that make it so. Remedy that situation with this simple, step-by-step book, the first devoted entirely to the topic. 256 illustrations. 224pp. 5⅜ x 8½. 0-486-40473-0

THE PICTURE OF DORIAN GRAY, Oscar Wilde. Celebrated novel involves a handsome young Londoner who sinks into a life of depravity. His body retains perfect youth and vigor while his recent portrait reflects the ravages of his crime and sensuality. 176pp. 5³⁄₁₆ x 8¼. 0-486-27807-7

PRIDE AND PREJUDICE, Jane Austen. One of the most universally loved and admired English novels, an effervescent tale of rural romance transformed by Jane Austen's art into a witty, shrewdly observed satire of English country life. 272pp. 5³⁄₁₆ x 8¼. 0-486-28473-5

THE PRINCE, Niccolò Machiavelli. Classic, Renaissance-era guide to acquiring and maintaining political power. Today, nearly 500 years after it was written, this calculating prescription for autocratic rule continues to be much read and studied. 80pp. 5³⁄₁₆ x 8¼. 0-486-27274-5

QUICK SKETCHING, Carl Cheek. A perfect introduction to the technique of "quick sketching." Drawing upon an artist's immediate emotional responses, this is an extremely effective means of capturing the essential form and features of a subject. More than 100 black-and-white illustrations throughout. 48pp. 11 x 8¼. 0-486-46608-6

RANCH LIFE AND THE HUNTING TRAIL, Theodore Roosevelt. Illustrated by Frederic Remington. Beautifully illustrated by Remington, Roosevelt's celebration of the Old West recounts his adventures in the Dakota Badlands of the 1880s, from roundups to Indian encounters to hunting bighorn sheep. 208pp. 6¼ x 9¼. 0-486-47340-6

THE RED BADGE OF COURAGE, Stephen Crane. Amid the nightmarish chaos of a Civil War battle, a young soldier discovers courage, humility, and, perhaps, wisdom. Uncanny re-creation of actual combat. Enduring landmark of American fiction. 112pp. 5³⁄₁₆ x 8¼. 0-486-26465-3

RELATIVITY SIMPLY EXPLAINED, Martin Gardner. One of the subject's clearest, most entertaining introductions offers lucid explanations of special and general theories of relativity, gravity, and spacetime, models of the universe, and more. 100 illustrations. 224pp. 5⅜ x 8½. 0-486-29315-7

REMBRANDT DRAWINGS: 116 Masterpieces in Original Color, Rembrandt van Rijn. This deluxe hardcover edition features drawings from throughout the Dutch master's prolific career. Informative captions accompany these beautifully reproduced landscapes, biblical vignettes, figure studies, animal sketches, and portraits. 128pp. 8⅜ x 11. 0-486-46149-1

THE ROAD NOT TAKEN AND OTHER POEMS, Robert Frost. A treasury of Frost's most expressive verse. In addition to the title poem: "An Old Man's Winter Night," "In the Home Stretch," "Meeting and Passing," "Putting in the Seed," many more. All complete and unabridged. 64pp. 5³⁄₁₆ x 8¼. 0-486-27550-7

ROMEO AND JULIET, William Shakespeare. Tragic tale of star-crossed lovers, feuding families and timeless passion contains some of Shakespeare's most beautiful and lyrical love poetry. Complete, unabridged text with explanatory footnotes. 96pp. 5³⁄₁₆ x 8¼. 0-486-27557-4

SANDITON AND THE WATSONS: Austen's Unfinished Novels, Jane Austen. Two tantalizing incomplete stories revisit Austen's customary milieu of courtship and venture into new territory, amid guests at a seaside resort. Both are worth reading for pleasure and study. 112pp. 5⅜ x 8½. 0-486-45793-1

THE SCARLET LETTER, Nathaniel Hawthorne. With stark power and emotional depth, Hawthorne's masterpiece explores sin, guilt, and redemption in a story of adultery in the early days of the Massachusetts Colony. 192pp. 5³⁄₁₆ x 8¼. 0-486-28048-9

THE SEASONS OF AMERICA PAST, Eric Sloane. Seventy-five illustrations depict cider mills and presses, sleds, pumps, stump-pulling equipment, plows, and other elements of America's rural heritage. A section of old recipes and household hints adds additional color. 160pp. 8⅜ x 11. 0-486-44220-9

SELECTED CANTERBURY TALES, Geoffrey Chaucer. Delightful collection includes the General Prologue plus three of the most popular tales: "The Knight's Tale," "The Miller's Prologue and Tale," and "The Wife of Bath's Prologue and Tale." In modern English. 144pp. 5³⁄₁₆ x 8¼. 0-486-28241-4

SELECTED POEMS, Emily Dickinson. Over 100 best-known, best-loved poems by one of America's foremost poets, reprinted from authoritative early editions. No comparable edition at this price. Index of first lines. 64pp. 5³⁄₁₆ x 8¼. 0-486-26466-1

SIDDHARTHA, Hermann Hesse. Classic novel that has inspired generations of seekers. Blending Eastern mysticism and psychoanalysis, Hesse presents a strikingly original view of man and culture and the arduous process of self-discovery, reconciliation, harmony, and peace. 112pp. 5³⁄₁₆ x 8¼. 0-486-40653-9

SKETCHING OUTDOORS, Leonard Richmond. This guide offers beginners step-by-step demonstrations of how to depict clouds, trees, buildings, and other outdoor sights. Explanations of a variety of techniques include shading and constructional drawing. 48pp. 11 x 8¼. 0-486-46922-0

SMALL HOUSES OF THE FORTIES: With Illustrations and Floor Plans, Harold E. Group. 56 floor plans and elevations of houses that originally cost less than $15,000 to build. Recommended by financial institutions of the era, they range from Colonials to Cape Cods. 144pp. 8⅜ x 11. 0-486-45598-X

SOME CHINESE GHOSTS, Lafcadio Hearn. Rooted in ancient Chinese legends, these richly atmospheric supernatural tales are recounted by an expert in Oriental lore. Their originality, power, and literary charm will captivate readers of all ages. 96pp. 5⅜ x 8½. 0-486-46306-0

SONGS FOR THE OPEN ROAD: Poems of Travel and Adventure, Edited by The American Poetry & Literacy Project. More than 80 poems by 50 American and British masters celebrate real and metaphorical journeys. Poems by Whitman, Byron, Millay, Sandburg, Langston Hughes, Emily Dickinson, Robert Frost, Shelley, Tennyson, Yeats, many others. Note. 80pp. 5³⁄₁₆ x 8¼. 0-486-40646-6

SPOON RIVER ANTHOLOGY, Edgar Lee Masters. An American poetry classic, in which former citizens of a mythical midwestern town speak touchingly from the grave of the thwarted hopes and dreams of their lives. 144pp. 5³⁄₁₆ x 8¼. 0-486-27275-3

STAR LORE: Myths, Legends, and Facts, William Tyler Olcott. Captivating retellings of the origins and histories of ancient star groups include Pegasus, Ursa Major, Pleiades, signs of the zodiac, and other constellations. "Classic." — *Sky & Telescope.* 58 illustrations. 544pp. 5⅜ x 8½. 0-486-43581-4

THE STRANGE CASE OF DR. JEKYLL AND MR. HYDE, Robert Louis Stevenson. This intriguing novel, both fantasy thriller and moral allegory, depicts the struggle of two opposing personalities — one essentially good, the other evil — for the soul of one man. 64pp. 5³⁄₁₆ x 8¼. 0-486-26688-5

SURVIVAL HANDBOOK: The Official U.S. Army Guide, Department of the Army. This special edition of the Army field manual is geared toward civilians. An essential companion for campers and all lovers of the outdoors, it constitutes the most authoritative wilderness guide. 288pp. 5³⁄₁₆ x 8¼. 0-486-46184-X

A TALE OF TWO CITIES, Charles Dickens. Against the backdrop of the French Revolution, Dickens unfolds his masterpiece of drama, adventure, and romance about a man falsely accused of treason. Excitement and derring-do in the shadow of the guillotine. 304pp. 5³⁄₁₆ x 8¼. 0-486-40651-2

TEN PLAYS, Anton Chekhov. *The Sea Gull, Uncle Vanya, The Three Sisters, The Cherry Orchard,* and *Ivanov,* plus 5 one-act comedies: *The Anniversary, An Unwilling Martyr, The Wedding, The Bear,* and *The Proposal.* 336pp. 5³⁄₁₆ x 8¼. 0-486-46560-8

THE FLYING INN, G. K. Chesterton. Hilarious romp in which pub owner Humphrey Hump and friend take to the road in a donkey cart filled with rum and cheese, inveighing against Prohibition and other "oppressive forms of modernity." 320pp. 5⅜ x 8½. 0-486-41910-X

THIRTY YEARS THAT SHOOK PHYSICS: The Story of Quantum Theory, George Gamow. Lucid, accessible introduction to the influential theory of energy and matter features careful explanations of Dirac's anti-particles, Bohr's model of the atom, and much more. Numerous drawings. 1966 edition. 240pp. 5⅜ x 8½. 0-486-24895-X

TREASURE ISLAND, Robert Louis Stevenson. Classic adventure story of a perilous sea journey, a mutiny led by the infamous Long John Silver, and a lethal scramble for buried treasure — seen through the eyes of cabin boy Jim Hawkins. 160pp. 5³⁄₁₆ x 8¼. 0-486-27559-0